Katharina von Knop, Heinrich Neisser,
Martin van Creveld (Hrsg.)

Countering Modern Terrorism

History, Current Issues and Future Threats

Proceedings of the Second International Security Conference
Berlin 15–17 December 2004

Bibliografische Information Der Deutschen Bibliothek

Die Deutsche Bibliothek verzeichnet diese Publikation in der Deutschen Nationalbibliografie; detaillierte bibliografische Daten sind im Internet über <http://dnb.ddb.de> abrufbar.

Herausgeber

Mag. Katharina von Knop
Leopold-Franzens-Universität Innsbruck
Institut für Politikwissenschaft
Universitätsstraße 15, 6020 Innsbruck, Österreich

Prof. Dr. Heinrich Neisser
Leopold-Franzens-Universität Innsbruck
Institut für Politikwissenschaft
Universitätsstraße 15, 6020 Innsbruck, Österreich

Prof. Dr. Martin van Creveld
The History Department, The Hebrew University
Jerusalem Israel 90105

© W. Bertelsmann Verlag GmbH & Co. KG, Bielefeld, 2005
Gesamtherstellung: W. Bertelsmann Verlag, Bielefeld

Das Werk einschließlich aller seiner Teile ist urheberrechtlich geschützt.
Jede Verwertung außerhalb der engen Grenzen des Urheberrechtsgesetzes ist ohne Zustimmung des Verlages unzulässig und strafbar. Das gilt insbesondere für Vervielfältigungen, Übersetzungen, Mikroverfilmungen und die Einspeicherung und Verarbeitung in elektronischen Systemen.
Printed in Germany.

ISBN 3-7639-3309-3

Bestell-Nr. 60.01.605

Tagungsleiter
Prof. Dr. Jan von Knop
Heinrich-Heine-Universität Düsseldorf

Dr. Boaz Ganor
The International Policy Institute for Counter-Terrorism
Herzliya, Israel

Mag. Katharina von Knop
Leopold-Franzens-Universität Innsbruck

Veranstalter
Heinrich-Heine-Universität Düsseldorf
International Policy Institute for Counter-Terrorism (ICT), Herzliya, Israel
Arbeitskreis Schutz von Infrastrukturen (AKSIS)
Deutscher Städtetag, Köln
Arbeitsgemeinschaft für Sicherheit der Wirtschaft e. V. (ASW), Berlin

Organisation
Ralf Schilberg, Universitätsrechenzentrum Düsseldorf
Harald Spiegl, Universitätsrechenzentrum Düsseldorf
Wilhelm Haverkamp, Universitätsrechenzentrum Düsseldorf

Satz
Friedhelm Sowa, LaTeX

Umschlaggestaltung
Ute Clames

Sponsoren
Deutsche Bank AG
Deutsche Forschungsgemeinschaft (DFG)
Heinrich-Heine-Universität Düsseldorf
Gesellschaft von Freunden und Förderern der Heinrich-Heine-Universität Düsseldorf e. V.
Diehl BGT Defence GmbH & Co. KG
Rheinmetall AG
Check Point Software Technologies GmbH
Lessing IRM GmbH
European Security Advocacy Group -ESAG-
The Bristol Group Deutschland GmbH
Steven Stern
Rafael Roth

Programmausschuss

Prof. Dr. Ulrich von Alemann, Heinrich-Heine-Universität Düsseldorf
Prof. Dr. Karsten Altenhain, Heinrich-Heine-Universität Düsseldorf
Prof. Dr. Michael Baumann, Heinrich-Heine-Universität Düsseldorf
Reinhard Bertram, Siemens Business Services, München
Prof. Dr. Martin van Creveld, Hebrew University, Jerusalem, Israel
Prof. Dr. Hans Dobbertin, Ruhr-Universität, Bochum
Prof. Dr. Claudia Eckert, Technische Universität Darmstadt
Bernhard Esslinger, Deutsche Bank AG, Frankfurt/Main
Dr. Johann Fichtner, Siemens, München
Ursus Fuhrmann, Deutscher Städtetag
Wilhelm Haverkamp, Heinrich-Heine-Universität Düsseldorf
Prof. Dr. Dr. Eric Hilgendorf, Universität Würzburg
Prof. Dr. Thomas Hoeren, Universität Münster
Karl-Heinz Holtz, Triaton GmbH, Frankfurt/Main
Prof. Dr. Patrick Horster, Universität Klagenfurt, Österreich
Prof. Dr. Hartwig Hummel, Heinrich-Heine-Universität Düsseldorf
Reinhard Hutter, IABG mbH, Ottobrunn
Dieter John, KPMG Wirtschaftsprüfungsgesellschaft, Köln
Mag. Katharina von Knop, Leopold-Franzens-Universität Innsbruck, Österreich
Dr. Rudolf Kreutzer, Allianz Zentrum für Technik GmbH, Ismaning
Kriminaloberrat Lothar Köhler, Bayerisches Staatsministerium des Innern, München
Peter Kraaibeek, BITKOM, Nordhorn
Prof. Dr. Gerd Krumeich, Heinrich-Heine-Universität Düsseldorf
Detlef Lannert, Heinrich-Heine-Universität Düsseldorf
Dr. Willy Marzi, Bundesverwaltungsamt, Bonn
Prof. Dr. Martin Mauve, Heinrich-Heine-Universität Düsseldorf
Prof. Dr. Heinrich Neisser, Leopold-Franzens-Universität Innsbruck, Österreich
Dr. h.c. Uwe Nerlich, IABG mbH, Ottobrunn
Jens Petersen, Deutsche Bahn AG, Berlin
MR Dr. Bernd Reuse, Bundesministerium für Bildung und Forschung, Bonn
Berthold Schweigler, Arbeitsgemeinschaft für Sicherheit der Wirtschaft, Berlin
Prof. Dr. Wolf Stock, Institut für Sprache und Information, Heinrich-Heine-Universität Düsseldorf
RA Dr. Berthold Stoppelkamp, Arbeitsgemeinschaft für Sicherheit der Wirtschaft, Berlin
Godehard Uhlemann, Rheinische Post, Düsseldorf
Wolfgang Weber, Bundesverwaltungsamt, Bonn
Prof. Dr. Gabriel Weimann, Department of Communication, University of Haifa, Haifa, Israel
Dr. Stephen D. Wolthusen, Fraunhofer-IGD, Darmstadt

Inhaltsverzeichnis / Table of Contents

Vorwort der Herausgeber 9
    Katharina von Knop, Heinrich Neisser und Martin van Creveld

I Herausforderungen / Challenges

Jihadi Networks of Terror 15
    Marc Sageman

The Power Resources of al-Qaeda and its Affiliates 31
    Katharina von Knop

The Intricacies of Funding the al-Qaida Network 69
    Michael E. G. Chandler

Hizballah Terror Organization of Global Reach 71
    Eithan Azani

Terror Online: How do Terrorists use the Internet? 87
    Gabriel Weimann

II Terrorismusabwehr / Counterterrorism

On Counterinsurgency 113
    Martin van Creveld

„Countering Terrorism" als Krieg der Weltanschauungen 131
    Bassam Tibi

Transition from "International Cooperation"
to a "Joint Counterterrorism Campaign" 173
    Boaz Ganor

How to Counter the Global Jihadists 181
  Peter S. Probst

Prävention und moderne Terrorismusformen 195
  Rudolf Adam

Die Rolle von Kultur in der Dynamik
und der Bekämpfung von Terrorismus 203
  Stephan Maninger

III Nationale und gemeinschaftliche Maßnahmen und Perspektiven / National and Common Measures and Perspectives

Maßnahmen der Europäischen Union zur Terrorismus-Abwehr 227
  Heinrich Neisser

A Hard Day's Night?
The United States and the Global War on Terrorism 239
  Thomas H. Johnson, James A. Russell

Gefährdet der Terrorismus den liberalen Verfassungsstaat? 273
  Sabine Leutheusser-Schnarrenberger

Terrorism and Germany: the Threat and the Response 289
  Joshua Sinai

Russian Prospectives,
International Terrorism Today, Retaliatory Measures 303
  A. S. Kulikov

Das Recht auf Selbstverteidigung im Kampf gegen den internationalen
Terrorismus 313
  Aleksandr A. Kovalev

Die Bedeutung multilateraler Konventionen für das Vorgehen
gegen den internationalen Terrorismus 321
  Ralph Alexander Lorz, Lars Mammen

IV Maßnahmen der Sicherheitsdienste / Measures of the Intelligence Agencies

Cooperation between National and International Security Services
in Countering Global Terrorism 339
   Ernst Uhrlau

Die Rolle des Bundesnachrichtendienstes bei
der Aufklärung des Internationalen Terrorismus 347
   August Hanning

Information Sharing in Support of Strategic Intelligence 353
   Peter J. Sharfman

V Risiko-, Krisen- und Katastrophenmanagement / Risk, Crisis, and Catastrophe Management

Non-Conventional Terrorism: Challenge & Response 361
   Yael Shahar

Bedrohungslage biologische Waffen –
Identifizierung biologischer Kampfstoffe 381
   Elisabeth Hauschild

Tools for Countering Future Terrorism 385
   Eric Herren

Forecasting Terrorists' Warfare: 'Conventional' to CBRN 397
   Joshua Sinai

Technologies against Terrorism 407
   Burkhard Theile

Anforderungen an Informationen zum Schutz
von kritischen Infrastrukturen 417
   Matthias Holenstein, Daniel Bircher

I³BAT and Nomad Eyes™ – Modeling the "Design of Death" and Incorporating Terrorist Thinking into Countermethods of Sensing and Preventive Response 423
    Martin Dudziak

VI   Maßnahmen der Wirtschaft / Economic Measures

Internationaler Terrorismus als Herausforderung
für die moderne Unternehmenssicherheit 441
    Christoph Rojahn

Risikomanagement und Sicherheitsstrategien in der Wirtschaft 453
    Günter Lessing

Wege zur Versicherung des Terrorrisikos 467
    Bruno Gas

VII   Lösung städtischer Krisen / Solutions of Urban Crisis

Bekämpfung von großen Schadensereignissen durch kommunale
Sicherheitsbehörden im Rahmen der föderalen Struktur Deutschlands 475
    Ursus Fuhrmann

Einsatzkonzept ÜMANV – „MANV überörtlich" 487
    Jörg Schmidt

Sicherheitsmaßnahmen in unterirdischen Verkehrsanlagen 491
    Peer Rechenbach

Autorinnen und Autoren / Contributors 497

Vorwort der Herausgeber

Mit den terroristischen Anschlägen des 11. September 2001 in den USA offenbarte sich die Substanz einer neuen Sicherheitsbedrohung. Diese Anschläge sind zu einem globalen Symbol des Schreckens und der Rücksichtslosigkeit des Terrorismus des 21. Jahrhunderts geworden. Die Allgegenwärtigkeit dieser Bedrohung wurde auch den Europäern schockartig durch die Anschläge in Madrid am 11. März 2004 bewusst.

Die Erscheinungsformen des modernen Terrorismus gefährden nicht nur das Leben von Menschen, sie bedeuten auch einen Angriff auf den Bestand und die Errungenschaften der freiheitlichen Demokratie. Der Kampf gegen den Terrorismus ist eine Herausforderung für jedes demokratische System, seine geistigen Grundlagen und seine fundamentalen Werte zu verteidigen. Diese Aufgabe kann von den einzelnen Staaten nicht allein bewältigt werden, es braucht dazu die Kooperation mit anderen Staaten und mit Staatengemeinschaften.

Die Bedrohung des modernen Terrorismus hebt die klassische Trennung von innerer und äußerer Sicherheit auf. Nur eine umfassende, nationenübergreifende, interdisziplinäre und interinstitutionelle Sicherheitsstruktur kann die neuen sicherheitspolitischen Herausforderungen bewältigen. Geleitet von diesem Handlungsimperativ veranstaltete die Heinrich-Heine-Universität Düsseldorf in Kooperation mit dem International Policy Institute for Counter-Terrorism (ICT), dem Deutschen Städtetag, dem Arbeitskreis Schutz von Infrastrukturen (AKSIS) und der Arbeitsgemeinschaft für Sicherheit der Wirtschaft e.V. (ASW) am 16. und 17. Dezember 2004 eine gemeinsame zweite internationale Sicherheitskonferenz. Diese Konferenz, die in den Räumen der Deutschen Bank AG in Berlin stattfand, stand unter dem Titel „Countering Modern Terrorism – History, Current Issues and Future Threats". Sie brachte hochrangige Experten aus Wissenschaft, Politik und Praxis zusammen. Die Referenten waren Regierungsvertreter, Diplomaten, Wissenschaftler, Führungskräfte der Wirtschaft und Sicherheitsbeamte aus Deutschland, Russland, den USA, Israel und Österreich. Dieser hochrangige, interdisziplinäre Expertenkreis wurde zu einem Forum für einen offenen und kritischen Gedankenaustausch, für die Analyse der aktuellen Sicherheitslage und für die Entwicklung geeigneter Handlungsoptionen sowie die Ausarbeitung künftiger Sicherheitsszenarien und der daraus abzuleitenden Anforderungen an Politik, Wissenschaft und Wirtschaft. Teilnehmer aus 16 Nationen kamen zu dieser Konferenz, um diesen Diskurs zu erleben und mitzuwirken.

Der moderne Terrorismus ist ein komplexes Phänomen, er ist durch ein noch nie da gewesenes Maß an Professionalität und Globalität charakterisiert. Auch die Terrorismusbekämpfung muss sich an komplexen und vielfältigen Zielen orientieren. Ihr vorrangiges Ziel ist der Schutz von Menschen, aber ebenso auch von Einrichtungen von Staat und Gesellschaft, vor allem der Erhaltung einer funktionierenden Infrastruktur. Antiterrorpolitik muss auch Schadensbegrenzung und Schadenswiedergutmachung gewährleisten. Es ist eine allgemeine Erkenntnis, dass Antiterrorismuspolitik im Besonderen auf Prävention ausgerichtet sein muss, das heißt auf die Verhinderung von terroristischen Aktivitäten. Im Bestreben, zukunftsorientierte, auf Prävention ausgerichtete Gegenstrategien zu entwickeln, müssen Antworten auf die Frage gefunden werden, weshalb radikale Weltbilder Unterstützung erfahren und sich Menschen für diese verachtenswerte Gewaltstrategie gewinnen lassen.

Schließlich ist Terrorismus nicht nur eine Gefahr für den einzelnen Menschen oder für Gruppen von Menschen, sondern für das System des Rechtsstaats, in dem bestimmte Werte der Gesellschaft zum Ausdruck kommen. Eine effektive Antiterrorismuspolitik muss daher die Werte einer Gesellschaft – Rechtsstaatlichkeit, Menschenrechte und Grundfreiheiten – respektieren und achten und gleichzeitig Terrorismus bekämpfen.

In einer asymmetrischen Bedrohungslage verlieren Analyseraster an Bedeutung, die von strukturell und taktisch ähnlich denkenden und handelnden Akteuren ausgehen. Deswegen sind Analyseraster, die auf die Dynamik und Klandestinität des Terrorismus eingehen, erforderlich. Terroristen planen und führen ihre Anschläge situationsabhängig nach den zur Verfügung stehenden Ressourcen durch. Dies erfordert ein hohes Maß an Aufmerksamkeit der Sicherheitsdienste und beansprucht intensive interinstitutionelle und nationenübergreifende Kommunikation.

Die zweite internationale Sicherheitskonferenz in Berlin orientierte sich an der Komplexität der terroristischen Bedrohung durch die Vielfältigkeit der behandelten Themen und durch den Perspektivreichtum der Analysen, wie Terrorismusabwehr konzipiert wird und wo Verbesserungen notwendig sind. Ursachen und Motive des modernen Terrorismus sowie organisatorische Strukturen wurden erschöpfend behandelt. Besondere Bedeutung kam neben Analysemethoden den Möglichkeiten der modernen Informationstechnologien sowie dem Wissensmanagement zu, das bei der Vernetzung von Behörden und Sicherheitsdiensten anzuwenden ist. Ebenso wurde die Reaktionsfähigkeit lokaler Sicherheitsbehörden und Rettungsdienste bei großen Schadensereignissen erörtert und die Rolle der Wirtschaftsunternehmungen in den neuen Bedrohungssituationen hinterfragt, im Besonderen auch im Hinblick auf die Rahmenbedingungen, die durch den Staat zu schaffen sind.

Die erwähnten Fragestellungen wurden von einer großen Zahl von Referenten behandelt, die überaus interessante und konstruktive Positionen ausdrückten. Im vorliegenden Tagungsband wurden die Beiträge thematisch gebündelt, um die Übersicht über die Themenvielfalt zu erleichtern.

Unter dem Titel „Herausforderungen" sind wissenschaftliche Analysen zusammengefasst, die sich intensiv mit der globalen Terrorismusorganisation, deren Bedrohungsspektrum und im Besonderen mit der intensiven Nutzbarmachung der modernen Kommunikationstechnologien befassen. Marc Sageman, Katharina von Knop, Michael E. G. Chandler, Eithan Azani und Gabriel Weimann haben hierfür umfassende und präzise analytische Studien erarbeitet.

Im folgenden Abschnitt, der die Bezeichnung „Terrorismusabwehr" trägt, werden strategische Positionen behandelt, die für den Kampf gegen den Terrorismus essenziell sind und von den ideologischen Wurzeln terroristischer Bedrohungen bis zu präventiven Aspekten der Antiterrorismuspolitik reichen. Martin van Creveld, Bassam Tibi, Boaz Ganor, Peter Probst, Rudolf Adam und Stephan Maninger beschäftigen sich seit Jahren mit diesen Fragestellungen und haben wissenschaftliche Expertisen zur Verfügung gestellt.

Die nationalen und gemeinschaftlichen Maßnahmen und Perspektiven sind in einem weiteren Kapitel zusammengefasst: Die kritischen Analysen beziehen sich dabei auf die Terrorismusabwehr innerhalb der Europäischen Union (Heinrich Neisser), in den USA (Thomas H. Johnson und James A. Russell), in Deutschland (Sabine Leutheusser-Schnarrenberger, Joshua Sinai) und in der Russischen Föderation (A. S. Kulikov, Aleksandr A. Kovalev). Eine völkerrechtliche Analyse der terroristischen Herausforderung wurde von Ralph Alexander Lorz und Lars Mammen erarbeitet.

Konkrete Überlegungen zu Maßnahmen der Sicherheitsdienste und deren ganzheitlichem und interdisziplinärem Aufklärungsansatz beinhalten die Beiträge von Ernst Uhrlau, August Hanning und Peter J. Sharfman, die ein eigenständiges Kapitel bilden.

Unter der Überschrift „Risiko-, Krisen-, und Katastrophenmanagement" tragen Yael Shahar, Elisabeth Hauschild, Eric Herren, Joshua Sinai, Burkhard Theile, Matthias Holenstein und Daniel Bircher sowie Martin Dudziak kenntnisreiche Untersuchungen bei, die nicht nur Bedrohungen und Schwachpunkte beleuchten, sondern auch Methoden zu deren Beseitigung zur Verfügung stellen. Dass die Wirtschaft durch jeden terroristischen Anschlag maßgeblich in Mitleidenschaft gezogen wird und dass hierfür ebenfalls neue Konzepte erforderlich sind, bestätigen die Beiträge von Christoph Rojahn, Günter Lessing und Bruno Gas in einem eigenen Abschnitt.

Da jeder terroristische Anschlag zuerst die lokalen Katastrophendienste fordert, widmet sich das Schlusskapitel dieses Tagungsbandes spezifischen Lösungen städtischer Krisen. Konstruktiv wurde dieses Thema von Ursus Fuhrmann, Jörg Schmidt und Peer Rechenbach behandelt.

Die eben beschriebene Gliederung macht die Komplexität sichtbar, die sowohl für das Phänomen des Terrorismus als auch für die Strategien der Bekämpfung desselben charakteristisch ist. Sie dient auch als Orientierung für die Entwicklung innovativer Denkansätze und Handlungsparameter. Wir hoffen, dass die Ergebnisse der zweiten internationalen Sicherheitskonferenz in Berlin nicht nur ein anregender nationen- und disziplinübergreifender Diskurs zwischen Wissenschaft und Politik waren, sondern auch eine neue Sensibilität in der Bekämpfung des modernen Terrorismus bewirken. Zum großen Erfolg dieser Konferenz gilt unser Dank jedem Referenten und im Besonderen der Deutschen Bank AG, die uns die Räumlichkeiten in Berlin zur Verfügung gestellt hat.

Katharina von Knop   Heinrich Neisser   Martin van Creveld

Herausforderungen

Challenges

Jihadi Networks of Terror

Marc Sageman, MD, PhD

University of Pennsylvania, USA

The Islamist terrorist threat to the Western world arises from a violent Islamist revivalist social movement, which is united by a utopian vision of justice and fairness. The effort to deal with this threat is hampered by common beliefs about terrorism. The conventional wisdom offers several explanations, which variously describe terrorists as: products of poverty and broken families; ignorant; lacking skills and opportunities, without occupational or family responsibilities; weak-minded, vulnerable to brainwashing; mentally ill psychopaths or sociopaths; plain criminals, religious fanatics or simply evil. The present study attempts to empirically test this conventional wisdom through accumulation and analysis of biographical data on the terrorists who wished to harm the United States. (Sageman, 2004).

Traditionally, the study of terrorism has been hampered by attempts to define terrorism. A common quip is that one man's terrorist is another's freedom fighter. So, the first task was to identify whom to include in this sample. This study focuses only in the terrorists connected to the perpetrators of the attacks of 9/11. Therefore, it excludes other terrorists such as the Palestinians or Tamil Tigers, whom many people lump together, but who are not linked to the anti-American perpetrators. In order to delineate who belongs in the sample, it is necessary to define the threat to the U.S.

The terrorists who flew into the World Trade Center, the Pentagon and crashed in the fields of Pennsylvania on 9/11/01 were part of al Qaeda. The term al Qaeda is confusing, because it refers both to a specific organization and to a more diffuse and global social movement at war with the U.S. Al Qaeda, the formal organization, is the vanguard of this violent Islamist revivalist social movement. This study is based on a sample of people belonging to this larger social movement, best labeled the global Salafi jihad, because many of the terrorists were not formally in al Qaeda, in the sense of swearing an oath of loyalty to Osama bin Laden, its leader, but were nevertheless fellow travelers with them.

In order to define who belongs to this social movement, it is important to understand its nature.

1 The evolution of the global Salafi jihad ideology

The terrorist social movement is held together by a common vision that arose in the context of gradual Muslim decadence over the past 500 years. During this period, Islam fell from its dominant position in the world. Because Islam claims to be the last and perfect revelation from God, this decline presents a problem. Many explanations, secular and religious, have tried to deal with this obvious mismatch between claim and reality. One of the more popular religious explanations is simply that Muslims have strayed from the righteous path. The source of strength of the original and righteous Muslim community was its faith and its practices, which pleased God. Recapturing the glory and grandeur of the Golden Age requires a return to the authentic faith of the ancient ones, namely the Prophet Mohammed and his companions, the Salaf – from the Arabic word for predecessor or ancient one. The revivalist versions of Islam advocating such a return are called Salafi. Their strategy is the creation of a pure Islamist state, which would create the conditions for the re-establishment of such a community.

Most Salafists advocate a peaceful takeover of the state, either through face-to-face proselytism or the creation of legitimate political parties. Their peaceful strategy was undermined by President Nasser's brutal crackdown in the name of a pan-Arabist socialist project, leading some people to conclude that Nasser would never give up power peacefully and preached his violent overthrow (Qutb, n.d.). They argued that Muslim countries had reached a state of decadence, injustice and unfairness, which was similar to the state of barbarism, *jahiliyya*, prevailing in the Arabian Peninsula just before the revelations of the Quran. This was due to a "crisis of values," namely greed, corruption and promiscuity, which could only be redressed from above, by capturing the state. Because their rulers were accused of having abandoned true Islam, they were branded apostates, and the Quranic punishment for apostasy was death. This violent overthrow of local rulers, the "near enemy," was the neglected duty of each Muslim, a sixth pillar of Islam (Faraj, 1986).

The Soviet invasion of Afghanistan internationalized the militant Islamist movement. Sheikh Abdallah Azzam, a Palestinian cleric and university professor in Saudi Arabia, came to Pakistan shortly after the Soviet invasion to support his fellow Muslims. From there, he launched a call for a traditional jihad against the Soviet invaders. Many militants from all over the Muslim world answered his call. As the Soviets withdrew, Azzam extended the defensive jihad into a more global one. He preached that all former Muslim lands dating back to the 15th century, from the Philippines to Spain, had to be liberated from the infidels. After the Soviet withdrawal from Afghanistan, these militants focused on the other lands under infidel occupation. They gathered in the Sudan where they held intense discussions about their failure to capture a core Arab state and transform it into an Islamist state. Some militants, led by Osama bin Laden, argued that this failure was due to the U.S. propping up the local regimes. The strategy that the most militant advocated was to switch priorities and fight the "far enemy" (the U.S. and the Jews) in order to expel them from the Middle East, so that they could overthrow the "near enemy," their own regimes. This argument split the Islamist militant community, for many did not want to provoke and take on a powerful enemy like the U.S. Osama bin Laden and his followers returned to Afghanistan and declared war on the U.S. (bin Laden, 1996). In February 1998, bin Laden extended his "Jihad against Jews and Crusaders" to civilians outside the Middle East, ruling that "to kill the Americans and their allies – civilians and military – is an individual duty for every Muslim who can do it in any country in which it is possible to do it" (bin Laden, 1998).

With the evolution of this ideology and social movement in mind, it is now possible to select the terrorists that belong in this sample. They are those who use violence against any foreign or non-Muslim government or population (the "far enemy") to establish an Islamist state in a core Arab region.

2   The history of the global Salafi jihad

The historical roots of the present terrorist Islamist revivalist social movement go back to Egypt in the 1970s, when President Anwar al-Sadat encouraged the formation of Islamic Societies at the universities to counter the leftist supporters of Nasser. Some of these militants adopted the radical views of Qutb and Faraj and turned against Sadat himself when he made peace with Israel. They were responsible for his assassination in 1981. Most of these militants were arrested and tortured in a crackdown after this assassination. Those not directly involved were released three years later and found their way to Afghanistan, in support of Sheikh Azzam's jihad against the Soviets.

The presence in Afghanistan and Peshawar of so many Islamist militants from all over the world transformed the jihad from a collection of local attempts to overthrow their governments into a more international movement to reclaim former Muslim lands lost to the infidels over the past five centuries. After the victory in Afghanistan, most of the foreigners returned to their country. But those who could not, mostly because of prior terrorist activities at home, stayed behind and became the nucleus of al Qaeda, the organization. After many Middle Eastern countries complained to Pakistan that it was harboring terrorists, Pakistan expelled them. The most militant went to the Sudan, invited by the new militant regime of Hassan al-Turabi, who tried to unify the disparate local Islamist terrorist movements under one umbrella. His greatest supporter in this enterprise was Osama bin Laden, who set up camps in the Sudan and Afghanistan for the training of terrorists coming from the whole world. It was during this Sudanese episode that the most militant terrorists switched priorities to target a common enemy, the U.S. The imposition of international sanctions on the Sudan after its support for a serious assassination attempt on Egyptian President Mubarak during a state visit in Addis Ababa forced it to expel the terrorists. The few who agreed with bin Laden's strategy of going after the "far enemy" returned to Afghanistan, and within two months of their arrival, declared war on the U.S. So the threat to the U.S. came from a process of self selection, in which the most militant of the most militant of the most militant switched their targets from their own governments to the U.S.

The return to Afghanistan heralded the start of a close collaboration with the Taliban leader Mullah Omar, who provided sanctuary to the now-global Salafi jihad, enabling Osama bin Laden to provide training camps, shelter, funding and logistic support to aspiring terrorists. This allowed bin Laden to gain control over this social movement, uniting various local Islamist terrorist groups that were scattered around the world. This gave the appearance of a hierarchical organization, with al Qaeda (Osama bin Laden's organization) at the top with strong command and control over the whole movement. During the five years leading to 9/11/01, this was mostly true, as bin Laden and his lieutenants provided training for local Islamist terrorists, housed them and their families in protected areas in Afghanistan, supported them with logistics and funds, and gave advice on their operations. In a sense, for about five years, Osama bin Laden achieved in Afghanistan what Turabi had tried to do in the Sudan.

However, the U.S. reaction to the 9/11 terrorist operation changed the movement. The elimination of sanctuaries in Afghanistan, the destruction of the training camps and the disruption of the financial "golden chain" for the jihad undermined bin Laden's and al Qaeda's control over the social movement, which degraded back into smaller local networks of operatives, now linked through the Internet. To the extent that these smaller clusters of terrorists respond to the Salafi vision and general guidance from al Qaeda, they are still part of this global Salafi jihad. There is no more need for a strong command and control structure. Now, this social movement is self-generated from below, very similar in structure and behavior to the World-Wide Web itself, which shows that there is no need for top-down control for the network to grow and prosper.

3 Methodology

The present study is based on the collection from open sources of biographical details of people who belong to this global Salafi jihad. The data suffers from several limitations. First, the terrorists selected are hardly representative of the global Salafi jihad as a whole. Journalists and scholars tend to focus on the unusual: leaders, people they can investigate and unusual cases. This bias toward leaders and unusual cases tends to ignore those who cannot be investigated and downplays the rank and file. Second, reliance on journalistic accounts is fraught with danger. In the rush to publish, the initial information may not be reliable. Lack of direct access to information feeds the wildest rumors, and journalists are born storytellers, who fill in the gaps in knowledge with their own ideas. These initial inaccuracies can be corrected by following the developing stories over time, rather than simply relying on initial reporting. Third, retrospective accounts from principals and witnesses are subject to the biases of self-report and flawed memory. These accounts were often the only available information, and were very occasionally able to be corroborated with existing contemporaneous documents. Finally, there is a lack of a relevant control group that would allow the generation of statements specific to the terrorists. It is difficult to make specific statements about these terrorists without comparison to a group of Muslims with similar backgrounds and activities who did not participate in terrorism despite having had an opportunity to do so.

Nevertheless, the hope is that even though each piece of information may be of questionable validity, the emerging pattern would be accurate given the large numbers involved. A description of the potential sample might be able to support or refute the conventional wisdom about al Qaeda terrorism. Using the definition of a terrorist elaborated in the previous section, I was able to identify 394 terrorists on whom there existed enough background information to include them in empirical generalizations as to age, origin, religious commitment and education. I was able to codify them into a matrix with 34 variables, most of which dealt with their relationships to each other and are not relevant to this chapter.

4 Profiles of the global Salafi terrorists

As mentioned above, the common stereotype is that terrorism arises among poor, desperate, naïve, single young men from third-world countries, vulnerable to brainwashing and recruitment into terror. Unpacking this formula, the geographical origins of the mujahedin should be not only the Third World, but some of the poorest countries of the Third World. It also implies that they come from the lowest socio-economic strata. Their naïve vulnerability implies that they either are brainwashed early into hatred of the West or are relatively uneducated and susceptible to such brainwashing as young adults. In this sense, they are relatively unsophisticated and local in their outlook. A broad experience of the world might be protective against the alleged brainwashing that presumably led to their conversion to terrorism. The desperation implies that their occupational opportunities are extremely limited. They are single, for any strong family responsibilities might prevent their total dedication to a cause that demands their ultimate sacrifice.

In fact, most of the global Salafi terrorists come from core Arab countries, immigrant communities in the West, Indonesia or Malaysia. They do not come from the poorest countries in the world, including Afghanistan. Surprisingly, there is no Afghan in my sample. In terms of socio-economic background, three fourths come from upper and middle class families. Far from coming from broken families, they grew up in caring intact families, mildly religious and concerned about their communities. In terms of education, over 60% have some college education. Most are in the technical fields, such as engineering, architecture, computers, medicine and business. This is all the more remarkable because college education is still relatively uncommon in the countries or immigrant communities they come from. Far from being immature teenagers, the men in my sample joined the terrorist organization at the age of 26 years, on average. Most of the terrorists have some occupational skills. Three fourths are either professional (physicians, lawyers, architects, engineers or teachers) or semi-professionals (businessmen, craftsmen or computer specialists). They are solidly anchored in family responsibilities. Three fourths are married and the majority have children. There was no indication of weak minds brainwashed by their family or education. About half of the sample grew up as religious children, but only 13%, almost all of them in South-East Asia, were madrassa educated. The entire sample from the North African region and the second-generation Europeans went to secular schools. About 10% were Catholic converts to Islam, who could not have been brainwashed into Islam as children.

Another popular set of explanations of terrorism centers on mental illness or innate criminality. Such popular explanations are based on the belief that "normal" people do not kill civilians indiscriminately. Such killing, especially when combined with suicide, is viewed as irrational. The mental illness thesis is dealt a strong blow by the fact that only 1% of the sample had hint of a thought disorder, which is below the base rate for thought disorder world-wide. A variant of the abnormality thesis is that terrorists are sociopaths, psychopaths or people with antisocial personality disorder. These terms are used to mean that terrorists are recidivist criminals, due to some defect of personality. Such recidivism implies that this personality defect had some antecedents in childhood. Out of the third of my sample where I had some fragment of childhood data, less than 8% showed evidence of a conduct disorder. The rest of this group seems to have had normal childhood without any evidence of getting in trouble with the law.

On a logical basis, although antisocial people might become *individual* terrorists, they would not do well in a terrorist *organization*. Because of their personalities, they would not get along with others or fit well in an organization, and indeed would be least likely to join any organization that would demand great sacrifices from them. They would be weeded out early if they attempted to join. Likewise, very few people in my sample had any criminal background. Those who did came from the excluded North African immigrant community in Europe and Canada, where they resorted to petty crime to survive. But there were no previously violent criminals in this sample. Therefore, it is more parsimonious to argue that in an organized operation demanding great personal sacrifice, those least likely to do any harm *individually* are best able to do so *collectively*.

The failure of mental illness as an explanation for terrorism is consistent with three decades of research that has been unable to detect any significant pattern of mental illness in terrorists. Indeed, these studies have indicated that terrorists are surprisingly normal in terms of mental health (Silke, 1998 & 2003).

5   Group dynamics

The above findings refute the conventional wisdom about terrorists. The global Salafi terrorists were generally middle-class, educated young men from caring and religious families, who grew up with strong positive values of religion, spirituality and concern for their communities. They were truly global citizens, conversant in three or four languages and skilled in computer technology. One of the striking findings of this sample is that three fourths of the terrorists joined the jihad as expatriates, mostly as upwardly mobile young men studying abroad. At the time, they were separated from their original environment. An additional 10% were second generation in the West, who felt a strong pull for the country of their parents. So a remarkable 84% were literally cut off from their culture and social origins. They were homesick, lonely and alienated. Although they were intellectually gifted, they were marginalized, underemployed and generally excluded from the highest status in the new society. Although they were not religious, they drifted to mosques for companionship. There, they met friends or relatives, with whom they moved in together often for dietary reasons. As their friendship intensified, they became a "bunch of guys," resenting society at large, which excluded them, developing a common religious collective identity and egging each other on to greater extremism. By the time they joined the jihad, there was a dramatic shift in devotion to their faith. About two thirds of those who joined the jihad did so collectively with their friends or had a long-time childhood friend already in the jihad. Another fifth had close relatives already in the jihad. These friendship or kinship bonds predated any ideological commitment. Once inside the social movement, they cemented their mutual bonds by marrying sisters and daughters of other terrorists. There was no evidence of "brainwashing": the future terrorists simply acquired the beliefs of their friends.

Joining this violent social movement was a bottom-up activity. Al Qaeda had no formal top-down recruitment program. There was neither a central committee with a budget dedicated to recruitment nor any general campaign of recruitment. There was no need for either. There were plenty of volunteers who wanted to join the jihad. Al Qaeda's problem was never recruitment but selection. It was akin to applying to a very selective college. Many apply but few are accepted. Likewise, al Qaeda was able to assess and evaluate potential candidates who showed a desire to join by coming to Afghanistan for training. It invited only about 15 to 25% of that group to join the jihad. However, this reliance on self-recruits had a drawback, namely gaps in the distribution of the jihad. One of the gaps was the U.S. The few volunteers from the U.S. who came to Afghanistan to join the jihad were shocked by the anti-Americanism in the training camps. This attitude was based on beliefs and ideas about the U.S. that they knew from personal experience to be false. Some, like the Lackawanna Six, tried to leave early or simply forget about this experience. Because of this gap, al Qaeda had to import terrorists from elsewhere to wage their war on U.S. soil. This was easier to do before 9/11 when there was easy access to Saudi citizens. But since 9/11, the U.S. has hardened the entry to the country and increased its vigilance against suspicious foreign activities, making such operations much more difficult. The lack of an indigenous terrorist population ("sleeper cells") and the hardening of the U.S. target account for the lack of major al Qaeda operations in the U.S. In contrast, most of the global Salafi jihad operations conducted elsewhere in the world after 9/11 relied heavily on indigenous global Salafi terrorists.

The process just described is grounded in social relations and dynamics. To look at it through individual lenses, as a Robinson Crusoe on a deserted island narrative, is to miss the fundamental social nature of this process. So far, the account of the global Salafi jihad seems to be a purely male story of heroic warriors fighting the evil West. Yet, women also play a critical role in this process. They provide the invisible infrastructure of the jihad. As influential parts of the social environment, they often encourage their relatives and friends to join the jihad. Many Christian converts or secular Muslims joined because of marriage to a committed wife. Indeed, invitation to join the Indonesian *Jemaah Islamiyah* depends on the background of the spouse of the applicant. And once in the jihad, single members often solidify their participation by marrying the sisters of other members. This further separates the new recruit from the rest of society and increases his loyalty to the social movement.

So far, this account has neglected the religious ideological contribution to the transformation of alienated young Muslims into fanatic terrorists. The specific interpretation of Islam that promoted this violent strategy with respect to the U.S. played a crucial role in this transformation. It provided the script to follow for these distressed cliques of men. Very few mosques world-wide preached this aberrant strategy to transform society using the utopian Salafi community as a model. Indeed, about ten mosques world-wide generated about 50% of my sample. This is a very small number, suggesting that the global Salafi jihad is a small collection of localized networks of people rather than a more widely and randomly distributed one.

This script stressing the justice and fairness of the original Muslim community appeals to gifted young men excluded from the higher rewards of society. Combined with natural group processes, it transforms their values to conform to those of their ever closer friends. Faith and commitment are grounded and sustained in intense small group dynamics, as friends and peers provide support and strength to help cope with any potential hardship. These born again believers welcome struggles in this life as a test of their faith. Over time, "authentic" Islamic spirituality and religious growth replace dominant "Western" values of career advancement and material wealth, which had contributed to their original feelings of exclusion, frustration, unfairness and injustice. They embrace Qutb's diagnosis that society faces a "crisis of values" for its main problems are not material but spiritual. The progressive detachment from the pursuit of material needs allows them to transcend their realistic frustrated aspirations and promotes satisfaction with spiritual goals more consistent with their limited resources and opportunities, relieving the malaise arising from their exclusion and marginalized status. Their sacrifice and participation in this Islamist vanguard provide them with a sense of moral superiority, optimism and faith in the collective future. Their activism and firm belief in the righteousness of their mission generate a sense of efficacy that enables them to overcome the apathy and fear that would otherwise inhibit high-risk terrorist operations. Over time, there is a general shift in values: from the secular to the religious; from the material to the spiritual; from short-term opportunity to long-term vision; from individual concerns to communitarian sacrifice; from apathy to active engagement; from traditional morality to specific group morality; and from worldly gains to otherworldly rewards. This transformation is possible only within intense small group face-to-face interactions. The values and fellowship of these groups not only forge intense bonds of loyalty and a collective identity, but also give a glimpse of what a righteous Islamist society could be like. The small size of these cliques and the mutual dedication of their members allow them to spontaneously resolve their problems among themselves. The quality of these small and dense networks promotes in-group love, transforming self-interest into self-sacrifice for the cause and comrades. The militants' experience in these groups deludes them into believing that social problems would also be spontaneously resolved in a righteous Islamist society, accounting for their curious lack of concern about what this ideal society would actually look like or how it might function politically or economically.

On a less positive perspective, these same group dynamics account for their hatred of Jews and the U.S., as illustrated from the police wiretaps of their apartments in Montreal, Hamburg and Milan. This hatred is grounded in their everyday experience of humiliating exclusion from society at large and promoted within the group by a vicious process of one-upmanship of mutual complaints about the alienating society. This "bunch-of-guys" phenomenon escalates resentment into a hatred and rejection of the ambient society itself. They express their hatred by cursing its symbols and legitimizing myths and by endorsing a conspiracy theory of Jews corrupting a now totally degenerate and unredeemable society. The wiretaps give a hint of this visceral hatred that seeks to destroy society even at the cost of their own lives. This virulent rejection of society finds a home in the doctrine of *takfir* or excommunication of society, which is popular in militant circles and sanctions the commission of crimes against infidels in the pursuit of the jihad.

The trajectory from low-risk participation with an increasingly closer set of friends to medium-risk proselytism for an ideal way of life, and to high-risk terrorist activities is a progressive and insidious one. This progression embraces an ideology that frames activism as a moral obligation demanding self-sacrifice and unflinching commitment to the jihad. This particular interpretation of Islam stands apart in challenging the validity of mainstream Islamic faith and practices, and it isolates the new adherents to this doctrine. Their self-sacrifice is again grounded in group dynamics. The terrorist is ready to show his devotion to his now exclusive friends, their group, and their cause by seeking death as a way to show his devotion to all of them. And group dynamics again helps in this ultimate sacrifice. Although each member of the "bunch of guys" might lack the courage to independently kill himself, group loyalty, support and encouragement help him overcome this hesitation, for refusing to participate in group suicide is the ultimate betrayal of the group. In-group love combined with out-group hate is a strong incentive for committing mass murder and suicide.

6 Network analysis

The above analysis suggests that this form of terrorism is an emergent quality of dense networks rather than an aberration based in individual pathology. Doing a qualitative social network analysis on this sample generates statements that simply cannot be generated from a more individualistic perspective.

The topology of the network representing the interpersonal links in the global Salafi jihad is divided into four major clusters of terrorists that evolved separately into four different structures. There are many links among members within a specific cluster, but very few spanning two large clusters. At the center is the Central Staff cluster, which used to connect to the rest of the clusters before the U.S. fall 2001 campaign against al Qaeda dramatically interfered with its communication to the social movement and broke its operational links to the other clusters. This Central Staff consists mostly of Egyptian Islamist militants who were released from prison after Sadat's assassination and went to Afghanistan to join the jihad against the Soviets. They formalized their bonds of friendship and kinship into al Qaeda proper after the Soviets announced their intention to withdraw. They provide the leadership, training and ideological guidance to the movement. The structure of this cluster is difficult to describe, as most of their relationships date back to the 1970s in Egypt. It is both an informal self-organizing group of friends forged during their militant activities in Egypt and during their fight against the Soviets and a hierarchical organization with bin Laden as its emir, supported by a *shura* composed of about a dozen members and dominated by Egyptians. The al Qaeda staff is divided into four committees consisting of finances, military affairs, religious affairs and public relations.

A second cluster consists of the South-East Asian part of the social movement, dominated by the *Jemaah Islamiyah*, which is hierarchically organized around the leadership of Abu Bakar Baasyir. This cluster evolved out of the recruitment of Baasyir's students at his two schools, *Pondok Ngruki* in Indonesia and *Pesentren Luqmanul Hakiem* in Malaysia. As would be expected from top-down recruitment of former disciples, it looks like a rigid pyramid, where all the significant decisions are taken at the top and showing very little local initiative. It is vulnerable to decapitation if the political will to destroy it existed. This cluster has been mostly eliminated in Malaysia through aggressive government counter-terrorist action but still exists in Indonesia due to internal political reasons. This type of structure may also promote splinter group formation in the future, as has been the case in the Philippines.

The other two clusters constitute the great majority of the global Salafi terrorist social movement. They consist of core Arabs coming out of core Arab countries from the Arabian Peninsula, Jordan and Egypt; and Maghreb Arabs coming out of Tunisia, Algeria, Morocco and their expatriate communities, mostly in France. These clusters organized themselves spontaneously around local charismatic members, often in the vicinity of very radical Salafi mosques. This preferential attachment to the jihad resulted in a small world or cellular structure, which is decentralized with much local initiative and flexibility. As such, it is very robust, resistant against random attacks, such as random arrests of its members or decapitation of its leadership.

This cellular structure provided for rapid diffusion of terrorist innovation through popular social hubs and flexible communication in all directions, rather than slow and vulnerable vertical communications required in strict hierarchical organizations. This communicative flexibility, based on pre-existing social bonds (kinship, friendship and later informal cliques), was a major contributing factor in the successful execution of terrorist operations. These informal communications bypassed the various rules of tradecraft advocated in the terrorist manuals, which reflected a more theoretical orientation to operational security, based on the "need-to-know" principle. This principle implies a hierarchical topology, with strict vertical communication. Such a communicative topology would ensure the failure of any operation because it would flood the vertical links of communication and prevent people in the field from talking to each other to overcome the inevitable obstacles arising in the field during the execution of a terrorist operation. Informal communications among intimates who knew each other, often from birth, and bypassed this security regulation violated this rule of tradecraft. This explains an apparent inconsistency found when comparing the actual execution of global Salafi terrorist operations to policies found in their manuals. The execution of their operations was characterized by very poor tradecraft on the part of the terrorists – leaving behind documents which would immediately identify them, not using aliases but real names, using their personal phones when they knew they could be monitored, and so on. Paradoxically, it is this poor use of tradecraft that made their success possible, especially when the authorities were not paying attention to the threat. In the new post-9/11 environment, this poor tradecraft makes their detection possible and hampers their operation.

After the U.S. intervention in Afghanistan eliminated al Qaeda command and control, this social movement reverted back to its original morphology. Now, its boundaries have become very fuzzy. These new terrorists no longer formally belong to a terrorist organization. They are often a "bunch of guys" inspired by al Qaeda messages on the Internet. There is no fixed number of terrorists. The pool of potential terrorists fluctuates according to local grievances and the world situation. Activated cliques of militant friends swarm together for a specific operation. They do not respond to central command and control anymore, but are self-organizing from the bottom up, fueled by local initiative. Like the Internet, they function very well with little coordination from the top. Gaps in the network don't last long but become opportunities for the most aggressive to step up and fill the voids created by the elimination of the old leadership. While the old leadership has been gradually eliminated through death and capture, a complete new leadership has been reconstituted, different from the old one. Aggressive new leaders, lacking the training and support of their predecessors, conduct more frequent, reckless and hurried operations. Often, the time between conception and final execution of the operation is just weeks, not years as was true before the 9/11 operation. The difficulty of communication between the central staff and these local groups has degraded the ability of the social movement to mount operations with the same degree of sophistication and coordination of 9/11 hijackings and 1998 East African embassies bombings. The wave of future terrorist operations will be similar in scale and execution to the bombings in Saudi Arabia, Casablanca, Istanbul and Madrid.

The distribution of the global Salafi jihad is based on the presence of militant mosques preaching the specific script advocating violence against Western civilians. This script interprets U.S. foreign political action and transforms local grievances into global ones. Groups of friends, who had no or very distant previous connection to the movement, may elect to answer these exhortations for violence and carry out terrorist operations. This makes them very difficult to detect beforehand, for the first indication of their participation in the jihad might very well be the successful execution of their operation. This has been the scenario in Casablanca, Istanbul and Madrid.

The global Salafi jihad is a unique terrorist social movement. Traditionally, terrorist organizations consist of people from country A living in country A and attacking the government of country A. The global Salafi jihad consists of people from country A living in country B and targeting country C. This imparts a very different dynamic to this terrorist social movement as opposed to more traditional ones. One of the major differences is that because the terrorists are completely disconnected from their target, they are not socially embedded in the society they target, as is the case of more traditional terrorist organizations. This embeddedness refers to the rich nexus of social and economic linkage between the terrorists and the society they live in. These multiple bonds act as a limit to the damages the terrorists can bring to their environment. The lack of such bonds frees them from these responsibilities and local concerns. Unrestrained by any responsibility to their target, this free-floating network is free to follow the logic of its abstract ideology and escalate the scale of terror, culminating in the 9/11 operations. This lack of embeddedness in the target society makes possible a strategy of vast devastation and damages against the target, including the use of weapons of mass destruction, which more traditional terrorists would avoid in order not to destroy their own society. This makes the global Salafi jihad especially dangerous to the U.S. and its allies.

New information technology has made the global Salafi jihad possible. Prior to the 1991 Sudanese exile, Osama bin Laden and his lieutenants could not have led this social movement from the remoteness of Afghanistan. By the time he returned in 1996, technology had solved his communication problems. Satellite telephones allowed him to speak extensively with his followers in Yemen, England and Saudi Arabia; facsimiles carried his press releases to his London public relations firm; laptops and e-mail made quick and extensive communication possible. The Internet also had a strong impact on the new more sophisticated recruits by diffusing the violent Salafi message of the jihad, bypassing traditional imams. Since most of these computer-savvy recruits had little prior religious training, they were most vulnerable to the appeal of such sites that encouraged a very aberrant interpretation of Islam and rejected traditional interpretations of it. The more traditional religious teachers simply could not compete with the more sophisticated militant websites, which did not require much knowledge in religion but a great deal of technical knowledge. The egalitarianism of chatrooms on these sites also fostered a feeling of unity with other members, creating a virtual Muslim community on the web, sustaining and encouraging extreme interpretation of the Quran and world events.

The vulnerability of the new electronic devices to interception has given the Internet more prominence in the global Salafi jihad. After the 1998 embassies bombings, bin Laden discovered through a media leak that the U.S. was monitoring his satellite phone conversations. He abandoned its use and communicated with his followers via his lieutenants. The post-9/11 crackdown further eroded his ability to communicate with their subordinates in the field. The old al Qaeda leadership started using Islamist websites on the Internet as indirect means of communication. This allows it to continue to provide general guidance even if it no longer exerts direct command and control over operations. For instance, it appears that the Madrid bombings were inspired by a document anonymously posted on the Internet advocating the use of bombs just before the Spanish election in order to influence the government to withdraw its troops from Iraq. In the future, this trend will continue and the leadership of the global Salafi jihad will rely more and more on the Internet to broadcast its message and to discuss tactics, as is already done in the proliferating virtual magazines. Since it is difficult to detect people who read these postings, identification of future terrorists will become even more difficult.

7 Conclusion

The global Salafi jihad has now become a fuzzy idea-based network, self-organizing from below, inspired by postings on the Internet. It will expand spontaneously from below according to international political developments, without coordination from above, except for general and blind guidance. From a counter-terrorist perspective, such a loose and ill-defined network does not present hard targets for military options. More subtle methods should be used to disrupt the formation of these networks by changing the social conditions promoting them and challenging the ideas encouraging mobilization into them.

For Germany, it is important to realize that a driving factor for the formation of a malignant "bunch of guys" is the experience of exclusion. In a sense, the two main attacks on U.S. soil, the failed Millennial Plot and the 9/11/01 operations, are a result of failed integration of the Muslim community in Western Europe. U.S. prominence in the world and U.S. foreign policy transform local grievances into global ones, directed at the U.S. Now, after 9/11, the U.S. has hardened its borders and increased its vigilance against Islamist terrorism and made it more difficult for the global Salafi network to strike on U.S. soil. This again shifts the threat from the continental U.S. to softer targets in Europe and elsewhere. 3/11s and not 9/11s are the threat of the future.

Fighting such a network requires the U.S. to address the ideology uniting this social movement. This is something that the American public is loath to do, as it believes in transparency, namely that the facts speak for themselves. Any attempt to engage in a war of ideas raises the specter of disinformation or propaganda. But the U.S. cannot afford to concede this ideological war, waged on the battlefield of interpretations, to the militant Islamists. It needs to develop a coherent and comprehensive strategy to deal with this new and unique threat.

This involves discrediting the legitimacy of the leaders and the ideology behind the global Salafi jihad and replacing it with an inspiring vision of a just and fair partnership with Islam. Unfortunately, the U.S. is poorly set up to wage such a war. Our free media broadcasts statements targeted for domestic consumption, which angers international audiences, for in politics the domestic agenda will always trump foreign concerns. Such an ideological war would also require the U.S. to regain the credibility that it has lost in the Muslim world in the past four years because of its lack of evenhandedness in the Israeli-Palestinian problem, its invasion of Iraq on false premises, and its support of repressive Muslim regimes. U.S. words, public diplomacy, would need to be matched with deeds to regain this lost trust and credibility. Otherwise, any statement, no matter how laudable, would simply be dismissed as hypocritical and further encourage the spread of the global Salafi jihad.

References

[1] Bin Laden, Osama, 1996, *Declaration of War against the Americans Occupying the Land of the Two Holy Places.* Published in al-Quds al-Arabi (London) on August 23, and found at http://www.pbs.org/newshour/terrrism/international/fatwa_1996.html.

[2] Bin Laden, Osama, et al., 1998, *Jihad Against Jews and Crusaders*, dated February 23, and found at www.fas.org/irp/world/para/docs/980223-fatwa.htm.

[3] Faraj, Muhammad Abd al-Salam, 1986, Al-Faridah al Ghaibah, in Johannes Jansen, *The Neglected Duty: The Creed of Sadat's Assassins and Islamic Resurgence in the Middle East*, New York: Macmillan, 159-234.

[4] Qutb, Sayyid, n.d., *Milestones*, Cedar Rapids, Iowa: Mother Mosque Foundation.

[5] Sageman, Marc, 2004, *Understanding Terror Networks*, Philadelphia: University of Pennsylvania Press.

[6] Silke, Andrew, 1998, "Cheshire-Cat Logic: The Recurring Theme of Terrorist Abnormality in Psychological Research," *Psychology, Crime and Law*, 4: 51-69.

[7] Silke, Andrew, ed., 2003, *Terrorists, Victims and Society: Psychological Perspectives on Terrorism and its Consequences*, Chichester, England: John Wiley & Sons.

The Power Resources of al-Qaeda and its Affiliates

Katharina von Knop

Leopold-Franzens-Universität Innsbruck
Institut für Politikwissenschaft
K.von-Knop@web.de

1 Introduction: Current Situation

No terrorist organization has been persecuted as capital-intensively, multilaterally and on such a high scale as al-Qaeda after 9/11, but today the frequency, deadliness and the internationality of these attacks are greater than at any other time in the history of this movement. In the past three years, there has been an increase in attacks on soft targets in countries with a large Muslim population: for example the bombings in Djierba, Tunesia (April 2002); Bali, Indonesia (October 2002); Mombassa, Kenia (November 2002); Casablanca, Morocco (May 2003); Riyadh, Saudi Arabia (May and November 2003); Jakarta, Indonesia (August 2003); Istanbul; Turkey (November 2003); Taba, Egypt (October 2004); Jedda, Saudi Arabia (December 2004). In many of those attacks Muslim civilians, among them women and children, were the primary victims. The first key question to be answered is what al-Qaeda stands for today. According to Marc Sageman, al-Qaeda is a formal organization and a global social movement at war with the US.

In fact al-Qaeda has lost important parts of its middle and upper leadership as well as of its operative powers. Numerous members of the Islamist terrorist group were killed or captured in the Afghan campaign. Painstaking investigative work led to some major arrests. International cooperation enabled antiterror agents to zero in on Abu Zubaydah, bin Laden's chief of operations, who was arrested in Pakistan in March 2002. Another one of the key planners of 9/11, Ramzi bin al-Shib, was seized in Pakistan in September of the same year. Also in 2002 British authorities arrested Abu Qatada, who was suspected of playing a major logistical role for al-Qaeda in Europe. Rahim al-Nashiri ended up in US custody in 2002. The Yemeni was not only a top financier for al-Qaeda, but he allegedly plotted suicide attacks in the Strait of Gibraltar. One of the biggest catches was Khalid Shayk Muhammed, the mastermind of the 9/11 attacks. Pakistani authorities arrested him in Rawalpindi in March 2003. Just a month later, the Pakistanis were also able to arrest Tawfiq bin Attash. He reportedly served as bin Laden's "personal intermediary," overseeing the October 2000 bombing of the USS Cole in Aden. The leader of the Saudi cell of al-Qaeda, Abdul Aziz al-Muqrin, died in a clash with the police in June that year. Just a month later, Mohammed Naeem Noor Kahn, who reportedly facilitated communication between al-Qaeda's leaders and subordinates, was arrested in Pakistan. Information derived from Khan himself led to more arrests in Pakistan, Britain and the United Arab Emirates. It was also possible to neutralize essential infrastructures like weapon arsenals, training camps and financial resources.

The US Treasury Department alone has seized 140 million US$ in funds belonging to al-Qaeda. Saudi Arabia has cracked down on the al-Haramain Foundation, a locally based charity considered one of al-Qaedas leading financial sponsors. But Islamist terrorist groups have proved adaptable. Al-Qaeda has trimmed back its own expenses, as by outsourcing operations to smaller local groups. The erosion of funding has hurt, but not pre-empted new terrorist attacks. The attacks carried out during the last three years have themselves been low-budget affairs. Suicide belts are not costly items, and the most valuable resource for a suicide attack, the terrorist, is not hard to recruit. When we examine the most recent attacks, we find that those who carried them out never spent time in a training camp; they were all volunteers. They were people with normal jobs, not full-time terrorists whose life was funded by an organization. At 10,000 US$, even the attack on Madrid commuter trains, in which backpacks filled with explosives were remotely detonated, was a relatively low-budget affair. Although the bombings were apparently inspired by al-Qaeda, the costs were borne by the Moroccan Islamic Combat Group.

On the other hand, al-Qaeda has developed new ways to obtain money. To an increased degree, al-Qaeda and its affiliates derive funding from various kinds of smuggling: drugs, guns, cigarettes and human trafficking. The movement is using cash, about 28 million US$ from the Afghanistan heroin market, to finance Osama bin Laden's life somewhere in the border area between Afghanistan and Pakistan.

A recently published Canadian intelligence report says that al-Qaeda is interested in acquiring nuclear capabilities in order to expand its attack arsenal.[1] On 23 November an unclassified CIA report said that the threat of terrorists using CBRN materials remained high. Many of the 33 designated foreign terrorist or-

---

[1] Canadian Intelligence Resource Centre, http://circjmellon.com/agencies/csis/ (accessed January 05, 2005).

ganizations and other non-state actors world-wide have expressed interest in using CBRN; however, most attacks will probably be small-scale, incorporating improvised delivery means and easily produced or obtained chemicals, toxins or radiological substances. Documents and equipment recovered from al-Qaeda facilities in Afghanistan show that al-Qaeda had conducted research on biological agents. The CIA believes that al-Qaeda's biological weapons program is primarily focused on anthrax for mass casualty attacks, although the group most likely will pursue opportunities to produce and use other biological agents in smaller-scale attacks. Although terrorist groups will probably continue to favor long-proven conventional tactics, such as bombings, shootings and kidnappings, the arrest of ricin plotters in London in January 2003 indicated that international mujahideen terrorists were actively plotting to conduct chemical and biological attacks.[2]

In mid October 2003, Spanish authorities dismantled an Algerian Salafist terrorist cell identified as part of al-Qaeda's European network with plans to blow up the national court in Madrid. The role of the Algerian Islamists in both the attacks on March 11th and the National Court terrorist planning suggests that Spain has become a new locus of operations for North African-based al-Qaeda terrorism. Algeria's two principal Salafist groups, which form part of al-Qaeda's North African network, are the Armed Islamic Group, known by its French acronym GIA, and a GIA off-shoot, the Salafist Group for Preaching and Combat (GSPC). The alignment of Algerian and other North African Salafist groups to al-Qaedas terrorist network in Spain and elsewhere in Europe represents a nexus of terrorist resources that will serve to strengthen al-Qaedas reach into the continent.[3]

The key geographic havens of al-Qaeda and its affiliates are the Caucasus region, including Chechnya as well as Iraq and South-East Asia. "The Caucasus is a training zone that has partially replaced Afghanistan," said Judge Jean-Louis Bruguiere, chief of the French antiterrorism unit, who has been at the forefront of the fight against terrorism for 20 years. With the Afghan territory out of Islamists' control after the US-led ousting of the Taliban in late 2001, Chechnya – which Bruguiere called "a jihad land" – and other parts of the Caucasus region

---

[2] CIA unclassified report: Unclassified Report to Congress on the Acquisition of Technology Relating to Weapons of Mass Destruction and advanced Conventional Munitions, 1 July-31 December 2003; Section Chemical, Biological, Radiological, and Nuclear Terrorism. http://www.cia.gov/cia/reports/721_reports/july_dec2003.htm (accessed January 04, 2005).

[3] Terrorism Monitor, Jamestown Foundation, "Algerian Salafists and the New Face of Terrorism in Spain," Vol. 2, No. 21, November 04. 2004. http://www.jamestown.org/publications_details.php?volume_id=3131&article_id=2368801 (accessed January 05, 2005).

"have taken on an enormous importance. It is a true international problem because the majority of the Chechen cause has been hijacked by al-Qaeda."[4]

Several thousands of surface-to-air missiles are missing in Iraq. Some US analysts figure that as many as 4,000 of those missiles, which at one time were under the control of Saddam Hussein's government, remain unaccounted for. That would raise the number of such missiles outside government hands world-wide to about 6,000. These new estimates are based on analysis done by the DIA and with the proliferation section of the CIA. US officials fear that the shoulder-launched missiles were among the items carried off by groups willing to sell them to terrorist organizations on the black market. Western intelligence officials have repeatedly warned of the desire of al-Qaeda to acquire the missiles for use against American and other airlines. The State Department estimated in 2003 that more than 40 aircraft have been struck by portable missiles since the 1970s, causing at least 24 crashes and more than 600 deaths world-wide.[5] Of course the US military has initiated a buy-back program for surface-to-air missiles in August 2003, but is somebody who seeks death to become a Shahid interested in 500 US$?

Judge Jean-Louis Bruguiere said that radical Islamic cells in Europe are using an ingenious way to finance terrorist networks that is virtually impossible to trace: they withdraw hundreds of thousands of dollars a month from ATMs with fake credit cards. The militant financing networks are small, scattered around the world and represent millions of dollars in fundraising for terrorists. The Islamic European networks finance themselves primarily through microfinancing systems. The technique appears to be similar to a sophisticated electronic scam that involved ATMs in Britain in March. There, police found cloning devices attached to the machines. The device, which is attached to the card slot of the machine, works by recording the details on the magnetic stripe of the card as it passes through. In the case of the Islamic militant cells, Bruguiere said they also purchase electronic equipment and resell it to help finance "large operations". In March 2004, France launched a judicial investigation after a former employee with a security company, Hassan Baouchi, claimed that he had been robbed of one million € which should have been used to refill ATMs. French authorities suspected the cash went into fund activities by the Moroccan Islamic Fighting

---

[4] Scheherezade Faramarzi, "Terrorists Using ATM Scheme to Fund Networks: French Judge Says Caucasus is Al-Qaeda Training Ground," in: Associated Press, December 10, 2004.

[5] Dana Priest and Bradley Graham, "Missing Antiaircraft Missiles Alarm Aids," in: *Washington Post*, November 07, 2004.

Group, which is blamed for the bombings in Casablanca. Bruguiere said that the problem is that judges who specialize in financial crimes are trained only in marcofinancing investigations – i.e. large sums involving banks. Therefore, little attention has been paid to this "fraudulent use of bank cards."[6]

The three years elapsed since the 9/11 attacks have made Osama bin Laden the most wanted man in the world, and he still remains much more than just an iconic figure-head of Islamic militancy. Today he sits in a hiding-place in the Hindu Kush mountain range on the Pakistani side of the Afghan-Pakistan border, well-protected and well-financed by a network of Pakistani tribesmen and foreign militants who operate in the impoverished border region. This structure enables him to maintain communication with major figures in his network and to transfer his video- and audiotapes to Al Jazeera. Pakistan does not permit American military and intelligence forces in Afghanistan to cross the border to catch bin Laden and his supporters. This prohibition on cross-border "hot pursuit" makes it relatively easy for Taliban and al-Qaeda fighters to initiate attacks on American bases in Afghanistan, and then quickly escape to the safety of Pakistan. The air operations with unmanned Predator drones conducted by the United States over Pakistan are authorized, but only with approval from the Pakistani military chain of command, which frequently leads to costly delays.

The power resources of al-Qaeda and its affiliates must have a very special quality, because they enable the movement to maintain great strength and redundancy even after three years of intense international pursuit.

When we talk about power resources we are referring to weapons, recruitment centres and bank accounts. But power is not something which exists in a vacuum. The power of one actor comes into being through its relationship with another actor. So what I am offering here is a different and very fruitful perspective to identify the power resources of this movement. Robert Keohane's theory of institutionalism – or, to be more precise, the theory of interdependence – provides us with a very fruitful perspective for finding the answer that we are looking for, because it helps us to analyze the relationship between this terrorist movement and the target states. This analysis is important, because power comes into being in the interaction between these two actors. With this perspective, we will be able to get a better understanding of the origins of the terrorist threat, and this will help us in developing better long-term strategies to counter terrorism more effectively.

---

[6] Scheherezade Faramarzi, "Terrorists Using ATM Scheme to Fund Networks: French Judge Says Caucasus is Al-Qaeda Training Ground," in: Associated Press, December 10, 2004.

So this paper has three themes: first, the theory of interdependence by Robert Keohane provides a fruitful framework to analyze the relationship between the target states and al-Qaeda with its affiliates. Second, the globalization of terrorism can be analyzed by exploring patterns of asymmetrical interdependences and their implications of power. Third, by identifying asymmetries in vulnerability interdependences it is possible to develop a better understanding of terrorism and in consequence this helps us to develop successful counter- and antiterrorism measures.

My argument is, following the theoretical framework of Robert Keohane, that the power of al-Qaeda does not come out of a suicide belt, but rather from asymmetries in vulnerability interdependences. With this approach I will identify seven asymmetries in vulnerability interdependences of information, belief, organizational structure, gender, learning, time and communication.

The present article starts with a description of the current situation. After a short explanation of the theoretical framework, the seven asymmetries in vulnerability interdependence will be identified. I will close this paper with some conclusions.

2   The Theory of Robert Keohane

It is surprising that the theory of interdependence by Robert Keohane,[7] which belongs to the theories of the international relations, could open an important window to understanding the most security-relevant threat of this century. In the ideal case of this theory, the international relations are complex interdependent. States and non-governmental actors are rational thinkers and the main actors in the international system. They are able to cooperate with each other on a basis of a cost-benefit analysis to guarantee their key goals: power, security and wealth.

A key reason for al-Qaeda's success is its strong ability to cooperate with other like-minded groups or states, such as Iran. The supporting tribal members and the militants of bin Laden may also have received help from officers in Pakistan's Inter-Services Intelligence, the country's powerful intelligence agency. The agency was the hidden power behind the Taliban's rise to power in Afghanistan and was close to al-Qaeda. In the past, Pakistani civilian security and police officials have complained that intelligence agency personnel have sometimes

---

[7] Robert O. Keohane, *After Hegemony, Cooperation and Discord in the World Political Economy*, Princeton, New Jersey, 1984.

interfered with their efforts to arrest al-Qaeda members.[8] It is this kind of cooperation that makes the threat against General Peervez Musharraf credible.

A variety of different kinds of actors, including states and non-states, develop transnational interactions. These interactions have features such as dependence and interdependence.

> In common parlance, dependence means an actor's being is determined or significantly affected by external forces. Interdependence means mutual dependence. Interdependence in world politics refers to situations characterized by reciprocal effects among countries or among actors of different countries.[9]

The networks of interdependence of al-Qaeda and its affiliates, involving transmission of informal violence, have now taken a genuinely global form.

This approach considers the political logic of actions in an increasingly interdependent international system from the perspective of observing asymmetries. "In our analysis, interdependence is frequently asymmetrical and highly political: indeed asymmetries in interdependences generate power resources for states, as well as for non-state actors,"[10] like al-Qaeda. Asymmetrical interdependences between the actors could lead to variable costs and benefits which induce variable effects. These effects could in turn lead to changes in particular power positions. Actors are affected by variances inside interdependent relations.[11] These costs are measured with the terms sensitivity and vulnerability:

> Sensitivity is the liability to costly effects imposed from outside before policies are altered to try to change the situation. [...] Vulnerability can be defined as an actor's liability to suffer costs imposed by external events even after policies have been altered.[12]

For our analysis, the term vulnerability is important because it identifies costs that still persist even after policies have been altered to reduce these costs.

---

[8] James Risen and David Rohde, "Intelligence: A Hostile Land Foils the Quest for Bin Laden," in: *New York Times*, December 13, 2004.
[9] Robert O. Keohane and Joseph S. Nye, *Power and Interdependence*, World Politics in Transition, Boston, 1977, 8.
[10] Robert O. Keohane, "Introduction: From Interdependence and Institutions to Globalization and Governance," in: *Power and Governance in a Partially Globalized World*, London, 2002, 2.
[11] Robert O. Keohane and Joseph S. Nye, *Power and Interdependence*, 2nd edition, Boston, 1989, 11.
[12] Ibid., 13.

In short, power does not simply come out of a suicide belt, but from asymmetries in vulnerability interdependences, since under these conditions power is the result of making others do what they would not do under different circumstances. Power is the ability to influence the results of relationships.

The networks of interdependence along which power can travel are multiple, and they do not cancel each other out. "Even a state that is overwhelmingly powerful on many dimensions can be highly vulnerable on others. We learned this lesson in the 1970s with respect to oil power; we are relearning it now with respect to terrorism."[13] Our mistake has been rather our failure to understand that the most powerful state that has ever existed on this planet could be vulnerable to a relatively small band of terrorists due to patterns of asymmetrical interdependences. The power is so strong that it could influence the outcome of elections, as we saw in Spain.

Until today and even after years and billions of US dollars of investments and intense legal developments, the target countries have not been able to reduce or neutralize the vulnerability of terrorist attacks or threats. Analyzing the relationship between the target states and al-Qaeda with this approach, seven asymmetries in vulnerability interdependences can be identified: information, belief, structure of organization, gender, time, learning and communication.

3 Asymmetry in the Vulnerability

3.1 Interdependence of Information

It seems paradoxical that information societies such as the ones of the contemporary United States and the European Union would be at an informational disadvantage when dealing with networks of individuals whose communication seems to occur largely through hand-written messages, face-to-face contacts and e-mails. However, an information society is also an open society. Potential terrorists always have good information about their targets, whereas the United States prior to 9/11 had poor information about the identity and location of terrorist networks. Until today it has been extremely challenging to follow the information flow of al-Qaeda and its affiliates and to prevent a terrorist attack. For example, the Royal Canadian Mounted Police (RCMP) has warned its investigators to be on the look-out for cleverly disguised messages embedded in al-Qaeda files which the police seize from terrorism suspects. An internal

---

[13] Robert O. Keohane, "The globalization of informal violence, theories of world politics, and the 'liberalism of fear'," in: *Power and Governance in a partially Globalized World*, London, 2002, 277.

report obtained by the Canadian Press gives credence to the long-rumored possibility that Osama bin Laden's terrorist network and other extremist groups are using steganography to hide the existence of sensitive communications. Simple computer-assisted steganography helps to apply such traditional methods in an electronic environment, the report notes. The messages may also be scrambled using cryptography to prevent them from falling into the wrong hands. The RCMP seems especially concerned, however, about digital steganography – the use of special computer programs to embed messages. "There now exist nearly two hundred software packages which perform digital steganography," the report says, but the success rate of tools designed to detect the use of this technology is limited.[14]

Hunting bin Laden, the CIA established a series of small, covert bases in the rugged mountain frontier of north-west Pakistan in late 2003. However, during all the time the bases were activated the CIA officers stationed there have been strictly supervised by Pakistani officials, who have limited their ability to operate and have escorted them wherever they travel in the Pakistani border region.[15] Considering the supposed connection of the al-Qaeda supporters to the Pakistani intelligence service, it has been virtually impossible for the Americans to gather intelligence effectively. Electronic surveillance of the border region by the National Security Agency (NSA) has proved frustrating. Bin Laden is believed to avoid using any electronic devices that could be monitored, and probably communicates only through trusted couriers. Without cell phone towers along the frontier, satellite pones and push-to-talk radios are widely used – often by drug smugglers –, making it difficult to zero in on al-Qaeda operatives who use the same kind of equipment. Many examples can be identified in which the information flow from the terrorists is blocked by institutional, human and technical shortcomings.

Equally important, the United States was unable to coherently process the information that its various agencies and institutions had gathered before 9/11. The same applies to the Madrid attacks. The Spanish intelligence agency was able to infiltrate the relevant cell, but it was impossible to prevent the attacks, in which 191 human beings lost their lives. Until today it has only been possible to achieve tactical successes with the allocation of security-relevant resources. Surely we cannot measure how many terrorist attacks have been prevented. We

---

[14] Jim Bronskill, "RCMP Suspect Al-Qaeda Messages," in: Canadian Press, CNews/Canoe, December 09, 2004, http://cnews.canoe.ca (accessed January 04, 2005).

[15] James Risen and David Rohde, "Intelligence: A Hostile Land Foils the Quest for Bin Laden," in: *The New York Times*, December 13, 2004.

can only observe that the network still carries out attacks, as for example in Jeddah in December 2004. After more than three years of intense institutional, human and technical developments, the asymmetry in the sensitivity interdependence of information, observed directly after the 9/11 attacks, continues to exist. This sensitivity has become a vulnerability, since we remain vulnerable in spite of intense of broad developments in suffering the costs of a deficit of terrorism-related information. Clearly, this is a vulnerability that must be addressed.

3.2 Interdependence of Belief

In order to identify an asymmetry in the vulnerability interdependence of belief, it is necessary to take a look at the ideology of al-Qaeda and its affiliates. The broadly-based ideology of al-Qaeda has its roots in the Egyptian Salafi jihad, and today it is articulated in the global Salafi jihad.

> The Salafi strategy is based on the following diagnosis: Islam became decadent because it strayed from the righteous path. The strength of the original and righteous umma flowed from its faith and its practices, for they were pleasing to God. Recapturing the glory and grandeur of the Golden Age requires a return to the authentic faith and practise of the ancient ones, namely the Prophet Mohammed and his companion.[16]

The term *jihad* has often been translated as "Holy War," a concept coined in Europe in the 11th century in reference to the Crusades. In the Middle East, the term *harb* and not *jihad* is used to describe wars. The word *jihad* is derived from *jahada*, which means "to make a substantial effort." *Jihad* has been defined in the Arabic dictionary as " to strive to attain something one loves" or "to save oneself from something one dislikes." There are many different interpretations of the concept of jihad, and none of these have found an all-embracing acceptance. However, the obligation of jihad for every Muslim has been clearly substantiated in the Quran, Sunnah and by the consensus of the umma. There are four ways for believers to fulfill a jihad: by the heart, the tongue, the hand and the sword. The one who dies in the battle against the infidels becomes a martyr, a Shahid, and he is guaranteed a place in paradise as well as certain privileges. Muslim law has divided the world into two entities, *dar al-islam*, the land of Islam, and *dar al-harb*, the land of war. The enemies of Islam are divided into two groups, the peoples of the book, *ahl ul-kitab*, and the pagans, *kafirun*. The first group, defined as Jews, Christians, Zoroastrians and Mandeans, only

---

[16] Marc Sageman, *Understanding Terror Networks*, Philadelphia, 2004, 4.

need to submit to an Islamic ruler, and live in peace with other Muslims to end the situation where jihad is the imperative.

For the purpose of this article, it should suffice to explain two different interpretations of the concept of jihad: the defensive and the offensive jihad against the *kufar*, the unbelievers. Defensive jihad implies *fard 'ayn*, an individual obligation for every Muslim to fight if the *kufar* attack the Muslims and force them into a defensive position. Such attacks are: when the unbelievers attack a country or city belonging to the Muslims, when they gain control of a Muslim country or when the unbelievers take Muslim captives. Additional attacks include: when a Muslim woman is held by the *kufar* and ensuring her freedom is the collective duty of the whole Muslim *ummah* as well as when the Imman orders the Muslims to wage jihad or when *kufar* and Muslims face each other on the battlefield.[17] In contrast, offensive jihad comes into being when the Muslims launch an offensive attack against the *kufar* on their territory. Offensive jihad is *fard kifaya*, a collective duty to bring the *kufar* and their territory under Islamic rule.

In Feburary 1998 Osama bin Laden published his fatwa "World Islamic Front against Jews and Crusaders" in the Arabic newspaper *al-Quds al Arabi* in London. Central to the creation of the ideology of al-Qaeda was bin Laden's declaration of "War against the Americans Occupying the Land of the Two Holy Places; Expel the *Mushrikeen* (infidels) from the Arabian Peninsula." In this declaration, bin Laden proclaims defensive jihad against the United States, the crusaders and the Zionists occupying the land of the two holy places and the route of the Apostle to the Furthest Mosque (Al Aqsa Mosque). "No other duty after belief is more important than the duty of jihad." Another fatwa, "Jihad against Jews and Crusaders," which bin Laden published in February 1998, added the concept of the offensive jihad to the previous ideology of the defensive jihad. The global Salafi jihad now carried the fight to the "far enemy" (the United States and the West in general) on its own territory or in third-country territory. The justification for this new type of jihad was that the United States' "occupation of Saudi Arabia, support for Israel, and the killing of Iraqi children was a clear declaration of war on Allah, his Messenger, and Muslims."[18]

As a result of the international campaign against al-Qaeda and the intense propaganda conducted over the Internet, smaller local groups were founded or declared their affiliation with al-Qaeda. Having in mind that not all of these groups have declared their connection with bin Laden, they share and operate under the broad-based ideology of the global Salafy jihad. The goal is to create

---

[17] *The Jihad Fixation*, Delhi, 2001, 22.
[18] Marc Sageman, *Understanding Terror Networks*, Philadelphia, 2004, 19.

an Islamic state which follows the pure Islam defined by the ideology of Salafi interpretation of the Quran and certain Fatwas.

In the course of relatively few years, the ideology of the global Salafi jihad has burgeoned from a low-key movement, seeking to oust corrupt regimes in the Muslim world, to a global phenomenon that seeks to eradicate Western influence from that world. The phenomenon today is not restricted to a particular group; it is rather a broad ideological movement to which many disparate groups – separated by geography, individual motivations and even immediate political goals – belong. The movement, which has been propelled by a number of events during the course of the past half-century, is now being driven forward by three factors. These are the decentralization of al-Qaeda, the proliferation of the ideology and the inability of the western world to use soft power as a long-term strategy. Self-motivation and a certain degree of autonomy are the key success factors of al-Qaeda. The organization has always been a relatively small one in comparison to the size of the movement it sought to inspire. Many of the training camps which al-Qaeda ran in Afghanistan following the Soviet war served, importantly, as a kind of ideological exchange program – a way of exporting the philosophy to the corners of the world. To this day, the collective experience of these camps remains a strong inspiration of the movement. In the online journals and printed pamphlets there are more ideological discourses than military essays, reflecting the constant need to justify acts with reference to their religious propriety. The principal Web-based journals *Sawat al-Jihad* (The Voice of Jihad) and *Mu'askar al-Battar* (The al-Battar military camp) illustrate this well. The first is almost exclusively doctrinal, while the second interweaves large doses of doctrine, quotes from the Quran and the Prophet's Hadith into the military instructions. Religious propriety is clearly a preoccupation. However, in the light of the recent events, this material may become scarcer. The number of jihadist scholars has been declining steadily. One important author, Al-'Ayyiri, was killed in 2003 as a result of a clash with Saudi security forces. There have also been high-profile recantations broadcast on Saudi television following the bombings in Riyadh on 12 May 2004 and the arrest of the high-ranking ideologues Shaykh Ahmad al-Khudayr, Shaykh Nasser al-Fahd and Shaykh Ahmad al-Khalidi. Shaykh al-Khudayr publicly distanced himself from all his previous and highly popular jihadist fatwas that supported the struggle against the authorities.[19] Shaykh

---

[19] Stephen Ulph, "Al-Qaeda's Ideological Hemorrhage," in: *Terrorism Focus*, The Jamestown Foundation, Vol. 1, Issue 2, August 20, 2004. http://jamestown.org/publications_details.php?volume_id=403&issue_id=3049&article_id=2368409 (accessed January 06, 2005).

Isa al-Áwshan, the author of many essays of al-Qaeda ideological literature, was killed in July 2004.[20]

Concluding, the robbing of the movement of its most important ideologues is an attack on what is essentially the movement's Achilles' heel. Military minds and willing volunteers step up to plate easily, but doctrinally trained and accepted leaders are considerably more difficult to replace.

The target countries do not share this kind of belief, and the populations have no experience with suicide attacks carried out by their own peoples for a transcendental goal in which civilians are the primary victims. Neither volunteering for suicide missions nor deliberately targeting civilians is consistent with the secular beliefs widely shared in the societies attacked by al-Qaeda. In different times and in different cultures, the tradition of suicide attacks has been argued with an *ad majorem dei gloriam*, but in contrast to these cases, the Islam-based method caused international crisis. Contrary to other suicide campaigns like the one carried out by the LTTE in Sri Lanka, which are responsible for the majority of suicide attacks in the last 20 years, the Salafi-based strategy asserts its claim to absoluteness of their ideology. This claim to absoluteness, which is necessary for its global reach, signifies in consequence the domination of the world. The stalwarts of this ideology have already reached a certain kind of world domination by the credible communication that anyone could be a victim of a suicide attack anywhere. Clearly, the suicidal nature of the attacks carried out by al-Qaeda and its affiliates made them more difficult to prevent and magnifies their potential for destructive power. Unlike the members of the global Salafi jihad, the target societies believe in the monopoly of executive power and its exclusive right to kill other people. However, this exclusive right has no impact on somebody who is seeking death. Terrorists are immune to this monopoly of power. That is the second source of power of al-Qaeda and its affiliates: namely the asymmetry in the vulnerability interdependence of belief. On both sides, the belief is not negotiable. The terrorists claim absoluteness for their ideology, and the states claim absoluteness for their institutional structure and power. Otherwise the states would negate the right of their existence and the right to be the biggest elements of the structure of the international system.

---

[20] Shaykh al-Áwshan's death was confirmed in a press release in *Sawat al Jihad*, Vol. 22, and is the subject of a "Conversation in Poetry" on page 44 in the same issue.

3.3 Interdependence of Organizational Structure

The organizational structure of the global Salafi Jihad shows substantial differences in comparison to the hierarchical institutional organization of national executive powers.

Several different stages of development can be identified in the evolution of this movement. At the beginning, the structure in Afghanistan could be described as a segmented, ideologically integrated network (SPIN). At that time, al-Qaeda's structure was already characterized by relatively flat hierarchies, decentralization, delegation of decision making authority and loose lateral ties between dispersed groups and individuals. Applying the network analyzes of John Arquilla and David Ronfeldt[21], the structure as it was during planning phases of the 9/11 attacks can generally be described as a hub or star network, whereas the entire structure of the cells represented a multiple hub network. After the military interventions in Afghanistan – the security measures carried out by many countries and the recruiting of affiliated groups and individuals – the structure changed to a complex polycentric multilevel system.

What we are confronted with today is what Marc Sageman defines as the global Salafi jihad.

> The global Salafi jihad is not a specific organization, but a social movement consisting of a set of more or less formal organizations, linked in patterns of interaction ranging from the fairly centralized (the East Africa embassy bombing) to the more decentralized (the two millennial plots) and with various degrees of cooperation (the Egyptian Islamic Jihad versus the Egyptian Islamic Group), resulting in more or less connected terrorists operations.[22]

What has been significant is the emergence of more regional and quasi-interdependent groups that act with little or no encouragement from al-Qaeda "prime" groups. Among them Jemaah Islamiyah in Southeast Asia, the semi-independent al-Qaeda cell in Saudi Arabia and even al-Zarqawi's virtually independent Jamaat al Taweed wa al Jihad (Monotheism and Fighting Group) in Iraq, which has renamed itself "Tandheem al-Qaeda fi Bilad al Rafidain" (Al-Qaeda Organization in the Land of the Two Rivers). We can identify two reasons of this dramatic change in organizational structure. First, al-Qaeda and its affiliates have been prosecuted multilaterally on a global scale for three years, and by success-

---

[21] John Arquilla and David Ronfeldt (ed.), *Networks and Netwars: The Future of Terror, Crime and Militancy*, RAND Cooperation, Santa Monica, 2001.

[22] Marc Sageman, *Understanding Terror Networks*, Philadelphia, 2004, 137.

fully providing its broad-based ideology world-wide, there is no more need for a strong command and control structure. Second, the organization switched to a movement which generates its strength form the impulses of the ongoing attacks, the military interventions in Iraq and the periodical surfacing of video- and audiotapes carrying messages of bin Laden and al-Zawahiri. Today, al-Qaeda is just a small organization within a larger social movement.

To understand the mode of operation of this movement the metaphor of the Orpheus Orchestra is very useful. Some highly successful organizations have adopted a pragmatic approach when they found that the role of the boss costs too much in team performance. That is, in some situations, the maintenance of the boss is too expensive by either draining the resources of the group as a whole or impeding the creativity within the team, even unintentionally. The Orpheus orchestra plays the most complicated music without a leader or a permanent hierarchical organization structure. Their recording legacy consists of nearly 70 albums. Their extensive catalog for Deutsche Grammophon includes Baroque masterworks of Händel, Corelli and Vivaldi, Haydn symphonies, Mozart symphonies and serenades, the complete Mozart wind concerti with Orpheus members as soloists and Romantic works by Dvorak, Grieg and Tchaikovsky.

The music produced by the Orpheus Orchestra method is analogous to the attacks carried out by global Salafi cells. The musicians play roles similar to those of the operatives of the terrorism movement. Both act without a personalized leadership in their respective concerts. Like Orpheus, al-Qaeda is a self-governing organization that is never static. Central to its distinctive personality is the Orpheus' unique practice of sharing and rotating leadership roles. Rather than an autocratic or charismatic conductor who determines the overall conception of a work and then dictates how each musician should perform the individual tasks, the Orpheus team generally selects a different "core group" for each piece of music, and the core group as a team works out the details of the piece – all without a leader. The 9/11 attacks show quite obviously the similarity between the methods of the Orpheus Orchestra and al-Qaeda. The core group, which was responsible for working out the details of the piece, was the Hamburg group. Analyzing the attacks carried out by al-Qaeda and its affiliates after the military interventions in Afghanistan, the organization was forced to develop its operative structure because of the loss of central operatives and infrastructure. By spreading its ideology over the Internet, the organizational structure became more flat and decentralized. Each time the members of the Orchestra intend to perform a piece, they select the concert-master and the principal players for each section. These players constitute the core group, whose role is to form the initial concept of the piece and to shape the rehearsal process. Verbal communication is rarely needed. For al-Qaeda, using the same method means that for each piece/attack there is one master, who is supported by the relevant operatives of at least one cell. For instance, Mohammed Atta was as the tactical commander of the 9/11 operation and also the head of the Hamburg group, whereas the mastermind of the operation was Khalid Shaykh Mohammed. The cells rarely communicate with each other, yet when their time of action comes they are able to play a perfectly choreographed concert. Al-Qaeda leaders may directly authorize specific attacks, as happened with the Bali bombing and the attacks on housing compounds in Riyadh. But in other attacks, local terror groups have acted relatively independently, as e.g. in Casablanca in May 2003. When a bomb goes off today, it does not matter if it was an al-Qaeda affiliate or al-Qaeda itself. Obviously the affiliated groups operate fairly locally and autonomously now, but they are still influenced by bin Laden's rhetoric. During the military interventions in Iraq, the US homeland adversary system was raised to the second highest terror warning level, but not a single attack took place. Without any direct communication flow, two clusters decided without direct communication flow that the perfect time to gain the highest public attention would be after the military interventions. The bombings happened on 12 May in Riadh and 16 May in Casablanca, two weeks after George W. Bush had declared the end of the military intervention.

Online magazines like *Mus'askar al Battar*, *Sawat al Jihad* and *al-Kansaah* communicate what work should be "played" right now. The reader of these online periodicals can obtain fighting strategies, knowledge of weapons, ideological advice as well as instructions on how to carry out attacks. The whole March 2004 issue of *Mus'askar al Battar* was on terrorism in large cities and how to select targets inside them; it also expounded the pros and cons of attacks on economic and political targets. The magazine stated explicitly that the target should be Jewish and Christian assets in Muslim Countries. Volume 10, published in May 2004, deals mainly with kidnapping. Various types of kidnapping are discussed, including secret and public kidnapping. The issue discusses hostage negotiations as well as how to implement the kidnapping operation. *Mus'askar al Battar* defines the goal of kidnapping operations as "putting the government in a difficult situation that will create a political embarrassment between the government and the countries of the detainees." It is easy to identify a strong correlation between the contents of these issues and the tactics used in Iraq during the time they were published.

Individual members of Orpheus have received recognition for solo performances, chamber music and orchestral performances. Each of them brings a diversity of musical experience to the orchestra, which constantly enriches and nurtures the musical growth of the ensemble, causing it to play better and better. Using the profiles made by Marc Sageman, it is easy to figure out that each of the global Salafi terrorists has certain skills that are useful for a specific kind of attack. For example, the members of the Hamburg group were not selected because of the religious knowledge. "The Hamburg group shared the anti-US fervor of other candidates for the operation, but added the enormous advantage of fluency English and familiarity in the West, based on years that each member of the group had spent living in Germany."[23] These skills enhance the abilities of the alliance and encourage its growth. Of the 18 string and 10 wind players who comprise the basic membership of Orpheus, many also hold teaching positions at prominent conservatories and universities in the New York and New England areas, including Juilliard, Manhattan School of Music, New England Conservatory, Montclair State University, Mannes College of Music and Columbia and Yale Universities. It is one of the core duties of the global Salafi jihad clutters to enlist additional members and like-minded groups and educate them according to their needs. The nucleus of the Hamburg cell was formed around Mohammed Belfa's study group at the al-Quds Mosque in Hamburg. One after the other, Mohamed Atta, Mounir Motassadeq, Abdelghani Mzoudi, Ramzi bin al-Shib, Said Bahaji, Zaid Amir and Marwan al-Sehhi joined the group. In November 1998, Bait al-Ansar, the house of the supporters, was founded by bin al-Shib and Bahaji and became the "conservatory" of the Hamburg cell. [24]

When considering the attacks in Madrid and Istanbul, spending time at a training camp was no longer a necessary condition for carrying out a successful attack, as it had been in the case of Atta. However, meeting points were still necessary, so the terrorists could educate each other in the right sound of the "music." Like the Orpheus Orchestra, al-Qaeda operatives are able to "play," in nearly every one their target countries. Like them, too, they always show their abilities in front of a large audience.

As the composer of the score, bin Laden's sound comes into being in the ideology of the Salafi jihad. He controls an élite terrorist cell from a presumed hiding-place on the Pakistani side of the Afghan-Pakistan border, which American intelligence officials say is devoted to preparing attacks within the United States. They contend that he personally oversees the group of al-Qaeda operatives, which he hopes he can use for another "spectacular" event, like the 9/11 hijacking plot. Counterterrorism analysts say this special al-Qaeda unit is prob-

---

[23] "The 9/11 Commission Report, Final Report of the National Commission on Terrorists Attacks Upon the United States," authorized edition, New York, 2004, 160.
[24] Marc Sageman, *Understanding Terror Networks*, Philadelphia, 2004, 103-105.

ably dispersed, though they do not know where. This "external planning group" can communicate with regional affiliates around the world to work with them when needed.[25] By spring 2002, South Waziristan had become the world-wide hub of al-Qaeda operations. Local religious leaders provided houses, while poor tribesmen collected handsome rents for their homes. They soon established a highly effective security system. A network of tribesmen, augmented by radios and satellite phones, acted as look-outs and notified them each time more than one vehicle left a new Pakistani army base in Wana.[26] Peter Bergen states that bin Laden's single major political goal is to overthrow the regime of the House of Sa'ud and to reduce Western influence in the Muslim world. Obviously, al-Qaeda has alienated a lot of people in Saudi Arabia. He suspects that the target selection is based on either one of those two things.

It is this unique structure, its flexibility, redundancy and its networking on a basis of a robust ideology, which enables this movement to maintain its enormous impact of power. This structure qualifies the movement to assure the international ability to carry out attacks and makes it at the same time so resistant against countermeasures. That is where our asymmetry in the vulnerability interdependence of organizational structure originates, because even after intense institutional developments like the creation of the Department for Homeland Security or the half-hearted Counterterrorism Center in Berlin, the structure and the communication flow between state institutions dealing with this threat are still too hierarchical to be successful.

Let me finish this paragraph with a quotation from *The New York Times* referring to a concert by the Orpheus Orchestra: "It is worth paying attention to almost anything these conductorless players put their collective hand, mind and heart to."

3.4 Interdependence of Gender

Analyzing the role of the women in the movement of the Salafi Jihad, it is easy to see that there are no reports with descriptions of the cases. There is no documentation on how these women are treated in these groups or how intense their participation is. The few reports we have about women and terrorism concern Palestinian and Chechen terrorist groups, and these reports have usually been conducted by male researchers and from a man's point of view, which might be

---

[25] James Risen and David Rohde, "Intelligence: A Hostile Land Foils the Quest for Bin Laden," in: *The New York Times*, December 13, 2004.
[26] Ibid.

inherently gender-biased, either consciously or unconsciously. The global Salafi jihad uses predominantly men for its attacks, and the people who deal with counterterrorism in the military, in politics and in science are also predominantly men. I therefore argue that the likelihood is extremely high that we overlook 50% of the power resources of the terrorist groups, namely the women. This likelihood seems to be confirmed when looking at the output of research analyzes dealing with the role of women in the business of terrorism. In consequence, the majority of scientific research still overlooks 50% of the resources of conflict and stability. Even when women do not carry out attacks personally but their role of supporting their relatives and educating their sons, is not less important in the process of effective and efficient counter- and antiterrorism. It is an error to believe that a terrorist movement that addresses its attacks to 100% of the target societies lives on just 50% of its potential resources, namely men.

Even if it is still seen as an exception when women carry out attacks in the movement of the global Salafi jihad, we are able to observe some interesting changes in other Islamist-based terrorist groups like the Hamas and the Palestinian Islamic Jihad (PIJ). In these groups, the involvement of women in terrorists attacks carried out by Islamist organizations is rare but not new. Using women as suicide bombers poses conflicts with some leaders' fundamental religious beliefs, while serving a tactical need for a stealthier weapon. In January 2002, Shaykh Ahmed Yassin, the spiritual leader of the Hamas, "categorically renounced the use of women as suicide bombers."[27] In March 2002, after the second Fatah bombing, he reported that "Hamas was far from enthusiastic about the inclusion of women in warfare, for reasons of modesty."[28] That position shifted dramatically in January 14, 2004, when the first Hamas female suicide bomber struck. Yassin defended this change as a "significant evolution in our fight. The male fighters face many obstacles,"[29] whereas women can more easily reach the targets. He concluded his statement by noting that "[w]omen are like the reserve army – when there is a necessity, we use them."[30] The Palestinian Islamic Jihad began to launch a public campaign to recruit women already in 2003:

> The PIJ was and is focusing its recruitment efforts in the northern part of the West Bank, particularly in the Jenin region, and has established a well-trained network of operatives, including some highly skilled

---

[27] Arnin Regular, "Mother of Two Becomes First Female Suicide Bomber for Hamas," Haaretz, January 16, 2004.
[28] Ibid.
[29] Ibid.
[30] Ibid.

women. The organization's first success in recruiting women was Heiba Daragmeh, a 19-year-old student in Quds Open University [...]. On 19 May 2003, she detonated an explosive device strapped to her body in front of a shopping mall in Afula, killing three civilians and injuring 83.[31]

Yoni Fighel states that the participation of women in Palestinian terrorism is increasing:

> Israeli forces are aware of as many as twenty cases in which women were involved in terrorist activity against Israeli targets; some of these women acted as facilitators in planning and carrying out terrorists attacks, while others operated at the most radical level, carrying out suicide bombings.[32]

Looking at the terrorist attacks carried out by Chechen terrorists between October 2002 and October 2003, 10 attacks can be identified in which women were among the suicide bombers. These female suicide bombers are in part a direct reaction to the Russian military tactics. Many of them are relatives of Chechens killed by the Russian military – that is the reason why they are called "black widows" in the Russian press. The human rights group Memorial adds that another contributing factor might be the routine rape of Chechen women by Russian soldiers. Many of the Palestinian female terrorists share the experience of having lost a male relative by the Israeli countermeasures. Mapping the biographies of the women who participated in the early history of Palestinian terrorism, we see that some of them were professional women with above-average education and training, while others were common young women with neither education nor career.

Analyzing the correspondence between the women who participate in Salafi study circles, similar observations emerge. The female members are well-educated, they have online access and they are able to write more or less fluently in German or English. Only a small part of the women in question have those languages as their native ones. At the other extreme, many members of the sisterhood who live in Pakistan and other countries are illiterate. I have not yet found out how strongly these sisters-in-belief are organized, but female Salafi study circles, the roots of which go back to the Egyptian-Syrian Muslim Sisterhood, are hosted in Germany and New Zealand. Some of the sisters-in-belief have converted to the Salafi ideology after their immigration to the West; this seems to be a similarity with the members of the Hamburg 9/11 cell. As far as

---

[31] Yoni Fighel, "Palestinian Islamic Jihad and Female Suicide Bombers," October 6, 2003; http://www.ict.org.il (accessed January 04, 2005).
[32] Ibid.

my current research indicates, the women in Germany seem to be more tightly organized than in other European countries. Some insights into the relationship between the members of the sisterhoods is provided by a Tawheed-aligned website for women. Surrounded by pink roses, this website calls for supporting the "Boycott Israel Campaign" with the words: "My brothers and sisters let us stand, and fight together without fears. [...] Pick up your rifles and set up your tanks, and with our people together we will fight. This war is for our land and is not a prank, so be ready for war with all your might"[33]

Sisters in Islam do more than greet each other, spend time socializing, make gifts on special occasions and cook for those who have a new baby. This is only the surface level of Sisterhood. Their special relationship goes much deeper than that to the level of the heart from which the bonds of Sisterhood emanate. The sisters describe this level as a unique type of love. "It is a feeling that is particularly extraordinary for those of us who are revert/converts to Islam. To really enjoy the beauty of this bond we need to completely comprehend the elements that are involved."[34] Indeed, in some respects females are considered to be the global Salafi jihad's most effective and loyal supporters. Members of the sisterhood are usually recruited by other females, especially relatives. In many cases, the sisters skilfully exploit a traditional moral prohibition. Analyzing the role played by females at the Islamic organization Hizb ut-Tahrir in Uzbekistan, similar observations can be made. They perceived the Hijab (veil) not as repression, but as an act of liberation, of faith and establish a female Muslim's life with honor, an aura of respect and dignity. It is also a symbol of power over their husbands as being a good Muslima who follows the true Islam. Their self-understanding is that the women are the other half of one pair.

While the sisters have not reached the same level of violence as their counterparts in the Palestinian areas, I argue that even when women are not used by the movement of the Salafi Jihad to carry out attacks directly, their role as supporters of their husbands and brothers and educators of their sons is no less important. The fatwas and some audiotapes of bin Laden express the role of the women very clearly. For the understanding of bin Laden's words it is important to keep in mind that the Quran defines the woman as the sister of the man and that they are created from a single being.

In the fatwa "Declaration of war against the Americans Occupying the Land of the Two Holy places, Expel the *Mushrikeen* (infidels) from the Arabian Penin-

---

[33] Meenara Khan: http://www.themuslimwomen.com (accessed January 04, 2005).
[34] The Muslim Women; http://www.themuslimwoman.com/sisterhood/Islam.htm (accessed January 04, 2005).

sula" bin Laden explains that women are playing an essential role as supporters, facilitators and promoters in carrying out the jihad:

> Our women had set a tremendous example for generosity in the cause of Allah; they motivate and encourage their sons, brothers and husbands to fight- for the cause of Allah in Afghanistan, Bosnia-Herigovina, Chechnya and in other countries. [...] May Allah strengthen the belief – Imaan – of our women in the way of generosity and sacrifice for the supremacy of the word of Allah. [...] our women instigate their brothers to fight in the cause of Allah. [...] Our women encourage Jihad saying: Prepare yourself like a struggler; the matter is bigger than the words.

However, in the fatwa "Jihad against Jews and Crusaders, world Islamic Front" published two years later, which became the manifesto of the fully-fledged global Salafi jihad, the role of the women seems to be alleviated. They are mentioned once and then just addressed as being the victims of the US and the Zionists: "[...] women and children, whose cry is: Our Lord, rescue us from this town, whose people are oppressors; and raise for us from thee one who will help!"

In the pledge of a training manual located by the Manchester Metropolitan Police during the search of an al-Qaeda member's home, women are also addressed as victims of the infidels: "To the sister believer whose clothes the criminals have stripped off. To the sister believer whose hair the oppressors have shaved. To the sister believer whose body has been abused by the human dogs." Above I have mentioned by explaining the ideology of the Salafi jihad that a reason to carry out the defensive jihad is when a Muslim woman is held by the *kufar* (infidels), to ensure her freedom is *fard* (duty) upon the whole Muslim *ummah* (world Muslim community). But the women are also addressed as supporters: "Covenant, O Sister [...]. To make them desire death and hate appointments and prestige" and perpetrators: "Covenant, O Sister [...] to slaughter them like lamb and let the Nile, al-Asi, and Euphrates river flow with their blood."

On an audiotape broadcast on Saturday 18 October 2003 by Al Jazeera, bin Laden said: "Our prudent Muslim women are also expected to play their role." These statements are strong indictors that women who follow the ideology of the global Salafi jihad have adopted a gender-specific interpretation of the jihad. The concept of female jihad connoted that the women carry out the jihad by educating, supporting and encouraging their sons, brothers and husbands. To reach this goal, they have to prepare themselves as a struggler. What is at least equally important for promoting the Salafi ideology is their role as the victims of the infidels to motivate their male relatives to carry out the jihad. Until today, women are rarely to be found among the suicide bombers of the global Salafi jihad. When terrorist groups find women useful in their operations, however, they will find or create something in the Islamic theology to justify it.

We do not know whether al-Qaeda and its affiliates will ever make the tactical decision to use women to carry out attacks on a common basis, but in September 2003, two 14-year-old girls, Imame and Sana Laghriff, were arrested in Rabat and sentenced for terrorist offences. According to various reports, the two were on their way to target a liquor store, with some sources suggesting this was a suicide attack plot. The teenagers were influenced by a branch of radical Islam advocates from a Salafia Jihadia cell. [35]

In 2004, several factors led the FBI to prepare for the possibility that al-Qaeda might recruit women. Recent intelligence has worried the FBI that al-Qaeda may be recruiting and training women to carry out terror attacks, trying to regain an element of surprise for a network thinned by arrests.[36] In March 2003, al-Qaeda reported the establishment of a women's suicide division, which is being led by a women named Umm Osama (the mother of Osama), a reference to al-Qaeda leader Osama bin Laden. In an online interview to the London-based *A-Sharq Al Awsat* daily on March 12, Umm Osama claimed that the unit trains women in suicide attacks:

> The idea gathered interests after female suicide missions in Palestine and Chechnya. [...] We are willing to take any Muslim woman, and we have Chechens, Afghans, and Arabs from all countries. We are preparing to carry out operations as our predecessors did in Palestine and Chechnya. [...] As a network and organization, we rely on the Internet for widest distribution."[37]

The woman asserted her job was "to oversee the training of the female mujahedeen affiliated with al-Qaeda and the Taliban." This statement is surprising because based on own observations members of the Salafi Sisterhood do not like the Taliban at all, because the latter perceive females as a threat and negate their abilities as Shahids. This fact would reduce the probability that the women

---

[35] "Girls guilty of terror charges," BBC News UK Edition, http://news.bbc.co.uk/1/hi/world/africa/3153110.stm (accessed January 04, 2005).

[36] "FBI Warns of Al-Qaeda Women," CBSNews.com; April 1, 2003 http:www.cbsnews.com/stories/2003/04/01/attack/main547237.shtml (accessed January 04, 2005).

[37] "Code Pink: Al Qaida announces women's suicide division," World Tribune.com, March 18, 2003 http://216.26.163.62/2003/me_terror_03_18.html (accessed January 04, 2005).

are even in loose contact with the Taliban. Later in this interview Umm Osama assured that "[w]e are building a women's structure that will carry out operations that will make the US forget its own name." Even when there are many reasons to have suspicions about this interview, in June 2003 the FBI started looking for a woman, the 31-year-old Aafia Siddiqui, for the first time since the war on terror began.[38] Together with her husband she had founded the Institute for Islamic Research and Teaching in 1999, and both were identified as suspected al-Qaeda agents. An indicator that the position of women is transforming could be the warrant for a Tunisian woman, Bentiwaa Farida Ben Bechir. As a member of a cell in Italy she was active in recruiting suicide bombers to be sent to Iraq.[39]

The reason why terrorist organizations could use women as suicide bombers is that they have many considerable advantages. First, they provide a tactical advantage: stealthier attack, an element of surprise, hesitancy to search for women and the female stereotype is perceived as non-violent. Second, the inclusion of women as suicide bombers would increase the number of combatants. Third, this would increase the publicity of an attack and finally the psychological effect is much higher. As we all know, suicide bombers provide a low-cost, low-technology, low-risk weapon that maximizes target destruction and instills fear – women are even more effective with their increased accessibility and media shock value than men.

So far, only few women have become operatives of the global Salafi jihad, and we should be careful in drawing generalizations from single cases mentioned above. Looking at videos made by embedded journalists in Afghanistan and Iraq Marines and other special forces usually let women mostly go and only arrest the men. This could be one reason why females can rarely be found in prisons. In the current situation, not enough information is available to understand the role of women who support their male relatives in joining the jihad and support other women to persuade their male relatives to do the same. We do not know how intense their role as facilitators is and how important they are in transmitting messages. What we know is that the Salafi jihad has its roses and they have sharp thorns. Marc Sageman found out that 70% of the 400 analyzed terrorists were married. Every terrorist has a mother, and many of them have at least one sister. Arranged marriages are a strong tradition in the Muslim world, and it would not be a mistake to assume that marriages in the Salafi Jihad world

---

[38] FBI, Seeking information, Aafia Siddiqui, http://www.fbi.gov/terrorinfo/siddiqui.htm (accessed January 04, 2005).
[39] "Italy terror suspects arrested," CNN, http://edition.cnn.com/2003/WORLD/europe/11/29/italy.terror/ (accessed January 04, 2005).

are not arranged by accident. Sidney Jones from the International Crisis Group in Jakarta states that the marriage alliances are the glue that holds Jemaah Islamiyah together:

> Oftentimes senior members of the organization will offer their sisters or sisters-in-law to new promising recruits so that they are not only drawn into the organization, but into the family as well. They have been in control of the finances in some cases. They play a role as couriers, in ensuring that, particularly after imprisonment, communication among different members of the organization is maintained. [...] It's not a role in actively talking part in bombing activities, the new way some of the women in Chechnya or in Sri Lanka have done. It's more ensuring that the organization stays solid.[40]

An analysis of the online periodical *al-Kansaah*, which is addressed to women who share the ideology of al-Qaeda, shows the importance of the female support very clearly. Al-Kansaah bint Omar was a poetess of the pre-Islamic period who converted to Islam during the time of the Prophet Muhammad, and she is considered "the mother of the Shahids." When her four sons died in the battle of Al-Qadissiya, she did not mourn but thanked Allah for honoring her with their death. The magazine indoctrinates that the goal of the woman is also to become a Shahid. An editorial in the magazine states: "[...] we love Allah and his Messenger. We march in a single path, the path of Jihad for the sake of Allah, and our goal is Shahada for the sake of Allah, and our goal is [to gain] the pleasure of Allah and His Paradise." The perception of the women is that they are standing shoulder to shoulder with their men, supporting them, helping them and backing them up. An article entitled "Obstacles in the Path of the Jihad Warrior Woman" written by Umm Badr includes indoctrination and guidelines for the women: "My noble sisters [...]. The woman in the family is a mother, wife, sister, and daughter. In society she is an educator, propagator and preacher of Islam, and a female jihad warrior." In the Muslim society, women have always had an extraordinary position. Expected to remain a virgin until she marries and expressing her respectability in her way of life and dressing she is responsible for the honour of the whole family, as a daughter, sister and wife. Mohamed Salah states that "[w]hat is new here is the use of the medium of the Internet to recruit women."[41]

---

[40] Kelly McEvers, "The Women of Jemaah Islamiah," BBC News World Edition http://news.bbc.uk/2/hi/asia-pacific/3382761.stm (accessed January 04, 2005).
[41] Rawya Rageh, "Islamist women use the Web for war with the infidels," in: *Washington Times*, http://www.washtimes.com/world/20040827-110032-4232r.htm (accessed January 04, 2005).

Based on my own fieldwork in religious girl schools in Herat, Kabul and Peshawar, the girls at these institutions are educated in this ideology from their first day of school. The head of a religious girl school in Peshawar told me that her pupils learn that their life is the female way of a Shahid. Having 8, 10 or 12 children and educate them to become a Shahid is their jihad. I have listened to songs of the school girls in which they praised the glory to be a Shahid by stepping on the flags of Israel and the US. For them their way of jihad is defective when it is according to which only men are responsible. Bearing arms in direct conflict with the enemy and carrying out suicide attacks is the jihad for the men. The women follow their own interpretation of the jihad. When a woman uses this male version of jihad, this perception is contrary to the truth. A Muslim woman is a female jihad warrior always and everywhere. She is a female jihad warrior who wages jihad by means of funding jihad. She wages jihad by means of waiting for her jihad warrior husband and when she educates her children to that which Allah loves. She wages jihad when she supports jihad, when she calls for jihad in word, deed, belief and prayer. When a woman enters the paradise not *quid pro quo* 70 male virgins are waiting for her, she will sit beside her husband. I conclude that when we talk about women and their role in the global Salafi jihad we should have in mind that the people of both sexes follow a gender-specific jihad.

The reason why women are rarely imprisoned for supporting terrorist groups is not that they do not play a role in this process. It is because we just do not look at them. If somebody transfers money to one of the critical aid organizations, this person will probably be in trouble if he or she is detected. However, if a mother educates her sons from their day of birth that they should become Shahids and that by doing so they would bestow the greatest possible honor on her, nothing will happen to stop her from continuing this education.

It is very difficult to understand the motivation of the female supporters of terrorism. It seems to be that the majority of the sisters in western countries converted to the Salafi ideology after they immigrated. On the other hand, the sisters in Pakistan are born into this ideology and have been indoctrinated from their first day. Others have had a traumatic experience with the "enemy," who has arrested, killed or tortured one of their male relatives. I would presume that there are a number of motivations working in concert.

I argue that terrorism is not just a male, but also a female issue. The difference is that the women follow a gender-specific jihad and that their interpretation of jihad is no less dangerous than that of the men. Because the women educate the next generation as mothers and support their husbands and brothers, they have a strong impact on the current generation. I would not generalize that every wife has an idea of what her husband is doing, but some do, and some of them support and persuade others of this dangerous war. The reason why we know so little about the women's role is that law enforcement, military, politics and science do not take a careful look at them. How many Islamic women organizations are infiltrated by female western intelligence agents? When we analyze terrorism, we make the mistake of seeing it in terms of the traditional fight man against man. We need to understand that the women are not always the victims of the radical Islamists, they are also perpetrators. To a large extent, the asymmetry in the vulnerability of interdependence of gender is rooted in our blindness related to the thorns of the Salafi jihad roses, the women.

3.5 Interdependence of Time

The goal of a terrorist attack is not primarily to kill people or destroy buildings; it is to undermine the monopoly of the executive power and to blame the state world-wide for not being able to guarantee the security of its citizens and national properties. Each terrorist attack forces the state to react immediately. The state is on the defensive, because it has an immediate need to communicate its legitimacy, its authority and its competence to exist on a global scale. Analyzing the timeline of terrorist attacks and US governmental actions, it is easy to figure out that the government starts its counter- and antiterrorism actions after a terrorism attack has been carried out. As always, policies are driven by a strong impulse. The Anti-Terrorism and effective Death Penalty Act was implemented after the Sarin Gas attack by the AUM Shinrikyo group in Tokyo in March 1995 and the Oklahoma City bombing in April of the same year. While the US embassy bombings in Kenya and Tanzania did not have an impact on legislation, three presidential directives, the PDD 62 Combating Terrorism, the PDD 63 Critical Infrastructure Protection and the PDD 67 Continuity of the Government, have been responses to these attacks.

The 9/11 attacks obviously had the largest impact on the US administration. The Supplemental Act for Response and Recovery, the Transport Safety and System Stabilization Act, the Aviation and Transport Security Act, the PATRIOT Act and its continuation, the National Defense Authorization Act, are all directly related to these attacks. The act with the greatest impact on US national law was the PATRIOT Act. This act grants federal officers greater powers to trace and intercept terrorist communication both for law enforcement and foreign intelligence gathering purposes. It reinforces federal money laundering laws and regulations in an effort to deny terrorists the resources necessary for future attacks. It tightens the US immigration laws to close the borders to foreign terrorists and expel those among the American population. Finally, it creates a few federal crimes, such as the one that outlaws terrorist attacks on mass transit, while increasing the penalties for many other crimes. The act also institutes several procedural changes, such as a longer statute of limitations for crimes of terrorism.[42] In the public debate that followed, the act was strongly criticized. Thus Jerry Berman, the President of the Center for Democracy and Technology, stated before the House Committee on Judiciary and the House Select Committee on Homeland Security, "Yet checks and balances were seriously eroded by the USA PATRIOT Act and Executive Branch actions."[43] By rapidly passing these legislative measures the Bush administration communicated to its population that the government was improving its capabilities and eliminating defects in the intrainstitutional communication on security-relevant information. In 2002, the Department of Homeland Security (DHS) was established as a capital and human resource-intense answer to solve the problems that had made the attacks possible. Today, the DHS has 183,000 employees and a budget of 33.8 billion US$.[44] under his command.

Operation Enduring Freedom in Afghanistan, which started on 7 October 2001, was a masterpiece of military creativity and finesse and the most intensive and publicly visible answer of the US to the attacks. At its peak, US forces involved in the war effort numbered no less than 60,000 (about half of which were stationed in the Persian Gulf), and Western allies added no less than 15,000. But the US-led military campaign has hardly been small in scale. By the end of January 2002, the United States had flown about 25,000 sorties in the air campaign and dropped 18,000 bombs, including 10,000 precision munitions. In addition, more than 3,000 US and French bombs were dropped on surviving enemy forces in March during Operation Anaconda, in which some 1,500 Western forces and 2,000 Afghans launched a major offensive against about 1,000 enemy troops in the mountain region of eastern Afghanistan. Through January 8, 2002, the

---

[42] Charles Doyle, Senior Specialist American Law Division, "The USA PATRIOT act: A Legal Analysis," in: CRS Report for the Congress, April 15, 2002, order Code RL31377, http://www.cdt.org/security/usapatriot/analyis.shtml (accessed January 05, 2005).

[43] Jerry Berman, "The Terrorist Threat Integration Center (TTIC) and its Relationship with the Department of Justice and Homeland Security," Statement of Jerry Berman, President Center for Democracy & Technology, before the House Committee on the Judiciary and the House Select Committee on Homeland Security, July 2003, http://judiciary.house.gov/media/pdfs/berman072203.pdf (accessed January 05, 2005).

[44] Office of Management and Budget, The Executive Office of the President, Department of Homeland Security, http://www.whitehouse.gov/omb/budget/fy2005/homeland.html (accessed January 04, 2005).

total costs had reached 3.8 billion US$, while the military costs of homeland security efforts in the United States had reached 2.6 billion US$.[45] This war was necessary for the US government to show the world what anybody could expect by attacking the most powerful state in the world. Even if the result of this war would be the birth of a second Colombia, and even the prospect of successfully countering the terrorists in the long run remains doubtful. The total costs worldwide for the counter- and antiterrorism measures instituted in response of the 9/11 attacks are uncountable.

The huge amount of money was needed in order to communicate to the world that the state and its system have the right and the ability to hold the monopoly of power. As the highest unit in the international system, it is unacceptable for a state that another group or movement undermine the national monopoly of power and aspire to become a sovereign. That bin Laden has this misperception of being a sovereign is shown very clearly in his speech broadcast by Al Jazeera on April 15, 2004. In this speech, bin Laden offers a peace treaty to those European countries that withdraw soldiers from Arab countries. However, with each attack terrorists define the time of action for the states. In contrast, the states think in parliamentary terms, terrorist groups and movements like the global Salafi jihad have no time pressure, they do not have to win elections. If the members cannot reach their goals in their lifetime, they will enter the paradise nevertheless, and others will follow and accomplish the mission. In addition, the groups of the global Salafi jihad have a different understanding of time. They have times of acceleration, in which they grow and carry out more attacks, and times of deceleration. For example, the current events in Iraq are a time of acceleration.

The different understanding of time, as well as the ability of the global Salafi jihad to define the point of time for national action, creates an asymmetry in the vulnerability interdependence of time between the global Salafi jihad and the target states. It is a vulnerability for the states, because even after important changes in legislation and many countermeasures, the asymmetry still exists, and the terrorists still know how to make use of it for their own purposes.

---

[45] Michael E. O'Hanlon, "The Afghani War: A Flawed Masterpiece," in: Robert Art and Kenneth Waltz (ed.), *The Use of Force, Military Power and International Politics*, 6th edition, Oxford, 2004, 270-281.

3.6 Interdependence of Learning

According to Robert A. Pape, three inherent general patterns of suicide terrorism can be identified. First, nearly all suicide attacks occur as part of organized campaigns, not as isolated or random incidents. Second, liberal democracies are uniquely vulnerable to suicide attacks. In the last two decades democracies have been the targets. Third, suicide campaigns are directed toward a strategic objective. When movements share so much of their core behavior, it is obvious that they share a tendency to learn from each other and that like-minded, less radical groups adopt the suicide attack tactic and undergo a spill-over effect. Excluding the ongoing insurgent campaign in Iraq, the data of the last 20 years show that the raw number of suicide attacks has increased, while the rates of other types of terrorism have actually declined.

In history, not only have terrorists often cooperated with each other, but suicide bombing, in particular, has demonstrated a contagion effect. We can discern the direct and indirect influences of suicide terrorism. "Arguments concerning demonstration effects assume that followers will learn only one kind of lesson – one that encourages further action, leading to repeated occurrences of the first event [...]."[46] In some instances, insurgent factions have been physically trained by other organizations and taught how to best use horrifying tactics with devastating effects, and these factions subsequently import the tactic far and wide. Edgar O'Balance alleges that the LTTE were being trained in Lebanon in the late 1980s and thus learned the tactic of suicide terror directly from the Hizballah's successes in 1983, and imported it back to Sri Lanka in 1987. Hizballah's success in expelling the Israeli military in southern Lebanon and the Beka'a Valley led to its imitation by Hamas and the Palestinian Islamic Jihad – then spreading further to secular organizations like Fatah's Tanzim, the Al'Aqsa Martyrs Brigade and the Marxist PFLP, who emulated the tactic. The domestic political situation in the Palestinian territories deteriorated in 2001 and led to an outbidding between rival Palestinian organizations. Several groups jumped on the suicide-bombing bandwagon, and previously secular groups adopted the language of jihad and martyrdom. Having proved relatively successful, suicide terrorism has spread throughout the Middle East, the Islamic world and places like Sri Lanka. There has also been an increase in the a number of regions, countries and non-state actors that utilize it as a tactic and strategy in the pursuit of their political

---

[46] Stephen M. Saidman, "Is Pandora's Box Half Empty or Half Full?" in: David Lake and Donald Rothchild, *The International Spread of Ethnic Conflict*, Princeton, 1998.

goals.⁴⁷ One reason why suicide terrorism has been rising so rapidly in the recent years is that terrorist groups have learned that the strategy pays off.

Important for the learning or contagion effect for al-Qaeda has been the collective experience in Afghanistan during the Soviet invasion. During this time, approximately 70,000 people from 47 countries passed through the training camps in the mid 1990s, where they were educated in making bombs. After the neutralization of these camps during the military invasion, al-Qaeda members taught individuals from other groups how to use the Internet to send messages and how to encrypt those communications to avoid detection. Bomb- and chemical manufacturing techniques have been passed on.⁴⁸ The intense learning process of the global Salafi jihad can be studied precisely by analyzing the shift in the financial structure of the movement:

> There is no longer a set pool of money from which the groups can draw. There is no longer a fairly knowable group of large donors or entities. Now groups in Indonesia raise money there. Groups in Malaysia raise money there [...]. Many of the local groups, unable to draw on the web of organizations and donors that have supported al-Qaeda, rely on petty crime, drug trafficking [...].⁴⁹

Today, there is no need anymore for the global Salafi jihad to send their recruits to training camps or to exchange knowledge with other terrorist groups, because they have learned to use the weapons of mass persuasion: the media and the Internet. Via live broadcast they are learning what works, because we are teaching them. The Internet in particular has become extremely important for providing them with know-how on carrying out a suicide attack. The comments on the online magazines *Sawat al Jihad* and *Mu 'saskar al Battar* have shown how organized they spread their knowledge. The diffusion of the ideology, the economic links and the use of the Internet are all inextricably linked to a form of contagion and learning of suicide terrorism.

In the past, the countries that had suffered from suicide attacks tended to respond with heavy military offensives, only to find that this tended to incite more attacks and stir public sympathy for the terrorists without hampering their networks.⁵⁰ Until today, terrorist groups have gained more by continuing their

---

⁴⁷ Robert A. Pape, "Dying to Kill Us," in: *The New York Times*, September 2, 2003.
⁴⁸ Douglas Farah and Peter Finn, "Al Qaeda's Terror Style Spreading," in: *Washington Post*, November 21, 2003.
⁴⁹ Douglas Farah and Peter Finn, "Al Qaeda's Terror Style Spreading," in: *Washington Post*, November 21, 2003.
⁵⁰ Robert A. Pape, "Dying to Kill Us," in: *The New York Times*, September 2, 2003.

brutal operations than by quitting them. Only by means of enormous investments and by transferring limited powers and autonomy rights to the Kurdish region was Turkey able to reduce the number of suicide attacks. Between 1996 and 1999, there were more than 20 suicide attacks throughout Turkey. However, over a few years they began to peter out. Today, apart from an isolated incident here and there, suicide bombings have largely disappeared from Turkish life. A combination of reasons were responsible for this development. First, the Turkish military hit the rebels hard, crushing the PKK, closing down international support for them and arresting its leaders. But the Army directed its fire at the rebels and not the surrounding population. In fact, the Turks worked very hard to win over the Kurds, creating stable governing structures for them, befriending them and providing them with social-welfare programs – to improve agriculture and women's education, for example. The Turkish government made a huge investment (totaling well over 32 billion US$) in the Kurdish southeast. On per capita basis, it has invested more in the Kurdish region than in any other part of Turkey. It also agreed to a number of Kurdish demands on language, cultural freedom and educational reforms. These concessions have been dramatically accelerated as a result of European pressure over the last few years.

Surely, we would be much better off if the global Salafi jihad had a Gerry Adams, but beside this issue there is also something to learn from the British campaign against the IRA. First, the long-term presence of strong and disciplined police forces in Northern Ireland was one important aspect of the British success. Second, the self and direct censorship of the British media was also a tactic with a positive impact on the conflict situation. On October 19th, 1988, Douglas Hurd introduced a notice under clause 13 (4) of the BBC Licence and Agreement and Section 29 (3) of the Broadcasting Act 1981 prohibiting the broadcast of direct statements by representatives or supporters of 11 Irish political and military organizations. The Broadcasting Ban, as it became known, was the first and, so far, the only use of this power to directly and overtly rule out a whole class of political viewpoints in the entire history of British broadcasting. In consequence, the IRA was not interviewed on British television between 1974 and 1994.

We treat suicide bombers as delusional figures, brainwashed by imams. But they are also products of political realities. Analyzing the conflicts of the Turks with the Kurds and the British with the Northern Irish population, there are lessons to learn that we still ignore. Until today, the members of the global Salafi jihad have learned faster then we have, even if set-backs have forced the movement to change its targeting pattern and focus on softer targets. This is the asymmetry in the vulnerability interdependence of learning.

3.7 Interdependence of Communication

Targets and attack forms are selected to generate the highest public attention. From the point of view of a terrorist, attacks are a perfectly choreographed news production aimed at an international audience. "Terrorism is aimed at the people watching, not at the actual victim. Terrorism is theatre."[51] Consequently the modern mass media are the most important channels for providing information about attacks and the interests of the movement. The military arm of al-Qaeda and its affiliates has only been able to develop this power with the power of the media arm. Terrorists know how to use the media for their purposes and the basic parameters of the mass media: live broadcast, timeliness pressure, pressure of competition and the high news value correspond perfectly with their interest in global communication. Compared with other terrorist groups like Hamas or Hizballah, Osama bin Laden has made the communication strategy of a terrorist attack perfect with the periodic publishing of audio- and videotapes of him and Ayman al-Zawahiri. With these videos, both figures continue to inspire fanatics. Since 9/11, they have surfaced with over a dozen of these videos and audiotapes in order to rally supporters. By means of these tapes, they keep influencing the terms of the debate. "When Ayman al-Zawahiri calls for an attack on Musharraf, the attack follows. And when bin Laden calls for attacks on coalition forces in Iraq, and you have things like Madrid happening. So, they retain a broader, strategic role," says Peter Bergen.[52] The media, especially TV channels, help them to communicate with their followers by broadcasting these tapes. With these tapes, the channels not only inform their audience about the news factor al-Qaeda, they also inform potential terrorists about the strength, the tactics, the strategy and the next steps of the terrorism movement.

Just how precisely al-Qaeda and the affiliated groups know the rules of dramaturgy was shown by the attacks on 12 and 16 May 2003 in Riadh and Casablanca. During the active combat operations in Iraq, the homeland adversary system used the color orange to indicate a high chance of a terrorist attack. But nothing happened during this time by al-Qaeda or its affiliated groups. The first attacks occurred exactly two weeks after the commander-in-chief landed on

---

[51] Jenkins M. Brian, "International Terrorism. The Other World War," in: Charles W. Kegley (ed.), *International Terrorism Characteristics, Causes, Controls*, New York, 1999, 30.

[52] Peter Bergen, "Three years after 9/11: an interview with Peter Bergen," in: *Jamestown Terrorism Monitor*, Vol. 2, Issue 10, September 13, 2004, http://jamestown.org/publications_details.php?volume_id=402&issue_id=3068&aricle_id=2368496 (accessed January 05, 2005).

the aircraft carrier USS Abraham Lincoln and declared that the major combat operations had ended. This time was chosen by the relevant cells to guarantee major public attention. If these attacks had been carried out during the combat operations, the media attention would not have been so high. Online magazines like *Sawat al Jihad* and *Mu'askar al-Battar* and provided tapes making the one-way flow of communication perfect. In an issue of the online journal *Mu'askar al-Battar*, which is considered to be affiliated with al-Qaeda, Abdul-Aziz al-Muqurin wrote that each cell is to plan and carry out attacks on its own, with bin Laden serving as an ideological leader, motivating and keeping the jihadist movement alive.

The videotape provided just two days before the presidential election in the USA was not placed by accident. The date was deliberately chosen in order to influence the American public. Al-Qaeda and its affiliates rely on rhetorical and ideological support in much the same way that they rely on financial and logistical support. Any small-scale regional activity that can be traced back to al-Qaeda only bolsters the image it seeks to create as a global entity representing the entire Muslim world. For this image, al-Qaeda needs main characters that both the western public and the existing and potential stalwarts of the movement will easily recognize. The rising celebrity of al-Zarqawi serves as a perfect example. Before the Iraq war he was an unknown, a fighter educated at a training camp in Herat in Afghanistan and now his name is almost as well known as that of bin Laden himself. Three key factors of his success can be identified. First, his contact to bin Laden does not seem to be that close, which may be one key factor of his success as a media star operating and being the al-Qaeda leader in a well-defined geographical region. The second key factor of his success is the universal applicability of his message, and, finally, there is the global media attention of this conflict region. All of his actions have received a news value as high as a videotape from al-Zawahiri. These three terrorists play the leading part in the theater of terrorism. They are the media stars, particularly if the next theater of operation should be repeated.

The manipulation of the public achieves its full impact with the permanent, credibly communicated threat that anyone could be a victim of a terrorist attack anywhere. This manipulation is so effective that it was able to influence the outcome of parliamentary elections in Spain, and the stock markets always suffer badly after an attack is carried out. The target states could only respond to this communication process with the same line of action, on a one-way basis with their counterterrorism and antiterrorism measures. Each terrorist attack communicated through the mass media forces the target country to react with stronger backlashes, and the helix of action and reaction rises. This is the point from which their vulnerability originates. All of the intense policy developments and the billions of dollars invested in security-relevant resources have not had an impact on the asymmetry interdependence of communication, and this is the reason why we are still vulnerable to terrorist attacks at this level; we still let them use the mass media as their platform. It is only with this vulnerability, which could be best described as the weapon of mass persuasion, that the other identified asymmetries in vulnerability interdependence of information, organizational structure, gender, learning and time are able to gain their full impact of power, since this vulnerability forces the states to do what they would not do under different conditions.

4   Conclusions

The objective of this paper was to look for the power resources of al-Qaeda and its affiliates. Surprisingly, a theory of international relations, Robert Keohane's theory of interdependence, provides a theoretical framework that allows us to identify seven resources of power of the strongest security-relevant threat of this century. After the 9/11 attacks, the world first reacted with sensitivity, and after intense policy developments and billions of dollars spent with the objective to change the situation, the liability of suffering the costs imposed by terrorism attacks still exists. In consequence, the sensitivities have become vulnerabilities, because all of these counter- and antiterrorism measures have not been able to neutralize or even reduce the costs.

Yet these asymmetries have been sufficient to give the terrorists at least a short-term advantage, and they make terrorism a long-term threat. Until now, each successful strike has empowered extremist elements and trained them because we use the wrong tools. If we want to be successful against terrorism, we have to turn our identified vulnerabilities of information, belief, organizational structure, gender, time, learning and communication at least into sensitivities. Surely not all identified vulnerabilities can be turned. For instance, the asymmetry in the vulnerability interdependences of belief cannot be turned because the system of the national state just only works if it applies to be absolute. An important step should be to reflect upon the mass media. I have mentioned how important this platform is for each terrorist group, and we should ask ourselves how important it is to show the public pictures of attacks or how important it is to show them the video- and audiotapes of al-Qaeda's key figures. The public would not lose information by not seeing these pictures and listening to the words of the ideological leaders, who define themselves as sovereigns and believe themselves to be on a level with our national governments, thus purporting to give them orders on what they are to do. Every communications scholar knows that the news value of pictures is very low and that the emotion value is in contrast extremely high. What do we gain by showing children being shot in their back, like in Beslan? We should always keep in mind that by broadcasting these pictures we not only emotionalize our public, but also support the followers of the global Salafi jihad and let them learn that terrorism pays off. When we are confronted with terrorists, the question is what needs a terrorist is satisfying with his actions. With an attack, a terrorist satisfies his need for publicity. With this publicity he or she gains power and satisfies the need to manipulate to have an impact on the largest powers in the world. Having in mind that all behavior is oriented toward the individual's needs, the need that is expressed in the ideology of the Salafi jihad is the powerlessness of the Arab countries. The GNP of all Arab countries combined is equal to that of Spain. The Salafi ideology argues that the reason for this weakness is, first, that the Muslim people do not follow the right, true and clean Islam and, second, the American capitalism. The result is a strong anti-Americanism.

Soft power in the terms of Joseph S. Nye is the ability to attract others by the legitimacy of US policies and the values that underline them. Survey data from the Pew Research Center shows that support for America has fallen in most of the Muslim countries:

> Negative views of the US among Muslims, which had been largely limited to countries in the Middle East, have spread to Muslim populations in Indonesia and Nigeria. Since last summer, favourable ratings for the US have fallen from 61% to 15% in Indonesia and from 71% to 38% among Muslims in Nigeria.[53]

"Success in the war on terrorism depends on Washington's capacity to persuade others without force, and that capacity is in dangerous decline."[54] The US decision to provide 350 million US$, plus logistical services of naval and air forces, to help the victims of the Tsunami disaster in Asia, with a focus on the Islamic parts of the region, is an important tactical and strategic move to increase the soft power of the United States. This help will contribute to the attractiveness of the United States, because the most important ally in the war on terrorism is the Islamic community. Even if an extremist comes here who is angry and isolated,

---

[53] The Pew Research Center, for the people and the press, Views changing World 2003, War With Iraq Further Divides Global Public, released June 3, 2003 http://people-press.org/reports/display.php3?ReportID=185 (accessed January 06, 2005).

[54] Joseph S. Nye, "The Decline of America's Soft Power," in: *Foreign Affairs*, May/June 2004.

our objective should be to ensure that the Islamic community is too integrated to provide any kind of reinforcement or protective cover for terrorists. These measures are important, having in mind that solid majorities in the Palestinian Territories, Indonesia and Jordan – and nearly half of those in Morroco and Pakistan – say they have at least some confidence in Osama bin Laden "do[ing] the right thing regarding world affairs." Fully 71% of the Palestinians say they have confidence in bin Laden in this regard.[55]

According to Joseph S. Nye, the use of hard power is necessary to combat already committed members of the global Salafi jihad. The successes of the Turks against the Kurds should teach us that the tens of millions of people who sympathize with bin Laden could be influenced with soft power measures. These soft power measures should be aimed specifically at the women, whose role in this conflict is still largely ignored.

---

[55] The Pew Research Center, for the people and the press, Views changing World 2003, War With Iraq Further Divides Global Public, released June 3, 2003 http://people-press.org/reports/display.php3?ReportID=185 (accessed January 06, 2005).

The Intricacies of Funding the al-Qaida Network

Michael E. G. Chandler

Chairman of the former UN Monitoring Group overseeing sanctions against the al-Qaeda network from 2001 to 2004

The Oxford English Dictionary defines "intricate" as "perplexingly entangled," "obscure" or "involved." The methods used to finance the al-Qaida network are all of these and more. It is also important to understand the extent and diversity of the network, which, today, comprises the threat from transnational Islamic terrorism – a network of loosely affiliated groups which, despite having diverse and individual objectives, are nonetheless capable of networking, operationally, when the situation warrants.

Long before 9/11 the importance of finance to terrorist groups was fully appreciated and the implications for the support it provided well understood. This understanding is reflected in the international conventions designed to suppress it and in UN Security Council sanctions-related resolutions which target it. However, the investigations into the attacks of "9/11" and subsequent atrocities committed by groups affiliated to al-Qaida have highlighted the diversity of funding used by the network not only for operations, but for recruiting, indoctrination, training and logistic support.

Efforts to counter the threat have to be "intelligence-led" if law enforcement and security agencies are to be able to catch the terrorists before they can carry out an attack. One of the most crucial threads in this intelligence tapestry is the financing, i.e. finding and/or following the money.

The 9/11 investigations uncovered the use by the terrorists of the commercial or formal banking system. Subsequent inquiries have indicated sources of financing terrorism from "deep pocket donors" to the downstream abuse of Islamic charities. The drug trade, particularly heroin and other opiates emanating from the cultivation of opium poppies in Afghanistan, provided and continues to provide a significant source of income to elements of the network, including the Taliban. "Shell" companies and offshore banks as well as legitimate businesses are used by the terrorists or their sympathisers to provide both a source of income and a convenient *bona fide* cover for the existence of logistic support cells.

Unlike 9/11, which is estimated to have cost as much as US$ 500,000 to mount, most of the subsequent terrorist attacks attributed to al-Qaida or its associated groups, e.g. in Djerba, Karachi, Bali, Mombasa, Jakarta, Casablanca, Riyadh, Istanbul and Madrid, have cost but a few thousand dollars to mount. In European countries, a pattern has emerged of cells being self-financing. Copying the indigenous criminals they have resorted to street crime, drug peddling and car theft and even attempted insurance scams. They have also become expert in credit card and bank cheque fraud and robbing ATMs, raising thousands of Euros a month.

It is against this diversity of financial mispractices that law enforcement and security services have to direct their efforts in order to develop and maintain the necessary hostile environment to disrupt the terrorists' operations. It is often a difficult judgement to find the appropriate balance between seizing assets, thus alerting the terrorists or their supporters to them being under investigation, and using finance as the scent that leads to the terrorists' lairs.

Hizballah Terror Organization of Global Reach

Col (res) Eithan Azani

International Policy Institute for Counter-Terrorism
Herzliya, Israel

1 The Threat

1.1 Background

The Hizballah of 2005 is a pragmatic terror organization which is far more dangerous than the Hizballah of the 1980s. The organization operates simultaneously both within the Lebanese political system and outside it. For over a decade the organization has been investing a great deal of effort in obscuring its terrorism image, by emphasizing its political activities and its legitimacy within the Lebanese political system on the one hand, and on the other, by hiding its military and security activities under a heavy cloak of secrecy.

The U.S., Australia, Canada, Israel, and recently also Holland, have defined the Hizballah as a terror organization and are acting accordingly. However, the European Union still perceives the Hizballah as a legitimate social organization, with representation in the Lebanese parliament, and they draw a distinction between the Hizballah and what they term "External Security Organizations".[1]

This is particularly salient in the light of the German Court ruling in December 2004 regarding the Hizballah. In December 2004, the German court (in Dusseldorf) confirmed the decision of the German security authorities and ordered the deportation of a Hizballah activist who had been living in Dusseldorf for several years. The court reasoned that the petitioner was a member of the Hizballah organization which supported international terrorism and attacked Israeli civilian targets outside Israel's borders. The court determined that the fact that the organization does not appear on the European Union's list of terror organizations is irrelevant, because the European Union list is determined according to the var-

---

[1] Nicholas Blanford, "Hizballah in the Firing Line", Middle East Report Online, April 28, 2003. see also: http://www.aipac.org/NotableException112904.htm. Notable Exception: Some European States are Unwilling to Label Hizballah a Terrorist Group, November 29, 2004. see also: http://www.crosswalk.com/news/1247108.html, Patrick Gooddenough, "Australian Muslim Leader praises Suicide Bombers".

ious political interests of the member-states, in accordance with their wishes and therefore is not legally obliging.[2]

The fundamental difference in the international community's definition of Hizballah, thwarts any possibility of directly or indirectly pressurizing the organization. While the U.S. and Israel are acting to eliminate the organization as a terrorist entity, European diplomats are meeting with its leaders. This international environment enables Lebanon, Syria and Iran to maneuver between the European position and American pressure. The lack of a uniform definition of the term "terrorism" prevents international cooperation in fighting the terror organizations. This fact, and the fear of the international community players of becoming too involved in areas saturated with violence and terrorism, where their interests could be harmed, play into the hands of Hizballah. Even in the 1980s, when Hizballah was active in perpetrating attacks against the international community, they found it difficult to cooperate in bringing effective pressure to bear against the organization. The conclusion is therefore: In the absence of a basic agreement that the organization is a terrorist organization, the international community influence on Hizballah is totally marginal.

The organization has been significantly active over the years and has established an international terror network based on activists enlisted from the Islamic population all over the world, both Shi'ites and Sunnis. This network is activated and controlled by the organization's headquarters in Lebanon and is active in various fields, including fundraising for the organization's operations in Lebanon, creating new financing sources by smuggling (drugs, cigarettes and munitions), money laundering, acquisition of munitions and enlisting new activists. These operations strengthen the organization's standing in the global village and improve its ability to perpetrate attacks within a short period of time, or alternatively to assist other terror organizations in the global arena.

1.2 Main Principals of Radical Shi'ite Thought

Shi'ite thought, and the principals by which Hizballah operates, were formulated by Khomeini and constitute the basis for the organization's operations until this very day:[3] They include:

---

[2] A photocopy of the German Court's decision was published on the site http://www.intelligence.org.il/sp/1_05/german_c.htm.

[3] Shaul Shai, Terror in the Name of the Imam: 20 Years of Shiite Terrorism 1979-1999. Interdisciplinary Center Herzliya, Israel 2001,pp. 23-28.

1. *Obtaining legitimacy for Shi'ite activism.* The Shi'ite community, which until Khomeini's time was passive and depressed due to its being a minority within the Moslem world, underwent a process of change under Khomeini's regime and became an active community which aspires to achieve political aims, including by violent means. He called for action of the depressed (the Shi'ites) against the oppressors.
2. *Creating de-legitimization of the corrupt Moslem regimes.*
3. Joining the Jihad against the corrupt Arab rulers and the West, as a means of advancing the vision of an Islamic nation.
4. *Defining the enemies.* Khomeini established two terms which defined the enemies of Islam. One, the "big Satan", which refers to the U.S.A. and the other term is the "little Satan", which relates to Israel.
5. *The principle of sacrifice.* This ideal of moving from total devotion to sacrificing the soul, within the framework of Jihad against the enemies of Islam, was the basis on which the suicide phenomenon developed, as a strategic means of terrorism to achieve its aims. Hizballah adopted the idea at its inception, by perpetrating the first suicide bombing attacks against the Americans, the French and the Israelis in Lebanon in 1983. This modus operandi was adopted later on by other terror organizations.
6. *The rule of the sages.* This idea, formulated by Khomeini, was that the religious sages should govern the Islamic state, because they are the only ones who know how to interpret the Divine Law. The Hizballah also religiously adhered to this principle, which was exclusive to the radical Shi'ite school of thought.

As a revolutionary Shi'ite organization with a universal Islamic vision, Hizballah carved three central goals onto its banner:

1. The application of Islamic law in Lebanon, as part of the worldwide Islamic revolution.
2. The banishment of foreign forces from Lebanon.
3. The extermination of Israel and the liberation of Jerusalem.

2 The Organization's Developmental Stages

The development of the Hizballah organization includes five different stages. Their development has been influenced by a number of systems around which it operated:

The Creation stage – Between the years 1975 and 1982. This stage is very important in order to understand the organization's growth. During this stage, the pre-movement groups developed on the fringes of the Shi'ite community and inside Amal.

The Establishment stage – Occurred during the years 1982 to 1983. This stage was essentially revolutionary and was characterized by unrestrained extreme terror attacks, perpetrated by groups and secret radical cells affiliated with the organizational framework.

The Consolidation stage – Between the years 1983 and 1985. During this stage the ideological framework was crystallized, the radical violence continued, led by the revolutionary charismatic pro-Iranian leadership.

The Expansion stage – Between the years 1986 and 1991. This was the stage where the buds of the embryonic institutional movement appeared, as a result of the increase in the number of activists, and the areas of operation. The radical violence continued simultaneously, peaking at the end of the 1980s, with the breakout of the struggle for control between the Shi'ite community and the Amal movement.

The Institutionalized stage – This is the stage in which the organization has been since 1992, when it integrated into the Lebanese political system. Its activities are characterized by pragmatism and political realism and they are motivated by profit and loss considerations.

2.1   The Hizballah Organization – Structure and Control

The organization is controlled by the Shura Council which is comprised of seven members, headed by Hassan Nasrallah, head of the organization since February 1992. In August 2004, the Council was re-elected to direct the organization's operations.[4] It is noteworthy, that all of its members, with the exception of Imad Mugnia, who is also responsible for the Jihad Council, are religious sages. The Council is responsible for the organization's operations on every level (social, political and military) and it is aware of all the organization's activities in the Middle Eastern and international arenas. The Council controls the following bodies: the Executive Council, the Political Council, the Military Council (Jihad council), and Nasrallah himself directly controls the Military Council. Iran and Syria influence the decisions of the Council, due to their relationship with Nasrallah and the other Council members. The head of the Jihad Council is Imad Mugnia, who

---
[4] Al-Safir, August 17, 2004.

is responsible for many of the terror attacks which the organization carried out in Lebanon and abroad from 1983 onwards. The Council is responsible for the resistance and attacks against Israel, for the organization's militia and its overseas operations. This body operates in complete secrecy and, as mentioned, the organization only stresses attacks against Israel, which, according to Hizballah, continues to violate Lebanese sovereignty in the Mt. Dov area, therefore, presenting legitimate action against them.[5]

2.2 The Hizballah organization is one body – Subordinate to one leadership

In contrast to the distinction which various countries make between the political arm of terror organizations and the military body of the organization, Hizballah explicitly declared, dating back to 1992, that its entrance into the Lebanese political system was aimed at advancing its resistance activities. Muhamed Fannish, a representative of the faction in Parliament for the town of Zur, declared in September 1992, that the armed struggle against Israeli occupation, is the tour de force of every type of resistance and added that "*our entry into Parliament is resistance on the political level, because it is natural for the resistance activists to have a political base behind them. This is because the armed struggle needs political assistance... our entry into Parliament constitutes a support factor in the armed struggle against the occupation*".[6]

In October 1994, Nasrallah declared that the "*AlWafa faction (the Hizballah faction in the Lebanese parliament) has become the mouthpiece of the resistance in parliament, inside and outside Lebanon*".[7]

In January 2002, in a speech televised on Al-Manar, Muhamad Fannish, Hizballah's representative in parliament, stated that "*Efforts are made to tempt the Hezbollah in order to hold it back. The objective is not to impair its political role; rather its military wing only. But I can say that no differentiation is to be made between the military wing and the political wing of Hezbollah*".[8]

3 Hizballah: Theatres of Operation

Hizballah is an independent terror organization which operates within a complicated environment. Over the years, the organization has shown a remarkable

---
[5] http://www.intelligence.org.il/eng/bu/hizbullah/chap_b.doc
[6] Interview with Muhamad Fannish, Al-liwaa, September 16 1992.
[7] Interview with Hassan Nasrallah, Al-Balad October 22, 1994
[8] Al-Manar television January 18, 2002.

resilience considering the direct and indirect efforts made to reign it in or disarm it. The organization developed new techniques and learned to adapt itself to changing circumstances. It operates in four different operational arenas, which interact within a dynamic reciprocal system which is influenced by them:

1. **The Shi'ite arena** – where the organization fights for control of the community against the national secular Amal movement.
2. **The Internal Lebanese arena** – where the organization conducts its struggles and acts to advance its interests on a number of levels: in Parliament, in the municipal system, and on the social-communal level and on the economic level.
3. **The Regional arena** – which includes the players in the Arab sub-system: Syria, Iran, Lebanon, the Palestinians and Iraq, against the Israeli sub-system.
4. **The International arena** – The arena where the organization operates a highly organized international terror network.

3.1 Hizballah and the Global Arena: Activity and Deployment Characteristics

Hizballah is an international terror organization. It has established an international network which cooperates with other Islamic terror organizations in the international arena and spreads the idea of the "Islamic Umma" in this arena. The organization is building a logistical and operational ability which will enable it to perpetrate attacks against targets in this arena within a short period of time. The organization's international network is controlled by the Shura Council headed by Nasrallah and specifically by Imad Mugnia the head of the Jihad Council. The organization's international operations are mostly directed towards Israeli, Jewish and American targets and are dependent on the organizational and logistic network, built up over the years, in over 40 countries worldwide.[9]

The roots of the complicated reciprocal system between Hizballah and the international network can be found in the late 1970s. During that time, Khomeini extolled his famous slogan "America is the Big Satan" and thereby gave expression to the winds of rage and frustration which was widespread in Islamic communities, against the background of the growing gap between the power of the Western societies and the continuing weakness of Islamic societies. The U.S. was perceived as the symbol of Western superiority and all the fundamentalist

---

[9] "IDF Intelligence Chief Views Hizballah-Syria Ties, PA Chaos, Saudi Stability". The Jerusalem Post, July 26, 2004.

arrows were pointed in their direction. Hatred of the U.S. was the common denominator between the various communities in Islamic populations and a means for social mobilization, and the enlistment of supporters and activists for direct action against American targets in Arab countries and against the pro-American rulers who governed them.[10]

The U.S. is ideologically perceived as Hizballah's primary enemy and it did not hesitate to declare this publicly in their attacks on American targets in Lebanon. For example, Nasrallah described the relations between his organization and the U.S. in February 1995 as *"The U.S. is the first evil. The Imam (meaning Khomeini) described it as the biggest Satan... we are hostile to the U.S. because they are hostile towards us... We only find adherence to oppressive aggression, and Satanism."* In 1998 he stated that *"the U.S. is the origin of all the calamities and destruction caused to our nation and all Arab nations. The Zionist murderous machine was built and financed by the U.S.".* [11]

In 1997, the U.S. defined the Hizballah as a terror organization whose operations constitute a threat to American interests. The man responsible for the Jihad Council, Imad Mugnia, appears at the top of the FBI's list of most wanted persons and the U.S. is willing to pay twenty five million dollars for information leading to his arrest.[12]

An American terror researcher cognizant of American action against Hizballah wrote in 2003 that "*Hizballah is a terrorist group of global reach, with an entrenched logistical support operating across Canada. The organization's reprehensible goals are clear, whether or not its officials actually articulate them. Hizballah should be banned not for its rhetoric, but for the terrorist activities – operational and logistical – that it conducts in Canada, the United States, South America, the Middle East and elsewhere.*"[13]

---

[10] Esther Webman. "Following 9/11 Islam and the West, Between Conflict and Making Peace", Moshe Dayan Center, Tel Aviv 2002, pp. 15-20.

[11] Interview with Nasrallah, Al-Manar February 20,1995. See also: Nasrallah Al-Safir February 24,1998.

[12] Matthew Levitt. "Banning Hizballah Activity in Canada." Peacewatch/Policywatch Anthology 2003. The Washington Institute for Near East Policy, pp. 102-104. Additional American researchers, including Robert Satloff carry the same opinion, and contend that the organization is a global player which is a threat to the U.S.

[13] Levitt, 2003. On the reference to Hizballah as a player of global reach, see Kenneth Katzman, "Narrowing options in Lebanon," in Stephen C. Pelletiere (ed.), Terrorism: National Security Policy and the Home Front Strategic Studies Institute May 15, 1995.

The organization enlists its activists from Islamic communities worldwide, and usually (but not only) from the Lebanese Shi'ite communities. The global network serves the organization in achieving and realizing the following goals:

1. Gathering operational intelligence on defined targets.
2. Keeping "sleeper" cells in field cells in various countries.
3. Raising funds for the organization's operations.
4. Smuggling – Cigarettes, drugs and diamonds. The organization operates independently or together with the Mafia in various places worldwide. This activity constitutes an important source of income for the financing of the organization's operations.
5. Acquisition and smuggling of weaponry.

The existence of this global network provides the organization with the ability to perpetrate terror attacks within a relatively short period from the time the decision is made by the Shura Council.

In October 2002, the U.S. under Secretary of Defense, Doug Feith, stated that *"one of the most highly developed and most dangerous networks, as Secretary Armitage suggested, is Hezbollah. . . . we recognize that. It is an organization that is functioning in many continents. . . its operations are based largely in Lebanon. It's supported by the Syrians and the Iranians. It has operations cells in Africa, in South America, in Asia. We are certainly watching it, conscious of it, and it is one of the key international terrorist networks; there's no question about that."* [14]

4 Changes in the Organizations Modus Operandi in the Global Arena

When analyzing the organization's operations in the global area, two different periods are plainly visible:

The first period is the decade of the 1980s, during which the organization carried out a series of terror attacks, which included suicide bombing attacks, hijacking aircraft and hostage-taking strikes of Westerners on Lebanese soil and abroad. During this period, the organization laid the foundations, with the aid of the Iranians, of its network of international activists and supporters.

---

[14] http://www.defenselink.mil/policy/speech/oct_8_02.html.

The second period is defined from the beginning of the 1990s and has continued until today. This period is characterized by the organization changing of its modus operandi abroad. It started to establish and expand its operational and logistic network abroad, while at the same time reducing the scope of its attacks in this arena against Western targets, focusing on "qualitative" targets, such as the U.S. army base in Dhahran in Saudi Arabia. Nineteen men were killed in that attack and more than 500 wounded. While the organization is conducting a continuous media campaign against the United States, it is encouraging attacks and even operating itself against U.S. interests in Iraq. During this stage, the organization has acted against Israeli and Jewish targets worldwide. Two of the most prominent attacks which it perpetrated took place in Argentina. On March 17th, 1992, the attack on the Israeli Embassy in Buenos Aires killed twenty nine people and wounded 250 others. The second attack was carried out on July 18th, 1994 in Buenos Aires against the Argentine Jewish Mutual Association (AMIA) during which 100 people were killed and dozens wounded.[15]

4.1 The Organization's Focuses and Operational Characteristics

4.1.1 In the Global Arena

The organization's global network is controlled from Lebanon by the Hizballah's Shura Council and directly by Imad Mugnia. The organization's operations abroad, as well as the formation of its network, are aided by Iran. The following are the main spheres of the organization's activities according to regions:

North America – In the year 2000 a network of activists was exposed. They were accused, inter alia, of aiding the organization, by purchasing weapons and money laundering. The organization operates within the Shi'ite communities in the United States and Canada, to raise funds for its activities. In 2001, a Hizballah activist was arrested and accused of supplying weapons to the organization. In December 2002, Canada defined the Hizballah as a terror organization and similar to the United States, is working to prevent fund raising for the organization by the Shi'ite communities in the country.[16]

---

[15] For the list of major Hizballah's terror attacks look at http://www.intelligence.org.il/eng/bu/hizbullah/pb/app4.htm.

[16] http://www.intelligence.org.il/eng/bu/hizbullah/chap_d.doc. See also: Ely Karmon "Fight on all Fronts, Hizballah the War on Terror and the War in Iraq". The Washington Institute Policy Focus, 2003. p. 8-11. See also: Yehudit Barasky, Hizballah the party of god, AJC, May 2003.

South America – The organization has a wide network of activists in the tri-border area of Argentina, Brazil and Paraguay, which are involved in crime, terrorism, logistic aid and financing activities. The organization's activists co-operate with the Iranians in perpetrating attacks, as well as with the activists of Al Qaida. The local authorities have difficulty in restraining or reducing the organization's activities from their territory. The organization is also active in additional countries on this continent including Colombia, Guatemala, Panama and Costa Rica.[17]

Europe – Europe is a comfortable activity base for Hizballah particularly due the fact that the organization does not appear on the European list of terror organizations. The organization dispatches its activists to perpetrate attacks against Israel via Europe. Between the years of 1996 to 2001 the following four activists of the organization were dispatched in this manner to Israel. 1. Hussein Mikdad (1996) – a Lebanese who was sent on a forged British passport. 2. Stefan Smirk (1997) – a German who converted to Islam, was sent to Israel on a German passport. 3. Fawzi Ayub (2000) – a Canadian of Lebanese origin was sent to Israel on a forged American passport. 4. Jihad Shuman (2001) a British citizen of Lebanese origin was sent to Israel on a British passport.[18]

In 2001, Sweden exposed a network of terrorism activists which was directly connected to Al Qaida and Hizballah. They were accused of transferring information, communications and funding.[19]

The organization raises funds for its operations in Europe through the activities of charitable organizations in Germany, Great Britain and Switzerland. This activity was particularly evident in Germany which in 2002, closed down two charitable organizations, the Alshahid Social Relief Institution and the Al Aqsa Fund, which were raising funds for Hizballah in Germany. The organization also operates, inter alia, in Russia, the Balkans, Turkey, Cyprus, Holland and Spain.[20]

Asia – Hizballah has a large organizational network in Asia, in particular in the Moslem countries in South-East Asia: Malaysia, the Philippines, Indonesia, Thailand, Korea and India. Reports relating to the activities of this network show that in 1995, plans existed to attack United States naval vessels and Israeli mer-

---

[17] Federal Research Division, Library of Congress, Terrorist and organized crime groups in the tri-border area (TBA) of South America.
[18] http://www.intelligence.org.il/eng/bu/hizbullah/chap_d.doc.
[19] Ely Karmon. "Fight on all Fronts, Hizballah the War on Terror and the War in Iraq". The Washington Institute Policy Focus, 2003. p. 11
[20] http://www.intelligence.org.il/eng/bu/hizbullah/chap_d.doc.

chant ships anchored in the Philippines. It was also reported that they gathered intelligence information relating to Jewish synagogues in Manila and the El Al offices in Bangkok. In 1994, an attempted car-bombing of the Israel Embassy in Thailand was foiled, due to an accident. Reports show that the organization is enlisting local activists in South East Asia, sending them to Lebanon for training, so as to enable them to perpetrate attacks in their countries of origin and in Australia.[21]

Africa – Hizballah and the Iranians operate a widespread active network in Africa amongst the Moslem communities. Wealthy Lebanese Shi'ite communities in Africa donate funds to the organization. The organization is active in the Ivory Coast, Nigeria, South Africa, Zaire, Zimbabwe, Uganda, etc. The organization's activists and the Iranians have created cooperative ties with Sudan and Bin Laden. It is noteworthy that the organization operates a network of diamond smuggling in Africa. In June 2004, the organization refuted American claims that it profits from the diamond trade in West Africa.[22]

5 American Activity in Eliminating/Restraining the Organization

From the second half of the 1980s, the United States has been striving to eliminate the Hizballah as an organizational entity of terrorism and to reduce its influence in the regional and international arenas, by pressurizing Syria and Iran and drying up the sources of income and aid given to the organization. These measures have not achieved significant results so far.[23]

In October 1997, the American administration published a list of organizations, which they defined as terrorist organizations, and Hizballah was included among

---

[21] Ely Karmon. "Fight on all Fronts, Hizballah the War on Terror and the War in Iraq". The Washington Institute Policy Focus, 2003. See also Matthew Levitt. "Hezbollah: A Case Study of Global Reach". The Washington Institute for Near East Policy. See also http://www.aijac.org.au/resources/aijac-media/cr-age-020603.html, Colin Rubenstein . "Australia is Right to Ban Hezbolla, Here's why", The Age, June 2 2003.
[22] http://www.intelligence.org.il/eng/bu/hizbullah/chap_d.doc.
See also: Al-Manar June 30 2004.
[23] Robert Satloff, "U.S. Policy Toward Islamism: A Theoretical and Operational Overview". The Council of Foreign Relations, Inc. New York, 2000, pp. 16-18. See also: Rensselaer Lee and Raphael Perl, "Foreign Affairs, Defense and Trade Division, Issues Brief for Congress Terrorism, the Future and U.S. Foreign Policy", Congressional Research Service, The Library of Congress, updated 12.12.2002.

them. The organization appears on this list to date. Recently, the organization's television station "Al-Manar" was added to the list and its broadcasts were banned in the U.S. and France. These steps were intended to make it difficult to raise funds in the U.S. for the organization's activities, to enable the freezing of its assets in the U.S. and to prevent any possibility of it influencing Moslem public opinion via the Al-Manar broadcasts. [24]

6 Hizballah and the Regional Arena

6.1 Hizballah's Relations with Iran

The relationship between Hizballah and Iran is that of a sponsor and a client, who share an Islamic Shi'ite common denominator, based on the higher religious authority in Iran. However, from the second half of the 1990s, as part of the effort to change its image, the organization declared that it was conducting an independent policy which was not influenced by Iranian decisions. Nasrallah himself several times stated that "*we are responsible to the spiritual leader which was in the past Khomeini and today is Ali Kahmenahi. We adhere to the principle of obedience to the teacher of religious law*". However, he added that "*a decision made by the Iranian government does not bind the Hizballah organization at all.*" The reality on the ground is not as clear and unequivocal as stated by Nasrallah. The organization has been aided many times by Iran, as a means of halting Syrian and other pressure to restrain the organization or disarm it.

Iran gives the organization 70-100 million dollars per year and supplies it with various weapons, mostly via the Damascus airport. In addition, it continues to support the organization's operations in the international arena. From Iran's point of view, Hizballah constitutes a means of perpetrating terror attacks to achieve Iranian interests on the one hand, and on the other as a major tool in the Islamic conflict with Isra[25]

---

[24] Al-Ahed, October 17 1997. see also: Al-Nur radio October 9, 1997. see also Al-Safir April 22, 1998. see also, Michel Gurfinkiel . "French ban of Anti-Semitic TV station shows impact of war on terror". New York Sun December 22, 2004. see also: Avi Jorisch and Matthew Levitt. " Banning Hizballah TV in America", December 17, 2004, http://www.washingtoninstitute.org/templateC05.php?CID=2207

[25] Tally Kritzman, "Arrest of Hizballah Supporters in the U.S.A: Successful anti-terrorist action or a drop in the bucket?", August 29, 2000, http://www.ict.org.il/articles/articledet.cfm?articleid=129. see also: Zohar Palti and Matthew Levitt. Special policy forum report Hizballah's west bank foothold, June,18 2004.

6.2 Hizballah's Relations with Syria

Syria acts as the landlord of Lebanon. In recent years, Syria mainly used diplomatic means to restrain Hizballah. It summoned Hizballah's leaders to Damascus for explanations, and involved Iran by asking it to use its influence with the organization. In certain cases, it even threatened to bring the organization under control. The "special" status which the organization enjoyed and the condoning shown by Syria, even when its interests were harmed as a result of Hizballah's actions, mainly emanated from the Syria's need to hold on to the strategic alliance with Iran.

During Assad Jr.'s time in power, a change occurred in the fundamental nature of the relationship between Syria and the organization. Hizballah became Syria's strategic partner in Lebanon. Since the withdrawal of the Israel Defense Forces from Lebanon June 2000, Syria supplies Hizballah with weapons on the one hand, and political support in the Lebanese and international arenas on the other.

6.3 Hizballah and the Jihad Arena in Iraq

The Hizballah leadership and the heads of the Shi'ite community in Iraq have had a close relationship dating back to the period when the leaders of the organization studied in the Shi'ite colleges in Najaf. The organization expresses its solidarity with the struggle of the radical Shi'ites in Iraq and finances the activities of the resistance against the Coalition and its Iraqi allies. The organization conducts a propaganda campaign against the Coalition in Iraq and endeavors to influence the Iraqis to join the opposition forces. Hizballah has opened an office in Iraq to advance the Shi'ite resistance, and its activists have even been arrested, according to one of the reports, on suspicion of being involved in terror activities, together with pro-Iranian activis[26]

6.4 Hizballah's New Front against Israel

In May 2000, the Israel Defense Forces withdrew from Lebanon and thereby terminated a chapter of 18 years on Lebanese soil and a decade, which fluctuated between extreme escalation in the operations against Hizballah, and the near signing of a peace agreement with Syria.

---

[26] "Iraqi Source Reports Arrest of Hizballah Captain, Massing of Iranian Troops" Al-Shark Al-Awsat, June 19, 2004.

Since the withdrawal the organization has changed its rhetoric and its policies, and has adapted them to the new situation. The organization has formed new ideas and goals and has developed the operational capability to enable it to realize its aims. At the same time, it has started carrying out direct attacks against Israel in the following manners:

1. Laying explosives.
2. Shooting at the Shebaa farm area which it claims is still occupied Lebanese territory.
3. Shooting at I.D.F. aircraft which penetrated Lebanese airspace.
4. Kidnapping Israeli soldiers.
5. Enlistment and operation of Israeli Arabs for activity inside the State of Israel, to gather intelligence information, and to carry out terror attacks.

The organization has acquired a considerable quantity of arms from Iran and Syria and has deployed them in Southern Lebanon in field cells exclusively controlled by the organization (Hizballah land). The Head of Israeli intelligence, Maj.Gen. Farkash, has stated that the organization has approximately 13,000 short-range rockets, about 500 medium-range rockets and several missiles with a range of 115-215 km/s. The organization sees these weapons as a means of deterrence against Israel and has even defined its policy on the iss[27]

Hizballah's leader, Nasrallah, feels secure in the organization's position in Southern Lebanon and therefore did not hesitate in September 2004 to define the reciprocity between his organization and the Lebanese army in the South, as follows: "In Lebanon there is an official Lebanese institution called the Lebanese army, and a popular resistance called the Resistance. Within on strategy, these two complement each other. They cooperate and share the roles in each, protecting and forming a fence around the homeland."[28]

6.5 Hizballah's New Front against Israel – Indirect Operations

The anarchy which has controlled the Palestinian Authority during the Intifada Al Aqsa, enabled Hizballah to become an influential organization within the West Bank and the Gaza Strip.

The organization set up a network of terror cells in these areas, instructed them, on several cases from their Lebanese training camps, on how to carry out at-

---

[27] "IDF Intelligence Chief Views Hizballah-Syria Ties, PA Chaos, Saudi Stability". The Jerusalem Post, July 26, 2004.
[28] Nasrallah speech, Al manar, September 4, 2004.

tacks, manufacture weapons, guerilla techniques, and pushed them to perpetrate attacks. In addition, according to Israeli intelligence reports, in 2004, Hizballah financed approximately 70-80% of the terror cells in the field amounting to 1,500,000 dollars a year. The organization was also involved in smuggling weapons to the Palestinians, for example the case of Karen A and the Santorini. These weapons were intended to increase the violence in the area to much higher levels. It is noteworthy, that Hizballah systematically acts to prevent any possibility of negotiations between the Palestinians and Israel by initiating violence and attac[29]

7 Hizballah and the Media

Hizballah operates a media empire, in comparison to other terror organizations. The leaders of the organization, who are aware of the power of rhetoric and the media on public opinion and the enlistment of activists, operate a number of mass media means:

1. Al Manar television – The main mouthpiece of the organization which is televised via satellite to millions of viewers worldwide. In December 2004, France banned the station's broadcasts by satellite in France, a week later, the United States also declared that the station was broadcasting propaganda in support of terrorism.

2. Radio Al Nur – Broadcasts from Lebanon and spreads the organization's messages.

3. Official internet sites of the organization, Nasrallah, and other bodies in the movement.

The media network serves to strengthen the organization's standing and that of its leaders within public opinion in Lebanon and outside Lebanon, to advance its ideology and strategic goals, to conduct a psychological war against its enemy and to spread propaganda to its other listeners. The organization used the media to advance the Palestinians' Intifada Al Aqsa as well as the resistance to the Americans in Iraq.

---

[29] Zohar Palti and Matthew Levitt . "Special policy forum report Hizballah's west bank foothold". June,18 2004. Nasrallah Speech, Al-Manar, October 30, 2004, see also: http://www.intelligence.org.il/sp/1_05/hezbollah.htm.

8 Summary

The Hizballah organization is an international terror organization, which makes use of its socio-political arm to present an image of a legitimate pragmatic Lebanese party, which operates guerilla warfare against a conquering army. In actuality, however, the organization also includes a covert terrorist arm which it uses against Israel, and western targets. The organization has not abandoned the idea of realizing an Islamic nation through Jihad, based on the principles of Khomeini and it is waiting for the right time to realize this goal. Hizballah presents a significant threat to the international arena. It has succeeded in establishing a global terror network which it utilizes to finance its activities, gather intelligence, aid and support other terror organizations includes Al-Qaeda, and to perpetrate terror attacks.

Terror Online:
How do Terrorists use the Internet?

Prof. Dr. Gabriel Weimann

Department of Communication, Haifa University, Israel
weimann@soc.haifa.ac.il

1 Introduction

Communication scholars conceptualize modern terrorism within the framework of symbolic communication theory. For example, Kraber argues that

> as a symbolic act, terrorism can be analyzed much like other media of communication, consisting of four basic components: transmitter (the terrorist), intended recipient (target), message (bombing, ambush) and feed back (reaction of target audience).[1]

Others have even argued that terrorism is theater, aimed not at the actual victims, but rather at the people watching on television.[2] Thus, modern terrorism can be understood as an attempt to communicate messages through the use of orchestrated violence.

The potential of the Internet for political purposes has fascinated many. Utopian visions of a 'virtual state' in which citizens hold daily common discussions, communicate needs and demands to their representatives, and vote by various referenda (all using communication by computers) have been raised by thinkers and researchers. However, this utopian vision was challenged by pornographic and racist content on the Internet, and it also became apparent that radical terrorist organizations of various kinds – anarchists, nationalists, separatists, revolutionaries, Neo-Marxists, and fascists – were using the network to distribute their propaganda, to communicate with their supporters, to create public awareness and sympathy, and even to execute operations. Paradoxically, the very decentralized structure that the American security services created out of fear of a

---

[1] Philip A. Karber, "Urban Terrorism: Baseline Data and Conceptual Framework," *Social Science Quarterly* 52 (1971): 529.

[2] Gabriel Weimann and Conrad Winn, 1994. *The Theater of Terror*. New York: Longman Publication; Gabriel Weimann, 1999. *The Theater of Terror: The Challenge for Democracy*. In R. Cohen-Almagor (ed.), Basic Issues in Israeli Democracy. Tel Aviv: Sifriyat Poalim (Hebrew).

Soviet nuclear attack now serves the interests of the greatest foe of the West's security services since the end of the Cold War, namely international terror. The nature of the network, its international character and chaotic structure, the simple access, the anonymity – all furnish terrorist organizations with an ideal arena for action. The present research focuses on the use of the Internet by modern terrorist organizations and attempts to describe the uses terrorist organizations make of this new communication technology.

2   The Advantages of the Internet for Modern Terrorism

The network of computer-mediated communication (CMC) is ideal for terrorists-as-communicators: it is decentralized, it cannot be subjected to control or restriction, it is not censored, and it allows access to anyone who wants it. The structure of modern terrorist organizations is making computer-mediated communication more important and useful for them. The loosely-knit network of cells and divisions and subgroups, typical to modern terrorists, makes the Internet an ideal and necessary tool for inter-group and intra-group networking. Al Qaeda, for example, has shown itself to be a remarkably nimble, flexible, and adaptive entity, mainly due to its decentralized structure.[3] The rise of networked terrorist groups is part of a broader shift to what Arquilla and Ronfledt have called "netwar."[4] Netwar refers to an emerging mode of conflict and crime at societal levels, involving measures short of traditional war in which the protagonists are likely to consist of small, dispersed groups who communicate, coordinate, and conduct their campaigns in an "internetted" manner and without a precise central command.

It is easy for terrorists to set up a website. Take for example the al Qaeda's long-lasting website, alneda.com. In the case of alneda.com, al Qaeda members created a fictitious organization, "The Center for Islamic Studies and Research," a bogus street address in Venezuela and a free Hotmail e-mail account to contact Emerge Systems, a Web hosting company in Malaysia, U.S. Intelligence officials

---

[3] Bruce Hoffman, "Al Qaeda, Trends in Terrorism, and Future Potentialities: An Assessment," *Studies in Conflict and Terrorism* 26 (2003): 427-440.

[4] John Arquilla and David R. Ronfledt, "Networks, Netwars, and the Fight for the Future" *First Monday* October 25, 2003 (Washington, DC, 2001); Arquilla and Ronfledt, "The advent of netwar (revisited)," in *Networks and netwars*, eds. Arquilla and Ronfledt (Santa Monica: RAND Corporation, 2001): 1-25; John Arquilla, David Ronfledt, and Michele Zanini, "Networks, Netwar and Information-Age Terrorism," in *Countering the New Terrorism*, eds. Ian O. Lesser, Bruce Hoffman, John Arquilla, David F. Ronfledt, Michele Zanini and Brian Michael Jenkins (Santa Monica: RAND Corporation, 2001).

say. The group then wired $87 to a Malaysian bank to pay for the cost of the website for a year. According to former CIA counterterrorism chief Vince Cannistraro, "Internet communications have become the main communications system among al Qaeda around the world because it's safer, easier and more anonymous if they take the right precautions, and I think they're doing that."[5]

Websites are only one of the Internet's services used by modern terrorism; there are many other facilities in the Net – e-mail, chat rooms, e-groups, forums, virtual message boards – that are used more and more by terrorists. Thus, for example, Yahoo! has become one of al Qaeda's most significant ideological bases of operation. They utilize several facets of the Yahoo! service, including chat functions, e-mail, and, most importantly, Yahoo! groups. Creating a Yahoo! group is free, quick, and extremely easy, and several terrorist groups and their supporters have used several Yahoo! groups.[6] Very often, the groups contain the latest links to other websites, serving as an online directory, and are sometimes the first to post communiqués to the public. Thus, by using Yahoo! groups, al Qaeda supporters chronicle the terrorist group's victories, disseminate hatred of non-Muslims, and provide multimedia Jihad frenzy for sympathetic viewers and other al Qaeda members.

The great virtues of the Internet – ease of access, lack of regulation, vast potential audiences, fast flow of information, and so forth – have been converted into the advantage of groups committed to terrorizing societies to achieve their goals. The anonymity offered by the Internet is very attractive for modern terrorists.[7] Due to their extremist beliefs and values, terrorists require anonymity to exist and operate in social environments that may not agree with their particular ideology or activities. The Internet provides this anonymity as well as easy access from everywhere with the option to post messages, to e-mail, to upload or download information – and to disappear into the dark.

3 Who are the Terrorists of the Internet?

These advantages have not gone unnoticed by terrorist organizations, no matter what their political orientation. Islamists and Marxists, nationalists and sep-

---

[5] Cited by Jack Kelly, "Militants Wire Web with Links to Jihad," *USA Today* (July 2002).
[6] Rita Katz and Josh Devon, "WWW.JIHAD.COM: E-Groups Abused by Jihadists," *National Review Online*, at: http://www.nationalreview.com/comment/comment-katz-devon071403.asp (2003).
[7] Marc Rogers, "The Psychology of Cyber-terrorism," in *Terrorist, Victims and Society*, ed. Andrew Silke (Chichester: John Wiley & Sons, 2003): 77-92.

aratists, fundamentalists and extremists, racists and anarchists: all find the Internet alluring. Today, all active terrorist organizations maintain websites, and many maintain more than one website and use several different languages. As the following illustrative list shows, these organizations and groups come from all corners of the globe. (This geographical categorization, it should be noted, reveals the geographical diversity but obscures the fact that many groups are truly transnational, and even transregional, in character.)

- *From the Middle East*, Hamas (the Islamic Resistance Movement), the Lebanese Hezbollah (Party of God), the Al Aqsa Martyrs Brigades, Fatah Tanzim, the Popular Front for the Liberation of Palestine (PLFP), the Palestinian Islamic Jihad, the Kahane Lives movement, the People's Mujahedin of Iran (PMOI – Mujahedin-e Khalq), the Kurdish Workers' Party (PKK); the Turkish-based Popular Democratic Liberation Front Party (DHKP/C), and the Great East Islamic Raiders Front (IBDA-C), which is also based in Turkey.
- *From Europe*, the Basque ETA movement, Armata Corsa (the Corsican Army), and the Real Irish Republican Army (RIRA).
- *From Latin America*, Peru's Tupak-Amaru (MRTA) and Shining Path (Sendero Luminoso), the Colombian National Liberation Army (ELN-Colombia), and the Armed Revolutionary Forces of Colombia (FARC).
- *From Asia*, al Qaeda, the Japanese Supreme Truth (Aum Shinrikyo), Ansar al Islam (Supporters of Islam) in Iraq, the Japanese Red Army (JRA), Hizb-ul Mujehideen in Kashmir, the Liberation Tigers of Tamil Eelam (LTTE), the Islamic Movement of Uzbekistan (IMU), Moro Islamic Liberation Front (MILF) in the Philippines, the Pakistan-based Lashkar-e-Taiba, and the rebel movement in Chechnya.

4 Methodology

The findings reported here come from a more general research project hosted and funded by the United States Institute of Peace that summarized seven years of monitoring terrorist presence on the Net[8]. The population for this study was defined as the Internet sites of terrorist movements as they appeared in the period between January 1998 and September 2004. We used the U.S. State Department's list of terrorist organizations which meet the accepted definition

---

[8] Gabriel Weimann, 2004a. *WWW.Terror.Net: How Modern Terrorism Uses the Internet*, Special Report, Washington, DC: United States Institute of Peace; Gabriel Weimann, 2004b. "Cyberterrorism: How real is the Threat?" Special Report, Washington, DC: United States Institute of Peace.

of terror.[9] Two earlier studies served as pilot studies for the present project: we applied a systematic content analysis to a sample of terrorist sites and repeated this analysis after three years.[10] These exploratory studies provided both the methodological tools as well as the first evidence of the diffusion of terrorism into the Internet and its growing sophistication. To locate the terrorist sites, frequent systematic scans of the Internet were conducted using the various keywords and names of organizations in the database. First, the standard search engines (Altavista, Lycos, Infoseek, Yahoo, Magellan, and Google) were used. The first search, conducted in January 1998, yielded 14 organizations and 16 Internet sites. Our scan of the Internet in 2003-4 revealed over 4,300 websites serving terrorists and their supporters. The Internet, as we found out, is a very dynamic arena – websites emerge and disappear, change addresses, or reformat. Throughout the years of monitoring the terrorist presence in the Net, we learned how to locate their new sites, how to search in chat rooms and forums of supporters and sympathizers for the new "addresses," and how to use links in other organizations' websites to update our lists. This was often a Sisyphean effort, especially since in certain instances (e.g. al Qaeda's websites) the location and the contents changed almost daily.

We have identified numerous, albeit sometimes overlapping ways in which contemporary terrorists use the Internet.[11] Some of these parallel the uses to which everyone puts the Internet – information gathering, for instance. Some resemble the uses made of the medium by traditional political organizations – for example, raising funds and disseminating propaganda. Others, however, are much more unusual and distinctive – for instance, hiding instructions, manuals, and directions in coded messages or encrypted files. In this report we focus on the use of the Internet as a virtual training camp, using the computer-mediated channels to train, teach, direct, and coordinate terrorists.

5   The Communicative Uses of the Internet by Terrorism

One of the enduring axioms of terrorism is that it is designed to generate publicity and attract attention to the terrorists and their cause. How do terrorist groups use the Internet to advance the organization's political and ideological agenda? We know that terrorist organizations are increasingly resorting to the

---

[9] Alex Schmid and Albert J. Jongman, 1988. *Political Terrorism*. Amsterdam: North-Holland Publishing; Gabriel Weimann and Conrad Winn, 1994. *The Theater of Terror*. New York: Longman Publication.
[10] Tzfati & Weimann, 1999; Tzfati & Weimann, 2002, op. cit.
[11] Weimann, 2004a, op. cit.

Internet to disseminate their views to a wider public, coming to the realization that establishing their presence in cyberspace is nearly just as critical to their long-term success as any military triumph or act of sabotage. Terrorist groups themselves can maintain webpages to "advertise" their ideology, to disseminate propaganda, and to recruit supporters. It is the first time that they have easily been able to reach the public directly and make their existence known on an international scale.

In the "conventional media," if some report was offensive to a government, the content of the report could be censored or filtered. However, governments cannot control the Internet to the same degree they could control newspapers, radio, and TV. The web allows an uncensored and unfiltered version of events to be broadcast world-wide. Chat rooms, websites, and bulletin boards are largely uncontrolled, with few filters in place. This climate, argues Thomas, is perfect for a radical group to explain its actions or to offset both internal and international condemnation, especially when using specific servers.[12] The Internet can target fence-sitters as well as true believers with different messages, oriented towards the target audience. Thus, for example, in the aftermath of the 9/11 attacks, al Qaeda operatives used the Internet to fight for the hearts and minds of the Islamic faithful world-wide. Several internationally recognized and respected Muslims who questioned the attacks were described as hypocrites by al Qaeda. Al Qaeda ran two websites, alneda.com and drasat.com, to discuss the legality of the attacks on 9/11. Al Qaeda stated that Islam shares no fundamental values with the West and that Muslims are committed to spread Islam by the sword. As a result of such commentary, several Muslim critics of al Qaeda's policies withdrew their prior condemnation.

What is the content of terrorist sites? They usually include information about the history of the organization as well as biographies of its leaders, founders, heroes, commanders, or revered personalities, information on the political and ideological aims of the organization, and up-to-date news. Most of the sites give a detailed historical review of the social and political background, a selective description of the organization's notable activities in the past, and its aims. National organizations (separatist or territorial) generally display maps of the areas in dispute: the Hamas site shows a map of Palestine; the Colombian site shows a map of Colombia; the Zapatista site has a map of Chiapas and information about it; the Tamil site presents a map of Sri Lanka.

---

[12] Timothy L. Thomas, 2003. "Al Qaeda and the Internet: The Danger of 'Cyberplanning'," *Parameters*, Spring, 112-123.

Almost all the terror sites detail the goals of the respective organisations in one way or another. The most common presentation of aims is through a direct criticism of their enemies or rivals. Thus, the terrorist sites do not concentrate only on information concerning their organizations; direct attack of the enemy is the most common strategy of the Internet terrorists. By contrast, almost all sites avoid presenting and detailing their violent activities. Although the organizations behind these sites have a record of bloodshed, they hardly ever record these activities on their sites. The exceptions are Hizbollah and Hamas, whose sites show updated statistical reports of its actions ('daily operations'), the number of dead 'martyrs,' along with the number of 'Israeli enemies' and 'collaborators' killed. However, this detailed depiction of violent action is unusual.

While avoiding the violent aspects of their activities, the Internet terrorists, regardless of their nature, motives, or location, usually stress two issues: freedom of expression and political prisoners. The terrorists appear to aim at Western audiences who are sensitive to the norms of freedom of expression and emphasize the issues that provoke sympathy in democratic societies. Restricted expression by political movements is contrary to the fundamental and sacred principles of democracy. This tactic works particularly well on the stage of the Internet, the symbol of absolutely free communication. Another theme is that of political detentions. The organizations' websites emphasize the anti-democratic measures employed against them. In so doing, they attempt to malign the authorities, appealing both to their supporters ('constituents') as well as to more remote audiences of 'bystanders.' Even among the community of their 'enemies,' namely the public that is naturally hostile to the organization, the terrorists try, by emphasizing the threats to democracy, to create feelings of uneasiness and shame.

Common elements on the terror sites are the organization's communiqués and the speeches and writings of its leaders, founders, and ideologists. The sites often present a word-for-word series of official statements by the organizations, which the visitor can browse through, along with selected announcements arranged by date. They tend to recycle materials distributed in the past through the mass media and other communication means. Some terrorist sites house a veritable online gift shop through which visitors can order and purchase books, video and audio cassettes, stickers, printed shirts, and pins with the organizations' badges.

The Internet is used by terrorists to deliver threats and messages to enemy governments and enemy populations. A Saudi radical Muslim group, the Brigade of the Two Holy Mosques, sent a threat to the House of Saud and its subjects in December 2003: "We are warning anyone who cooperates with the authorities or gives the tyrants information leading to the arrest of one of the mujahideen. He will be liquidated." The next day, a man identifying himself as "Daleel Al-Mojahid" (meaning "guide for the Jihad warrior") and claiming affiliation with the Taliban and al Qaeda issued his own warning to those participating in the previous weekend's Loya Jirga council in Afghanistan: "We [. . .] assure you and send you our coming news that we will start killing all the (Loya Jerga) council that is due to start elections, we have sent them all messages warning them that if any of them show up in the elections they will be killed directly on our hands." Both of these threats were delivered through the Internet. More than a year later, in June 2004, al Qaeda posted an alarming threat to Americans and Western airlines through a warning to Muslims:

> We are hereby renewing our call and warning to our Muslim brothers against associating [mingling] with the Crusaders: Americans, Westerners, and all the Polytheists in the Arab Peninsula. Muslims must keep away from them, their residences and compounds, and all their means of transportation [. . .]. We do not wish for any of our Muslim brothers to bring it upon himself, and allow his killing by keeping company with the enemy that must be fought. We have no other lawful choice but to fight and exterminate them. Everything related to those Crusaders: Compounds, bases, means of transportation, especially Western and American airlines – will soon be the target of our future operations with the help and assistance of God, in our course for the Jihad that we shall continue in the upcoming period in particular.

This statement was issued by "al Qaeda of the Arabian Peninsula" on an Islamic website known to be an al Qaeda mouthpiece and on several Arabic language Jihad forums. This quote is part of a general threat advising Muslims to avoid being in close proximity to Americans and other non-Muslims in order to avoid being caught up in the coming wave of attacks. The message was posted by an individual with a history of providing credible information regarding the activities of al Qaeda in Saudi Arabia. The group, al Qaeda in the Arabian Peninsula (or Arabian Island), is the same group that conducted attacks on oil facilities and on the Oasis Residential Complex in Saudi Arabia during 2004.

The Internet can be used also to harm the credibility of enemy media, enemy officials, and the establishment. In this case the target audience is the enemy population, but the attack is on its official media credibility. One example comes from the Chechen separatist rebels fighting the Russian army; in their propaganda war with the Russians, Chechen fighters have been using the Internet. In May 2000, Russian forces sought to cast doubt on claims by Chechen rebels who said that they had shot down a Russian SU-24 jet fighter bomber. But when a picture of Chechen fighters holding parts of the plane's wreckage appeared on the rebels' Internet website, the Russians were forced to admit the claim was probably true. The rebel website – kavkaz.org – had proved its effectiveness again. It might seem odd that bedraggled partisans moving among mountain hideouts in a country desolated by war would use computers and sophisticated Internet technology to communicate with the world, but the Chechens had already launched their website before the Russians imposed an information blockade. The site is particularly important during the current fight against the Russians, because unlike in the earlier conflict, these times there are far fewer foreign journalists able to report from the Chechen side. Because the Chechen site is primarily designed to influence foreigners, it appears in Russian, English, and a handful of other languages, but not in Chechen. Journalists or government officials interested in finding out about the war use this website, which offers news and interviews with Chechen leaders, fighters, and civilians. Photographs published on the site are often used to back up Chechen claims, displaying images of the dead on both sides as well as of Russian prisoners. The Russians removed the site from a U.S. server. The site, however, has since moved among several other servers and now seems safely entrenched.

6 The Rhetoric of Terror on the Internet

As Weimann and Winn argued in their study on *The Theater of Terror*, one of the central problems facing modern terrorism is to justify the use of violence.[13] It is clear that this problem also preoccupies the operators of the terror Internet sites. At most sites significant efforts are devoted to vindicating the use of violence. Four rhetorical structures are used on the terrorist sites to justify violence. The first one is the "no-choice" motive. Most sites aver that they do not reject a peaceful solution. Violence is presented as a necessity foisted on the weak as the only means to deal with an oppressive enemy. Thus the Tamil Tigers argue that their use of violence is legitimized by the Sri Lankan rejection of the rights of the Tamil minority. They cite the UN Universal Declaration of Human Rights and various reports of external observers (usually from human rights organizations) about the right of the Tamil people to self-determination, the Geneva Convention, and UN Security Council resolutions. All these lead to the conclusion that "the armed struggle of the Tamil people is both right and legal because the rule of law for the Tamil people has ceased to exist." The site points out that the

---

[13] Weimann and Winn, op. cit.

Tamil struggle developed only as a last resort after the Tamils had endeavored to realize their rights peacefully.

The ELN notes that the armed struggle is legitimate, for

> with or without the guerrilla, violence reigns in our world day by day: hunger, repression, rape, crime [...]. The violence of our organization is the result, not the cause, of this reality. This is the attempt of the weak to free themselves [...]. Therefore, the ELN will not abandon the armed struggle until the causes of our struggle have passed [...]. We are fighting because we long for a society without violence.

The Hizbollah site argues that the Islamic resistance is a response to Zionist aggression and the Zionist aim of mastery over southern Lebanon, and that "as noted in the Declaration of Human Rights, it is our right to fight until our rights and our land are restored to us." Hamas argues that "just as the French resistance movement fought the Nazis in the forties, Hamas is a movement [...] composed of patriots seeking self-determination and struggling to free their homeland, Palestine."

A second rhetorical structure related to the legitimacy of the use of violence is the demonizing and de-legitimization of the enemy. The members of the movement or organization are presented as freedom fighters, forced against their will to use violence because a ruthless enemy is crushing the rights and dignity of their people or group. The enemy of the movement or the organization is the real terrorist, many sites insist, and 'our violence is dwarfed in comparison to his aggression' is a routine slogan. The Hamas site directs the visitor to a page bearing the heading 'Who Is A Terrorist?' and showing an illustration of Israeli soldiers holding a child (caption: 'We have captured a terrorist, Sir!'), another of Israeli soldiers in an armored troop carrier, with the bodies of women and children visible through the gun sights (caption: 'I have won, Levi! I shot three of those creatures'), and others of Israeli soldiers shooting and beating women and children, accompanied by cynical headings presenting the Israelis as inhuman brutes. The message is that the Palestinians are the victims of the Zionists, who are the real terrorists, devoid of moral restraint and ready to hurt women and children. The Hamas site is replete with many facts whose purpose is the de-legitimization of Israel. These include 'facts' about the connection between Zionist and British imperialism, quotations from Zionist leaders about 'Zionist expansionist aims,' and examples of brutal and violent acts committed by Israelis.

The Hizbollah site similarly stresses that the Israelis are the terrorists. It shows lurid pictures of the killings in the Kana disaster, deaths that in fact were caused by mistake by Israeli artillery. A historical survey of the 'development of the Islamic resistance' quotes from speeches of Zionist leaders (including Herzl) who held that to ensure water sources for the Jewish state, its northern border had to be the Litani River (today deep in Lebanese territory). The site presents detailed information about 'Israeli terrorism': information about the 'birth of the Zionist entity,' 'Israel's daily aggression,' and 'Israeli acts of slaughter'.

The argument at the Turkish DHKP/C site is that

> the ruling classes have adopted a policy of terror and slaughter, hardly to be found anywhere in the world [...]. Every day thousands of revolutionaries are murdered by the fascist forces of the state [...]. In the prisons hundreds of prisoners are tortured. Villages and forests are wiped out and thousands of people are driven off their land and herded into concentration camps. Almost every day the state raids the unions and workers' organizations [...]. At the same time, members of the ruling class are found almost every day involved in corruption or other scandals. Most of the senior officials of the state, including the president and the prime minister, depend on and are under the thumb of the Mafia and are linked to acts of bribery and corruption.

The Shining Path site gives information about "the crimes of the Fujimori regime, supported by the United States." According to this site,

> from the start the popular struggle was obliged to face the most evil brutality that the Peruvian government could apply – from the slaughter and annihilation of whole villages to the execution of hundreds of revolutionaries and of the Chairman of the organization Gonzalo [...]. The Peruvian army conducted a campaign of genocide [...]. For all that, the revolution continued to advance.

Terrorist rhetoric tries to shift the responsibility to the opponent, displaying his brutality, his inhumanity, and his immorality. The violence of the 'freedom' and 'liberation' movements is dwarfed in comparison with the cruelty of the opponent.

The third rhetorical tactic is to emphasize weakness. The organizations attempt to substantiate the claim that terror is the weapon of the weak. As noted earlier, despite the ever-present vocabulary of 'the armed struggle' or 'resistance,' the terror sites avoid mentioning or noting how they victimize others. On the other hand, the actions of the authorities against the terror groups are heavily stressed, usually with words such as 'slaughter,' 'murder,' 'genocide,' and the like. The organization is constantly being persecuted, its leaders are subject to assassination attempts and its supporters massacred, its freedom of expression is curtailed, and its adherents are arrested. This tactic, which portrays the organization as small, weak, and hunted down by a power or a strong state, turns the terrorists into the underdog. Hizbollah differs somewhat from other organizations in that it highlights its military achievements, gloating over enemy victims (showing pictures of funerals of murdered Israelis), and publishing detailed statistics about its military successes. The motive for this unique approach has been Hizbollah's attempt to influence the public debate in Israel about withdrawal from Lebanon. The organization has stated explicitly that its aim has been to exert pressure in Israel in favor of withdrawal. The organization knows that many Israelis visit the site, whose address is published in Israeli media. Hizbollah publishes its records of murdered Israelis, maintains electronic mail connections with Israelis, and appeals to Israeli parents whose sons serve in the Israeli army, all with the aim of causing demoralization.

Finally, some of the terror sites are replete with the rhetoric of non-violence, messages of love of peace, and of a non-violent solution. Although these are violent organizations, many of their sites claim that they seek peaceful solutions, diplomatic settlements, or arrangements reached through international pressure. Two organizations state that they are not violent at all – the Basques, who present themselves as searching for a peaceful resolution, and the ELN. The latter does indeed call for armed struggle, but the site writers argue that their organization is not militarist and that talk of the goal of the organization being a military revolution is idle gossip put about by the authorities.

Terrorist rhetoric on the Internet tries to present a mix of images and arguments in which the terrorists appear as victims forced to turn to violence to achieve their just goals, in the face of a brutal, merciless enemy, devoid of moral restraints. Demonizing the enemy, playing down the issue of terror victims, shifting blame for the use of violence to the enemy, and proclaiming peace-loving messages are strategies utilized on most terror sites. Is this rhetoric qualitatively different from that of terror organizations in other communication channels? It appears that the terror organizations that have turned to the Internet use patterns of rhetoric similar to those used by their spokespersons in the 'conventional' media. The justification of violence, the demonizing and de-legitimization of the enemy, and the rhetoric of weakness – all was found in press releases by the terror organizations, in the broadcasts of their radio and television stations, and in speeches and books by their leaders (see Cordes, 1988; Weimann & Winn, 1994).

However, the online version of terrorist rhetoric differs from the conventional media strategy of terrorists in that in the latter, the organizations took responsibility for violence, and did not avoid it. The rhetoric used by media-oriented terrorism in the early 1970s threatened the existing order altogether and did not hint at the possibility of diplomatic or peaceful solutions, as so many of the current organizations do on their websites. It is probable that perceptions of the medium (the Internet) and of the target audience (web surfers) dictate this more pacifist rhetorical strategy.

7 The Instrumental Uses of the Internet by Terrorism

In addition to communicative uses of the Internet, terrorists use the medium for instrumental purposes. It may serve them as an excellent source of useful information. The World-Wide Web alone offers about a billion pages of information, much of it free – and much of it of interest to terrorist organizations. Terrorists, for instance, can learn from the Internet about the schedules and locations of targets such as transportation facilities, nuclear power plants, public buildings, airports and ports, and even counterterrorism measures. Dan Verton, in his book *Black Ice: The Invisible Threat of Cyber-Terrorism* (2003), explains that

> al Qaeda cells now operate with the assistance of large databases containing details of potential targets in the U.S. They use the Internet to collect intelligence on those targets, especially critical economic nodes, and modern software enables them to study structural weaknesses in facilities as well as predict the cascading failure effect of attacking certain systems.[14]

Numerous tools are available to facilitate such data collection, often called datamining, including search engines, e-mail distribution lists, and chat rooms and discussion groups. Many websites offer their own search tools for extracting information from databases on their sites. Word searches of online newspapers and journals can likewise generate useful information for terrorists; some of this information may also be available in the traditional media, but online searching capabilities allow terrorists to capture it anonymously and with very little effort or expense. One captured al Qaeda computer contained the engineering and structural architecture features of a dam, enabling al Qaeda engineers and planners to simulate catastrophic failures.[15] According to Secretary of Defense Donald Rumsfeld, speaking on January 15, 2003, an al Qaeda training manual recovered in Afghanistan tells its readers, "Using public sources openly and without

---

[14] Dan Verton, *Black Ice: The Invisible Threat of Cyber-Terrorism* (New York: McGraw-Hill Osborne Media, 2003).
[15] Barton Gellman, "Cyber-Attacks by Al-Qaeda Feared," A01.

resorting to illegal means, it is possible to gather at least 80% of all information required about the enemy."[16]

Like many other Internet users, terrorists have access not only to maps and diagrams of potential targets but also to imaging data on those same facilities and networks that may reveal counterterrorist activities at a target site. Terrorists can use the Internet to learn about counterterrorism: word searches of online newspapers and journals allow a terrorist to study the means designed to counter his actions, or the vulnerabilities of these measures. For example, recent articles reported on attempts to slip contraband items through security checkpoints. One report noted that at Cincinnati's airport, contraband slipped through over 50% of the time. A simple Internet search would uncover this shortcoming and offer the terrorists an embarkation point for their next operation. Several reports on various Internet sites noted that U.S. law enforcement agencies were tracing calls made overseas to al Qaeda cells from phone cards, cell phones, phone booths, or Internet-based phone services. Exposing the targeting techniques of law enforcement agencies allows the terrorists to alter their operating procedures.

The Internet has become a networking device for modern terrorists. Modern terrorism has transformed into segmented networks instead of the pyramidal hierarchies and command-and-control systems (no matter how primitive) that have governed traditional insurgent organizations. The advantage of this operational structure is that surveillance, penetration, or capture of operatives do not lead the intelligence agency to other cells or the central control structure. In addition, cell members can be dispersed quickly and the organization dismantled when one member is captured, due to the flexible and ad hoc nature of the organization.[17] RAND's experts on modern terrorism, John Arquilla, David Ronfeldt, and Michele Zanini, point to the emergence of new forms of terrorist organization attuned to the Information Age. They contend, "Terrorists will continue to move from hierarchical toward information-age network designs. More effort will go into building arrays of transnational internetted groups than into building stand alone groups."[18]

Several reasons explain why modern communication technologies, especially the Internet, are so useful for modern terrorists in establishing and maintaining networks. First, new technologies have greatly reduced transmission time, enabling

---

[16] From "Citing Al Qaeda Manual, Rumsfeld Re-Emphasizes Web Security," *InsideDefense.com*, http://www.insidedefense.com/ (January 15, 2003).
[17] Hoffman, "Plan of Attack."
[18] Arquilla et al., 1999, 41.

dispersed organizational actors to communicate swiftly and to coordinate effectively. Second, new technologies have significantly reduced the cost of communication. Third, by integrating computing with communications, they have substantially increased the variety and complexity of the information that can be shared. Also, the Internet connects not only members of the same terrorist organizations but also members of different groups. For instance, dozens of sites exist that express support for terrorism conducted in the name of Jihad. These sites and related forums permit terrorists in places such as Chechnya, Palestine, Indonesia, Afghanistan, Turkey, Iraq, Malaysia, the Philippines, and Lebanon to exchange not only ideas and suggestions but also practical information about how to build bombs, establish terror cells, and carry out attacks.

> Thus, information-age technologies are highly advantageous for a netwar group whose constituents are geographically dispersed or carry out distinct but complementary activities. In addition, information technology (IT) can be used to plan, coordinate and execute operations. Using the Internet for communication can increase speed of mobilization and allow more dialogue between members, which enhances the organization's flexibility, since tactics can be adjusted more frequently.[19]

The latest communications technologies are thus enabling terrorists to operate from almost any country in the world provided they have access to the necessary infrastructure. Some analysts have argued that networked terrorists may have a reduced need for state support – indeed, governmental protection may become less necessary if technologies such as encryption allow a terrorist group to operate with a greater degree of stealth and safety.[20]

Terrorists may use the Internet to provide information to fellow terrorists, including maps, photographs, directions, codes, and technical details of how to use explosives. The World-Wide Web is home to dozens of sites that provide information on how to build chemical and explosive weapons. Many of these sites post the *Terrorist's Handbook* and *The Anarchist Cookbook*, two well-known manuals that offer detailed instructions of how to construct a wide range of bombs. Another manual, *The Mujahadeen Poisons Handbook*, written by Abdel-Aziz in 1996 and 'published' on the official Hamas website, details on 23 pages how to prepare various homemade poisons, poisonous gases, and other deadly materials for use in terrorist attacks.

---

[19] Ibid., p. 36.
[20] Kevin, J. Soo Hoo, Seymour E. Goodman and Lawrence T. Greenberg, "Information Technology and the Terrorist Threat", *Survival* 39, no. 3 (1997): 135–155.

The Hamas organization has launched an Internet course in the production and assembly of explosives. Hamas, which claims responsibility for the lion's share of Palestinian suicide bombing attacks, has established an Internet site that offers Muslims instructions in the production of bombs, rockets, and light aircraft. News of the site has spread throughout the West Bank and Gaza Strip. The instructions can be found on the website of Hamas's Izzedin Kassam military wing. The site, called "Military Academy," offers 14 lessons in bomb-making as part of what the Islamic group says is a campaign to expand the pool of bomb-makers. The courses include lessons on the production of a belt filled with explosives that can be worn by a suicide bomber. Other courses demonstrate how to manufacture plastic explosives from RDX, a material that is said to be difficult to detect. The Hamas online course also provides instructions on preparing regular bombs as well as methods to identify targets. Izzedin Kassam said the process of producing suicide bombs requires three people: a bomb expert, an electrician, and a tailor to sew the belt to the proportions of the suicide attacker. The Hamas site is interactive, and those taking the course can correspond with the movement's bomb instructors. However, the military wing warned that those who miss one lesson will not be allowed to continue the course. The site said those who ask a question about a lesson that already was given would be removed from the course. Those taking the course would also be required to take tests after each stage.

For al Qaeda, the Internet serves as a virtual training camp. When American forces in Afghanistan shut down al Qaeda terrorist training camps, the terror group moved its base of operations to the Internet. The Internet has become a valuable tool for the terrorist organization, not just to coordinate operations and launch attacks, but also as virtual training camps, a tool of indoctrination and recruitment. Actually the Internet has turned for al Qaeda to be what experts call an "online terrorism university." The prospect of self-taught terrorism suggests that personal initiative and decentralization may soon provide additional elements of chaos to the already difficult-to-detect web of terror groups and individuals. "It is not necessary [...] for you to join in a military training camp, or travel to another country, [...] you can learn alone, or with other brothers, in [our arms] preparation program," announced al Qaeda leader Abu Hadschir Al Muqrin, as cited by *Der Spiegel Online*, the Internet version of the weekly German newsmagazine.[21] In 2004, al Qaeda launched its online *Al Battar Training Camp. Al Battar* takes its name from the "Sword of the Prophets," currently

---

[21] Toby Westerman, "Terror training online: Al Qaeda franchises out," *International News Analysis* (April, 23 2004), at http://inatoday.com/terror\%20training\%20online\%2042304.htm.

located in the Topkapi Museum in Istanbul. In an effort to maintain the tradition of victory that is associated with the phrase *Al Battar*, the authors go into extensive detail each month, providing explicit directions in a wide range of topics that are essential for the well-prepared *mujhad*, or warrior. In early 2004, al Qaeda published the first issue of *Al Battar Training Camp*.[22] The introduction to the issue states:

> Preparing [for Jihad] is a personal commandment that applies to every Muslim [...]. Because many of Islam's young people do not yet know how to bear arms, not to mention use them, and because the agents of the Cross are hobbling the Muslims and preventing them from planning [*Jihad*] for the sake of Allah – your brothers the Mujahideen in the Arabian peninsula have decided to publish this booklet to serve the Mujahid brother in his place of isolation, and he will do the exercises and act according to the military knowledge included within it [...]. The basic idea is to spread military culture among the youth with the aim of filling the vacuum that the enemies of the religion have been seeking to expand for a long time. Allah willing, the magazine will be simple and easy, and in it, my Muslim brother, you will find basic lessons in the framework of a military training program, beginning with programs for sports training, through types of light weapons and guerilla group actions in the cities and mountains, and [including] important points in security and intelligence, so that you will be able [...] to fulfill the religious obligation that Allah has set upon you.

Like many other political organizations, terrorist groups use the Internet to raise funds. Al Qaeda, for instance, has always depended heavily on donations, and its global fundraising network is built upon a foundation of charities, non-governmental organizations, and other financial institutions that use websites and Internet-based chat rooms and forums to solicit and gather funds. The fighters in the Russian breakaway republic of Chechnya have likewise used the Internet to publicize the numbers of bank accounts to which sympathizers can contribute. (One of these Chechen bank accounts is located in Sacramento, California.) In October 2003, a *Washington Post* correspondent reported that the FBI was probing Wahhabi Muslim websites and that, "FBI and Treasury officials said they believe some Islamic conferences, as well as Web sites that extol radical Islam, are vehicles in the United States for recruitment and fundraising by

---

[22] At http://www.hostinganime.com/battar/b1word.zip.

terrorist groups."²³ According to Thomas, the Internet is also used "to put together profiles": Internet user demographics (culled, for instance, from personal information entered on online questionnaires and order forms) allow terrorists to identify users with sympathy for a particular cause or issue.²⁴ These individuals are then asked to make donations, typically through e-mails sent by a front group (i.e. an organization broadly supportive of the terrorists' aims but operating publicly and legally and usually having no direct ties to the terrorist organization).

Another example comes from Lashkar e-Taiba. Literally meaning "Army of the Pure," the Lashkar e-Taiba has proved to be the most brutal terrorist group presently active in Jammu and Kashmir. The group also uses the Internet for fundraising: "Allah gives you the opportunity to take part in the struggle for Muslim rights – Jihad," proclaims the English-language website. "Even if you cannot take part physically in the Jihad, you CAN help us by the means of financial aid." The site provides readers with the numbers of two bank accounts in Karachi, Pakistan, to which they can send donations, and it offers an e-mail address they can write to if they need assistance.

Finally, the Internet can be used to recruit and mobilize supporters to play a more active role in support of terrorist activities or causes. In addition to seeking converts by using the full panoply of website technologies (audio, digital video, etc.) to enhance the presentation of their message, terrorist organizations capture information about the users who browse their websites. Users who seem most interested in the organization's cause or well suited to carrying out its work are then contacted. Sophisticated methods are used by terrorists to refine or customize recruiting techniques on the Net:

> Using some of the same marketing techniques employed by commercial enterprises, terrorist servers could capture information about the users who browse their web sites, and then later contact those who seem most interested. Recruiters may also use more interactive Internet technology to roam online chat rooms and cyber cafes looking for receptive members of the public, particularly young people. Electronic bulletin boards and user nets can also serve as vehicles for reaching out to potential recruits. Interested computer users around the world can be

---

[23] Susan Schmidt, "Spreading Saudi Fundamentalism in US," *Washington Post* (February 10, 2003): a1, a8.

[24] Thomas, "Al Qaeda and the Internet: The Danger of Cyberplanning", 112-123.

engaged in long-term "cyber relationships" that could lead to friendship and eventual membership.[25]

The Site Institute, a Washington, DC-based terrorism research group that monitors al Qaeda's Internet communications, has provided chilling details of a high-tech recruitment drive launched in 2003 to recruit fighters to travel to Iraq and attack U.S. and coalition forces there. Potential recruits are bombarded with religious decrees and anti-U.S. propaganda, provided with training manuals on how to be a terrorist, and – as they are led through a maze of secret chat rooms – given specific instructions on how to make the journey to Iraq.[26] Rita Katz, the Site Institute's director and author of the book *Terrorist Hunter* (2003), argues, "Al Qaeda's use of the Internet is amazing. We know from past cases – from captured al Qaeda fighters who say they joined up through the Internet – that this is one of the principal ways they recruit fighters and suicide bombers."[27]

8 Who are the Target Audiences?

Whom do the Internet terrorists target on their sites? Are they appealing to potential supporters, to their enemies (namely the public who is part of the opposing socio-political community in the conflict), or are they targeting international public opinion? While it is impossible for us to identify the actual users of the sites, an analysis of their contents indicates an attempt to approach all three audiences. Reaching out to supporters is evinced from the fact that the sites offer appropriate items for sale, including printed shirts, badges, flags, and video and audio cassettes. The slogans at these sites also appeal strongly to the supporter public. Of course, the sites in local languages target these audiences more directly. These sites include much more detailed information about recent activities of the organizations and elaborate in detail on internal politics (the relationship between local groups).

But an important target audience, in addition to supporters of the organizations, is the international "bystander" public and surfers who are not involved in the conflict. This is evident from the presentation of basic information about the organization and the extensive historical background material (with which the supporter public is presumably familiar). Similarly, the sites make use of English in addition to the local language of the organization's supporters. Most of the sites offer versions in several languages in order to enlarge their international

---

[25] Zanini and Edwards, "The Networking of Terror in the Information Age," 43-44.
[26] Niles Lathem, "Al-Qaeda Terror.com," *New York Post* (September 16, 2003), a12.
[27] See site at http://www.siteinstitute.org/.

audience. The Basque movement site offers information in Castilian, German, French, and Italian; the MRTA site offers Japanese and Italian in addition to its English and Spanish versions; the Uzbeki site offers information in Arabic, English, and Russian.

Judging from the content of many of the sites, one might also infer that journalists constitute another bystander target audience. Press releases by the organizations are often placed on the websites. The detailed background information might also be useful for international reporters. One of Hizbollah's sites (Hizbollah's press office) specifically addresses journalists and invites them to interact with the organization's press office via email.

Approaches to the "enemy" audiences are not as clearly apparent from the content of many sites. However, in some sites the desire to reach this audience is evident by the efforts to demoralize the enemy or to create feelings of guilt. When the terror sites show pictures of their enemies performing acts of killing, enemy police aiming their weapons at women and children, or evidence of torture of detainees by those enemies, they are meant not only to mobilize support and to promote sympathy among neutral visitors, but also to arouse feelings of unease, guilt, and remorse in audiences belonging to the opposing political or social group. The organizations try to utilize the websites to change public opinion in their enemies' states, to weaken public support for the governing regime, to stimulate public debate, and of course to demoralize the enemy.

From the words of the Hizbollah leader quoted at the beginning of this article we gather that the movement indeed wishes to enter "the homes of Israelis, creating an important psychological breakthrough." In 1999, Hizbollah succeeded in this goal when, on its Internet site, it showed details about the return of the bodies of Israeli marine commandoes who had fallen in Lebanon. The organization stated that the one returned coffin contained not only the body of one of the fallen soldiers, Itamar Ilya, but also body parts of other fighters. The statement aroused a furor among the families of the dead soldiers and a bitter confrontation with the IDF authorities. The 'dialogue' that the Hizbollah organization wants to open with the Israelis by means of the Internet is also evident in the inclusion of appeals to the parents of Israeli soldiers stationed in Lebanon (with publication of an interview originally aired in Israel with four mothers of Israeli soldiers in Lebanon, under the headline "I don't want my son to die in Lebanon"). In an article in *Yediot Aharonot* (16 December 1998, p. 7) many Israelis, particularly parents of soldiers serving in Lebanon, reported that they visit the Hizbollah site to get an update on the news ("I regard these sites as a legitimate source of information," said one Israeli father). The Hizbollah site even offers to answer anyone who sends questions by e-mail, and does indeed reply to Israeli questioners, sending information and news to their e-mail addresses.

Do the terror organizations try to enroll supporters through the network? Analysis of the sites revealed a few attempts to enlist new recruits into an active circle of support, but there was no attempt to mobilize visitors for any actual violence. Kahane Lives (in which the suggestion appears under the title "How can I help the struggle: A few suggestions"); the Shining Path ("Action alert: What you can do"); the Basque movement; and the IRA site seeking economic support (including a page for contributions through credit cards) are examples of pages seeking readers' active support. The Zapatista site calls on its visitors to assist the struggle in several ways: to approach members of the Mexican government (the site offers links to the e-mail address of the President of Mexico), and to

> send letters of support to ENLZ or local refugees. Educate your friends [. . .]. Join protest marches outside embassies or diplomatic missions of Mexico near you, or organize such a rally yourself [. . .]. Send humanitarian aid to Mexico (link to humanitarian organizations) [. . .]. Donate money to the organization.

In contrast to the absence of appeals for active violence, there is a highly conspicuous effort at many terror sites to obtain supporters for non-violent activity, especially through the signing of petitions.

Though no direct calls for violence were found, some of the content on the websites could be viewed as encouraging violence indirectly. The Hamas site included calls for Jihad ('Jihad is victory or martyrdom,' 'an eye for an eye,' 'the Jihad will continue till judgment day'). Of course, the legitimization and justification of violence can also be interpreted as an indirect call for violence. Glorification of martyrs (and the very use of the word "martyr"), for example, signals that the perpetrators of violence are rewarded. However, as mentioned above, this is only the subtext. Most sites' contents ignore violence, and some of the organizations even imply that they seek non-violent solutions.

Another activity frequently suggested by the terror sites to their visitors is to navigate to other web pages through links appearing on the site. The sites provided are usually those ideologically close to the organization (its journals, its solidarity groups, etc.). In addition, links can be found to organizations offering information on subjects related to topics of interest to the terror groups – human rights bodies in the case of some of the revolutionary organizations; Islamic groups in the case of the Islamic and Palestinian sites; nationalist movements in the case of groups engaged in political struggle (e.g. the Hamas site to the Pal-Net Palestinian site).

9 Conclusion

The Internet may be the most perfect embodiment of the democratic ideals of free speech, open communication, and the "marketplace of ideas" that has ever existed. As the American Supreme Court has written, online "any person with a phone line can become a town crier with a voice that resonates farther than it could from any soapbox." Unfortunately, freedom on the Internet is far from secure – in fact, it is under challenge from numerous directions, as the present article has attempted to show.

The Internet is clearly changing the landscape of political discourse and advocacy. It offers new and inexpensive methods for collecting and publishing information, for communicating and coordinating action on a global scale, and for reaching out to world public opinion as well as decision makers. The Internet benefits individuals and small groups with few resources as well as organizations that are large or well-funded. It facilitates activities such as educating the public and media, raising money, forming coalitions across geographical boundaries, distributing petitions and action alerts, and planning and coordinating events on a regional or international level. It allows activists in politically repressive states to evade government censors and monitors. It is inexpensive to use and increasingly pervasive, with an estimated 250 million online. The Internet offers several channels whereby advocacy groups and individuals can publish information (and disinformation) to further policy objectives. Thus the Internet could have become a peaceful and fruitful forum for the resolution of conflicts. And yet, as this article reveals, it has become also a useful instrument for terrorists.

Modern terrorists use the Internet for various functions, from communicative purposes such as propaganda and distribution of information to instrumental uses such as recruitment, coordination of actions, hacktivism, and cyberterrorism. Many violent groups with a long record of victimization, bloodshed, and destruction have entered the Internet. Their use of this liberal, free, easy-to-access medium is indeed frightening. The September 11, 2001 attacks by Bin Laden's terrorists promoted the fear and the call for radical countermeasures. And yet, one should consider that the fear that terrorism inflicts can be – and has in the past been – manipulated by politicians to pass questionable legislation, undermining individual rights and liberties, that otherwise wouldn't stand a chance of being accepted by the public. It is important to assess the real threat posed by terrorist groups using the new information technology, keeping in mind that governmental action against it could easily go beyond acceptable limits.

Across a wide range of battlefields, privacy is on the retreat. Many high-tech surveillance tools that were deemed too intrusive before September 11, including the FBI's "Carnivore" Internet eavesdropping system, are being unleashed. Pre-attack legislation aimed at protecting people from unwanted privacy invasions has been shelved, while new anti-terrorism laws give the authorities broad new powers to wiretap, monitor, and invade Internet activity. These developments could wind up having profound implications for democracies and their values, adding heavy prices in terms of civil liberties to the destructive effects of terrorism on the Internet.

Terrorismusabwehr

Counterterrorism

On Counterinsurgency

Martin van Creveld

The History Department, The Hebrew University
Jerusalem Israel 90105

This paper falls into four parts. The first, "How We Got to Where We are," is a brief history of insurgency since 1941 and of the repeated failures in dealing with it. The second, "Two Methods," focuses on President Asad's suppression of the uprising at Hama in 1983 on the one hand and on British operations in Northern Ireland on the other, presenting them as extreme case studies in dealing with counterinsurgency. The third, "On Power and Compromises," craws the lessons from the methods just presented and goes on to explain how, by vacillating between them, most counterinsurgents have guaranteed their own failure. Finally, part four of the paper presents my conclusions.

1   How We Got to Where We Are

At a time when much of the world is either engaging in counterinsurgency, preparing to do so, or writing about it, something is rotten in the kingdom of Denmark. Just when the rot began is not entirely clear, but a good starting point is provided by the 6th of April 1941. On that day the German Wehrmacht, assisted by Italian, Hungarian and Bulgarian formations, launched its offensive against Yugoslavia. Opening with a ferocious bombardment of Belgrade that left much of the city in ruins, the attack developed very rapidly, indeed more rapidly even than the 2003 American campaign in Iraq. The Yugoslav Army was 800,000 strong. During World War I it had given an excellent account of itself and made itself famous for its bravery. However, it hardly possessed any heavy modern weapons and was still dependent on oxcarts for transportation. As a result, it was scarcely able to mobilize and, coming under attack from several directions at once, was easily cut to pieces. Two weeks later Hitler was able to proclaim victory. At the cost, to the Wehrmacht, of no more than 400 dead.

As was later to happen in other occupied countries as well, however, the end of major combat operations in Yugoslavia did not mean that the war was over. Resistance – whether one calls it guerrilla, or terrorism, or banditry (as the Germans did) – got under way in a matter of weeks; as early as May 1941, Belgrade had to witness the first partisans being executed. Repeatedly, Wehrmacht soldiers on patrol, escorting supply convoys, and similar detached forces were attacked, stabbed, shot, or blown up. At peak, no fewer than 29 Axis divisions were deployed in the country[1] and engaged in harsh reprisals. Far from those reprisals serving to quell the uprising, though, resistance grew and grew until it developed into the mother of all ulcers.

Over the next three and a half years the Wehrmacht, ably assisted by such kindhearted organizations as the Waffen-SS, the Gestapo, and other exotic Nazi formations, did what it could. It used every weapon at its disposal, tanks, heavy artillery, and dive-bombers not excluded. It tortured tens of thousands, laid waste to entire districts, and lashed about with such ferocity that an estimated 800,000 Yugoslavs died – many of them in internecine warfare between Croats, Serbs, Chetniks, Communists, and other resistance groups. Yet in the end Yugoslavia became the only Nazi-occupied country to rid itself of its conquerors before it could be overrun by one of the major allied belligerents, a fact whose significance for the post-war world was very great. So much, then, for suppressing terrorism by the most brutal means.

While the Yugoslavs were exceptionally quick off the mark, to a greater or lesser extent the same experience was repeated throughout occupied Europe. The Poles, the Russians, the Greeks, the Italians, the French, even the civilized Danes and Dutch – all found themselves engaging in armed resistance. Some of the resistance movements took less time to get organized, some more. Some were more effective, others less. None succeeded in emulating the Yugoslavs by liberating their countries before outside help was able to reach them. On the other hand, by the time outside help did reach them none was even close to being suppressed. Most were becoming more and more effective, Greece, Italy, and France being particularly good examples of this.

By way of an intellectual exercise, suppose the Germans had "won" the war in some sense. To do this, they would first have had to break the USSR as a functioning polity, a task that, towards the end of 1941, did not seem out of reach. Next, building up their navy and air force, they would have had to fight Britain and the USA to a standstill, a task which, given that they would have had the entire resources of Europe at their command, may not have been out of reach either. Even so, no country, not even Nazi Germany, can permanently keep ten percent of its population in uniform – the more so because those ten

---

[1] See, for the order of battle, M. F. Cancian, "The Wehrmacht in Yugoslavia: Lessons of the Past?" *Parameters*, 21, 3, autumn 1993, p. 78.

percent invariably comprise the healthiest, economically most productive part of the available manpower. Had the Germans "won" the war, then presumably about 80 percent of their armed forces would have been demobilized and sent home. Even assuming twice as many men would have been kept on active duty as were available in the pre-1939 peacetime Wehrmacht, their number would only have stood at 1.5 million. Their task would have been to hold down an entire continent; an area which, reaching from Brest to the Ural Mountains and from Narvik at least as far as the Brenner Pass and the Peloponnese, had a population of approximately 200 million. Let others calculate the resulting ratio of German troops to occupied people and square kilometers of land. In all probability it could not have been done. Given ten or twenty years, most of the subject peoples would almost certainly have risen, engaged in extensive terrorism and guerrilla warfare, and made the continent so ungovernable as to virtually liberate themselves; albeit at the cost of millions of civilian lives lost; and albeit at the cost of physical destruction as great as, or greater than, that which actually took place.

Far from being exceptional, the German experience only acted as a prelude for countless similar defeats to come. In Palestine, the British with 100,000 men tried to hold down a population of 600,000 Jews – of whom no more than a few hundred were active terrorists – and failed; yet this was as nothing compared to what was to follow. Partly because the British considered the Jews a "semi-European" race,[2] partly because they had to operate in full view of world opinion, which, then a now, took a special interest in the Holy Land, their operations there were relatively civilized. No such limits applied to subsequent counterinsurgency operations in Malaysia and Kenya, where the exchange rate was a hundred blacks killed to every white farmer slain; the attempts to keep Cyprus and Aden also failed. Other counterinsurgents were no more successful. The French in Indo-China and Algeria used hundreds of thousands of troops to kill hundreds of thousands of Vietnamese and Arab "natives," but to no avail. The Dutch, the Belgians, and the Portuguese all lost their Empires. By the time the latter finally gave up in 1975, additional hundreds of thousands had been killed.

Then it was the Americans' turn. For some ten years on end, over two million GIs saw service in South-East Asia, the peak being reached in 1968-69, when there were over half a million of them. They used every available technological means, from heavy bombers to people sniffers and from remotely piloted vehicles to

---

[2] Field Marshal John Dill, Chief of the Imperial General Staff, 1941, quoted in C. L. James, *Imperial Rearguard: Wars of Empire, 1919-1985*, London, Brassey's, 1981, p. 96.

napalm. And yet, after six million tons of bombs had been dropped – more than twice as many as were used against Germany and Japan combined during all of World War II –, 1,500 helicopters lost, over 55,000 troops killed, and $ 125 billion spent, they too were forced to concede failure. In 1975, the world was treated to the spectacle of the last Americans hanging on to their helicopters' skids as they fled from the roof of their embassy in Saigon.

As long as it was "Western" powers that went down to defeat, people attributed their failures at least in part to the moral scruples under which those powers had labored; although, in truth, such scruples were not much in evidence either in Algeria or in Vietnam. But no scruples could be, or were, attributed to the Red Army operating in Afghanistan. The Soviet invasion of Afghanistan started in late 1980, when eight mechanized divisions, perfectly armed with everything that the largest military-industrial complex in history until then could provide, drove south by way of the Khyber Pass towards Kabul. Next, having set up a puppet government, they spent eight years trying to "pacify" the country against various groups of *mujahedin*, or holy warriors. Doing so, they killed perhaps a million Afghans and sent perhaps another five million fleeing across the border into neighboring Pakistan. Hardly a weapon in the Soviet arsenal that was not deployed; from time to time there were even reports of chemical and biological warfare ("yellow rain"),[3] though these were never substantiated. However great the Kremlin's efforts, in the end it too was forced to concede failure. Having suffered 13,000 casualties in dead alone and abandoned much of their equipment, finally its divisions reeled back the way they had come. As they did so, they were jeered by the *mujahedin*, who did not even bother to open fire at them.

To list all the other countries that, starting in 1941, have tried but failed to put down guerrilla and terrorism would be tedious. Even a short list would have to include the Vietnamese (in Cambodia), the Indians (in Sri Lanka and Kashmir), the South Africans (in Namibia), the Indonesians (in East Timor), the Philippines (in the south), and the Russians (in Chechenya). Some of these would-be counterinsurgents were as ruthless as ruthless can be, the Indonesians in East Timor killing perhaps half a million people. Others, such as the Israelis in Lebanon and the Occupied Territories, deployed some of the world's best troops and the most modern available technologies to no visible gain. Having spent 32 years

---

[3] State Department, "Legal Issues Associated with Formally Charging the Soviet Union with Violation of the BWC," 1982, available at http://www.gwu.edu/~nsarchiv/NSAEBB/NSAEBB61/Sverd20.pdf; Director, CIA, "Use of Toxins and other Lethal Chemicals in South-East Asia and Afghanistan," 2 February 1982, available at http://www.gwu.edu/~nsarchiv/NSAEBB/NSAEBB61/Sverd21.pdf

fighting in Lebanon, during which they even occupied Beirut, the Israelis were unable to cope with Hizbollah and finally found themselves back at their starting positions. After 16 years, during which Israel did what it could to put down the first and second Palestinian uprisings, Ariel Sharon, a hard-liner if ever one there was, reached the point where he felt he had no choice but to pull out of the Gaza Strip.[4] Yet only a few years had passed since a former deputy chief of staff, General (ret.) Mathan Vilnai, had referred to the terrorists Israel was facing in Gaza as "bird-brained"; one does not know whether to laugh or cry.

As these lines are being written in the summer of 2004, the uprising against the Americans in Iraq is also spreading. Having taken just three weeks to break Saddam's Army – the same which, back in 1991, had been advertised as the fourth largest in the world – and occupy Baghdad, the Americans hoped to be welcomed as liberators. Instead, right from the beginning, they met with resistance. As in Vietnam, the Americans are totally at loss amidst a foreign culture where it is virtually impossible to tell friend from foe and where every translator may be a spy. Much more than in Vietnam, where the opponent was first the Viet Cong and then the North Vietnamese Army, they are unable to discover who is behind the uprising. Be it former members of a mysterious Iraqi intelligence organization known as M-14;[5] or Al Qaeda; or the Sunnis; or the Shi'ites. In both cases their intelligence was or is limited to what they can photograph, intercept, or learn from low-level prisoners. With the exception of Saddam Hussein, so far no senior terrorist leader has been captured.

As a result, they thrash about wildly. They do what they used to do in Vietnam: publishing statistics, some of which are probably bogus, on how well the "war for hearts and minds" is going; calling for additional troops in order to defend hopelessly overextended supply lines; and, when meeting with resistance, showing little restraint in using their immensely superior firepower in places such as Faluja and Najaf. So far the ratio of Iraqi insurgents killed to dead American troops is said to be approximately ten to one. Even though, and again with Vietnam, Afghanistan, and similar "non-trinitarian" conflicts in mind, there is very good reason to suspect that most of the Iraqi dead are actually civilians who happened to be around when the fight broke out.

As the German and American experiences prove, many of those who tried their hands at the counterinsurgency game during the period in question were, for their time, the most modern, most powerful, most heavily armed, best trained,

---

[4] See his own account in *Yediot Achronot*, weekend supplement, 16 April 2004, p. 2.
[5] T. Shanker, "Saddam's Secret Service Planned for Insurgency, Pentagon Finds," *New York Times*, 30 April 2004.

and most experienced on earth. Quite a few were also utterly ruthless, to the point that they did not hesitate to kill millions of people and turn entire districts into deserts; in the case of the Americans in Vietnam, this was done by spraying defoliant gases over the jungle. Yet in case after case the forces in question went down to defeat. Very often those defeats were inflicted by small, if highly determined, groups of men and women who, certainly at the beginning and often even at the end of the campaign, did not even have one percent of the military power their opponents did. In many places in Asia and Africa a large percentage of the insurgents could barely read. On other occasions they wore sandals with bottoms cut out of old tires or else went barefoot. Often they were without a strong organization, untrained, inexperienced, and lacked any but the most rudimentary medical care.[6] What they did do was to prove themselves prepared to fight and die; in the end, that was what mattered.

Each time a counterinsurgent army went down to defeat, legions of military and civilian experts engaged on a *post-mortem* analysis to find out what had gone wrong. To focus on Vietnam, perhaps the most analyzed counterinsurgency of all, the following are some of the reasons adduced. The political leadership did not provide adequate direction, never telling the armed forces what their mission was[7] but instead tying their hands – as when imposing limits on the targets that could be bombed – and trying to micro-manage the war from the White House.[8] The public, misled by those nefarious characters who had taken over the media, did not understand the importance of the war and, unwilling to make sacrifices, withdrew its support.[9] The number of agencies that tried to fight the war was too large and coordination among them deficient or non-existent. Not enough men, money, and machines were allocated to finish the job. The strategy adopted ("attrition") was wrong. The tactics adopted ("search and destroy") were also wrong. The war was not waged ruthlessly enough, or else, to the contrary, it was waged in such a ruthless manner as to be counterproductive. The war for hearts and minds was not given as much priority as it deserved. Concerned with their own promotion and failing to provide leadership, the commanders were to blame.[10] Unwilling to fight, unfamiliar with the country, and increasingly coming under the influence of drugs, the rank and

---

[6] "Iraqi doctors watch helplessly after days of war in Fallujah," Yahoo! News, 19 April 2004.
[7] See H. Summers, *On Strategy*, Novato, California, Praesidio, 1982, pp. 133-49.
[8] B. M. Jenkins, "The Unchangeable War," RAND Paper RM-6278-ARPA, Santa Monica, California, RAND, 1972, pp. 8-9.
[9] W. Westmoreland, *A Soldier Reports*, New York, Dell, 1972, pp. 82-3, 89, 553-58.
[10] R. Gabriel and P. Savage, *Crisis in Command*, New York, Hill and Wang, 1976.

file were to blame. The South Vietnamese were to blame, given that they mostly stood aside, allowing the Americans to do their work for them while at the same time enriching themselves as much as they could. The demonstrators who burnt their country's flag and wished departing troops that they would come to an early grave were to blame. The draft resisters were to blame. Everybody was to blame. Nobody was to blame.

By the time the War in Vietnam reached its inglorious end, each of these explanations was quite old. At the time it started, each of them was already quite old; see, for example, the excuses offered by the commanders of the British Army concerning the reasons behind their failure to hold on Palestine in 1944-48.[11] As an American defeat in Iraq appears all but certain, no doubt we shall hear more such explanations in the future, and already now some pundits are sharpening their pens. Yet as the repetitive character of the explanations and the continuing failures prove, little is to be gained from continued work along these lines. Instead I propose to break new ground by focusing on two modern counterinsurgency campaigns that succeeded; to wit, the one conducted by late President Hafez Asad in Hama, 1982, and the British one in Northern Ireland.

2 Two Methods

In early 1982, President Hafez Asad's (In Arabic, Asad means "Lion") regime in Syria was twelve years old and was meeting with growing opposition that did not make its future appear rosy.[12] Part of the opposition came from the members of various ethnic groups who took issue with the fact that Asad, like his most important collaborators, was an Alawite. Now the Alawites are one of the less important Islamic sects, traditionally poor and discriminated against. Many in the Islamic world do not even regard them as true Moslems and claim that, instead of Allah, they worship the moon and the stars; it is as if Germany had been ruled by a Sorbic Mafia or Italy by a Greek one.

Even more dangerous was the Islamic priesthood, or *Ulama*. During the early years after seizing power, Asad had made some concessions to them, promoting priests, increasing their salaries, and even giving them limited freedom of speech. They, however, saw the secular Ba'atist state as opposed to everything they themselves believed in and were determined to wage holy war against it.

---

[11] See A. Nachmani, "Generals at Bay In Post-War Palestine," *Journal of Strategic Studies*, 4, 6, December 1983, pp. 70ff.

[12] The following is based on M. Maoz, *Assad: The Sphinx of Damascus*, New York, Grove Weidenfeld, 1988, pp. 149-63.

To make things worse for Asad, for a number of years a large part of his Army had been involved in Lebanon. Originally its mission was to put an end to a vicious civil war that had broken out in 1976. That proved hard to do, and the Syrians found themselves trying to run the country; which, early in 1982, was also being threatened by a possible Israeli invasion.

As the Muslim Brothers, a religious terrorist organization with branches in practically every Arab country, mounted a well-organized and effective terrorist campaign against him, Asad's response was similar to, though perhaps more brutal than that of countless others before and since. His first move was to abolish what limited civil liberties existed – compared to its predecessors, originally his regime had been relatively liberal. Next he used his Army and secret police to persecute, arrest, and torture thousands, going so far as to order the inmates of entire prisons stood against the wall and shot. Nothing worked, and the bombings, in which hundreds lost their lives, went on.

With his regime disintegrating and his own life increasingly threatened, the Syrian leader resorted to desperate measures. Though clashes between terrorists and the security forces took place all over the country, the center of the rebellion was known to be the city of Hama, called "the head of the snake." Even as the repression campaign continued in full swing, 12,000 soldiers, commanded by Asad's brother Rifat, surrounded Hama. The way the Syrian newspapers told the story later on, they started combing the city house by house, making arrests. As they did so, about 500 *mujahidun*, or holy warriors, launched a counterattack. Perhaps they were deliberately provoked by Rifat's forces. Perhaps they were hoping that the Army's Suni troops would desert from their units and, possibly, join their uprising. Either way, they emerged from hiding, took up their weapons, and engaged in open warfare, reportedly killing some 250 civil servants, policemen, and the like.

Whether or not it had been planned that way, the uprising provided Rifat and Hafez with the excuse they had been waiting for. Relying mainly on their most powerful weapon, heavy artillery, the Syrian troops surrounding Hama opened fire. Anywhere between 10,000 and 30,000 people, many of them women and children, were indiscriminately killed. What followed was even more important than the killing itself. Far from apologizing for his action, Rifat, asked how many people his men had killed, deliberately exaggerated their number. As his reward, he was promoted to vice-president for national security; several of his fellow butchers were also promoted or decorated.[13] Later, survivors told horrifying

---

[13] Statement by Syrian Human Righs Committee, 18 February 1999, available at http://www.shrc.org.uk/data/aspx/d1/1121.aspx.

tales of buildings that had collapsed on their inhabitants and trenches filled with corpses. They also described how, in an attempt to get at jewelry, Syrian troops did not hesitate to cut off people's fingers and ears.[14]

Hama's great mosque, one of the best known in all of Syria, was razed to the ground and later became a parking lot. Years afterwards a journalist, Scot Peterson of the *Christian Science Monitor*, who had visited the city, told me that when people passed the place they still looked away and shuddered. Some of them were so terrified that they did not even dare pronounce the word "Alawite"; instead, pointing at the hills, they spoke of "those people there."[15] In the words of Asad's Israeli biographer, Prof. Moshe Maoz,[16]

> the terrible crushing of the Hama revolt not only broke the military backbone of the Muslim Brothers but also served as a vivid warning to them, as well as to other opposition groups, against further acts of disobedience. And although in recent years small groups of Muslim Brothers have occasionally conducted guerrilla attacks on army units, the *mujahidun* ceased for the time being to be a threat to Assad.

Having fallen out with his brother, Rifat had to flee abroad. Not so Hafez, who went on ruling Syria with an iron fist. His son, Bashir, continues to so today.

The other successful counterinsurgency campaign worth examining in some detail in the present paper is, as already said, the British one in Northern Ireland.[17] The "troubles" in Ireland have a long history. They go back all the way to the Irish struggle for independence (1916-21), King William III, Oliver Cromwell, and even King Henry II (reigned 1154-89), who was the first English monarch to campaign in the island. In January 1969 they broke out again and quickly escalated as bombs demolished parts of the infrastructure – electricity pylons and water pumps – and opposing demonstrators fought street battles with each other. The Royal Ulster Constabulary (RUC, a locally recruited riot police consisting largely of Protestants) was unable to contain the violence, and so the British Army became heavily involved from the summer on.

---

[14] Material on the massacre will be found at http://reformsyria.org/Baath/Terrorism/the_hama_massacre.htm.

[15] Scot Peterson, "How Syria's Brutal Past Colors Its Future," 20 June 2000, available at http://csmonitor.com/cgi-bin/durableRedirect.pl?/durable/2000/06/20/p1s3.htm.

[16] Ibid., pp. 162-63.

[17] Much of what follows is based on M. Dewar, *The British Army in Northern Ireland*, London, Arms and Armor Press, 1985.

From this point, the situation went from bad to worse. In a single night's "battle" (Belfast, 14-15 August 1969), four policemen and ten civilians were killed whereas 145 civilians were wounded. Property damage was also extensive, amounting to no fewer than 150 houses destroyed by fire. The violence, the like of which had not been seen in the region for almost 50 years, seems to have dampened the enthusiasm of both sides. However, memories proved short, and there was another outbreak of even greater violence in August of the next year. From this time on things deteriorated as the British troops, whose number now exceeded 10,000, vainly sought to prevent mobs of Protestant and Catholic demonstrators from clashing with each other and destroying as much property as they could. Behind their backs terrorism also escalated as 37 explosions rocked the district in March 1971, 47 in April, and 50 in June. From January to August of that year the total number of bombings was 311, causing over 100 injuries. In 1972 the number rose to well over 1,000; the IRA also extended its operations from Ireland into the United Kingdom proper. A temporary peak was reached on 30 January 1972, when Street fighting in Londonderry led to 13 people dying at the hands of British troops trying to quell yet another riot. An event which is remembered as "Bloody Sunday."

Had things been allowed to continue in the same way, no doubt the British attempt to hold on to Northern Ireland would have ended as so many others since 1941 had, i.e. in complete defeat followed by elaborate analyses as to why it had taken place. If, for a change, this did not happen and the outcome did not correspond to the usual pattern, then perhaps there are some things to be learnt from the effort. This article is hardly the place to detail all the many different things the Army did during its 30-year involvement, let alone follow the immensely complicated political process with all its twists and turns. Instead, all I can do is provide a short list of the things that the British Army, having used "Bloody Sunday" to reconsider its actions, did *not* do.

First, never again did the British open indiscriminate fire into marching or rioting crowds; in the future, however violent the riots and demonstrations that faced them, they preferred to employ less violent means that led to a far smaller number of casualties. Second, and in marked contrast to most other counterinsurgents from the Germans in Yugoslavia to the Israelis in the Occupied Territories, not once in the entire struggle did they bring in heavy weapons such as tanks, armored personnel carriers, artillery, or aircraft to repulse attacks and inflict retaliation. Third, never once did they inflict collective punishments such as imposing curfews, blowing up houses, destroying entire neighborhoods to open up fields of fire, and the like; by posing as the protectors of the population, not its tormentors, they were able to prevent the uprising from spreading.

Fourth and most important, by and large the Army stayed within the law. Partly because they restrained themselves, partly because there were other, less conspicuous organizations to do some of the dirty work for them, they were able to refrain from arbitrary imprisonment, torture, and illegal killings.

From time to time, this rule was infringed upon. Even without breaking the law, interrogation techniques could be intimidating enough. Here and there were clear violations of civil liberties, as torture as well as false accusations were used in order to elicit information and obtain convictions. A few known IRA leaders, identified and tracked in foreign countries, were shot, execution-style, in what has since become known as "targeted killings." On the whole, however, the British played by the rules. This remained true even after terrorists had blown up the 79-year-old Earl of Mountbatten, the Queen's uncle, in his yacht; even after they had planted a bomb that demolished part of a Brighton Hotel where Ms. Thatcher was due to speak; and even after they had used a van to fire mortar rounds at a Cabinet meeting at 10 Downing Street.

Passing over the details, which would suffice to fill many volumes, the real secret behind the British success seems to have been extreme self-control – whatever else might happen, they did not allow themselves to be provoked. I myself began to get an inkling of that fact during my numerous visits to the Army Staff College at Camberley. Each time I went there I discussed the situation in Northern Ireland with as many officers as I could; people whose names I cannot remember, but to all of whom I am grateful. What I still consider the most important insight, however, was given to me not at Camberley, but over dinner in Geneva some time in the early 1990s. My interlocutor was a British lieutenant colonel who had done several tours of duty in Northern Ireland but whose name, alas, I cannot remember either. What he told me can be summed up as follows. Look at almost any one of the 100 or so major counterinsurgency campaigns that have taken place all over the world since 1945 (or, if you wish, 1941). However great the differences between them, they have one thing in common. In every known instance, the "forces of order" killed far more people than they lost; often by an order of magnitude, as is the case in Iraq, where the Americans always emphasize how many more Iraqis have died; and often in such an indiscriminate manner (in counterinsurgency, whenever heavy weapons are used, the results are bound to be indiscriminate) as to make the result approximate genocide. By contrast, up to that date the struggle in Northern Ireland had cost the United Kingdom 3,000 casualties in dead alone. Of the 3,000, about 1,700 were civilians, most of them innocent bystanders who had been killed as bombs exploded at the time and place they happened to be. Of the remaining 1,300, 1,000 were

British soldiers and no more than 300 were terrorists, a ratio of three to one. And that, he ended his exposition, is why we are still there.

3   On Power and Compromises

According to the well-known proverb, success has many fathers whereas failure is an orphan. However true this may be in respect to every other aspect of life, in the case of counterinsurgency clearly it does not apply. As noted, entire libraries have been written on counterinsurgency campaigns that failed. Often the authors were the very people who had participated in, or were responsible for, the failures in question. For example, the term "low intensity war" itself was invented by the British General Frank Kitson; having taken part in a whole series of them, he was finally made commandant of the Staff College so he could teach others how it should be done.[18] Very great efforts have been made to analyze the reasons and suggest ways to avoid a repetition. Judging by the way the Americans are conducting themselves in Iraq, to no avail.

By comparison, very little has been written about counterinsurgency campaigns that succeeded. One reason for this is because, since 1941, the number of such successes has been so limited that nine out of ten people cannot even remember them. Another is because the methods used may be so unsavory as to make it difficult for *soi-disant* civilized persons to write about them or, which is probably even worse, attract research money for them. Here again I may call on my own experience as a military scholar. Years ago, I spent months trying to interest people in and around the Pentagon in the way Asad *pere* had operated, first in Hama and then in putting an end to the Lebanese civil war and bringing that country under his control. Had such a study been available today, it might actually have done some good; however, nobody cared.

Thus, whoever will look to the modern literature on the subject will do so almost entirely in vain. Nevertheless, for those who, instead of feeble excuses, want real answers, an excellent short analysis of how it should be, and has been, done is readily available. In chapters viii and xvii of *The Prince*, the sixteenth-century writer, Niccolo Machiavelli, explains the way a ruler should use cruelty when necessary. To prevent misunderstanding, let it be said that there *are* such circumstances; and that no one who does not recognize this should ever aspire to rule any country except Disneyland.

---

[18] F. Kitson, *Low Intensity Operations: Subversion, Insurgency, Peacekeeping*, Hampden, Connecticut, Archon Books, 1971.

This much having been conceded, what Machiavelli, using examples from the ancient world as well as his own time, has to say boils down to four points. First, should you feel you have no choice left but to resort to cruelty, then the blow should be sudden. The more like a thunderbolt out of a clear sky it comes, the greater the effect; therefore, continue to talk softly while secretly completing your preparations. Second, having made up your mind to strike, you cannot strike hard enough. Better to kill too many people than too few. Strike so hard as to make sure you do not have to strike again; or else, the very fact that you have to do so will weaken the impact of your original blow. Besides, you must consider the effect a repetition will have on your troops. However well-trained and hard-bitten they may be, if they are made to commit one atrocity after another (and very likely resort to alcohol or drugs in order to muster the necessary will), it will only be a matter of time before they become demoralized.

Facing an organization most of whose operations are covert, it is an illusion to think that you can ever "get" all or even most of them at once – something not even Saddam Hussein, using gas against the Kurds, succeeded in doing. Even if you do, chances are that, like the mythological hydra, the organization in question will re-constitute itself. Witness the French interception and arrest of the entire FLN leadership back in 1956.[19] Just six years later, the same people were sitting across their captors at Evian and negotiating the independence of their country. To prevent this from happening, while aiming to kill as many insurgents and their leaders as possible your true target should be the spirit of the population from whom they draw their support and without whom they cannot exist. To put Mao on his head: you must refuse to admit a distinction between "active" fish and the "passive" sea in which they swim.

In other words, the true objective of your strike is less to kill people than to display your ruthlessness and your willingness to go to *any* lengths to achieve your objective – a war on hearts and minds, only in reverse. Von Clausewitz once wrote that war is a moral and physical contest by means of the latter.[20] The same is even more true of the massacre that accompanies a war; if you do it right, it may even prevent a war. Careful consideration should therefore be given to the means. Forget about infantry, it is too slow. Riding in APCs, it cannot see anything. Riding in soft vehicles, it is too vulnerable (currently the war in Iraq is

---

[19] See on this episode A. Horne, *A Savage War for Peace; Algeria 1954-1962*, London, MacMillan, 1977, pp. 159-60.
[20] C. von Clausewitz, *On War*, Princeton, New Jersey, Princeton University Press, 1976, p. 127.

causing a whole literature to develop about this subject).[21] Its weapons are small and will only kill people one by one. Besides, if the enemy has similar weapons and fights back, then the process is going to be very expensive. Early in April 2004, five days' fighting cost the U.S. Marine Brigade at Fallujah ten percent of its troops in casualties (killed and wounded). Yet when the operation ended, the Brigade had only re-taken ten percent of the city; had the Marines continued in this way, it might have become a second Stalingrad.

Airpower and missiles are much better, but still problematic because they are deployed from a distance so that the victims, being unable to see who is massacring them, will not be properly impressed by your determination. Modern airpower also has two other disadvantages. First, it is too fast. Fighter-bombers appear out of nowhere. They discharge their weapons and disappear. Just as a colony of ants that is stirred with a stick will quickly recover, so their disappearance permits the opponent to recover their breath. Second, most of the "precision-guided" weapons it uses carry relatively small warheads and can only do limited damage to selected targets. For example, following a three months' continuous bombardment by 1,000 NATO aircraft, 95 percent of Belgrade still stood. To inflict real damage, old-fashioned, heavy, "dumb" iron bombs are much superior. The problem is that only one country, i.e. the U.S., still retains the kind of bomber force that can carry them in any numbers; and even in its case that force is down to one sixth of what it used to be.

Everything considered, and recalling Asad at Hama, the weapon of choice should probably be artillery. Heavy guns are sufficiently accurate to be aimed at individual targets, especially, as is desirable, if they can be made to fire point-blank. At the same time they are sufficiently powerful to do just the kind of spectacular damage you want; to see the results, search the Internet for pictures of Hama. Unlike aircraft, they can fire non-stop for hours, even days. Still their greatest advantage is that they can be deployed in such a way that, before being blown to hell, the victims can look straight into the muzzles of the guns that are trained at them. When Napoleon famously spoke of a whiff of grapeshot, he knew what was he was talking about.

Third, do what you have to do openly. At any cost, prevent the media from messing with your operations while they are going on. Once you are done, though, you should not try to hide them or explain them away; indeed you should do exactly the opposite. There should be no apologies, no kwetching about collateral damage caused by mistake, innocent lives regrettably lost, "excesses" that

---

[21] J. Higgs, The Killer Ride, Soldier of Fortune, 2004, available at http://www.military.com/soldiertech/0,14632,Soldiertech_Stryker2,,00.html.

will be investigated and brought to trial, and similar signs of weakness. Instead, make sure that as many people as possible can see, hear, smell, and touch the results; if they can also taste them, e.g. by inhaling the smoke from a burning city, then so much the better. Invite journalists to admire the headless corpses rolling in the streets, film them, and write about them. Do, however, make sure they do not talk to any of the survivors so as not to arouse sympathy.

Fourth and last, do not command the strike yourself, but have somebody else do it for you – if at all possible, without ever giving him written orders. This method has the advantage that, if your designated commander succeeds, you can take the credit. Presenting yourself to the world, you will offer no regrets and shed no tears. Instead you will explain why it absolutely had to be done and make sure everybody understands that you are ready to do it again at a moment's notice. But what if, for one reason or another, your deputy fails and resistance, instead of being broken, increases? In that case, you can always disown him and try another course such as negotiation.

Whether Asad read Machiavelli is doubtful. Be that as it may, by his operations in Hama he gave clear proof that he knew what he was doing. Of course his actions deserve to be called horrible, barbaric, cruel, inhuman, and what not. Yet not only did he die peacefully in his bed, but he probably saved Syria from a civil war in which far more people might have died; over twenty years later, the results continued to speak for themselves. Events at Hama have not been forgotten and continue to be denounced when and where opportune. Still, as far as Asad's international standing goes, they did him little damage. If he was perceived as a brutal dictator, at any rate the greatest crime he committed was in the past; there was no need for an endless series of small crimes, as with those who take a more gradual approach. He emerged as an effective ruler with effective forces at his command with whom it was possible to do business. Provided you have what it takes to do what is necessary, the Asad method promises better, and certainly faster, results than any other.

If, on the other hand, one reason or another prevents you from emulating him, then the other approach is the British one in Northern Ireland. However, doing so is very hard and the method may not be practical for the troops of certain nations who simply do not possess the necessary mind-set. For example, the Americans combine aggressiveness with impatience. Putting blind faith in technology and using far more firepower than is needed, they regularly end up alienating whomever they face – as happened in Vietnam, Somalia, and now in Iraq. Or take the Israelis. As anyone who has been to Israel knows, they are the least disciplined people on earth. As long as they fought Blitzkrieg campaigns against external enemies, this factor worked in their favor, given that individual soldiers often displayed high courage, initiative, and resourcefulness. However, faced with a struggle in which self-restraint is everything, they are apt to make a mess of it. A long legacy of persecution, culminating in the Holocaust, also causes Israelis to combine self-pity with the shedding of crocodile tears.[22] As Ms. Meir supposedly said, "we are angry with the Palestinians for forcing us to shoot them." Whoever feels like this will hardly win a counterinsurgency campaign.

The first indispensable condition for adopting the British method is to have truly excellent troops and even better officers to command them and keep them in line. Next come professionalism, strict discipline, and endless patience. Yet none of these will be of any avail if there is not also present a certain mixture of phlegmatism and pride. Only pride will prevent one from hitting innocent people who are far weaker than you, thus making new enemies faster than you can kill the old ones and creating a situation where, sooner or later, you are no longer able to look at yourself in the mirror. Only phlegmatism can make a unit take casualties and keep going, if necessary for years. Until the other side, realizing it will *never* be able to provoke you or cause you to disintegrate, will finally be ready to sit down with you and talk about peace.

On the surface of things the two approaches, the Asad one and the British one in Northern Ireland, are so different as to constitute direct opposites. This is true, but it is also true that, at a deeper level, they have something very important in common. As the demoralization and progressive disintegration of so many counterinsurgent forces – from the French in Algeria through the Americans in Iraq[23] – shows, the greatest problem they face is time. In an asymmetric struggle the insurgent, so long as he does not lose, wins; his very presence acts as the best possible proof that the counterinsurgent does not have thing well in hand.[24] The situation of the counter- insurgent is just the opposite. As long as he does not win, he loses; as sure as night follows day, the result will be demoralization. Which, of course, is the prelude to defeat.

Each in its own way, both the Asad approach and the one the British, after much trial and error, adopted in Northern Ireland represent a way of dealing with

---

[22] See on these problems M. van Creveld, *The Sword and the Olive: A Critical History of the Israel Defense Force*, New York, Public Affairs, 2nd ed., 2002, pp. 344-45.

[23] R. Randal, A.P., "At Least 17 U.S Troops Have Committed Suicide in Iraq," 22.11.2003, available at http://www.truthout.com/docs_03/112403D.shtml

[24] See the excellent analysis of this problem in M. Begin, *The Revolt*, New York, Dell, 1977 [1950], p. 92.

this problem. The former forestalls demoralization by reducing the campaign to a sharp, powerful blow, after which most of the troops will hopefully be able to wash their hands and go back to their barracks. The latter inculcates them with such strict self-control as to prevent them from losing their pride, thus enabling them to sustain their morale for a long time, perhaps forever. Both approaches, the second perhaps even more than the first, require enormous courage and strength if they are to be consistently applied. Such being the case, it is no wonder that the vast majority of counterinsurgents tried to apply now one policy, one another, until they fell between two stools.

Take, as a perfect case in point, the Americans in Vietnam. Right from the beginning, President John F. Kennedy announced his determination to bear any burden in the cause of liberty. However, the approach that he, and after him Lyndon B. Johnson, took belied their words. With domestic considerations in mind, neither President was prepared to go to the point where the domestic economy would be affected. Johnson's slogan, indeed, was "guns *and* butter"; engaging in Vietnam, he was trying to win the war on poverty as well. Partly for this reason, partly because they feared Chinese intervention as had happened in Korea, both he and Kennedy adopted an approach that was reactive and incremental. Being reactive and incremental, to all the world it signified hesitancy, weakness, and a lack of will; and how could it be otherwise, given that most Americans had never even heard of Vietnam? At times, the American desire to treat war as an instrument of politics looked as if they were begging their opponents to negotiate. Meeting a stony silence on Hanoi's part, now they tried to bomb North Vietnam into surrender, now they called a unilateral halt to bombing. Now they fought all out, now they declared a holiday and agreed to a truce. Now they took over from the South Vietnamese, now they "Vietnamized" the war. While this was going on, they were constantly defending their record, trying to conceal the extent of the devastation they were inflicting – which, of course, came out nevertheless – and inventing excuses to explain why their troops were killing as many civilians as they did.

Against such a background it is scant wonder that the entire world, the Viet Cong and North Vietnamese leadership presumably not excluded, soon understood that the U.S. had no idea as to what it wanted to accomplish.[25] Not having an idea, it allowed its course of action to be determined by the means at its disposal, putting the cart before the horse. As to the rest of the story and

---

[25] See, for example, the strictures of Moshe Dayan, who visited Vietnam in July 1966: M. Dayan, *Vietnam Diary* [Hebrew], Tel Aviv, Dvir, 1977, *passim*.

all the glorious deeds the Americans committed before pulling out, lo they are written on the Vietnam Memorial in the Mall in Washington, DC.

4 Conclusions

In conclusion, and as the countless defeats suffered by would-be counterinsurgents since 1941 prove without a shadow of doubt, something has gone very, very wrong indeed. This applies both to Western nations and, as the Soviet defeat in Afghanistan showed, former Communist ones; both to developed nations and to many undeveloped ones; both to those who, like the Germans in Yugoslavia, were utterly ruthless and to those who, like the Israelis in the Occupied Territories, only killed four or five enemies for every casualty they suffered. Each time a failure occurred, rivers of ink were spilt trying to explain the reasons, to no avail. One might almost apply Hegel's words: the only thing one can learn from history is that people do not learn from it.

A spoon, plunged into salt water, will rust. To prevent this from happening, it is possible to do either of two things. One is to scoop out all the water and withdraw the spoon, wipe it clean, and return it to the cupboard where it belongs. The other is to stir the water very carefully and, by so doing, prevent it from becoming even saltier than it already is. Assuming the two methods are equally effective in principle, seen from a humanitarian point of view the British one is undoubtedly superior. There may, however, be circumstances when it cannot be applied: either because the uprising has already gone too far, or else because the character of the nation and the instruments of power at its disposal do not permit it. Under such circumstances, Bismarck's dictum that politics is the art of choosing between the bad and worse applies. Unless you are prepared to recognize this fact and draw the consequences, perhaps the best course is to stay out of the counterinsurgency game in the first place.

„Countering Terrorism" als Krieg der Weltanschauungen

Der djihadistische Terrorismus als eine neue totalitäre Herausforderung an die europäische Demokratie*

Bassam Tibi

Harvard University und Cornell University

Zu den wichtigsten Spielarten des Terrorismus des 21. Jahrhunderts gehört der religiös legitimierte Terror, der in allen Religionen vorkommt.[1] Darunter ragt der Djihad-Terrorismus als neuer Totalitarismus hervor; er wird nicht von einem Staat, sondern von einer Bewegung getragen. Dieser islamistische Djihadismus bedient sich des modernen Terrorismus nur als ein Instrument bei der Verwirklichung eines politischen Zieles. Es gibt noch keine klare Strategie, die für ein „countering" dieser Bedrohung der offenen Gesellschaft geeignet wäre. Der Terrorismus[2] stellt diese Bedrohung dar. Die Auseinandersetzung des demokratischen Europa mit den bisherigen Totalitarismen, also Kommunismus und Fa-

---

* Dieser Beitrag ist im Herbst 2004 während der Beurlaubung von der Universität Göttingen im Rahmen meiner „Affiliation" an der Harvard University/Center for Middle Eastern Studies als „Visiting Scholar" entstanden.
[1] Mark Juergensmeyer, *Terror in the Mind of God. The Global Rise of Religious Violence*, Berkeley 2000. Zur islamischen Spielart Bassam Tibi, *Der neue Totalitarismus. Heiliger Krieg und westliche Sicherheit*, Darmstadt 2004, besonders Kapitel III, in dem eine Analyse über den islamistischen Terror-Djihadismus (S. 106-137) enthalten ist.
[2] Unter den zahlreichen Arbeiten zum Terrorismus vor und nach dem 11. September 2001 sind lesenswert: Richard Chasdi, *Tapestry of Terror. Portrait of Middle Eastern Terrorism*, New York 2002; Philip Heyman, *Terrorism and America*, Cambridge, Massachusetts, 1998; Bruce Hofman, *Inside Terrorism*, New York 1998; David Whittaker, Hg., *The Terrorism-Reader*, London 2001; Paul A. Pillar, *Terrorism and US-Foreign Policy*, Washington, DC, 2001 und nicht zuletzt Walter Reich, Hg., *The Origins of Terrorism*, Cambridge 1990. Der anstehende Gegenstand ist nicht neu, so dass unter den älteren Arbeiten folgende ebenso empfehlenswert bleiben: Christopher Dobson, Ronald Payne, *The Never Ending War. Terrorism in the 1980s*, New York 1987 und Grant Wardlaw, *Political Terrorism. Theory, Tactics and Counter Measures*, Neuausgabe Cambridge 1989. Eine wichtige Neuveröffentlichung zum Thema „Countering Terrorism"

schismus,[3] erforderte nicht nur eine militärische Sicherheitspolitik, sondern auch einen geistigen Einsatz für die Verteidigung der Freiheit. Dies gilt auch in einem erhöhten Maße für die neue Bedrohung, wenngleich mit dem großen Unterschied, dass der Gegner unsichtbar ist; er ist weder ein Staat noch ein Militärblock.

Erschwerend kommt hinzu, dass die neue Bedrohung aus einer anderen Zivilisation kommt. Die „Armeen der al-Qaida"[4] bestehen aus irregulären, aus dem Untergrund agierenden, also nicht sichtbaren Kriegern. Unter den Bedingungen „globaler Migration" nisten sich die Terroristen vor allem in westlichen Gesellschaften, vorrangig in der westeuropäischen Islam-Diaspora, ein; sie treten äußerlich betrachtet wie „normale" Bürger auf und leben unauffällig. Die von der Islam-Diaspora aus agierenden Islamisten beanspruchen Zivilrechte für sich, und es gelingt ihnen sogar mit Hilfe von „Human Rights" und „Asylgruppen", demokratische Freiheiten des Rechtsstaates für sich zu instrumentalisieren. Dies ermöglicht den Djihadisten, Europa als „Ruhezone" zu verwenden[5] – eine Problematik, die beim „Countering Terrorism" kaum erhellt wird, weil viel Vernebelungsideologie – von Multikulti bis zur Romantik fremder Kulturen – vorherrscht.

1   Einführung

Der historische Hintergrund des djihadistischen Terrorismus ist die Entstehung des politischen Islam im 20. Jahrhundert. Auf der Basis eines ein Vierteljahrhundert andauernden Studiums dieses Phänomens habe ich viele Arbeiten[6] über diesen Gegenstand vorgelegt, die diese Analyse untermauern. Die Entwicklung beginnt mit der Gründung der ersten fundamentalistischen Bewegung im Islam,

---

   ist: A.K. Cronin, James Ludes, *Attacking Terrorism. Elements of Grand Strategy*, Washington, DC, 2004.
[3] Dazu Hannah Arendt, *Elemente totaler Herrschaft*, Frankfurt am Main 1962 (Original: Origins of Totalitarism, 1955), darin zum Totalitarismus als Bewegung Teil III, S. 455ff.
[4] Jonathan Schanzer, *Al-Qaeda's Armies. Middle East Affiliate Groups & the Next Generation of Terror*, Washington, DC, 2005; vgl. auch Anm. 56 unten.
[5] Mehr hierzu in Kapitel IV über Deutschland als „Ruhezone" in Bassam Tibi, *Die fundamentalistische Herausforderung. Der Islam und die Weltpolitik*, 4., völlig neu überarbeitete und erweiterte Ausgabe, München 2003, S. 184-214.
[6] Darunter zentral Bassam Tibi, *The Challenge of Fundamentalism. Political Islam and the New World Disorder*, Berkeley 1998, aktualisierte Neuausgabe nach dem 11. September 2001, Berkeley 2002. Deutsche Übersetzung mit neuer Einleitung, *Die neue Weltordnung*, Berlin 1999 (mehrere Neuauflagen nach dem 11. September 2001).

nämlich der Bewegung der Muslim-Bruderschaft[7] im Jahr 1928. Dieser politische Islam ist der neue Totalitarismus, der sich von den früheren Totalitarismen durch die religiöse Legitimation des Terrorismus als irregulärer Krieg unterscheidet (vgl. Anm. 1). Dieser islamisch legitimierte Djihad-Terror geschieht nicht aus Besessenheit mit Gewalt und seine Vertreter sind keine „Bande von Verrückten/*Crazed Gang*", wie der Kritiker des Orientalismus Edward Said einst falsch unterstellte; vielmehr findet die Anwendung von Gewalt als Djihad aus religiöser Überzeugung statt. Aus diesem Grunde und auch, weil der Djihadismus eine politische Ordnungsvorstellung der „Gottesherrschaft/*Hakimiyyat Allah*" vertritt, ist er eine politisch-militärische Erscheinung, die nicht mit Kriminalität zu verwechseln ist. Dies zeigt, wie Konflikte in der postbipolaren Politik oft eine religiöse Dimension annehmen, die nur wenige Sozialwissenschaftler im Westen verstehen.[8] Weil die Djihadisten – wie angeführt – als nichtstaatliche Akteure auftreten, sind ihre Handlungen schwer vorauszusagen und auch kaum zu berechnen.

Aus den bisherigen Ausführungen geht hervor, dass es bei der militärischen und geistigen Auseinandersetzung mit dem djihadistischen Totalitarismus mehr um einen Einsatz für die Freiheit als um Kriminalitätsbekämpfung geht. Der neue Totalitarismus ist zudem keine Erfindung eines Ersatzes für einen mit dem Ende des Ost-West-Konflikts verloren gegangenen Feind für den Westen. Niemand würde den Begründer der gesellschaftskritischen Frankfurter Schule, Max Horkheimer, verdächtigen, ein Kalter Krieger zu sein, weil er gegen Ende seines sehr erfüllten Lebens dazu aufrief, das freiheitliche Europa gegen jede Bedrohung zu verteidigen. Er hatte den Totalitarismus „Hitlerscher oder Stalinscher Varianz"[9] im Blick. Ich schließe mich diesem Aufruf an[10] und sehe, in dieser Tradition stehend, im totalitären Islamismus den neuen Feind der offenen Gesellschaft Europas. Der

---

[7] Vgl. den Klassiker hierzu: Richard Mitchell, *The Society of the Muslim Brothers*, Oxford 1969. Der Enkel des Begründers der Muslimbruderschaft (Hasan al-Banna) ist der ägyptische Schweizer Tariq Ramadan. Der von ihm behauptete „europäische Islam" ist keiner, weil er in der Tradition der Muslimbruderschaft steht, die falsch als antikoloniale Bewegung gedeutet wird. Bis heute bleibt diese international vernetzte Bewegung die wichtigste Einrichtung des politischen Islam, ja seine Herkunft.

[8] Darunter fast als einzige Ausnahme in Deutschland Wilfried Röhrich, *Die Macht der Religionen. Glaubenskonflikte in der Weltpolitik*, München 2004.

[9] Max Horkheimer, *Kritische Theorie*, 2 Bände, hierzu Band 1, Frankfurt am Main 1968, hier S. XIII.

[10] Dies tue ich, indem ich dieses Zitat von Horkheimer in meinem Buch *Europa ohne Identität?*, München 1998, Neuausgabe mit dem neuen Untertitel: *Leitkultur oder Wertebeliebigkeit*, München 2002, anführe, um ihm, meinem Lehrer, dieses Buch zu widmen. Darin argumentiere ich gegen die falsche Toleranz, gegen den Islamismus und für eine europäische Leitkultur zur Verteidigung der offenen Gesellschaft.

militärische Djihad-Zweig des irregulären Krieges, der nicht nur auf die USA hinzielt, hat seine Logistik in Westeuropa. Bei den Anschlägen vom 11. März 2004 in Madrid wurde sehr deutlich gezeigt, dass Europa auch auf der Feindesliste steht. Dabei besteht die Bedrohung nicht nur für die westliche Sicherheit, sondern auch für das friedliche Zusammenleben mit der stets wachsenden europäischen Islam-Diaspora. Die Auseinandersetzung mit dieser Bedrohung muss daher im Mittelpunkt jeder Strategie des „Countering Terrorism" stehen. Die erste hierfür erforderliche Voraussetzung ist darin zu sehen, dass dieses neue Phänomen des Djihadismus angemessen zu verstehen ist. Ein Hindernis auf diesem Wege stellen die Fesseln der PC-Zensur dar. Lange haben Multikulturalisten ein ideologisches Verbot für eine solche Debatte durchgesetzt. Von dieser Zensur sind im Krieg der Ideen und Weltanschauungen Analysen über die religiösen Wurzeln der Gewalt betroffen. Das Denkverbot wurde mit Klischees wie „Orientalismus" und „Feindbild Islam" verhüllt, die als Totschlagsargumente gegen die Kritiker dienen; ihnen wird „Fremdenfeindlichkeit" und Ähnliches mehr unterstellt, um jede Aufklärung über die anstehenden Gefahren für die Freiheit durch den Djihadismus zu verhindern. Beim Nachdenken im Rahmen der Erforschung des islamischen Djihad-Terrorismus darf man sich von dieser PC-Zensur nicht einschränken oder einschüchtern lassen.

Die folgende Arbeit versucht sich in zwei Schritten dem Gegenstand anzunähern: Erstens wird der Islamismus in einem größeren Kontext als eine religiös begründete Weltanschauung einer totalitären Ordnung eingeordnet. Diese wird zur ideologischen Orientierung einer Bewegung, die sich des Terrorismus bedient. Der zweite Schritt wird durch die Deutung des Djihadismus als neues Muster des irregulären Krieges vorgenommen. Somit beruht die erste Stufe auf einer geistigen Auseinandersetzung, während die zweite eine neue Sicherheitspolitik erfordert.

Natürlich bekennen sich nicht alle Islamisten zum Djihad. Es gibt auch friedliche, in demokratischen Institutionen arbeitende Islamisten, die dasselbe Ziel, aber ohne Gewalt erreichen wollen. Vor ihnen haben Kommunisten und Faschisten Vorbilder für die Unterwanderung demokratischer Einrichtungen durch den Totalitarismus gegeben. In der vorliegenden Studie werden die „institutionellen Islamisten" nur am Rande erörtert. Die Djihadisten, die einen irregulären Krieg gegen Ungläubige außer- und innerhalb der Welt des Islam führen, sind der Gegenstand der Analyse, weil es hier um „Countering Terrorism" geht. Im Gegensatz zum zwischenstaatlichen Krieg ist dieser djihadistische Terrorismus kaum berechenbar. Deshalb erfordert „Countering Terrorism" von der offenen Gesellschaft[11], sich sowohl weltanschaulich mit der Ordnungsvorstellung der Gottesherrschaft als auch sicherheitspolitisch mit den neuen Mustern des irregulären Djihad-Krieges auseinander zu setzen. Dies sind die bereits angeführten zwei Ebenen der folgenden Analyse.

In den Rahmen der vorliegenden Analyse fügt sich die bestialische Hinrichtung des niederländischen Filmemachers Theo van Gogh. Direkt danach haben „Tauhid-Brigaden" als djihadistische Bewegung in der westlichen Islam-Diaspora den Europäern mit dem Djihad-Krieg gedroht, sollten Repressionen gegen Islamisten folgen. Europäer bildeten sich nach den Anschlägen vom 11. September 2001 in den USA ein, sie seien nicht betroffen, aber der 11. März 2004 und die van-Gogh-Lynchjustiz haben Besseres gelehrt. Denn auch in Europa findet der Djihad-Krieg statt; er ist mitten in den Westen hineingetragen worden.[12] Wer dies nicht einsieht, versteht nicht nur nicht, was in Europa vor sich geht, sondern verkennt auch die neue Welt des 21. Jahrhunderts. Wer im Gegensatz dazu die Grundzüge des neuen Phänomens erkennt, tritt dafür ein, dass eine Strategie zum „Countering Modern Terrorism" erforderlich ist. Diese darf sich nicht auf rein polizeiliche oder im größeren Rahmen sicherheitspolitische Fragen beschränken; sie muss auch die geistigen Grundlagen des Djihadismus einbeziehen. Denn der djihadistische Islamismus, der – wie angeführt – der neue Totalitarismus des 21. Jahrhunderts ist, hat Anhänger, die nicht nur Terroranschläge ausüben; sie verbreiten den Geist eines weltanschaulichen Krieges gegen die Grundwerte der westlichen Zivilisation mitten im Westen. Somit richtet sich der Djihad-Islamismus gegen die Demokratie als säkulare Ordnung. Doch bedient er sich in einer zynischen Weise westlicher Werte, nämlich der Toleranz, und greift hierbei sogar auf Moden wie die des Multikulturalismus zurück.[13]

Beim Nachdenken über „Countering Terrorism" beziehe ich mich auf die Arbeit von Hannah Arendt, weil sich ihre Ansätze für die geistige Auseinandersetzung mit der beschriebenen Herausforderung sehr gut eignen. Sie hat politische Systeme totaler Herrschaft untersucht, in denen die Trennung zwischen öffentlicher

---

[11] Karl Popper, *Die offene Gesellschaft und ihre Feinde*, 2 Bände, 7. Auflage, Tübingen 1992.
[12] Udo Ulfkotte, *Der Krieg in unseren Städten. Wie Islamisten Deutschland unterwandern*, Frankfurt am Main 2003. Statt Islamisten, über die im Ulfkotte-Buch aufgeklärt wird, zu verfolgen, ging die deutsche Justiz auf der Basis vieler islamistischer Klagen, die noch vom Sozialstaat finanziert wurden, gegen den Autor vor, wodurch er beruflich ruiniert wurde; vgl. Anm. 13.
[13] Alice Schwarzer, *Gotteskrieger und die falsche Toleranz*, Köln 2002, darin das Kapitel von Bassam Tibi, „Die verordnete Fremdenliebe", auf S. 105-120.

und privater Sphäre abgeschafft wird.[14] Das ist ein zentraler Inhalt der Ideologie des Totalitarismus, die eine totalitäre Herrschaft anstrebt. In diesem Sinne ist der Islamismus eine Vision einer totalitären Herrschaftsform. Die Djihadisten als Vertreter einer Bewegung betreiben den Djihad nicht als „action directe", im Sinne von Georges Sorel, sondern sie sind religiös und nicht säkular orientiert; sie wollen schließlich eine Gottesherrschaft errichten. Daher erfordert ein „Countering Terrorism" bei diesem Gegenstand eine Doppelstrategie: Ein Einsatz für die offene Gesellschaft gegen den Totalitarismus und zugleich eine Suche nach einem Konzept für „new security"[15] gegen die unmittelbare Gewalt des Djihad-Terrorismus.

Aus den vorangegangenen Ausführungen geht hervor, dass die folgende Analyse von der Annahme ausgeht, dass der Islamismus mit seinem djihadistischen Zweig mehr als ein schlichter Terrorismus ist; er ist das Instrument einer totalitären Bewegung. Heute bestehen hierdurch vergleichbare Gefahren zu den früher von Hannah Arendt und Sir Karl Popper erkannten Bedrohungen für die Demokratie (vgl. Anm. 3 und 11). In diesem Kontext stehe ich in der Tradition beider Vordenker, Arendt und Popper, die die NS-Terrorherrschaft erlebt haben. Sie haben auf der Basis dieser Erfahrung die Grundlinien bei der Erkenntnis von Bedrohungen der Freiheit gelegt. Im 21. Jahrhundert bewahren sich diese Arbeiten ihre Relevanz bei der Verteidigung der Demokratie und bleiben wegweisend. Karl Popper hatte einmal argumentiert, dass es nicht zur Toleranz gehöre, die Intoleranz totalitärer Kräfte zu tolerieren. Wie gezeigt, hat Hannah Arendt sowohl für die Bewegungen dieser Kräfte als auch für die Herrschaftsform, die sie vertreten, den Totalitarismusbegriff geprägt. Der Islamismus ist eine politische Ideologie einer Bewegung, die eine totale Diktatur anstrebt, die jedoch mit der Religion legitimiert wird.

Die Toleranz, die gegenüber der beschränkt toleranten Religion des Islam gelten soll, darf nicht auf den intoleranten Islamismus und seinen Djihad-Terrorismus übertragen werden. Dies wäre der Selbstmord Europas als ein Kontinent islami-

---

[14] Zur Trennung von öffentlich und privat in einer freien Gesellschaft: Hannah Arendt, *Viva Activa oder vom tätigen Leben*, München und Stuttgart 1960, zweites Kapitel sowie Anm. 3 oben.

[15] Hierzu Lenore Martin, Hg., *New Security*, New York 2000 und die Neuausgabe von Bassam Tibi, *Conflict and War in the Middle East. From Interstate War to New Security*, unter Harvard-Sponsorship in New York 1998 erschienen; dazu im neuen Teil von Kapitel 12 besonders den Abschnitt: „Understanding, Fundamentalism in Security Terms", S. 223ff.

scher Migration. Im Konfliktherd Toleranz[16] muss man klare Positionen gegen die Feinde der offenen Gesellschaft beziehen. Diese Einsicht gehört in die Überlegungen zur Entfaltung einer Strategie für „Countering Modern Terrorism". Der neue Totalitarismus bedroht mit seiner Djihad-Gewalt nicht nur den Westen, sondern auch freiheitsliebende Muslime, die gegenüber der Demokratie und der offenen Gesellschaft aufgeschlossen sind. Daher sind die „Faultlines/Bruchlinien" nicht zwischen Islam und Europa, sondern zwischen der „offenen Gesellschaft und ihren Feinden" in der Tradition von Popper zu ziehen. Das muss man nicht nur aus einer aufgeklärten Geisteshaltung der Offenheit anderen Religionen gegenüber anstreben; auch ist dies aus strategischen Gründen erforderlich, weil zwischen dem Islam als Religion und dem Islamismus als der islamischen Spielart des religiösen Fundamentalismus unterschieden werden muss.[17] Aus dieser Unterscheidung muss die Einsicht als Schlussfolgerung erfolgen, dass kein Generalverdacht gegen die Masse der Muslime entstehen darf, eben weil dieser nur dem Djihadismus zugute kommt. Vielmehr soll man Muslime vor dieser Polarisierung schützen und sie gewinnen. Denn die Polarisierung erzeugt ein Klima, das für eine falsche Solidarität in den Kollektiven genutzt werden kann.

2 Die Herausforderung des Djihad-Islamismus als neuer Totalitarismus

Der Djihad-Terrorismus beruft sich auf den Islam, jedoch im Rahmen einer „Erfindung der Tradition"[18]. Diese Erkenntnis hat eine doppelte Bedeutung: erstens, dass die Islamisten nicht außerhalb des Islam stehen, weil sie sich auf seine Tradition berufen; zweitens, dass ihr Denken jedoch neu ist, eben weil sie die Tradition neu definieren. Daraus ergibt sich, dass wir es mit einer neuen Erfindung zu tun haben, die nicht dem Islam schlechthin anzulasten ist, obwohl sie sich islamisch versteht. Die „Erfindung von Tradition" verhält sich somit wie neuer Wein in alten Schläuchen. In diesem Sinne hat der Begründer der Muslimbru-

---

[16] Vgl. Michael Kessler, Hg., *Konfliktherd Toleranz*, Tübingen 2002, hierzu das Kapitel von Bassam Tibi, „Toleranz zwischen Kulturpluralismus und multikultureller Wertebeliebigkeit", S. 173-192.

[17] Bassam Tibi, „Ist der Islam eine politische Religion? Über den Unterschied zwischen Islam und Islamismus", in: *Religion-Staat-Gesellschaft*, Band 5 (2004), S. 77-112.

[18] Hierzu vgl. Erich Hobsbawm, Hg., *The Invention of Tradition*, Neuausgabe Cambridge 1996, darin besonders die Einleitung. Zur Verwendung dieses Bezugsrahmens der Beitrag von Bassam Tibi, „Ist der Islam eine politische Religion? Die Möglichkeit eines interreligiösen Pluralismus unter den Bedingungen des Zivilisationskonfliktes", in: Georg Pfleiderer, Ekkehard W. Stegemann, Hg., *Politische Religion. Geschichte und Gegenwart eines Problemfeldes*, Zürich 2004., S. 223-253, zu diesem Thema S. 229ff.

derschaft, Hasan al-Banna, eine Neudeutung des Djihad vorgenommen, die die Bedeutung des klassischen islamischen Djihad erheblich verändert hat. Die Bewegung der Muslimbrüder gilt als Pionier des Djihad-Islamismus; ihr Begründer, Hasan al-Banna, ist der Großvater des „Doppelagenten" (*Die Zeit*) Tariq Ramadan. Der Djihadismus ist die islamische Spielart des irregulären Krieges.[19] Somit ist al-Banna der Vorläufer des Kampfes für eine Verwirklichung islamistischer totalitärer Herrschaft und nicht ein „Freiheitskämpfer gegen Kolonialherrschaft", wie sein Enkelkind Tariq Ramadan falsch behauptet und die westliche Öffentlichkeit täuscht. Die US-Regierung hatte einen Grund, Ramadan ein Visum und somit die Einreise in die USA 2004 zu verweigern. Doch ist Ramadan nur ein gemäßigter Islamist und nicht, wie sein Großvater, ein Djihadist. Was ist denn Djihadismus? Um dies zu erklären, müssen wir auf seinen Ursprung, nämlich die islamische Djihad-Doktrin, zurückgreifen und dabei die oben gemachte Erkenntnis der doppelten Bedeutung stets im Auge behalten.

Der klassische islamische Djihad lässt sich unterschiedlich deuten. Es ist aber falsch, manchmal auch eine bewusste Täuschung, wenn manche den Djihad alleine als eine „friedliche Anstrengung" darstellen, denn laut Koran ist er mit „*qital*/Kampf" verbunden, wodurch er Gewaltanwendung einschließt.[20] Doch schreibt der Koran strenge Regeln für die Durchführung des Djihad als „*qital*/Kampf" gegen Ungläubige vor, er ist also kein irregulärer Krieg ohne Normen. Die für den Djihad vom Koran vorgeschriebenen Einschränkungen sind bei allen Terroranschlägen der islamistischen Djihadisten vom 11. September 2001 bis zum 11. März 2004 missachtet worden. So sind die Angriffe ohne Vorwarnung erfolgt, so wie der Koran es festlegt, und haben sich gegen Zivilisten gerichtet, was der klassische Djihad verbietet. Die Urheber des neuen Djihad ohne Regeln tun dies in Anlehnung an Hasan al-Banna und verstehen sich selbst als „die wahren Muslime" unserer Gegenwart.

Die Unterscheidung zwischen Islam und Islamismus dient nur der Differenzierung. Darüber hinaus öffnet sie eine Perspektive dafür, dass beim „Countering Terrorism" eine Zusammenarbeit mit Muslimen möglich wird, weil der „War on Terror" ohne dies nicht zu gewinnen ist. Bei westlich-islamischen Dialogen in In-

---

[19] Hasan al-Banna, „Risalat al-Djihad", abgedruckt in seiner Essaysammlung *Madjimu'at Rasa'il al-Imam al-Shahid*, neue legale Edition (so im Impressum) Kairo 1990, S. 271-292.

[20] Zur Erklärung des klassischen islamischen Djihad-Begriffes vgl. Bassam Tibi, *Der wahre Imam. Der Islam von Mohammed bis zur Gegenwart*, Neuausgabe, München 2002, Kapitel 2, S. 83-99 (zuerst 1996). Vgl. ferner mein Kapitel „War and Peace in Islam" in: Terry Nardin, Hg., *The Ethics of War and Peace. Religious and Secular Perspectives*, Princeton, New Jersey, 1996 (neu 1998), S. 128-145.

donesien habe ich argumentiert, dass Muslime aufgefordert sind, sich nicht nur an einem „Aufstand der Anständigen" gegen den Terror der Djihadisten zu beteiligen, sondern auch beim „War on Terrorism" mitzumachen.[21] Allein dadurch kann dafür gesorgt werden, dass keine Huntingtonschen „Faultlines" zwischen dem Islam und dem Westen als „fulfilled prophecy" (erfüllte Prophezeiung) entstehen.[22] Anders verfahren Islamisten, wenn sie in ihrem „Krieg der Anschauungen" jedes „Countering Terrorism"-Unternehmen propagandistisch als einen „War on Islam" verfemen. Aus diesem Grunde muss jede Strategie zur Bekämpfung des Djihad-Terrorismus diese Dimension als Kampf der Weltanschauungen einschließen. Sicherheitspolitik schließt somit eine geistige Auseinandersetzung ein. Dies erfordert ein Verständnis für den „cultural turn" (kulturellen Wechsel) in unserer Zeit und für den Stellenwert von Weltbildern und Weltanschauung in der postbipolaren Weltpolitik.[23]

Wie bereits angeführt, ist der Islamismus ein vielschichtiges Phänomen, das nicht grob mit dem Djihad-Terrorismus gleichgesetzt werden soll. Ich habe bereits die institutionellen Islamisten genannt, die einen gewaltlosen Marsch durch die Institutionen anstreben. Dagegen beanspruchen Djihadisten, eine auf Djihad-Gewalt basierende „islamische Weltrevolution"[24] zur Islamisierung der Welt zu tragen. Die allgemeine „Revolte gegen den Westen"[25] ist der zeitgeschichtliche Kontext dieser Weltrevolution. Diesen westlichen Begriff verwendet Sayyid Qutb.

---

[21] Zu den westlich-islamischen Dialogen in Indonesien, an denen ich die Sicherheitsproblematik als Dialogthema hervorgehoben habe, vgl. die Bände von Chaider S. Bamualim u. a., Hg., *Islam and the West. Dialogue of Civilizations in Search of Peaceful Global World Order*, Jakarta 2003 (Tibi, S. 15-26 und S. 249-254) sowie von Karolina Helmantia u. a., Hg., *Dialogue in the World Disorder. A Response to the Threat of Unilateralism and World Terrorism*, Jakarta 2004; darin der US-Botschafter in Jakarta, R. L. Boyce (S. 9-24), sowie der iranische Botschafter (S. 149-158) und meine Antwort auf beide, „Islamic Civilization and the Quest for Democratic Pluralism", S. 159-203.

[22] Samuel P. Huntington, *The Clash of Civilizations*, New York 1996, und dagegen Roman Herzog u. a., *Preventing the Clash of Civilizations*, New York 1999, Hg. von H. Schmiegelow, darin Bassam Tibi, „International Morality and Cross-Cultural Bridging", S. 107-126.

[23] Vgl. das erste Kapitel über den „cultural turn" und die Bedeutung der Weltanschauung in meinem in Anm. 1 nachgewiesenen Buch *Der neue Totalitarismus*, besonders S. 43-51.

[24] Sayyid Qutb, *al-Salam al-Alami wa al-Islam*, 10. legale Ausgabe (laut Impressum) Kairo 1992, darin zur „islamischen Weltrevolution" S. 172-173.

[25] Hedley Bull, „The Revolt against the West", in: Hedley Bull, Adam Watson, Hg., *The Expansion of International Society*, Oxford 1984, S. 217-228.

Die Entwicklung der Doktrin vom klassischen Djihad zum Djihadismus ist die Tradition, in der auch der 1957 geborene Osama Bin Laden steht. Er hat über seinen Lehrer Abdullah Yousuf Azzam[26] die Ideen des 1966 gehenkten Sayyid Qutb aufgenommen und dann selbst entwickelt. Letzterer ist der geistige Vater der Idee der „*Hakimiyyat Allah*/Gottesherrschaft"[27], also der politischen totalitären Ordnung, die durch den Djihad als „Weltrevolution" verwirklicht werden soll.

Sowohl früher in den einstigen al-Qaida-Camps in Afghanistan vor ihrer Zerstörung im Krieg 2001 als auch heute in einigen Schulen der Moscheevereinskultur in Europa gelten die Schriften Qutbs, in denen zu einer „totalen Revolution zur Verwirklichung der Gottesherrschaft" aufgerufen wird, als Pflichtlektüre. Nach Qutb könne es nur dann Frieden geben, wenn der Islam global vorherrsche; somit sei „eine Weltrevolution mittels Djihad" als Voraussetzung für den islamischen Weltfrieden erforderlich. Ein Pluralismus, in dessen Rahmen Europa und der Islam unter gegenseitigem Respekt in Frieden zusammenleben könnten, wird durch die djihadistische Zweiteilung der Welt in eine der Gläubigen und eine andere der Ungläubigen ausgeschlossen. Das Prinzip lautet: entweder wir Gläubige oder sie, die Ungläubigen, und nicht: leben und leben lassen. Zum „Countering Terrorism" muss ein Verbot der Verbreitung dieses Gedankengutes in der Diaspora und in der Welt des Islam als Volksverhetzung gehören.

Mit al-Banna, Qutb und Azzam sind drei Figuren der djihadistisch-islamischen Herausforderung an Europa genannt worden. Die Schriften dieser geistigen Führer bilden die Quellen dieses heute populär gewordenen Islam-Verständnisses des Islamismus. Zentral ist hierbei das Denken Qutbs. Seine Sicht lässt sich mit seinen eigenen Worten wie folgt zusammenfassen: Nach seiner Darstellung der Dichotomie *Iman*/Glaube versus *Kufr*/Unglauben schreibt er: „Daraus folgt, dass der Islam einen permanenten Djihad führt, der nicht nachlässt, bis die Gottesherrschaft, d. h. die wahre Ordnung Wirklichkeit wird"[28]. Dies ist bis heute das lebendige Erbe des Ägypters Qutb, das der Saudi-Yemenit Bin Laden vom Palästinenser Azzam übernommen hat. Neu an Bin Laden ist, dass er den „permanenten Djihad" von Qutb zu einem „*al-Djihad al-alami*/globalen Djihad" weiterentwickelt hat. Seine in vielen Reden wiederholte neue Formel lautet: Die Muslime

---

[26] Zu Azzam vgl. Yossef Bodansky, *Bin Laden. The Man Who Declared Ward On America*, Rocklin, Kalifornien, 1999.

[27] Zur Quelle der Herrschaftsform „*Hakimiyyat Allah*" vgl. Sayyid Qutb, *Ma'alim fi al-Tariq*, 13. legale Ausgabe (laut Impressum) Kairo 1989; zur Erklärung des Konzepts vgl. Kapitel 5 in Bassam Tibi, *Fundamentalismus im Islam. Eine Gefahr für den Weltfrieden*, 3. aktualisierte Auflage 2002, S. 73-86.

[28] Zitat aus Sayyid Qutb, *al-Salam al-Alami wa al-Islam* (wie Anm. 24).

müssen einen „*al-Djihad al-alami*/globalen Djihad" des Glaubens gegen den „*al-kufr al-alami*/globalen Unglauben" führen. Damit meint Bin Laden die schon von Qutb entworfene islamische Weltrevolution gegen den Westen als Zivilisation. Ich habe bereits den Ursprung der Ideen des Neo-Djihad, nämlich den Ägypter Hasan al-Banna, benannt (vgl. Anm. 19). Dieser wurde 1949 ermordet. Die Gewalt richtete sich gegen ihren eigenen Prediger.

Nach diesen Erläuterungen möchte ich noch einmal auf die geistige Selbstzensur der Political Correctness zurückkommen, die verbietet, den politischen Islam und seinen Djihadismus offen als Gefahr anzusprechen. In den USA richtet sich diese Selbstzensur gegen einen Buhmann, den man westlichen Orientalismus nennt und sehr scharf kritisiert. Die in der beschriebenen Tradition stehenden Djihadisten wurden nach dem 11. September 2001 von Edward Said als „crazed gang" bezeichnet, und auf diese Weise wurde die islamische Legitimation ihrer Aktion heruntergespielt. Said war der geistige Vater der Kritik am Orientalismus. Unter „westlichem Orientalismus" verstand der 2003 verstorbene Palästinenser die „westliche Sicht des Orients", die ihn „orientalisiert". Bei allem Respekt vor Edward Said[29] müssen wir die Kultur der Political Correctness überwinden, um uns die Freiheit zu nehmen, über den Geist des Djihadismus und sein Endziel der „*Hakimiyyat Allah*/Gottesherrschaft" als totalitäre Ordnung nicht nur für die Welt des Islam, sondern auch für den Rest der Welt aufzuklären. Wenn diese Aufklärung als ein „Orientalismus" verfemt wird, dann haben wir es nicht nur mit einer Verhinderung von „Countering Terrorism" zu tun, sondern auch den geistigen Krieg gegen den Djihad-Terror verloren.

Eines muss klar gemacht werden: Verständnis für eine fremde Religion zu haben kann nicht heißen, blind gegenüber der Bedrohung der Islamisten zu sein, die eine „islamische Weltrevolution" als Djihad für eine neue Ordnung für die gesamte Welt beabsichtigen. Das ist der Inhalt des globalen Djihad, der kein Aufstand von Unterdrückten ist, sondern im Dienst eines neuen Totalitarismus geschieht. Der Islamismus ist zwar vom Geist eines toleranten und vernunftorientierten Islam weit entfernt, aber die Schriften von Qutb und al-Banna haben heute in der Welt des Islam großen Einfluss; jeder jugendliche Muslim kennt sie, nicht aber jene des toleranten Mystikers al-Arabi oder des Rationalisten Ibn Ruschd/Averroës. Diese großen Geister der islamischen Zivilisation sind im dunklen Zeitalter des Islamismus in kollektive Vergessenheit geraten.

---

[29] Edward Said, *Orientalism*, New York 1978. Über die daraufhin international entfachte Orientalismusdebatte vgl. Bassam Tibi, *Einführung in die islamische Geschichte*, Darmstadt 2001, Kapitel IV, S. 136-190.

Beim „Countering Terrorism" muss man auch mit dem Spiel Schluss machen, dass dies alles gar nichts mit dem Islam zu tun habe. Es ist eine Tatsache, dass der djihadistische Totalitarismus sich islamisch legitimiert; er steht deshalb nicht außerhalb des Islam. Zudem genießt er unter der jungen Generation eine hohe Popularität. Hierfür brachte ich bereits die Deutung von der Erfindung der Tradition. Ich möchte zusätzlich seine Nähe zum Faschismus und Stalin-Kommunismus feststellen. Den Vergleich mit den früheren Totalitarismen unternimmt sogar der Pakistani Abu al-A'la al-Maududi (1903-1979), der wie Qutb zu den Vätern des Islamismus zählt. In seiner Schrift „Die islamische Sicht der Politik" schreibt er, dass der Islam einen islamischen Staat vorschreibe, der, ohne Trennung von Öffentlichem und Privatem, alle Bereiche des Lebens regle. Es gehe also um einen – so fährt er fort –

> totalitären Staat (*daula schamilah*) [...], gegenüber dessen Vorschriften keiner das Recht hat, Opposition zu leiten, etwa mit dem Argument, dies sei eine persönliche Angelegenheit [...]. Dieser Staat hat eine gewisse Ähnlichkeit mit der faschistischen und kommunistischen Regierungsform, wenngleich im islamischen Staat der despotische oder hegemoniale Charakter jener Formen deshalb nicht vorhanden ist, weil der islamische Totalitarismus (*Schumuliyya*) Vorschriften gehorcht, die von Allah stammen.[30]

Das ist genau das Regierungssystem, das Qutb „*Hakimiyyat Allah*" nennt und das durch globalen Djihad zu verwirklichen ist. Das System selbst ist noch keine Realität, wohl aber die djihadistische Bewegung, die dafür eintritt, dass es eine gesellschaftliche Realität wird. Diese Bewegung hat ihre Logistik in Europa, wo ihr Geist in bestimmten Kreisen der Moscheevereinskultur blüht; diese Erkenntnis leitet zum nächsten Schritt über.

3 „Islamismus in Deutschland. Warum hat der Staat zu spät reagiert?"

Unter dieser Ankündigung fand am 7. April 2003 ein internes Symposium für Sicherheitsexperten auf Einladung des Innenministers des Landes Rheinland-Pfalz statt. Dort sollte erklärt werden, warum in Europa die Herausforderung des Djihad-Islamismus nicht angemessen wahrgenommen wird. Man stellte sich die Frage, welcher Hintergrund diesen Sachverhalt bedingt. Ich führte dort folgendes

---

[30] Das ist ein Zitat von Abu al-A'la-al-Maududi Maudoodi, *Nazariyat al-Islam wa hadiyat fi-al-siyasa wa-l- Qanun wa-l- dastur*, Kairo (o. D.) S. 44. Vgl. auch Hartmut Kraus, *Faschismus und Fundamentalismus*, Osnabrück 2003, besonders S. 89ff.

Beispiel an, das die Situation veranschaulicht: Als die Alfred-Herrhausen-Gesellschaft für Dialog im Sommer 2002 eine Veranstaltung in Berlin über Toleranz und Pluralismus durchführte, um mit dem Islam in einen Dialog einzutreten, suchte man vergebens nach einem europäisch denkenden Imam in Deutschland. So musste als islamischer Geistlicher schließlich ein Imam aus Frankreich eingeladen werden. Es war der Obermufti S. Ben-Cheich, der eine europäische Orientierung hat und aus Marseille eingeflogen wurde. Dabei gibt es in Deutschland Imame in 2.400 Moscheen und Gebetsräumen. Warum befindet sich unter ihnen kein einziger vom Geiste Ben-Cheichs? Von diesem stammt der Spruch: „Jedes Land in Europa bekommt den Islam, den es verdient". Ein laizistischer, mit religiösem und kulturellem Pluralismus vereinbarter Islam hat religiöse Vertreter unter den Muslimen in Frankreich, nicht aber in Deutschland. Für einen mit Europa kompatiblen Islam habe ich in Paris die Formel „Euro-Islam" geprägt.[31] In Deutschland finden wir in der Moscheevereinskultur keine Befürworter eines Euro-Islam. Es fällt auf, dass führende Köpfe unter den Djihadisten des 11. September aus der deutschen, nicht aus der französischen Islam-Diaspora[32] kamen. In diesem Lande liegt die Führung des organisierten Islam weitgehend in den Händen der Islamisten oder orthodoxen Salafisten. Wer verschuldet diese Situation? Warum ist die Integration der islamischen Zuwanderer gescheitert[33] und warum sind die Islamisten in der deutschen Islam-Diaspora überproportional stark vertreten? Diese Fragen dürfen nicht unterdrückt werden.

Eine Erklärung des Sachverhalts bietet die Tatsache, dass Deutschland eine auf den Staat fixierte Tradition hat, obwohl dieser erst 1871 entstanden ist. Mit diesem Hintergrund sprechen deutsche Sicherheitsexperten auf ihren Konferenzen – wie z. B. in Mainz – von der Formel „Hat der Staat zu spät reagiert?" Nach der Gesellschaft, die dies verschuldet, wird kaum gefragt. Im Gegensatz zu dem Fachtreffen des Ministeriums des Inneren in Mainz würde man im Französischen eher fragen: Was ist in der Zivilgesellschaft schief gelaufen? So denkt man in Paris, obwohl der französische Staat viel älter als der historisch relativ junge deutsche ist und weit mehr Autorität genießt.

---

[31] Zum Konzept des Euro-Islam und zu seiner Entstehung vgl. das neue, nur in der Neuausgabe enthaltene Kapitel in Bassam Tibi, *Im Schatten Allahs*, Neuausgabe, München 2003 (Original 1994), Kapitel 12, S. 491-529. Vgl. auch Ursula Spuler-Stegemann, *Muslime in Deutschland*, Neuausgabe, Freiburg im Breisgau 2002.

[32] Zur Hamburger Zelle vgl. Rohan Gunaratna, *Inside al-Qaida. Global Network of Terror*, New York 2002, S. 129-134.

[33] Hierzu vgl. Bassam Tibi, *Islamische Zuwanderung. Die gescheiterte Integration*, München 2002.

Ein weiterer Faktor, der eine Verhinderung eines angemessenen Umgangs mit dem Islam bedingt, ist die geschichtliche Belastung der NS-Gewaltherrschaft. Dadurch fühlen sich Deutsche befangen, wenn demokratie- und verfassungsfeindliche Aktivitäten von Ausländern, nicht von Deutschen, ans Licht kommen. Offen gesagt: In Deutschland verfolgt man Djhadisten nicht wie Neo-Nazis, obwohl sie einen ähnlichen Geist haben, also auch nachweisbar Antisemiten sind.[34] Hierfür soll folgendes Beispiel angeführt werden: Als im Oktober 2000 die Synagogen in Düsseldorf und Essen geschändet wurden, rief Bundeskanzler Schröder mit Recht zu einem „Aufstand der Anständigen" auf, und die Nation schrie auf. Nachdem Sicherheitsbehörden herausgefunden hatten, dass die Täter islamistische Muslime waren, schwiegen „die Anständigen", die Medien, die Politiker und mit ihnen die ganze Nation. Ich hatte große Schwierigkeiten, eine Zeitung für meinen Artikel „Islamismus ist genauso gefährlich wie Rechtsradikalismus" zu finden. Erst als im Januar 2001 jugendliche Islamisten auf offener Straße in Berlin einen Rabbiner zusammenschlugen, war *Die Welt* bereit, ihn zu veröffentlichen (Ausgabe vom 15. Januar 2001, S. 2). Dies erklärt, warum Islamisten Deutschland bevorzugen, um ihre logistische Basis und Ruhezone aufzubauen: weil sie dies ohne Widerstand tun konnten und immer noch können (vgl. Anm. 5 und 12). Die *New York Times* schrieb nach dem 11. September 2001, terroristische Islamisten finden in Deutschland einen „safe haven", eine sichere Freizone, vor, und ich veröffentliche am 12. August 2002 in der Zeitung *Die Welt* den Artikel „Der Rechtsstaat schützt die Islamisten". Es ist auch erwähnenswert, dass bisher kein einziger Djihadist in Deutschland von einem Gericht verurteilt worden ist. Das Prinzip gilt: *In dubio pro Islamico*. Die Zivilgesellschaft und der Rechtsstaat haben versagt. Warum diese Blauäugigkeit?

Statt aufzuklären, wurde bisher in vielen Medien, Kirchen und Gewerkschaften ein Widerstand dagegen geleistet, einen Zusammenhang zwischen religiös motiviertem Extremismus als Gewaltorientierung, Zuwanderung und bestimmten Einrichtungen in der europäischen Islam-Diaspora zu sehen. Jeder, der wagte, in diese Richtung vorzupreschen, auch wenn er wie ich ein Muslim ist, erntete den Vorwurf, „Angst zu schüren", und wurde des „Feindbildes Islam" bezichtigt, ja sogar inkriminiert. Dabei wird die Unterscheidung zwischen Islam als Religion der Toleranz und Islamismus als Spielart des islamischen Rechtsradikalismus als neuer Totalitarismus zugunsten der Islamisten unterschlagen. In dieser vergifte-

---

[34] Über den Islamismus als die Quelle des neuen Antisemitismus vgl. Phyllis Chesler, *The New Antisemitism*, San Francisco 2003. Vgl. ferner Bassam Tibi, „Der importierte Hass. Antisemitismus ist in der arabischen Welt weit verbreitet", in: *Die Zeit* vom 6. Februar 2003, S. 9. Wieder abgedruckt in: Michael Thumann, Hg., *Der Islam und der Westen*, Berlin 2003, S. 97-106.

ten Atmosphäre sprechen Gutmenschen ohne Differenzierung bei jeder Kritik am Islamismus vom „Feindbild Islam" und verordneter „Fremdenliebe". Dabei muss die Formel lauten: „Toleranz und Dialog dem Islam, wehrhafte Demokratie und Sicherheitspolitik dem Islamismus". Dies war schon vor dem 11. September 2001 meine Empfehlung an den deutschen Staat und seine Behörden sowie an die Zivilgesellschaft.

In der deutschen Zivilgesellschaft herrschen zu viele Tabus, und bei der Bevölkerung lässt sich kein Bewusstsein für die Gefährdungslage durch Aufklärung herstellen, weil diese durch die Medien verhindert wird. Generalbundesanwalt Kai Nehm hat dies mehrmals beklagt. Nicht nur der Staat und seine Justiz, sondern auch die Zivilgesellschaft trägt Mitschuld an diesem Missstand. Bereits im ersten, einführenden Teil dieser Untersuchung wurde argumentiert, dass die erste Grundlage für eine Strategie zum „Countering Terrorism" ein genaues Verständnis des Phänomens sein muss. Wenn jedoch die Freiheit, hierüber offen sprechen zu können, untersagt wird und eine rezeptive Umwelt für ein solches aufgeklärtes Unternehmen fehlt, sind die primären Voraussetzungen für „Countering Terrorism" nicht vorhanden. Beide Voraussetzungen fehlen in unterschiedlichem Maße. Es hat sich zwar nach dem Mord an Theo van Gogh vieles geändert. So veröffentlichte *Der Spiegel* beispielsweise eine Titelgeschichte über die Unterdrückung der Frau im Islam, und die *Frankfurter Allgemeine Zeitung* sprach offen von der „islamischen Herausforderung".[35] Dennoch gibt es viel Nachholbedarf, um dieses Projekt des „Countering Terrorism" einen Schritt weiter zu bringen.

4 Der Djihad-Terrorismus als eine Militarisierung der fundamentalistischen Herausforderung

Die Politisierung des Islam zu einem Islamismus bringt die Forderung nach einer Gottesherrschaft mit sich. Das ist die Herausforderung. Wird sie mit Djihad verbunden, dann haben wir es mit einer Militarisierung zu tun. Djihad im Islam ist zwar mit Gewalt verbunden, doch habe ich bereits gezeigt, dass der klassische Djihad deshalb kein Terrorismus ist, weil er an Regeln gebunden ist. Djihadismus erfolgt dagegen ohne Regeln, und er ist eine Begleiterscheinung der Politisierung des Islam. Der übergeordnete Rahmen ist die fundamentalistische Herausforderung (vgl. Anm. 5). Was ist der Hintergrund?

---

[35] Vgl. das Themenheft „Allahs rechtlose Töchter in Deutschland. Muslimische Frauen in Deutschland", *Der Spiegel* 47 vom 15. November 2004, und Nils Minkmar, „Die islamische Herausforderung", *Frankfurter Allgemeine Sonntagszeitung* vom 14. November 2004, S. 27.

In seinen Anfängen war der politische Islam mehr oder weniger Ausdruck einer defensiv-kulturellen Protestbewegung gegen die Hegemonie des Westens.[36] In der Verbindung mit dem Djihadismus hat sich der Charakter des politischen Islam von einer defensiven zu einer offensiven Bewegung verändert. Die Setzung eines „ismus" hinter den klassischen Begriff des *Djihad* (im Arabischen: Djihad bzw. *Djihadiyya*) zeigt zugleich eine zentrale Inhaltsveränderung an. Im Koran bedeutet *Djihad* Anstrengung, die durch *Qital* (Kampf) gewaltförmig werden darf. Wie bereits angegeben, ist dies jedoch stets an strenge Regeln gebunden. Im geschichtswissenschaftlichen Werk *Kreuzzug und Djihad* (1999) habe ich gezeigt, dass sich der *Djihad* im Verlauf der islamischen Geschichte seit dem 7. Jahrhundert zu einem konventionellen Welteroberungskrieg entwickelt hat und sich vom Neo-Djihad unterscheidet, weil die Neubestimmung des Djihadismus (*Djihadiyya*) kein regulärer Krieg, sondern ein „irregulärer Krieg" ist. Die Grundlagen hierfür bieten in den islamischen Realitäten viele islamistische Gruppen, die den Namen *Djihad* in ihrem Titel tragen. Als Beispiele hierfür möchte ich nur wenige anführen: *Djihad Islami* in Palästina, *Tauhid wa Djihad* im Irak, *Djihad Commando* in Kaschmir oder Laskar Djihad in Indonesien. Wir haben es mit einem globalen Djihad zu tun, der nicht mehr nur ein Aufruf ist – wie es bei Qutb noch der Fall war –, sondern eine politische Realität geworden ist, die zu „Countering Terrorism" herausfordert. Das ist auch ein Kriegszustand.

Die vielen Gruppen des Djihad sind gut informierten Experten schon länger bekannt. Zu Prominenz in der Weltöffentlichkeit gelangten diese jedoch erst nach den Anschlägen vom 11. September 2001.[37] Seitdem ist dieser djihadistische „irreguläre Krieg" Alltag in der Weltpolitik geworden. Im Jahre 2002 fanden die Terroranschläge auf Djerba (Tunesien), Bali (Indonesien) und in Moskau (die Geiselnahme des gesamten Theaterpublikums im Oktober 2002) statt. In den darauf folgenden Jahren wurden zahlreiche *Djihad*-Anschläge verübt, wenngleich nicht alle auf das Konto des globalen al-Qaida-Netzwerkes gehen. Was für die USA mit dem 11. September gilt, ist im Jahr 2004 vergleichbar der 11. März von Madrid für Europa.[38] Die Behauptung, Europa stehe außerhalb des Terrorkrieges, ist eine Legende. Die Sicherheitsexperten, die mit dem Phänomen vertraut sind, deuten dies als die militarisierte Form der fundamentalistischen Herausfor-

---

[36] Über diese Zusammenhänge Bassam Tibi, *Die Krise des modernen Islam*, München 1980, völlig neue und erweiterte Ausgabe Frankfurt am Main 1991.
[37] Vgl. Anm. 36.
[38] Stefan Aust, Cordt Schnittben, Hg., *Spiegel-Buch 11. September. Geschichte eines Terrorangriffs*, München und Stuttgart 2002; zum 11. März vgl. Bassam Tibi, „The Open Society and its Enemies Within", in: *Wall Street Journal Europe* vom 17. März 2004, S. A10.

derung; sie wird uns in den nächsten Jahrzehnten begleiten und ist somit keine tagespolitische Eintagsfliege. Man darf sie nicht schnell vergessen und zur Tagesordnung übergehen. Im Sinne der Political Correctness werden diese Anschläge, selbst die Lynchjustiz an Theo van Gogh, heruntergespielt; so wird statt vor dem Djihadismus vor einem „Feindbild Islam" gewarnt. In dieser Situation ist die Tatsache Besorgnis erregend, dass die Vertreter des organisierten Islam, sei es in der Welt des Islam, sei es in der Diaspora, – bis auf ein paar Ausnahmen – schweigen und einen Anschluss an einen Aufstand der Anständigen gegen den Terrorismus schuldig bleiben. Aus diesen Kreisen bekommt man nur zu hören, dass das alles nichts mit dem Islam zu tun habe. Es ist jedoch ein empirischer Fakt, dass der Djihadismus auf einer islamistischen Deutung basiert, eine entsprechende Legitimation bietet und großen Anreiz unter den Jugendlichen in der Welt des Islam hat.

Wenn die islamische Legitimation des Djihadismus als Terrorbedrohung problematisiert wird, ist nicht die Rede von der Religion des Islam, sondern von einer weltpolitischen Realität, die auch alle Muslime angeht. Denn der Terror wird im Namen ihrer Religion vollzogen, und somit ist eine glaubwürdige Distanzierung erforderlich. In diesem Zusammenhang wird von der europäischen Islam-Diaspora und von islamischen Ländern für eine erfolgreiche Strategie zum „Countering Terrorism" weit mehr als Zusicherungen und Lippenbekenntnisse benötigt; es bedarf einer tatkräftigen islamischen Beteiligung am „Countering Djihad-Terrorism", weil dieser allein mit Worten nicht bekämpft werden kann.[39]

Im Gegensatz zum zwischenstaatlichen Krieg hat der neue, irreguläre Krieg eine nicht festmachbare logistische Basis (vgl. *Financial Times Deutschland* vom 8./10. November 2002), die sich mitten im Feindesgebiet, also in Westeuropa, befindet und die Form eines in der Islam-Diaspora untergebrachten „supporting system" annimmt. Parallelgesellschaften dieser Islam-Diaspora existieren als „islamische Enklave in Europa, die aber nicht zum Westen gehört."[40] Im Rahmen einer Auseinandersetzung mit dem Islamismus als Ausdruck des politischen Islam ist es erforderlich, hierüber offen zu sprechen und Camouflage-Taktiken im

---

[39] In Jakarta habe ich beim westlich-islamischen Dialog in diese Richtung argumentiert und die These untermauert, dass auch ein „Security Dialogue" zu diesem Unternehmen gehört. Nachweise dazu oben in Anm. 21. Vgl. auch Bassam Tibi, „Between Islam and Islamism: A Dialogue with Islam and a Security Approach vis-à-vis Islamism", in: Tami A. Jacoby, Brent Sasley, Hg., *Redefining Security in the Middle East*, New York 2002, S. 62-82.

[40] John Kelsay, *Islam and War*, Louisville, Kentucky, 1993, spricht von islamischen Parallelgesellschaften als Enklaven (S. 118). Zum islamischen Anspruch auf eine islamisch geprägte Weltordnung vgl. S. 117.

geistigen Krieg zu entlarven, weil die Sicherheitspolitik sonst nicht erfolgreich betrieben werden kann. Es gibt Übereinstimmung unter Experten, dass während des Irak-Krieges 2003 die französische Außenpolitik eben von dieser Enklave bestimmt wurde; ein Autor spricht von „Algeria in France"[41]. Mit Toleranz und formaler Rechtsstaatlichkeit kann man den neuen Herausforderungen, die eine Gefahr für die Sicherheit Europas implizieren, nicht beikommen. Denn in den „Banlieus de l'Islam" gilt französisches Recht nicht, ebenso wenig wie deutsches Recht in bestimmten Teilen Berlins nicht befolgt wird.

Die symbolträchtige Hinrichtung Theo van Goghs als Ungläubiger illustriert die neue Gefahr, auch wenn diese weder mit dem 11. September noch mit al-Qaida direkt zu tun hat. Doch hat Craig Smith in der *New York Times* (25. November 2004) die islamistische, weit über die Niederlande bestehende Vernetzung des Mörders Mohammed Bouyeris nachgewiesen. Der Terrorismus ist jedoch weit mehr als solche Einzelmorde, weil er ein irregulärer Krieg mit Hunderten von Opfern ist, wie etwa der Anschlag von Bali zeigte. Noch einen Monat zuvor wollten indonesische Politiker am Jahrestag des 11. September 2002 bei einer Dialogveranstaltung als Initiative zur Friedenspolitik zwischen den Zivilisationen in der indonesischen Hauptstadt Jakarta nicht einsehen, dass der Dhijadimus auch mit Sicherheitsfragen und Terrorismus zu tun hat. Die politische Elite Indonesiens verurteilte zwar Bin Laden und sein Netz und bekundete ihr Mitgefühl mit den Opfern des Terrorismus, jedoch bestritten die Politiker noch 2002, dass ihr Land irgendetwas damit zu tun habe. Ebenso stellten sie damals wie heute in Frage, dass der al-Qaida-Terrorismus irgendetwas mit dem Islam zu tun habe. Ich habe eine entgegengesetzte Sicht in den indonesischen Medien verbreitet. Auf diese Einstellung stieß ich auch in der Türkei und mehrfach in anderen islamischen Ländern. Unbeirrt davon stelle ich auf dem Boden der Tatsachen fest: Der Djihadismus ist die neue Gewaltform innerhalb des Islamismus, und er repräsentiert heute eine zentrale Strömung der Revolte in der islamischen Zivilisation, die gleichermaßen Popularität genießt und eine islamische Legitimation auf der Basis einer neuen Deutung des Djihad hat. Die al-Qaida-Anschläge von Bali 2002 und Istanbul 2003, die von ihren Urhebern als Djihad definiert wurden, strafen jede Einstellung Lügen, dass dieser Terrorismus außerhalb des Islam steht. Er ist die Militarisierung des Islamismus.

In Indonesien wirken djihadistische Gruppen mit Verbindungen zu al-Qaida, zu denen vorrangig die *Laskar Jihad* (die Soldaten des Djihad) und noch mehr die *Jama'a Islamiyya* des Imams Abu-Bakr Bashir gehören. Es ist erwiesen, dass der

---

[41] Vgl. Paul A. Silverstein, *Algeria in France. Transpolitics, Race and Nation*, Bloomington, Indiana, 2004.

bewaffnete Arm der *Jama'a Islamiyya* hinter dem Terroranschlag von Bali stand, ebenso wie andere djihadistische Akte, z. B. in Istanbul, lediglich Glieder in einer Kette sind. Diese reicht von Djerba bis Moskau.

Den Geist der Djihadisten, der hinter diesen Handlungen der al-Qaida steht, kann man in einem Text der Gruppe, die kurz vor dem Bali-Anschlag im Sommer 2002 einen Angriff auf einen französischen Ölfrachter vor Jemen ausführte, vernehmen. Darin heißt es, dass jene al-Qaida-Zelle unter der falschen Annahme gehandelt habe, das Angriffsziel sei ein US-Schiff. Es wird jedoch hinzugefügt, dass trotz der Fehlinformation die Handlung als solche richtig gewesen sei. Die Begründung hierfür lautet, „Millet al-Kufr" (die Gemeinschaft der Ungläubigen) sei überall dieselbe und gegen sie gelte es, Djihad zu führen. Entsprechend mache es keinen Unterschied, ob die Ungläubigen bzw. Opfer US-Amerikaner, Franzosen, überwiegend Australier, z. B. wie auf Bali, oder wie zuvor auf Djerba Deutsche seien. Der Geist des Djihad-Terrorismus geht von einer Orientierung aus, die gegen den Westen als „Zivilisation des Unglaubens" gerichtet ist. Die Begründung ist islamistisch. Daher staune ich über einige Deutsche, die „den Krieg gegen den Terrorismus" als eine „amerikanische Angelegenheit" diffamieren. Selbst ein großer deutscher Philosoph, Jürgen Habermas, klagt die USA, nicht den Islamismus an, den er überhaupt nicht versteht.[42] Islamisten nutzen den hier verbreiteten Antiamerikanismus und setzen ihn erfolgreich in ihren Dienst.

Es gehört zur Täuschung, wenn der Außenminister der islamistischen AKP-Partei in der Türkei behauptet: „Wir sollen uns davor hüten, die Anschläge vom 11. September als religiöse Handlung zu deuten." (*Der Spiegel* vom 11. November 2002) Hiermit wird bestritten, dass al-Qaida eine Weltanschauung hat, die auf einer bestimmten Interpretation des Islam aufbaut. Ich wiederhole die sehr wichtige Erkenntnis: Die islamistische Deutung des Djihad zu einem Djihad-Islamismus durch al-Qaida hat also religiöse Grundlagen und steht nicht außerhalb des real bestehenden Islam. Der Islam ist nicht nur Text, auch ist er Realität, ein „fait social". Die Militarisierung des Islamismus durch den Djihad-Terrorismus ist ebenso ein „fait social".

Obwohl der „War on Terror" im Zentrum der US-Präsidentschaftswahl 2004 stand und Bush zum Sieg verholfen hat, kann den Strategien des US-Präsidenten nicht bescheinigt werden, das Konfliktpotenzial des Djihadismus zu verstehen. Wäre es anders, wäre unnötige Polarisierung – wie z. B. im Irak-Krieg – vermieden worden, weil dies nicht dem Westen, sondern eben den Djihad-Terroristen zugute kommt. Bei jeder Polarisierung mobilisieren Djihadisten weiteres Fußvolk,

---

[42] Bassam Tibi, „Habermas and the Return of the Sacred", in: *Religion-Staat-Gesellschaft*, Band 3 (2002), S. 264-296.

vor allem unter der frustrierten Jugend, wodurch ihre Anhängerschaft sich stets vergrößert. Das ist keine Aussage gegen Gewalt als Mittel gegen den Terrorismus. Anders als pazifistische und sich durch ihre Äußerungen als „Gutmenschen" qualifizierende deutsche Intellektuelle und Kulturprotestanten stimme ich der Deklaration der 60 führenden amerikanischen Denker – darunter u. a. Michael Walzer, Amitai Etzioni und Jean Elshtain – zu, die in der New York Times unter dem Titel „What are we fighting for?" veröffentlicht wurde (deutsche Übersetzung in der Neuen Zürcher Zeitung vom 23/24. Februar 2002), in der die militärische Gewalt gegen den Terrorismus im Afghanistan-Krieg als „just war" legitimiert wird. Aber ein solcher Krieg ist nicht immer als strategisches Instrument für „Countering Terrorism" geeignet. Dies zeigt der Irak-Krieg. Durch seine Folgen ist die militärische Form der fundamentalistischen Herausforderung gestärkt, nicht abgeschwächt worden. So war der Irak-Krieg ein totaler Fehlschlag im „War on Terror". Es war nach einer US-Formel ein „War of Unnecessity", ein unnötiger Krieg, der den Irak von einer Saddam-Despotie in eine Spielwiese des Terrors verwandelt hat. Er hat zudem eine Polarisierung herbeigeführt, die sich für „Countering Terrorism" als schädlich erwiesen hat. Dadurch wurde die ohnehin weit verbreitete islamische Wahrnehmung „War on Terrorism is War on Islam" und somit die kollektiv-zivilisatorische Haltung der Selbstviktimisierung bei den Muslimen verstärkt, die al-Qaida zugute kommt.

Diese Hinweise zeigen, dass „Countering Terrorism" im Djihad-Krieg oft ein Unternehmen nichtmilitärischer Natur ist. Die Moscheevereinskultur, die viele Europäer weder verstehen noch wahrhaben wollen, bietet sich im Zeitalter der Migration in Europa als Logistik für die Djihadisten. Die westeuropäische Islam-Diaspora ist das Gewässer, in dem Djihadisten der al-Qaida glauben, sicher wie die Fische zu schwimmen. Michael Radu hat unterstrichen, dass „al-Qaida ihre Kämpfer unter nicht assimilierten islamischen Migranten in Westeuropa rekrutiert, die Europa in den vergangenen zwei Dekaden hineingelassen hat."[43] Radu fügt hinzu, dass viele europäische „Menschenrechtsgruppen" sich in naivster Weise für die Handlungsfreiheit dieser Islamisten einsetzen. Damit hängt die von Generalbundesanwalt Nehm auf einem Symposium für Terrorismusexperten beklagte Tatsache zusammen, „dass in der Bundesrepublik nach wie vor ein Bewusstsein für die Gefahr, die von islamistischen Gruppen ausgeht, fehlt." (Die Welt vom 8. Juli 2002) Die Öffnung für andere Kulturen und die Gefährdung durch eingesickerte Djihadisten werden bei dem allgemeinen Gerede über Toleranz durcheinander gebracht, mit der Folge, dass – bis zur bestialischen Abschlachtung von van Gogh – den Gotteskriegern Toleranz entgegengebracht wurde.

---

[43] Michael Radu, „Terrorism After the Cold War. Trends and Challenges", in: Orbis 46/2 (2002), S. 275-287.

„Countering Terrorism" kann nicht erfolgreich mit der Bush-Doktrin verfolgt werden, die lautet: „Kampf gegen Terroristen und gegen die Länder, die sie beheimaten". Es gibt ca. 55 Länder, viele davon in Europa, in denen sich die Logistik der Islamisten befindet. Wie können islamistische Zellen, die Deutschland beherbergen, von US-Streitkräften bekämpft werden? Mit Flächenbombardierung und traditionell-militärischer Muskelschau kann der „War on Terror" nicht gewonnen werden. Dies gilt auch für die USA selbst. Daniel Pipes hat dies in seinem Buch *Militant Islam Reaches America* (2003) gezeigt. Im Buch von Stephen Schwarz über den Wahhabismus wird belegt, dass etwa 80% der US-Moscheen wahhabitisch unterwandert sind.[44] Mit diesen Hinweisen will ich das Argument untermauern, dass die für „Countering Terrorism" benötigte neue Sicherheitspolitik weit über das Militärische hinausgehen muss. Zudem ist es äußerst wichtig, mit der höchst sensiblen islamischen öffentlichen Meinung, die eher Bin Laden als den USA zuneigt, entsprechend behutsam umzugehen. Andernfalls schießt man ein Eigentor und trägt durch falsche Politik zu der ohnehin bestehenden großen Popularität des Bin Ladismus in der islamischen Welt bei. Anders formuliert: Beim Nachdenken über eine geeignete Reaktion auf die terroristische Bedrohung muss auch die islamische Wahrnehmung mit einkalkuliert werden. Diese sowie die antiamerikanische Einstellung in der islamischen Welt dürfen Europäer nicht dazu verleiten, im Islamismus einen gerechten Widerstand gegen die von den USA kontrollierte Globalisierung zu sehen. Gerade Europäer müssen wissen, dass der Djihadismus in antisemitischer Manier sich auch gegen eine unterstellte „jüdische Verschwörung" richtet, die ebenso in Europa verortet wird. Der „new Antisemitism"[45] kommt aus diesen Kreisen des politischen Islam.

Die Abwehr des Djihadismus als Militarisierung der fundamentalistischen Herausforderung ist keine zeitlich begrenzte Schlacht, die leicht zu gewinnen ist. Wir müssen uns die „limits" des „Countering Terrorism" bewusst machen. Das Ziel von US-Präsident Bush, „to eradicate terrorism", also die Bedrohung völlig auszurotten, ist schlicht nicht erreichbar; es hört sich wie eine Wahlkampfparole an. Nach realpolitischer Einschätzung kann irregulärer Krieg eingedämmt, nicht aber in einem Kriegsakt gewonnen werden. Es ist aber durchaus machbar, eine der wichtigsten Stützen des Terrorismus im Rahmen von „countering", nämlich dessen „supporting systems" (dazu gehört die nichtmilitärische Logistik der al-Qaida in Westeuropa), zu unterminieren. In dieser Frage vertrete ich eine Position, die in Westeuropa höchst unpopulär ist, zu der es jedoch keine

---

[44] Vgl. Daniel Pipes, *Militant Islam Reaches America*, New York 2003, sowie Stephen Schwarz, *The Two Faces of Islam*, New York 2003, der über den Wahhabismus schreibt.
[45] Vgl. Anm. 34 oben.

Alternative gibt. Zwar darf der Rechtsstaat auch im Kampf gegen den Terrorismus keinen Schaden nehmen, aber die Bewahrung rechtsstaatlicher Standards ist nicht mit Rechtsformalismus, so wie wir diesen in der Justiz Deutschlands kennen, gleichzusetzen. Ein rein rechtsformalistischer Umgang mit den al-Qaida-Zellen und ihren Kombattanten kommt nur den Djihadisten im Westen zugute: *In dubio pro Islamico*. Machen wir uns nichts vor: Die Islamisten sind weltanschaulich gegen den Rechtsstaat und gegen seine Demokratie, sie haben aber keine Hemmungen, dasselbe für sich zu ihrem Selbstschutz zu instrumentalisieren. In diesem Sinne habe ich einmal in einem Kommentar argumentiert: „Der Rechtsstaat schützt die Islamisten" (*Die Welt* vom 12. August 2002). Die Terrorismusbekämpfung zwingt die Demokratie zu Abstrichen, die hingenommen werden müssen, wenn der Terrorismus effektiv bekämpft werden soll. Der Rechtsstaat muss in der Auseinandersetzung mit der djihadistischen Form der fundamentalistischen Herausforderung die Zähne zeigen und nicht durch Rechtsformalismus und falsche Toleranz den Djihadisten zuschauen, während sie aus Europa eine Ruhezone machen. Craig Smith hat in seiner *New-York-Times*-Recherche über den van-Gogh-Mord gezeigt, dass die niederländischen Sicherheitsbehörden alles wussten, aber nicht handeln konnten, weil das Recht dies nicht erlaubt (25. November 2004). Eine Woche zuvor konnte ich mich mit dem niederländischen Justizminister in Washington in einem Dialog hierüber austauschen, der eben dieses Problem einräumte. Ein Bericht der *Frankfurter Allgemeinen Zeitung* aus Den Haag nach der Hinrichtung van Goghs trägt die Überschrift: „Niederländische Politiker sehnen sich einmütig nach dem zu bessernden Rechtsstaat" (*Frankfurter Allgemeine Zeitung* vom 15. November 2004, S. 3). Am 19. November konnte ich diese Einstellung beim niederländischen Justizminister zur Kenntnis nehmen.

5 Die offene Gesellschaft lässt sich nicht formaljuristisch gegen Djihad-Terror verteidigen

Es ist politisch inkorrekt, aber sicherheitspolitisch dringlich, den Zusammenhang zwischen Migration und Terrorismus und in diesem Kontext den Missbrauch der Demokratie und der Zivilrechte durch die Djihadisten der Islam-Diaspora in Europa[46] anzusprechen. Sie instrumentalisieren sie und fühlen sich in ihren Paral-

---

[46] François Revel, *Democracy Against Itself*, New York 1993, Kapitel „Fundamentalismus und Terrorismus", S. 199-224. In dem Buch von Michael Teitelbaum und Jay Winter, *A Question of Numbers. High Migration, Low Fertility and the Politics of National Identity*, New York 1998, S. 221-240, wird der Zusammenhang Migration/Fundamentalismus erläutert.

lelgesellschaften sicher. Dasselbe tun sie mit dem Rechtsstaat, der sie schützt. Nach dem Freispruch für die in Afghanistan ausgebildeten und deshalb des Djihad-Terrorismus verdächtigen M. al-Motassadeq und seinen Kompagnon Mzoudi in Hamburg habe ich als Euro-Muslim Grund, dem Formalismus des deutschen Rechtsstaates zu misstrauen. Das Berliner Landgericht hat im Fall des deutschen Komplizen des Terroristen Carlos, also Johannes Weinrich, den Angeklagten unter ausdrücklicher Berufung auf das Urteil des Bundesgerichtshofes bei der Aufhebung der Verurteilung Motassadeqs, trotz der Belastung mit 22 Mordversuchen und sechs Morden im Anklagesatz, freigesprochen. Ein solcher Staat kann auf diese Weise die offene Gesellschaft nicht schützen. Im Gegenteil: Er schützt ihre Feinde. Der ehemalige Richter des Bundesverfassungsgerichtes und heutige Rektor des Berliner Wissenschaftskollegs, Dieter Grimm, hat in einem *Welt*-Interview in diesem Geist argumentiert, dass der Rechtsstaat „auch Ablehnung von Demokratie und Rechtsstaat erlaubt. Das ist eine Stärke, keine Schwäche"[47]. Dies kann ich nicht nachvollziehen – und denke auch, Popper hätte es nicht gekonnt. Grimm räumt zwar ein, dass man sich wehren muss, wenn „einem ein Ordnungsmodell aufgezwungen wird [...], die Frage ist allein, welche Mittel" (ebd.). Bei dem Prozess gegen Weinrich in Berlin wurde aber vom Nebenkläger bemängelt, dass in Deutschland „nachrichtendienstliche Terrorismusbekämpfung nicht automatisch in rechtsstaatliche Standards gegossen werden kann." Dies zeigt, dass das Wissen des Staates über die Gefahren nicht zur Justiz gelangt, die dann keine Verfolgung der Djihad-Terroristen vornimmt, sie im Gegenteil sogar vor einer Verurteilung schützt; man lässt sie dann mangels Beweisen schlicht laufen. Die folgende Frage drängt sich auf: Kann man nach der öffentlichen Hinrichtung des Filmemachers van Gogh als Schari'a-Bestrafung in einem Djihad-Akt weiterhin so argumentieren, dass die offene Gesellschaft ihre Feinde, die Lynchjustiz befürworten, verkraften muss? Wie kann der Rechtsstaat die „offene Gesellschaft" gegen Djihad und Schari'a, die von ihren Feinden vertreten werden, schützen, wenn er sich selbst die Kraft hierzu versagt?

Wenn eine Ausbildung zum Djihad-Terrorismus in al-Qaida-Camps in Afghanistan vor deutschen Gerichten nicht als Beweis gilt, um Djihadisten, die für eine andere Ordnung als die der offenen Gesellschaft eintreten, zu verurteilen, dann frage ich mich, wie djihadistische Islamisten vom Rechtsstaat verfolgt werden können. Es ist ein Fakt, dass sich Parallelgesellschaften, in denen sich Islamisten verschanzen[48], dem Rechtsstaat entziehen. In der Moscheevereinskultur der islamischen Diaspora agieren die Islamisten und verfemen jeden Verdacht dagegen als Aus-

---

[47] Dieter Grimm im Interview mit Andrea Seibel, in *Die Welt* vom 14. August 2004, S. 2.
[48] Zur Problematik der Parallelgesellschaft Bassam Tibi, *Islamische Zuwanderung* (wie Anm. 33), Kapitel 3 und 4.

druck eines „Feindbildes Islam"[49]. Teile der deutschen Öffentlichkeit sowie der Medien machen bei diesem Spiel mit. Ich unterstelle, dass in der deutschen Justiz kaum Sachwissen über den Gegenstand besteht, man also dort auch nicht mit dem Unterschied zwischen Islam und Islamismus vertraut ist. Auf dieser Annahme basierend, will ich vor der Entfaltung meiner Argumente die Problematik an drei konkreten Beispielen veranschaulichen, wie bestehende Rechtsstrukturen im übergeordneten Zusammenhang des Bedarfs an „Countering Terrorism" aussehen. Diese Beispiele lassen sich jeweils durch ein Stichwort festhalten:

- *Schari'a für den Westen*: In der Islam-Diaspora fordert man ein eigenes Recht für die Migranten. In Toronto ist die Führung der Islamgemeinde ehrlicher als in Deutschland und stellt diese Forderung in aller Offenheit; sie wird von Erfolg gekrönt sein, weil sie sich der Unterstützung von Multikulturalisten sicher sein kann. Eine Rechtsprechung der Muslime nach der Schari'a gilt als Voraussetzung für die Durchsetzung des Minderheitenprivilegs. Wenn dies Schule macht und die Schari'a als Rechtsgrundlage für Muslime im Rahmen des Multikulturalismus eingeführt wird, so wie in Toronto, kann die Existenz einer Parallelgesellschaft als islamische Enklave auch im Rechtsbereich zementiert werden. Das ist das Ende des demokratischen Rechtsstaates. Die Ablehnung dieses Modells richtet sich nicht gegen den Islam, weil es viele Muslime gibt, die ein einheitliches Recht für alle fordern. Die Islamisten jedoch, die die Moscheevereinskultur kontrollieren, wollen die Schari'a; sie betreiben Djihad für die Durchsetzung dieses Ziels und instrumentalisieren hierfür den Multikulturalismus, der nicht zu den Verbündeten beim „Countering Terrorism" gehört.

- *Doppelstrategie*: Der Islamist Hani Ramadan (Bruder des berüchtigten Tareq Ramadan) fordert in der Schweiz die Anwendung der eindeutig menschenrechtswidrigen körperlichen Strafen der Schari'a (das *Hudud*-Recht). Er wird deshalb als Lehrer aus dem Schuldienst entlassen. Daraufhin greift er auf das bestehende Schweizer Recht zurück, das er weltanschaulich ablehnt, um seinen Einsatz für die Schari'a rechtsstaatlich zu schützen. Welch ein Widerspruch! Auch die Nazis nutzten die Demokratie, um sie abzuschaffen. In einem in Frankreich veröffentlichten Buch von Caroline Fourset, *Frère Tareq*, wird gezeigt, wie Nils Munkmar in der *Frankfurter Allgemeinen Sonntagszeitung* (14. November 2004, S. 27) zusammenfasst, welches Doppelspiel auch Tareq Ramadan betreibt: „[D]urch ein geschicktes double language"

---

[49] Dies tun auch J. Hippler und A. Lueg, Hg., *Feindbild Islam*, Neuausgabe Hamburg 2002.

verdeckt der als „Reformer des Islam" auftretende Tareq Ramadan, dass er „in Wahrheit ein missionarischer Fundamentalist ist". Mit diesem Doppelspiel verfahren die meisten Führer des in der europäischen Islam-Diaspora organisierten Islam, weshalb ich den von diesen geführten Dialog als solchen der Verlogenheit bezeichnet habe[50].

- *Duales Rechts- und Justizverständnis*: In Deutschland hielt Metin Kaplan noch vor seiner mühsam durchgesetzten Abschiebung einmal dem ihn anklagenden Gericht vor, er sei Muslim und für ihn gelte deshalb nur die Schari'a, weshalb er diesem das Recht absprach, über ihn zu urteilen. Zur selben Zeit hatte er jahrelang alle Rechtsmittel des Rechtsstaates, den er ablehnt, ausgeschöpft, um erfolgreich seine Ausweisung zu verhindern. Das Doppelspiel ging erst 2004 zu Ende. Zuvor hatte der „Sozialhilfeempfänger" Kaplan vom Sozialstaat umfangreiche Summen empfangen und ließ seine Rechtskosten von diesem übernehmen, bis die Polizei Bargeld in sechsstelliger Höhe in seiner Wohnung beschlagnahmte.

In allen drei Ländern und Fällen schützt der Rechtsstaat seine Feinde, er ist der Verlierer und trägt nicht zu „Countering Terrorism" bei. Gewinner dagegen sind die Djihad-Islamisten. Ein Islamist sagte zu mir einmal innerislamisch auf meine Verteidigung des europäischen Rechts hin: „Wir können das Recht dieser Ungläubigen für die *Da'wa* des Islam einsetzen; kannst du dir vorstellen, dass sie die Schari'a gegen uns einsetzen können". Er hat Recht.

Diese Denkweise der Islamisten (den Rechtsstaat verachten, aber ihn zum eigenen Schutz heranziehen) bleibt vielen Europäern verschlossen. Beim „Countering Terrorism" geht es nicht nur um die Abwehr von Gewalt, sondern vielmehr um Handlungsbedarf bei einer Erscheinung, der der Amerikaner Mark Juergensmeyer mit dem Titel seines Buches *The New Cold War* einen Namen gab. Dieser ist ein weltanschaulicher Krieg zwischen religiösen – hier islamischen – Schari'a- und Djihad-Ordnungsvorstellungen und säkularer Rechtsstaatlichkeit. Die zwei konkurrierenden Ordnungsmodelle Demokratie und Gottesherrschaft beruhen auf einander ausschließenden weltanschaulichen Einstellungen, die auch das Rechtsverhältnis einschließen. In dieser Situation wirkt die Forderung der weltanschaulichen Neutralität an den Rechtsstaat, der das Recht nur formaljuristisch – sozusagen als wertfreie Technik – anwenden darf, nicht nur naiv, sondern auch als eine Behinderung des „Countering Terrorism". Diese Einstellung ist für die Verteidigung der offenen Gesellschaft gegen ihre Feinde schädlich und ihr ab-

---

[50] Bassam Tibi, „Selig sind die Belogenen", *Die Zeit* vom 29. Mai 2002, S. 9, neu abgedruckt in: Ursula Spuler-Stegemann, Hg., *Feindbild Christentum im Islam*, Freiburg im Breisgau 2004, S. 54-61.

träglich. Wenn der Rechtsstaat sich nicht wehrt, geht er unter. Von Sir Karl Popper stammt die eine Handlungsanweisung enthaltende Weisheit, es gehöre zur Toleranz, keine Intoleranz im Namen der Toleranz zuzulassen. Analog zu Popper könnte man argumentieren, dass es zur Rechtsstaatlichkeit gehört, rechtsstaatsfeindliche Gesinnung (also nicht nur Taten, wie der ehemalige BVG-Richter Grimm argumentiert) im Vorfeld abzuwehren. Schließlich befinden wir uns mitten in einem „weltanschaulichen Krieg der Zivilisationen"[51], in dem die Gegenseite für eine andere Ordnung und für anderes Recht kämpft und für diesen Djihad den Rechtsstaat instrumentalisiert. Wer nicht begriffen hat, dass der Djihadismus nicht ein bloßer Terrorismus ist, sondern einen weltanschaulichen Krieg führt, der hat bereits im Konflikt verloren. Der Mord an Theo van Gogh in Form einer Hinrichtung war ein Anschlag auf alle Werte der freiheitlichen Zivilgesellschaft. Hier beginnt das Denken über „Countering Terrorism".

Europa steht vor einer massiven Herausforderung, die viele Europäer nicht verstehen oder nicht verstehen wollen. Jenseits des Atlantiks war es an der University of California, Berkeley, in einer multikulturell zusammengesetzten Gruppe unter der Leitung zweier Berkeley-Professoren, die zugleich Migranten sind – ein ägyptischer Muslim und ein christlicher Spanier –, möglich, das Projekt „Islam and the Changing Identity of Europe" durchzuführen. Die zunehmende islamische Migration verändert die demographische Zusammensetzung der Bevölkerung. Dadurch wandelt sich die Identität Europas, aber in welche Richtung? Das aus dem angeführten Projekt hervorgegangene, in New York und Berkeley erschienene Buch beantwortet diese Frage bereits im Titel: *Muslim Europe or Euro-Islam?*[52] Das heißt, entweder wird der Islam europäisiert oder Europa wird islamisiert. Ohne diese Forschung zu kennen, hat Bernard Lewis in einem *Welt*-Interview düster prophezeit: „Europa wird Ende des 21. Jahrhunderts islamisch sein"[53]. Er begründet diese Prognose mit Migration und Demographie (vgl. Anm. 46) und stellt fest, dass Europa eine mehrheitlich islamische Bevölkerung haben wird. Selbst einer dieser islamischen Migranten, argumentiere ich, dass das Problem nicht darin besteht, ob die Mehrheit der Europäer islamisch sein wird. Vielmehr geht es darum, welcher Islam, Schari'a-Islam oder Euro-Islam, in Europa dominieren wird. In diesen innerislamischen Konflikt, der auch die Europäer betrifft, ist der Djihad-Terrorismus eingebettet. Die von Lewis ausgelöste Debatte

---

[51] Bassam Tibi, *Krieg der Zivilisationen*, Hamburg 1995 (3., um ein Kapitel über Huntington erweiterte Taschenbuchausgabe München 2002).
[52] N. Al Sayyad, M. Castells, *Muslim Europe or Euro-Islam?*, Berkeley und New York 2002, darin das Euro-Islam-Kapitel von Bassam Tibi, S. 31-52.
[53] „Europa wird am Ende des Jahrhunderts islamisch sein", Interview mit Bernard Lewis, in *Die Welt* vom 28. Juli 2004, S. 6.

machte international Schlagzeilen[54]. Eine Strategie für „Countering Terrorism", die nicht nur auf die Eindämmung der Gewalt hinzielt, sondern auch gegen jene gerichtet ist, die für die Islamisierung Europas kämpfen, muss dies würdigen. Das betrifft die im Mittelpunkt dieses Abschnitts stehende Problematik: Welches Recht gilt in Europa, positives Recht oder die Schari'a?

Es muss in diesem Zusammenhang klargestellt werden: Nicht mit einem Generalverdacht gegen die zunehmende Zahl islamischer Migranten in Europa (1950 nur knapp eine Million, heute 17 Millionen, 2025 voraussichtlich ca. 40 Millionen), sondern mit einer Politik der Europäisierung des Islam kann man die Gefahr abwenden. Deswegen ist „Countering Terrorism" weit mehr als eine sicherheitspolitische Perspektive. Das Modell einer angemessenen Strategie in diese Richtung bietet das deutsche Verständnis vom Rechtsstaat nicht. Dieser schützt eher die Kombattanten der Schari'a-Islamisierung, denn die Richter entscheiden formaljuristisch in ihrer Rechtsprechung *in dubio pro islamico* und lassen Djihadisten laufen, die Demokratie und Rechtsstaat gefährden. Diese werden langfristig bei einem Highjacking der Islam-Diaspora den von Bernard Lewis vorausgesehenen Trend eines „islamischen Europa" kaum erleben. In der Welt des Islam nennt man den Geist, der durch die zitierte Passage des ehemaligen Verfassungsrichters Dieter Grimm zum Ausdruck kommt, „byzantinisch". Der historische Hintergrund hierfür ist folgender: Während byzantinische Rechtsgelehrte und Mönche mit dem Debattieren über Formeln beschäftigt waren, nahm Sultan Mehmet II. Konstantinopel ein und verwandelte es in Istanbul.[55] Daraufhin bekam er den Titel *Fatih*/Eroberer. Ist es ein Zufall, dass viele türkische Moscheen in Europa den Namen „Fatih" tragen? Zwei Großmoscheen in Deutschland – in Pforzheim und in Bremen – bekennen sich durch ihren Namen *Fatih*-Moschee zu dieser Tradition. Auch in den Niederlanden wird diese Tradition durch Moscheen vertreten, die ihrerseits *Fatih*/Eroberer heißen. Ohne zu wissen, was das bedeutet, hat die Evangelische Kirche die Beleuchtung für die Pforzheimer Moschee aus Toleranz gespendet. Eben vor dieser Toleranz hat Sir Karl Popper gewarnt, weil die offene Gesellschaft sich nicht von allein bewahrt; sie muss von Demokraten gegen ihre Feinde, die als *Fatih*/Eroberer auftreten, verteidigt werden. Islamisten scheuen es nicht, den formaljuristischen Rechtsstaat in ihren Dienst zu nehmen. Das muss im Dienste der Freiheit verhindert werden. „Countering Terrorism" erfordert Wis-

---

[54] So im *International Herald Tribune*-Leitartikel von John Vinocur, „Trying to Put Islam on Europe's Agenda", 21. September 2004, S. 2. Diese Diskussion ist auch eingegangen in den Artikel von Christopher Caldwell im *Standard Weekly* vom 4. Oktober 2004, S. 15-16, worin unter Bezug auf meinen Artikel in der *Welt am Sonntag* vom 5. September 2004 zur Thematik die Gegenposition zu Lewis zitiert wird.
[55] Sir Steven Runciman, *The Fall of Constantinople 1453*, Cambridge 1990.

sen über die Sache und worum es geht. Während die neuen Byzantiner Europas über „Islam-Unterricht" fürsorglich zum Schutze der Identität der islamischen Zuwanderer debattieren, betreiben die anderen tatkräftig ihre Islamisierung, auch die des Rechts. Die „Toleranz" dieses Musters wendet sich gegen die „offene Gesellschaft" selbst.

6 Al-Qaida und der Missbrauch der europäischen Islam-Diaspora

6.1 Die Logistik des Djihad in Westeuropa als Freizone

Aus der vorangegangenen Analyse geht hervor, dass der djihadistische Islamismus ein größeres und verästeltes Phänomen ist, aus dem der islamistische Terror hervorgeht. Er ist umfassender als al-Qaida[56] selbst, die nur ein Glied in einer übergeordneten Kette bildet. Beim „Countering Terrorism" muss man aber nicht nur den allgemeinen Rahmen analysieren, sondern auch konkret spezifische Gefahren ansprechen. Wenn wir bei al-Qaida bleiben, ist es schmerzlich, auf die Tatsache hinzuweisen, die man realisieren muss: Bis auf wenige Ausnahmen (z. B. Westiristan/Tribal Area Nordpakistan) befindet sich die Logistik der al-Qaida und des Djihadismus in Westeuropa, das sich als Ruhezone des Terrorismus anbietet (vgl. Anm. 5). Zwar werden die Terroranschläge, die in kurzen Zeitabständen weltweit zwischen New York, Djerba, Rabat, Palästina, Moskau, Indonesien, Madrid, Beslam und anderswo stattfinden, in Europa wahrgenommen, wenn die Presse hierüber tagespolitisch-sensationell berichtet, aber kurz darauf geht man jedes Mal schnell zur Tagesordnung mit der Geisteshaltung „business as usual" über. Wenn die „roots of terrorism" thematisiert werden, kommen die Altmarxisten mit ihrem Schnee von gestern und servieren den Kaffeesatz der Ungerechtigkeiten der kapitalistischen Globalisierung als Ursache der Djihad-Anschläge. Selbst die Kriegshandlung vom 11. März 2004 blieb, bis auf den Rückzug vom Krieg gegen den Terror und die Abwahl der spanischen Regierung, ohne große Folgen. Damit wurden die Bedingungen von al-Qaida erfüllt.

Bisher vertrauten Europäer darauf, dass al-Qaida und andere Djihad-Islamisten nicht in den Teller spucken werden, aus dem sie essen. Um es zu wiederholen: Jeder gut informierte Journalist weiß, dass die gesamte Logistik der Unterstützersysteme (supporting systems) des islamischen Djihadismus in den vergangenen Jahren dank der „falschen europäischen Toleranz gegenüber den Gotteskriegern" (vgl. Anm. 13) in Westeuropa aufgebaut worden ist. Mancher Experte ver-

---

[56] Zu al-Qaida vgl. Gunaratna (wie Anm. 32) sowie Schanzer (Anm. 4) und Peter Berger, *Heiliger Krieg*, Berlin 2002, sowie Jane Corbin, *al-Qaeda*, New York 2002.

mutete: Ein Terroranschlag in Europa könnte diese Freizone für die Djihadisten stören, ja gefährden, deswegen würden diese in Europa nichts unternehmen. Wenn dem so wäre, warum hat der 11. März stattgefunden? Die Antwort ist klar: Seit dem Afghanistan-Krieg gegen al-Qaida von Oktober 2001 hat diese djiadistische Internationale ihr Zentralkommando eingebüßt. Dadurch haben ihre global verstreuten Netze an Autonomie gewonnen. Dies gilt gleichermaßen für Europa und Nahost, wie der Anschlag vom 11. März in Madrid, die Anschläge in Djerba und Casablanca und die Aktivitäten der *Tauhid-wa-Djihad*-Bewegung von al-Zaraqawi im Irak veranschaulichen. In Bezug auf Europa muss gefragt werden, wie sich die europäische Zuwanderungspolitik nach dem djihadistischen Terroranschlag vom 11. März in Madrid und auch der Lynchjustiz eines Islamisten in Amsterdam ändern muss; ähnlich, wie sich zuvor in den USA nach dem 11. September die Migrationpolitik wandelte. Auch wenn manche unbelehrbaren Köpfe es bestreiten, der 11. März 2004 ist die europäische Spielart des amerikanischen 11. September; auch ist der Mord an van Gogh weder eine Einzeltat, noch betrifft er allein die Niederlande.[57] Weil Djihad-Terrorismus als ein Protest gegen die amerikanisch dominierte Globalisierung gedeutet wurde, argumentiert man bisher diesseits des Atlantiks, dass der 11. September eine US-Angelegenheit sei. Daraus wurde die Schlussfolgerung gezogen, Europa sei sicher und habe mit dieser Gefahr wenig zu tun. Zu Beginn der Anschlagserie des Weltdjihad 2001 rissen die von al-Qaida durchgeführten djihadistischen Terroranschläge vom 11. September auch die Europäer mit und riefen Empörung über den Djihadismus hervor. Diese hielt jedoch nicht lange an. Bereits ab 2002 begann die europäische Solidarität mit den USA, nicht nur wegen des zu Recht kritisierten US-Unilateralismus der Bush-Administration in der Irak-Politik, zu zerbröckeln. Der traditionelle Antiamerikanismus[58] bekam einen Auftrieb, Verschwörungsbestseller wucherten. *Der Spiegel* befasste sich in seinem Themenheft zum 11. September 2003 zwei Jahre nach dem Ereignis auf dem Cover mit der populären Wahrnehmung einer „Verschwörung 11. September" in Deutschland. Diese Wahrnehmung findet man in zahlreichen Bestsellern, die diese Sicht verbreiten. Der Untertitel des *Spiegels* lautete: „Wie Konspirations-Fanatiker die Wirklichkeit auf den Kopf stellen." Ich selbst habe am 11. September 2003 in der *Financial Times Deutschland* die Kolumne schreiben dürfen: „Verschwörungstheorien lenken ab". Richtig ist, dass sowohl der 11. September 2001 als auch der 11. März 2004 nur durch In-

---

[57] Der investigative US-Journalist Craig Smith hat in seiner in der *New York Times* vom 25. November 2004 veröffentlichten Recherche die islamistische Vernetzung des Mörders Mohammed Bouyeri nachgewiesen.
[58] Dan Diner, *Feindbild Amerika. Über die Bestätigung eines Ressentiments*, München 2002.

strumentalisierung der im Rahmen der islamischen Zuwanderung in den Westen entstandenen Parallelgesellschaften der Islam-Diaspora überhaupt durchführbar waren.[59] Beim „Countering Terrorism" muss man sich von Verschwörungstheoretikern abwenden und erforderliche Wachsamkeit an den Tag legen, begleitet von der Erkenntnis, dass al-Qaida nun eindeutig europäische Politik, sogar Wahlergebnisse (z. B. Spanien), mitdiktiert. Ohne den Anschlag vom 11. März wäre der Wahlsieg der Sozialisten, woraufhin der Abzug Spaniens aus dem Irak im Sinne von al-Qaida stattfand, wahrscheinlich nicht möglich gewesen. Auch kurzfristig hat sich der Djihadismus des 11. März ausgezahlt.

Unter Wiederholung der Warnung vor Generalverdacht sowie vor irgendwelchen Ausgrenzungen der europäischen Islam-Diaspora müssen die Europäer es wagen, die Führer der westeuropäischen Islamgemeinde zur eindeutigen Zusammenarbeit bei der Abwehr des Djihad-Terrorismus zu bewegen. Sie sind aufgefordert, sich mit den über die islamische Zuwanderung nach Europa gelangten al-Qaida-Zellen auseinander zu setzen, wenn sie nicht unter einen gefährlichen Generalverdacht geraten wollen. Auf Drohungen vom Abbruch des „Dialogs", wie dies von islamischer Seite in Deutschland als Reaktion auf solche Forderungen geschah, soll man gelassen reagieren und entschieden auftreten, statt sich einschüchtern zu lassen.

Jenseits der Multikulti-Seligkeit weiß man seit dem großen Werk des bedeutenden Migrationsforschers Myron Weiner, *The Global Migration Crisis*[60], in der Fachwelt, dass ein Zusammenhang zwischen Migration und Sicherheit besteht. Diese Erkenntnis schien noch Mitte 2004 nicht bis in die Chefetagen der Politik, z. B. in das deutsche Bundeskanzleramt, oder in einflussreiche Redaktionen gelangt zu sein. Denn auf die Forderung nach dem 11. März 2004, die Sicherheitsproblematik in das in der Bundesrepublik zur Debatte anstehende Einwanderungsgesetz hineinzuschreiben, reagierte Bundeskanzler Gerhard Schröder laut Presse mit der Aussage, er lehne „eine Vermischung des Terrors mit dem Zuwanderungsgesetz ab [...] man soll das eine nicht mit dem anderen vermengen." Diese Aussage belegt nicht nur das Fehlen von staatsmännischer Kompetenz, sondern eine schlechte Beratung. Dies geschah noch im Vorfeld der Verabschiedung des Zuwanderungsgesetzes. Darin sind sowohl durch den Einsatz von Otto Schily, der die Situation besser als Schröder und die Grünen kennt, als auch unter Druck der Opposition Sicherheitsklauseln enthalten. Diese reichen allerdings nicht aus. Man muss sich mit den durch Zuwanderung nach Europa gelangten Djihadisten auseinander setzen. Bei der Aufgabe, die Djihadisten abzuwenden,

---

[59] Dazu ausführlich Bassam Tibi, *Islamische Zuwanderung* (Anm. 33).
[60] Myron Weiner, *The Global Migration Crisis*, New York 1995.

müssen europäische Politiker Einwanderung und Sicherheit miteinander in einen Zusammenhang bringen. Darüber nachzudenken ist weder eine Vermengung von Themen, die nicht zueinander gehören, noch ein Beitrag zu einem „Feindbild Islam", wie propagandistisch behauptet wird. Nach der Hinrichtung von Theo van Gogh muss man den Islamisten deutlich sagen: „Das Spiel ist aus!" In der *Frankfurter Allgemeinen Zeitung* erschien in dieser Richtung der Artikel „Die multikulturelle Gesellschaft zerbröckelt".

Zu der Einstellung „Das Spiel ist aus!" muss man mit dem Märchen Schluss machen, dass Djihad im Islam nur „Anstrengung" heiße und nichts mit dem Terror zu tun habe. Hier ist die Berücksichtigung der schon erläuterten Entwicklung des Djihad zum Djihadismus im Rahmen der Erscheinung des politischen Islam von zentraler Bedeutung. Weder die Islamkunde noch ihre Philologie der islamischen Quellen können das Phänomen erklären. In der arabischen Presse wird der Begriff „*Djihadi*/Djihadist" synonym mit „*Mutatarif*/Extremist" bzw. „*Irhabi*/Terrorist" verwendet. Die Erkenntnisse der Europäer diesbezüglich sind so gering, dass bewusste Täuschung der Islamisten bei argloser Blauäugigkeit des Gutmenschentums gelingt, den Djihad des politischen Islam mit dem einseitigen Hinweis auf die koranische Bedeutung als „Anstrengung" herunterzuspielen. Manch deutscher Islamkundler – wie die „verspätete Nation" – hat die Entwicklung nicht mitbekommen. Jene, die als Motiv für ihre Haltung „Offenheit" angeben, wollen Vorurteile bekämpfen, ohne dabei zu merken, dass hierdurch über die aus dem Djihadismus hervorgehende Gefahr des Terrorismus hinweggetäuscht wird. Die Absicht ist gut, die Wirkung dagegen fatal. Wer nicht mitmacht, wird mit der Keule des „Feindbildes Islam" erschlagen und mundtot gemacht. Selbst Muslime – wie der Verfasser – werden dieser Verfemung ausgesetzt.[61]

Experten vermuten, dass al-Qaida in 55 bis 60 Ländern dieser Welt Basen bzw. Zellen hat, auf denen ihr islamistisches globales Netzwerk fußt. Seit dem Afghanistan-Krieg 2001 ist sie ohne Kopf, d. h., sie ist weitgehend durch die Zerstörung ihrer afghanischen Zentrale dezentralisiert. Bin Laden, der vermutlich in Nordpakistan (in dem Stammesgebiet/„tribal area von Wesiristan") versteckt lebt, hat nicht mehr die Bedeutung, die ihm die USA zuschreiben. Wenn seine Verhaftung gelingt, wird der Djihad-Terror – ähnlich wie bei der Verhaftung von Saddam – nicht zum Ende kommen. Die allgemeine Strömung des Djihadismus sowie al-Qaida entwickeln sich in Richtung einer dezentralen Bewegung, die nach einem möglichen Verschwinden ihrer symbolischen Figuren aktiv bleiben kann. Außer dem Saddam-Beispiel kann man ein weiteres anbringen: Nach dem Mord an Scheich Yassin in Gaza wurde die Hamas-Bewegung in ihrem Djihad nicht im

---

[61] Zum Feindbild Islam vgl. Anm. 49 oben.

Geringsten geschwächt, vielmehr ist sie dezentraler und weitaus gefährlicher geworden.

Wie bereits mehrfach erläutert, geht der Djihadismus aus dem Islamismus als Weltanschauung einer Revolte gegen den Westen hervor, wenngleich er mit diesem nicht identisch ist. So ist beispielsweise die türkische AKP islamistisch, wohl aber nicht djihadistisch. Ich erinnere nochmals daran, dass der Djihad in der islamischen Geschichte zwar kriegerisch, aber eindeutig kein Terrorismus im Sinne des heutigen post-Clausewitzschen irregulären Krieges war. Die djihadistischen Islamisten betreiben eine Gewaltform des Djihadismus, die eine zeitgeschichtliche Erscheinung ist. Zwar ist der djihadistische Islamismus aus einer liberal-islamischen Perspektive eine Fehlinterpretation des Islam. Er ist jedoch – ebenso wie der liberale Islam selbst – eine aus einer Interpretation hervorgetretene Position. Beide nehmen den Islam als Grundlage für sich in Anspruch. Wenn man diese Vielfalt verleugnet oder herunterspielt, dass Djihadisten sich auf den Islam berufen, verschließt man sich dem Verständnis des Phänomens. Anders formuliert: Sowohl liberale Muslime als auch islamistische Djihadisten berufen sich auf den Islam. Was tun? Zum „Countering Terrorism" sollte man den Djihad-Islamismus mit den Argumenten eines liberalen Islam bekämpfen, nicht nur um islamische Verbündete zu gewinnen, sondern auch, um der propagandistischen „Kampf-der-Kulturen-Polarisierung" die Spitze zu nehmen und die islamistische Behauptung zu widerlegen, der „War on Terror" sei ein „war on Islam".

Die Erkenntnis für die europäische Politik nach dem „11. März" und nach dem van-Gogh-Mord muss darin bestehen, dass Einwanderung und Sicherheitspolitik miteinander verquickt sind. Ein kleiner Schritt in diese Richtung ist in Deutschland mit dem neuen Zuwanderungsgesetz getan worden. Die Verbindung von Islamismus und Sicherheitspolitik ist also zwingend und muss zu den zentralen Themen einer neuen europäischen Innenpolitik gehören. Einzelne europäische Staaten können mit einer nationalen Politik kein „Countering Terrorism" erfolgreich betreiben. Europäer müssen unter der neuen sicherheitspolitischen Herausforderung erkennen, dass der Rechtsstaat die offene Gesellschaft gegen die Islamisten, die vorwiegend aus dem Untergrund agieren, verteidigen muss, statt ihnen wie bisher rechtsformalistisch Schutz vor Verfolgung zu bieten.

Darüber hinaus ist der irreguläre Krieg des Djihadismus auf der Ebene der internationalen Politik eine neue Erscheinung nichtstaatlicher Akteure, die im 21. Jahrhundert zunehmend an Signifikanz gewinnt. Staaten haben jeweils ihre kalkulierbaren Nationalinteressen, weil sie an international gültigen Regeln gemessen werden. Daher zeichnen sich ihre außenpolitischen Handlungen durch ein Mindestmaß an Berechenbarkeit aus, weil das Abweichen von den Regeln Sanktionen nach sich ziehen kann. Nichtstaatliche Akteure, wie etwa ethnisch-nationalistische oder religiös-fundamentalistische Djihad-Bewegungen des irregulären Krieges, sind dagegen unberechenbar. Gegen Staaten, die sich nicht an internationale Regeln halten, etwa Schurkenstaaten, kann man Sanktionen verhängen, ja sogar – wie etwa im Irak-Konflikt und zuvor in Afghanistan – Kriege führen, die in einen – wie auch immer gearteten – Regimewechsel münden können. Gegenüber global vernetzten djihadistischen Bewegungen des politischen Islam wie al-Qaida ist eine solche Strategie schlicht und einfach nicht praktizierbar. Man ist ihnen gegenüber machtlos. „Countering Terrorism" ist daher eine äußerst komplexe und schwierige Aufgabe. Die Entwicklung der al-Qaida zu einer dezentralisierten Bewegung erschwert die Situation zunehmend und stellt neue Herausforderungen an die Sicherheitspolitik.

In der Dreiecksbeziehung zwischen Europa, der Welt des Islam sowie ihrer Diaspora tritt eine veränderte weltpolitische Lage ein, mit der europäische Politiker konfrontiert werden. Dazu gehört der nach Europa über die islamische Zuwanderung gelangte Djihadismus. Die Gefahr geht nicht nur aus Djihad-Gewalt hervor, sondern auch aus der Bedrohung der Freiheit der offenen Gesellschaft. Die Integration der islamischen Zuwanderer als europäische Bürger könnte einen entscheidenden Beitrag für die Sicherheit leisten. Das ist der Grund dafür, warum die Islamisten diese behindern. Das „Countering" des djhadistischen Islamismus ist somit über das militärische Sicherheitsverständnis hinaus auch für den Schutz der Demokratie sowie für den inneren Frieden europäischer Gesellschaften von Relevanz. Deswegen spreche ich in diesem Zusammenhang von der djihadistischen Bedrohung als neuem Totalitarismus, der auch politisch für die offene Gesellschaft die größte weltpolitische Herausforderung des 21. Jahrhunderts darstellt (vgl. Anm. 1). Der von den Islamisten angestrebte Gottesstaat als Grundlage für eine neue Weltordnung ist eine Gefahr für den Weltfrieden. Es muss in Europa möglich sein, offen ansprechen zu dürfen, dass Islamisten das Ziel verfolgen, Europa zu islamisieren. Es ist ihre Vision, dass die Mehrheitsbevölkerung Europas durch die Migration islamisch sein wird. So besteht die Alternative für die Zukunft Europas darin: Entweder europäisieren die Europäer den Islam (ein Euro-Islam ohne Djihad und Schari'a), oder die Islamisten islamisieren Europa (vgl. Anm. 52).

Die angeführte Problematik – Europäisierung versus Islamisierung – ist auf eine langfristige Perspektive zugeschnitten und wird seit dem *Welt*-Interview mit Bernard Lewis international kontrovers diskutiert. Konkret besteht kurzfristig der Bedarf an „Countering Terrorism" als sicherheitspolitische Abwehr des Islamismus, auch zum Schutz der offenen Gesellschaft als westliche Lebensart.

7 Der Islamismus als weltpolitische Bedrohung der offenen Gesellschaft

Angesichts der bestehenden Behinderungen kann man nicht oft genug wiederholen, dass eine Strategie für „Countering Terrorism" nur ohne Selbstzensur entfaltet werden kann. Das freie Denken über den Gegenstand beginnt damit, darüber zu sprechen, dass die Islamisten Deutschland als Ruhezone benutzen. Sie berufen sich dabei stets auf Rechtsstaat und Religionsfreiheit und kommen damit gut an. Beide gehören aber nicht zu ihrer Weltanschauung. Was ist nun unter Religionsfreiheit zu verstehen? Gilt sie auch, wenn sie für politische, gegen die Demokratie gerichtete Weltanschauungen in religiösem Gewand instrumentalisiert wird? Der Islamismus, ich wiederhole es aus gegebenem Anlass, ist wohl nicht der Islam als Religion – es ist eine religiös legitimierte Weltanschauung, die als neuer Totalitarismus eingestuft werden kann.

Als ein Beispiel für die Bedrohung der offenen Gesellschaft kann die Bewegung für einen Kalifatstaat des inzwischen nach langem Spiel mit der Justiz in die Türkei abgeschobenen Islamisten Metin Kaplan angeführt werden. Dieser hat sich einst mit Bin Laden in Afghanistan getroffen und vertritt offen eine totalitäre Weltanschauung. Das Bundesverfassungsgericht war sehr mutig, als es die Verfassungsbeschwerde des Islamisten Kaplan abwies und entschied, das Grundrecht auf Religionsfreiheit stehe dem Verbot dieser Bewegung nicht entgegen (Az: 1BvR 536/03). Weiter heißt es in der Urteilsbegründung: Wenn eine Gruppe in kämpferisch-aggressiver Weise gegen die Demokratie, den Rechtsstaat und die Menschenwürde agiere, sei ein Verbot gerechtfertigt. Das, was das BVG hier beanstandet, findet sich im Geist des Islamismus wieder. Es verwirrt jedoch, dass nicht alle Islamisten ihren totalitären Geist so offen zur Schau tragen, wie Kaplan es getan hat. Andere, auch sunnitische Islamisten, haben von den Schiiten die Praxis der *Taqiyya* (Täuschung durch Verstellung) gelernt und präsentieren sich als brave Demokraten, die Dialog und Toleranz predigen und vom Djihad als friedlicher Anstrengung sprechen. Nun ist der Weg vom Djihad zum Djihadismus als totalitärer Ideologie heute sehr kurz. Er ist seit al-Qaida eine Weltrealität, nicht nur eine Geisteshaltung. Im Rahmen von „*Ilham*/Täuschung" der Ungläubigen wird die sunnitische Spielart der schiitischen *Taqiyya* sehr erfolgreich geübt.

Gegen die falsche multikulturelle Toleranz, die nichts anderes als Wertebeliebigkeit und Indifferenz ist, muss man im Sinne der Freiheit demokratisch für einen „zivilen Islam" eintreten. Sonst geschieht genau das Gegenteil. In ihren Kreisen deuten Islamisten den Islam totalitär als Gottesherrschaft (die Lehre von der *Hakimiyyat Allah*), ohne dass Europäer der Multikulti-Front dies verstehen. Den früheren Einsatz für Freiheit gegen zwei Totalitarismen – Kommunismus und Faschismus – haben viele vergessen. Heute ist der politische Islam mit seiner Ordnungsvorstellung des Gottesstaates sowie seinen Kampfmethoden des Djihadismus die neueste Spielart des Totalitarismus. Er gefährdet die europäische Sicherheit, was eine neue Countering-Strategie erfordert.

Der Islamismus benutzt die wertebeliebig gewordene postmoderne Demokratie (der Franzose Jean-Francois Revel nannte sie „Demokratie gegen sich selbst"), um sich formaljuristisch durchzusetzen. Nicht immer verhält sich die deutsche Justiz wie das Bundesverfassungsgericht beim Kaplan-Kalifatstaat-Verbot. Zuvor hatte dieses Gericht in zwei Urteilen (zum Schächten und Kopftuch-Urteil) die Schari'a durch die Hintertür der Religionsfreiheit in Deutschland zugelassen. Damit konnte der Islamismus mit Hilfe des Rechtsstaates mehrmals Oberhand gewinnen. Journalisten, die aufdecken, werden verklagt und verurteilt, nicht aber Islamisten, die auf Kosten der Steuerzahler mit Armenrecht ihre Kritiker verklagen (vgl. Anm. 12). Worin besteht also nun das Problem?

Faktisch hat der Wettbewerb zwischen konkurrierenden Ordnungen für unsere Welt auch die Islam-Disapora erreicht. Meinen Studenten an der islamischen Hidayatollah State University Jakarta im größten islamischen Land der Erde, Indonesien, erklärte ich kürzlich als ihr Gastprofessor: Die Welt im 21. Jahrhundert steht vor drei alternativen Modellen: erstens einer amerikanisch dominierten Weltordnung (Pax Americana), zweitens, als Gegenmodell, einer Erweiterung von *Dar al-Islam* (Haus des Islam) auf die gesamte Erde als so genanntes islamisches Friedensmodell (*Pax Islamica*) oder drittens einem pluralistischen Frieden zwischen den Demokratien, also dem Kantschen Modell des demokratischen Friedens. Ich fragte, was sie bevorzugen würden. Die Antwort meiner aufgeklärten muslimischen Studenten war eindeutig für den demokratischen Frieden. In Indonesien herrscht ein „civil Islam"[62]. Auch dort gibt es Djihad-Terrorismus, jedoch schützt der Zivil-Islam Indonesien vor der weltanschaulichen Infiltration der al-Qaida. (Eine persönliche Anmerkung: Dies würde ich etwas vorsichtiger ausdrücken)

Eine andere Antwort geben die Islamisten, die, anders als die indonesischen Verfechter eines liberalen „civil Islam", leider international das Gesicht des Islam prägen. Wie mehrfach angemerkt, ist dies kein offener Islam, sondern ein neuer Totalitarismus. Es ist bedauerlich, wie Islamisten naive Europäer missbrauchen, um ihr demokratiefeindliches Anliegen im falschen Rahmen der Religionsfreiheit voranzutreiben. Sie stoßen dabei auf Gleichgültigkeit, die ihnen als Toleranz entgegengebracht wird. Ungewollt entsteht ein unheiliges Bündnis zwischen sala-

---
[62] Robert Hefner, *Civil Islam*, Princeton, New Jersey, 2000.

fistisch-orthodoxen Wahhabiten, halbmodernen Islamisten und Multikulti-Werterelativisten sowie Antiglobalisten im Namen falsch verstandener Religionsfreiheit und Gerechtigkeit. So werden in der saudischen Fahd-Akademie in Bonn – laut *Spiegel* – islamische Kinder im Geiste des Djihadismus erzogen, ohne dass der Rechtsstaat etwas dagegen tut. Die „Akademie" existiert fort, den Rechtsstaat verspottend. „Countering Terrorism" hat unter diesen Bedingungen kaum eine Chance. Deshalb ist die offene Gesellschaft nicht nur durch die Islamisten in Gefahr, sondern auch durch wertebeliebige Europäer selbst.

Wann wachen die Europäer auf, sehen die neue Gefahr und erkennen den Bedarf an einer Countering-Strategie? Wann hören sie auf, das Vorurteil Feindbild mit Aufklärung über Gefährdung gleichzusetzen? Wer die Aufklärung über den neuen Totalitarismus der Islamisten als Gefahr für die offene Gesellschaft und Verbreitung eines „Feindbildes Islam" verfemt, der unterminiert jede Countering-Strategie und spielt der Islamisierung Europas in die Hände. Dagegen hat die Verteidigung von Freiheit und Demokratie gegen die totalitären Vorstellungen des politischen Islamismus gar nichts mit „Feindbild Islam" zu tun. Man sollte darauf achten, nicht in die Propagandafalle der Islamisten zu geraten. Vor der Djihad-Gefahr für die Freiheit zu warnen heißt in der Tradition von Popper, Arendt und Horkheimer, als demokratischer Aufklärer zu stehen. „Countering Terrorism" ist daher weit mehr als eine Sicherheitspolitik.

7.1 Schlussfolgerungen: Die bisherigen Lehren aus dem „Countering Terrorism"

Nach der bisherigen Analyse des Djihad-Terrorismus sowie seiner politischen Deutung als neuer Totalitarismus mit der Feststellung, dass ein Bedarf an einer Countering-Strategie besteht, fasse ich die Ergebnisse zusammen. Ich habe den djhadistischen Islamismus als eine Herausforderung an die westliche Demokratie und ihre offene Gesellschaft, die auch mittels der Gewalt des Djihad-Terrorismus als irregulärer Krieg geführt wird, dargestellt. Im Sinne von neuer Sicherheitspolitik, die ihren Blick nicht auf das Militärische beschränkt, wird der Djihadismus in einen großen Rahmen eingeordnet, nämlich den Wettbewerb zwischen den Ordnungsmodellen der totalitären Gottesherrschaft und der pluralistischen Demokratie. In diesem Licht ist die Abwehr der neuen Gefahr im Rahmen von „Countering Terrorism" in einem Krieg der Weltanschauungen eingebettet. Ich vertrete die Auffassung, dass dieser weltpolitische Konflikt weitgehend den Verlauf des 21. Jahrhunderts bestimmen wird. Dieser Prozess hat längst begonnen.

Nach diesen Ausführungen möchte ich zu einem Rückblick auf den 11. September (USA) und 11. März (Europa) übergehen, die den Übergang vom 20. zum 21.

Jahrhundert begleitet haben. Ich beginne mit der Forderung, das Spiel zu beenden, dass die Bedrohung der westlichen Zivilisation durch den Djihadismus nicht existiere und dass es sich bei der Debatte hierüber nur um die Konstruktion eines „Feindbildes Islam" handele, das die Medien im Geiste des Orientalismus pflegen. Auch muss man die deutsche, in vielen Bestsellern verbreitete Version von einer „Verschwörung 9/11" aufgeben. Der Djihad-Terrorismus ist im Zeitalter des „irregulären Krieges" weder eine Erfindung noch eine tagespolitische Sensation. Im Gegensatz zu den Autoren der Bestseller über Verschwörungstheorien spricht sogar der deutsche Bundesaußenminister Fischer von der djihadistischen Bedrohung im Rahmen eines strukturellen Konfliktes. Er vertritt also eine Idee, die ich in mehreren Veröffentlichungen erläutert habe; auch hat er in seiner Princeton-Vorlesung meinen Begriff vom „neuen Totalitarismus" übernommen. Am Ende des Jahres 2004, mehr als drei Jahre nach jener djihadistischen Kriegserklärung an die westliche Zivilisation vom 11. September, die im Jahr 2004 am 11. März in Madrid erneuert wurde, lassen sich drei weltpolitisch für die Zukunft relevante Lehren in Bezug auf „Countering Terrorism" ziehen.

Die erste Lehre basiert auf der Tatsache, dass al-Qaida nicht nur weiterhin am Leben ist, sondern heute ihre durch den Afghanistan-Krieg vom November 2001 geschädigte, aber nicht in vollem Umfang zerschlagene Schlagkraft wiederhergestellt hat. Die im Computer des im August 2004 in Pakistan verhafteten al-Qaida-Funktionärs Mohammed N. Khan vorgefundenen Dokumente belegen diese Vermutung. Sicherheitsdienste wissen heute, dass die durch Verhaftung und Tötung ausgefallenen Führungskräfte der al-Qaida bereits voll ersetzt worden sind. Zudem haben sich die Kader verjüngt, womit der Verlust ausgeglichen worden ist. Einige Monate vor der Verhaftung Khans veröffentlichte das Londoner Institute for Strategic Studies einen, durch die Presse bekannt gewordenen Bericht, in dem die Deutung enthalten ist, dass al-Qaida sich nun in vollem Umfang wieder von den Afghanistan-Rückschlägen erholt hat. Wir lernen daraus, dass al-Qaida nicht die Person Bin Laden, sondern eine global vernetzte Bewegung ist, die auch nach der Verhaftung oder Tötung ihres Gründers mit Sicherheit fortbestehen wird. Es sei an die Ausführungen aus der Geschichte des politischen Islam erinnert, die zeigen, dass die Ermordung des Begründers des Djihadismus, Hasan al-Banna (Großvater von Tariq Ramadan), im Jahre 1949 der 1928 gegründeten Muslimbruderschaft keinen Schaden zufügte. Der Mord an al-Banna hatte damals kaum etwas angerichtet, denn die Muslimbruderschaft (z. B. in Deutschland vertreten durch die Islamische Gemeinschaft Deutschland) existiert weiter und ist heute stärker denn je. Dieselbe Beobachtung lässt sich auf al-Qaida, die für den djihadistischen, d. h. terroristischen Islamismus steht, übertragen. Daraus folgt, dass der irreguläre Krieg der al-Qaida uns in den folgenden

Jahrzehnte weiterhin begleiten wird. Der Westen muss sich darauf einstellen und eine neue Sicherheitspolitik entwickeln. „Countering Terrorism" ist für Europa eine Aufgabe des Überlebens im Weltkonflikt.

Die zweite Lehre betrifft die Propagandakomponente im terroristischen Djihad-Krieg. Der Westen steht vor der Aufgabe, die „hearts and minds" der Muslime, besonders in der westlichen Diaspora, sowie diese selbst als Verbündete zu gewinnen. Die Verhaftung von Khan in Pakistan hat zu Enthüllungen verholfen, die zu Verhaftungen in Großbritannien, darunter der eines großen al-Qaida-Fisches namens Abu Musa al-Hindi, führten. Dazu gehört auch die Schließung einer Moschee und Arrestierung ihres Imams in Albany, New York. Kaum waren diese Maßnahmen als „Countering Terrorism" ergriffen, wurde eine PR-Kampagne von gewissen Institutionen der europäischen Islam-Diaspora gestartet, die die massive Anschuldigung enthält, hinter diesen Verhaftungen stünden – wie gewohnt – die Vorwürfe „Feindbild Islam"; auch wurde eine „kollektive Diskriminierung von Muslimen" unterstellt. Diese Propaganda liest man u. a. in den Londoner *The Muslim News*. In Großbritannien haben Islamisten Rückenwind von „Human Rights Groups" bekommen. Diese Fakten zeigen, wie prekär die Lage des Westens und wie moralisch machtlos dieser im Krieg gegen den Djihad-Terrorismus ist. Einerseits muss sich Europa verteidigen und nicht nach der christlichen Devise handeln, dass man nach dem ersten Schlag die zweite Wange bietet (so denken viele Muslime über Christen); andererseits muss Europa den Propagandakrieg der Islamisten sehr ernst nehmen und darf seine Wirkung nicht unterschätzen. Bis auf wenige mittelständische Strukturen der europäischen Islam-Diaspora – vor allem Frankreich und Großbritannien – gehören die meisten in Europa lebenden Muslime zu den sozial marginalisierten Schichten der Bevölkerung. Diese reagieren hierauf mit Selbstethnisierung, wodurch ethnisch organisierte Parallelgesellschaften entstehen. Erst nach der Hinrichtung van Goghs durch einen Islamisten hat man in den Niederlanden und Europa diese Problematik der Parallelgesellschaften als islamische Enklaven[63] und der in ihnen lebenden ethnisch-religiösen Randgruppen erkannt. Der Wahhabismus[64] dringt in die Moscheevereinskultur dieser Parallelgesellschaften und stärkt sie mit saudischer Unterstützung.

Die Integration der Muslime steht nicht im Interesse der al-Qaida, weil integrierte Muslime für sie nicht rekrutierbar sind. Aber der Propagandakrieg stößt in den Parallelgesellschaften, in denen ihre Djihadisten wie die Fische im Wasser

---

[63] Zu den Parallelgesellschaften vgl. Kap. 3 und 4 in meinem in Anm. 33 nachgewiesenen Buch.
[64] Zum Wahhabismus vgl. Stephen Schwarz (wie Anm. 44).

schwimmen können, auf fruchtbaren Boden; er hat großen Anreiz. Die muslimischen Jugendlichen – ein Großteil von ihnen sind Schulabbrecher, die Arbeitslosenquote liegt zwischen 40 und 60% Prozent und ein Abdriften in die Kriminalität ist nahe liegend – lassen sich für den Djihad mobilisieren, denn sie haben als Marginalisierte das Bedürfnis, sich an Europa zu rächen. Der Westen muss im „Krieg der Weltanschauungen" jeden Eindruck entkräften, dass der Krieg gegen den Terrorismus indirekt ein Krieg gegen den Islam ist. Nur durch eine erfolgreiche Politik der Integration kann sich dieser Verdacht verflüchtigen. Die Aufgabe ist immens schwer. Die Schuldzuweisungen der Islamisten an Europa gehen einher mit Selbstbezichtigungen mancher Europäer, die sich in diesem Krieg auf die Seite der Islamisten schlagen. Diese Form des verlogenen Dialogs muss zugunsten anderer Formen des Dialogs als Konfliktlösung aufgegeben werden.

Die dritte Lehre hängt mit dem Charakter des neuen Krieges, für den ich den Begriff „irregular war" geprägt habe, zusammen. In Deutschland gibt es andere Autoren, die diese Begriffe in unterschiedlichen Varianten beschlagnahmt haben und in den Feuilletonseiten Zustimmung fanden, obwohl sie die internationale Diskussion umgehen, aus der diese Ideen entnommen sind. Im irregulären Krieg ist der Feind nicht sichtbar, es gibt keine klaren Fronten und man weiß nicht, wie und wann die Djihadisten zuschlagen werden. Sicher ist nur, dass der Feind angreifen wird. Die dritte Lehre zwingt dazu, das bisherige Muster des zwischenstaatlichen Krieges und die mit ihm verbundene Sicherheitspolitik zu überdenken. Der ehemalige britische General Sir Michael Rose hat auf der Basis seiner bosnischen Erfahrung, auch angesichts der US-Lehre vom „Regime Change" als Grundlage des Irak-Krieges, die Formel geprägt: „Change attitudes not regimes" (IHT vom 4. August 2004) beim „War on Terror". Trotz aller anders lautenden Zusicherungen von George W. Bush hat die Beseitigung des Regimes des Despoten Saddam Hussein die Welt nicht sicherer gemacht, sondern genau das Gegenteil ist der Fall. Der im Afghanistan-Krieg geschwächte Djihadismus nutzte den Irak-Krieg, um noch kräftiger zu werden; seine Propaganda kommt heute besser an. Die Lehre für Politiker und Strategen heißt daher: Beim „Countering Terrorism" ist ein Wechsel in der Sicherheitspolitik, nicht notwendigerweise der Regime, vonnöten. Hierfür muss man den Charakter des „irregulären Krieges" des Djihadismus verstehen. Drei Experten, der Israeli Martin Creveld, der Kanadier Kalvi Holsti und ich, haben in ihren englischsprachigen Arbeiten diesen neuen Krieg lange vor dem 11. September 2001 beschrieben und über ihn aufgeklärt. Das Gerede von der Verteilung der Macht und den asymmetrischen Kriegen in bestimmten deutschen Büchern lenkt nur von dieser Substanz ab. Der Krieg gegen den Djihad-Terrorismus in einem postbipolaren und post-Clausewitzschen Zeitalter kann ohne neue Lernprozesse nicht gewonnen werden. Die angeführten drei

Lehren drei Jahre nach „September 11" sind zentral für die benötigte Strategie des Westens für „Countering Terrorism".

Bei einer abschließenden Schlussfolgerung, die mit Zukunftsperspektiven verbunden ist, lässt sich festhalten, dass die zentrale Idee des vorliegenden Beitrags darin besteht, dass der Djihadismus, der aus dem Islamismus (wohl nicht dem Islam) hervorgetreten ist, die Weltpolitik des 21. Jahrhunderts verändert hat und die nächsten Jahrzehnte weiterhin bestimmen wird. Der Djihad-Islamismus wird als ein Terrorismus des irregulären Krieges gedeutet, dem mit einer passenden Countering-Strategie begegnet werden muss. Hierbei geht es nicht alleine um sicherheitspolitisch-militärische Belange, sondern auch um einen Krieg der Weltanschauungen in einem Zivilisationskonflikt. Von höchster Wichtigkeit ist es, dass man nicht in die Hände der Terroristen arbeitet und Bruchlinien zwischen den Zivilisationen meidet. Die Linie soll nicht zwischen dem Islam und dem Westen, sondern zwischen den Anhängern und den Feinden der offenen Gesellschaft gezogen werden. Kurz: „Countering Terrorism" erfordert „a new security" und eine offensive Werteorientierung der offenen Gesellschaft im Krieg der Weltanschauungen, die von der bisherigen Wertebeliebigkeit als kulturelle Schwäche Europas Abschied nimmt.

Im Zentrum der vorliegenden Abhandlung stand der Versuch, die weltanschauliche Dimension des islamistischen Djihad-Terrorismus zu beleuchten und sie in einen weltpolitischen Kontext einzuordnen. Es wurde deutlich gemacht, dass der Neo-Djihad kein klassischer islamischer Djihad mehr ist, auch weil er auf einer „Erfindung von Tradition" (vgl. Anm. 18) basiert. Nicht behandelt wurde die Problematik der Verbindung der untersuchten Erscheinung zur modernen Wissenschaft und Technologie.[65] Die Djihadisten vom 11. September waren technisch versiert. Als die Nachricht von den Terroranschlägen Kairo erreichte, kommentierte der Scheich der al-Azhar, Sayyid al-Tantawi, er schließe aus, dass Muslime hinter der Tat stünden, weil die Anschläge auf einem hohen, technisch perfekten Niveau durchgeführt worden seien; dies könnten keine Muslime gewesen sein. Ein Harvard-Professor, den ich mit diesem Kommentar konfrontierte, erwiderte, dass dies „ein Ausdruck des Orientalismus" sei. Dass die zitierte Aussage aber nicht von einem westlichen Orientalisten, sondern von einer hohen islamischen Autorität stammt, interessierte ihn nicht. Jenseits des Orientalismus und seiner Umkehrung steht fest, dass die Djihadisten ihren Neo-Djihad auf einem hohen Niveau der Technologiebeherrschung austragen. Zwar lehnen sie westliche Werte und somit die kulturelle Weltsicht der Moderne ab, adoptieren sie jedoch vollen

---

[65] Bassam Tibi, *Islamischer Fundamentalismus, moderne Wissenschaft und Technologie*, Frankfurt 1992 (neu gedruckt 2001).

Herzens als techno-wissenschaftliche Instrumente. „Den Feind mit den eigenen Waffen bekämpfen", lautet ihre Devise. Der Neo-Djihad ist ein Techno-Djihad[66], der sich auch der modernen Kommunikationstechnologie, vor allem des Internets, in voller Perfektion bedient.

---

[66] Zum Interneteinsatz der Djihadisten vgl. Gary R. Bunt, *Islam in the Digital Age, E-Jihad, Online Fetwas and Cyber Islamic Environments*, London 2003, besonders das Kapitel „The Digital Sword? E-Jihad", S. 25ff.

Transition from "International Cooperation" to a "Joint Counterterrorism Campaign"

Boaz Ganor, PhD

Executive Director, The International Policy Institute for Counterterrorism
Deputy Dean, Lauder School of Government,
The Interdisciplinary Center, Herzliya, Israel

1 Introduction

On September 11, 2001, the face of international terrorism changed. From that point on the world faced a new kind of threat, of a scope and severity that was heretofore unknown.

The problem of international radical Islamic terrorism is not the problem of one individual – Osama Bin Laden – or of a single organization – al-Qaida, but rather a matter of a vast international terrorist network with global reach. This network encompasses activists from many different backgrounds, who live and work in Arab and Muslim nations, as well as Western states and Third World countries.

The international radical Islamic terrorist base poses an unprecedented threat to the enlightened world, if for no other reason than the dangerous combination of characteristics that are unique to this group.

One such characteristic is the fundamentalist belief in the divine command, which calls on the network's members to disseminate their radical Islamic world view across the globe, through the use of extreme violence and terrorism. The belief in *jihad* (holy war) makes these activists particularly dangerous because if this is the will of God, then neither argument nor compromise is acceptable. What is needed is all-out war.

In addition, this network's global reach is based on many Islamic fundamentalist terrorist organizations, as well as dormant cells in various countries – Arab states, Islamic states and Western states.

The members of the radical Islamic networks are not novices. Rather, in many cases, they are battle-seasoned warriors who gained their combat experience during the Afghan campaign.

Nor do members of this network hesitate to use suicide terrorism, the modern terrorist method that has been proven more effective than any other. As a result of their extreme religious beliefs, they are even happy to undertake this type of attack, out of their conviction that with such action they will not die at all, and they are certainly not committing suicide (which is forbidden by Islamic religious law), rather, they are carrying out a sacrifice for the sake of martyrdom (*ishtishad*), guaranteeing them eternal life in Paradise.

Statements made by leaders of the international radical Islamic terrorist network indicate that these terrorists have no qualms about using non-conventional means if necessary – chemical, biological or even nuclear weapons – in order to achieve their goals. A number of foiled attack attempts by others belonging to this system tend to support this.

The combination of all these characteristics creates an unparalleled level of postmodern threat and danger to the entire enlightened world. So great a threat requires the international community to unite its efforts, combine forces and formulate a new international strategy to fight terrorism.

This international campaign must be carried out simultaneously and on a global level against all those who belong to, or support, the radical Islamic terrorist network, because the scope of the threat necessitates an urgent and significant reduction of their operational capability. An essential and fundamental condition for the campaign's success is honest and close cooperation between the greatest possible number of Western and Third World nations. This cooperation should include the following steps:

1. The creation of a shared normative-legal platform for the international struggle against terrorism;
2. Bilateral and multilateral cooperation in transmitting intelligence information and cumulative offensive and defensive experience;
3. Establishment of joint international frameworks for fighting terrorism.
4. The creation of a joint, legal-normative platform to combat terrorism

2 The international legal platform

As stated, the first step in formulating a joint international counterterrorism policy is to create a normative common denominator in the form of an accepted definition for the term "terrorism." This definition must be as narrow and limiting as possible so that it represents the broadest possible basis for shared agreement, and makes a distinction between the goals of terrorists and their modes of operation, that is *deliberate injury to civilians*. Such a definition will enable the formulation of international charters for combating terrorism.

These international charters must include:

- Provisions requiring nations to act against infrastructures of foreign terrorist organizations located on their territory, and against communities that aid terrorist organizations operating on their soil;
- Charters that obligate nations to fight terrorist financing – raising funds aimed at terrorist activity, money-laundering and camouflaging funds under the guise of philanthropic social welfare activities;
- Charters that compel banks to divulge information to security forces regarding terrorist organizations or those suspected of involvement in terrorist activity;
- Treaties for extraditing terrorists and their associates;
- Treaties that prohibit membership in terrorist organizations and perpetrating various types of terrorist acts – suicide bombings, extortion attacks, killing and sabotage;
- Treaties that establish a nation's right to carry out counter-terrorist activity against terrorist organizations on the territory of another nation under certain circumstances.

3 Bilateral and multilateral cooperation in transmitting information and cumulative experience in combating terrorism

The experience garnered by various nations in fighting terrorism could be used to help other nations that lack the relevant experience in this sphere, making their struggle more effective. Information about these issues can be transmitted via joint training activities: shared counterterrorism courses, exchange programs for officers and operatives, tactical drills, strategic education, etc.

Another form of cooperation has to do with sharing technological knowledge. There should be a united effort to develop a variety of technological means: methods of identifying and neutralizing terrorists from a distance; intelligence equipment for wiretapping, surveillance, command and control; means for locating and neutralizing explosives, as well as chemical and biological agents; methods for supervising crowds and restoring order. A joint international technological effort in all of these areas can help improve the final outcome, reduce development costs, and shorten time frames. Joint technological teams can more easily overcome typical technical problems and obstacles on the road to product development, while basing their efforts on technological experience gained in various countries.

4 Establishing joint international counterterrorism frameworks

It has already been mentioned that the scope and nature of terrorism at the dawn of the third millennium constitutes a tangible threat to the peace of modern Western civilization, and poses a serious challenge to the enlightened world. As such, there is a primary need for a new level of international cooperation in the effort to confront radical Islamic terrorism. It is no longer enough to improve and enhance international cooperation on the basis of familiar formulae; rather, we must develop a joint international counterterrorism campaign. *The transition from international cooperation to a joint counterterrorism campaign* is not merely a semantic change, but rather, it entails a new understanding of the essence of the struggle and the means needed for coping on an international scale. Naturally, the transition to a joint international campaign does not preclude the need to enhance cooperation as described above. At the same time, it demands that we establish joint frameworks of action for a more effective international effort, which relate to almost all spheres and elements of counterterrorism:

Intelligence – An international intelligence body should be established, to which real-time warning data can be channeled, as well as information concerning the movements, intentions, capabilities and characteristics of terrorist operations. This information will be made available to the coalition of nations committed to the uncompromising struggle against international terrorism, and which will use it to foil potential attacks. This international entity is also likely to employ its own independent intelligence sources against terrorist agents throughout the world.

In the offensive domain – A joint intervention unit should be established, as well as international counterterrorism units, which will be available at short notice to nations under attack to carry out anti-terrorist missions – to capture terrorists, rescue hostages, etc. Concomitantly, there should be an international unit to handle negotiations with terrorists in cases of extortion. The unit members must be well acquainted with all aspects of radical Islamic terrorism, including the culture, language, religious, decision-making processes, and intellectual characteristics of its adherents.

In the defensive domain – International security units should be introduced to help nations contending with an ongoing terrorism threat, and to demonstrate international determination and solidarity in the war on terrorism. The units will be equipped with the most advanced technological means and will be deployed *ad hoc* in sensitive areas within any nation requesting such assistance. They will also help train a security and preventive network in these nations, so that after a certain time local units will be able to replace the international ones.

Legislative and judicial action – An international court for terrorist crimes should be established. The idea is to fill the lacuna that presently exists since the establishment of the International Court of Justice in the Hague, regarding which it had already been stipulated that the court would be authorized to try any person – leader and common citizen alike – but only for criminal acts or war crimes, without any mention of terrorist activity. Instead, an international court for terrorism would focus on trials for terrorists, and would be based on an accepted definition of terrorism and international charters ratified accordingly. This court could also recommend that international institutions develop new international charters, if necessary.

Civilian activity – Terrorism is an interdisciplinary issue more than any other phenomenon. Almost every academic discipline is relevant to one aspect of terrorism or other – political science, international relations, Middle Eastern studies, sociology, psychology, economics, computer science, law, biology, chemistry, physics, and many more. For this reason, coping with terrorism demands the broadest possible perspective and the greatest analytical ability. The academic system must be prepared by making available all relevant knowledge and information. As part of this effort, an international academic research network should be set up with the finest academic minds, directing them towards research questions that are particularly relevant for prevention agencies, providing them with the necessary financial resources, forging links between different researchers from around the world and conducting working meetings, and helping to build joint academic databases. Such a network has recently been established by this author – ICTAC, the International Academic Community – and it includes about a dozen academic research institutes and professionals from various countries.

Educational and informational activity – To enlist international public opinion in the vital struggle, informational and educational activities must be dovetailed in nations coping with terrorism, and other nations as well. An international framework of experts should be established to formulate joint public relations and educational policies, and to work with education systems in the different nations. It is especially important that this framework offer assistance to education and information systems in Muslim countries as part of the effort to counter radical Islamic indoctrination. International teams will provide Muslim nations with all the help they need to develop curricula and to hold educational activities promoting tolerance, pragmatism, and humanism.

Establishing a "League of Nations Fighting Terrorism" – To promote effective action against terrorist organizations and the states that support them, a permanent, international anti-terrorism institution must be given the authority to identify nations and organizations considered to be involved in terrorism, and determine sanctions and actions to be taken against them. This institution would operate on the basis of a clear and approved mandate. It would include experts from different countries who would study global terrorism and on the basis of their findings, would publish an annual list of nations supporting terrorism. International sanctions could then be adopted against countries included on that list, in accordance with the scope of their support, so as to force them to stop or limit their involvement.

This is an especially challenging task and, as mentioned, would require a broad international consensus regarding the definition of terrorism, and a classification of the different levels of involvement. Most likely any international effort in this direction would be doomed to fail, although perhaps some of the goals can be achieved through the establishment of a "League of Nations Fighting Terrorism" by a few countries, with others joining later on.

Ideally, the United Nations should fulfill this role, but past experience has shown that it cannot be expected to lead an effective campaign against international terrorism, and certainly not against specific sponsors of terrorism.

5 Conclusion

It seems that so long as the world does not change its balance of interests with regard to terrorism, it will not be possible to mount an effective joint international campaign against it. Only when the nations of the free world understand that their interest in fighting international terrorism is more important than any other interest, will it be possible to begin coordinated and effective steps to force nations such as Iran, Syria and Lebanon to limit their involvement in terrorism and stop sponsoring such organizations. This step could change the cost-benefit equation for terrorist organizations, and allow the world to fight global terrorism more effectively. However, the nations' balance of interests will change only when terrorism crosses a certain level of damage and the threat increases significantly. In other words, it may be that only if "things get worse" will the nations of the world take the initiative. Perhaps the September 11 attacks in the United States served as the watershed in international terrorism. But as of this writing it would appear that, except for the American leadership, and perhaps the British as well, the world has yet to awaken from its complacency.

It appears that only when waves of multi-victim terrorist attacks wash over the nations currently choosing to ignore the severity of the problem, or when there are sufficient signs that the level of global terrorism has increased (with the use of non-conventional weapons), will the risk to world peace becomes more tangible. Only then can we expect the nations of the free world to unite together in a genuine and uncompromising struggle against international terrorism.

How to Counter the Global Jihadists

Peter S. Probst

Vice President
Institute for the Study of Terrorism and Political Violence
Washington, DC, USA

1 Introduction

The full scope and threat represented by Global Jihad has yet to be fully recognized by the western democracies. We are currently engaged in a protracted conflict which is much different and in many ways more challenging than conventional war. This asymmetric form of conflict and the accompanying terrorism is much more than the bomb, the gun and the carnage. It is what the British used to call 'Political Warfare,' and it extends across the spectrum of conflict.

2 The Nature and Scope of the Challenge

Global Jihad has emerged as a strategic threat, with conflicts being fought on multiple geographic fronts. Confrontations are not only military in nature, but, also and more significantly, involve sustained campaigns that are political, economic and psychosocial – the conventional use of military power playing a relatively subordinate role and its employment, too often, proving counterproductive. Global Jihad has largely been personified by Osama Bin Laden and al Qaeda, but they represent only a part of the story, and an increasingly marginal one.

A vulnerability shared to varying degrees by the democracies is that we have adopted the lexicon and mindset of political correctness, a development that undermines our ability to successfully meet the Jihadist challenge. We are living in an age of political correctness run amok wherein it is considered bad form to pay undue attention to young Arab males of Saudi extraction, the suggestion being that to do so would be to practice religious and ethnic bigotry despite the fact that 15 of the 19 hijackers on 9/11 were Saudi nationals. No one would suggest that if the police were hunting down a rapist they should focus on 70-year-old nuns rather than young adult males, but in this age of political correctness a focus on young adult males of Middle East extraction ends up in media castigation and law suits charging discrimination.

Our failure to correctly identify the adversary and the nature of the threat has caused confusion not only within my country, but among Europeans as well. We characterize the current conflict as a War on Terrorism, which is a terrible misnomer. Terrorism is a tactic and one does not declare war against a tactic. To talk in terms of a War on Terrorism makes as much sense as a "War on Frontal Assaults" or a "War on Ambushes."

The protracted conflict in which we are engaged is primarily one of ideas and ideology. During the 1930s and 1940s, the ideology that confronted the democracies was fascism, which stoked a rampant and racist imperialism. The ideological challenge of the Cold War was international communism, which drove a rampant and malignant imperialism that sought to pit class against class and race against race. The current ideological threat that stokes a particularly vicious form of religious crusade is militant Wahhabism, a form of political Islam that harbors dreams of world conquest and a determination to destroy all who fail to embrace its particularly poisonous tenets. Fascism was the ideological engine of Nazi Germany. Communism was the ideological glue of the Soviet Union. And today, militant Wahhabism is the latest in a long line of tyrannical, anti-democratic, ideological exports, and Saudi Arabia is its principal advocate and promoter.

3 Scrambled Syntax

I also have a particular problem when people refer to this Protracted Conflict as a "war." The term "war" creates false expectations and causes us to adopt premises and make assumptions many of which are irrelevant or, even worse, counter-productive.

I think of wars as normally having a defined beginning and end, but this current conflict could well last for generations. Wars take place between formal, organized armies with an established chain of command. In this conflict, the Jihadists are increasingly decentralized, with the threat moving beyond systems of networks or even definition as a movement. Increasingly, Global Jihad has become a "state of mind," with its practitioners moving towards a concept known as "leaderless resistance."

In conventional warfare, soldiers wear uniforms or, at least, some sought of identifying insignia. Terrorists, in contrast, seek to blend with the civilian population and, unlike armies in conventional warfare, purposely target non-combatants with deliberate brutality. In conventional war, the adversaries are subject to the laws of war, and usually seek to abide by them. Terrorists, in contrast, purposely and systematically violate conventional norms, attacking not only military targets but innocent civilians with ferocious brutality, their aim being to terrorize all who would oppose them. In terrorism – and particularly the Jihadi terrorism we face today – there are neither front lines nor a relatively safe rear area. All are vulnerable and all are targets – men, women and children. The enemy is within the gates and walks among us.

4 Know Thy Enemy

If we are to prevail in this protracted conflict, it is absolutely essential that we understand the enemy so we may more efficiently destroy him while, at the same time, avoiding counter-productive tactics and strategies that would only serve to strengthen his hand and broaden his appeal.

In this form of conflict, the terrorists' conventional military capabilities are important but pale in comparison to their ability to psychologically intimidate. Their aim, despite being militarily inferior, is to break the will of the targeted groups. Their most effective weapons are neither the RPG nor an improvised explosive device. Their most effective weapon systems are the camcorder, the fax machine, the Internet and the media, which serve as force multipliers and imbue their operations with disproportionate impact. Terrorism is psychological warfare writ large.

To successfully counter Jihadist terror, we need to view it in the broader contexts of communications, perception, group dynamics and mindset. To be successful, we need to understand the ideas and forces that motivate radical Islamists; how best these may be countered, and their legitimacy and drawing power undermined and discredited. In other words: the true adversary is not the Jihadists but, rather, the ideology that motivates them. Discredit the ideology and morale flags. And once morale falters and the theocratic justifications for violence no longer hold water, the steam goes out of the movement and the threat will dissipate.

To do this effectively, we must understand what makes the Jihadist tick, and how best we can leverage that knowledge to our advantage. We need to better understand what our adversary values, what he fears, how he sees himself – his strengths, his weaknesses and his vulnerabilities. We need to better identify his operational predilections and the rational and irrational factors that motivate him and drive his operational and decision-making calculus.

Of equal importance we need to understand how he sees us. In other words: we need to see ourselves through the eyes of our terrorist adversary so we may better and more rationally allocate our limited resources. We need to determine what he sees as our strengths, weaknesses and our preferred responses to his tactics. His assessment may differ markedly from our own self-assessment and surprise us.

It really does not much matter whether the terrorist's perceptions are right or wrong. In the world in which we operate perception is reality; and it is this subjective 'reality' on which the terrorist will base his strategies, tactics and operations. It is therefore in our interest to shape or bend his reality to our advantage so that the terrorists ultimately play to our strengths rather than focusing on our weaknesses. It is a contest in which deception and dissimulation play a critical role.

Reality is in the eye of the beholder, and we must learn to see the world through lenses of the terrorist – lenses that have been framed by the terrorist's culture, his history and his personal experiences. Once we understand the reality on which the terrorist bases his actions, we can better anticipate his choice of tactics, targets and strategies and more effectively deploy our assets to counter and, then, destroy him.

5 Know Thyself

But to be effective, there is one other critical factor. We must subject ourselves and our decision-making processes to similarly rigorous analysis. This last task is perhaps the most daunting, as it calls for the intellectual honesty, rigor and courage to separate objective fact from wishful thinking and jingoistic rhetoric. It demands our seeing the world as it really is, not as we would wish it to be. It calls for a willingness to explore new approaches and technologies, and re-examine the lessons of past conflicts such as the Vietnam War and the Soviets' Afghan debacle to glean what lessons may be learned, tailored and have relevance to the current challenge.

Students of the Algerian War for Independence and the Vietnam conflict have commented that the French lost the War for Algeria in the streets of Paris, and the Americans lost the Vietnam War in the streets of Washington. Undermining the adversary's morale is a prime goal of the terrorist and the insurgent, and it must be ours as well.

Their goal is to break our will to resist. Maintenance of home-front morale is absolutely crucial, as the Algerian and Vietnam conflicts so cruelly demonstrated. Victory or defeat hangs in the balance. It hangs on how well we and friendly governments inoculate our populace against the scourges of panic, paranoia, despair and defeatism – particularly in the face of a second 9/11 attack, which most believe is inevitable.

6 The Changing Threat

The nature of the terrorist threat has changed markedly since 9/11, and we have failed to keep pace. What we are facing is much more than al Qaeda. It is what I call Global Jihad, of which al Qaeda has been its most visible manifestation.

Since 9/11, al Qaeda essentially has morphed from a highly organized, centralized, hierarchical organization to primarily a skein of networks and, more recently, into a movement or even something more amorphous and internalized – what I would characterize as a state of mind.

It is important to recognize that al Qaeda is only one of several Jihadist groups and is not in a position to dictate to compatriot organizations. I think in terms of the old confederation of major mafia families, with Al Qaeda being the first among equals. These groups may cooperate. They may engage in mutually supportive or even joint operations; but they also maintain their own independence and pursue their own individual agendas. This is the model that I think most accurately approximates the current reality.

Al Qaeda and organizations of like-minded Jihadists have proven much more adaptable and aggressive than we ever imagined. The threat has metastasized, and we are engaged in a series of conflicts on multiple fronts that take multiple forms.

Increasingly ubiquitous, the Jihadists operate not only in the Gulf, Middle East and North Africa, but in locations as far-flung as Indonesia, the Philippines, Southern Thailand, Chechnya, Uzbekistan, China, Turkey, the triborder area of Latin America, Canada and, of course, here in Europe and in the United States.

Mosques and madrasses built with Saudi money and staffed by Wahhabi-trained Imams serve as ideological incubators for the movement, providing haven, ideological direction, facile explanations and financial and other resources. They serve as magnets for the alienated, the disaffected, the fanatic and, on occasion, the deranged.

7 Countering the Threat

A first step in countering the Jihadist threat is to close down radical mosques and madrasses or, at the very least, ensure a wholesale removal of radical staff and texts to be replaced by those Imams and texts that reflect a more mainstream form of Islam, and then aggressively monitor the results to ensure against backsliding. The aim is to deprive the Jihadists of the two prime mechanisms they use for indoctrination, recruitment and training. It is true that radical religious services and education would then likely migrate to private homes, but this is better than the current situation and, I believe, advantageous to the security services, as they would likely face fewer constraints.

Germany faces a dilemma that is shared by most of the Western democracies. The 7 December edition of the *Wall Street Journal* recounts the role of the King Fahd Academy in Bonn, which is described as a center for Jihadist training. Opened some nine years ago and funded by a 15 million Euro donation by King Fahd, the academy was reportedly described by a senior German police official as a "training ground for religious war." A German television news program secretly taped a teacher telling the children that they must learn "to throw a spear, swim and ride, to be strong and brave" so they will be willing to join the Jihad. And according to a study, two thirds of the texts being used at the academy teach the students to hate non-Muslims; one in five praises martyrdom, urges violence against non-Muslims or threatens hell for minor infractions against Muslim ritual. Some parents and school staff reportedly are under investigation for involvement in terrorist activities including contacts with the 9/11 hijackers and those involved in the synagogue bombings in Tunis. Both the Saudi government and the school have made promises that radical indoctrination would cease and then have systematically violated their pledges.

This has been part of an established pattern, which has been repeated time and again not only here in Europe, but in the United States as well. The Saudis have become very aggressive against Jihadist elements carrying out operations on Saudi soil, but continue to encourage and facilitate the export of Jihad to other countries. The duplicity is well documented, but rarely discussed. Such discussion would be impolite and impolitic. It would violate the norms of political correctness. There are, as we are all too well aware, self-imposed political and economic constraints that further act to stifle debate and run counter to European and American democratic values and humanistic traditions.

At virtually every terrorism conference I have attended, speakers talk about the root causes of Jihadi terrorism in terms of lack of options, poverty and humiliation, but these conditions in my view only predispose an individual to embrace radical Islam. They may be contributing causes, but are not the root cause. Most are loathe or too fearful to note that the root cause of Jihadi terrorism is the Wahhabi religious establishment and the government of Saudi Arabia.

Until we address this issue head-on, Jihad and the Jihadists will continue to prosper. Too often, we mistake the symptom for the disease. The most evident symptom is Jihadist terrorism, but the root cause is the Wahhabi teachings that provide ideological justification for terror and the governments that fund and actively promote it. We are not engaged in a War on Terrorism. Terrorism is a tactic, and one does not declare war on a tactic. What we are engaged in is a war against the militant Wahhabi and those who support them. The enemy has a name, and we should not shrink from using it.

We compound our problems in other ways as well. What I see today is political correctness run amok, and a failure of courage by intellectuals and too many political figures. Political sophistry masquerades as political sophistication, and when militant Islamist community leaders talk in terms of building bridges between the faiths and the co-existence of the three great religions, we are mesmerized by words we desperately wish to believe. We fail to look behind the veil. We take their utterances at face value. In private and in the security and sanctity of their radical mosques, however, they preach hatred, violence and Jihad.

Meanwhile, truly moderate Muslim leaders are marginalized, and their followers intimidated because they are unable to compete with the well-funded and politically powerful radical Wahhabi establishment and those they have co-opted. Muslim moderates also are marginalized because we fail to support them. I think it is shameful. What we are seeing is a battle for the soul of Islam, which is, perhaps, the most important struggle of the new century. And for the most part we stand by, wring our hands and, essentially, do nothing.

8   The Enemy Within

Just one example from my own country – the case of Abduraham Alamoudi, the founder and former Executive Director of the American Muslim Council (AMC). For years, Mr. Alamoudi was regarded as a prime spokesman for the American Muslim community. He had direct and frequent access to both the Clinton and Bush White House as well as powerful members of Congress. In a true travesty, he was invited as a representative of the American Muslim Community to the 9/11 memorial services held at our National Cathedral. He also is credited with being the moving force behind the founding of the Pentagon's much troubled Muslim chaplain's program.

But why be so suspicious of Mr. Alamoudi's intentions?

There is another side to Mr. Alamoudi that was well known, but until 9/11 assiduously ignored. At the 28 October 2000 Jerusalem Day Rally held across from the White House, Mr. Alamoudi let the mask slip, and was caught on video exhorting his followers to support Jihad and loudly proclaiming his support for Hizballah and Hamas. In January 2001, Alamoudi was photographed in Beirut where he was attending a terrorist summit together with representatives from HAMAS, Palestinian Islamic Jihad, Hizballah and al Qaeda. It was all terribly damaging, but only in the post-9/11 context.

Mr. Alamoudi was not unmasked by the FBI or the CIA. His cover was blown and his true loyalties documented by a private citizen, Rita Katz, Director of the SITE Institute, who filmed him in front of the White House exhorting his followers to support Hizballah and Hamas and other terror groups. This video, taken at the 2000 Jerusalem Day Rally, was released to major television news networks, where it was broadcast on the prime-time evening news, and encouraged others including some in government to more closely scrutinize the activities of Mr. Alamoudi and the American Muslim Council. However, for the most part, Mr. Alamoudi's access and influence was only marginally affected.

More recently, however, Mr. Alamoudi was arrested for trying to illegally bring into the United States some $345,000 of Libyan money, and subsequently he has been implicated in a plot to assassinate Crown Prince Abdullah of Saudi Arabia. This is a man who purports to be a moderate and to represent the American Muslim community.

And why do I worry about the Pentagon's Muslim chaplain's program? My concern, of course, is that people such as Mr. Alamoudi are manipulating the process to ensure that Muslim chaplains who share Mr. Alamoudi's views are hired to minister to our young Muslim troops in Iraq and elsewhere. What could be a better way to spot, assess and recruit potential Jihadists who already are combat-trained than to serve as their spiritual guide? The reason I raise this is I have little doubt that the military of many European countries are being similarly targeted through similar mechanisms.

There is more to Jihad than meets the eye. And Jihadist political action operations is one area that has been largely ignored. Terrorism may be the most blatant Jihadist weapon, but Political Action represents the other side of the coin. In most cases, the latter is rarely detected and in my view may ultimately prove far more damaging.

Another factor contributing to the Jihadist rise is the readiness of the Western democracies to compromise their long-term security interests for short economic advantage. Too often greed masquerades as "realpolitik," and too often we have permitted rampant greed to cloud our judgment and, thereby, facilitate the growth of a cancer within the body politic.

This struggle is being fought in geographically disparate areas of the world by groups and organizations that have adapted the broad principles of Global Jihad, which they have tailored to respond to local needs, local grievances, local traditions and perceived historic injustices.

9 The War on Terrorism

In the immediate aftermath of 9/11, the US seemed to make all the right moves. Our people acted as one, and a brilliant campaign was launched that combined conventional and non-conventional military and intelligence assets. It resulted in the crushing of the Taliban and the decimation of the al Qaeda core leadership with over three fourths killed or captured. Al Qaeda was on the run and – many thought – on the ropes.

However, things are not always what they seem. Al Qaeda, although wounded and in retreat, did not atrophy or throw in the towel. And our opening of a second front in the War on Terror in the form of our war against Iraq provided al Qaeda and the Taliban a new lease on life. I regard it as our Christmas gift to Bin Laden.

Many of our highly specialized military and intelligence assets that had been running al Qaeda to ground in Afghanistan were shifted to Iraq. The diminished numbers and capabilities left us unable to deal a death-blow to Bin Laden and the remaining al Qaeda core. Al Qaeda survived, and the Taliban have reasserted themselves. Throughout the Muslim world the fact of their survival – the mere fact of their survival – is seen as a 'victory' and a harbinger of the ultimate triumph of Radical Islam over the military and technological superiority of the United States and the West.

Moreover, the resistance in Iraq did not capitulate. It seems the longer we stay, the stronger it grows. Iraq has also become a magnet for foreign Jihadists answering the call to resist the American occupation; much the way some two decades earlier an older generation had joined the anti-Soviet Jihad to drive the Russians from Afghanistan. What we are facing today is a full-blown insurgency that has the potential to expand far beyond the borders of Iraq and further destabilize countries such as Jordan, Egypt, Saudi Arabia and the Gulf States.

In this new, more dangerous and complex world, Bin Laden has become increasingly irrelevant – except, perhaps, as a symbol and martyr. In fact, Bin Laden dead may be more dangerous than Bin Laden alive. A captured Bin Laden may be broken and discredited, but myths, legends and martyrs are notoriously hard to kill.

Currently, we are engaged in a conflict in which there are no front lines. The enemy walks and lives among us – quietly. And in coming years, the typical Jihadist will not look like the typical Middle Easterner. Many of these Jihadists will be blond-haired and blue-eyed. They will carry American and European passports and, thereby, be free to travel the world. They will be recruited from college campuses, from prisons, from radical mosques and from our military – the four prime recruitment targets of Jihadist cadre.

As long as the ideology of Global Jihad resonates in the hearts of millions, we are going to find ourselves increasingly besieged.

Whether we like it or not, this has become primarily a war of ideas, ideology and a struggle for the soul of Islam. Until we better understand how best to compete in this particular arena of conflict and how best to constructively support mainstream Islam and Muslim moderates, Global Jihad will continue to gain adherents and garner success.

My educational background is anthropology. As a result, I see each terrorist group as an essentially unique social system having its own mores, operational code and world-view – separate and apart from the society from which it may have sprung. It therefore follows that any counterstrategy must be tailored to each specific group. One size does not fit all. Measures that are effective against one group may well prove counter-productive against another.

To effectively counter the Jihadists, all aspects of national power must be employed. These are the political, economic, psycho-social and military, with conventional military power often being the least effective and, too often, proving to be counter-productive.

Our future planning must involve the development of intelligent systems that can mimic and predict how a particular terrorist group and its decision makers are likely to perceive a particular situation, weigh their options and respond to a particular challenge. It calls for the development of tools and mechanisms that will enable us to influence and skew terrorist perceptions and steer our adversaries to make choices that will be the most disadvantageous to their survival. It calls for imaginative operations that change the configuration of the battlefield and alter the parameters of conflict.

To provide an example of what I mean: we have heard at this conference that the Jihadists use the Internet as their primary means of communication and as a device for recruitment, fundraising, training, etc. In my view, the Internet has become the new arena of conflict, something like the Wild West, in which there is no law and no code of conduct. The Jihadists use the Internet for propaganda, fundraising, recruitment, training and even for operational communication. The terrorists recognize its potential and are seeking to increase their exploitation of the medium. They are experimenting with net warfare, denial of service attacks, wholesale identify theft and a raft of other strategies to disrupt economies and diminish public confidence in the ability of governments to preserve and protect the interests of its citizens. In the future, decisive engagements and many forms of psychological operations are likely to take place in cyberspace.

But we too can use the Internet to disrupt and dismantle terrorist groups. To more fully explain: because it is so difficult to identify potential terrorist recruits and operatives, we should explore means to encourage them to self-identify. Because so many potential recruits come to the Internet seeking out Jihadist sites and chat rooms, we should consider creation of a number of militant sites and chat rooms that mimic the genuine article. Once someone contacts such sites they are fair game, and through technical means, the security services can determine the individual's identity and location.

This approach is commonly used by governments to identify child pornographers and pedophiles. Such a program has the salutary effect of discouraging sex offenders from using the Internet to pursue their interest in the sexual exploitation of children. Potential Jihadists can similarly be discouraged in their quest to link up with groups and like-minded individuals.

Of course, use of such tactics would ultimately become public knowledge, but this is not a bad thing as the Internet increasingly would become viewed as "compromised." It would no longer be regarded as a permissive environment in which to operate or relatively secure means of communication. It would be extremely difficult for the Jihadist to determine which militant site is genuine and which is a honey pot being used as a lure and run by the security services. Such tactics would also serve to fuel terrorist paranoia, which renders them less effective as they expend time and energy watching their back rather than engaging in operations.

Most students of terrorism will tell you that virtually all terrorist groups suffer from a surfeit of paranoia. It is endemic and pervasive. It is part and parcel of the clandestine existence. Our aim should be to feed terrorist paranoia so as to cause the organization to turn inward on itself. When the terrorist is busy watching his back, he has less time and energy to focus on his primary goal – our destruction. In such a climate, the terrorist not only fears the security forces, he also begins to fear his compatriots, their ambitions and their jealousies. Promoting suspicion and distrust erodes group cohesion, induces operational paralysis, and diminishes effectiveness. It is, therefore, a goal well worth pursuing.

For example, an intelligence service might want to pit a brilliant and ambitious terrorist lieutenant against the organization's leader. Even where there is little hard intelligence, this can still be accomplished. Such a dynamic could be promoted through a series of speculative media placements emanating from several different outlets in different countries that echo variations of the theme that the talented charismatic operative has leadership ambitions and is really the moving force behind the organization. The much revered leader, in contrast, would be portrayed as past his prime, having become little more than a figure-head – something of a telegenic dilettante who is rolled out whenever an important pronouncement needs to be aired. Wounded vanity often leads to precipitous acts, and has been the downfall of many men. It is a lever to be exploited.

Credibility of such themes may be enhanced by salting the stories with one or two nuggets of information that have special resonance for the targeted individuals. The irony is that even if both targets believe that hostile forces are trying to manipulate them, each also may fear that his ostensible rival believes, at least in part, that his position is being threatened and, therefore, has little choice but to strike pre-emptively to preserve his position and even his life.

Despite face-to-face meetings and mutual pledges of fealty, once the seeds of distrust have been planted, they are virtually impossible to extinguish.

Mutual suspicion grows, and each move made by the other, no matter how innocent, is viewed through lenses distorted by fear and suspicion. Even the best-intentioned overtures are viewed as provocative and further indication of disloyalty. Often one or the other decides to play it safe and strike first. The result can be that the organization loses either an invaluable operative or, perhaps, even its leader. Even if neither succumbs, their standing within the organization may be severely eroded. The friction that ensues also can fracture the organization's cohesion, induce paralysis and propels it down the path to self-destruction. Trust is ephemeral, and paranoia is highly contagious. This is what I call the "Othello Gambit."

Such approaches have been used successfully to weaken and dismantle criminal conspiracies, particularly drug gangs. Similar stratagems can be used to isolate and separate the hard-core terrorists from the organization's less committed members, potential recruits, sympathizers and their natural constituencies.

10   Conclusion

The nature of the protracted conflict in which we are now engaged cannot be won by a frontal military assault or the conventional use of military power. Our future will largely depend on how well we fight the war of ideas. This is not a war of leaflet drops and loud speakers. To succeed, we must be more sophisticated and imaginative. This is what the British have called 'Political Warfare,' and what I am talking about is the world of Covert Action and the world of the Special Operator.

The challenge of Global Jihad calls for the development of new and imaginative approaches that integrate sophisticated information technologies with the traditional soft sciences. It calls for an educated and engaged public to provide a nation a defense in depth. It also demands of our leadership uncommon courage, tenacity, patience as well as coolly rational decision-making in the face of unconscionable terrorist provocations that foment public rage and hysteria. It also demands the development of viable and effective options that game out probable secondary and tertiary consequences; as well as a clear recognition that the game has changed and old assumptions, solutions and constructs need to be reassessed and well may no longer apply. How quickly we recognize the rapidly changing nature and scope of the challenge and how resourcefully and energetically we respond will ultimately determine the winners, the losers and the price paid by each.

Prävention und moderne Terrorismusformen

Rudolf Adam

Präsident der Bundesakademie für Sicherheitspolitik
Schlossanlage Schönhausen, Ossietzkystraße 44/45, 13187 Berlin

Weshalb ist Prävention von so zentraler Bedeutung?

Es gibt keine andere wirksame Strategie. Terror zielt auf psychologische Zermürbung. Er ist eine Taktik der Ermattung und der Polarisierung, um eigene Schwäche mit den Verwundbarkeiten des Gegners zu kompensieren. Jeder erfolgreiche Terroranschlag ist in sich schon ein Sieg. Freilich kann im militärischen Sinn nicht von einem Sieg des Terrors gesprochen werden. Al Qaida wird weder die USA noch Europa erobern und unterwerfen können.

Aber das ist auch nicht das Ziel. Das Ziel ist vielmehr, einen psychologischen Wahrnehmungs- und Gefühlsprozess in Gang zu setzen, der zu einer Verschiebung der Gewichte und damit der Einflusssphären führt. Es ist eine Schlacht um Köpfe und Gefühle, um Ideen und Werte, nicht um Territorium, Wirtschaftsressourcen oder sonstige Ziele, wie sie klassischen militärischen Strategien zugrunde liegen.

Usama bin Laden denkt prozessual, nicht in Ergebnissen. So lange er nicht verliert, gewinnt er, solange der Westen nicht gewinnt, verliert er.

Lassen Sie mich vier Aspekte aus Usama bin Ladens neuem Ansatz hervorheben:

1. Er will den Selbstbehauptungswillen des Westens untergraben. Seine Ziele sind Einschüchterung, Selbstzweifel, Verunsicherung; das Gefühl, einem übermächtigen, unbekannten Gegner ausgeliefert zu sein, der jederzeit, überall, ohne erkennbare Begründung oder Zielauswahl zuschlagen und Tod und Schrecken verbreiten kann. Damit soll der Weg geebnet werden für einen Rückzug der westlichen Präsenz aus der arabisch-islamischen Welt und für erweiterte Freiräume für radikal-militante Vertreter der Jihad-Ideologie im Westen. Der Sieg ist nicht auf dem Schlachtfeld zu gewinnen, sondern in den Parlamenten, in der öffentlichen Debatte innerhalb der westlichen Gesellschaften.

2. Al Qaida will provozieren und polarisieren. Einerseits sollen durch das Gefühl der Unbesieglichkeit Sympathisanten und Unterstützer gewonnen werden.

Andererseits soll der Westen dämonisiert werden in der Hoffnung, er werde durch Überreaktion sich selbst diskreditieren und seine moralische Glaubwürdigkeit zerstören. Deshalb sind die Vorgänge in Abu Ghraib von solch enormer Bedeutung: Sie vertiefen in der arabischen Welt den Eindruck, dass der Anspruch der westlichen Welt, für zivilisatorisch überlegene Werte einzustehen, hohl und verlogen ist. Darüber müssen wir uns immer wieder klar sein: In diesem Kampf sind Perzeptionen und Gefühle viel wichtiger als materielle Realitäten. Wenn es Usama bin Laden gelingt, sich als ebenbürtig und gleichrangig mit dem Präsidenten der Vereinigten Staaten darstellen zu lassen, ist dies ein fast größerer Sieg für ihn als ein erfolgreiches Attentat. Al Qaida ist mit einem Franchising-Unternehmen verglichen worden – nicht zu Unrecht, wie ich finde. Dann muss aber auch klar sein, dass ein Franchising-Unternehmen von seinem Image, seiner Trademark, seinem Goodwill – oder sollte ich hier lieber von *bad will* sprechen – lebt.

3. Al Qaida plant nicht Einzelaktionen, sondern den kumulativen psychologischen Effekt von Serien. Vordergründig ist der materielle Schaden bei vier Einzelattentaten nicht größer als bei vier synchronisierten. Auf der psychologischen Ebene aber erzeugt die generalstabsmäßige Koordinierung solcher Schreckensereignisse ein Stimmungsklima der Einschüchterung, der Hilflosigkeit, des Ausgeliefertseins. Umgekehrt wird in der arabisch-islamischen Welt ein Stimmungsklima der Unbesiegbarkeit, des Triumphes und der Siegeszuversicht erzeugt. Usama bin Laden begnügt sich nicht damit, einzelne Terroranschläge zu konzipieren und zu planen. Er zielt auf einen Bewusstseinswandel in der Welt, auf eine terroristische *levée en masse* in der islamischen Welt. Den *clash of civilisations* will er provozieren durch Polarisierung, Schüren von Vorurteilen und emotionale Antagonisierung.

4. Schließlich: Al Qaida hat die Ökonomie des Terrors entdeckt. Die Anschläge in New York und Washington vom 11. September 2001 haben maximal 2 Mio. US$ gekostet. Der durch sie ausgelöste volkswirtschaftliche Gesamtschaden wird auf ca. 70 Mrd. US$ geschätzt – eine Hebelwirkung von 1:35.000! Auch Selbstmordattentate stellen – mit wissenschaftlich-nüchterner Emotionslosigkeit betrachtet – eine rationale Taktik für denjenigen dar, der aus einer Gemeinschaft mit hohem Bevölkerungswachstum gegen eine Gemeinschaft mit schrumpfender Bevölkerung ankämpft. Einfache, aber effektive Flugabwehrraketen sind für 100.000 US$ zu beschaffen. Sie können damit ein Flugzeug im Wert von 100 Mio. US$ abschießen – wie dies wiederholt versucht worden ist und wohl auch künftig versucht werden wird. Authentische Äußerungen von Usama bin Laden und aus seinem Umkreis legen dar, dass diese Terrorökonomie dort nicht unbekannt ist.

Deshalb ist jeder erfolgreiche Terroranschlag einer zu viel. Die IRA fasste diese Asymmetrie der Erfolgschancen in die Worte: „We only have to be successful once, but you have to be lucky all the time." Gegen zum Selbstmord entschlossene Terroristen versagen klassische Abschreckungsinstrumente. Wie also ist Prävention zu leisten?

Einer Tat zuvorkommen heißt, sie einerseits zu antizipieren, mögliche Täter und mögliche Ziele im Voraus benennen zu können, heißt aber auch, immer aufgrund von Vermutungen, Hypothesen, Szenarios zu operieren, also in einem Umfeld mit hoher Ungewissheit.

Prävention setzt Aufklärung voraus: Aufklärung über potenzielle Täter, ihre Motive, ihre Vorgehensweise, ihre Zielauswahlkriterien und eventuell konkrete Anschlagsvorbereitungen. Die Aufklärung wird um so besser sein, je stärker die entsprechenden Kapazitäten weltweit vernetzt werden und kooperieren. Die Herausforderung ist global, deshalb kann die Antwort auch letztlich nur global gegeben werden.

Was heißt Prävention nun konkret? Ich sehe hier vier Felder:

- Schutz der Infrastruktur,
- Vorbereitung auf den *worst case*,
- täterbezogene Aufklärung und Überwachung sowie
- Unterbindung der Rekrutierung von Terrornachwuchs.

Lassen Sie mich das in aller Kürze ausführen:

Terror lebt von unserer Verwundbarkeit. Also müssen wir unsere Verwundbarkeiten identifizieren und minimieren. Die Bundesregierung hat nach dem 11. September 2001 in einer groß angelegten Aktion sämtliche Infrastrukturbereiche einer solchen Prüfung unterzogen und entsprechende Maßnahmen getroffen. Die verstärkten Sicherheitsvorkehrungen an den Flughäfen und die verstärkte Bewachung amerikanischer, israelischer und britischer Institutionen gehören dazu – hier ist nicht Platz für mehr Einzelheiten. Zwei Bemerkungen sind mir jedoch wichtig:

1. Wir sollten Sicherheitsvorkehrungen optimieren, nicht maximieren: Sicherheit – das sind die Dämme, die wir gegen Gefahrenfluten aufwerfen. Es macht wenig Sinn, diesen Damm an einer Stelle übermäßig hoch und verstärkt auszubauen, wenn er an anderen Stellen vernachlässigt wird. Das Wasser wird dort durchbrechen, wo der Damm am schwächsten und am niedrigsten ist. Und wir sind gut beraten, den Terroristen so viel Geduld und

Intelligenz zu unterstellen, dass sie die Stellen, an denen die Dämme am schwächsten sind, relativ schnell und zuverlässig herausfinden. Was will ich damit sagen? Wir müssen Systeme als Ganzes betrachten und sollten uns nicht auf den sichtbaren Sektor konzentrieren: Passagierkontrollen beispielsweise machen im sicht- und fühlbaren Sektor nur dann Sinn, wenn auch Gepäck und Fracht im unsichtbaren Sektor ebenso stringent kontrolliert werden.

2. Es gibt keine 100%ige Sicherheit. Wir können das Anschlagsrisiko reduzieren, aber nicht eliminieren. Offene, mobile, global vernetzte Gesellschaften wie die unsere bleiben verwundbar. Wir können Flughäfen nicht zu Hochsicherheitstrakten umbauen. Wir können auch nicht die dort praktizierten Kontrollen auf alle Bahnhöfe ausweiten – geschweige denn auf alle Kino-, Konzert- und Theatersäle, Einkaufszentren, Weihnachtsmärkte usw. Und wir wissen seit dem Frankfurter Prozess gegen die Meliani-Gruppe: Gerade ein solcher Anschlag auf einen Weihnachtsmarkt war geplant.

Damit bin ich bei meinem zweiten Punkt: Vorbereitungen auf einen *worst case*. Weil es 100%ige Sicherheit nicht geben kann, müssen wir trotz allem Vertrauen in unsere Abwehrfähigkeiten damit rechnen, dass irgendwann ein katastrophaler Anschlag gelingt. Schon die statistische Wahrscheinlichkeit spricht dafür. Ich persönlich gehe davon aus, dass die Gefährdung durch eine militant-fundamentalistische Jihad-Ideologie noch auf Jahre hinaus bestehen wird. Damit wächst die statistische Wahrscheinlichkeit, dass wir eben nicht, wie die IRA meinte, „lucky all the time" sein können. Wir müssen deshalb Anschlagsrisiken analysieren und entsprechende Vorkehrungen treffen. Auch hier gilt: Wir können unmöglich auf *alle* Szenarien *maximal* vorbereitet sein. Was immer wir an gesicherten Erkenntnissen über Zielauswahlkriterien, Vorgehensweisen und konspirative Strukturen gewinnen können, dient als Grundlage für Planungen und Vorbereitungen, wie die Wirkungen eines Anschlags eingedämmt und bewältigt werden können. Experten in Katastrophenhilfe und Bevölkerungsschutz müssen wissen, was zu tun und zu beachten ist. Sie müssen realitätsnah üben und trainieren. Sie müssen hinreichend ausgerüstet sein, um auch unkonventionelle Szenarien bewältigen zu können. Wir können im europäischen Verbund planen; einige Mitgliedstaaten können und sollten Spezialfähigkeiten entwickeln und pflegen, die sie im Ernstfall anderen zur Verfügung stellen. Der Verfassungsvertrag sieht diese innergemeinschaftliche Solidarität ausdrücklich vor. Nicht jeder wird überall alles tun können. Im einheitlichen Raum der Sicherheit, der Freiheit und des Rechts wird es ohnehin keinen Raum für nationale Alleingänge geben. Wichtig bleibt, dass unsere Aufklärung ein realistisches Bild von Fähigkeiten und Absichten der Terroristen behält. Wir müssen uns dem annähern, was Terroristen denken, wir müssen ihre Planungen zu antizipieren lernen. Die Zukunft ist niemals eine Wiederholung der Vergangenheit. Insofern stimmt die Warnung, dass Generäle in Gefahr sind, immer noch einmal den letzten Krieg zu planen, und Polizisten, immer noch einmal Vorkehrungen gegen den letzten Anschlag zu treffen. Gerade Al Qaida hat ein ungewöhnliches hohes Maß an Kreativität und kühner Vision gezeigt. Dennoch gilt: Wie sonst, wenn nicht in sorgsamer Analyse aus der Vergangenheit und der Herausarbeitung von Mustern, Trends, typischen Konstellationen usw. lässt sich Zukunft halbwegs plausibel und damit planbar machen? Auch dem Terror wohnt eine Eskalationslogik inne. Der 11. September 2001 hat einen Maßstab gesetzt, der schwer zu übertreffen ist. Wenn er übertroffen werden soll, müssen die Schreckensdimensionen gesteigert werden. Und wenn wir uns hier umschauen, sind wir bald im unkonventionellen Bereich. Diese unkonventionelle Dimension verleiht der Prävention eine zusätzliche Dringlichkeit. Bislang haben wir derartige Gefahren durch Abschreckung abgewehrt. Künftig werden wir auf Abschreckung immer weniger bauen können.

Das bringt mich zum dritten Punkt: Prävention ist letztlich nur zu gewährleisten durch eine möglichst nahe, auf potenzielle Täter ausgerichtete Aufklärung. Terrorverdächtige müssen rechtzeitig identifiziert, Tatvorbereitungen frühzeitig erkannt, konspirative Netzwerke möglichst lückenlos aufgedeckt werden. Denn Klandestinität und Überraschungsmoment sind essenzielle Faktoren in der psychologischen Anschlagswirkung. Ein Anschlag, der rechtzeitig aufgedeckt, vereitelt oder durch geeignete Gegenmaßnahmen ins Leere gelenkt wird, ist die einzige Form einer Niederlage, die dem Terrorismus zugefügt werden kann. Verhaftung oder gar Exekution von Terroristen wirkt dagegen häufig nur anstachelnd oder radikalisierend, weil Märtyrer und sichtbare Opfer geschaffen werden. Durch nichts kann die Aura von Überlegenheit und mysteriöser Omnipräsenz des Terrors besser zerstört werden als wenn sich erweist, dass auch Terroristen Fehler machen, dass sie in Planung und Ausführung ihrer Taten versagen, dass sie – in einem Wort – inkompetent sind.

Die bisherige Bilanz von Aufklärung und Verfolgung ist eindrucksvoll: Führende Terroristen sind gefasst oder getötet worden. Die organisatorische Struktur von Al Qaida ist weitestgehend zerstört, Netzwerke sind zerrissen. Wir haben erfolgreich eine große Anzahl von Anschlagsplanungen und -vorbereitungen aufgedeckt. Das Problem besteht darin, dass Al Qaida von Anfang an ein elusives Konzept war, eine bewusst ambivalent angelegte Organisation mit proteusartiger Wandlungsfähigkeit. Als hierarchisch strukturierte Terrororganisation ist Al Qaida schwer angeschlagen. Als ideologische Bewegung ist sie stärker als zuvor. Usama bin Laden kann kaum noch operieren; aber als Inspirator und Motivator ist er umso wirkungsvoller. Heute machen nicht die Terroristen Sorge, die von ihm instruiert sind, sondern die, die von ihm inspiriert sind und ihn vielleicht niemals gesehen haben. Wir haben es mit der dritten Terroristengeneration zu tun: Usama bin Laden und sein Führungszirkel stellen die erste Generation dar; die Anhänger, die er in den Lagern in Afghanistan ausgebildet und indoktriniert hat, die zweite. Seit der Operation „Enduring Freedom" hat sich diese zweite Generation in alle Welt zerstreut. Einige haben sich zurückgezogen, andere haben Ruheräume aufgesucht, wieder andere vagabundieren durch die Welt, predigen den fanatisierten Hass und verbreiten ihre terroristische Expertise und die Netzwerkverbindungen, wo immer sie auf Gleichgesinnte stoßen. Und von denen gibt es dank des Irak eine wachsende Anzahl. Wer hätte gedacht, dass der säkulare Irak eine solche Serie von Selbstmordattentätern produzieren würde? Keiner von denen, die sich in den letzten Wochen im Irak in die Luft gesprengt haben, dürfte Usama bin Laden gesehen haben oder ihm religiös besonders nahe stehen; aber sie alle lassen sich von seinem unbeugsamen Widerstandswillen, seinem brutalen Fanatismus und seinem zynischen Zerstörungskalkül inspirieren.

Damit zum letzten Punkt. Bislang habe ich über taktische Prävention einzelner Anschläge gesprochen. Strategische Prävention muss sich darüber hinaus auf die militante Jihad-Bewegung als Ganzes beziehen. Niemand kann die Hydra besiegen, solange ihr immer wieder neue Köpfe nachwachsen. Deshalb lässt sich Terror nicht allein durch Militär oder Polizei bekämpfen. Es muss eine zweite Dimension von Aufklärung hinzukommen: Aufklärung verstanden im Sinne Kants und Voltaires, als Überwindung selbstverschuldeter Unmündigkeit.

Niemand wird als Terrorist geboren. Zum Terroristen wird man durch fehlerhafte Bildung, Überzeugung oder Indoktrinierung. Wichtig ist, dass wir hinter den terroristischen Anschlägen den wirklichen Gegner erkennen: Hinter der Terrorbewegung steht die gewaltbereite, fanatische und militante Jihad-Ideologie. Wir müssen die morbide Faszination von Todesverachtung und sadistischer Brutalität gegenüber „Ungläubigen" durchbrechen, wir müssen schon im Sprachgebrauch verhindern, dass die, die wir als Selbstmordattentäter bezeichnen, in ihrer eigenen Sprache als „shaheeds", als Märtyrer gefeiert werden, d. h. als Helden, die selbstlos für den Glauben und zum Ruhme Allahs gefallen sind. Wir müssen dem Terror die Wurzeln abgraben, aus denen er immer wieder neue Lebenskraft saugt. Wie kann das gelingen? Neben den praktizierenden Terroristen müssen Prediger von Hass und Gewalttaten, diejenigen, die manichäisch zwischen der Brüderlichkeit der Gläubigen und der Verworfenheit der Ungläubigen unterscheiden, die vier Fünfteln der Menschheit die Menschenwürde absprechen, weil sie nicht der Botschaft des Koran folgen, als nicht weniger gefährlich erkannt werden. Taten werden durch Gedanken und ideologische Indoktrinierung vorbereitet. Also gilt es, diese Indoktrinierung zu verhindern.

Nichts trifft Terroristen härter, als wenn sich das Umfeld von Sympathisanten und Unterstützern von ihnen abwendet. Die Terrorbewegungen in Europa sind erloschen, nicht weil die Terroristen alle gefasst wurden, sondern weil der Nachwuchs ausblieb und sich die Gesellschaft abwandte von Gewalttätern dieser Art. Wenn wir die extreme Brutalität einzelner Extremisten zum Anlass nehmen für Pauschalurteile über den Islam insgesamt, sind wir bereits in Usama bin Ladens Falle gegangen. Dann polarisieren auch wir. Deshalb muss die Gegenstrategie gegen den Terror folgende Elemente umfassen: die extremen, gewaltbereiten Jihadis innerhalb der muslimischen Umma isolieren; darauf hinwirken, dass religiöse Autoritäten die militante Jihad-Interpretation klar und eindeutig verurteilen; liberale, weltoffene Strömungen im Islam ermutigen; Länder stützen, die islamisch, aber doch modern, kosmopolitisch und tolerant sind, wie z. B. Malaysia oder Bangladesch. Letztlich sind es doch die moderaten, weltoffenen und friedfertigen Muslime, die am meisten einen Triumph einer talibanähnlichen Bewegung in der islamischen Welt zu fürchten haben. Also müssten sie natürliche Verbündete der westlichen Welt sein. Aufklärung im Sinne von Toleranz, Rationalität, Fähigkeit zur Selbstkritik und kritischer Suche nach Wahrheit, nicht die doktrinäre Arroganz von Orthodoxie und Dogmatismus sollte in arabischen Schullehrplänen mehr Raum erhalten. Ohne Zuschauer, die applaudieren, ohne Sympathisanten, die finanziell und organisatorisch unterstützten, ohne radikale Prediger und Ideologen, die die Ungleichheit der Menschen predigen und verkünden, das Abschlachten unschuldiger Menschen sei ein gottgefälliges Werk, wird auch die gewalttätige Jihad-Bewegung allmählich erlöschen. Dabei sollten wir in Europa nicht vergessen: Das Problem kommt nicht von außen zu uns; es hat seine Wurzeln auch mitten unter uns. Wahrscheinlich geht die Zuspitzung dieser Bewegung sogar auf die Modernisierungskrise zurück, die entsteht, wenn traditionsgeprägte Muslime unvorbereitet mit westlichen Lebensformen konfrontiert werden und dann in eine totalitäre Verweigerungshaltung ausbrechen. Der Radikalismus der Jihad-Ideologie wäre dann in funktionaler Analogie zu Faschismus, Nationalsozialismus und Kommunismus, also den totalitären Modernisierungskrisen Europas, zu sehen.

Der militante, radikale Extremismus der Jihad-Bewegung bedroht die moderate Welt des Islam stärker als den Westen. Wirkungsvolle Prävention wird uns nur gelingen, wenn wir auch mit solchen moderaten Kräften in der islamischen Welt bei Aufklärung und Bekämpfung dieser Tendenzen zusammenarbeiten. Die jüngsten Terroranschläge erfolgten überwiegend in islamischen Ländern, die Zahl der getöteten Muslime übersteigt die der westlichen Ausländer um ein Vielfaches. Deswegen müssen entscheidende Impulse zur Prävention aus dem moderaten Teil der islamischen Welt kommen.

Die Rolle von Kultur in der Dynamik und der Bekämpfung von Terrorismus

Dr. Stephan Maninger

„Kultur ist die Mutter, die Institutionen sind die Kinder."
Daniel Erounga-Manguelle

1 Einleitung

Oben zitierte Erkenntnis bezüglich des Stellenwertes von Kultur im wirtschaftlichen Verhalten der Menschen ist gleichermaßen übertragbar auf deren Konfliktverhalten. Die mit der Globalisierung verbundenen Konvergenztheorien werden zunehmend ergänzt durch ein wachsendes Bewusstsein, dass Kultur ein wesentlicher Faktor ist, der bisher ungenügend berücksichtigt wurde.[1] Tatsächlich zeigt die momentane Konfliktkonfiguration des „Krieges gegen den Terror", dass die ideologischen Erklärungsmuster der Vergangenheit überholt sind und die kulturellen Bruchlinien sich als die entscheidenden, wenn auch nicht alleinigen Faktoren erwiesen haben.

Trotzdem zeigen Politik und Wirtschaft eine gewisse Beharrlichkeit, was Vertrauen und Erwartungen bezüglich der Universalität bzw. der transkulturellen Übertragbarkeit von Werten betrifft. Dies zeigt sich dann in der festen Überzeugung, dass der liberalen Demokratie und Marktwirtschaft nur wenige globale „Hürden" im Wege stehen, keineswegs jedoch dauerhafte kulturelle Grenzen gesetzt sind. Verfassungen und die Konstruktion von „Verfassungspatriotismus" sollen auch auf die Migrationsströme, die verstärkt die Industriestaaten prägen und demographisch verändern, identifikationsstiftend wirken und die engeren Identifikationsradien wie „Volk" oder „Nation" ersetzen. Dieser Konstruierungsansatz („social engineering") versteht sich als ein Schmelztiegel der Vernunft, moralisch überlegen und als utilitaristisches Ordnungsmodell daher vermeintlich unwiderstehlich. Hier sollen, im klassischen Sinne eines ideologischen „Topdown"-Ansatzes, die Institutionen die „Mutter" sein und die Kultur die „Kinder".

---

[1] Wobei der Autor an dieser Stelle betonen möchte, dass Kultur keine unabhängige Variable ist, sondern sich durch Faktoren wie Geographie oder Klima beeinflussen lässt und dabei durchgehend verändert und anpasst. Kulturen lassen sich allerdings nicht beliebig und nach gewünschtem Tempo verändern.

Dieser verfassungspatriotische Optimismus erinnert stark an die Euphorie im Europa des frühen 20. Jahrhunderts. Damals erklärten die global denkenden Wirtschaftseliten Krieg als unwahrscheinlich aufgrund der wirtschaftlichen Verzahnung europäischer Großmächte. In seinem einflussreichen Bestseller *The Great Illusion* vertrat Norman Angell 1910 sogar die Position, dass Krieg zwischen den Großmächten „unmöglich" sei.[2] Dieser Ansatz beruhte auf einem teils romantisch-idealistischen, teils rational-utilitaristischen Menschenbild. Heute beruht das Vertrauen in globaler Kulturkonvergenz hauptsächlich auf der Reduzierung des Kulturbegriffes auf Trachten und Kulinarisches ohne Berücksichtigung der im Kernwertesystem verankerten menschlichen Einstellungen, Glaubens-, Denk- und Motivationsstrukturen. Denn Kultur ist, wie auch mittlerweile multinationale Firmen zur Kenntnis genommen haben[3], die Art und Weise, in der Menschen als Individuen und in Gruppen ihre Probleme identifizieren, nach Prioritäten ordnen und lösen, d. h. die Welt interpretieren und verstehen. Dadurch unterscheiden sich Kulturen, auch wenn sie sich in einem permanenten Veränderungsprozess befinden, mehr oder weniger voneinander. Kultur ist, nach der Definition von Trompenaars und Turner, „[...] the way we do things around here"[4]. Dies betrifft alle Fassetten des Lebens und somit auch die Art und Weise, in der Konflikte entstehen und gelöst werden, und schließt die Fragen des Terrorismus mit ein.

2 Die Säulen von Kultur

Vereinfacht betrachtet beruht der Begriff „Kultur" auf drei tragenden Säulen, nämlich Religion, Sprache und gemeinsame Vergangenheit, die im Zusammenspiel ein komplexes Wertesystem darstellen und identifikationsbildend und somit abgrenzend wirken.

Religion: Religion wird als ergiebigste Quelle von Werten betrachtet, deren moralisches Gerüst das Handeln von Menschen maßgeblich beeinflusst.[5] Die Auswirkungen betreffen alle Bereiche, und schon Max Weber sah z. B. im Protestantismus die Wurzeln des wirtschaftlichen Erfolges und Wohlstandes. Als Glaubensgerüst bietet Religion nicht nur moralische Rechtfertigung für Konfliktver-

---

[2] Friedman, G. und Friedman, M., *The Future of War*, St. Martin's Griffin, New York, 1998, S. 6-7.
[3] „Intercultural Management" ist mittlerweile ein weit verbreitetes Phänomen bei Firmen, die sich als „Global Players" verstehen und ihr Personal für die kulturellen Realitäten vorbereiten.
[4] In *Riding the Waves of Culture*, Nicholas Brealy Publishing, London, 1997, S. 2.
[5] Werte bilden den ethischen Bereich von Kultur.

halten, sondern auch eine methodisch-moralische Dimension, was die Vorgehensweise anbetrifft, denn „das Verhalten eines Menschen, der aus Achtung vor einem intrinsischen Wert handelt, den er freiwillig akzeptiert und zu seinem Leitbild gemacht hat, nennt man ‚moralisch'."[6] Da Glaubensfragen seltener an die Vernunft appellieren und weniger rationale als emotionale Zugänge bieten, scheint es kaum verwunderlich, dass religiöse Symbole und Rituale in der Geschichte der Menschheit eine hohe Schlachtfeldpräsenz zeigten bzw. zeigen. Momentan wird in diesem Zusammenhang weltweit der radikale Islam hervorgehoben als Beispiel für eine besonders hohe Gewalt- und Aufopferungsbereitschaft. Dabei schildert der weit verbreitete Satz von Bernard Lewis die Komplexität des Problems: „Die meisten Muslime sind keine Fundamentalisten und die meisten Fundamentalisten sind keine Terroristen, aber die meisten heutigen Terroristen sind Muslime und behaupten, stolz darauf zu sein". Muslime erklären sich verantwortlich für 80% der weltweiten Terrorangriffe und sind involviert in 75% der Kriege, wobei zu erwähnen ist, dass ein signifikanter Teil dieser Gewalt sich auch gegen Muslime richtet, da der Islam eine multidimensionale und in sich zerstrittene Religion darstellt. Von 36 terroristischen Organisationen, die das US-Außenministerium weltweit als solche identifiziert, behaupten 17, sie handeln im Namen des Islam, während sechs weitere von überwiegend muslimischen Mitgliedern betrieben werden.[7] Der Genozidforscher Gunnar Heinsohn[8] erklärt die legitimierende Rolle von Religion in der Gewaltentfaltung folgendermaßen: „Es stimmt schon, dass der Religionsstifter des Islam als siegreicher Heerführer und Machtpolitiker vor die Welt tritt, während der christliche als Wanderprediger hingerichtet wird. Der eine tötet siegreich, der andere vergibt seinen Henkern."[9] Der Religionsstifter des Islam war also auch Kriegsherr, dessen Vorgehensweise in den 29 Kriegen, die er zur Unterwerfung der arabischen Völker führte, für jeden Gläubigen als richtungsweisend oder vorbildlich gilt, während christlich begründete Gewalt, von den Kreuzzügen bis zum Nordirlandkonflikt, inzwischen insgesamt auf Kritik und Ablehnung innerhalb des mittlerweile humanistisch geprägten Christentums der Gegenwart stößt.[10]

---

[6] Grondona, Mariano, „Eine kulturelle Typologie der wirtschaftlichen Entwicklung", in: Harisson, Lawrence und Huntington, Samuel, *Streit um Werte – Wie Kulturen den Fortschritt prägen*, Europa Verlag, 2003, S. 77.
[7] Frumm, David and Perle, Richard, *An End to Evil – How to Win the War on Terror*, Random House, New York, 2003, S. 41.
[8] *Söhne und Weltmacht*, Orell Füssli Verlag, Zürich, 2003, S. 31.
[9] Heinsohn sieht allerdings in seiner Analyse nur graduelle Unterschiede in der Gewaltentfaltung der beiden Religionen.
[10] Wobei das Erlöschen von Kriegsbereitschaft in christlich geprägten Kulturkreisen durch den Geburtenschwund und die geringere Anzahl junger Männer begünstigt wird.

Beobachter scheinen weniger daran zu zweifeln, dass die Mehrzahl der Menschen muslimischen Glaubens friedliebend seien, sondern vielmehr beunruhigt zu sein über deren relatives Schweigen gegenüber dem im Namen ihrer Religion verübten Terrorismus.[11] Es wird allgemein akzeptiert, dass es in allen Kulturen gute und böse Menschen gibt, nur wirkt es beunruhigend, dass ein „Aufstand der Anständigen" unter Muslimen, bis auf formelles Bedauern und Distanzierung, größtenteils ausbleibt.[12] Hierin zeigt sich eine Kluft im jeweiligen Moralitätsverständnis, denn viele Handlungen des Westens oder westlicher Menschen sind für viele Muslime oftmals außerhalb der eigenen moralischen Parameter. Daher sehen sie den Kampf gegen den „unmoralischen" und „dekadenten" Westen als legitimen kulturellen Abwehrkampf.[13] Dabei sind es die als Bedrohung wahrgenommen Werte und Veränderungen, die mit „Verwestlichung" innerhalb des eigenen Kulturkreises verbunden werden.

Westliche Politiker reagieren auf das oben geschilderte Stimmungsbild, indem sie versuchen, die Terroristen von deren populärer Machtbasis zu trennen und somit zu isolieren. Dabei nutzen sie jede Gelegenheit, die muslimische Weltbevölkerung daran zu erinnern, dass auch Muslime dem Terror zum Opfer gefallen sind. Die Nachricht soll lauten: „Seht, sie töten rücksichtslos, auch euch Muslime". Damit wird die Hoffnung verbunden, den Terrorismus in dessen Ursprungsländern zu bekämpfen. Aber implizit lautet die Nachricht auch, wenn auch nicht beabsichtigt, dass man befürchtet, die Muslime könnten sich möglicherweise weniger für den „Krieg gegen den Terror" interessieren, solange es „nur" Nichtmuslime, d. h. Ungläubige, betrifft. Die implizierte Botschaft kann möglicherweise zutreffender sein als die beabsichtigte.

Tatsächlich unterscheidet sich hier das moderne Christentum in zweierlei Hinsicht vom Islam, nämlich:

1. durch das universale Menschenbild, d. h. durch den aus dem Judentum stammenden, von der Gottesebenbildlichkeit abgeleiteten Gedanken einer abso-

---

[11] Im Islam gibt es 73 Glaubensvarianten, ohne eine zentrale Hierarchie, wie dies z. B. bei den christlichen Kirchen der Fall ist. Die zahlenmäßig stärkste Gruppierung, die zugleich die älteste ist, sind die Sunniten mit ca. 80 bis 90%. In Deutschland gibt es eine signifikante Anzahl (ca. 500.000-700.000) Aleviten, die eine relativ gemäßigte Glaubensrichtung bilden und sich nicht der Integration verweigern.

[12] Im Vergleich schien die Empörung der in Deutschland lebenden Türken zur geplanten CDU-Unterschriftenaktion und der Ablehnung eines so genannten „Christenclubs" weitaus heftiger als die bisherige Distanzierung vom bzw. Verurteilung des internationalen Terrors.

[13] Dies bestätigt auch der Bundesverfassungsschutzbericht 2003 (2004: 165).

luten Menschenwürde, die dem Islam in dieser Form fremd ist. Seine Würde erlangt der Mensch, indem er sich dem Willen Gottes ausliefert. Die Brüderlichkeit und Feindesliebe des gepredigten Christentums der Gegenwart weicht stark ab von der klaren Trennung des Islam zwischen „Gläubigen" und „Ungläubigen", was die schon erwähnte mangelnde Verurteilung des in seinem Namen ausgeübten Terrors erklärt. Hier ist auch der Koran deutlich: „Nehmt keinen von ihnen zum Freund [...]. Und so sie den Rücken kehren, so ergreift sie und schlagt sie tot, wo immer ihr sie findet."[14] Wo Muslime dem Terror zum Opfer fallen, kann sich der Terrorist psychologisch entlastet fühlen, indem er sich ebenso auf den Koran beruft: „Und nicht ihr erschluget sie, sondern Allah erschlug sie."[15] Demgegenüber scheint, bis auf wenige Randerscheinungen[16], das moderne Christentum stets bemüht, die Ökumene zu fördern, und verteidigt gar gelegentlich die Fundamentalisten gegen die vermeintliche „Kreuzrittermentalität" von Sicherheitsexperten;[17]

2. durch die Trennung von Gott und Staat. Gunnar Heinsohn[18] erklärt: „Religion und Staatsgewalt liegen im Islam von Beginn an in einer Hand, während die christliche Kirche gegen die römische Herrschaft heranwachsen musste und auch danach nur in Ausnahmefällen die Regierung stellt." Für den Islam kann Staatsgewalt nicht vom Willen des Volkes abgeleitet werden, sondern ausschließlich von Gott und seinem im Koran offenbarten Willen. Der Islam lehnt die Trennung zwischen Staat und Religion, zwischen irdischer und überirdischer Macht, grundsätzlich ab.

Ein weiterer Faktor im modernen Terrorismus, bei dem Religion eine außerordentliche Rolle spielt, ist dessen apokalyptische Dimension. Wie der U-Bahn-An-

---

[14] Sure 4, 91.
[15] Sure 8, 17.
[16] Die Gewaltbereitschaft bzw. -wahrscheinlichkeit ist selbst bei „christlichen Fundamentalisten" gering und wird vermutlich dauerhaft auf Randerscheinungen begrenzt sein, weil die philosophisch-moralische Grundlage einer breiteren Unterstützung entgegenwirkt.
[17] Die Church of England hob beispielsweise lobend und als vorbildlich das Verhalten von Rachel Corrie hervor, die durch einen israelischen Bulldozer irrtümlich begraben wurde, als dieser einen Tunnel für Waffenschmuggler in Gaza zuschüttete. Elf Tage nach deren Tod wurde ein bewaffnetes Mitglied des „Islamischen Dschihad" in den Büroräumen von Corries Organisation „International Solidarity Movement" (ISM) verhaftet. Die gleiche Organisation bewirtete den britischen Selbstmordterroristen Omar Khan Sharif fünf Tage vor dessen Anschlag auf einen israelischen Nachtclub am 30. April 2003 (Frumm and Perle, 2003: 81).
[18] *Söhne und Weltmacht*, 2003 S. 31.

schlag in Tokio zeigte, bezieht sich dies nicht nur auf den Islam. Apokalyptischer Terrorismus unterscheidet sich in zweierlei Hinsicht maßgeblich vom praktischen Terrorismus der Vergangenheit. Zum einen sind politische Ziele oft zweitrangig und klassische politische Reaktionen begrenzt in ihrer Fähigkeit, Terroristen zu beeinflussen oder zur Zurückhaltung zu bewegen. So waren die Vorbereitungen für den 11. September 2001 am intensivsten, als die USA eine wichtige und für die Palästinenser günstige Rolle im Friedensprozess spielten.[19]

Zum anderen bietet die moderne Welt viel mehr Möglichkeiten zum Massenmord als jemals zuvor. Der 11. September 2001 verursachte mehr Tote als 35 Jahre IRA-Terrorismus. Apokalyptische Terroristen fühlen sich dem quasi-fatalistischen Glauben verbunden, ein „heiliges Werkzeug" in einem göttlichen Plan zu sein. Dies beinhaltet eine emotional stärkere Zielbindung, als es beim praktischen Terroristen der Fall ist, dessen „höheres Ideal" durch politische Veränderungen erreichbar ist und der selten überirdische Ziele verfolgt. Im schlimmsten Falle sehen sich apokalyptische Terroristen als „Racheengel", deren Gewalt nicht die Methode, sondern das eigentliche Ziel ist.[20] Gegen deren Endzeitmentalität sind die herkömmlichen Sicherheits- und Abwehrmaßnahmen oft unzureichend.[21]

Sprache: Sprachen transportieren Werte und Bedeutung, wobei Kulturen naturgemäß nicht immer die gleichen Bedeutungen teilen. Denn Sprache existiert in einem größeren kulturellen Kontext und „Kommunikationsfeld". Der Diskurs über kulturelle Grenzen hinweg wird kompliziert durch die Tatsache, dass die akustische Verständigung allein nicht unbedingt ausreichend ist; man kann z. B. nur schwer kommunizieren, was man nicht kennt. Außerdem sind grundsätzliche Begriffe wie „Terrorismus", „Demokratie" und „Frieden" einer kulturspezifischen Bedeutung bzw. bewertenden Interpretation unterworfen. So stellt sich bei letztgenanntem Begriff die Frage, ob das westliche Verständnis von „Frieden", nämlich die *Abwesenheit von Gewalt*, gemeint ist oder das Nichtwestliche, bei dem die *Abwesenheit von Gegnern* oftmals einen höheren Stellenwert genießt. Wo westliche Gesellschaften „Gott" und „Staat" teilen und das Christentum sich, vereinfacht gesprochen, von der mittelalterlichen Inquisition zum pazifistischen Humanismus wandelte, ist dies in anderen Regionen so nicht der Fall. Wiederum sind es grundlegende Kernbegriffe, die aufgrund der Religion un-

---

[19] Simon, Steven und Benjamin, Daniel, „The Terror", *Survival*, Winter 2001, S. 12.
[20] Morgan, Mathew, The Origins of the New Terrorism, Parameters, Spring 2004, S. 34.
[21] Peters, Ralph, „When Devils Walk the Earth – The Mentality and Roots of Terrorism, and How to Respond", Study for the Center For Emerging Threats and Opportunities, 2003, S. 2.

terschiedlichen Definitionen unterliegen. Bassam Tibi[22] postuliert beispielsweise, dass mit dem Begriff „Krieg" („Harb") eine Handlung gemeint ist, die von außen auf die islamische Welt ausgeführt wird. Bei eigener Gewaltausübung, mit dem Ziel der Verbreitung des Islam, wird euphemistisch der Begriff „Öffnung" („Futuhat") verwendet. Zusätzlich erschwerend ist dabei laut Jörn Brauns, dass „die reich entwickelte Synomie der arabischen Sprache die Abweichung von der Regel der aristotelischen Logik in sich birgt. Nach dieser Regel ist das Denken in synonymen Begriffen nicht zulässig."[23]

Wie wenig die Wirkung von Sprache von westlichen Nachrichtendiensten berücksichtigt wurde, zeigt deren Serie von Irrtümern in der Lageeinschätzung, angefangen beim Umsturz im Iran 1978/79 bis zum Versagen bei Terroranschlägen und unlängst im Irak.[24] Der Mangel an Agenten mit den notwendigen Sprachkenntnissen führt dazu, dass westliche Nachrichtendienste sich gezwungenermaßen sehr stark auf die einheimischen Dienste verlassen müssen.[25] Gleichzeitig wird Kultur in Lageberichten größtenteils ausgeklammert, weil der Gedanke abgelehnt wird, dass Menschen aufgrund ihrer unterschiedlichen Werte- bzw. Glaubenssysteme ebenso diverse Handlungsmotive und -muster haben könnten. Dies wird als insgesamt anrüchig betrachtet, und entsprechend liegen die Analysten möglicherweise öfter falsch, weil sie eben nicht kulturelle Faktoren ausreichend berücksichtigen.[26]

Gemeinsame Vergangenheit: Dabei handelt es sich nicht nur um das generationsübergreifend gemeinsam Erlebte, das „kollektive Gedächtnis" der Gruppe. Die Geschichte ist nicht nur „Werteschaffer", sondern definiert in der Regel die Inhalte und interpretiert das Geschehene durch die „Brille" der schon vorhandenen Werte. Der Kampf um die Geschichte, d. h. die Inhalte der Überlieferung und deren Interpretation, ist ebenso wichtig wie der Verlauf des beschriebenen

---

[22] Tibi, Bassam, *Krieg der Zivilisationen*, Hoffman und Campe, Hamburg, 1995, S. 58.
[23] Brauns, Jörn, „Europa vor dem Bürgerkrieg – Der Islam – Thema seit 11.9.2001", unveröffentlicher Vortrag, Carl Crantz Gesellschaft, 2003, S. 2.
[24] Das volle Ausmaß der Versagensserie erklären Frumm und Perle (2003: 201-209).
[25] Die Abhängigkeit von einheimischen Diensten, verschleiert unter dem Euphemismus „Kooperation", führt dazu, dass westliche Nachrichtendienste grundsätzlich von Maßnahmen abraten, die die Kooperationsbereitschaft gefährden könnten. Die Risiken liegen auf der Hand, da die Zusammenarbeit spätestens dann problematisch wird, wenn sie gegen die Interessen der einheimischen Regierungen gerichtet ist. Fehl- und Desinformation beeinträchtigt die Verwertbarkeit der Information und kann zu Manipulationen führen, für die der KGB in Zeiten des Kalten Krieges berühmt wurde.
[26] Frumm, David und Perle, Richard, *An End to Evil – How to Win the War on Terror*, Random House, New York, 2003, S. 206.

Ereignisses selbst[27], denn sie definiert Gut und Böse, Täter und Opfer, Sieger und Verlierer.[28] Es ist die gemeinsame Vergangenheit und Geschichte – das Erlebte und Geschaffene –, die die individuelle Identität zur kollektiven Schicksalsgemeinschaft erweitert. Aus ihr entspringt oftmals ein kollektives Selbst- und Sendungsbewusstsein. Dies bezieht sich sehr stark auf subjektive Selbsteinschätzungen und beruft sich daher auch auf das emotional verwurzelte, gemeinschaftliche Verlangen nach kultureller Kontinuität. Gemeinsame Allianzen oder vergangene Feindschaften können eine ausschlaggebende Rolle in der Bestimmung der interkulturellen Beziehungen spielen. Auch hier sind mehr als tausend Jahre kriegerische Beziehung zwischen Islam und Christentum ein belastender Faktor. Das historische Trauma der Muslime mag die Belagerung von Jerusalem (1099) durch die Kreuzritter oder die „Reconquista" (1492) sein. Währendessen mag das Trauma der Christen bei der Abwehrschlacht von Tours (732) liegen oder bei der Belagerung von Konstantinopel (1453) oder Wien (1529) zu finden sein.[29] Wenn auch im kollektiven Gedächtnis des Westens diese Ereignisse kaum mehr eine Identifikationsrolle spielen, so spielen vor allem die Kreuzzüge bei arabischen und türkischen Muslimen sehr wohl eine Rolle und finden bei Predigten und Rechtfertigungen immer wieder Erwähnung. Die kollektive Erinnerung bleibt lebendig und beeinflusst das Verhalten in der Gegenwart.

3 Bruchlinien

Die oben genannten Faktoren prägen die Wertesysteme maßgeblich. Bruchlinien zwischen Kulturen finden sich dort, wo die realen oder wahrgenommenen kulturellen Unterschiede zwischen den Menschen größer sind als die Gemeinsamkeiten. Ernsthafte und nachhaltige Bruchlinien entstehen, wenn die jeweiligen kulturellen Eigenschaften (auch „Kulturkapital" genannt) sich mehr stören als ergänzen, was nicht den kulturellen Austausch ausschließt, aber dennoch die Konfliktträchtigkeit des Miteinanders dermaßen erhöht, dass die Abgrenzungstendenzen überwiegen und sich existenzielle Fragen stellen. In der Praxis bestehen sichtbare Bruchlinien zwischen den jeweiligen Wertesystemen meistens aus folgenden Aspekten:

---

[27] Lepore, Jill, *The Name of War*, Alfred A. Knopf Publishers, New York, 1998, S. 10
[28] Wo der Sieger den Verlierern seine Version des Geschehens aufzwingen kann, entsteht ein doppelter Sieg. Denn ein Geschehen durch die psychologische Brille des anderen zu sehen legitimiert dessen Auftreten und Verhalten gegenüber der eigenen Gruppe.
[29] Während die Kreuzzüge gerne angeführt werden als der Sündenfall des Christentums, zeigt die historische Analyse, dass die Muslime sich bis zur Schlacht von Tours in der strategischen Offensive befanden und die Christen in der Defensive, also bereits dreihundert Jahre vor Beginn der Kreuzzüge.

3.1 Das individuelle „Selbst" gegenüber dem kollektiven „Selbst"

Während der Westen den Individualismus betont und Demokratie ohne Individualismus kaum vorstellbar ist, findet sich in vielen nichtwestlichen Ländern eine stärkere Betonung der kollektiven Entscheidungsmuster, die sich oftmals an den Interessen der Familie, des Clans oder der Volkszugehörigkeit orientieren. Engere Identifikationsradien verhindern, dass Menschen sich bereitwillig dem westlichen Universalismus anschließen oder Demokratie als moralisch hochwertigste Gesellschaftsform anerkennen und annehmen. Während der als erfolgreich erklärten Wahlen in Afghanistan und im Kosovo 2004 zeigte sich, dass ganze Gebiete sich geschlossen hinter Kandidaten stellten, die zumeist auch die De-facto-Machthaber waren. Ähnliche Muster, d. h. Clan- oder ethnoreligiöses Wahlverhalten, sind auch im Irak zu erwarten, wobei sich die Frage stellt, ob die Grundvoraussetzungen für westliche Demokratie bestehen und ob es realistisch ist, an diesem strategischen Ziel als Exportschlager festzuhalten. Kollektive Entscheidungsmuster werden auch nicht zwingend abgelegt, wenn sich Menschen aus solchen Kulturen in den Westen begeben.

3.2 Zeitbegriffe

Während westliches Zeitverständnis sich auf die unmittelbare Zukunft konzentriert und sich dies im wirtschaftlichen und politischen Tagesablauf spiegelt, zeigen andere Kulturen oft eine Orientierung, die sich weiter in der Zukunft oder Vergangenheit befindet.[30] Während man japanische Geschäftspläne belächelte, die 200 Jahre im Voraus planten, so zeigt sich selten ein Verständnis für das lange kollektive Gedächtnis vieler Kulturen. Begriffe wie „Kreuzzügler" vermitteln einen Eindruck darüber, wie weit dieses Gedächtnis zurückreichen kann und welche Assoziationsketten bestehen. Währenddessen kennt der Durchschnittsbürger der Industrienationen selten weder den genauen Zeitraum der Kreuzzüge, noch teilt dieser das augenscheinliche Empfinden seines muslimischen Gegenübers bezüglich deren historischer Signifikanz. Wenn die Forderungen der Terroristen sich daher gelegentlich an taktischen Zielen orientieren, wie beispielsweise dem Abzug von US-Truppen aus Saudi-Arabien, so liegt deren Kriegsgrund viel weiter zurück. Demnach sind die Ereignisse des Mittelalters von einer Relevanz, wie sie im westlichen Kollektivgedächtnis nur schwer vorstellbar scheint.

---

[30] Auch die Reihenfolge der Abläufe ist davon betroffen. So ist wirtschaftlich ein eindeutiger Unterschied zwischen monochromem und synchronem Zeitverständnis zu beobachten.

3.3 Kontext

So genannte „High-context"-Kulturen beziehen sich stärker auf Veränderungen im Umfeld als die weitaus regelorientierteren „Low-context"-Kulturen. Letztgenannte versuchen, vermeintlich universalgültige Regelsysteme aufrechtzuerhalten, sehen darin die Quelle von Ordnung und Stabilität. Nur so scheint ihnen die Welt berechenbar und setzen sie ihr Vertrauen in Institutionen wie die UNO. „High-context"-Kulturen setzen stärker auf Beziehungen, vor allem auf Familie, Clan und Volkszugehörigkeit. Sie halten auch Abkommen nur für so lange gültig, wie die Bedingungen konstant bleiben, fühlen sich jedoch nicht mehr an diese gebunden, wenn Veränderungen eingetreten sind. Daraus entstehen Einschränkungen in der Bildung von Friedensstrukturen und Abkommen. Alle moralisch hochwertigen Intentionen der Politik zur friedlichen Konfliktlösung stoßen hier an eine Grenze der Zuverlässigkeit. Erschwerend ist dabei laut Jörn Brauns[31], dass der Islam das Täuschen, durch den Einsatz des so genannten Takiya, ausdrücklich erlaubt, wenn es denn der Sache dient. Dem wiederholten Kollaps von Abkommen zwischen Aufständischen und US-Truppen im Irak wie auch zwischen Letztgenannten und den von ihnen aufgestellten irakischen Sicherheitskräften während der Stabilisierungsoperationen mag daher eine Mischung aus mehreren Faktoren zugrunde liegen.

3.4 Status

Während der ausgeprägte Individualismus einen hohen Grad an individualleistungsbezogener sozialer Mobilität in westlichen Ländern gewährleistet, ist dies in vielen anderen Teilen der Welt bisher noch begrenzt. Dort wird Status eher zugewiesen, beruht stärker auf Herkunft und Beziehungsgeflechten. Allein durch die Geschlechterrollen sind Frauen in ihrer sozialen Mobilität stärker eingeschränkt und mehr oder weniger strukturell benachteiligt in ihren Entfaltungsmöglichkeiten. Ein Aufbrechen solcher kulturellen Strukturen wird erschwert, wenn der Impuls dazu zu einem erheblichen Teil aus einer Nachbarkultur kommt, z. B. Kopftuchdebatte, und so gibt es trotz kultureller Modernisierungsprozesse nach wie vor weit verbreitet Ehrenmord und für Frauen oft tödliche Ehebruchgesetze. Des Weiteren führen die hohen Geburtenraten in muslimischen Ländern dazu, dass der hohe Bevölkerungsanteil von jungen Männern sich stark auf die gesellschaftliche Konflikt- bzw. Kriegsbereitschaft auswirkt. Deren gesellschaftlicher Status, unter Berücksichtigung der Tatsache, dass diese nicht in postheroischen Gesellschaften sozialisiert wurden, sondern in so genannten „Machokultu-

---

[31] Brauns, Jörn, „Europa vor dem Bürgerkrieg – Der Islam – Thema seit 11.9.2001", unveröffentlichter Vortrag, Carl Crantz Gesellschaft, 2003, S. 18.

ren", kann durch deren Gewalt- bzw. Aufopferungsbereitschaft erhöht werden. Dies zeigt das Ansehen von „Märtyrern".[32] Während Selbstmord im Islam grundsätzlich abgelehnt wird, weil er als Flucht und Rückzug gilt, ist der Selbstmordterrorist laut Scheich Jussuf-el-Karadawi (Islamstudiendekan an der Universität Katar) eben kein einfacher Selbstmörder, sondern ein Mensch, der eine „Märtyreroperation" durchführt und somit beim Vormarsch und im Angriff stirbt.[33] Diese Art des Selbstmordes, bei dem gerade zivile Ziele vorrangig angegriffen werden, kann sich dabei auf das historische Vorbild der radikal-schiitischen Assassinen des 11. und 12. Jahrhunderts berufen.[34] Das Sozialprestige des Täters und dessen Angehöriger steigt durch seine Tat, während ein vergleichbares Verhalten in postheroischen Überflussgesellschaften kaum auf Verständnis stoßen, geschweige denn positiv bewertet werden würde. Dort wäre die Selbstaufopferung beim Angriff auf eindeutig und ausschließlich zivile Ziele eher mit einem Statusverlust verbunden.[35]

Diese Bruchlinien spielen eine Rolle im alltäglichen interkulturellen Kontakt und sind auf allen gesellschaftlichen Ebenen vorhanden, da es sich um Verhaltensmuster handelt, die aus Kernwerten und Normen abgeleitet und dadurch nachhaltig sind. Die Kompatibilität oder Inkompatibilität der jeweiligen Wertesysteme zeigt sich beim direkten interkulturellen Kontakt, weil gerade dadurch die Bruchlinien am stärksten in den Vordergrund treten. An ihnen entscheidet sich, ob die Kulturen sich bereichern, wie oft dies der Fall war und ist, oder ob sie sich stören und dem Konflikt widmen, was ebenfalls oft der Fall ist. Insgesamt dominiert

---

[32] Vgl. Heinsohn, Gunnar, *Söhne und Weltmacht – Terror im Aufstieg und Fall der Nationen*, Orell Füssli Verlag, Zürich, 2003, S. 15.
[33] http://www.memri.org/bin/articles.cgi?Page=subjects&Area=jihad&ID=SP54203.
[34] Meigs, Montgomery, „Unorthodox Thoughts about Asymmetric Warfare", *Parameters*, Sommer 2003, S. 4.
[35] Während die Selbstaufopferung bei der Bekämpfung militärischer Ziele in der Vergangenheit bekanntlich ebenso zu erhöhtem Status beigetragen hat, kann durch zu viele „Kollateralschäden" der ganze Konflikt in Frage gestellt werden und gesellschaftliche Widerstände mobilisieren. Selbstaufopferung für militärische Ziele ist keineswegs selten in der Militärgeschichte und unter fast allen Kulturen vorzufinden. Seltener ist allerdings die offensive Selbstaufopferung bei Angriffen auf primär zivile Ziele, denen man aus westlicher Sicht einen hohen Grad an Menschenverachtung unterstellen kann. Christliche Märtyrer opferten sich bekanntlich aus anderen Überlegungen heraus, nämlich zur Rettung von Mitmenschen oder „heidnischer Seelen" bzw. mit dem Zweck der Bekehrung durch imponierende Leidensbereitschaft. Im Gegensatz zum christlichen Glauben ist daher auch die Bereitschaft unter Muslimen zur Selbstaufopferung eine, die zielstrebig auf die Vernichtung des Gegners und den damit verbundenen Zuwachs an Status zielt.

diesbezüglich in westlichen Ländern allerdings der Glaube, dass der interkulturelle Kontakt grundsätzlich dem Abbau von Vorurteilen dienlich sei und Menschen dadurch auf ihre Gemeinsamkeiten aufmerksam würden, was wiederum das gegenseitige Verständnis erhöhe. So edel dieser Gedanke auch ist, so falsch hat er sich erwiesen, und interkulturelle Kontakte haben meist das Gegenteil bewirkt, weil sie sogar die Einstellungen in vielen Fällen eher negativ beeinflusst haben.[36] Menschen werden sich dadurch nicht nur ihrer Gemeinsamkeiten, sondern auch ihrer Unterschiede bewusst. Vorurteile werden somit nicht nur widerlegt, sondern einige auch bestätigt. In der Tat sind kulturelle Konflikte zwar meist, aber keineswegs immer, das Produkt von „Missverständnissen" oder „Verständnisproblemen". Manchmal sind sich Parteien einig, dass beide das Gleiche wollen – nur auf ähnliche Art, wie die Könige von England und Frankreich sich einig waren, dass sie beide Nordamerika für sich haben wollten und zu diesem Zweck vier Kriege auf dem Kontinent gegeneinander führten. Israelis und Palästinenser befinden sich auch nicht im „Missverständnis", sondern sehen sich beide vor die existenzielle Frage gestellt. Ohne Ausweichmöglichkeiten, geografisch oder durch Abwanderung, haben Bruchlinien oft zu Konflikten geführt und sind multikulturelle Gebilde, bestehend aus inkompatiblen Kulturen, generell Konfliktgebilde.[37] Durch die Anwesenheit mehrerer Kulturen stellt sich in Krisenzeiten viel einfacher die Frage „*Wer* hat uns das angetan?" als „*Was* haben wir falsch gemacht?"[38] Der Verlust jener Konsensfähigkeit, die gerade die kulturell relativ homogenen Gesellschaften zu wirtschaftlich und politisch erfolgreichen Nationen gemacht hat, wirkt sich destabilisierend aus, indem die Transformation zu einer multikulturellen Minoritätengesellschaft auch den Wohlstand und die Regierbarkeit in Frage stellen kann.

4 Eigenschaften der neuen Konfliktmuster

Die Bruchlinien zwischen Kulturen trennen nicht nur Erdteile kulturell auf, sondern zeigen sich durch die Migrationsmuster transferierbar. So sind vergleichbare Bruchlinien mittlerweile durchaus in den meisten europäischen Städten zu finden und ganze Stadtviertel zu Brennpunkten geworden. Folgende Dimensionen sind dabei zu berücksichtigen:

---

[36] Connor, Walker, *Ethnonationalism – The Quest for Understanding*, Princeton University Press, Princeton, 1995, S. 67-68.
[37] Untersuchungen der Weltbank haben gezeigt, dass multiethnische bzw. -kulturelle Staaten kürzere und niedrigere Wachstumskurven haben als monokulturelle.
[38] Vgl. Harrison, Lawrence und Huntington, Samuel (Hrsg.), *Streit um Werte – Wie Kulturen den Fortschritt prägen*, Europa Verlag, Hamburg, 2002.

Schwindende Integrationskraft des Staates: Die erhöhten Integrationsbemühungen, die als wichtigste Maßnahmen betrachtet werden, stoßen an gewisse Grenzen der Machbarkeit. Die Globalisierung schwächt den Nationalstaat und bietet Terroristen Vernetzungsmöglichkeiten und Mobilitätsvorteile ungekannten Ausmaßes. Die kulturelle Inkompatibilität und das ausgeprägte kollektive Selbstbewusstsein mancher Migrantengruppen kommen stärker zur Geltung durch die gleichzeitig schwindende Integrationskraft des Staates. Der „Hunger nach Sinn", der bis Ende des Kalten Krieges durch die nationale Ordnung und deren „Wir-Bewusstsein" gestillt werden konnte, ist zunehmend das Terrain extremistischer Organisationen. Die These, dass der technologische Fortschritt, vor allem dessen Einwirkung auf die Kommunikationswege, die Welt „immer näher zusammenbringt", enthält daher eine selten genannte Schattenseite. In der Tat ermöglichen nämlich gerade diese technologischen Fortschritte ethnischen oder religiösen Minderheiten, den Kontakt zum eigenen Herkunftsland nachhaltiger zu pflegen, als dies früher möglich war. Untersuchungen des Zentrums für Türkeistudien zufolge schauen türkische Jugendliche in Deutschland via Kabel und Satellitenfernsehen fast ausschließlich türkische Programme.[39] Eine Folge ist, dass die deutschen Sprachkenntnisse der Türken der dritten und vierten Generation in Deutschland schlechter sind als die der zweiten, während die Ergebnisse der Integrationsbemühungen sich als ebenso rückläufig erweisen.[40] Eine weitere Folge ist, dass die modernen Medien (Satellitenfernsehen und Internet) auch einen integrationshemmenden Einfluss auf die Einstellungen, Ansichten und folglich das Verhalten ganzer Bevölkerungssegmente haben, dessen Ausmaß und Umfang sich schwer beurteilen lässt, aber denkbar in Konflikt geraten kann mit denen der einheimischen Mehrheit (siehe unten).

Kulturelle Distanz bestimmt emotionale Distanz: Dabei zeigt sich angesichts der Größe der Bruchlinien, dass es durchaus auch kulturelle Grenzen der Integrationsfähigkeit bzw. -bereitschaft gibt. Die Konfliktbereitschaft orientiert sich ebenso an der kulturellen Distanz. Trotz aller Versuche, einen „Kulturkampf" nicht anzuerkennen, gibt es Hinweise, dass ein solcher sich abzeichnet. Umfragen ergeben eine wachsende Skepsis gegenüber dem Islam unter Europäern, während die schon erwähnte Rückläufigkeit der Integrationsindikatoren die Desintegrati-

---

[39] *Der Spiegel*, 14. April 1997, S. 91.
[40] Vgl. Scholl-Latour, Peter, *Allahs Schatten über Atatürk*, Siedler Verlag, Berlin, 1999, S. 267-268. Ebenso Beer-Kern, Dagmar, „Sprachvermögen von Deutsch-Türken", Arbeitsstab der Beauftragten der Bundesregierung für Ausländerfragen, Mai 2001 (http://www.integrationsbeauftragte.de/themen/sprachvermoegen.htm).

onstendenzen verstärkt.[41] Untersuchungen zeigen: Je ausgeprägter die Religiosität unter muslimischen Jugendlichen ist, desto geringer ist deren sprachliche und soziale Integration (siehe unten) in westliche Gesellschaften. In einer Umfrage unter britischen Muslimen im März 2004, jenem Monat des Anschlages in Madrid, erklärten 13%, dass ein weiterer Anschlag durch Al Kaida gerechtfertigt sei.[42] In Deutschland stimmten schon lange vor dem 11. September 2001 57% der türkischen Jugendlichen im Alter zwischen 15 und 21 Jahren der These zu, die wörtlich lautet: „Das Türkentum ist unser Körper, unsere Seele ist der Islam. Ein seelenloser Körper ist ein Leichnam." Gleichzeitig vertraten 41% die Ansicht, dass Gewalt als legitimes Mittel zur Durchsetzung religiöser Ziele für sie akzeptabel wäre, während jeder Vierte der Aussage zustimmte: „Wenn jemand gegen den Islam kämpft, muss man ihn töten."[43] Der Glaube verringerte somit offenbar die Bereitschaft, sich zu integrieren und den Wertepluralismus zu akzeptieren. Auch die Neigung zur Intoleranz und Gewalt unter Jugendlichen nimmt demnach parallel zur islamischen Religiosität zu. Dagegen scheint es, dass sich die Gewaltbefürwortung bei Jugendlichen senkte, je stärker diese sich dem christlichen Glauben zugehörig fühlten.[44]

Die Verbindung zwischen kultureller und emotionaler Distanz zeigt sich auch anderswo. Es entstehen Allianzen unter ehemals befeindeten muslimischen Gruppen, die die Kulturkampfkritiker zuvor nicht für möglich hielten. Im Juni 2002 fand in Teheran ein Führungstreffen von Hizbollah, Hamas, Islamischer Dschihad und der Volksfront zur Befreiung Palästinas statt.[45] Ähnliche Solidarität zeigte der Iran gegenüber den ansonsten verhassten Taliban.[46]

---

[41] Vgl. Heitmeyer, Wilhelm und Anhut, Reimund (Hrsg.), *Bedrohte Stadtgesellschaft – Soziale Desintegrationsprozesse und ethnisch-kulturelle Konfliktkonstellationen*, Juventa, Weinheim und München, 2000.

[42] *Time Magazine*, 20 September 2004, S. 42.

[43] Der Spiegel, 14. April 1997, S. 88. Der Sozialarbeiter Ali Cakir vertrat deshalb schon Mitte der Neunzigerjahre die Meinung, dass deshalb „jeder türkische Jugendliche" in Deutschland eine „Zeitbombe" sei (*Süddeutsche Zeitung*, 7. August 1996, S. 5).

[44] Brauns, Jörn, „Europa vor dem Bürgerkrieg – Der Islam – Thema seit 11.9.2001", unveröffentlichter Vortrag, 2003, S. 2.

[45] Dass sich hier Sunniten und Schiiten zusammen mit Marxisten trafen und die beabsichtigte Vernichtung Israels besprachen, zeigt, dass die durchaus signifikanten inneren Spannungen muslimischer Gesellschaften angesichts eines gemeinsamen Feindes nicht übertrieben werden sollten.

[46] 250 hochrangige Taliban- und Al-Kaida-Mitglieder, darunter Saad bin Laden, ältester Sohn von Osama, fanden nach dem afghanischen Umsturz im November 2001 Unterschlupf im Iran. Behauptungen der iranischen Regierung, denen zufolge die Flüchtigen interniert seien, haben sich als unwahr erwiesen.

Konflikttransfer: Die Migrationsmuster einer sich globalisierenden Welt führen zu einer Verpflanzung von Konflikten, die unter und zwischen den Zuwanderern ausgetragen werden oder sich gegen die Politik des neu beheimateten Staates richten. Die Reaktion der Bundesregierung im Falle Öcalan 1998/99 hat gezeigt, dass dies den politischen Willen und die Rechtsstaatlichkeit im unmittelbaren Interesse der inneren Sicherheit aushebeln kann. Es ist außerdem angesichts der oben erwähnten Meinungsbilder zu beobachten, dass sich dort, wo Zuwanderer sich als Diasporagemeinden verstehen und sich eine gewisse Brückenkopfmentalität etabliert, mehr als nur Sympathie für Terroristen mobilisieren lässt.[47] Der Terrorexperte Walter Laqueur[48] lässt wenig Zweifel aufkommen, welches Konfliktpotenzial die kulturelle Dimension aus seiner Sicht für die westlichen Gesellschaften birgt, wenn er schreibt: „The second and third generation of 'guest workers' – North Africans in France, Turks in Germany, West Indians and Africans in Britain – could be particularly susceptible to the appeal of terrorism [...]". In der Praxis bedeutet dies die Destabilisierung westlicher Innenstädte, die sich immer stärker zu ethnokulturellen „Festungen" entwickeln und für die Ordnungshüter als „no-go areas" zusehends schwerer zugänglich werden. Dies hauptsächlich deswegen, weil sie kaum Rückhalt in einer Bevölkerung haben, die ihr immer mehr zu einem signifikanten Anteil von der gesamten Wertvorstellung her fremd erscheint und sich auf alternative Strukturen verlässt, um als Parallelordnung den Alltag zu regeln. Dadurch werden solche Gebiete zu idealen Rückzugsgebieten, Vorbereitungsräumen und Rekrutierungszentren moderner Terroristen. Gleichzeitig haben Ausschreitungsserien in anderen europäischen Vor- oder Innenstädten auf die Zentrifugalkräfte und schwindende Konsensfähigkeit multikultureller Gesellschaften aufmerksam gemacht.[49] Deren Zusammenstellung, d. h., welche Kulturen sich treffen, bestimmt größtenteils die Stabilität. Der Hinweis des Verfassungsschutzes[50], der zum Thema islamischer Extremismus lautet: „lediglich eine Minderheit (rund 1%) hat sich islamistischen

---

[47] Vgl. Tibi, Bassam, „Zuwanderung muss strenger geregelt werden", *Focus*, 1. November 2004, S. 140.

[48] Laqueur, Walter. *The New Terrorism – The Fanaticism and Arms of Mass Destruction*. Oxford 1999, S.228

[49] Das alljährliche Eid-el-Kabir-Fest der algerischen, marokkanischen und tunesischen Einwanderer im Süden Frankreichs führt dazu, dass rund 8.000 Tiere auf offener Straße rituell geschlachtet werden. Der Einwand der Tierschutzvereine und eine Klage bei der Europäischen Union führten dazu, dass die Franzosen die EU warnten, sie zum Handeln zu zwingen, weil dies zum „Kampf der Religionen" ausarten könne. Schon seit Jahren sind die arabischen Stadtteile französischer Städte de facto islamische Inseln, in denen der Staat nur noch beschränkt Einfluss hat (*Die Welt*, 22. Februar 2000, S. 1).

[50] Verfassungsschutzbericht 2003, Bundesregierung, 15. Mai 2004, S. 170.

Organisationen angeschlossen", deutet eher auf eine massive Bedrohung hin als darauf, dass die Aussage als Beruhigung dienen kann. Denn wären „nur rund 1%" der einheimischen Bevölkerung dem Extremismus uzuordnen, hätte man in Deutschland mit 650.000 bis 750.000 Extremisten zu tun anstelle der rund 28.000, die zurzeit in Erscheinung treten.

Destabilisierung der Sicherheitsorgane: Eine besondere Eigenschaft, die sich bei vergleichbaren Kulturkonflikten erkennen lässt, ist deren Auswirkung auf Sicherheitsorgane, d. h. die Fähigkeit des Staates, seine stabilisierende und konfliktregulierende Rolle zu spielen und die Bedrohung abzuwehren. Abgesehen von deren Schwierigkeiten, ethnoreligiöse Terrororganisationen zu infiltrieren (so berichtet der Verfassungsschutz 2003, z. B. die Anhängerschaft der „Arabischen Mujahedin" sei „für Deutschland nicht bezifferbar") und zuverlässige Quellen bzw. Informationen zu gewinnen, werden sie selbst unterwandert oder gar zum Ziel.[51] Unter Berücksichtigung der besonderen, oben erwähnten Art des modernen Terrorismusphänomens sind folgende Auswirkungen zu befürchten:

1. Effektivitätsverluste unter den Sicherheitskräften: Ethnokulturelle Loyalitäten penetrieren erfahrungsgemäß alle staatliche Strukturen und Institutionen. Hatte das Militär in der Vergangenheit in manchen Ländern für zugewanderte Gruppen sogar als Integrator fungiert, so zeigen sich heute Loyalitätskonflikte bzw. Infiltrationsmuster, die kohäsionsschwächend wirken. Hinzu kommen außerdem die bereits erwähnten Vorbehalte gegenüber der Berücksichtigung von Kultur. Diese kommen Denkverboten gleich, denn die Unvorstellbarkeit des Unvorstellbaren verbindet sich mit der Gewissenlosigkeit des guten Gewissens. Frumm und Perle[52] schreiben dazu: „The CIA is blinded too by the squemishness that many liberal minded people feel about the dark side of third world cultures." Die Konsequenz ist eine verminderte Fähigkeit des nachrichtendienstlichen Frühwarnsystems, die Absichten und Vorgehensweisen von Terroristen rechtzeitig zu erkennen. Für die Spezial- und Kernstreitkräfte bieten sich dadurch weitere Herausforderungen, die nicht zuletzt mit einer Fortsetzung des oben besprochenen Problems zusammenhängen, nämlich der Rolle interkultureller Akteure. Deren interkulturelle Kompetenz wird zweifelsohne benötigt in der Bekämpfung des Terrors. Doch haben sich historisch betrachtet gerade diejenigen, die das westliche Wertesystem sehr gut kannten, als dessen leidenschaftlichs-

---

[51] Schon jetzt müssen Polizeikräfte besondere Vorkehrungen treffen, um ihre Unternehmen geheim halten zu können, was immer seltener gelingt.
[52] Frumm, David und Perle, Richard, *An End to Evil – How to Win the War on Terror*, Random House, New York, 2003, S. 201.

te und gefährlichste Gegner erwiesen. Im Westen gebildete Männer wie Gandhi oder Ho Chi Minh waren die Sieger der Dekolonisierung, weil sie ihren Gegner bestens kannten und gerade durch ihren intensiven Kontakt zum Westen dessen Kultur ablehnten.[53] So standen unlängst im US-Militär Hauptaufklärer gegen den fundamentalistischen Terror in Verbindung mit Al Kaida. Andere Sicherheitsorgane erleben vergleichbare Probleme.[54] Abgesehen von diesen Loyalitätsfragen bestehen keine sicheren rückwärtigen Gebiete mehr. Die Sicherheit der Spezialkräfte sowie deren Familien und Kasernen wird eine größere Herausforderung darstellen als zuvor, und solches Personal ist praktisch immer weniger in der Lage, zwischen „Einsatzgebiet" und „Heimatgebiet" zu unterscheiden, da Letztgenanntes durch demographische Verschiebungen immer mehr zu Erstgenanntem wird.

2. Justiz und Strafvollzugsinstitutionen: Während für die Justiz ähnliche Sicherheits- und Penetrationskriterien gelten, verdichten sich die Anzeichen für eine Verbindung zwischen Islamismus und Gewalt, die nicht begrenzt ist auf die klassische Bruchlinienproblematik, sondern sich ins kriminelle Milieu erstreckt. So behaupten Vertreter des Staatsschutzes, dass ihnen Fatwas vorliegen, „nach denen Muslime sich keine Sorgen machen müssten, wenn sie die angeblich dekadente westliche Gesellschaft der Ungläubigen mit Straftaten überziehen."[55] Unter Berücksichtigung aller bisherigen Erkenntnisse ergeben sich hier demnach drei Problemschwerpunkte, nämlich:

- *Erosion des Rechtsstaates* durch dessen multidimensionale Unterwanderung und aufgrund eines unzureichenden Maßnahmekataloges. Dabei entstehen Fragen um Strafmaß, Bürgerrechte und Zeugenschutz. Wo kulturell relativ homogene Gesellschaften im Westen bisher als liberale

---

[53] Dies ist kein Phänomen der Moderne, denn auch Arminius der Cherusker besiegte die Römer, weil er zuvor selbst als römischer Offizier das notwendige Wissen und das Vertrauen seiner späteren Opfer gewonnen hatte. Die Anführer des Tschetschenenaufstandes haben ähnliche Lebensläufe als ehemalige Sowjetoffiziere, während selbst das US-Militär die Nachhaltigkeit ethnoreligiöser Loyalitäten unterschätzt hat, weil es sich auf die Integrationserfahrungen des 2. Weltkrieges stützte, was sich als nachteilig erwies. Deutsch- und Japanoamerikaner dienten während des Krieges treu ihrer neuen Heimat ohne jegliche spektakuläre oder signifikante Ausnahmen. Eine aus amerikanisierten Japanern bestehende Division kämpfte in Italien.
[54] Das FBI erlebte bei einer Untersuchung die Verweigerung eines Agenten, Gamel Abdel-Hazif, der als eingebürgerter Amerikaner Glaubensgründe anführte, weshalb er sich nicht in der Lage sah, als Zivilfahnder gegen muslimische Terroristen ein Tonbandgerät an seiner Person einzusetzen. Ab Februar 2001 bis zu seiner Beurlaubung Mitte 2003 diente er daraufhin in Saudi-Arabien.
[55] *Der Spiegel*, 44/2004, S. 68.

Konsensgesellschaften bestehen konnten, entwickelt sich in multikulturellen Gesellschaften wegen ihrer inneren Turbulenzanfälligkeit ein stärkeres Bedürfnis nach Recht und Gesetz, das wiederum von einem oder mehreren der kulturellen Komponenten abgelehnt oder subjektiv als „Unrecht" empfunden werden kann. Je multikultureller, desto stärker bilden die schon besprochenen Zentrifugalkräfte Herausforderungen an den Staat – bis hin zu ernsthaften Desintegrationstendenzen.

- *Einschränkung der Rechtsprechung* durch direkte Bedrohung der Justizbeamten. So werden in den USA die Justizbeamten des ersten Anschlages auf das World Trade Center (1992) dauerhaft beschützt aufgrund der hohen Wahrscheinlichkeit, dass sie durch ihren Beitrag zur Verurteilung nun zu den Anschlagszielen der Glaubensbrüder der Täter zählen. Im Gegensatz zu ähnlichen Maßnahmen bei Fällen mit organisierter Kriminalität stellt das Ausmaß und die Dauerhaftigkeit des modernen Terrorismus den Staat hier vor eine viel größere Herausforderung.
- *Destabilisierung der Vollzugsanstalten*, wobei diese nicht nur zunehmend als Rekrutierungszentren genutzt werden[56], sondern sich auch die Frage stellt, ob diese dauerhaft unter Kontrolle gehalten werden können. Selbst oder gerade bei wachsendem Fahndungserfolg wird sich zeigen, ob der Rechtsstaat in der Lage sein wird, die Vollzugsbeamten bzw. deren Familien gegen Erpressung, Nötigung oder andere Repressalien zu schützen.

5 Die Zukunft

Angesichts der bisher geschilderten Sachlage lassen sich die Möglichkeiten der Terrorismusbekämpfung zunächst stark einschränken. Des Weiteren verdichten sich die Hinweise, dass die postmultikulturelle Phase der Beziehungen zwischen den Kulturen in Europa erreicht ist und potenziell destabilisierende Machtverschiebungen stattfinden. Die von manchen propagierte „Gelassenheit" bezüglich des destabilisierenden Potenzials von Terroristen, die sich innerhalb ethnoreligiöser Brückenköpfe signifikante Unterstützung und operative Bewegungsspielräume geschaffen haben und die von den europäischen Sicherheitsbehörden nur begrenzt beobachtet werden können, ist unangebracht. Würde sich in vergleichbarer Größe ein europäisches Gegenpotenzial heranbilden und mit der gleichen Offenheit Gewalt propagieren und praktizieren, wäre von „Gelassenheit" wohl keine Rede.

---

[56] Eine große Anzahl bekannter Terroristen wurde in Gefängnissen rekrutiert (*Der Spiegel*, 44/2004, S. 67).

Gleichzeitig setzt das europäische Wertesystem Grenzen, was die Terrorismusbekämpfung betrifft. Einerseits der Glaube des „Therapeutischen" oder die Einsicht des Anderen durch Toleranz und Diskurs, gepaart mit den Erklärungsmustern der Ursachen, denen zufolge jede Schandtat irgendwie ein „Hilfeschrei" des Gegners ist. Anderseits können Hendryk Broders „Terroristenversteher" sich auf einen gefestigten Kausalitätsrahmen verlassen, demzufolge „Armut" oder „mangelnde Bildung" allem Bösen zugrunde liegt. Die westlichen Erklärungsmuster zeigen sich auch hier als unzureichend. Zwischen Juli 2001 und August 2002 ausgeführte Selbstmordangriffe gegen Israel zeigten folgendes Täterprofil: Zwei Drittel waren unter 23 Jahre alt, nur wenige über 30. Nur 14% waren verheiratet, alle stammten aus kinderreichen Familien, und immerhin 77% hatten einen Oberschul- bzw. Hochschulabschluss.[57] Demographie, Religion und Statusbedürfnis sind die eigentlichen Faktoren, die sich aus diesen Zahlen erkennen lassen, nicht Armut. Wie sooft scheitern die westlichen Beobachter an ihren universalistischen Annahmen und verweigern sich der kulturellen und demographischen Realität, die hier im Zusammenspiel den Großteil der treibenden Kraft darstellt. Doch selbst diese Erklärungsmuster sind ein Beleg für die kulturelle Kluft, denn sie interpretieren das Geschehene durch die eigene „Wertebrille" und verwechseln bei ihrer Erklärung von Selbstmordanschlägen die postheroische oder christliche Opferbereitschaft mit der heroischen und nichtchristlichen.

Im Gegensatz zu ihren Gegnern setzten westliche Staaten auf das Prinzip der gezielten, begrenzten oder minimalen Gewaltanwendung – treu den individuellen Verantwortlichkeitsgrundsätzen und der daraus abgeleiteten Differenzierung bzw. Trennung der „Bösen" von den „Guten". Sie sind durch die überwiegend pazifistische Werthaltung ihrer Bürger auch kaum in der Lage, anders zu handeln, auch wenn sie eine strategische Notwendigkeit schärferer Gegenmaßnahmen erkennen würden. Selbst israelischer Gewalteinsatz orientiert sich an diesen Maßstäben. Eine Studie des International Policy Institute for Counter-Terrorism[58] zeigt, dass 55% der getöteten Palästinenser Kämpfer oder gewalttätige Demonstranten waren, während 80% der israelischen Opfer eindeutig zu den Nichtkombattanten zählten.[59] Obgleich Zivilisten durch israelische Maßnah-

---

[57] Laqueur, Walter, *Krieg dem Westen – Terrorismus im 21. Jahrhundert*, Ullstein Verlag, Berlin, 2004, S. 130.
[58] http://www.ict.org.il
[59] Wobei zu berücksichtigen ist, dass konventionelle Streitkräfte in bebauten Gebieten grundsätzlich eine Gefahr für Nichtkombattanten darstellen, allein schon durch die ballistischen Realitäten. Werden der Einsatz von Kindern und anderen Nichtkombattanten zur Intifada oder als menschliche Schutzschilde für gesuchte Terroristen berücksichtigt, zeigt sich ein anderes Bild. Walter Laqueur (2004: 171) weist darauf hin, dass die

men umkommen, unterscheidet sich dies von der Gegenseite insofern, als dass dies nicht ausdrücklich beabsichtigt wird.

6 Schlussfolgerungen

1. Die Ursachen des heutigen Konfliktes sind im Zusammenspiel der kulturellen Inkompatibilität, der unterschiedlichen demographischen Entwicklung und der durch Globalisierung beschleunigten Migrationsbewegung zu finden. Ein Einstellungswandel und eine Abnahme der terroristischen Bedrohung steht erst in Aussicht, wenn Nordafrika und der Nahe Osten den demographischen Übergang vollzogen haben. Bis dahin gilt die alte Erkenntnis, dass Völker, deren Präferenzen eher in der Familiengründung und Kriegsführung liegen, kaum zum interkulturellen Diskurs neigen, d. h. zunächst ihre Interessen mit Macht durchsetzen.

2. Die Erfahrungswerte aus dem 19. Jahrhundert als Modell zur Integrationsprognose modernerer Zuwanderungswellen führen zu unzulässigen Verallgemeinerungen, weil die jeweiligen Bestimmungsfaktoren der beiden Vorgänge zu unterschiedlich sind, als dass ein Vergleich zutreffend wäre. Die Erfahrung zeigt, dass manche Kulturen sich gegenseitig bereichern, andere sich jedoch bekämpfen. Die Anwesenheit vieler Kulturen bedeutet somit nicht zwingend die Anwesenheit von viel Kultur. Ausdruck dieser Fehlschlussfolgerung ist das Modell „Verfassungspatriotismus" als identitätsstiftendes Alternativkonstrukt, das Herkunft und Kultur theoretisch irrelevant machen soll, weil alle die „Spielregeln" anerkennen und respektieren. Verfassungen sind zwar Regelsysteme, aber keineswegs in sich werteneutral, sondern eben zutiefst kulturspezifisch. Weder die Universalität der Verfassungsliebe noch die Werteuniversalität einer Verfassung, die das Modell unterstellt, lassen sich erkennen, wo die zu integrierenden Kulturen nicht ohnehin schon in ihrem Kern wertekompatibel sind. Es bestehen daher Grenzen der Übertragbarkeit, die sich größtenteils an der kulturellen Distanz messen lassen. Es zeigt sich, dass wenn eine Gesellschaft zum Zweck der Integration besondere Strukturen schaffen muss, sie meist schon gescheitert ist.

Tendenz, Frauen und Kinder als Schutzschilde einzusetzen oder die des Gegners willkürlich zu töten, eine Kerneigenschaft des modernen islamischen Terrorismus ist, und schreibt: „In den Augen der Terroristen des 19. Jahrhunderts wäre es feige gewesen, Frauen und Kinder als Schutzschild zu benutzen oder, ganz allgemein, wahllose, also nicht gegen ein bestimmtes Ziel oder Opfer gerichtete Anschläge zu verüben. Doch solche Skrupel stammen aus einer anderen Zeit und Kultur und von einem anderen Kontinent."

3. Die Eindämmung oder Bekämpfung des Phänomens wird politisch behindert durch die zurzeit üblichen Hoffnungen auf die Integration inkompatibler Kulturen. Der erhoffte Wertekonsens eines solchen Ansatzes orientiert sich zwangsläufig am kleinsten gemeinsamen Nenner aller beteiligten Kulturen. Und der bietet zu wenig, um als ernsthafte Alternative gegenüber Radikalismen wirken zu können.

4. Eine grundlegende Verbesserung der Zuwanderungskontrolle ist unvermeidlich. Das sicherheitspolitische Ziel muss dabei sein, die Verbindungswege für Terroristen finanziell und physisch zu stören und ihnen gleichzeitig die im Text erwähnten Rekrutierungszentren zu entziehen. Technologie, insbesondere biometrische Daten, bietet diesbezüglich eine der wenigen ernsthaften Vorteile, die den westlichen Staaten noch zur Verfügung stehen.

5. Die Abkehr von einer Außenpolitik, die darauf abzielt, multikulturelle Konstrukte zu jedem Preis zu erzwingen, wie z. B. in Bosnien, im Kosovo oder in Afghanistan. Dies führt zu einer Bindung von sicherheitspolitischen Ressourcen an überlebensunfähige Strukturen. Territoriallösungen zu fördern bietet größere Möglichkeiten, denn sie entflechten die befeindeten Gruppen und führen zu staatlichen Akteuren mit legitimen (nicht unbedingt demokratischen) Vertretern und berechenbaren Interessen. Territoriallösungen haben sich bisher als die besseren Konfliktregulierer erwiesen – und zwar nicht, weil sie alle Konflikte lösen, sondern weil sie ihnen Strukturen spenden, die größere politische Einflussmöglichkeiten bieten. Dadurch haben sie sich als nachhaltiger und humaner erwiesen als die von Dauerkonflikten und externer militärischer Dauerpräsenz gezeichneten multikulturellen Konstruktionen.[60]

6. Unser Handeln sollte sich an der Moralität des Resultats und nicht an der Moralität der Intention messen.

---

[60] Kaufman, C., „Possible and Impossible Solutions to Ethnic Civil Wars", *International Security*, 20(4), 1996, S. 160-161.

Nationale und gemeinschaftliche Maßnahmen und Perspektiven / National and Common Measures and Perspectives

Maßnahmen der Europäischen Union zur Terrorismus-Abwehr

Prof. Dr. Heinrich Neisser

Leopold-Franzens-Universität Innsbruck, Institut für Politikwissenschaft

Es gibt keinen Zweifel, dass die terroristischen Anschläge vom 11. September 2001 in den USA innerhalb der Europäischen Union der Terrorismusbekämpfung einen neuen Stellenwert gegeben haben. Sie führten zu einer erneuerten Solidarität zwischen den transatlantischen Partnern im Kampf gegen den Terrorismus und verliehen dem Counter-Terrorismus eine Priorität auf der politischen Agenda der Europäischen Union. Neben einer verstärkten Kooperation im internationalen Bereich verstärkte die Gemeinschaft der europäischen Staaten ihre Anstrengungen, im eigenen System präventiv dem Terrorismus zu begegnen.

Einen noch größeren Schock bewirkten die Ereignisse in Madrid. Die Terroranschläge im März des Jahres 2004 führten den Europäern deutlich vor Augen, dass auch der europäische Kontinent Zielscheibe des Terrorismus ist. Sie haben den europäischen Politikern in drastischer Weise klar gemacht, dass sie um die Erhaltung jener Werte kämpfen müssen, die das geistige Fundament des europäischen Einigungsprozesses sind: Freiheit, Demokratie, Menschenwürde, Menschenrechte und Rechtsstaatlichkeit. Fast scheint es, dass Madrid im März 2004 Europa und die Europäer noch mehr wachgerüttelt hat, als dies nach dem 11. September 2001 der Fall war.

1 Die Entwicklung einer europäischen Anti-Terrorismus-Politik

Die europäische Anti-Terrorismus-Politik wurzelt in einer Entwicklung, die in den 70er Jahren des 20. Jahrhunderts begann. Damals wurde Terrorismus zwar als gemeinsames, aber doch vorwiegend internationales Problem angesehen, das durch zwischenstaatliche Abkommen zu bekämpfen ist (z. B. Konvention zur Terrorismusbekämpfung 1977). Die Bekämpfung des Terrorismus war eine Aufgabe der wechselseitigen Hilfe der Staaten („legal assistance"). Schritte gegen terroristische Gruppierungen oder Personen waren daher reaktiv und nicht präventiv.

Seit dem Vertrag von Maastricht wurde diese Kooperation zur justiziellen und polizeilichen Integration vertieft. Durch die dritte Säule („Zusammenarbeit in den Bereichen von Justiz und Innerem") wurde die Kooperation durch eine gemeinsame Rechtsetzung ersetzt. Strafbarkeit und Strafausmaße terroristischer Straftaten wurden vereinheitlicht, die grenzüberschreitende Verfolgung und die Auslieferungen wurden vereinfacht. Das Auslieferungsverfahren wurde durch einen gemeinsamen Haftbefehl ersetzt und damit die Überstellung an das zuständige Gericht außerordentlich vereinfacht.

Anti-Terrorismus-Politik – das ist jedenfalls der gegenwärtige Stand – ist ein Spezialfall zur Bekämpfung der organisierten Kriminalität, sie wird der justiziellen Kooperation zugeordnet. Im Rahmen dieser Möglichkeiten hat der Rat schon vor dem 11. September 2001 eine Reihe von Beschlüssen und Aktionsplänen akzeptiert, die dem Aufbau eines Raumes der Freiheit, der Sicherheit und des Rechts gegen den Terrorismus dienen sollten. Sie betrafen beispielsweise die Einrichtung eines Europäischen Justiziellen Netzes mit Befugnis bei terroristischen Straftaten oder die Zusammenarbeit bei der Bekämpfung der Finanzierung von terroristischen Gruppierungen.

2 Der 11. September 2001 als Katalysator der europäischen Anti-Terrorismus-Politik

Die Ereignisse vom 11. September 2001 in den USA hatten eine Katalysatorwirkung für die gemeinsamen europäischen Bemühungen in der Terrorismusbekämpfung. Bestehende unterschiedliche Auffassungen wurden zumindest vorübergehend durch kooperative Anstrengungen überdeckt. Schon am 13. September 2001 machte die Kommission einen Vorschlag für einen europäischen Haftbefehl und eine gemeinsame Terrorismusdefinition. Am 20. September diskutierte der Rat einen generellen Plan für die zukünftige Anti-Terrorismus-Politik. Bei Europol wurde eine spezielle Gruppe eingesetzt. Die Europäische Union und die USA gaben eine gemeinsame Erklärung ab. Am Tag darauf erörterte der Rat der Justiz- und Innenminister eine „Anti-Terrorismus-Road Map", die Anfang Dezember beschlossen wurde. In gemeinsamen Standpunkten des Rates vom 27. Dezember 2001 über Maßnahmen zur Terrorismusbekämpfung wurden weitere Schritte gesetzt, erstmals wurde eine „Terroristenliste" veröffentlicht.[1]

Die Verwirklichung von substanziellen Maßnahmen nahm allerdings Zeit in Anspruch. Erst am 13. Juni 2002 wurden vom Rat der Justiz- und Innenminister

---

[1] Verlautbart im Amtsblatt der Europäischen Gemeinschaften vom 18. Dezember 2001 (2001/931/CFSP) L344/93.

zwei richtungsweisende Rahmenbeschlüsse akzeptiert. Der Rahmenbeschluss „zur Terrorismusbekämpfung"[2] enthält strafrechtliche Bestimmungen, der Rahmenbeschluss „über den Europäischen Haftbefehl und die Übergabeverfahren zwischen den Mitgliedstaaten" normiert die Abschaffung der Auslieferung zwischen den Mitgliedstaaten und ersetzt diese durch ein System der Übergabe zwischen den Justizbehörden.[3]

Im erstgenannten Rahmenbeschluss wird nachdrücklich betont, dass der Terrorismus einer der schwersten Verstöße gegenüber den Grundsätzen der Europäischen Union (Würde des Menschen, Freiheit, Gleichheit und Solidarität, Demokratie und Rechtstaatlichkeit sowie Menschenrechte und Grundfreiheiten) sei. In weiterer Folge werden konkrete Straftaten (Angriffe auf das Leben einer Person, die zum Tode führen können; Entführung oder Geiselnahme; Kapern von Luft- und Wasserfahrzeugen oder von anderen öffentlichen Verkehrsmitteln und Gütertransportmitteln; Störung oder Unterbrechung der Versorgung mit Wasser, Strom oder anderen lebenswichtigen natürlichen Ressourcen, wodurch das Leben von Menschen gefährdet werden kann) aufgezählt, die als terroristische Straftaten einzustufen sind, wenn sie mit folgenden Zielen begangen werden:

- die Bevölkerung auf schwerwiegende Weise einzuschüchtern,
- öffentliche Stellen oder eine internationale Organisation rechtswidrig zu einem Tun oder Unterlassen zu zwingen oder
- die politischen, verfassungsrechtlichen, wirtschaftlichen oder sozialen Grundstrukturen eines Landes oder einer internationalen Organisation ernsthaft zu destabilisieren oder zu zerstören.

Ausdrücklich wird hervorgehoben, dass die Verfolgung dieser Straftaten nicht die Pflicht berühre, die Grundrechte und die allgemeinen Rechtsgrundsätze des Artikels 6 des Unionsvertrages[4] zu achten.

Neben der Konkretisierung des Begriffes der terroristischen Straftaten wird der Begriff „terroristische Vereinigung" definiert: Diese ist ein auf längere Dauer angelegter organisierter Zusammenschluss von mehr als zwei Personen, der dazu dient, terroristische Straftaten zu begehen. Die Mitgliedstaaten verpflichten sich, dass Anführer von terroristischen Vereinigungen und die Beteiligung an

---

[2] Verlautbart im Amtsblatt der Europäischen Gemeinschaften vom 22. Juni 2002 (2002/475/JI) L164.
[3] Verlautbart im Amtsblatt der Europäischen Gemeinschaften vom 18. Juli 2002 (2002/584/JI) L190.
[4] Die Prinzipien dieser Vertragsbestimmung sind: „Freiheit, Demokratie, Wahrung der Menschenrechte und Grundfreiheiten sowie Rechtstaatlichkeit."

Handlungen einer terroristischen Vereinigung unter Strafe gestellt werden. Sie verpflichten sich zur Normierung der Strafbarkeit von Anstiftung, Mittäterschaft und des Versuchs terroristischer Straftaten. Auch juristische Personen müssen verantwortlich gemacht werden. Zu erwähnen ist noch, dass der Rahmenbeschluss auch ausdrücklich den Schutz und die Unterstützung der Opfer erwähnt: Die Mitgliedstaaten verpflichten sich, alle Maßnahmen zu ergreifen, die „zur angemessenen Unterstützung der Familie des Opfers durchführbar sind" (Artikel 10).

Beide Rahmenbeschlüsse sind zweifellos bemerkenswerte Schritte auf dem Weg der Europäischen Union zu einer wirksamen Anti-Terrorismus-Politik. Sie entsprechen der im Unionsvertrag im Bereich der justiziellen Zusammenarbeit in Strafsachen vorgesehenen Ermächtigung, eine schrittweise Annahme von Maßnahmen zur Festlegung von Mindestvorschriften über die Tatbestandsmerkmale strafbarer Handlungen und die Strafen in den Bereichen der organisierten Kriminalität, des Terrorismus und des illegalen Drogenhandels zu verwirklichen.[5]

Der Werdegang dieser Rahmenbeschlüsse macht aber auch den komplizierten Entscheidungsprozess sichtbar, der innerhalb der Europäischen Union abläuft. Mehr als neun Monate nach den Vorfällen des 11. September 2001 – die Rahmenbeschlüsse traten am 23. Juni bzw. am 7. August 2002 in Kraft – wurde zumindest eine teilweise Antwort auf die Herausforderungen des Terrorismus gegeben. Dieser relativ lange Zeitraum liegt in der Verfahrensweise begründet, mit der die Europäische Union reagiert: Die primäre Reaktion erfolgt durch den Europäischen Rat, der im Regelfall die Notwendigkeit neuer Maßnahmen verkündet und meist gleichzeitig die Kommission auffordert, Vorschläge zu machen. Die Kommission arbeitet aufgrund dieser Aufforderung Vorschläge für Maßnahmen aus, die dem Rechtsetzungsverfahren zugeführt werden müssen.[6] Dem endgültigen Beschluss des Rates geht im Regelfall eine Reihe von Kontaktnahmen voraus; das Europäische Parlament hat das Recht, eine Stellungnahme abzugeben.[7]

---

[5] Vergleiche Artikel 31 Absatz 1 lit.EUV. Es ist dies ein Teil eines gemeinsamen Vorgehens im Bereich der justiziellen Zusammenarbeit in Strafsachen (so genannte Dritte Säule im Vertrag von Maastricht). Andere Bereiche des gemeinsamen Vorgehens sind beispielsweise die Erleichterung der Auslieferung zwischen den Mitgliedstaaten, die Vermeidung von Kompetenzkonflikten zwischen den Mitgliedstaaten sowie die Erleichterung und Beschleunigung der Zusammenarbeit zwischen den Behörden der Mitgliedstaaten.

[6] Vergleiche dazu Artikel 32 EUV.

[7] Nach Artikel 39 Absatz 1 EUV hat der Rat vor der Beschlussfassung eines Rahmenbeschlusses das Europäische Parlament zu hören. Das Europäische Parlament gibt seine Stellungnahme innerhalb einer Frist ab, die der Rat festsetzen kann und die mindestens

Angesichts der Gefahr zunehmender terroristischer Aktivitäten in der Zukunft scheint es durchaus sinnvoll zu sein, ja geradezu notwendig, über Reformen nachzudenken, die eine raschere Reaktion der Europäischen Union möglich machen und ihr einen breiteren Handlungsspielraum einräumen.

3 Die Madrider Ereignisse vom März 2004 – Schock und Herausforderung

Die Terroranschläge in Madrid im März 2004 haben Europa wachgerüttelt und dem europäischen Kontinent bewusst gemacht, dass auch er jederzeit zum Schauplatz blutigen Terrorismus werden kann. Die Reaktionen erfolgten daher prompt. Noch Ende März einigten sich die Staats- und Regierungschefs der Union auf einem Gipfeltreffen in Brüssel, schärfere Maßnahmen zur Terrorbekämpfung einzusetzen. Sie beauftragten einen Terrorismuskoordinator, der in Zukunft die unterschiedlichen Maßnahmen der Mitgliedstaaten abstimmen soll. Der Holländer de Vries, der diese Aufgabe wahrnimmt, arbeitet beim Ministerrat der Europäischen Union. Dort wurde auch eine Geheimdienst-Schaltstelle eingerichtet, die Informationen über den Terrorismus, die von Polizeidienststellen oder Geheimdiensten stammen, verarbeiten soll. Die Kommission wurde aufgefordert, bis Ende 2004 die Vorschläge über einen Austausch von DNA-Daten und Fingerabdrücken im Rahmen der Ermittlung gegen mutmaßliche Terroristen vorzulegen. Biometrische Daten sollen bis Ende 2005 in Pässe und Visa aufgenommen werden. Für die Speicherung von Daten von Telefongesprächen sowie über die Weiterleitung von Fluggastdaten sollen besondere Regeln ausgearbeitet werden. Ebenso werden Vorschläge darüber ausgearbeitet, wie die Sicherung von Trinkwasser, Strom und Telefonnetzen sowie der Lebensmittelversorgung erfolgen soll.

Im Juni 2004 einigte sich der Europäische Rat auf einen Aktionsplan, der eine enge Zusammenarbeit zwischen nationalen Behörden vorsieht und über 100 Initiativen enthält, die während der niederländischen, luxemburgischen und britischen Präsidentschaft (d. h. von Mitte 2004 bis Ende 2005) umgesetzt werden sollen.

Die Gesamtheit der Maßnahmen lässt sich in vier Schwerpunkten zusammenfassen, die Priorität besitzen:

---

drei Monate beträgt. Ergeht innerhalb dieser Frist keine Stellungnahme, kann der Rat beschließen.

1. Informationsaustausch:Ziel ist ein systematischer Austausch von Informationen und geheimdienstlichen Kenntnissen. Voraussetzung dafür ist eine reibungslose Zusammenarbeit zwischen den Sicherheits- und Informationsdiensten. Diese Informationen müssen dem Rat zur Verfügung gestellt werden unter Anschluss strategischer Analysen und Auswertungen. Europol spielt dabei eine wichtige Rolle.

2. Kampf gegen die Terrorismusfinanzierung:Die Zerstörung der Finanzierungsmechanismen ist ein wesentlicher Beitrag zur Terrorbekämpfung. Die Union hat Listen von Personen und Gruppen angelegt, deren Konten eingefroren werden sollen. Da Terroristen für finanzielle Transaktionen kaum noch das normale Bankensystem benützen, braucht man eine verstärkte Kontrolle der Überweisungen. Einbezogen werden muss dabei auch der Kampf gegen die Geldwäscherei. Die verschärfte Geldwäscherichtlinie dehnt bereits die Meldepflicht für Banken bei verdächtigen Transaktionen aus (auf Notare, Wirtschaftstreibende und dergleichen) und bezieht auch die Finanzierung terroristischer Aktivitäten in das Verbot der Geldwäscherei mit ein.[8]

3. Verstärkte Einbeziehung der Terrorismusbekämpfung in die Außenbeziehungen der Union:Terrorismus als globales Phänomen verlangt eine breite, internationale Zusammenarbeit, um ihn zu bekämpfen. Die Vereinten Nationen sind dabei ein wichtiger Partner in vielen Bereichen. Sie haben zwölf Konventionen beschlossen, die den Kampf gegen den Terrorismus betreffen. Lediglich 57 von 191 Mitgliedstaaten dieser internationalen Organisation haben alle zwölf Vereinbarungen ratifiziert, 47 Staaten haben weniger als sechs dieser Übereinkommen ratifiziert. Es ist ein Ziel der Gemeinsamen Außen- und Sicherheitspolitik der EU, auf eine vermehrte Ratifikation hinzuwirken.Weiters ist eine verstärkte Zusammenarbeit zwischen der EU und den Vereinten Nationen notwendig, um sich gegenseitige Hilfe und technische Unterstützung zu geben.Im Besonderen soll der Dialog mit der Dritten Welt, vor allem mit den besonnenen Muslimen intensiviert werden.Schließlich ist eine Zusammenarbeit zwischen den USA und Europa eine wichtige Dimension einer EU-Strategie der Terrorismusbekämpfung.

4. Verbesserter Schutz der zivilen Bereiche und der Infrastruktur (Verkehr, Energie, Kommunikation):Die Kommission hat angekündigt, im Jahr 2005 ein Programm vorzuschlagen, das den Schutz der Infrastruktur mit grenzüberschreitender Perspektive betrifft. Ebenso soll ein Warnsystem im Rahmen eines Netzwerkes von Experten errichtet werden.

---

[8] Vergleiche RL 2001/97/EG vom 28. Dezember 2001, verlautbart im Amtsblatt der Gemeinschaften 2001 L344,76-81.

Da die Hauptverantwortung für die Anti-Terrorismus-Politik weiterhin bei den Mitgliedstaaten bleibt, hat der Rat der Justiz- und Innenminister ein Evaluierungssystem vorgeschlagen, das im Zusammenwirken zwischen den Behörden der Mitgliedstaaten die Qualität der nationalen Terrorismuskonzepte überprüfen soll. Diese Methode des Peer Review ermöglicht eine schrittweise Verbesserung der nationalen Anstrengungen zur Terrorismusbekämpfung.

4 Die Europäische Verfassung und Terrorismusbekämpfung

Am 29. Oktober 2004 unterzeichneten die Regierungsvertreter der Mitgliedstaaten den Vertrag über eine „Verfassung für Europa". Diesem Ereignis war ein langes und intensives Ringen vorausgegangen, das zunächst in einem eigens zur Vorbereitung eingesetzten Konvent zur Zukunft Europas stattfand. Dieser Konvent begann seine Beratungen am 28. Februar 2002 und legte dem Europäischen Rat von Thessaloniki am 20./21. Juni 2003 sein Abschlussdokument vor. Nach einigen Ergänzungsarbeiten beendete er am 10. Juli 2003 seine Tätigkeit. Die im Herbst 2003 begonnene Regierungskonferenz, die den Verfassungsvertrag beschließen sollte, war mit kontroversiellen Positionen konfrontiert, so dass erst am oben genannten Datum der Verfassungsvertrag unterzeichnet werden konnte. Er muss noch dem Ratifikationsverfahren unterzogen werden, wobei in einigen Mitgliedsländern der EU neben der parlamentarischen Genehmigung noch Referenden durchzuführen sind.

Schon die Konventsdiskussion zeigte, dass die Bereiche ESVP und GASP umstritten waren. Der Verfassungsvertrag brachte jedoch substanzielle Fortschritte in der Begründung einer europäischen Verteidigungspolitik. Mit der so genannten Solidaritätsklausel (Artikel I-43 der Europäischen Verfassung) wird eine klare Antwort auf die Bedrohungen des Terrorismus gegeben: „Die Union und die Mitgliedstaaten handeln gemeinsam im Geiste der Solidarität, wenn ein Mitgliedstaat von einem Terroranschlag, einer Naturkatastrophe oder einer von Menschen verursachten Katastrophe betroffen ist." In diesem Fall sind alle zur Verfügung stehenden Mittel, einschließlich der militärischen Mittel, zu mobilisieren, um terroristische Bedrohungen im Hoheitsgebiet von Mitgliedstaaten abzuwenden, um im Besonderen die demokratischen Institutionen und die Zivilbevölkerung vor Terroranschlägen zu schützen und im Falle eines Terroranschlages einen Mitgliedstaat auf Ersuchen seiner politischen Organe innerhalb seines Hoheitsgebietes zu unterstützen – ebenso im Falle einer Naturkatastrophe oder einer von Menschen verursachten Katastrophe, wenn die Organe des Staates dies wünschen.

Diese Solidaritätsklausel, die durchaus auch als „Terrorismusklausel" bezeichnet werden kann, ist eine späte politische Konsequenz der Ereignisse vom 11. September 2001. Sie ist eine Beistandsklausel, die zu Folgendem verpflichtet:

- handeln im Geiste der Solidarität, wenn ein Mitgliedstaat von einem Terroranschlag bedroht ist;
- die Union mobilisiert im Falle einer terroristischen Bedrohung alle zur Verfügung stehenden Mittel (auch militärische);
- ein besonderer Schutz ist den demokratischen Institutionen und der Zivilbevölkerung zu gewähren;
- auf Ersuchen der politischen Organe der betroffenen Mitgliedstaaten sind diese innerhalb ihres Hoheitsgebietes zu unterstützen.

Diese Solidaritätsklausel signalisiert einen Neubeginn einer Entwicklung in der Europäischen Union. Terrorismusbekämpfung ist zur Verfassungsaufgabe geworden; es ist dies eine Entwicklung, die im Jahr 2001 nicht denkbar gewesen wäre. Diese Beistandsklausel ist in einem Abschnitt enthalten, der die Regelungen über die Gemeinsame Außen- und Sicherheitspolitik zum Gegenstand hat. Das ist zumindest ein Indiz dafür, dass die Anti-Terrorismus-Politik schwergewichtig in den internationalen und militärischen Bereich verlagert wird. Sie gehört nicht mehr nur in den Bereich der Dritten Säule des Vertrages von Maastricht (polizeiliche und justizielle Kooperation). Damit beginnt offensichtlich eine zunehmende Verlagerung in den Bereich der Außen- und Sicherheitspolitik. Terrorismus wird nicht mehr als bloß internes Problem angesehen. Die Verpflichtung zur uneingeschränkten Solidarität ist ein Schritt in Richtung militärische Beistandsklausel. Diese „Militarisierung" der Terrorismusbekämpfung wird noch dadurch unterstrichen, dass die in der Europäischen Verfassung vorgesehenen Missionen[9] zur Bekämpfung des Terrorismus beitragen können, unter anderem auch durch die Unterstützung für Drittländer bei der Bekämpfung des Terrorismus in ihrem Hoheitsgebiet.

Die eben beschriebene stärkere Verbindung zur ESVP bedeutet, dass der europäische Standpunkt immer näher an den der USA heranrückt, wonach Terrorismus primär eine militärische Bedrohung ist, dessen Bekämpfung der Außen- und

---

[9] Artikel III-309 sieht vor, dass Missionen, bei deren Durchführung die Union auf zivile und militärische Mittel zurückgreifen kann, gemeinsame Abrüstungsmaßnahmen, humanitäre Aufgaben und Rettungseinsätze, Aufgaben der militärischen Beratung und Unterstützung, Aufgaben der Konfliktverhütung und der Erhaltung des Friedens sowie Kampfeinsätze im Rahmen der Krisenbewältigung einschließlich Frieden schaffender Maßnahmen und Operationen zur Stabilisierung der Lage nach Konflikten betreffen.

Sicherheitspolitik zuzuordnen ist. Dies hat unter anderem der Hohe Vertreter der GASP, Solana, in seinen Leitlinien für die europäische Sicherheitspolitik deutlich gemacht, worin Terrorismus als strategische Bedrohung bezeichnet wird und dagegen eine offene Verteidigung eingesetzt werden kann; d. h., dass präventive militärische Aktionen gegen Terrorismus auch außerhalb des Gebietes der Europäischen Union möglich sind.

5 Die europäische Herausforderung

Die bisherigen Ausführungen haben gezeigt, dass die Anschläge vom 11. September 2001 als Katalysator einer europäischen Anti-Terrorismus-Politik wirkten. Die Vorgänge vom September 2001 haben Diskussionen ausgelöst, die zur Verwirklichung einer Reihe von einzelnen Maßnahmen führten. Echte Impulse für eine Vergemeinschaftung der Terrorismusbekämpfung wurden jedoch nicht ausgelöst. Die nationalen Staaten bleiben weiterhin der Bezugsrahmen der Anti-Terrorismus-Politik. Angesichts der neueren Bedrohungsszenarien des Terrorismus konzentriert man sich im Bereich der Sicherheitspolitik zunächst auf die Ebene der nationalen Staaten und verstärkt die intergouvernementale Kooperation. Howorth hat diese Reaktion treffend wie folgt charakterisiert: „The most immediately notable feature of European responses to 11th September was renationalisation of security and defense reflexes."

Obwohl die Ereignisse in Madrid im März 2004 einen neuerlichen Schock auslösten, änderte sich an der grundsätzlichen Tendenz nichts. Wohl gibt es Ansätze für eine militärisch und außenpolitisch orientierte Vorgangsweise gegen terroristische Bedrohungen, doch gehört die ESVP nach wie vor zum Bereich der intergouvernementalen Zusammenarbeit. Die Erwartungen konzentrieren sich auf die in der Europäischen Verfassung enthaltene Solidaritätsklausel, deren Umsetzung nach dem Willen einiger Europapolitiker vorgezogen werden sollte, noch bevor der schwierige und in seinem Ergebnis noch unbestimmte Ratifikationsprozess dieses Verfassungswerkes beendet wurde.

Die Effektivität einer Anti-Terrorismus-Politik der Europäischen Union leidet in dreifacher Hinsicht unter strukturellen Mängeln:

- Anti-Terrorismus-Politik ist keine Gemeinschaftspolitik, sie basiert auf dem Prinzip der intergouvernementalen Kooperation. Hinter gemeinsamen Absichtserklärungen steht die Dominanz nationaler Politik.

- In der in der Dritten Säule des Vertrages von Maastricht angesiedelten Terrorismusbekämpfung dominieren die Regierungen. Die demokratische Kontrolle durch das Europäische Parlament hat wenig Bedeutung.[10]

- Die Wahrung der Grundrechte und Menschenfreiheiten ist ein fundamentales Prinzip der EU (Artikel 6 Absatz 1 EUV). Bei allen Maßnahmen zur Bekämpfung der terroristischen Bedrohung (europäischer Haftbefehl, Terroristenliste, Terrorismusdefinition) ist dieser Schutz zu beachten. Besondere Erfordernisse ergeben sich in diesem Zusammenhang für den Datenschutz.

Die globale Reichweite des Terrorismus verlangt auch eine Globalisierung im Bereich der europäischen Außen- und Sicherheitspolitik. Die GASP bedarf daher einer Neuorientierung. Eine Kooperation mit den USA ist unerlässlich. Voraussetzung dafür ist eine engere verteidigungspolitische Kooperation zwischen den Mitgliedstaaten.

Weiters ist eine länderübergreifende Organisation aller Maßnahmen notwendig. Die Durchlässigkeit der Binnengrenzen verlangt ein höheres Maß des Zusammenwirkens von Justiz und Polizei. Dies gilt im Besonderen für die Maßnahmen des Zivilschutzes (Ausbau eines Seuchen-Frühwarnsystems, Herstellung und Verfügbarkeit von Impfstoffen).[11]

Zusammenfassend muss darauf hingewiesen werden, dass Europa in der Anti-Terrorismus-Politik erhöhte Anstrengungen unternehmen muss. Obwohl ein breites Spektrum von Instrumenten zur Bekämpfung des Terrorismus vorhanden ist, fehlen die notwendigen militärischen Mittel. In entscheidenden Bereichen bleibt Europa auf die Zusammenarbeit und Unterstützung der USA angewiesen. Terrorbekämpfung verlangt von der Europäischen Union Reaktionsschnelligkeit, ein Maximum an Kooperationswilligkeit und eine Flexibilität in den möglichen Antworten. Ob dies allein durch ein System gewährleistet werden kann, das sich an den Grundsätzen der intergouvernementalen Zusammenarbeit orientiert, ist fraglich.

---

[10] Nach Artikel 39 EUV ist das Europäische Parlament vor einer Maßnahme vom Rat zu hören. Das Europäische Parlament kann Anfragen und Empfehlungen an den Rat richten.

[11] Vgl. Burkard Schmitt, „Der 11. September 2001 – Herausforderung für die europäische(n) Sicherheits- und Verteidigungspolitik(en)", in: Gustav E. Gustenau (Hg), *Zur Theorie des Terrorismus, Studien und Berichte zur Sicherheitspolitik* (4/2002), Schriftenreihe der Landesverteidigungsakademie des Österreichischen Bundesheeres, 135-140.

Der Terrorismus hat neue Qualitäten entwickelt. Die Gefahr, dass sich Terroristen nukleares Material beschaffen – ein Schwarzmarkt für radioaktive Substanzen existiert – ist durchaus realistisch. Auch Asylwerber mit Terrorismushintergrund können eine Gefahr bilden. Die Bekämpfung solcher Phänomene unter Wahrung der tragenden Prinzipien der Europäischen Union, im Besonderen der Verpflichtung zum Schutz der Grundfreiheiten und Menschenrechte, wird zur Gratwanderung zwischen gegensätzlichen Zielen und Interessen. Gerade darin wird jedoch die Bewährungsprobe der Europäischen Union in Zukunft liegen.

A Hard Day's Night? The United States and the Global War on Terrorism

Thomas H. Johnson and James A. Russell

Department of National Security Affairs
Naval Postgraduate School
Monterey, California
thjohnso@nps.edu, jarussel@nps.edu

1 Introduction

Throughout much of the 20th Century, the international system has exhibited the characteristics, in social science parlance, of a "system dominant system".[1] Interaction of actors within the broader system was governed by the nature of dominant actors themselves. In the post-World War II era, superpower interactions defined and categorized the nature of the overall international system, defined by political scientist as "bipolarity".

During the era of bipolarity, behavioral norms among state actors became routinized around a series of normative rule sets or steady states. The rule sets consisted of a series of explicit and implicit agreements reached by the United States and the Soviet Union. Bipolarity induced a certain aura of confidence by the two dominant actors and the bulk of most other states in the system

---

[1] For Systems Theory, see: J.G. Miller, *Living Systems* (New York: McGraw-Hill, 1978); Ludwig von Bertalanffy, *General System Theory* (London: Allen Lane, 1968); Boulding, K., "General System Theory – The Skeleton of Science." *General Systems* (Yearbook of the Society for the Advancement of General Systems Theory, 1956). For an introduction to general system in the social sciences, see: Walter Buckley, *Sociology and Modern Systems Theory*, (Englewood Cliffs, N.J.: Prentice-Hall, 1967).

For systems theory applied specifically to international relations see: Deutsch K.W, *The Nerves of Government: Models of Communication and Control* (New York: Free Press, 1963); Charles A. McClelland, *Theory and the International System* (New York, Macmillian, 1966); Kenneth Boulding, *Conflict and Defense: A General Theory*, (New York: Harper, 1962); Morton A. Kaplan, *System and Process in International Politics*, (New York: J. Wiley, 1957). For a discussion of the pros and cons of the use of systems theory as a "tool for concept formulation" for the study of international relations see: Mathias Albert, "Observing World Politics. Luhmann's Systems Theory of Society and International Relations". *Millennium: Journal of International Studies*, vol. 29 no. 2

that were either co-opted or willfully joined one of the two camps during the Cold War. Cognitive comfort and consistency flowed from an interstate bargaining framework supported by mirror imaging that created a sense that interstate communications and interactions were bounded by this normative rule set. Conflict erupted when actors violated the established rule sets, most of which were enforced by the superpowers.

Since the demise of the Soviet Union, the global system has increasingly reflected a process of defining a new interactive dynamic that thus far suggests a more important role for subsystems – actors and dynamics seemingly outside of the direct and explicit control of the superpower(s). During the 1990s (and some would argue as early as the 1960s), evidence of the growing salience of subsystem forces emerged as it became steadily more difficult for the remaining hegemon, i.e., the United States, to manage the international environment. Actors engaged in ethnic genocide and other heinous acts that shocked the "civilized" world. When confronted by the United States, instead of submitting to the hegemon's military might, the actors adopted asymmetric tactics as part of a cognitive paradigm that showed little "respect" for the hegemon's statistical superiority or its formidable military capabilities.

Starting roughly in the 1980s, political scientists and historians posited a number of explanations that essentially described the obvious trends in subsystem dynamics. Various schools of thought subsequently emerged that attempted to dissect and understand the dynamics. Samuel Huntington, for example, defined civilizations or cultures as the dominating feature of the international system[2]. and the principal cause of friction within the global environment. A variety of scholars identified resource scarcity and environmental factors as prominent causes of subsystem friction.[3] During the 1990s, the world looked on in horror at the genocide in Rwanda and the brutal ethnic sectarian conflict in the Balkans. Reacting to these events, a school of international relations theory known as "neo-realism" gathered steam. The neo-realists took a dark view of the world– believing that the international system was devolving into the Hobbesian state of nature, where the strong survive and the weak are subjugated.[4] The neo-realists

---

[2] Samuel P. Huntington, "The Clash of Civilizations" *Foreign Affairs, Summer 1993 vol. 72, no. 3, p. 28-50*

[3] Homer-Dixon, Thomas. "http://www.library.utoronto.ca/pcs/thresh/thresh1.htm" *International Security*, vol. 16, no. 2 (Fall 1991) pp. 76-116. Homer-Dixon; Also see Michael Klare, http://www.henryholt.com/2001s-hh/resourcewars.htm (Henry Holt, 2001).

[4] See Robert Kaplan's *Warrior Politics: Why Leadership Demands a Pagan Ethos*, Random House 2002, 198 pp.

argued that the United States should adopt a more muscular and aggressive approach to impose order. To these events, the "realist" school more or less shrugged its shoulders, continuing to believe that no matter how chaotic the international environment that the states remained essentially in a self-help system and remained motivated by self interests and pursued security based on their assessment of those national interests.[5]

The 1990s and the technological revolution created by the internet and personal computers supported the phenomenon of globalization, which became an increasingly powerful force shaping the international system. The increased pace of interaction between states, not-state actors and individuals around the globe layered yet another level of theoretical complexity over the realist arguments.[6] These theoretical distinctions notwithstanding, it is a truism that we live in a globalized, virtual world where physical boundaries between states are declining in importance. Physical distance is becoming less important, but global interconnectivity is creating new, three dimensional spaces and networks that have introduced a new level of complexity to the international system.

Globalization's interconnectivity has created its own systemic dynamic that does not easily fit within existing theoretical models of the international system. With the global system no longer anchored in bipolarity, subsystem dynamics are exerting an increasingly powerful and important role in the international environment. Global networks promise to continue growing as the movement of data, money and people throughout the international system accelerate in the years ahead. But while globalization governed by normative rule sets has made physical boundaries less important in a virtual sense, states remain defined by these physical boundaries and they still exist in identifiable geographic areas. The virtual state is not yet a reality.

But as highlighted by realist theory, it seems clear that protection and oversight over these geographic spaces remain pre-eminent imperatives for states. States inhabit physical spaces and remain charged with protection of these spaces from

---

[5] For statements on realist thought see, Hans Morgenthau, *Power Among Nations* (New York, Knopf, 1966); E. H. Carr, *Twenty Years' Crisis: 1919-1939*, (Perrenial Press, April 1964); For more recent treatments of realism and neorealism see the scholarship of Kenneth Waltz, *Theory of International Politics*, (McGraw Hill, 1979); Also see Waltz's *Man, the State and War*, (Columbia University Press, 2001); John J. Mearsheimer, *The Tragedy of Great Power Politics*, (W.W. Norton 2003); Alexander Wendt, *Social Theory of International Politics*, (Cambridge University Press, 1979).

[6] Lars-Erik Cederman, *Emergent Actors in World Politics*, (Princeton University Press, 1997), 258pp.

internal and external threats. States have addressed defense of their geographic spaces in a variety of different ways, depending on threat perception, the means available for protection, and their evaluation of the overall security environment. Belgium, for example, does not see the necessity of defending itself per se, and has simply integrated itself within the security umbrella offered by its participation in North Atlantic Treaty Organization. In the Persian Gulf, the smaller Gulf States have turned responsibility for their self-defense to the United States. After spearheading the global defense system that outlasted the Soviet Union, the major industrialized states are in the process of restructuring their defense policies to further their interests and offer protection and security to their citizens. This is particularly the case in the United States, which, in the aftermath of the September 11th attacks, has proclaimed a dramatically redefined global security environment and is taking equally dramatic steps to try and realign its internal organizational structures to better address emerging threats.

While it is true that the reorientation of United States defense policy can be tied to the September 11th attacks, it can also be argued that these changes were in fact long-overdue, reflecting a changed international system where new and emerging subsystem dynamics have emerged to drive the overall nature of the broader international framework. What the September 11th attacks simply showed, was how wide the delta had become between the threat environment and governmental institutions that were designed to protect the nation. These dominant institutions remained rooted in behavioral and organizational dynamics that reflected the paradigm of a system dominant system. Stated another way, these institutions continued to reflect the Cold War intellectual paradigm, which had morphed into a sister concept of the United States as global hegemon.

Throughout the decade, U.S. thinking on defense policy, planning and budgeting remained essentially rooted in its historic Cold War experience, but the nature of conflict and warfare had moved on both for state and non-state actors. It is now suddenly a cliché to assert, for example, that campaign-style conventional force-on-force wars are being replaced in the lexicon of the United States security community by a new scheme of conventional conflict called "effects based operations", or "shock and awe" by the press. This scheme of warfare offers the prospect of using force at reduced physical and monetary costs, lower collateral damage and an integrated targeting scheme designed to undermine the opponent's will to fight.

Non state actors have also moved on, with various terrorist organizations embracing a global organizational structure, innovative marketing and fund-raising techniques, and new technologies designed to enhance the lethality of their operations and increase the efficiency of their operational structures. Some terrorist organizations now appear interested in acquiring capabilities to cause mass casualties and disruptions to strategic effect. At least as practiced by Al Qaeda, tactical and localized attacks intended to exert leverage in pursuit of a narrowly defined political objectives seem to have been overtaken by what many describe as a global insurgency.[7]

The changing nature of conflict and the changing nature of actors populating the international environment all bespeak to a changed global security environment. While armed great power conflict is thankfully absent from the international system, chronic instability in the form of ethnocentric and sectarian conflict seems as pervasive as ever. Proliferation of weapons of mass destruction, the continued existence of states operating outside global behavioral norms (the so-called "rogues") and emergent globally-networked terrorist organizations receive particular emphasis in a wide variety of the Bush Administration's strategy documents.

It must be admitted that the United States is still struggling to conceptually bound and define the security environment. While some applaud the Bush Administration's moral clarity in drawing distinctions between good and evil, critics assert that that the so-called Global War on Terrorism (GWOT) remains a conceptual morass that has intuitive appeal for domestic political purposes but which is practically useless as a basis on which to develop strategic guidance that can be used to build plans, policies and programs.[8]

Arguments about the applicability of specific policies, plans, and procedures miss a broader point: that the United States remains conceptually and institutionally mired in a paradigm of a system dominant system that has seen bipolarity replaced by unipolarity, i.e., the U.S. as hegemon. The shift to unipolarity is reflected by continual references in policy and academic circles asserting the salience of U.S. Statistical superiority relative to other states with the accompanying assertions of unparalleled dominance relative to other actors. This statistical dominance, it is argued, affords the United States unparalleled global power

---

[7] See Daniel Byman, "Measuring the War on Terrorism: A First Appraisal", *Current History*, December 2003, vol. 102, Issue 668. Byman notes "As such, Al Qaeda is probably best defined as a religiously inspired, global insurgent movement that often uses terrorist tactics". Also see, "Anonymous" *Imperial Hubris: Why the West is Losing the War on Terrorism*, (Brassey, 2004) for a similar argument.

[8] Jeffery Record, *Bounding the Global War on Terrorism*, (U.S. Army War College, Carlisle, PA, December 2003).

and influence. Data to support this view is readily at hand. The U.S. $11 trillion gross domestic product accounts for nearly 1/3 of the world's total; U.S. defense spending represents half of global totals and far outdistances the combined total spending of any combination of its potential rivals. The United States since 9-11 has experienced the most rapid surge in military spending since the Korean War. No other country in the world can afford a single fighter aircraft that will cost between $250-$325 million each.[9]

Given these irrefutable indicators, it is perhaps not surprising that the instruments of power, organizational and behavioral structures remain rooted in assumptions that the international framework is still defined by its dominant actor, i.e., the United States. This is simply an extension of Cold War logic. But this logic is now disconnected from the system it was originally designed for and does not account for the growing influence of subsystem dynamics. Intellectually, it means the United States is left trying to fit a two dimensional square peg into a three-dimensional undefined space. Hence the United States metaphorically faces the incongruent Lennon/McCartney "Hard Day's Night".

This disconnect is creating a palpable sense of unease in policy and academic elites due to the apparent inability of the United States to translate its position of global dominance upon subsystem dynamics. After all, why can't the United States and its 1.2 million person military (supported by a budget that could top $500 billion in 2005) control the 13-mile road from the Baghdad airport into the city? And why don't the tribal leaders along the impoverished Northwestern frontier of Pakistan and Afghanistan (that has historically witnessed kidnappings and ransoms as a regular social dynamic) avail themselves of the $25 million reward for Osama bin Laden (rumored to be frequenting these climes)?

The troubling implications to these and other subsystem issues suggest that the United States faces a number of profound intellectual and strategic challenges if it is to effectively exercise power and influence the reconfigured global environment: (1) Acknowledgement of the importance of subsystem dynamics as a defining criterion of the evolving international environment; (2) Assessing the threats to U.S. interests based on a corresponding series of assumptions that accept the dominance of subsystem dynamics; (3) Restructuring the nation's institutions to protect and further its interests in such an environment; and (4) Having the political and societal will to execute policies, plans and resources that reflect the realities of a new environment.

---

[9] Estimates for the F-22 drawn from *Tactical Aircraft: Changing Conditions Drive Need for New Business Case*, General Accounting Office, Washington, DC, GAO Report-04-391

The purpose of this paper is to assess the threats the United States faces in the so-called global war on terrorism, or GWOT. In assessing the nature of this threat, this paper will examine a series of implications and characteristics that the threat poses for U.S. policies and counterterrorism strategies and tactics. In defining the nature and characteristics of the threat, this paper will provide a terrorist perspective on the relevant religious, cultural, political, and military domains of the GWOT.[10] Consideration of this perspective can offer a radically different paradigm for suggesting policy prescriptions and implications when compared to those commonly used in policy circles that remain driven by bi- and unipolar assumptions and prescriptions.

Understanding the threat from the perspective of the "terrorist" is challenging and troubling. As will be evident below, such a perspective challenges modal assumptions concerning American prestige, power, and influence as well as the underlying structure of the international system. Indeed, the connotations of many of terrorist perspectives seem to imply that while the United States may very well win each military campaign associated with the GWOT this does not equate with winning a broader war being driven by powerful subsystem dynamics.

2 A New American Strategic Imperative – Counterterrorism

The United States has embraced the idea that there is a new and overriding threat to its interests. Following the September 11th attacks, the Bush Administration released a series of strategy documents all of which indicate that the "global war on terrorism" is now the principal security problem facing the United States, replacing the Cold War as a unifying theme for national security strategy. As noted by President Bush in the introduction of National Security Strategy report: "Enemies in the past needed great armies and great industrial capabilities to endanger America. Now shadowy networks of individuals can bring great chaos and suffering to our shores for less than it costs to purchase a single tank. Terrorists are organized to penetrate open societies and to turn the power of modern technology against us".[11]

---

[10] For a similar methodology and approach to the research question, see: Anonymous, *Through Our Enemies' Eyes: Osama bin Laden, Radical Islam, and the Future of America*, (Washington, DC, Brasseys, 2003).

[11] *The National Security Strategy of the United States of America*, (The White House, Washington, DC, September 2002).

The National Strategy to Combat Terrorism identifies a variety of critical national goals and objectives in the context of the struggle against terrorism: (1) Identify and locate terrorists, terrorist organizations and their command and control and support infrastructure; (2) Deny sponsorship, support and sanctuary to terrorists and ending state sponsorship of terrorism; (3) Establish and maintain an international standard of accountability; (4) Strengthen and sustain the international effort to fight terrorism; (5) Interdict and disrupt material support; (6) Eliminate terrorist sanctuaries and havens; (6) Diminish the underlying conditions that terrorists seek to exploit.[12]

If terrorism represents the principal threat facing the United States, that makes the mission of counterterrorism a pre-eminent organizing principle to build relevant capabilities for those government agencies that have a role in the fight. The United States' counterterrorism policy consists of 4 basic positions: (1) Make no concessions to terrorists and strike no deals; (2) Bring terrorists to justice for their crimes; (3) Isolate and apply pressure on states that sponsor terrorism to force them to change their behavior; (4) Bolster the counterterrorism capabilities of those countries that work with the U.S. and require assistance.[13]

Implementation of counterterrorism policy falls across the variety of different governmental agencies. But it seems clear that the U.S. Military and the Department of Defense will assume prominent roles in execution of the GWOT. Chairman of the Joint Chiefs of Staff, General Richard Myers, unequivocally states that the war on terrorism is the military's top priority in the introduction to the National Military Strategy:

> First while protecting the United State we must *win the War on Terrorism.* The attacks of 11 September 2001 demonstrated that our liberties are vulnerable. The prospect of future attacks, potentially employed weapons of mass destruction, makes it imperative that we act not to stop the terrorists before they can attack again. We must continue to root out transnational terrorist networks, sever their connections with state sponsors, eliminate their based of operations, counter dangerous proliferation and establish a global anti-terrorism environment.[14]

---

[12] *National Strategy for Combating Terrorism*, (The White House, Washington, DC, February 2003), pp. 15-18.

[13] See these objectives as listed by the State Department's Counterterrorism Office at http://www.state.gov/s/ct/.

[14] *National Military Strategy of the United States of America 2004: A Strategy for Today; A Vision for Tomorrow*, Joint Chiefs of Staff, Department of Defense, Washington, DC, May 13, 2004.

While the Bush Administration's strategy documents also universally note that the fight against terrorism will require an integrated government-wide approach using law enforcement, diplomacy, international organizations, strategic communications, and other capabilities, it is fair to say that much of the responsibility for prosecuting a sustained global campaign against terrorists will fall to the United States military – dubbed by one commentator as the new "sheriff" in the international system.[15]

A variety of factors will drive the military's pre-eminent counterterrorism role. The first overriding imperative is that the United States is not conducting a defensive battle that relies on containment and deterrence. All of the Bush Administration's strategy documents clearly indicate the desire to preemptively take the fight to the enemy wherever it is and attack terrorist groups before they can threaten the American homeland. That means fighting forward.

The military's forward deployed global posture developed during the Cold War will figure prominently in a variety of counter-terrorist missions. The Quadrennial Defense Review (QDR) and the National Military Strategy highlight the critical and increasingly important role that these forces will play. The QDR notes that: "Over time, [forward deployed] U.S. forces will be tailored increasingly to maintain favorable regional balances in concert with U.S. allies and friends with the aim of swiftly defeating attacks with only modes reinforcement and, where necessary, assuring access for follow-on forces".[16] Echoing this theme, the National Military Strategy notes: "Combatant commanders, employing a mix of forward stationed rotational and temporarily deployed capabilities tailored to perform specific missions, improve our ability to act within and across borders, strengthen the role of partners and expand joint and multinational capabilities. Posture and presence enhancements also serve to assure our friends, improve the ability to prosecute the WOT [war on terrorism]; deter, dissuade and defeat other threats; and support transformation".[17] The Defense Department is in the process of realigning its global military posture to better address threats in the so-called "arc of crisis" that are widely seen as part of GWOT. As part of the plan, the United States has developed operating areas in the Central Asian Republics and Pakistan, which complement the existing infrastructure in the Persian Gulf.

---

[15] Colin Gray, *The Sheriff: America's Defense of the New World Order*, (University Press of Kentucky, March 2004), 195 pp.

[16] *Quadrennial Defense Review Report*, Department of Defense, (Washington DC, September 30, 2001), p. 20.

[17] *National Military Strategy of the United States of America 2004: A Strategy for Today A Vision for Tomorrow*, op. cit., p. 10.

A second powerful reason driving the U.S. Military's counterterrorism role is means. The Bush Administration's fiscal year 2005 defense budget that will exceed $500 billion (including anticipated requirements for operations in Iraq and Afghanistan) now represents about half of all global defense spending, providing the United States military with resources available to no other country and no other part of the federal government. The U.S. Military remains one of the only organizations in the world capable of conducting sustained operations simultaneously in far-flung parts the globe on the scale that is required. The U.S. Military can do global logistics like nobody else.

A third reason that is defining the U.S. Military counterterrorism role is domestic politics. The United States public is being told by its political leadership that the nation is "at war". By drawing upon a "war" metaphor, the nation's political leadership creates an understandable perception and expectation that the military is engaged in operations to defeat the adversary and defend the homeland. Such an approach seemed clear the day after the September 11th attacks when the Navy was ordered out to sea to patrol the nation's coastlines – although the presence of these ships on the day of the attacks could not have foiled Mohammed Atta and his fellow conspirators. The domestic political pressure to keep the military continuously engaged shows no sign of letting up. And, it has to be noted that, the public wants to know that the billions of dollars lavished on their nation's military are being used to forestall adversaries and protect the homeland – a mission that U.S. Military institutions are embracing with reluctance.

A fourth reason is history. The historical experience and expertise gained during the Cold War in conducting coalition warfare is relevant for combating terrorist groups around the world. The conflict will require a sustained long-term, even open-ended commitment, that will require coalition partners providing access to military facilities and joint operations that will build interoperability on an ongoing basis. The United States constructed these partnerships all over the world during the Cold War – partnerships that will have to be resurrected and maintained over long periods just as they were in the post World War II period. In parallel, the United States will have to re-energize its programs to build host-nation military capabilities through foreign military sales and training – programs that will need to be coordinated through training missions manned with military officers and trained civilians. Building these military-to-military relationships will also involve exchanges in professional military education as well as joint exercises and training, which will again replicate activities developed during the Cold War.

The collective documentation and reorientation of the country's security establishment as highlighted in the Bush Administration's various strategy documents is impressive. But despite the rhetorical embrace of battling new and shadowy enemies, it remains unclear that the cold war security paradigm has in fact been banished to the dustbin of history. The same strategy documents that proclaim the dawn of a new era in the global security environment also proclaim unbridled confidence that the United States maintains its ability to shape and mange and ultimately control the dynamics of the international environment. The documents essentially assert a belief in U.S. hegemonic power.

Interestingly, in 1991 President George H. Bush flirted with the idea of embracing fundamental and structural change in the international environment. Months after the conclusion of the first Gulf War on September 11, 1991 in his "New World Order" Speech, Bush suggested that

> Out of these troubled times... a new world order can emerge: a new era – freer from the threat of terror, stronger in the pursuit of justice, and more secure in the quest for peace... Today that new world is struggling to be born. A world quite different from the one we've known. A world where the rule of law supplants the rule of the jungle. A world in which nations recognize the shared responsibility for freedom and justice. A world where the strong respects the rights of the weak.[18]

In this speech, President Bush expressed intuitive recognition that the era of dominate system actors was drawing to a close – a dramatic departure from the model that have drove the U.S. national security establishment for the last 60 years. Bush's speech recognized and accepted that global subsystems would become the main driver in international dynamics. But this speech was soon forgotten amidst an election campaign fought on domestic issues. The inability of the United States to embrace his ideas has created an overriding sense of confusion and cognitive dissonance that continues to this day. Describing the nation's Cold War adversary seemed relatively straightforward and became intellectually comfortable as this description became part of an overall cognitive belief structure. Today the international environment is characterized not by cognitive consistency but by cognitive dissonance.

President Bush's speech proved prescient. During the 1990s, the ascendancy of subsystem dynamics became apparent. In Somalia, the United States confronted

---

[18] Speech as reprinted in George Bush and Brent Scowcroft, *A World Transformed*, (New York, Knopf, 1998) p. 370.

a discombobulated landscape and a foe that appeared manifestly unimpressed by U.S. Military capabilities. Aideed's militias showed no regard for the human cost of confronting the United States, bloodied the U.S. Military's nose using asymmetric tactics and convinced President Clinton that further intervention was pointless. With the searing experience of Somalia still figuring prominently, the United States stood on the sidelines in Rwanda and again watched in disbelief as one tribal actor turned on another in a brutal genocide. In the Balkans, the United States once again confronted a subsystem dynamic that defied the Cold War rule sets, though it did eventually lead an international coalition to stop the conflict by deploying force to separate the warring parties. The rest of the decade saw the U.S. Military engaged around the world in what became derisively known (in the military) as Military Operations Other than War, or MOOTW. During the election campaign in 2001, candidate George W. Bush indicated his commitment to put an end to these messy and open-ended operations that were chewing up manpower, money and equipment.

The September 11 attacks of course changed this approach. In his address to a joint session of Congress nine days after September 11 attacks, President George W. Bush suggested that the world envisioned by his father 10 years earlier had been turned upside down and he darkly warned states harboring terrorists to:

> Deliver to the United States authorities all the leaders of al Qaeda who hide in your land. Release all foreign nationals, including American citizens, you have unjustly imprisoned. Protect foreign journalists, diplomats and aid workers in your country. Close immediately and permanently every terrorist training camp in Afghanistan, and hand over every terrorist, and every person in their support structure, to appropriate authorities. Give the United States full access to terrorist training camps, so we can make sure they are no longer operating.... Every nation, in every region, now has a decision to make. Either you are with us, or you are with the terrorists.[19]

Bush's stark words provided a harbinger of the initial conceptual outlines of what would become known as GWOT – the central priority of U.S. national security policy. Two weeks after delivering this speech, the U.S. attacked the Taliban and al Qaeda – initially named *Operation Infinite Justice*. Protests from Muslim countries lead to the changing of the mission's name to *Operation Enduring Freedom* (OEF) on 25 September 2001.

---

[19] George W. Bush, Address to a Joint Session of Congress and the American People, September 20, 2001. http://www.whitehouse.gov/news/releases/2001/09/20010920.html (Accessed November 15, 2004).

The initial overwhelming international support for OEF and the United Nations' endorsement of a renewed global effort against terrorists seemed to signal a new global coalition lead by the United States to reimpose order in the international system. Today, however, the United States finds itself in a position of international isolation and even obloquy. It seems inconceivable to many that United States policies based on President Bush's formulation that "Freedom is the non-negotiable demand of human dignity; the birthright of every person — in every civilization"[20] are not being embraced around the world. Instead the United States is confronted by powerful subsystem dynamics manifesting as an ideology that casts what seem like noble, moral and universal truths as secondary to imperial ambition, cultural and religious subjugation and support for tyrants and dictators.

In short, the United States remains intellectually suspended between competing universes that are defined by fundamentally opposed views of the nature of the global system. The United States believes in itself as the hegemon, while much of the rest of the world marches to the beat of the global subsystem drummer. The intellectual bridge between these competing universes lies for the United States in returning to Sun Tzu's age-old strategic axiom of "know thy enemy".

3   Understanding the Threat

> "Jihad" is as essential to Islamic identity and self-definition as the Mass is to Catholicism
> - *Historian Malise Ruthven*[21]

> "The focus of the U.S. is against the concept of jihad. Jihad in Islam is one of the greatest actions to repulse tyranny and to restore justice and rights"
> - *Dr. Mohammed Abd al-Hali, Cairo's al-Azhar University*[22]

> "[Global trends] are working against the notion that a nation strongly armed is adequately shielded against all threats to it and its interests. . . Even today, knowledge of one's enemy and his culture and society may be more important than knowledge of his order of battle".
> - *Retired Vice ADM Arthur Cebrowski*[23]

---

[20] National Security Strategy Report, foreword as signed by President Bush.
[21] Malise Ruthven, *A Fury for God: The Islamicist Attack on America*, (London: Granta Books, 2002), p. 246.
[22] Dr. Mohammed Abd-al-Halim Umar, "The United States has begun its War against Islam", *Lailatalgdr* (internet version), March 21, 2002.
[23] *Inside the Pentagon*, 28 October 2004.

The United States has only recently begun to recognize the nature of the threat it is facing in GWOT. As argued in the 9-11 Commission Report, prior to September 11th attack the U.S. did not understand its enemy and did not give significant weight to the terrorist threat.[24] While significant improvement has been realized in threat recognition since the 9-11 report, the Bush Administration still appears confused about the nature and implications of the *jihad* or Muslim insurgency. The most realistic and best official description of the phenomenon appears in the recent draft *Joint Operational Concept for Defeating Terrorist Organizations (JOC-DTO)* 14 November 04.[25] This is a planning document being drafted by the Special Operations Command in Tampa, Florida. Once finalized, the document will form the basis for the development of joint capabilities throughout the Defense Department to defeat terrorist organizations. These capabilities will, in turn, form the basis for programs and budgets. The JOCs being developed throughout the nation's military institutions are part of the Defense Department's implementation of capabilities-based planning.

There is little argument that the United States is facing a *jihad* that is perceived by its proponents as a holy and just war to defend the Muslim faith. This *jihad* is a world-wide, primarily Arab[26], insurgency that is *not* based on merely terrorist acts or acts of criminality. Nor is this *jihad* based on or represented by oft repeated Bush Administration rhetoric that the "terrorist evil doers" act because of their hate for democracy or American freedoms. Such beliefs represent not only impoverished and inaccurate views of the threat but also trivialize the threat implications and obscure appropriate policy prescriptions and actions.[27]

A more nuanced view is being developed by the Special Operations Command, or SOCOM. The *JOC-DTO* states, "Despite the use of modern technologies by all parties, the fundamental nature of this war is an insurgency – a struggle for popular perceptions of political legitimacy and control over Islamic civilization

---

[24] "The 9-11 Commission Report: Final Report of the National Commission on Terrorist Attacks Upon the United States," (W.W. Norton and Co, 2004).

[25] Draft Joint Operational Concept for Defeating Terrorist Organizations (JOC-DTO) 14 Nov 04, Special Operations Command, Tampa, FL. We will refer to this document as the JOC-DTO.

[26] Bin Ladin's message appeals mostly to Sunni Muslims and Arabs.

[27] Much of the argument here is based on the controversial thesis developed by Michael Scheuer, a 22-year veteran of the CIA and once head of the agency's Osama bin Laden Unit and published in Anonymous, "Imperial Hubris: Why the West is Losing the War on Terrorism," (Washington, DC, Brass, 2004). Also see: Daniel Benjamin and Steven Simon, "The Age of Sacred Terror: Radical Islam's War Against America," (Random House, 2003).

that extends beyond national borders".[28] SOCOM's realization of the nature of the threat provides a healthy and welcome departure from simplistic sound-bytes delivered in press conferences and talk shows by senior administration officials.

Intellectual precision as to the nature of the threat and difficulties facing the United States in mitigating the threat is critical. Taking a cue from the adversary could be instructive.

> *The true believers fight for the cause of Allah, but the infidels fight for the devil. Fight then against the friends of Satan.*
>
> Koran 4:75

For example, bin Laden has been extremely precise when he states that he is waging a holy war against the United States.[29] This war is not necessarily directed at American freedoms, liberty[30], or democracy[31]. However, from the perspective of many Muslim theocrats democracies and socialist governments undermine Islam in traditionally Muslim countries/areas.[32] The goal of these adherents is to see Allah's religion reign supreme over the entire world. That means the establishment of Muslim theocracies. In order to do such democracies, socialist and any other form of government must eventually be destroyed. Key to understanding the *jihadists'* beliefs is their view that polices of the United States and its apostate Muslim friends[33] are directly aimed

---

[28] *JOC-DTO*, 14 November 2004 pp. 7.

[29] For example see his, "Declaration of War Against the Americans Occupying the Land of the Two Holy Places", Originally published in *Al Quds Al Arabi*, August, 1996 and redistributed in 1998.

[30] Muslim *jihadists* and theocrats do desire the elimination of some of the western "liberties" because such are perceived as sin and wickedness such as alcohol, illicit sex, promiscuity on T.V.and in movies, magazines, etc.

[31] Bin Laden desires the establishment of Muslim theocracy/theocracies. In that sense, he is against Western concepts of democracy, especially in traditionally Muslim held regions. But he and other Muslim theocrats are not confined to commonly recognized borders. The establishment of Muslim theocracy anywhere and everywhere is a goal.

[32] Muslim theocrats hate both U.S. actions and those western values that are perceived as sin/wickedness. From a Muslim theocrat's perspective there is no separation between values or beliefs and actions. A person's or society's values or beliefs guide its actions. If the values or beliefs are wrong or wicked then the actions will be wrong or wicked.

[33] According to Al Qaeda the following Muslim leaders are considered apostate Sadat, Hosni Mubarak, Gadafi, Hafez Assad, Saleh, and Fahed. See: The Al Qaeda Training Manual, UndatedUK/BM-8 Translation. (The manual was located by the Manchester (England) Metropolitan Police during a search of an *al Qaeda* member's home. The manual was found in a computer file described as "the military series" related to the "Declaration of Jihad".)

at harming and undermining "true" Islam and its faithful.[34] Muslim extremists primarily hate and attack the United States because of their perception of U.S. actions not American values.[35]

Bin Laden and other *jihadists* sincerely believe that the West and primarily the United States represents a mortal danger to Islam. In the *jihadist's* eyes U.S. policy and actions irrefutably confirm this belief. The United States supports and mandates the Zionists to continue their occupation of Palestine[36]; U.S. troops remain in Saudi Arabia, the land of the two holy shrines; the United States supports apostate tyrants[37]; the United States "occupies" Afghanistan and Iraq and threatens Syria and Iran; the United States is establishing bases in the Middle East, the Gulf, and South and Central Asia; the United States steals Muslim natural resources, most prominently oil, and; quite simply American and Western corruption threatens Muslim souls. In the eyes of *jihadists*, the United States has become the restorer of European 19th and 20th Century colonialism and *jihad* is the only antidote to the United States and its explicitly hostile policies towards Islam. Bin Laden and other *jihadist* insurgents "mean exactly what they say: to them America is the font of all evil, the 'head of the snake,' and it must be converted or destroyed".[38]

> *Prophet rouse the faithful to arms.*
>
> Koran 8:65

---

[34] Examples cited by bin Laden and other *Jihadists* include: Hindu India in Kashmir; Catholic Filipinos in Mindanao; Orthodox Christian Russians in Chechnya; Uzbek ex-communists in Uzbekistan; Chinese communists in Xinjiang Province; Apostate al-Sauds in Arabian Peninsula; Israeli Jews in Palestine.

[35] See: Anonymous, *Imperial Hubris*. Op. cit.

[36] The importance of U.S. Middle Eastern policy promoted over the last 30 years to the present GWOT cannot be overstated. Pakistani President Musharraf, for example has recently argued that the United States must more aggressively press for resolution of the Israeli-Palestinian conflict which "is the source of all problems". He has argued that the resolution of this very difficult and long-standing problem is key to defusing tensions in Iraq, Afghanistan and elsewhere in the Islamic world (*Washington Post*, December 5, 2004, p. A22).

[37] Apostate and corrupt Islamic Governments cited by *jihadists* include: Kuwait; The UAE; Egypt; Jordan; Pakistan; and Saudi Arabia.

[38] *The 9-11 Commission Report*, p. 362. op. cit.

What makes the *jihadists'* convictions so threatening and problematic are that they are based on the belief that they are fighting a defensive *jihad* against the United States and its allies.[39] Moreover, this defensive *jihad* is revealed by *Allah* in the Koran and the *Sunnah* [40] and thus not subject to interpretation. Islam has been attacked and it is the personal duty and responsibility of every Muslim to fight back to the death if necessary. A lack of a response to this attack by an individual Muslim in the eyes of bin Laden and other *jihadist* insurgents is tantamount to sin and eternal damnation. These are powerful motivating forces and cannot be taken lightly by policy responses, strategies or organization.

> *Never think that those who were slain in the cause of Allah are dead. They are alive and well provided for by their Lord...*
>
> Koran 3:169

The JOC-DTO analyses the nature of the threat in a similar fashion, but while it argues that the GWOT is really a war against a global insurgency, the JOC-DTO states that the individual *jihadist* does not view him or herself as an insurgent. The DoD defines an insurgent as a "Member of a political party who rebels against established leadership".[41] The JOC-DTO argues that individual *jihadists*

> "[d]o not see themselves as terrorists or even as political insurgents, but rather as holy warriors engaged in a heroic and epic struggle inspired by an all-encompassing religious *mythos*. [The *jihadists*] are motivated by a different morality than we are accustomed to in the Western world. They interpret Islamic law literally and without regard for its historical context. They do not recognize international (Western) laws of war or any Western notions of morality that contradict Islamic law. [They] believe that:
>
> [1] Uniquely Islamic rhythms of history compel them to pursue violent change to restore Islam after generations of corruption.
>
> [2] Islam is under attack by the West and that it is their holy obligation to defend their faith against this attack.
>
> [3] Their cause is just and right-minded and that their victory is preordained and inevitable.
>
> [4] The act of struggle itself is a triumph that unites them with God; they cannot be defeated, as the West defines the term, so long as they continue the perpetual struggle.

---

[39] *JOC-DTO* p. 9 refers to the conflict as a "defensive jihad designed to protect Islam from Western attack".

[40] The Sunnah is the sayings and traditions of the prophet Mohammed.

[41] Joint Publication 1-02 , *DoD Dictionary of Military Terms.*

[They] do not recognize the Western concept of statehood or the Western concept of state monopolies on the legitimate use of political violence. [They] do not recognize any distinction between religion and politics. [And they] do not apply Islamic prohibitions against unlimited warfare to those Muslims or non-Muslims who live their lives outside our enemies' literal and intolerant interpretation of Islamic law".[42]

American Islamic scholar Professor Bernard Lewis has argued that "Islam is not only a matter of faith and practice, it is also an identity and a loyalty – for many an identity that transcends all others".[43] The United States faces a *jihadist* mentality that transcends the individual and which reflects the *jihadist's* views of the tenets of his core faith and personage. The unalterable law of *Allah* is the source of response.

> *Believers, when you encounter infidels on the march, do not turn your backs to them in flight. If anyone on that day turns his back to them, except for tactical reasons, or to join another band, he shall incur the wrath of Allah and Hell shall be his home: an evil fate.*
>
> Koran 8:15

What more powerful motivating temporal or spatial force could the United States face? And militarily conquering a state or occupying a nation's capital cannot defeat this force. For this is truly a transnational *jihadist* movement. It is not contained within any border or borders. This *jihadist* mentality some argue reflects the style of pre-Islamic warfare on the Arabian Peninsula and results in a perpetual condition of warfare and not a finite undertaking of a war. This conception flies in the face of western linear conceptions of conflict and war.

> *Make war on them until idolatry shall cease and Allah's religion shall reign supreme.*
>
> Koran 8:39

The Bush Administration's statements that terrorists are motivated primarily by their hate of our freedoms and democracy are matched to a public diplomacy and information campaigns directed at "educating" the Muslim masses of the true nature of the United States.[44] This public diplomacy campaign is destined

---

[42] *JOC-DTO*, pgs. 8-9.
[43] Bernard Lewis, "The Crisis of Islam: Holy War and Unholy Terror," (New York: The Modern Library, 2003), p. 17.
[44] There is also a public diplomacy campaign not directed at the Muslim theocrats but at the "apostate" governments and "apostate" Muslims. It is designed to keep the

for failure, since it fails to reflect an appreciation for the subsystem dynamics that are defined by the *jihadist's* hate that, from the U.S. perspective, can only be met by direct and violent military actions.

> *Whether unarmed or well equipped, march on and fight for the cause of Allah...*
>
> *Koran 9:41*

The *Jihadists* initial aim is deterring the United States militarily (including WMD) from attacking things they love – their faith, brethren, and land. There is little convincing evidence to suggest that they view violence and conflict as an end in itself.

Do Muslim theocrats want peace? Absolutely. But peace is not defined as the absence of armed conflict. Violence and conflict is one side of the *jihad*. Converting and establishing theocracies is another side of the *jihad*. There can be no peace for the Muslim theocrat while wicked sinners and idolatrous religions and secular governments exist. Peace is the resultant that occurs after the enemies of Allah have be killed or converted and Allah's religion reigns supreme. From the Muslim theocrat's perspective only then will there be peace. This is the nature of the threat that the U.S. faces.

4 Reactions to the Threat

On 16 October 2003 Defense Secretary Donald Rumsfeld raised a series of critical questions concerning the United States and the GWOT to the Defense Department's senior staff.[45] Rumsfeld's memo expressed concern about the ability of the U.S. to execute and win the GWOT. The well-formulated and profound questions in fact reflect a deeper intellectual confusion over the nature of the threat and its implications for strategy, policy and organizational structure. Rumsfeld, for example, asked:

- Are we winning or losing the Global War on Terror?
- Is DoD changing fast enough to deal with the new 21st century security environment?
- Can a big institution (such as DoD) change fast enough?

"apostates" from joining the Muslim theocrats hence, diminishing the support to and size of the Muslim theocratic movements.

[45] See: Secretary of Defense Donald H. Rumsfeld, Memo on the *Global War on Terrorism* published in U.S. Today On-Line http://www.usatoday.com/news/washington/executive/rumsfeld-memo.htm (Accessed 10/21/2003).

- Is the United States government changing fast enough?[46]

Implicitly recognizing the immense implications of GWOT on the U.S. Military and defense strategy, Rumsfeld comments that, "DoD has been organized, trained and equipped to fight big armies, navies and air forces. It is not possible to change DoD fast enough to successfully fight the global war on terror; an alternative might be to try to fashion a new institution, either within DoD or elsewhere – one that seamlessly focuses the capabilities of several departments and agencies on this key problem"[47]. Months earlier Rumsfeld raised similar issues when he wrote in the *Transformation Planning Guidance* that "[t]he war on terrorism is a transformational event that cries out for us to rethink our activities, and to put that new thinking into action". Rumsfeld defined transformation as "a process that shapes the changing nature of the military's competition, capabilities, people and organizations that exploit our nation's advantages and protect against our asymmetric vulnerabilities".[48]

The implications of Rumsfeld's queries remain important. The assumptions underlying his questions are central to the argument of this paper: that the United States remains intellectually and organizationally rooted in an outmoded view of the international system. Rumsfeld's disquiet, it could be argued, flows from an intuitive recognition that the structure of the international system has moved on, creating the mismatch between that system and U.S. institutions designed to manage that system.

5 A Military Conundrum: Missions and Requirements

Despite the relevance of certain aspects of the Cold War experience, the U.S. Military faces a much more complicated and even contradictory set of mission requirements as part of GWOT. These basic missions can be summarized as follows:

- Deny sanctuary to terrorist groups afforded by state sponsors and geographic areas outside the control over central governments. This latter category entails operations in some of the most remote and lawless areas of the world, such as the tri-border region in South America, the Horn of Africa, the Central Asian Republics and the tribal border areas of Pakistan and Afghanistan. It also means maintaining a series of active and ongoing

---

[46] Ibid.
[47] Ibid.
[48] Secretary of Defense Donald H. Rumsfeld *Transformation Planning Guidance*, April 2003.

military activities in support of a political coercive and compellant framework designed to prevent states from supporting terrorist groups.

- Identify, track and destroy terrorist groups before those groups can mount attacks on the U.S. homeland. This mission will be accomplished by forward-deployed surveillance assets, allowing quick targeting and destruction of identified targets – preferably at standoff ranges using the new family of precision guided munitions, and, if necessary force-on-force engagements using special operations forces or forward deployed conventional forces.
- Work with coalition partners in forward operating areas to defeat terrorist groups, with particular emphasis on those countries being threatened by insurgents.
- Engage in psychological and information operations that will discredit Islamist ideologies that are at the core of the insurgent ideology.
- Help create conditions in which terrorist groups lose their legitimacy and base of support within the broader population. This returns the military to its MOOTW functions, involving the military in law enforcement, road building and other so-called "stability" operations.
- Retain the flexibility to engage in a variety of forms of warfare, ranging from conventional military operations to "irregular" or counterinsurgency operations.
- Collect intelligence that in all the targets in forward operating areas.

These mission sets create a series of problems for the U.S. Military. The fundamental contradictions in any counterinsurgency strategy are clearly evident in the military requirements. The military is being directed to conduct information operations to delegitimize the adversary while it must simultaneously destroy the adversary using tactics and techniques that undermine the ability to conduct the information side of the campaign. This phenomenon is on vivid display in Iraq right now. The fundamental counterinsurgency conundrum is also exacerbated by the widespread view that battling the Al-Qaeda ideology is considered not primarily a military problem.

Despite efforts to elevate the role of special operations forces, the U.S. Military remains largely organized, equipped and trained to fight a large-scale conventional war. The GWOT requirement to exert control over remote geographic spaces necessitates conducting widespread stability operations inside these divergent locations in order to mitigate the conditions where terrorist grow and flourish. These operations cannot be accomplished on the scale necessary with the current organizational structure. The U.S. Military resembles a vat with its tap located at the top; each time the vat is tapped for those forces that are needed the most in MOOTW missions – military police, civic affairs specialists and training experts. The bulk of the "combat" force remains underutilized, while those elements at the top of the vat and needed for the GWOT are overburdened, under funded and ill equipped for the mission. Despite Secretary Rumsfeld's efforts to "transform" the military, the organizational structures remain grounded in a platform-centric approach to conflict and warfare. Platforms continue to drive planning, programming and budgeting within the $500+ billion Defense Department budget.

The United States military remains ill prepared to conduct operations in culturally opaque regions in the world. Fifty years of Soviet-centric study and education have left an education and training structure that must be geared up to provide language and cultural awareness on a wide-scale for intelligence analysts, officers and enlisted personnel. In Iraq, for example, commanders still face shortages of translators and personnel grounded in the region's history and culture. Correcting these steps on an institutional level will take no less than a paradigm shift for the U.S. Military, which currently de-emphasizes regional and cultural expertise. In most U.S. Military organizations, seeking this expertise is a career-limiting move for personnel.

GWOT requirements entail nearly continuous operations conducted on a global scale, straining the readiness of forces that are equipped for campaign-style linear operations that have a beginning and an end. This is particularly the case in the Navy, which has historically been driven by a maintenance cycle founded upon the idea that aircraft carriers could remain at sea for 6 months, followed by an 18-months of in-port maintenance. The Navy is now moving towards something called global CONOPS, or global concept of operations, in which this historic cycle has been broken. It is unclear whether and how long the Navy can function in an environment requiring continuous operations and maintenance-intensive high readiness levels and correspondingly difficult manning and personnel issues.

6 Implications of the Threat

There is little doubt that the GWOT involves a threat domain radically different to those traditionally faced by U.S. Military that at its root is based on new subsystem dynamics within the international system. And as Secretary Rumsfeld implies in the aforementioned memo as well as in his "transformation planning guidance", the threats and associated dynamics of the GWOT require new institutional, doctrinal, and structural changes within DoD.[49] The purpose of the next section of this paper is to assess the implications these threats represent to U.S. counter terrorism policy and policy instruments.

Relevant Beliefs and Perception are Zero-Sum Games. The United States was originally founded by refugees of religious persecution. The basic belief that society and polity is best served by a separation between church and state has become an engrained staple of American political and social belief. Islam, the source of the *jihadists*, however, has a radically different view. For the average Muslim, and profoundly for the *jihadist*, religion is the source of all moral support, the basis for regulating conflict and the foundation for all governmental organization and law, and ultimately the justification for war. Indeed, for the Muslims the separation of religion and government is apostasy for the simple and seemingly profound reason that only *Allah* makes laws not man. Bin Laden clearly suggested the differences in the two belief systems when he wrote in his "2002 letter to Americans" that "[Americans] rather than ruling by the law of Allah, chose to implement your own inferior rules and regulations, thus following your own vain whims and desires. You run a society contrary to the nature of mankind by separating religion from your politics".[50]

Al-Qaeda's Training Manual addresses its belief on the congruency of the entirety of religious and political life when it states:

> "Allah realized that Islam is not just performing rituals but a complete system: Religion and government, worship and Jihad [holy war], ethics and dealing with people, and the Koran and sword. The bitter situation that the nation has reached is a result of its divergence from Allah's course and his righteous law for all places and times. That Allah realized that Islam is not just performing rituals but [bitter situation] came about as a result of its children's love for the world, their loathing of death, and their abandonment of Jihad [holy war]".[51]

---

[49] Secretary Rumsfeld was recently quoted: "The enemy is operating in smaller cells with every bit as lethal capabilities as we have, but they can turn on a dime. . . . We've got to find ways to be much swifter and more adept" at everything from attacking enemy fighters to spending money to build local security forces and reconstruction projects. Quoted in Greg Jaffe, "Rumsfeld's Gaze is Trained Beyond Iraq", *Wall Street Journal*, December 9, 2004, p. 4.

[50] Bin Laden's Letter to America, 2002.

[51] *The Al Qaeda Training Manual*, UndatedUK/BM-8 Translation. (The manual was located by the Manchester (England) Metropolitan Police during a search of an *al Qaeda*

In the context of such conflicting belief systems, perceptions concerning all aspects of social and political life become absolutely critical. Consider, for example, the case of Islamic educational centers or *madrassas*. While the United States advocates what it believes to be the reasonable reform of *madrassas'* curriculum that it believes ferments hatred of modernity and the West, such policy prescriptions are viewed by many Muslims as American demands for Muslim's to abandon Allah's law for man-made law. When the United States asks Pakistan and Saudi Arabia and other Muslim regimes to limit, track, and control Muslim tithing that assists the poor, refugees, or embattled brethren, *jihadists*, as well as moderate Muslims, perceive such a policy as inhibiting *zakat* – one of the five pillars of Islam.[52] When the United States understandably incarcerates and declares *jihadists* as criminals, bin Laden argues that the American state challenges *Allah's* word and holy disciples and martyrs. "Islam does not coincide or make a truce with unbelief; but rather confronts it".[53]

In social science parlance, these contradictory positions are truly zero-sum games; there is no room for rational diplomacy with the *jihadists* only nonnegotiable demands and positions.[54] The United States still has difficulty recognizing this fact. It gives us no solace to posit that the primary way to win (and we are not even sure what "win" means in this context) the GWOT war is through violent and aggressive military means.

It is important to recognize that bin Laden's and other *jihadists'* political positions are based on their understanding and beliefs concerning Islam. Indeed, even

---

member's home. The manual was found in a computer file described as "the military series" related to the "Declaration of Jihad".)

[52] *Zakat* – The seriousness of *Zakat*, the obligatory charity, to a Muslim is reflected in *Hadith Zakat*: Allah's Apostle said, "Whoever is made wealthy by Allah and does not pay the Zakat of his wealth, then on the Day of Resurrection his wealth will be made like a baldheaded poisonous male snake with two black spots over the eyes. The snake will encircle his neck and bite his cheeks and say, 'I am your wealth, I am your treasure.'" Then the Prophet recited the holy verses: "And let not those who covetously withhold of that which Allah has bestowed on them of His Bounty (Wealth) think that it is good for them (and so they do not pay the obligatory Zakat). Nay, it will be worse for them; the things which they covetously withheld shall be tied to their necks like a collar on the Day of Resurrection. And to Allah belongs the heritage of the heavens and the earth; and Allah is Well Acquainted with all that you do." (3:180) [Hadith Vol 2:#486] as quoted http://www.road-to-heaven.com/fr15.htm (Accessed 20 December 2004).

[53] *The Al-Qaeda Training Manual*, UndatedUK/BM-8 Translation, op. cit.

[54] A principal recommendation of the 9-11 Report was negotiations with this enemy are useless.

trying to separate politics from religion in the *jihadist's* eyes is a grave misnomer and as well as a blasphemy.

Yet the U.S. also represents an opportunity to the *jihadist*. It presents bin Laden and other *jihadists* with a common enemy and hence, can represent a basis of unity for radical Islamists. The U.S. and the West, in general, as an enemy allows the *jihadists* to harness local commitment to their global struggle and in so doing promotes, in their perspective, the continual unification of Muslim *Umma* (community). Fighting the *jihad* not only benefits the individual because of the religious obligation associated with it[55]; it also benefits the larger Muslim community through united pious action against its enemies.

How does the United States deal in such a zero-sum world? It appears unlikely that the *jihadists* will modify their behavior; for they remain unaffected by the West's perceptions of their actions other than the widespread sense of vulnerability they hope it instills in the public. The United States, however, must continually assess actions and policies as to how they will be perceived by more moderate sectors of the Islamic world – those that the Muslim theocrat consider to be "apostate". Modification of the *jihadist* or theocrats' views is nonsense; since the Muslim theocrats are at war with the U.S. because the U.S. is an enemy of Allah reviewing actions and policies for Islamic perceptions could be argued is a waste of time. All the actions and policies of the U.S. will be perceived as wrong or evil because the U.S. has rejected Allah, His Laws, His Prophet and follow man's laws.

This ideological war is a war for hearts and minds, but not as traditionally conceptualized. The challenge for the United States is to merely hold its ground in the eyes of the moderate Muslim World and avoid any disastrous public relation nightmares. The actual control of the relevant hearts and minds by the United States is something that probably will not happen. As the Defense Department's new counter-terror guidance cogently notes: "Ultimately, however, winning the ideological war will depend on the individual and collective ability of the Armed Forces to wage "culture-centric warfare" in which understanding indigenous people and their culture is at least as important as tactical military victories".[56]

---

[55] Jessica Stern compares and draws parallels of this uncompromising, "true belief" of the *jihadist* to the abortion clinic bombers in the United States. See: Jessica Stern, "Terror in the Name of God: Why Religious Militants Kill," (Harper Collins, 2003).

[56] *JOC-DTO*, p. 18, op. cit.

Cultural and Religious Intelligence and Sensitivity Becomes Critical. As suggested above, while winning the ideological war will be next to impossible by the United States this does not mean that it can ignore cultural and religious issues. Secretary Rumsfeld was recently quoted as stating: "Transforming is as much about culture and people [as about programs]".[57] Quite the contrary; it is critical that U.S. policies and actions are developed and pursued with an explicit view as to how these will be viewed by the Muslim World. The U.S. will never win over the *jihadists* but it must at least hold its own relative the Muslim moderates and masses. And to accomplish this, the U.S. must continually be aware of its moral standing. This is especially true now that the Arab and Muslim press such as *al Jazeera* has expanded its coverage of regional and world affairs. As the 9-11 Commission Report suggests, the U.S. GWOT policies "should be accompanied by a preventive strategy that is as much, or more, political as it is military. The strategy must clearly focus on the Arab and Muslim world, in all its variety".[58]

This also implies that the United States must demonstrate moral leadership and occupy the moral high ground, but this can be a daunting task during a war and post-9-11 world environment. Events such as U.S. prisoner abuse at Abu Ghraib have damning short- and long-term implications and indeed represent a gift to the *jihadists* because such events have the capacity to confirm their views of the moral bankruptcy of the United States and motivate their supporters and influence fence sitters. Fighting terror with terror is not only unproductive; it can also enhance the insurgent's popular support.

The United States must sensitize its policy makers and war fighters to Muslim cultural and religious matters. Such sensitivity to include appropriate language skills has the added value of enhancing and the development of actionable intelligence. Without such skills U.S. troops will not be able to adequately interact with the population and indigenous troops. As bluntly stated by U.S. Brigadier General Caret Ham, who commands the task force for Mosul area in northern Iraq, "We don't lack for people to go thump in the night; the challenge is getting the intel".[59] Hence, cultural and religious knowledge has both strategic and tactical significance.

The importance of understanding American culture, which they despise, is surely not lost on the *jihadists*. While the U.S. needs to understand the Muslim culture to avoid making disastrous policy choices as well enhancing its possibility for collecting actionable intelligence, the *jihadists* struggle to understand Western

---

[57] *Wall Street Journal*, 8 November 2004.
[58] *The 9-11 Commission Report*, p. 364, op. cit.
[59] *Washington Post*, December 6, 2004, p. A18.

culture because it has important tactical implications. For example, the arrival of the *jihadists* from Hamburg (Mohammed Atta, et. al.) was a godsend for al-Qaeda because of the group's relative familiarity with Western culture and their considerable English language skills.[60] These skills are much sought after by bin Laden and have been critical in the formulation of *jihadist* attack cells and their strategies.

Sheer Numbers can be Daunting. With approximately 1.3 billion followers worldwide Islam is the second most popular and fastest growing religion in the world. Muslims reside in every country of the world. These demographics have important implications for the GWOT, especially in the context of bin Laden wanting a clash of civilizations. In addition the *jihadist* ideology has proven to be "a widely-appealing ideology that legitimizes the movement while it generates all types of support and new recruits".[61]

It is relatively clear that the majority of the world's Muslims are not proponents or supporters of bin Laden's *jihad*. Nevertheless, the size of the Muslim world population theoretically means that the *jihadists* have a vast reservoir of potential recruits. This potential reservoir of recruits and supporters, as suggested above, are a major impetus for al Qaeda actions. The JOC-DTO suggests that the "global insurgency" is already "supported by millions of sympathizers and enablers among the world's Muslim population".[62]

This presents a particular dilemma for the Untied States. The U.S. pursuit of the GWOT can have the very real consequence of creating recruits for the *jihadists*. The U.S. war and occupation of Iraq is a recent and instructive illustration of this dynamic. It has been argued by some that the war and occupation was a blessing for bin Laden and has served as a recruiting poster for the *jihadists*.[63] It has opened up a new front for the *jihad* and has provided a new radicalizing and bonding experience for young recruits.[64] Recent estimates suggest that the Iraqi insurgency is comprised of more than 200,000 people, with an estimated 40,000 hard-guerilas engaged in operations against U.S. forces.[65] Moreover, Iraq is

---

[60] See, *The 9-11 Commission Report*, op. cit.
[61] *JCO-DTO*, p. 9.
[62] *JOC-DTO*, p. 7.
[63] See Anonymous, "Imperial Hubris: Why the West is Losing the War on Terrorism." Op. cit.
[64] See Brian Jenkins, *The Operational Code of the Jihadists*, A Briefing Prepared for the Army Defense Science Board, April 1, 2004.
[65] United Press International, "Iraqi Insurgents Outnumber U.S. Forces", January 4, 2005. The report quotes the director of Iraq's newly created Intelligences Service, Gen

proving to be valuable ground for the insurgents and *jihadists* to gain valuable field experience and test new tactics, techniques, and procedures (TTPs). Some have gone as far as to argue that the U.S. failure to achieve a quick military and political victory in Iraq, is giving the *jihadists* exactly the type of conflict – an insurgency – they desired.[66] We have seen a similar phenomenon in Afghanistan where there are troubling reports that the Taliban are regrouping to challenge the perceived U.S. occupation and President Karzai's regime that is presumed to be an American puppet.

Muslim states generally have been very reluctant to join the American "coalition of the willing" primarily because of the assumed domestic repercussions. Many of these regimes have volatile internal problems that are difficult enough to control without opening the door to the possible consequences resulting from explicitly supporting U.S. war efforts. Hence, explicit support of the GWOT is viewed a harbinger for regime threatening domestic instability. It is interesting to note that the combined gross domestic product of the 22 countries in the Arab League is less than the GDP of Spain.[67] Domestic problems abound in this world and its leaders are constantly avoiding sparks that might ignite a greater fire.

The insurgency in Iraq, of course, has demonstrated how difficult it can be for moderate Muslim leaders, in this case interim leaders, to govern in the face of a determined jihadist opposition. From 1 October 2004 to 4 December 2004, according to U.S. Military figures, a total of 338 Iraqis working with the new Iraqi governing structures had been assassinated, including 35 police chiefs, mayors, and middle-ranking officials.[68]

The silence of support offered to U.S. in their campaigns against the jihadists by the moderate Muslim international community has been deafening. Few Muslim leaders with the exception of Pakistan's President Musharraf have had the gumption or commitment to the GWOT to commit significant resources and explicit policies to support the United States. And in the case of Musharraf, he only committed his support after being given a series of nonnegotiable demands by the Bush Administration in the immediate days after 9-11 and before the U.S. Afghanistan campaign commenced.[69] And, of course, since lending his

---

Muhammad Abdullah Shawani on these estimates. The number of so-called "jihadists" within this population is believed to number below 1,000.

[66] See Brian Jenkins, The Operational Code of the Jihadists. Op. cit.
[67] *The 9-11 Commission Report*, p. 379.
[68] *Washington Post*, December 6, 2004, p. A18.
[69] Bob Woodward, "Bush at War," (Simon and Schuster, 2002), pp. 58-59.

support to the United States, Musharaff has been the target of two assassination attempts.

Ultimately, a key indicator of the eventual success of the GWOT is how U.S. policies and actions are perceived by moderate Muslim Community and how successful the U.S. is at physically separating the *jihadist* organizations from the societies in which they operate and from which they draw their resources.

How should one interpret the fact that over the last few years Osama has become one of the most popular names for Muslim male infants? Or consider recent opinion polls of Arab Muslim populations as to their perspectives of the United States. American engagement in much of the world is resented. For example only 15% of the Egyptian and 12% of the Saudi Arabian population has a favorable opinion of the United States. Moreover, in 2003 two-thirds of those polled in countries from Turkey to Indonesia were very or somewhat fearful that the U.S. might eventually attack them.[70]

While it would be a fallacy to judge the naming of an infant or the results of an opinion poll as definitive data as to the popularity of the *jihadists* or the negative image of the United States, it does suggest that there are troubling undercurrents in the Arab Muslim community. Recent Islam history is not marked by an abundance of internationally popular and revered figures. Michael Scheuer argues that while the average Muslim will not been found in the streets protesting for Osama bin Laden, they still have incredible respect for his veracity to challenge the position of the United States. Scheuer argues that bin Laden may be the most respected, loved, charismatic figure of the last 150 years of Islamic history.[71] If this is indeed the case and more Muslims eventually embrace bin Laden's *jihad* or just silently support it, the subsystem dominance of the international system will intensify. As Benjamin and Simon suggest, "Islamists may not control parliaments or government palaces, but they have occupied the popular imagination"[72].

The United States Cannot Go it Alone. During the Cold War the United States built a great alliance to confront the Soviet Union and its allies. While the alliance was available to support the policies and campaigns of the United States, because the U.S. was the dominant actor in the international system defined by

---

[70] For polling data see: James Zogby, "What Arabs Think: Values, Beliefs, and Concerns," (Zogby International, 2002). For fear of U.S. attacks see: Pew Global Attitudes Project Report, Views of a Changing World: June 2003 (Pew Research Center, 2003), p. 2.
[71] *Imperial Hubris*, pp. 103-5, 118-26. op. cit.
[72] Benjamin and Simon, Op. cit. p. 173.

the dominance of its power it could always act alone to counter Soviet actions if the circumstances called for it. Today this is not the case.

The international system of today is being dominated and driven by less dominant actors – the *jihadist* insurgents. And while the United States claims and has demonstrated that it is willing to confront the insurgents alone if necessary, this is not a receipt for success. In a subsystem dominated international environment concerted effort by multiple actors are required to change the system. Moreover the U.S. assistance that "you are either completely with us or against us" leaves no middle ground for policy debate and positions amongst allies. In this instance, U.S. policies and actions ignored the concerns of its traditional European allies and eventually alienated them. It is a sad state of affairs for the United States when fear of a protest by members of parliament negates an address to Parliament by President Bush or when he is met by widespread protests when he visits his northern neighbor, Canada. Such a reaction to the President in the lands of two traditional U.S. friends – one being America's most prominent supporter in the GWOT – suggests a very troubling environment for U.S. action and maneuver. Going it alone will not suffice.

The *jihadists* envision a conflict consisting of battles and isolated engagements spread over time and space. While traditional campaigns against a much weaker foe would usually allow the U.S. to go it alone, the nature of its enemy in the GWOT requires a concerted effort by a broad coalition. As suggested by the 9-11 Commission Report, the United States needs to take the lead role in a broad coalition to stop Islamic terrorists and insurgents.[73]

Easy Solutions and Initial Impulses are Probably Wrong. During the Cold War the United States had a pronounced enemy that U.S. policy makers came to know well. A large percentage of the U.S. national security infrastructure during this period was devoted to exclusively analyzing every aspect of the USSR and its intentions. The U.S. and the USSR, while extremely powerful, both had a lot to lose in a superpower conflict. The potential for massive loses resulting from any head-to-head conflict enabled each to deter the other. In many respects an eerie tranquility was realized as the two super powers maneuvered the international system. Communications and interactions between the U.S. and USSR became routinized and this steady state defined the international system equilibrium. While surprises and crises (i.e., disturbances to the routine or equilibrium) surely occurred during the Cold War period such events were the exception rather than the rule of this system dominated system.

---

[73] See *The 9-11 Commission Report.* Op. cit.

In the Cold War environment decision makers had a clear range of alternative policies to enact. Moreover, the nature of the Cold War international system made policy prescriptions and foreign policy actions relatively easy. This is surely not the case in the present GWOT dominated international present system, where U.S. policies cannot only alienate moderate Muslims but also traditional friends and allies.

Today's system is characterized by threats that can and have emerged very quickly. And these threats are anything but routine. In addition the *jihadists* have proven themselves to be extremely clever. This, of course, was tragically witness on 9-11 when al Qaeda employed airplanes as missiles, a threat in which there were no NORAD protocols to address it.[74]

The *jihadist* threat, unlike the Cold War Soviet threat, is also relatively vague. The threat is not characterized by national boundaries and it cannot be bargained or negotiated with. Such a vague and amorphous threat can result in vague goals towards it. And vague goals are often defined by initial impulses and easy solutions instead of informed and thorough analysis. Moreover such goals and respective policies aimed at their realization are often misguided. For example the notion that Iraqi democracy will domino across the entire Middle East, or that the U.S. must differentiate between the "Old Europe" and "New Europe" or that Saddam Hussein was intimately involved in 9-11, or that there was an explicit link between Iraq and al Qaeda[75] are all impulses that might sound good and reinforce American desires, but ultimately represent simple reductionist responses to complex problems.

Time Isn't Necessarily on our Side. The patience of al Qaeda as well as other *jihadists* is possibly their most problematic dimension of the threat they pose to the United States. The al Qaeda training manual states that:

> [The member] should have plenty of patience for [enduring] afflictions if he is overcome by the enemies. He should not abandon this great path and sell himself and his religion to the enemies for his freedom. He should be patient in performing the work, even if it lasts a long time.[76]

---

[74] Ibid.

[75] For a discussion of: President Bush's view that Saddam was connected to 9-11 or Secretary Rumsfeld's commitment to hitting Hussein at the same time as Bin Ladin or Deputy Secretary Wolfowitz view that Iraq was the source of the GWOT problem or that General Tommy Franks' concern about a connection between Iraq and Al-Qaeda, see: Bob Woodward, "Bush at War" or the *9-11 Commission Report*. Op. cit.

[76] *Al Qaeda Training Manual*, UK/BM-16.

The GWOT unfortunately has the potential to last well beyond our children's lifetime and fought in a global arena that increasingly involves the U.S. homeland. The JOC-DTO suggests that the GWOT will last "decades or generations".[77]

Is the United States prepared for decades of violent warfare spread over the entire globe and involving its homeland? Will the U.S. public draw war weary as the *jihadists* continue their war of attrition?

A recent Washington Post-ABC News poll, for example, suggests that there is deep and growing skepticism concerning the war in Iraq.[78] This poll reveals a solid majority of U.S. citizens believing that the war is a "mistake" and has led 56% of those polled to conclude that the conflict given the associated human and financial costs is "not worth fighting". [79]

7 Conclusions

The United States is only starting to recognize the true nature of the *jihadist* threat and its wider implications for strategy and policy. The principal argument of this paper is that the *jihadist* ideology as manifested by bin Laden really reflects the continuing and growing salience of international subsystem dynamics – a system with characteristics that do not respect the primacy of U.S. power, position or national interests. Before addressing the strategic challenge and taking steps to address the threat, the United States must come to terms with the primacy of subsystem dynamics and intellectually divorce itself from the ideas of bi-and uni-polarity that have been used as the basis to assert U.S. hegemony.

While roundly derided in the fields of international relations theory, Samuel Huntington's *Clash of Civilizations* correctly identified the growing impact that subsystem dynamics would play in the international system. Bounding these dynamics with concepts such as "culture" and "religion" left Huntington open to understandable attacks due to the inherent difficulty of defining these concepts – not to mention the politically charged nature of his argument. These issues miss the broader point of his argument, which we believe has been borne out in events throughout the 1990s to today's environment. Subsystem dynamics, driven by a variety of different forces, are the defining feature of the international environment.

---

[77] *JCO-DTO*, 14 Nov 2004, p. 12.
[78] *Washington Post*, December 21, 2004, A4.
[79] Ibid.

A neo-realist view of the world asserting that the United States must assume the mantle of sheriff or policeman in the absence of effective international institutions is doomed to failure. Institutions designed around assumptions of hegemony and unipolarity remain fundamentally mismatched to the broader environment. The temporal and spatial nature of the global *jihad* makes it virtually impossible for the U.S. to tackle the enemy alone. The U.S. does not have the forces, organization, equipment and it is doubtful that the U.S. public has the will to commit the resources that would be necessary to conduct a long and dispersed conflict. The limits of U.S. resources are vividly on display in Iraq.

Even when the *jihad* or insurgency is confined to a bounded space such as Iraq the strains on U.S. resources and strategy are obvious. While the attacks on the insurgent stronghold in Fallujah appeared successful, the insurgents also seem to have successfully dispersed, forcing U.S. forces into more reactive focused raids in a variety of other cities. The response of the insurgents to the Fallujah attacks was to raise the level of violence, which in turn has lead to calls for more troops.[80]

The thinking expressed in SOCOM's draft guidance seems in line with Rumsfeld's own intuitive thinking. Both actors seem to realize the incongruity between the threat of the *jihadists* and DoD's organizational structures. Both actors are on the right track but face formidable obstacles in not just tackling the daunting organizational an operational challenges facing the Defense Department. The mature organizational structures within the Defense Department remain locked in organizational behavior that is devoted to self-preservation as a defining principle. These organizational rhetorically embrace the ideas of change, but simply "wait out" the leadership calling for fundamental structural change. The "values" of the system remain tied to platform driven planning and budgeting and the endless bureaucratic battles for resources. . But perhaps their most daunting challenge remains the most intractable one: convincing the political leadership to embrace the need to fundamentally reorient the nation's organizational structures to meet the demands of subsystem primacy. The stakes of the issue are enormous: failing to address the intellectual and organizational challenge will ensure that the United States may win battles in the GWOT, but it can never win the wider war.

---

[80] *Washington Post*, December 6, 2004, pg A1 and A28.

Gefährdet der Terrorismus den liberalen Verfassungsstaat?

Sabine Leutheusser-Schnarrenberger MdB, Bundesministerin a.D.

FDP-Bundestagsfraktion

Terrorismus und innere Sicherheit markieren die Reizwörter in einer innenpolitischen Debatte, die um den richtigen Weg der Terrorbekämpfung ringt.

Vieles ist in den letzten drei Jahren diesseits und jenseits des Atlantiks an gesetzgeberischen Maßnahmen vollzogen worden. Ich möchte mich heute darauf konzentrieren, die Gefahren dieser Entwicklung zu skizzieren. Mit der Fragestellung meines Vortrages, „Gefährdet der Terrorismus den liberalen Verfassungsstaat?", möchte ich eine Perspektive wählen, die den Umgang demokratischer Staaten mit Terrorismus – und insbesondere den der Bundesrepublik – in den Mittelpunkt rückt. Meine These ist, dass wichtige Maßnahmen in ihrer übergeordneten Tendenz in den Vereinigten Staaten wie in der Bundesrepublik einen gefährlichen Trend markieren, der den liberalen Rechtsstaat auszuhöhlen droht.

Ich möchte diese These in vier Schritten entwickeln und erläutern. Zunächst werde ich kurz auf die Entwicklung in den Vereinigten Staaten eingehen, um allgemeine Entwicklungszusammenhänge aufzuzeigen. Im nächsten Schritt werde ich die gefährdeten Grundlagen des Rechtsstaats skizzieren. In einem dritten Teil werde ich auf die innenpolitischen Maßnahmen eingehen, die ergriffen worden sind. Abschließend möchte ich vor diesem Hintergrund die innenpolitische Agenda analysieren. Welche Trends und Entwicklungen hieran aufgezeigt werden können, ist Bestandteil meines Fazits.

1 Trends und Entwicklungen in den Vereinigten Staaten

Seit dem 11. September 2001 sind zahlreiche legislative Maßnahmen in den Vereinigten Staaten vollzogen worden.

Bereits am 26. Oktober 2001 kam der so genannte „Patriot Act" zustande. Dahinter verbergen sich bekanntlich in hohem Tempo verabschiedete Novellen von

Gesetzen der Inneren Sicherheit. Zusammengefasst: Diese Novellen schränken die Bürgerrechte der Amerikaner massiv ein. Bank- und Arztgeheimnis sind so gut wie aufgehoben; die Akten von Universitäten, Psychiatern und Kreditinstituten können von den Behörden ohne gerichtliche Genehmigung eingesehen werden; Einzahlungen von über 10.000 Dollar fallen automatisch in die Kategorie verdächtiger Finanzbewegungen; der Große Lauschangriff ist auf Telefon und Internet mit minimaler Kontrolle durch Gerichte erlaubt; Hausdurchsuchungen dürfen ohne Hausdurchsuchungsbefehl auch in Abwesenheit der Bewohner durchgeführt werden; der Auslandsgeheimdienst darf auch im Inland spionieren.

Der „Patriot Act" ermächtigte unter anderem den Justizminister, Ausländer auf unbestimmte Zeit zu inhaftieren, wenn deren Abschiebung bis auf weiteres nicht möglich oder absehbar erscheint oder wenn diese Ausländer nach seinem Ermessen eine Gefahr für die nationale Sicherheit der Vereinigten Staaten darstellen, die allgemeine Sicherheit oder die Einzelner bedrohen.

Der Justizminister ist also autorisiert festzulegen, ob es sich bei einem Ausländer um einen gefährlichen Terroristen handelt, der Angriffe plant oder unterstützt. Seine Ermessensentscheidung kann sich auch auf geheime Beweismittel stützen, die dem Inhaftierten bzw. dessen Anwälten nicht bekannt gemacht werden müssen. Diese Beweismittel dürfen bei der späteren Rechtsfindung nicht herangezogen werden; sie bilden dennoch die Legitimationsgrundlage für einen Freiheitsentzug zum Zwecke der Prävention terroristischer Akte.

Dieses Beispiel ist bezeichnend für die in den USA zu beobachtende Tendenz, die Rolle des Staates grundlegend neu zu interpretieren: Der amerikanische „Patriot Act" ist ein Paradigmenwechsel, der vollzogen wird.

Aus Sicht der Exekutive hat die Präventionsfunktion des Staates Vorrang vor der Rechtsfindungs- und Rechtsstaatsfunktion. Die Inhaftierung ohne konkreten Tatvorwurf, die Versagung anwaltlichen Beistands und die Aussetzung der US-amerikanischen Jurisdiktion sind die Merkmale dieser Entwicklung.

Guantánamo Bay ist trauriger und beschämender Höhepunkt dieser Entwicklung. Es ist ein Symbol für Terrorismusbekämpfung, bei dem oft die Grenzen des Völkerrechts überschritten werden.

Leider gibt es wenig Grund zu der Hoffnung, dass sich dies schnell ändern wird. Der Supreme Court (Rasul et al. vs Bush et al.) stellte fest, dass den zwölf kuwaitischen sowie den zwei australischen in Guantánamo Bay inhaftierten Gefangenen, die den Fall vor den Gerichtshof gebracht hatten, gemäß der Verfassung und den Gesetzen der USA der Zugang zu den US-Bundesgerichten zwecks

Überprüfung ihrer Haft nicht mit dem Argument der Unzuständigkeit verwehrt werden darf.

Die Antwort des Supreme Court – das Verhalten der Staatsgewalt gegenüber US-Bürgern wird geprüft – ist ausschließlich dem innerstaatlichen Recht der USA entnommen und nicht dem Völkerrecht. Sie ist zudem nur der erste Teil der gerichtlichen Bearbeitung, denn endgültig „geformt" wird die Entscheidung über die zu beurteilende Praxis durch die unteren Gerichte und möglicherweise durch die künftige Gesetzgebung.

Mit viel rhetorischem Aufwand begleitet, wurde 2002 das Ministerium für Heimatschutz (engl. "Department of Homeland Security") gegründet, das einige vorher unabhängige Institutionen umfasst, so zum Beispiel die Sicherheitskontrollen an den US-Flughäfen, den Zoll und die Küstenwache. Entgegen den ursprünglichen Plänen unterstehen ihm jedoch nicht FBI und CIA.

Was sind die allgemeinen Entwicklungszusammenhänge, die in den Vereinigten Staaten deutlich werden?

Erstens: Das „Heimatschutzministerium" ist Ausdruck einer ungeheuren Zentralisierungstendenz, die durch die jetzt beschlossene Reform der Geheimdienste verstärkt wird. Zweitens: Prävention wird zulasten individueller Freiheit derart gestärkt, dass die Grundfesten des Rechtsstaats existenziell bedroht werden. Drittens: Mit dem Internierungslager Guantánamo Bay sind rechtsfreie Räume entstanden, die völkerrechtswidrig sind – die leider weiter bestehen bleiben.

2 Gefährdete Grundlagen des Rechtsstaats

Die weltweiten „Anti-Terror-Gesetze", die von Regierungen rund um den Globus als Reaktion auf die Anschläge innerhalb weniger Monate auf den Weg gebracht und von zahlreichen Parlamenten auch verabschiedet worden sind, ergänzen dieses Bild. „Reporter ohne Grenzen" kritisierte bereits knapp vier Monate nach den Anschlägen 15 Staaten für die von diesen Maßnahmen ausgehenden Beschränkungen der Presse-, Meinungs- und Informationsfreiheit.

Diese Maßnahmen, so wird uns immer wieder von Sicherheitspolitikern jeglicher Couleur versichert, schaffen Sicherheit und damit mehr Freiheit. In einem demokratischen Rechtsstaat, so heißt es, gebe es immer ein Spannungsverhältnis zwischen der Wahrung der Freiheitsrechte der Bürger und dem ebenfalls von den Bürgern geforderten Recht auf ein Mindestmaß an Sicherheit. Gerade jetzt müsse man die Trennlinie neu definieren.

Diese Argumentation ist nicht nur falsch, sie ist schlichtweg gefährlich.

Freiheit, Gleichheit und Brüderlichkeit sind die zentralen Leitwerte moderner, demokratischer Legitimität. Freiheit ist im liberalen Rechtsstaat eine kategoriale Zielbestimmung: Staatliches Handeln ist diesem Ziel normativ verpflichtet. Sicherheit ist somit eine Möglichkeit der Bedingung von Freiheit. Nur wer sein Leben ohne mögliche Beeinflussung von Leib und Leben führen kann, ist in der Lage, es frei zu gestalten.

Soweit besteht wohl Konsens. Problematisch ist eine zweite Argumentationsfigur, die gerade hier ansetzt: Deswegen müsse eine freiheitliche Verfassung das Grundrecht auf Sicherheit gewährleisten. Nur wer in Sicherheit lebe, könne überhaupt frei sein.

Staatliches Handeln kann per se nicht partnerschaftlich Sicherheit schaffen, da grundsätzlich ein Spannungsverhältnis zwischen Freiheit und Sicherheit besteht.

Zu Spannungen zwischen dem Streben nach Freiheit und dem nach Sicherheit kommt es grundsätzlich da, wo demokratische Rechtsstaaten es als ihre Aufgaben ansehen, ihren Bürgern beides zu garantieren. Das ist ein ehrgeiziges Ziel und ein hoher Anspruch, dem sich in dieser Form nicht alle demokratischen Rechtsstaaten stellen, oder besser gesagt, dem sich nicht alle Politiker und Regierungen demokratischer Rechtsstaaten stellen. Aber dem sie sich alle stellen müssen.

Dieses Spannungsfeld macht auch deutlich, dass dem Anspruch, Sicherheit und Freiheit gleichermaßen zu garantieren, nie entsprochen werden kann. Am Ende steht immer ein Abwägungsprozess zwischen mehr Sicherheit und weniger Freiheit oder umgekehrt. Selbst ein Rechtsstaat, der seine Grundlagen aufgeben würde, der also u. a. die Grundrechte der Bürgerinnen und Bürger bis zur Unkenntlichkeit aushöhlen würde, selbst dieser autoritäre Schutzstaat könnte keine absolute Sicherheit gewähren. Ein Blick in Staaten, die keine gewachsenen demokratischen und rechtsstaatlichen Traditionen und Strukturen besitzen, belegt dies. Man denke nur an die GUS-Staaten, an lateinamerikanische Staaten oder an den asiatischen Raum.

Um keine Missverständnisse aufkommen zu lassen: Selbstverständlich ist der Schutz vor Kriminalität und terroristischen Anschlägen Teil der staatlichen Verantwortung. Daraus kann aber kein Grundrecht auf Sicherheit abgeleitet werden. Es gibt kein solches Grundrecht im Grundgesetz. Gäbe es dieses Grundrecht auf Sicherheit als Anspruchsrecht gegen den Staat, dann wäre es um die Freiheitsrechte nicht mehr gut bestellt. Denn bei der verfassungsrechtlichen Abwägung zwischen zwei Grundrechten würden im Zweifel die Freiheitsrechte der Bürger den Kürzeren ziehen.

Um des vermeintlichen Freiheitsschutzes willen werden dabei immer intensivere Eingriffe in die Freiheit Aller ganz selbstverständlich in Kauf genommen. Der Schutz der Privatsphäre vor staatlichem Zugriff ist auf einmal nicht mehr Grundbedingung für die individuelle Freiheitsentfaltung. Im Gegenteil: Der Schutzstaat, der immer stärker in die Privatsphäre eindringt, erscheint geradezu als Garant für die Freiheit Aller.

Für die moderne liberale Demokratie ist der zentrale Ansatzpunkt, dass Staat und Gesellschaft nicht identisch sind, dass die Gesellschaft, die Bürgerschaft, den Staat lediglich stellvertretend beauftragt, Aufgaben und Verantwortung zu übernehmen – Aufgaben, die sie nicht selbst übernehmen kann. Deswegen schreibt der Staat den Bürgern Rechte zu, die die Tätigkeit des Staates begrenzen und zugleich die Freiheitsräume des Einzelnen schützen. Diese vom Staat zugeschriebenen Rechte sind in den modernen demokratischen Verfassungen die Grundrechte.

Diese Sichtweise unserer Verfassung und implizit auch der Bedeutung unserer Grundrechte ist nachhaltig von der Rechtsprechung des Bundesverfassungsgerichts gestärkt worden, erstmalig 1958 in dem nach einem Prozessbeteiligten benannten Urteil („Lüth"-Urteil). Das Gericht erklärte damals sinngemäß, dass die Grundrechte vor allem dem Schutze des Einzelnen vor Eingriffen des Staates dienen.

Absolute Sicherheit gibt es nicht einmal im absoluten Polizeistaat. Sicher ist dort nur eines, nämlich dass die Presse dort weder über die Kriminalität noch über die Verletzung der Würde des Menschen berichten darf.

Natürlich wissen wir: Freiheit ohne Sicherheit bedeutet das Ende von Freiheit. Was würde es bedeuten, wenn das Spannungsverhältnis zuungunsten von Freiheit aufgelöst würde?

Der große Moralist Karl Jasper hat darauf eine einprägsame Antwort gegeben:

> Die menschlichen Dinge gestatten keine absolute Sicherheit. Freiheit kann sich nur durch Freiheit im Risiko behaupten. Wer absolute Sicherheit will, will die Unfreiheit und den politischen Tod. Der Wille zur absoluten Sicherheit drückt eine Gesinnung aus, die die Wirklichkeit des menschlichen Daseins nicht anzuschauen wagt.

Dieses Zitat mag manche Zuhörer erstaunen. Ist das die Agenda, die heute angesichts der Bedrohungen des internationalen Terrorismus diskutiert wird?

Lassen Sie mich auf ein Zitat von Walter Scheel hinweisen, das aus seiner berühmten Rede im Bundestag nach der Ermordung Hanns Martin Schleyers am

26. Oktober 1976 stammt. Angesichts des damaligen furchtbaren RAF-Terrors wählte er bedächtige Worte, um auf die langfristigen Gefahren hinzuweisen: „Unsere Aufgabe ist es, unser Bild der Freiheit vor Entstellungen zu bewahren". Er mahnte angesichts des RAF-Terrors an, dass der Terrorismus nur dann erfolgreich an seiner Wurzel bekämpft werden kann, wenn seine Ursachen bekannt sind.

Wie sieht es damit heute aus? Wie wirksam ist die Bekämpfung des Terrorismus, wenn umfangreiche Kenntnisse über seine Wurzeln nicht vorliegen? Die Intervention in Afghanistan hat die AlQuaida-Strukturen dort, nicht aber ihre weltweiten Strukturen zerstört.

Die neue Qualität des internationalen Terrorismus besteht ja nicht in der Blindwütigkeit, mit der er operiert. Sie besteht in den Ressourcen und der Art der Organisation. Al Quaida kann heute leider nicht als zerschlagen gelten. Wie eine schallende Ohrfeige muss daher das Videoband bewertet werden, das Bin Laden kurz vor der amerikanischen Präsidentenwahl veröffentlichte. Nicht nur, dass damit aller Welt demonstriert wurde, wie wohlauf der berüchtigtste Terrorist der Welt ist. Es zeigt auch, wie dringend notwendig eine Auseinandersetzung mit den Ursachen des Terrorismus ist.

Das Weltbild, das Bin Laden dort offenlegt, ist erschreckend und verstörend. Es muss aber genau analysiert werden. Was sind die Motive dieser Menschen, die sogar bereit sind, ihr eigenes Leben zu opfern? Was ist das Welt- und Menschenbild, und wie entsteht es? Wie wird dieses Menschenbild verbreitet bzw. warum findet es überhaupt Verbreitung?

Diese schwierigen Fragen werden zu selten gestellt. Die nationale wie internationale Politik muss sich stärker um die richtigen Antworten bemühen. Es reicht einfach nicht aus, diese Menschen verachtende, lebensfeindliche Ideologie zu bewerten; das macht sie selbst. Wir brauchen einen viel breiteren Ansatz, um dann konkrete Handlungsstrategien entwickeln zu können. Es reicht einfach nicht aus, wie eine Heilsbotschaft den demokratischen Lebensentwurf zu predigen; Handeln und Rhetorik müssen zusammenpassen. Die liberale Demokratie muss sich an ihren eigenen Maßstäben messen lassen.

Leider kann ich an dieser Stelle auch nicht die Frage diskutieren, ob und, wenn ja, in welchem Maße die Innere Sicherheit in Deutschland durch religiös motivierten Extremismus und Terrorismus bedroht ist. Erlauben Sie mir aber einige kursorische Anmerkungen.

Ich möchte mir keine Zahlen zu Eigen machen, aber z. B. auf die Zahlen des Terrorismusexperten Kai Hirschmann verweisen, der davon ausgeht, dass etwa

5 % der hier lebenden Muslime radikalislamisches Gedankengut unterstützen; gewaltbereit seien sogar etwa 1 %. Danach handelt es sich also wirklich um eine Minderheit.

Der Präsident des Bundesamtes für Verfassungsschutz, Klaus-Dieter Fritsche, hat jüngst darauf hingewiesen, dass es nach Erkenntnissen des Verfassungsschutzes ein kleines „Mujahedin-Potenzial" mit internationalen Kontakten gebe. Deutschland sei bisher eher Ruhe- und Vorbereitungsraum für diese Gruppierungen, allerdings auch durchaus ein potenzielles Ziel.

Die Bedrohungslage, wie sie öffentlich diskutiert wird, ist also alles andere als eindeutig. Zusätzlich wird sie vor dem Hintergrund konkreter Ereignisse oft „verschärfend" diskutiert. So war nach den Terroranschlägen gewaltbereiter Islamisten in den Niederlanden in der deutschen Presse die Befürchtung von Trittbrettfahrern zu lesen.

Der Präsident des Bundeskriminalamts (BKA), Jörg Ziercke, wies in dem Zusammenhang darauf hin, dass islamistische Terroristen jederzeit in Deutschland zuschlagen könnten.

Solche Hinweise müssen erlaubt sein, daran besteht kein Zweifel. Einzelne Ereignisse dürfen nicht den Blick auf die Bedrohungslage verstellen; die Bedrohungslage darf weder von kurzfristigen Stimmungen noch von einzelnen Ereignissen abhängig gemacht werden.

Hinzu kommt ein wesentlicher Aspekt, der oftmals sträflich vernachlässigt wird: Islamistische Terroristen versuchen durch ihre Gewalttaten, eine harte, repressive Gegenreaktion des Gegners zu provozieren. Das bedeutet: Die Gegenreaktion ist ein wichtiger Bestandteil der terroristischen Strategie. Sie soll Polarisierung bewirken und Unterstützung für die eigene Sache schaffen. So brutal sich das anhören mag – einer rationalen Analyse darf dies nicht im Wege stehen: Die direkten Opfer werden von Terroristen nur als Mittel zum Zweck betrachtet. Dieses Kalkül muss in eine nüchterne Bedrohungsanalyse mit einfließen.

Umso wichtiger ist es, Antworten in der Tradition des liberalen Verfassungsstaats zu suchen. In der öffentlichen Debatte fehlt die Vorstellung teilweise vollständig, dass Sicherheit kein Selbstzweck ist.

Trotz dieser widrigen Umstände hat sich der Rechtsstaat bislang in seinen Grundfesten nicht erschüttern lassen. Es ist der bundesdeutschen Rechtsprechung zu verdanken, dass der liberale Verfassungsstaat immer wieder gestärkt wurde, zuletzt mit dem Urteil des Bundesverfassungsgerichts zum „Großen Lauschangriff".

Mit diesem Urteil hat das Bundesverfassungsgericht einen entscheidenden Beitrag zum Schutz der Intim- und Privatsphäre geleistet, indem ein unantastbarer Kernbereich anerkannt wurde, in den überhaupt nicht eingegriffen werden darf, auch nicht nach einem Abwägungsprozess des Staates. Der Gesetzgeber muss bei der Neuformulierung des „Großen Lauschangriffs" das Bundesverfassungsgerichtsurteil ernst nehmen, das auch Entscheidungen der Rechts- und Innenpolitik der letzten Jahren betrifft. Dies gilt nicht nur für die Bundesgesetzgebung, sondern im gleichen Umfang für Polizeigesetze der Länder.

Im Bereich des Polizeirechts verschieben sich die Schwerpunkte immer mehr von der klassischen Aufgabe der Verfolgung begangener oder der Verhütung konkret bevorstehender Straftaten zur präventiven Gefahrenabwehr, zu deren Zweck die Polizei immer öfter ohne konkreten Anlass eingreift.

Das dieser Entwicklung zugrunde liegende Prinzip hat niemand besser beschrieben als Lewis Caroll in *Alice hinter den Spiegeln*:

> „Woran könnt ihr euch erinnern?", fragte Alice vorsichtig. – „Ach, an Verschiedenes, was übernächste Woche geschah", versetzte die Königin leichthin, „da ist zum Beispiel der königliche Läufer. Er sitzt gerade seine Strafe ab im Kerker; und der Prozess fängt erst Mittwoch in acht Tagen an; und das Verbrechen kommt natürlich erst ganz zum Schluss". – „Angenommen, er begeht das Verbrechen gar nicht?" sagte Alice. – „Umso besser! Oder etwa nicht?" sagte die Königin.

Die deutsche Gesetzgebung der letzten drei Jahre unterliegt in einem erschreckenden Maße dieser präventiven Funktionslogik, die Lewis Caroll so prägnant beschrieben hat. Zu dieser Gefährdung durch die präventive Funktionslogik kommt eine Gefährdung des liberalen Verfassungsstaats, die seine Grundfesten massiv bedroht: die öffentliche Diskussion über die Aufweichung des Folterverbots.

Damit spiele ich nicht auf den konkreten Fall des Vizepräsidenten der Frankfurter Polizei, Wolfgang Daschner, an. Ich meine vielmehr die gefährliche Tendenz, in der öffentlichen wie in der akademischen Diskussion das Folterverbot zu relativieren. Ich möchte gar nicht weiter auf die absurde Vorstellung einer „formalisierten Folter" eingehen, da es für Folter geradezu typisch ist, keine rechtlichen Schranken anzuerkennen und den Gefolterten der schrankenlosen Willkür des Folterers auszuliefern. Nein, ich sehe in der Folterdiskussion einen Angriff auf den Konsens einer wie auch immer begründeten, für alle Menschen gültigen Menschenwürde. Sie durfte und darf auch dem schlimmsten Verbrecher nicht abgesprochen werden.

Die Frage, ob eine auf die Menschenwürde verpflichtete Gesellschaft ihre Ordnung sowie Leben und Freiheit ihrer Glieder durch Negation der Menschenwürde Anderer verteidigen kann, verlangt eine kategorische Antwort: Wenn man zu denselben Mitteln greift wie die Terroristen, ist der liberale Verfassungsstaat am Ende.

3 Innenpolitische Maßnahmen: Was ist geschehen?

Die konkrete innenpolitische Bilanz der vergangenen drei Jahre gibt in mehrfacher Hinsicht ebenfalls Anlass zur Besorgnis.

Am 14. Dezember 2001 wurden 17 Gesetze in einem die parlamentarisch-demokratische Willensbildung missachtenden Verfahren vom Bundestag gegen die Stimmen von FDP und PDS verabschiedet, die die Sicherheitsarchitektur unseres Staates grundlegend zugunsten eines Präventionsstaates verändern.

Das Terrorismusbekämpfungsgesetz verändert die Sicherheitsarchitektur zugunsten eines Staates, der seine Bürger massiven Misstrauens- und Überwachungsmaßnahmen aussetzt, um Sicherheitsrisiken angeblich zu minimieren – und dies ohne konkreten Tatverdacht. Und diese Entwicklung entspricht genau jenem Trend, der in den USA identifiziert werden kann.

In den letzten Jahre konnten sich kriminalpolitische Konzepte durchsetzen, in denen die Beobachtungs-, Überwachungs- und Ermittlungstätigkeit der Sicherheitsbehörden immer weiter nach vorne verlagert wurden. Konzepte, die also vom konkreten Verdacht als rechtsstaatliche Voraussetzung für staatliches Eingriffshandeln Abstand nehmen und die Grenze zwischen polizeilicher und geheimdienstlicher Tätigkeit immer weiter verwischen.

Den genannten und anderen Maßnahmen – man denke etwa an die uferlos ausgeweitete Rasterfahndung – liegt die fundamental mit dem Rechtsstaatsprinzip kollidierende Vorstellung zugrunde, terroristische Gefahren präventiv, das heißt weit im Vorfeld jedweder Strafbarkeit durch Beobachtung, Kontrolle oder Überwachung großer Teile der Bevölkerung besser ausschließen zu können.

Besorgnis erregend ist, dass die Schily-Gesetze in ihrer Gesamtheit das Verhältnis des Bürgers zum Staat verändern. Vor allem findet so gut wie keine öffentliche Erfolgskontrolle aller dieser Maßnahmen statt, und sie wird auch von den zuständigen Bundesländern als zu arbeitsintensiv abgelehnt.

Einige Gesetzesmaßnahmen, die in der Folge nach 2001 verabschiedet wurden, verstärken diese Tendenz: das Gesetz zur Neuregelung von Beschränkungen des Brief-, Post- und Fernmeldegeheimnisses (G-10 Gesetz von 2001), das Finanzmarktförderungsgesetz (2002), das Gesetz zur Förderung der Steuerehrlichkeit (Oktober 2003), das Telekommunikationsgesetz (Mai 2004) und das Übereinkommen zwischen der EU und den USA zur Verfassung und Verwendung von EU-Passagierdaten (Mai 2004).

Das Luftsicherheitsgesetz vom Juni 2004 enthält dazu auch noch Maßnahmen, die gegen grundlegende Verfassungsprinzipien verstoßen. Die Kritik richtet sich in erster Linie gegen die Ermächtigung des Bundesverteidigungsministers zur Anordnung eines Flugzeugabschusses. Dabei wird das Grundrecht der Besatzungsmitglieder und der Passagiere auf Leben zugunsten Dritter missachtet. Ein vorbeugender Flugzeugabsturz, der sich auf eine Prognose stützt und der zahlreiche Unverdächtige, die für die Gefahrenlage keine Verantwortung tragen, tötet, verkennt, dass eine Abwägung von Leben gegen Leben verfassungsrechtlich unzulässig ist. Eine gesetzliche Regelung kann dazu führen, durch entsprechende Definitionen die Einsatzschwelle herabzusetzen.

Bereits heute deckt Art. 35 GG die vorausschauende Abwehr von Gefahren und räumt damit auch im Extremfall den Abschuss eines als Tatwaffe genutzten Flugzeugs ein. In extremen Einzelfällen kann auf die seit langem anerkannte Rechtsfigur des übergesetzlichen Notstands als „Ultima Ratio" zurückgegriffen werden.

4 Innenpolitische Maßnahmen: Was soll geschehen?

Die Besorgnis erregende Tendenz der Gefährdung des liberalen Verfassungsstaats ist in der aktuellen innenpolitischen Debatte weiterhin sichtbar.

Ohne hier die Ebene der Europäischen Union weiter analysieren zu können, möchte ich auf die diskutierte EU-Vorratsdatenspeicherung hinweisen.

Die Europäische Union hat Anfang Dezember 2004 eine Arbeitsgruppe eingerichtet, die die Voraussetzungen einer EU-weiten Vorratsspeicherung von Telekommunikationsverbindungsdaten vorbereiten soll. Eine pauschale, maximal dreijährige, umfassende Speicherung von Datentypen – wie u. a. Short Message Services (SMS) und Internet-Protokolle einschließlich E-Mail, Datenübertragungs- und Netzübertragungsprotokoll, Sprachübermittlung über Breitband sowie Daten zur Umsetzung der Netzadresse – greift unverhältnismäßig stark in die Privatsphäre der Nutzer ein. Die erheblichen Auswirkungen für Bürger und Unternehmen stehen in keinem Verhältnis zu einem nicht erwiesenen Effekt für die Strafverfolgungsbehörden.

Der Vorschlag, der von Frankreich und Großbritannien in der EU angestoßen wurde, wird von Bundesinnenminister Schily unterstützt. Der Bundesinnenminister orientiert sich in diesen Fragen fast immer an den Vereinigten Staaten. So trommelt er seit Wochen für eine neue zentralisierte Sicherheitsarchitektur: Mehr Macht für das BKA und die Stärkung des Verfassungsschutzes sind die Kernbestandteile seiner Forderung.

Bundesinnenminister Schily will noch unbedingt vor Weihnachten sein Zentralisierungsprojekt durchsetzen. Es ist schon der zweite Anlauf: Denn bei der Innenministerkonferenz vor einigen Wochen hatten selbst SPD-Kollegen aus den Ländern gegen die Zentralisierung votiert.

Für solche Pläne müsste das Grundgesetz geändert werden, denn die Polizei ist bekanntlich Ländersache. Der Verfassungsschutz ist streng von der Polizei getrennt, und das BKA besitzt eine „Zentralstellenfunktion".

Diese historisch gewachsene Sicherheitsarchitektur wird jetzt als besonders ineffizient dargestellt. Die, wie es der ehemalige Präsident des Bundesamts für Verfassungsschutz, Eckart Wertebach, ausdrückt, „asymmetrische Bedrohungslage" erfordere „neue unkonventionelle Sicherheitsstrategien".

Was bedeutet dies konkret?

Zunächst geht es um die Ausweitung der Ermittlungskompetenz des BKA. Der Bundesinnenminister will dem BKA die zentrale Zuständigkeit für die Bekämpfung von Terrorismus und Organisierter Kriminalität übergeben; das BKA soll eine Weisungsbefugnis gegenüber den Landeskriminalämtern (LKAs) erhalten.

Schily lässt auch nicht locker, was die so genannte „Iniativermittlungskompetenz" des BKA betrifft. Damit könnte das BKA fast nach Belieben etwa „suspekte Islamisten" ausforschen. Dieses Projekt ist schon bei den Beratungen vor drei Jahren gescheitert, u. a. am Widerstand des Bundesjustizministeriums.

Die Einführung einer Kompetenz des Bundeskriminalamts für „Vorfeldermittlungen" – wie sie der Bundesinnenminister propagiert – wäre ein Verstoß gegen bewährte Grundsätze des deutschen Polizeirechts. Ein Weisungsrecht des BKA gegenüber den LKAs kommt nicht in Frage. Polizeihandeln setzt die Abwehr oder Verfolgung konkreter Straftaten voraus. „Vorfeldermittlungen" bergen die Gefahr in sich, dass ohne klare Abgrenzungskriterien Eingriffe in die Bürgerrechte erfolgen. Deshalb hat der Bundestag schon bei den Beratungen zum Anti-Terrorismus-Gesetz „Schily II" nach dem 11. September 2001 Vorfeldkompetenzen des BKA abgelehnt.

Ein wichtiger Hinweis sei erlaubt: Eine Zentralisierung der Sicherheitsarchitektur bedeutet nicht automatisch mehr Effektivität. Ein Herausbrechen der LKAs aus der Sicherheitsarchitektur kann Löcher in die enge Zusammenarbeit mit der

Polizei vor Ort reißen. Gleiches gilt für die Anbindung der Landesämter für Verfassungsschutz als Außenstellen an das Bundesamt für Verfassungsschutz.

Hinter den Vorschlägen Schilys steht das große Vorbild USA: Eine Bundespolizei nach dem Vorbild des FBI, das hätte der Bundesinnenminister am liebsten. Den Anfang hat er zumindest sprachlich gemacht; der Bundesgrenzschutz wird Anfang Januar 2005 in Bundespolizei umbenannt.

Zugunsten dieser propagierten Zentralisierung der Sicherheitsarchitektur sollen bewährte Grundsätze des Grundgesetzes preisgegeben werden. Zu diesen Grundsätzen zählt insbesondere das nach dem 2. Weltkrieg eingeführte Gebot der Trennung von Polizei und Geheimdiensten.

Buchstäblich in letzter Minute ist Bundesinnenminister Schily von seinem ursprünglichen Plan abgekommen, Polizei und Geheimdienst in einem gemeinsamen Analysezentrum zusammenzufassen. Beide Bereiche werden nun in unterschiedlichen Gebäuden als „Piaz" (Polizeiliches Informations- und Analysezentrum) und „Niaz" (Nachrichtliches Informations- und Analysezentrum) nebeneinander arbeiten.

Unter Wahrung dieser grundgesetzlichen Tradition ist eine effektive Terrorismusabwehr möglich. Die gesetzlichen Voraussetzungen für einen verbesserten Datenaustausch zwischen den Sicherheitsbehörden sind längst existent. Sie müssen nur voll angewandt werden.

Das Ziel kann nur sein, eine effektive Terrorismusabwehr bei Wahrung grundgesetzlicher Strukturen zu erreichen. Nicht alles, was vermeintlich effektiv und effizient im „Kampf gegen den Terrorismus" zu sein scheint, ist rechtsstaatlich durchsetzbar.

Wir brauchen bei der Terrorismusbekämpfung endlich klare, rechtsstaatliche Maßstäbe. Lassen Sie mich dies abschließend in einigen Thesen zusammenfassen.

Erstens: Wir müssen verstärkt und mit Augenmaß und Sachverstand Bedrohungen ernst nehmen und entschieden bekämpfen. Das gelingt nur, wenn wieder ein Klima entsteht, das die politische Bedeutung von Grundrechten und Grundfreiheiten ernst nimmt. Grundrechte und Grundfreiheiten sind die Pfeiler einer freiheitlich verfassten Gesellschaft. Sie müssen für jeden Einzelnen erfahrbar sein, sonst drohen sie wertlos zu werden.

Zweitens: Die Gefahren unserer Zeit werden verharmlost, wenn fragwürdige, ineffektive und für den Rechtsstaat gefährliche Instrumente entwickelt werden.

- Lassen Sie mich ein meiner Meinung nach mehr als fragwürdiges Beispiel anführen: die Ausweitung der so genannten „Sicherungshaft". Es geht dabei um Personen mit Terrorismusbezug, denen aber weder eine Straftat noch die konkrete Vorbereitung einer Straftat nachgewiesen werden kann. Selbstverständlich ist es erlaubt und bei entsprechenden Anhaltspunkten notwendig, solche Personen mit polizeilichen Mitteln zu überwachen. Solange die Überwachung aber keinen Hinweis auf eine konkret von den Personen ausgehende Gefahr ergibt, ist eine Inhaftierung unzulässig.

Drittens: Weitere Eingriffsrechte dürfen nur Folge der Erkenntnis sein, dass auf der praktisch-operativen Ebene Verbesserungen nicht mehr möglich sind. Zu den praktisch-operativen Verbesserungen gehören:

- Die personelle Ausstattung der Polizei muss schnell und substanziell verbessert werden. Die Streichung tausender von Polizeistellen in den vergangenen Jahren war falsch. Die organisatorische Ausstattung der Polizei muss in allen Bereichen von Büroorganisation bis zur Einführung des Digitalfunks schnellstmöglich verbessert werden.
- LKAs und BKA müssen vertikal besser vernetzt werden. Ein optimierter Datenaustausch ist angesichts der föderalen Struktur der Sicherheitsbehörden unerlässlich. Datenschutzgrundsätze sind strikt einzuhalten.

Viertens: Eine rationale, auf die Auswertung von Tatsachen und Erfahrungen mit den bereits bestehenden, weit reichenden Gesetzen gestützte Innenpolitik muss endlich zum Durchbruch kommen. Die FDP-Bundestagsfraktion hat seit langem gefordert, die Erfahrungen mit den Anti-Terrorismus-Gesetzen „Schily-I" und „Schily-II" auszuwerten.

- Die einzelnen Maßnahmen des Sicherheitspaketes II müssten daraufhin überprüft werden, inwieweit sie dazu beigetragen hätten, die Terroranschläge vom 11. September 2001 zu verhindern oder die unauffällig in Deutschland als „Schläfer" lebenden Terroristen rechtzeitig dingfest zu machen, wenn sie zu diesem Zeitpunkt bereits in Kraft gewesen wären.
- Grundsätzlich gilt, dass bei allen zu kaltblütigen und blutrünstigen Taten bereiten Kriminellen, zu denen auch die Terroristen gehören, immer Probleme des rechtsstaatlichen Umgangs bestehen. Dies gilt für legal in Deutschland lebende „Schläfer" erst recht. Ob die Neuauflage der Rasterfahndung mit Blick auf diese Tätergruppe größere Erfolge zeitigen wird als der berühmte Kommissar Zufall und als riesige Datenberge, bleibt abzuwarten. Doch der absehbare Nebeneffekt, dass Menschen, die muslimischen Glaubens sind, von ihren Nachbarn, Berufs- oder Studienkollegen verdächtigt werden, be-

hindert die Integration von Zuwanderern und kann zu Stigmatisierung und Gettoisierung führen. Das Klima des internationalen Zusammenlebens wird schlechter. Das kann unmittelbare Auswirkungen haben, etwa indem bei Teilen der islamgläubigen Minderheit die Gewaltbereitschaft steigt.

Fünftens: Wir sind gut beraten, an der klaren Trennung der Aufgaben von Polizei, wozu auch die Bereitschaftspolizei und der Bundesgrenzschutz gehören (innere Sicherheit), und Bundeswehr (äußere Sicherheit einschließlich der Überwachung des Luftraums) festzuhalten.

- Die Bundeswehr ist für polizeiliche Aufgaben weder ausgebildet noch ausgerüstet. Dagegen erfordert die moderne Polizeiarbeit eine hoch spezialisierte (Fachhochschul-)Ausbildung; eine solche Tätigkeit kann daher nicht einfach von anderen Berufsgruppen übernommen werden. Schließlich ist es auch nicht Aufgabe der Bundeswehr, Kosten für die Polizeiarbeit, die im föderalen Staat bei den Bundesländern anfallen, zu übernehmen.

Sechstens: Der liberale Verfassungsstaat ist wehrhaft, so wie er besteht.

- Die Verhinderung des geplanten Anschlags gegen den irakischen Ministerpräsidenten Allawi ist ein Beleg dafür, dass die Sicherheitsarchitektur funktioniert.

- Ich will an dieser Stelle nicht „en detail" auf den Fall Metin Kaplan eingehen. Das Urteil des Bundesverwaltungsgerichts vom 7. Dezember 2004 zeigt aber, dass der Rechtsstaat wehrhaft ist – allen Unkenrufen zum Trotz. Es stellt außerdem unmissverständlich klar, dass Folter und unmenschliche Behandlung ein Auslieferungshindernis darstellen. An diesen Grundsätzen muss festgehalten werden. Da Metin Kaplan eine menschenunwürdige Behandlung in der Türkei nicht droht und nach den Zusagen der türkischen Regierung ein faires Verfahren gewährleistet erscheint, konnte er keinen Abschiebungsschutz geltend machen. Dies hat das Bundesverwaltungsgericht auch eindeutig klargestellt.

Wir leben seit den schrecklichen Anschlägen vom 11. September 2001 in einer Gesellschaft, die durch ein erhöhtes Schutzbedürfniss vor Terroranschlägen und eine gewachsene Furcht vor permanenter Bedrohung gekennzeichnet ist.

Der Ruf nach strengeren Gesetzen, die schärfere Kontrollen, präzisere Aufklärung und härtere Strafen ermöglichen, ist meist prompte Folge von Anschlägen, die die Öffentlichkeit erschüttern. Diese reflexartigen Reaktionen verstellen oft den Blick auf die Grundlagen des liberalen Rechtsstaats.

Mit dem skizzierten Verständnis des liberalen Rechtsstaats können wir den Herausforderungen unserer Zeit begegnen. Das gelingt nur, wenn wieder ein Klima entsteht, das die politische Bedeutung von Grundrechten und Grundfreiheiten ernst nimmt.

Fangen wir heute an und ändern dies.

Terrorism and Germany: the Threat and the Response

Dr. Joshua Sinai

Senior Terrorism Analyst, ANSER, Shirlington, Virginia, USA
Joshua.sinai@verizon.net

Although no terrorism attacks have recently taken place in Germany, the preconditions for terrorism have been created in the country over the past several years. After the September 11, 2001 terrorist attacks against the U.S., which were planned in Germany, the German government acknowledged that Germany was used as a base by terrorists to prepare attacks on other countries and was also a target of potential attacks.[1] Three of the pilots in the 9/11 attacks, for example, had been students in Hamburg, including the plot's leader, Mohammad Atta. More recently, German authorities foiled a plot by Iraqi exiles to assassinate Iyad Allawi, the Iraqi interim prime minister, who visited Berlin in November 2004. With Germany becoming a center for radical Islamic activities, its government since 2001 has implemented a variety of new security laws, regulations and organizational structures to combat terrorism, and engaged in a series of operations against Islamic terrorists and their sympathizers based in Germany.

Germany, like other European nations, has faced a terrorism challenge since the 1970s, although its character has changed over the years. In the 1970s and 1980s, Germany's terrorism threat emanated from left-wing groups, such as the Red Army Faction (RAF). The RAF was an outgrowth of the Baader-Meinhof Gang. The RAF was eventually succeeded by a small grouping of some 20 to 30 terrorists, who carried out attacks against United States and NATO military officials and bases as well as prominent German officials and business executives. In August 1992, however, the RAF renounced armed struggle. By the early 1990s, terrorism in Germany was characterized by neo-Nazi and other xenophobic right-wing fringe groups, whose violence was fueled by the growing presence of large numbers of foreign workers, mostly from Turkey, and large numbers of aliens

---

[1] Hugh Williamson, "German Security Services to Improve Cooperation," *Financial Times*, December 16, 2004.

seeking political asylum in the country. By the late 1990s, these groups were superseded by Middle Eastern terrorist organizations, who received support from the country's growing Muslim community.

1 General Overview

The Federal Republic of Germany is Europe's most populous nation and has its largest economy. It is a key member of the continent's economic, political, and defense organizations. In 1949, with the advent of the Cold War, two German states were formed: the western Federal Republic of Germany (FRG) and the eastern German Democratic Republic (GDR). The end of the Cold War resulted in German unification in 1990. Since then, Germany has expended considerable funds to integrate, revitalize and raise the economic standards of the former East Germany, with the unified Berlin serving as the nation's capital.

As suggested by its name, Germany is a federation of 16 individual states (Bundesländer). Each state is endowed with its own powers and its own republican and democratic state constitution, as laid out in the country's constitution (Grundgesetz). The states elect representatives to the federal council (Bundesrat). However, the major responsibility for governance resides in the federal diet (Bundestag), which is the country's parliament. It is by the Bundestag that the Chancellor, the country's head of state, is elected, while the President, who is elected by the Bundesrat, serves as ceremonial chief of state. As discussed later in this article, this federal structure has imposed restrictions and constraints on the country's anti-terrorism posture, due to a contest of wills between the federal and state levels, so that even federal agencies involved in countering terrorism may lack control over their state bureaus.

2 Radical Islamists in Germany

Muslims constitute the largest religious minority in Germany. Some 82.4 million people lived in Germany according to a July 2004 estimate. Approximately 9%, 7.3 million, of the German population are foreign nationals. Germany's foreign population ratio is one of the highest in Europe. Approximately 3 to 3.5 million Muslims live in Germany. More than one quarter (28.7%; 1,998,534) of the foreign community in Germany, and a majority of the country's Muslims, come from Turkey. In recent years, the proportion of persons from the former Yugoslavia, especially Bosnian refugees, has risen markedly, to some 727,204 persons (10.1%), making them the second largest Muslim community in the country. Of the remaining foreign population, some 608,500 (8.4%) are Italians and 363,000 (4.9%) are Greek. The Turkish and Bosnian Muslims are not considered to pose a terrorist threat in Germany. The major threat comes from North African and Middle Eastern expatriates, and, in particular, the Moroccan immigrants, who tend to be more radical in their religious beliefs than the Turkish or Bosnian Muslims. The cities where radical Islamic activity proliferates reportedly include Munich, Berlin, Aachen, Dortmund and Bonn.

Foreign nationals in Germany also include refugees and asylum seekers. In 1999-2000, Germany received the highest number of asylum applications in Europe, numbering some 1,958,153 (for comparison purposes, the United Kingdom received 574,769, the Netherlands 366,090, France 335,990, Switzerland 300,381 and Sweden 261,292). German asylum policy, however, is considered lenient, so radical Islamists have taken advantage of it and settled in Germany, where they benefit from social-welfare programs and conduct their radical activities. Some of the most notable examples include Ramzi bin al Shibh, Shadi Abdallah and Rabei Osman el Sayed Ahmed, recently arrested in Milan and extradited to Spain.

The radicalization of the German Muslim community is the product of several factors. One of the main problems is the failure of German integration policy directed at the Muslim community. Although many first- and second-generation immigrants may have gradually adjusted to their lack of complete integration, feelings of being excluded from German society have led to the radicalization of many of the younger members of these communities. Within the large Turkish community, for example, the first two generations may be relatively secular, but according to a recent poll, some 20 percent of the members of the third generation now identify themselves as fundamentalist Muslims. There is concern that if the situation were to deteriorate in Turkey, this third generation might become increasingly militant and violent in its opposition activities.

With German immigrant communities coming from numerous Muslim countries, many of the world's Islamic radical and terrorist groups are similarly represented in Germany, including the Palestinian Hamas, the Lebanese Hizballah, the Turkish PKK, and al Qaida and its affiliates.

In its 2003 annual report, issued in May 2004, Germany's domestic intelligence service, the Office for the Protection of the Constitution (BfV), warned that Islamic extremists and foreign terrorist groups posed the greatest danger to the country's security.[2] As explained by the Minister of the Interior Otto Schily, "Un-

---

[2] "German Intelligence Says Islamists Present Major Threat," Deutsche Welle (http:\\www.dw-world.de), May 18, 2004.

fortunately we still face diverse dangers in Germany of which Islamic terrorism and Islamic extremism form the focal point."[3] Referring to the recent terrorist attacks in Madrid in March 2004, Schily added that "We can't assume that Germany lies outside the reach of such targets," because Germany was viewed by Islamic terrorists as allied with the U.S. and Israel and was involved in the peacekeeping operation in Afghanistan.[4]

The BfV report considered 57,300 foreign individuals as "radical," with about 31,000 active in 24 Islamist organizations with extremist ties.[5] The largest membership was in six Turkish organizations, which had a total of 27,300 followers.[6] The BfV, according to Schily, believed that extremist Islamic groups commanded a large number of covert sympathizers and had extended their influence to a wider proportion (swathe) of the Muslim population than a year ago. He added that Islamist groups, which he described as religiously "fanatic," were reaching many more people in mosques and community centers through "disintegrative activities" that were attracting a younger following.[7]

The largest Islamic organization in Germany is Milli Görüs. It operates legally in the country, but is on the BfV watch list because it tried to indoctrinate Muslims living in Germany, especially the youth, in anti-western and anti-democratic notions.[8]

The report stated that the Islamists who advocated jihad or holy war posed one of the most potent dangers to the country.[9] It mentioned the militant Islamist Abu Mussab al Zarqawi, whose al Qaida affiliated Jordanian-based al Tawhid group was accused of carrying out attacks on Jewish targets in Berlin and Dusseldorf. According to the BfV, Zarqawi also plays a central role in the radical Islamic Kurdish group Ansar al Islam, which in 2003 was supported logistically by members in Germany.[10]

The BfV estimates that there are about 100 supporters of Ansar al Islam in Germany.[11] Counter-terrorism officials believe that the group attempts to recruit

---

[3] Ibid.
[4] Ibid.
[5] Ibid.
[6] Ibid.
[7] Ibid.
[8] Ibid.
[9] Ibid.
[10] Ibid.
[11] Richard Bernstein, "3 Arrested in Suspected Plot to Attack Iraqi Prime Minister," *The New York Times*, December 3, 2004.

new members in Germany to go to Iraq to fight the Americans. (It also has a presence in Italy, France, Spain and Britain.)[12]

The report also included the groups such as Hamas, which has about 300 members in Germany, and the Lebanese Hizballah, which is believed to have around 800 sympathizers in Germany.[13]

Also mentioned was the banned Islamic organization led by Metin Kaplan, the so-called "Caliph of Cologne," which had 800 members before it was disbanded at the end of 2001.[14] The BfV believes that former members are attempting to re-start the group's organizational structures despite the ban.[15]

Another problem Germany faces is the existence of "hate preachers" – Islamic radicals who make virulent public pronouncements against Israel, the United States, and Western values. These preachers are considered a threat but have never been implicated in any terrorist acts. According to veteran terrorism expert Paul Wilkinson, these organizations are "very smart in walking the very fine line between propaganda and incitement to terrorism."[16]

Although not implicated directly in terrorism, groups such as Hizb-ut-Tahrir have been banned in Germany. The controversy over Hizb-ut-Tahrir erupted in October 2002, when a student group affiliated with the movement organized a conference at Berlin's Technical University which was also attended by several leaders of the extreme right-wing National German Party (NPD), including Udo Voigt, its chairman. The meeting provoked outrage in the press against "Islamists and neo-Nazis" uniting to deliver anti-Semitic harangues in an educational institution. In January 2003, the Minister of the Interior Schily banned the group, saying it was "spreading hate and violence" and was calling for the killing of Jews.[17] A member of the group was expelled from Germany for alleged ties to one of the 9/11 hijackers.[18]

---

[12] Ibid.
[13] Ibid.
[14] Ibid.
[15] Ibid.
[16] Sophie Lambroschini, "Germany: Court Appeal by Hizb Ut-Tahrir Highlights Balancing Act Between Actions, Intentions," Radio Free Europe/Radio Liberty, October 26, 2004.
[17] Ibid.
[18] Ibid.

According to publicly available estimates, some 250 to 300 suspected radical Islamists are currently being monitored by the BfV.[19] A further challenge is presented by radical Islamists who have left Germany to fight with the insurgents in Iraq. Reports that some of them are starting to trickle back into Germany are causing concern among German security services. The BND, for example, is monitoring members of this group for indications of potential terrorist activity on German soil.

3   Islamic and Right-Wing Extremists

German authorities are also concerned about potential alliances between Islamic militants and right-wing extremists.[20] Despite their religious and philosophical differences and the xenophobic attacks by neo-Nazis and skinheads against immigrant Muslims and other foreigners for spoiling their dream of a pure German state, security officials are concerned about the growing attraction between the two. (So far, no links have been found suggesting that they are collaborating on terrorism-related activities.) One reason why the right-wingers may be attracted to Islamic radicals is the latter's tenacity and patient planning, as exemplified by the 9/11 attacks in striking the icons of American capitalism and military prowess.[21] As mentioned earlier, Udo Voigt, the chairman of the NPD, attended the conference of Hizb-ut-Tahrir in October 2002. Voigt also supports Ahmed Huber, a Swiss far-right leader who espouses closer ties with Muslim radicals.[22]

4   Terrorist Threats

With the largest terrorist threat to Germany posed by the Hamburg cell which carried out the 9/11 attacks, German law-enforcement officials have conducted numerous operations to arrest or ban suspected terrorists, their organizations and sympathizers. However, even before 2001 radical Islamic groups had attempted to carry out terrorist activities in the country. In December 2000, four Algerians and a Moroccan were accused of planning to set off a bomb hidden in

---

[19] "Überforderte Ermittler," *Die Zeit*, May 6, 2004, cited in Francis T. Miko and Christian Froehlich, "Germany's Role in Fighting Terrorism: Implications for U.S. Policy," *CRS Report for Congress*, December 27, 2004.
[20] Jeffrey Fleishman, "East, West Radicals Find Unsettling Bond," *Los Angeles Times*, January 6, 2003.
[21] Ibid.
[22] Ibid.

a pressure cooker in the Strasbourg Christmas market. The bomb did not detonate. The defendants were alleged to be part of the "Frankfurt cell" network. They were tried in April 2003 in Frankfurt, and four members were sentenced to 10 to 12 years in prison for their role in plotting the attack.

In October 2001, authorities arrested Abdelghani Mzoudi for allegedly supporting the al Qaida cell in Hamburg involved in the 9/11 attacks. The following month, Mounir el Motassadeq, a Moroccan student, was arrested in Hamburg for membership in the Hamburg cell, including managing its finances. He admitted to being Atta's friend and attending an al Qaida training camp in Afghanistan.[23] Motassadek was convicted in early 2003, but a retrial was underway as of early 2005, after an appeals court had overturned the earlier conviction. As a result, it is still unclear whether German legal authorities will succeed in gaining convictions against Mzoudi or Motassadek.

On April 23, 2002, German police arrested nine members of a Palestinian organization suspected of plotting attacks.[24] The organization, known as al Tawhid, is a Sunni Palestinian movement supporting Islamic jihad. The detainees were suspected of involvement in providing fake identity documents and seeking donations in support of terrorism.[25]

In March 2003, German investigators in Berlin detained five alleged Islamist terrorists on suspicion of planning an attack to coincide with the start of the war in Iraq.[26] Germany's general federal prosecutor charged the five with having founded a terrorist organization in Berlin "at the behest of the international network of violent Islamists," to recruit Arab students for future bomb attacks.[27] Among the premises searched was a building that houses the al-Nur mosque.

Also in March, German authorities arrested Ihsan Garnawi, a Tunisian, for planning bombing attacks in Berlin and other cities and seeking to create an al Qaida sleeper cell in Germany.[28] Garnawi was arrested with five other Islamists at Berlin's al Nur mosque. While the others were subsequently released, Garnawi remained in custody. Garnawi had reportedly been trained in the use of weapons and explosives at an al Qaida camp in Afghanistan and was acquainted

---

[23] Mary Louise Kelly, "Profile: Al Qaeda Cells in Germany," National Public Radio, October 19, 2004.
[24] Jonathan Fighel," International Terrorism in Germany: An Ongoing Threat," ICT, May 1, 2002.
[25] Ibid.
[26] John Hooper, "Al Qaida Suspects Detained in Berlin," *The Guardian*, March 21, 2003.
[27] Ibid.
[28] "New Terror Trial Opens in Berlin," Deutsche Welle, April 4, 2004.

with Usama bin Laden.[29] According to the indictment, he arrived in Germany in January 2003, on a fake passport, to "recruit Muslim students and refugees and train them in terrorist fighting techniques and strategy."[30] A search of his apartment uncovered bomb-making materials as well as a flight-simulator game, a handbook on poisons and aerial photographs of German cities, including nuclear and chemical plant sites.[31] Prosecutors believed that Garnawi had been planning a mass casualty attack to humiliate the West and that it had been due to coincide with the protest demonstrations against the war in Iraq.[32]

German police thwarted a possible terrorist attack when they arrested a Turkish male and an American female suspected of attempting to bomb the US military base in Heidelberg.

In mid-September 2004, German authorities banned "The First Arab Islamic Congress in Europe," a controversial Islamic conference that was to be held in Berlin in early October. In addition, they deported Fadi Madi, the organizer of the conference, to his home country of Lebanon for his alleged radical anti-Israel and anti-U.S. views.[33]

In October 2004, Metin Kaplan, leader of the banned Hilafet Devleti (Caliphate State) movement, was deported from Germany to Istanbul.[34] Kaplan, known as the "Caliph of Cologne," was deported because of his association with Islamic extremists in Germany and was also wanted in Turkey for terrorism charges.[35]

In late November 2004, a German court banned the Al Aqsa Foundation for collecting funds for Hamas.[36] This followed a raid on the Islamic charity's offices in the western city of Aachen, where "important documents" were confiscated.[37]

On December 3, 2004, German police arrested three Iraqis suspected of planning to assassinate Iraqi interim prime minister Ayad Allawi, who was in Berlin at the time for talks with chancellor Gerhard Schröder. The three, who had been under surveillance for several months, were believed to be members of Ansar

---

[29] Ibid.
[30] "Bin Laden 'Associate' Faces Charges," E Expatica, January 16, 2004.
[31] Ibid.
[32] "New Terror Trial Opens in Berlin."
[33] "Berlin Deports Islamic Conference Organizer," Associated Press, September 19, 2004.
[34] Germany Extradites Islamist Leader to Turkey," ICT, October 13, 2004.
[35] Ibid.
[36] "German Police Raid Offices of Charity With Links to Hamas," *Jerusalem Post*, December 3, 2004.
[37] Ibid.

al-Islam, the Iraqi terrorist group responsible for numerous suicide bombings in Iraq.

As of late 2004, the German Justice Ministry was involved in some 80 preliminary proceedings against 170 persons suspected of involvement in Islamic terrorism.[38]

5 Right-Wing Extremism

Political extremism is Germany is not limited to the radical Islamists. Interestingly, the rise in radical Islamism has been accompanied by, although not directly linked with, a slight decline in right-wing extremism. The BfV's 2003 annual report claimed an 8% drop in membership among right-wing extremist groups in the country to 41,500 individuals.[39] This was the first significant decrease in nine years and was accompanied by a 10% decrease in politically motivated right-wing crimes and violent acts.[40] At the same time, however, the report claimed a 15% rise in the number of neo-Nazis, adding up to 3,000 persons.[41] The Minister of the Interior Schily said that Skinhead music fueled by the Internet is "the number one gateway drug" for many young people, with anti-Semitism being their distinguishing mark.[42]

6 Germans killed by Terrorism

German nationals have been killed by terrorist acts overseas, although they were not the prime targets. In April 2002, 11 German citizens were killed in a suicide attack against a synagogue on the Tunisian island of Djerba. In October of that year, six German citizens were killed in the bombing of a Bali nightclub.

7 Anti-Terrorism Legislation

In the wake of the 9/11 attacks, the German government began implementing a new series of anti-terrorism laws. In November 2001, "Security Package I"

---

[38] Federal Minister of Justice Brigitte Zypries in *Süddeutsche Zeitung*, June 11, 2004, cited in Miko and Froehlich, "Germany's Role in Fighting Terrorism: Implications for U.S. Policy."
[39] "German Intelligence Says Islamists Present Major Threat."
[40] Ibid.
[41] Ibid.
[42] Ibid.

took effect, amending existing laws by closing loopholes in German law that enabled terrorists to operate and raise funds in Germany, revoked the immunity of religious groups and charities from governmental investigation or surveillance, allowed for the prosecution of terrorists living in Germany even if their organizations operated only abroad, and strengthened border and air traffic security to make it difficult for terrorists to enter the country.[43] On January 1, 2002, under "Security Package II," new anti-terrorism security laws and regulations took effect in Germany, pertaining to the rights of foreigners. The new laws were intended to prevent the entry of terrorists into the Federal Republic and to enable the authorities to identify extremists already residing in Germany and contain their activities. Provisions included using biometric characteristics in passports and personal Ids, making visa-relevant data available to security authorities, upgrading background checks on security-related employees, ensuring that asylum seekers and temporary residents received Ids that cannot be counterfeited, and using sky marshals to prevent hijackings.[44] In August 2002, a new law was passed allowing the government to lift the country's strict legislation protecting religious organizations if they are deemed to promote extremism or ideals that could be linked to terrorism. However, a more sweeping series of new laws, known as "Security Package III," was initiated by the Minister of the Interior Schily in November 2004, but was rejected by the Länder of Germany because it would have shifted the balance of power to the central state.

8 Governmental Organizations to combat Terrorism

The Minister of the Interior Otto Schily is chief of Germany's war on terrorism. He has held this post since 1998 and is widely respected in Germany and internationally for his stalwart commitment to countering terrorism. His tenure has been marked by efforts to overhaul the country's complex network of independent state-run police and intelligence services at the federal and state levels, which he believed hampered effective counterterrorism. For example, three national intelligence services are charged with gathering information on domestic and foreign extremist and terrorist groups active in Germany, but they are not collocated with each other. The headquarters of the Office for the Protection of the Constitution (BfV), which gathers domestic intelligence and monitors the jihadists, is located in Cologne; the headquarters of the counterterrorism unit of

---

[43] Miko and Froehlich, "Germany's Role in Fighting Terrorism: Implications for U.S. Policy."
[44] German Embassy, Washington, DC, "Counter-Terrorism Laws Take Effect," January 2002.

the Federal Criminal Police (BKA) is located in Wiesbaden; and the headquarters of the Federal Intelligence Service (BND) is located in Pullach near Munich.[45] The BKA and the BfV both have offices in each Land and operate under the federal government. The BND also has offices throughout Germany and foreign countries. Of the three, the BND is the only intelligence service in Germany to send its reports directly to the government. However, all three services have very limited counterterrorism powers as defined by the Grundgesetz, so that the communications flow regarding terrorism-related information is at times too slow to disseminate information in a timely manner.

As a result, following the March 2003 bombings of the Madrid transportation system, the Minister of the Interior Schily had to hold crisis meetings by telephone, which made him realize that effectiveness in combating terrorism required a radical overhaul of the country's federalist system. An optimal solution was to create a strong federal intelligence agency and put the 16 state offices under its control, giving the BKA and the BfV greater investigative powers and moving the agency to Berlin.[46] However, the states refused to cede any power to the federal government and would only grant improved cooperation, not centralization. To resolve the dispute, Mr. Schily created a commission to propose a new plan. As a result of the commission's recommendations, in mid-December 2004, Germany established a new counterterrorism coordination and command center in Berlin to improve coordination between federal and state security services. The center includes more than 100 federal criminal police (BKA) and 15 BfV domestic intelligence officers and BND officers, with additional staff expected to be added in 2005.[47] In accordance with their constitutionally-specified separation of powers, the three intelligence services are located in three different buildings in the new compound. Besides providing opportunities for the exchange of information between the BfV, BND and BKA, e.g. by maintaining a central database on Islamist extremists, the center is also expected to cooperate with security organizations such as the state police forces and border police.[48] Counterparts from security services in other European countries and the United States would also work in the counterterrorism center.[49]

The center represents an unusual degree of centralization in Germany, where policing remains the responsibility of 16 regional states. Germany's division

---

[45] Ibid.
[46] Ibid.
[47] "Germany Creates New Terror Center," Deutsche Welle, December 14, 2004.
[48] Ibid.
[49] Williamson, "German Security Services to Improve Cooperation."

between police and intelligence work arose as a post-war reaction to Nazi-era abuses by security forces. As a result, the police were banned from gathering domestic intelligence, with each state creating its own intelligence agency.[50] These coordinated with the other agencies, but only reported to their own state government. The Minister of the Interior Schily decided that if the BKA and other agencies would not report to him, the next best thing was to centralize intelligence collection and analysis at the BfV.[51] He also wanted to move the part of the BKA that collects and analyzes information to Berlin.

Even in this new organizational structure, however, Germany's traditionally strict division between the political and intelligence services will persist. The center will focus on information exchange and analysis of terrorism rather than joint anti-terror activities and will maintain the constitutionally based division between intelligence services and the police, with neither allowed to jointly gather information.[52]

9 German-American Cooperation

As part of strengthening German-American cooperation in countering terrorism, on August 1, 2002, Germany and the U.S. signed a declaration to improve bilateral cooperation on shipping container security. The container security initiative is designed to prevent terrorists from smuggling weapons of mass destruction in sea cargo containers. Under the initiative, cargo containers would be pre-screened in the German ports of Bremerhaven and Hamburg before they arrive in U.S. ports, with German and U.S. customs agents stationed in each other's countries.[53]

In mid-June 2003, the Minister of the Interior Schily met with U.S. government officials to discuss cooperation on counterterrorism. Schily and Tom Ridge, U.S. Secretary for Homeland Security, reached an agreement on bilateral co-operation for the protection of computer systems and networks with the goal of defending vital infrastructures such as power supplies, transportation and telecommunications in both Germany and the U.S.[54] In summer 2003, the first

---

[50] Boston, "The Intelligence Test."
[51] Ibid.
[52] Ibid.
[53] German Embassy, Washington, DC, "Agreement on Container Security Strengthens Cooperation in Fight Against Terrorism," August 2002.
[54] German Embassy, Washington, DC, "The Week in Germany: Politics; Schily: Close Cooperation on Counterterrorism is Key," June 20, 2003.

German-American workshop on IT dependency of critical infrastructure was held in Berlin.[55]

10 Conclusion

Although Germany so far has been immune from major terrorist attacks by radical Islamists on its soil – even though the country has been used to plan attacks against other countries and several plots targeting Germany have been thwarted –, the German government is concerned that the underlying currents are present for future attacks. As a result, Germany has become a major player in the international fight against terrorism. Nevertheless, radical Islamic subcultures that serve as breeding grounds for terrorist activities are reported to be active in the country. The Minister of the Interior Schily is keenly aware of such threats and has attempted to implement the necessary bureaucratic steps at the federal level to effectively counter such challenges. However, he has been stymied by opposition in the government and the federal states to greater centralization and coordination of counterterrorism, which would upgrade the nation's capabilities to combat terrorism. Another issue is that information on suspects is generally collected through intelligence means, yet it cannot be used in court because such information is collected covertly.[56] Moreover, the police are prohibited from collecting intelligence type information on suspects; they can only initiate an investigation once it can be proven that a crime has been perpetrated or is being planned.[57] Thus, if legal authorities lack a reasonable probability in terms of appropriateness of the evidence collected to convict a suspect, he or she must be released. This has been the case with several recent suspects. In a further problem area, in keeping with the tradition of upholding the rights of religious expression, the government is reluctant to block radical influences at Islamic educational institutions such as the Saudi Arabian-financed King Fahd Academy, which was founded in Bonn in 1995 and has been criticized in the international media for supporting martyrdom operations. Thus, to upgrade the country's counterterrorism capability, the constitutionally sensitive balance between maintaining a security state and allowing for greater civil liberties still needs to be resolved. Answering such questions looms large in

---

[55] German Embassy, Washington, DC, "Bridging US-European Homeland Security Concerns," May 10, 2004 (remarks by Otto Schily at 2004 Roundtable on Transatlantic Cooperation in Homeland Security, in Washington, DC).
[56] Miko and Froehlich, "Germany's Role in Fighting Terrorism: Implications for U.S. Policy."
[57] Ibid.

German counterterrorism and legal circles because the radicalization currently taking place among segments of the Muslim community may result in the creation of a new cadre to carry out future terrorist operations in that country or, as in 9/11, against other countries.

Russian Prospectives, International Terrorism Today, Retaliatory Measures

A. S. Kulikov

Deputy Chairman
Committee on Security
The State DUMA of the Russian Federation
General of the Army

1 International Terrorism today

The conception of "international terrorism", though generally accepted and used, does not precisely reflect the essence of this new and rapidly developing as a chain reaction threat.

Terrorism is merely a tactics, but not a political program or ideology. The roots of the problem lie in the inner contradictions of the Moslem world, fermented by contacts with the globalization. In real life it has found dramatic and visible confirmation.

It is possible to extract three main reasons of the growing international terrorist activities at the beginning of the 21st century.

Firstly, along with the USSR-USA confrontation end the extremist forces – and first of all national liberation, religious and other movements, which earlier were financed and armed by those superpowers, as well as directed and restrained by them, in their majority have become ownerless. But they have not disappeared and moreover – along with the strengthening of the American hegemony the process of protesting, violence and terror has begun to speed up in the developing world.

Secondly, in the countries of the third world, or as they are called now, "the failed states', the process of transition to the free market relations in economy and to the liberalization in politics has been speeded up as well. The neo-liberal model absorbs nation-states, brings new values, especially in cultures, destroys traditional life-styles and thus causes protest and constitutes a powerful source of terrorism.

Thirdly, globalization, which provides the possibility to bring terrorism into every household in any region of the world.

From the end of the 1990ties terrorism from a second rate factor of the world politics has moved to the first place among the global challenges and threats of the world community.

It is evident, that the real enemy of the USA and the European countries is the radical Islamism. Today there exist many points of view concerning its values orientation: from the explosion of uncontrolled emotions, blind urge to cause maximum pain to the West, to the realization absolutely rational strategy of setting up an Islamic "caliphate". The majority of those orientations are concentrated around problems of the Near and Middle East. Russia, the USA and the European countries have different vision on solving those problems. Conditional unity on Israeli-Palestinian settlement is neigbouring with serious disagreements on Iran and Iraq. There are already several years that one of the obstacles on the road to the closer Russian-Western co-operation is Chechnya. The situation appeared when from the US and the EU stand on Chechnya depend in fact not only the character of the Russian participation in anti-terrorist coalition, but also a quality of the relations between Russia and yhe West in general.

Tragic events in Madrid, as well as with Russian aircraft, psychological attacks on the governments of a number of European states, originated in Iraq, and last but not the least – the tragedy in Beslan – have put Europe on the first line of the anti-terrorist war.

In this connection let us look closely at the conceptions with which the Old and New Worlds have at this stage.

Three years after 9/11 under the US leadership and according to the non-alternative credo of President Bush – "those who are not with us, are against us" – the world has formed the first anti-terrorist coalition. George Bush did not conceal, that this credo is absolutely American. The fact that this credo will become the one of the coalition, did go without saying.

But, alas, it has not. And while the experts were looking for the guilty ones – the over-confident America herself, her obstinate allies or the resourceful enemies of the Western democracies – the history and the geopolitics have put everything on its place.

The enemies are not eternal. Having received American scolding, Afghan talibs forever disappeared from political scene.

The same goes for the regime of Saddam Hussein. Some more candidates for the execution were already mentioned – Iran, Libya, Syria, the North Korea – "if they do not reform themselves". And they are doing it: at the order of the Head of the Libyan Peoples Jamahiria, Colonel Kadaffi, all the nuclear installations in that country have been suddenly dismantled and sent to the USA in carefully numerated boxes. Why to the USA?

Why not to IAEA, authorized to prevent the possession of nuclear bludgeon by any dictator? Apparently the authoritarian regimes digest the slogan –"those who are not with us, are against us"- much more rapidly and much better than the Western democracies, preoccupied with the human rights.

The partners are not stable. Joining the anti-terrorist coalition, Russia, for instance, was sure: it is now at last on the ground of common struggle with the world evil the USA and her allies will find corresponding legal definitions of the Chechen armed separatism. For to the whole world were demonstrated the facts, that the bandit formations in Chechnya are financed by extremist funds, screened by Islam, and that in their ranks fight the "soldiers of fortune" not only from Arab, but even from European countries. But everything was in vain: up until now the Chechen terrorism is been refused to be considered as a part of international one. They say, "this is a Russian internal problem". No one among the partners from anti-terrorist coalition have reacted to the Russian demands to extradite criminals, on whose hands is the blood of dozens and hundreds of innocent people. And when such a demand after long and difficult polemics has been met by Georgia, she was reproached by the Council of Europe.

In general it is necessary to recognize, that the European allies of the USA at the anti-terrorist coalition have found themselves in a rather ambiguous position. Some of them are copying the American model of confronting terrorism so thoroughly, that very soon they may surpass it. For instance, if all the proposals on the toughening of anti-terrorist legislation in the Great Britain are to be realized, she will become the most repressive in Europe.

In other words, back home the European democracies defend themselves against terrorism absolutely American way – the same bet on a fist even if it requires to sacrifice the civil rights, even sometimes the basic human rights. At the same time it is evident, that the membership in the NATO and inter-allied organizations with the USA, for the majority of the European countries gladly retreat to the background , if they feel risking to be involved into dangerous international shady enterprises.

It means, I think, that the EU as a whole and every European government feel the public opinion in their countries much better and much more readily take it into account.

Summing up this brief analysis, I would like to stress the following.

Apparently the Western governments prefer to separate the problems of anti-terrorist coalition from the problem of internal situation in Russia, including that of Chechnya. All the same the problem of Chechnya and the Northern Caucasus should be solved by Russia herself.

In this connection it is rather interesting to look at the materials of one intellectual gathering with the participation of a number of influential European political personalities, which was held at the end of February this year in the "Monaco Club".

The participants were around 40 influential persons (former Prime-ministers and Foreign ministers of the Mediterranean, including some highly placed people from Israel and the Palestine). The Chairperson of this gathering was former UN General Secretary Butros Butros-Gali, the main speaker – the famous French investigator Jean-Louis Brugier, no doubt, one of the best experts on terrorism in Europe.

During the proceedings was undertaken a serious analytic brainstorm on the problems of confronting modern terrorism. As a result there were formulated some conclusions and recommendations, which are quite close to those of my colleagues from the WAAF.

Here I shall cite six such conclusions:

1. The main feature of modern terrorism – its ability to mutate. In essence, it presents a threat of a virus type: the epidemics is approaching, the nature of disease is known, but it is not clear, when it strikes and where it will be the most painful. As a rule, virus penetrates most easily into a weak organism. That is why it is necessary to be saved from an illusion that local and international terrorism exists separately from each other, not touching each other.

2. The Al Qaida conception as it is today demonstrated to the public opinion, is so lightweight and inconsistent, that only obscures the complexity of radical Islamic threat. Even arresting Ussama bin Laden will not change anything. He is in fact a mythical personage without real power in any of the known terrorist structures.

3. The main nursery of the real terrorist threat today is situated in Pakistan as a result of a merger of the Al Qaida old core with local radical Islamic groups. At the time they were created by the Islamabad special forces for fanning anti-Indian feelings and mutinies in Kashmir, but lately came out of the obedience to them. Today their attention is concentrated on Singapore, Indonesia and Australia. But it is no doubt, that the regrouping of forces is going on and very soon the terrorist attacks will be redirected to the West.

4. A dangerous source of terrorism in Russia has become Chechnya, which now serves as a transit point for radical Islamists from different countries. From there they are secretly transferred to Europe, where they are trained to use chemical and bacteriological weapons. The threat of the use of the weapons of mass destruction in terrorist purposes is not already a fantastic nightmare, but a quite realistic possibility.

5. The use of force in Iraq, which as Washington thinks, has helped to liquidate along with the regime of Saddam Hussain the dangerous center of terrorist threat – is a strategic blander. This war has awoken the jihad of a new type, earlier unknown in the Arab East. If the Iraqi problem is not solved in the earliest time, it is quite possible, that the world will confront a "new Afghanistan".

6. The only guarantee of successful struggle against terrorism lies in constant co-operation of the intelligence organs, police forces and the law of all the countries of the world. It is interesting to note, that even in the most dramatic moments of the polemics between Paris and Washington on the Iraqi crisis, the co-operation of the French and American special forces was not ceased.

If to analyze very thoroughly these six conclusions, we can come to another and the most important one.

> After the Eastern crusade the first anti-terrorist coalition has ceased to exist to the accompaniment of the Madrid bombs thunder. Is there a coalition, based on the co-operation of special forces and economic support of civic regimes in the Arab world to be born?

Quite possible that it is in this context we should analyze the events, essential to the present and future development of the world society under the conditions of growing terrorist threat.

And I would like to stress one more point.

Fanaticism of Islamic businessmen and managers goes together with their high professionalism and even more with their skill in terrorist acts planning. Religious passion and professional calculation is a very dangerous mixture indeed.

The rich together with intellectual traditionalists and quite civil professors with the university education give not only money. They contribute also corresponding ideology, pattern of thinking, which become the possession of dozens if not millions of their co-religionists. For these purposes institutes, centers, the whole system of education are been set up and due to it the Moslems receive access to the modern interpretation of Salafiya (the most radical doctrine of Islamic ideology in the Middle ages).

And the participants in "global jihad" enjoy understanding and sympathy, and if it is not love, it is in any case respect.

That is why confronting terrorism, the West cannot count on the understanding of its actions from Moslem community.

Thus , religious extremism, which constitutes the spearhead of the terrorist influence on the world society, needs not only a surgical intervention: the "amputation" of bin Laden or Zavahiri will not be the final fight with terrorism.

The medicinal treatment is also needed. It is evident, that at the same time the world society should take into account, that a dead shaheed is somewhat more dangerous than alive "prophet".

2 Retaliatory Measures

The question how to confront new challenges and threats is urgent and stays unanswered.

It is necessary to accept, that neither the world community, nor separate coalitions of the nation-states have found nowadays effective means of defending themselves against terrorist threat. But the fact, that to defeat modern terrorism in a visible prospective does not seem possible, is not a justification for the total pessimism.

It is worth noting, that globalization and the "flourishing"of accompanying it deep deformations (terrorism, narco-business, smuggling, human trade etc.) show that excessive orientation on formal economic indices, unfounded and unjust distribution of resources, socially non-adopted models of political and economic, as well as social development are the main catalysts of political radicalization, based on religious extremism.

The virus of terrorism has a chance to penetrate and fix itself first of all there, where the immunity of the society has been weakened, and where the people are not ideologically, culturally, socially and politically consolidated.

The social and cultural breaks and "voids", in the countries, where the state power and international mechanism of political and legal regulation are weakened, become nutrient medium for all kinds of radicalism.

From the beginning of the 21st century Russia remains the most vulnerable among all the big countries from the point of view of international terrorist actions. And the terrorist offensive of August-September 2004 showed, that the enemy has reached the new level of operational planning and their realization.

The initiative is still on his side.

Under those conditions and proceeding from their own interests, the Western powers should cease to play the hypocrite on the situation around Chechnya, begin to actively co-operate with Russia and propose their real help in the struggle against terrorism.

Urgent is the problem of setting up a united world anti-terrorist center, which could accumulate all the experience aquired in the world on the struggle against terrorism and work out the strategy and tactics of such struggle.

And such world center already does exist. It is the World Interpol with the participation of 180 countries. It should be noted, that it is the police forces of different states, that today most effectively co-operate with each other.

But, of course, the work of the Interpol should be modernized , and for this the Charter of the organization, which remains basically unchanged since the middle of the last century, should be updated.

It is evident, that international terrorism cannot develop separately, without close ties with other forms of transnational crime (narco-traffic, trade in arms and human beings etc). That is why the activities of the world anti-terrorist center cannot be limited to the struggle against terrorism only. Possibly, we must talk about setting up an anti-terrorist and anti-criminal center.

Apart from this, it is necessary to search for more effective mechanism of all the states and non-government anti-terrorist and anti-criminal forces of the world community with the purpose to work out new approaches to the struggle against terrorism.

In this connection in order to realize the aims of the WAAF, I think, that a complex of retaliatory measures on the following directions should be urgently worked out.

1. Development of a unified conceptual apparatus.

   In order to understand each other it is necessary to communicate on the basis of unified terminology.

2. "Inventarisation" of international terrorist organizations, criminal groups and their infrastructures. The concentration of efforts on finding out and liquidation in the first place the organizations, providing financing, training, arms, technical appliances and their transportation.

3. Widening of diplomatic missions co-operation and improvement of effectiveness of diplomatic channels.

   (Russian experience of the 19th century).

4. Development of approaches to the struggle against international crime and corruption as an integrated part of the whole complex of measures against international terrorism.

   And really, the struggle against terrorism is impossible without confronting organized crime and corruption. (Examples: bribing Russian officials before terrorist acts on the aircraft and in Beslan).

   And it is interesting, that more and more often terrorists do not take responsibility for the terrorist acts, and at the same time criminals apply the terrorist tactics of frightening the public (use explosive devices, open murders of important businessmen etc.).

5. Attracting the sensible part of the Moslem clergy to leading the explanatory work among Moslem community.

   The representatives of the radical Islamic ideology could be classified as follows:

   - inspirers ("the people of thoughts");
   - Moslem masses ("the people of emotions");
   - Performers ("the people of actions").

   The importance of attracting the sensible part of the Moslem clergy towards explaining the real meaning of "the people of thoughts" schemes and the harms of radical ideology is absolutely evident. One should not fear to give them opportunity to do this important job on TV screens, in mass media (example – Chechnya: "Let us speak up for the people are tired of war".)

   But today we are trying to influence only "the performers".

6. Working out the optimum combination and correlation of the measures, directed at the effective functioning of the security systems, on one hand, with the rights of the society and the individuals, on the other.

   The WAAF has to continue the formulation of proposals on reasonable use and coordination of measures, providing for the effective security and guarding the basis of democracy.

7. Revision of the role and place of mass media in providing the system of active confronting terrorism, professional approach to the subjects of terrorism and crime, correct co-operation with power structures and the society in objective reflection of tragic events.

   One can observe the evident distortions in the activities of mass media under the banner of struggle against terrorism: showing the portraits of shaheed-suicides, circulating the statements of the terrorist organizations leaders, publications about terrorist actions preparation and realization plans etc., which promotes the existence of "false terrorists" of different kinds (false telephone calls, threats etc.).

   Sometimes the impression appears, that mass media turn terrorist acts into shows, which are readily demonstrated for the public. And the Ichkerian bandits and terrorists are called there "field commanders and fighters" and the Russian servicemen – "federals", not to mention Western born terms "rebels" and "freedom fighters".

8. Mobilization of the civil society potential fer the formation of the state priorities system with the subordination of departamental, corporate, national and other interests to the aims and purposes of struggle against terrorism.

And in fact, while there is evident, that there exist urgent necessity to consolidate all the efforts of the civil society on the struggle against terrorism and crime, very often the priorities and preferences are given to the departamental and corporate interests.

So that is, in my opinion, a far from complete list os possible directions of our organization structures for working out and realization of a complex of retaliatory measures to confront international terrorism.

In conclusion I would like to attract your attention to the following.

During three years from the creation of the WAAF there goes difficult process of the formation of the model to confront international terrorism based on the concept, which could unite the efforts of all strata of the society on national and international level.

The WAAF is not an alternate body, but in essence a symbiosis of the potentials of the academic, mass media and NGOs, directed at helping the organs of the state management on the front of the common struggle agaist international terrorism.

For the discussions and further working out the modern approaches to the realization of our ideas and plans we should use any possibility, including the potential of the participants of our broadened "Round table".

Das Recht auf Selbstverteidigung im Kampf gegen den internationalen Terrorismus

Prof. Dr. jur. Aleksandr A. Kovalev

Lehrstuhlinhaber für Internationales Recht der Diplomatischen Akademie des Außenministeriums der Russischen Föderation

Die Terroranschläge vom 11. September 2001 in den USA waren Ausdruck einer neuen Epoche in den Fragen zur internationalen Sicherheit. Obwohl es terroristische Aktionen schon in der zweiten Hälfte des letzten Jahrhunderts gegeben hatte, unterschieden sich die Anschläge vom 11. September von den früheren sowohl in ihrem Ausmaß als auch von der Vorgehensweise her. Die Zahl der menschlichen Opfer und der materiellen Verluste war außerordentlich erschreckend. Die Übertragung der Anschläge und ihrer Auswirkungen in den Massenmedien verstärkte zudem noch die ohnehin schon verheerenden psychischen Auswirkungen auf die Menschen.

Der Terrorakt vom September 2004 in Beslan (Nordossetien), der den Tod von 330 Menschen, davon zum größten Teil Kindern, zur Folge hatte, zeigte noch drastischer das unmenschliche Antlitz, das der internationale Terrorismus im 21. Jahrhundert trägt. Mit herkömmlichen Methoden kann er kaum erfolgreich bekämpft werden.

Terroranschläge müssen verhindert werden, gleichgültig, an welchem Ort, zu welchem Zeitpunkt und zu welchem Zweck sie verübt werden. Nicht selten kommt es dabei jedoch vor, dass die Opfer von Terroranschlägen selbst zu ungesetzlichen und überzogenen Maßnahmen greifen, um sich zu schützen. Bei der Ausarbeitung von Strategien und Taktiken im Kampf gegen den Terrorismus müssen aber die internationalen Rechtsnormen, auch diejenigen, die unmittelbar internationale Militäreinsätze betreffen, beachtet werden.

Bekanntlich bilden zwölf überregionale und sieben regionale Abkommen sowie die Statuten der Generalvollversammlung und des UN-Sicherheitsrates die international gültige rechtliche Grundlage im Kampf gegen den internationalen Terrorismus. Die internationalen Abkommen reglementieren aber nicht den Kampf gegen den Terror im allgemeinen, sondern lediglich das Vorgehen gegen dessen jeweilige Erscheinungsform, wie z. B. die Entführung von Flugzeugen, Fluss- oder Seeschiffen, Übergriffe auf Personen, die unter internationalem Schutz stehen, Geiselnahmen, den Einsatz von Sprengstoff zu terroristischen Zwecken usw. Die jeweiligen regionalen Statuten, wie z. B. das Europäische Abkommen bezüglich Maßnahmen zur Bekämpfung des Terrorismus aus dem Jahre 1977 oder auch der Vertrag von Schanghai über den Kampf gegen den Terrorismus, Separatismus und Extremismus von 2001, beziehen sich lediglich auf gesetzwidrige Handlungen, die als Terrorismus eingestuft werden.

In der Fachliteratur wird der Begriff „Internationaler Terrorismus" unter drei Gesichtspunkten betrachtet, erstens als Straftat mit internationalem Hintergrund, zweitens als internationales Verbrechen und drittens als Angriff unter Einsatz von Waffengewalt. Wenn der internationale Terrorismus als Straftat mit internationalem Hintergrund eingestuft wird, werden die Tatverdächtigen strafrechtlich nach der nationalen Gesetzgebung verfolgt[1].

Viele Juristen betrachten Terroranschläge nicht nur als internationales Verbrechen, sondern auch als Verbrechen gegen die Menschlichkeit[2]. Mit dieser Definition stimmen auch der UN-Generalsekretär K. Annan und der ehemalige UN-Hochkommissar für Menschenrechte M. Robinson überein[3]. Zahlreiche russische Wissenschaftler (so z. B. N.W. Ždanov, I.I. Karpez, E.I. Skakunov u.a.) erachten Terroranschläge als Akt indirekter Aggression. Sie begründen dies damit, dass die Terroristen von einigen Staaten unterstützt würden[4]. Dieser Ansatz lässt allerdings außer acht, dass die Anschläge von Einzeltätern bzw. Terroristischen Organisationen verübt werden. Sie lassen keine Rückschlüsse darauf zu, welcher Staat der Urheber der Anschläge sein soll und gegen wen sich die Abwehrmaß-

---

[1] Vgl.: "Terrorism an the International Legal Order," ed. by Van Krieken. The Hague: T.M.C. ASSER Press, 2002. P.17. O'Connell M. E., "Evidence of Terror," *Journal of Conflict and Security Law*. V. 7 (April 2002), Nr. 1. P. 32. Fedjanin W. Ju. "Aktuelle Fragen bzgl. der Sicherstellung der Verantwortung für den Terrorismus im internationalen Strafrecht" [Aktual'nye voprosi obespečenija otvetstsvennosti za terrorizm v meždunarodnom ugolovnom prave], *Moskauer Zeitschrift für internationales Recht* [Moskovskij žurnal meždunarodnogo prava]. 2001. Nr. 3. S. 161-162.

[2] Vgl. Byers M. "Terrorism, the Use of Force and International Law after 11 September 2001" *International and Comparative Law Quaterly*. V. 51 (April 2002), Part. 2. P. 413.

[3] zit. in: Juan M. A. U. "Testing the Legality of the Attack in Afghanistan," *Ateneo Law Journal*, V. 47 (September 2002), Nr. 2 P. 503. Cassese A. Op. Cit. P .413.

[4] Vgl.: Prokofjev N. W. "Zur Frage, wie der internationale Terrorismus auf dem Territorium anderer Staaten bekämpft werden kann" [K voprosu o bor'be s meždunarodnym terrorizmom na territorii inostrannych gosudarstv]. *Moskauer Zeitschrift für internationales Recht* [Moskovskij žurnal meždunarodnogo prava]. 2003. Nr. 1. S. 49.

nahmen des angegriffenen Staates richten sollen. Bekannt ist hingegen, dass die UN-Charta den gesetzlichen Rahmen vorgibt, wenn es darum geht, einen militärischen Angriff als Akt direkter oder indirekter Aggression einzustufen. Eine entscheidende Rolle kommt dabei dem UN-Sicherheitsrat zu.

In Art. 2, Abs. 4 der Charta wird eines der Grundprinzipien des internationalen Rechts wie folgt formuliert: „Alle Mitglieder unterlassen in ihren internationalen Beziehungen jede Androhung oder Anwendung von Gewalt, die gegen die territoriale Unversehrtheit oder politische Unabhängigkeit eines Staates gerichtet ist, da dies mit den Zielen der Vereinten Nationen unvereinbar ist."[5] Es ist klar, dass jede Missachtung des Prinzips, die Androhung und Anwendung militärischer Gewalt zu unterlassen, die Grundlagen des internationalen Rechts und der internationalen Beziehungen gefährdet.

Das internationale Recht kennt drei Ausnahmen von diesem Prinzip: Den folgenden Beschluss des UN-Sicherheitsrates:

- Wenn der Sicherheitsrat feststellt, dass der Frieden bedroht ist oder gebrochen wurde oder dass es zu einem Angriff gekommen ist, legt er die Maßnahmen fest, die zu ergreifen sind. Dies kann bis hin zu einem militärischen Einsatz gehen (Art. 42 der UN-Charta).

- Die Selbstverteidigung mit militärischen Mitteln (sowohl als Maßnahme eines Einzelnen als auch als gemeinsames Vorgehen) sowie das Recht eines Staates, sich gegen den Aggressor zu verteidigen (Art. 51 der UN-Charta).

- Den Fall des Krieges zum Zwecke der Befreiung einer Nation. Er kann im Grunde genommen als militärisches Mittel angesehen werden, um das Recht auf die Selbstbestimmung für alle Völker zu erlangen.

Was nun konkret mein Thema „Das Recht auf Selbstverteidigung im Kampf gegen den internationalen Terrorismus" angeht, so möchte ich auf die Frage eingehen, was unter Selbstverteidigung zu verstehen ist. Art. 51 der UN-Charta sagt folgendes aus: „Bei einem bewaffneten Angriff gegen der Mitglied der Vereinten Nationen schränkt diese Charta in keiner Weise das naturgegebene Recht auf individuelle oder kollektive Selbstverteidigung ein, bis der Sicherheitsrat die Maßnahmen getroffen hat, die erforderlich sind, um den Frieden in der Welt und die internationale Sicherheit zu gewährleisten. Maßnahmen, die ein Mitglied in Ausübung dieses Rechts auf Selbstverteidigung trifft, sind dem Sicherheitsrat sofort anzuzeigen. Sie berühren in keiner Weise die auf dieser Charta beruhende

---

[5] zit. in: UN-Charta in: http://www.runiceurope.org/german/charta/charta.htm. (Anm. d. Übersetzer)

Befugnis und Pflicht des Sicherheitsrates, zu jeder Zeit die Maßnahmen zu ergreifen, die er für erforderlich hält, um den Frieden in der Welt und die internationale Sicherheit zu wahren oder wiederherzustellen."[6]

Der Begriff des „bewaffneten Angriffs" lässt sich aus Art. 2 Abs. 4 der UN-Charta ableiten. Bei der Anwendung von Gewalt, die sich gegen die territoriale Unversehrtheit oder die politische Unabhängigkeit eines anderen Staates richtet, gilt der bewaffnete Angriff als Verletzung dieses Artikels. Im Internationalen Recht gibt es allerdings keinen gesetzlich definierten Begriff des bewaffneten Angriffs. Zu diesem Ergebnis kam auch das Internationale Gericht der UNO in seinem Urteil zum Prozess „Nicaragua gegen die USA" vom 27. Juni 1986. Allerdings hielt es einige Merkmale für einen bewaffneten Angriff fest. Demnach muss z. B. die reguläre Armee am bewaffneten Angriff beteiligt und über die Staatsgrenze in das Territorium des Angegriffenen eingedrungen sein. Der Angreiferstaat kann außerdem bewaffnete Banden oder Söldner in seinem Auftrag den Angriff durchführen lassen, die dann als reguläre Armee gelten können.

Lassen Sie uns nun untersuchen, inwieweit die Anwendung von Gewalt im Kampf gegen den Terrorismus in den Territorien anderer Staaten gesetzmäßig ist.

Der internationale Terrorismus lässt sich nach folgenden Gesichtspunkten unterscheiden, die sich alle danach richten, wer der Ausführende ist:

- Es handelt sich um „Staatsterrorismus", wenn der Ausführende ein Staat ist.
- Es handelt sich um andere Formen des Terrorismus, wenn die Ausführenden Einzelpersonen oder Gruppen sind, bei denen nicht nachgewiesen werden kann, dass ein Staat als deren Auftraggeber fungiert hat.

Betrachtet man nun die Vorgehensweisen des so genannten „Staatsterrorismus", dann lassen sich wiederum drei Erscheinungsformen feststellen:

- der Terrorismus, den die Streitkräfte eines Staates gegen einen anderen Staat in Form eines bewaffneten Angriffs verüben.
- der Terrorismus, der sich in Form von Verbrechen gegen das eigene Volk richtet.
- der Terrorismus in Form geheimer Operationen, die von Sicherheitsdiensten durchgeführt werden.

Jede diese Erscheinungsformen lässt sich als Akt der Aggression definieren. Infolgedessen hat der angegriffene Staat gemäß Art. 51 der UN-Charta das Recht,

---
[6] Ebenda (Anm. d. Übersetzer).

sich allein oder gemeinsam mit anderen zu verteidigen. Allerdings muss dann zunächst gesichert festgestellt werden, ob der angegriffene Staat in Ausübung dieses Rechts auch berechtigt ist, nicht nur die über die Grenzen in sein eigenes Territorium eingedrungenen Terroristengruppen in seinem eigenen Land zu bekämpfen, sondern darüber hinaus auch militärische Operationen gegen den Staat zu führen, der diese Banden geschickt hat. Zu diesem Problem gehen die Meinungen der Juristen auseinander.

Wie bereits erwähnt, ist es das Ziel der Selbstverteidigung, entweder einen bewaffneten Angriff abzuwehren, oder im Falle der indirekten Aggression, das eigene Territorium zu befreien, oder die fremden Militärtruppen, die in das Gebiet des angegriffenen Staates eingedrungen sind, zu vernichten. An dieser Stelle soll auf die Ansichten einiger Juristen eingegangen werden. So vertritt E. Skakunov die Auffassung, dass bei der Verteidigung gegen einen Angriff die Ausweitung der Militäroperationen in das Gebiet des Aggressors hinein als Vorbeugungsmaßnahme nicht ausgeschlossen werden kann. Demzufolge habe ein angegriffener Staat das Recht, Lager im fremden Territorium, die der Ausbildung irregulärer/geheimer Militärtruppen dienten, anzugreifen. Die Streitkräfte des angegriffenen Staates könnten über die Grenze einrücken, um die Infrastruktur zu zerschlagen. Vom Standpunkt des internationalen Rechts (gemäß Art. 2 und weiterer Artikel der UN-Charta) aus gesehen, ist es aber kaum möglich, derartige Militäroperationen auf dem Boden des Angreiferstaates zu rechtfertigen, obwohl die Doktrin eine solche Möglichkeit nicht ausschließt. Die Vorgehensweisen, die im Kampf gegen den Terrorismus angewandt werden, sind sehr vielfältig. So unterstützte Russland im Jahr 1993 den Raketenangriff der USA auf Bagdad (angeblich hatte die irakische Regierung ein Attentat auf den Präsidenten George Bush Senior vorbereitet) mit der Begründung, dass „ ... die Maßnahmen der USA gerechtfertigt sind, weil sie aus dem Recht, sich allein oder gemeinsam mit anderen im Sinne des Art. 51 der UN-Charta zu verteidigen, abgeleitet werden"[7]. Andererseits kritisierte Russland die Raketenangriffe der USA auf die Terroristenlager in Afghanistan und im Sudan, weil sie die internationale Lage destabilisiert hätten.

Bei der zweiten Erscheinungsform des „Staatsterrorismus" handelt es sich um den im Inneren eines Landes der sich sowohl gegen die eigenen Bürger als auch gegen Ausländer richtet die sich dort aufhalten. In diesem Fall ist das Problem aufs engste mit dem Konzept der „humanitären Intervention" verbunden. Unter dem Begriff „humanitäre Intervention", wie er im internationalen Recht de-

---

[7] Diplomatisches Informationsblatt Außenministerium Russlands. [Diplomatičeskij vestnik. MID Rossii]. 1993. N° 13-14, S. 40.

finiert ist, versteht man „ ... die Androhung oder die Anwendung von Gewalt seitens eines oder mehrerer Staaten auf dem Territorium eines anderen Staates mit dem einzigen Ziel, die Missachtung der Menschenrechte und elementaren Freiheiten, unabhängig von der Staatsangehörigkeit der betroffenen Bürger, zu beenden oder ihr vorzubeugen, wenn eine solche Missachtung bereits gegeben ist oder wenn es abzusehen ist, dass sie in absehbarer Zeit gegeben sein wird. Das gilt auch dann, wenn die erforderliche Ermächtigung durch den UN-Sicherheitsrat nicht vorliegt, oder wenn die Regierung des Staates, in dessen Gebiet die Intervention stattfindet, ihre Erlaubnis verweigert."[8] Obwohl diese Doktrin die Anwendung von Gewalt zum Zwecke des Schutzes von Menschenleben sowie zur Durchsetzung ihrer Grund- und Freiheitsrechte dann zulässt, wenn diese missachtet werden (wie z. B. im Jahr 1971 in Ostbengalen, im Jahr 1978 in Kambodscha, im Jahr 1979 in Uganda, im Jahr 1991 in Somalia und im Jahr 1997 im Kongo), gilt gemäß des internationalen Rechts der bewaffnete Übergriff, auch der mit einer humanitären Mission, auf die inneren Angelegenheiten eines anderen Staates als rechtswidrig.

Bei der dritten Form geht es um die Selbstverteidigung gegen die indirekte Aggression. Wie bereits erwähnt, sehen die Artikel 2 (Abs. 4) und 51 das Recht zur alleinigen (und kollektiven) Selbstverteidigung im Falle eines bewaffneten Angriffs vor. Dabei ist es wichtig festzustellen, welche Maßnahmen gemäß des internationalen Rechts zu ergreifen sind, wenn ein bewaffneter Angriff oder ein Terroranschlag offensichtlich bevorsteht. Beinhaltet der Begriff „bewaffneter Angriff" im Sinne des Art. 51 auch die Vorbereitung, Festlegung von Ort und Zeit und weitere Maßnahmen, die von Terroristen in der Vorbereitungsphase getroffen werden? Berücksichtigt man den technischen Fortschritt auf dem Gebiet der Massenvernichtungswaffen, wie z. B. auch atomare Waffen, so ist die Frage, wo der Beginn eines bewaffneten Angriffs anzusetzen ist, von außerordentlicher Bedeutung. Das russische Konzept von R.A. Mjulerson und das westliche Konzept von E. Himenes de Arechaga gehen davon aus, dass die derzeitige Einsatzbereitschaft von Kernwaffen und ihre zerstörerische Wirkung es zulassen, die Vorbereitungen zu ihrem Einsatz, wie z. B. Die Festlegung ihres Einsatzortes, mit dem Beginn des bewaffneten Angriffs gleichzusetzen. Dementsprechend soll der Staat – als potenzielles Opfer – das Recht zur Selbstverteidigung bekommen. Allerdings muss dieser Staat noch vor der Anwendung von Gewalt die Rechtmäßigkeit seines Vorgehens nachweisen. Dabei müssen die Belege dem UN-Sicherheitsrat unverzüglich vorgelegt werden. Darüber hinaus übernimmt

---

[8] zit. in: Černišenko S.W., *Die Theorie des Internationalen Rechts* [Teorija meždunarodnogo prava]. M.: NIMP, 1999, Bd. 1, S. 472.

der Staat, der behauptet, im Sinne präventiver Selbstverteidigung zu handeln, die volle Verantwortung für seine Maßnahmen.

Die USA gehen gemäß ihrer neuen „Strategie der nationalen Sicherheit" im Kampf gegen den internationalen Terrorismus vom Konzept der Präventivschläge auf Terroristenlager aus. Die russische Regierung erklärte ebenfalls ihre Entschlossenheit, unter bestimmten Voraussetzungen derartige Militärschläge anzuwenden.

Es ist durchaus möglich, dass eine Einzelperson oder eine Gruppe Terroristen sein können und auf eigene Faust handeln, also keine Verbindungen zu irgendeinem Staat haben. Wenn derartige Verbindungen nicht nachzuweisen und die Terroristen einzelne Personen oder Organisationen sind, dürfen sich Anti-Terror-Maßnahmen ausschließlich gegen die unmittelbar Beteiligten richten, nicht aber gegen andere Staaten.

Im Zusammenhang mit dem Statut des internationalen Rechts ist auch die Frage interessant, wie Gewalt gegen ein Regime, wie das der Taliban in Afghanistan, anzuwenden ist. Das Regime war von der internationalen Staatengemeinschaft nicht als legitime Regierung anerkannt worden. Bekanntlich bestätigte der Sicherheitsrat in seinen Resolutionen Nr. 1368 und 1373 das Recht der Staaten auf Selbstverteidigung – angesichts der Gefahren, die der internationale Terrorismus mit sich bringt, und im Hinblick auf die von den Staaten zu treffenden Maßnahmen zur Vorbeugung und Verhinderung von Terroranschlägen ausschließlich im jeweils eigenen Territorium. In der Resolution Nr. 1378 musste der Sicherheitsrat dann jedoch einräumen, dass die Terrorgefahr aus dem Gebiet, das sich unter der Kontrolle der Taliban befand, drohte.

In Anbindung an das internationale Recht darf ein Staat einen anderen weder bedrohen noch angreifen, wenn vom Territorium des letzteren aus ein Terroranschlag verübt werden sollte. Dies würde dem Prinzip des Art. 2 der Charta widersprechen, wonach die Androhung und Anwendung von Gewalt zu unterlassen ist. Obwohl derartige Situationen in der Charta nicht vorgesehen sind, ist zu vermuten, dass die Grundsätze des Art. 51 dann übertragbar sein können, wenn die Regierung desjenigen Staates, von dessen Gebiet aus ein Terroranschlag verübt wurde, den Terroristen Unterschlupf gewährt. Wie im Aufsatz von O. N. Chlestov und M.L. Myšljaeva dargelegt, muss aber vor dem Einsatz militärischer Präventionsmaßnahmen folgendes geprüft worden sein:

- die Beteiligung an einem bereits verübten Terroranschlag oder an dessen Vorbereitung seitens des Staats bzw. der Regierung, der dieses Gebiet untersteht und gegen die möglicherweise Gewalt angewendet werden soll.

- deren Einverständnis, die Terroristen auszuliefern bzw. deren Auslieferung.
- deren Einverständnis, Maßnahmen gegen die Benutzung des Staatsgebietes zu terroristischen Zwecken zu ergreifen und diese umzusetzen[9].

An dieser Stelle ist es angebracht, den Artikel 25, Abs. 1 des Status zu den Grundlagen der internationalen Verantwortung der Staaten durch die Kommission für internationales Recht zu erwähnen. Im Artikel wird als gegeben vorausgesetzt, dass eine Situation unter außerordentlichen Umständen äußerst gefährlich werden kann und das „ureigenste Interesse" einen Staat zu einem Verhalten zwingt, das seinen internationalen Verpflichtungen nicht mehr entspricht. Die Sicherheit der eigenen Bürger stellt nach meiner Meinung ein solches „ureigenstes Interesse" dar. Gesetzt den Fall, die Bürger eines Staates würden als Geiseln genommen und in ein anderes Land verschleppt, wäre in einem solchen Fall eine Anti-Terror-Operation in Form eines bewaffneten Angriffs seitens des angegriffenen Staates zulässig? In der heutigen Zeit kann das internationale Recht auf diese Frage keine eindeutige Antwort geben. Ich bin der Meinung, dass der Staat zum Zwecke der Verteidigung und der Wahrung der Sicherheit seiner Bürger, die als Geiseln in einem Staatsgebiet festgehalten werden und in akuter Lebensgefahr schweben, ein eingeschränktes Streitkräftekontingent einsetzen darf. Dabei müssen das Vorgehen und der Rahmen solcher Anti-Terror-Operationen festgelegt werden.

Abschließend möchte ich betonen, dass die Geschichte auch viele Beispiele für den Missbrauch des Rechts auf Selbstverteidigung kennt. Offensichtlich besteht aber eine Notwendigkeit, dafür ein Kontrollverfahren zu festzulegen. In Fällen, in denen Lebensgefahr für die eigenen Bürger im Ausland besteht, in denen es um die Befreiung von Geiseln geht oder in denen die Notwendigkeit besteht, lebenswichtige Interessen zu verteidigen, ist es bislang noch nicht zulässig, das Recht auf Selbstverteidigung umzusetzen.

---

[9] Vgl. Chlestov O.N., Myšljaeva M. L., "Der bewaffnete Kampf gegen den Terrorismus" [Vooružennaja bor'ba protiv terrorizma], *Moskauer Zeitschrift für Internationales Recht* [Moskovskij žurnal meždunarodnogo prava]. 2001. Nr. 4, S. 20.

Die Bedeutung multilateraler Konventionen für das Vorgehen gegen den internationalen Terrorismus

Ralph Alexander Lorz und Lars Mammen

Heinrich-Heine-Universität Düsseldorf

"The War on Terror Will not Be Fought on the Battlefield"
Andrew Ayers[1]

1 Ausgangslage

Die Völkerrechtsordnung sieht sich seit dem Ende der bilateralen Weltordnung in den 1990er Jahren vor neue Herausforderungen gestellt. Von nichtstaatlichen Akteuren und insbesondere von grenzüberschreitenden Terrornetzwerken gehen in zunehmendem Maße Gefahren für die internationale Sicherheit aus. Der Sicherheitsrat der Vereinten Nationen hat dies in seinen als Reaktion auf die Terroranschläge vom 11. September 2001 erlassen Resolutionen anerkannt und die terroristischen Akte „as a threat to international peace and security" verurteilt[2]. Bedingt durch die als ‚Globalisierung'[3] bezeichnete Entwicklung ist das internationale System zahlreichen Veränderungen unterworfen, die eine zunehmende Verflechtung internationaler Strukturen und damit einhergehend einen Bedeutungsverlust nationalstaatlicher Grenzen bewirken[4]. Terroristische Organisationen konnten diese Entwicklung zum Aufbau globaler Netzwerke nutzen, die

---

[1] Andrew Ayers, „The Financial Action Task Force: The War on Terror Will not Be Fought on the Battlefield"; in: *New York Law School Journal of Human Rights* 18 (2002), 449-459.

[2] Seit dem 11. September 2001 ständige Resolutionspraxis hinsichtlich terroristischer Anschläge. Siehe beispielhaft S/Res/1368 vom 12. September 2001 oder die die Anschläge von Istanbul (S/Res/1516 vom 17. November 2003) oder Madrid (S/Res/1530 vom 12. März 2004) verurteilenden Resolutionen.

[3] Siehe statt vieler Ernst-Otto Czempiel, *Weltpolitik im Umbruch*, 2003, 20 ff.

[4] John F. Murphy, „The Impact of Terrorism on Globalization and Vice-Versa", in: *International Lawyer* 36 (2002), 77-89, 78 f.; Thomas Risse-Kappen (Hrsg.), „Bringing Transnational Relations Back In", 1995, 4.

es ihnen ermöglichen, ihre Aktionen unabhängig von staatlichen Begrenzungen zu planen sowie durchzuführen[5]. Spätestens die Anschläge vom 11. September 2001 haben gezeigt, welche schrecklichen Folgen transnationale terroristische Gewalt für den Staat und die internationale Gemeinschaft hat. Dabei bleibt der Wandel der internationalen Strukturen nicht ohne Auswirkungen auf die völkerrechtliche Ordnung. Bei den Staatenvertreter setzt sich zunehmend die Erkenntnis durch, dass der internationale Terrorismus nicht mehr allein mit Mitteln des nationalen Rechts wirksam bekämpft werden kann. Aufgrund seines grenzüberschreitenden Charakters versprechen nur Maßnahmen, die auf der Grundlage des internationalen Rechts vorgenommen werden, eine erfolgreiche Bekämpfung der verschiedenen terroristischen Erscheinungsformen. In den vergangenen Jahren kann daher eine Zunahme der internationalen Anstrengungen zur Bekämpfung des Terrorismus verzeichnet werden. Insbesondere internationale Konventionen stellen ein wirksames Mittel im Vorgehen gegen den grenzüberschreitenden Terrorismus dar, weshalb ihre Bedeutung im vorliegenden Artikel näher dargestellt wird.

In diesem Zusammenhang gewinnt zudem ein zweiter Aspekt entscheidend an Bedeutung: Der Erfolg völkerrechtlicher Instrumentarien hängt zentral davon ab, inwieweit das Recht in der Lage ist, die sich verändernde faktische Entwicklung zu erfassen. Der globale Terrorismus stellt die internationale Rechtsordnung dabei vor eine besondere Herausforderung, da er in verschiedenen Erscheinungsformen auftritt und die technologischen Entwicklungen gezielt für die Erreichung seiner Zwecke nutzt. Neben dem biologischen oder nuklearen Terrorismus stellt der computerbezogene Terrorismus eine besondere Gefährdung für die westlichen Industriegesellschaften dar, die durch ihre zunehmende Abhängigkeit vom Internet[6] leicht verletzbar sind. Durch Angriffe auf Datenver-

---

[5] Allgemein zu den Entwicklungsstufen des internationalen Terrorismus: Christopher Daase, „Terrorismus – Begriffe, Theorien und Gegenstrategien", in: *Die Friedenswarte* 2002, 55-79, 61 f.; Jost Delbrück, „The Fight against Global Terrorism: Self-Defense or Collective Security as International Police Action", in: *German Yearbook of Int'l Law* 44 (2001), 9-24; Thomas Bruha, „Gewaltverbot und humanitäres Völkerrecht nach dem 11. September 2001", in: *Archiv für Völkerrecht 40* (2002), 383-421, 384; umfassend auch Petra Bendel/Mathias Hildebrandt (Hrsg.), *Im Schatten des Terrorismus. Hintergründe, Strukturen, Konsequenzen des 11. September 2001*, 2001.

[6] *United Nations Manual* on the Prevention and Control of Computer Crime, 1999, http://www.uncjin.org/Documents/eightCongress.html (Zugriff am 04. 12. 2004); Cheri Ganeles, „Technological Advancements and the Evolution of Terrorism", in: *ILSA Journal of Int'l and Comparative Law* 8 (2002), 617-659, 635; Michael N. Schmitt, „Angriffe im Computernetz und das ius ad bellum", in: *Neue Zeitschrift für Wehrrecht* 1999, 177-195, 177 f.; Murphy (Fn. 5), 81 f.

arbeitungssysteme wichtiger Wirtschaftszweige – etwa die besonders computerabhängigen Bereiche der Luftverkehrskontrolle, der Telekommunikation und des Energiewesens (vor allem Kernkraftwerke) – können erhebliche Schäden verursacht werden[7]. Der gezielte Einsatz virtueller Befehle oder Computerviren gegen ein bestimmtes Objekt reicht häufig aus, um Schäden von erheblichem Ausmaß anzurichten[8]. Ein erhöhter physischer Kraftaufwand oder die Anwesenheit am Tatort ist dazu in der Regel nicht erforderlich, was den computerbezogenen Terrorismus um so gefährlicher werden läßt. Auch wenn die von ihm ausgehenden Gefahren zu einem großen Teil noch hypothetischer Natur sind, stellt der Cyberterrorismus eine ernst zu nehmende Bedrohung für die nationale sowie internationale Sicherheit dar. Wie kaum eine andere Form des Terrorismus zeichnet er sich durch die Loslösung von territorialen Bezügen aus, sodass ein Vorgehen ausschließlich mit Mitteln des nationalen Rechts nicht mehr ausreichend erscheint[9]. Vielmehr ist es notwendig, auch völkerrechtliche Instrumentarien zur Bekämpfung des Cyberterrorismus heranzuziehen. Damit ist zugleich der zweite Aspekt des vorliegenden Beitrags umrissen, der die Anwendbarkeit des internationalen Rechts auf die spezielle Form des computerbezogenen Terrorismus untersucht. Darüber hinaus lässt sich daran exemplarisch demonstrieren, inwieweit die Völkerrechtsordnung in der Lage ist, wirksam auf neue Erscheinungsformen des internationalen Terrorismus zu reagieren.

2 Versuch einer begrifflichen Bestimmung

Die rechtliche Auseinandersetzung mit dem Terrorismus steht zunächst vor der Schwierigkeit, diesen Begriff definitorisch zu bestimmen. Wenn mit Mitteln des Völkerrechts wirksam gegen den Terrorismus vorgegangen werden soll, bedarf es einer klaren Erkenntnis darüber, was der Gegenstand der Maßnahmen sein soll. Vor allem hinsichtlich des Regelungsgehalts internationaler Konventionen ist

---

[7] Siehe auch *Council of Europe*, Committee of Experts on Crime in Cyberspace, Explanatory Memorandum to the Convention on Cybercrime vom 25. Mai 2001, http://www.conventions.coe.int/Convention/en/Reports/HTML185.htm (Zugriff am 04. 01. 2005).

[8] Schmitt (Fn. 7), 178; Ganeles (Fn. 7), 635 f.

[9] Shannon L. Hopkins, „Cybercrime Convention: A Positive Beginning to a Long Road Ahead", in: *Journal of High Technology Law* 2 (2003), 101-108, 101; Joel P. Trachtman, *Global Cyberterrorism, Jurisdiction and International Organizations*, 1-36, 21, vom 20. Juli 2004, abrufbar unter: http://ssm.com/abstract=566361 (Zugriff am 14. 12. 2004); zu den sich ergebenden Jurisdiktionskonflikten Susan W. Brenner/Bert-Jaap Koops, „Approaches to Cybercrime Jurisdiction", in: *Journal of High Technology Law* 3 (2004), 3-45.

eine Definition unumgänglich, da nur so ihr Geltungsumfang bestimmt werden kann. Eine allgemeine und international akzeptierte Definition des Begriffs ‚Terrorismus' existiert jedoch bislang nicht[10]. Der viel zitierte Aphorismus *„one man's terrorist ist another man's freedom fighter"* zeigt, welche Schwierigkeiten bei der Bestimmung des Begriffs bestehen. Vor allem die Abgrenzung zu Freiheitskämpfern, die sich zur Legitimation ihrer Gewaltanwendung auf das Selbstbestimmungsrecht eines durch sie repräsentierten Volkes berufen, hat bisher eine allgemein akzeptierte Festlegung auf internationaler Ebene verhindert[11]. Allerdings setzt sich zunehmend der Ansatz durch, dass bestimmte Formen von Gewalt unabhängig von ihrer konkreten Zielsetzung unter keinen Umständen zu rechtfertigen sind. Damit soll die schwierig zu führende Diskussion um die Rechtmäßigkeit der ausgeübten Gewalt für den spezifischen Zweck der Bekämpfung bestimmter terroristischer Erscheinungsformen ausgeklammert werden[12]. Vielmehr gibt es danach bestimmte Formen von Gewalt, die aufgrund ihrer Intensität und Zielrichtung *per se* völkerrechtlich verboten sind. Dazu zählt in erster Linie die gegen Zivilisten ausgeübte terroristische Gewalt. Was genau unter terroristischer Gewalt zu verstehen ist, kann durch die Herausarbeitung typologischer Merkmale näher bestimmt werden. So lässt sie sich objektiv als diejenige krimi-

---

[10] Als kleine Auswahl aus der rechtswissenschaftlichen Diskussion vgl.: John Dugard, „Towards the Definition of International Terrorism", in: *American Society of Int'l Law Proceedings* 94 (1973), 94-100; Robert A. Friedländer, „Terrorism", in: Rudolf Bernhardt (Hrsg.), *Encyclopedia of Public Int'l Law*, Bd. IV, 2000, 845-857, 846; Michael P. Scharf, „Defining Terrorism as the peace time equivalent of war crimes", in: *Journal of Int'l & Comparative Law* 7 (2001), 391-398, 392 f.; Robert Keeley, „Trying to define terrorism", in: *Middle East Policy* 9 (2002), 33-39; Christian Walter, „Defining Terrorism in National and International Law", in: ders./Silja Vöneky/Volker Röben/Frank Schorkopf (Hrsg.), *Terrorism as a Challenge for National and International Law: Security versus Liberty?*, 2004, abrufbar unter: http://edoc.mpil.de/conference-on-terrorism/index.cfm (Zugriff am 4. 12. 2004); sowie stellvertretend für die politikwissenschaftliche Diskussion: Katharina von Knop, *Die Quellen der Macht von Al Qaida*, 2004, 38-43. Eine besondere Schwierigkeit bei der Begriffsbestimmung liegt zudem darin, dass der Terminus sowohl in der wissenschaftlichen als auch in der tagespolitischen Berichterstattung Verwendung findet.

[11] Siehe dazu nur Malvina Halverstram, „The Evolution of the UN-Position on Terrorism: From Exempting National Liberation Movements to Criminalizing Terrorism", in: *Columbia Journal of Transnational Law* 41 (2002), 573-583.

[12] Die Frage nach dem Gerechtigkeitsbezug von Gewaltanwendung ist so alt wie das Völkerrecht selbst. Für einen rechtshistorischen Überblick siehe Michael Bothe, „Friedenssicherung und Kriegsrecht", in: Wolfgang Graf Vitzthum (Hrsg.), *Völkerrecht*, 2004, 592 f. Rn. 3. Zu der wiederbelebten Diskussion Michael Walzer, *Just and Unjust Wars: A Moral Argument with Historical Illustrations*, 1992.

nelle Gewaltanwendung definieren, die sich gegen (Zivil)Personen oder materielle Güter richtet und durch eine besondere Intensität auszeichnet[13]. Zusätzlich zum objektiven bestimmt sich der Terrorismus aber auch durch ein subjektives Element. Demnach dient seine Gewaltanwendung primär der Einschüchterung oder Zwangseinwirkung gegenüber der Bevölkerung mit dem Ziel, eine Regierung oder andere Staatsorgane zu einem bestimmten Verhalten zu veranlassen[14]. Opfer unter der Zivilbevölkerung werden als Teil seiner Strategie bewusst in Kauf genommen, um den Druck auf die Regierungen zu erhöhen. In einer „Working Definition" ausgedrückt, ergibt sich daraus folgende Begriffsbestimmung:

> „Terrorism is defined as threat or use of violence in order to create extreme fear and anxiety in a non-combatant target group so as to coerce a government or other state organs to meet political objectives of the perpetrator."[15]

Unter Berücksichtigung der jüngsten Entwicklung zeichnet sich auf internationaler Ebene ein Konsens über eine Bestimmung des Begriffs des Terrorismus ab, der die hier herausgestellten Elemente enthält. In einem vom Generalsekretär der Vereinten Nationen, Kofi Annan, eingesetzten *High-Level Panel on Global Security Threats*[16] werden vergleichbare Kriterien zur Bestimmung des Terrorismus herausgearbeitet[17].

Der Vorteil einer Beschränkung auf die grundlegenden Merkmale zur Charakterisierung des Phänomens des Terrorismus wird auch deutlich, wenn man die abgeleitete Definition auf die Erscheinungsform des Cyberterrorismus anzuwenden versucht. Zusätzlich zu den allgemeinen Kriterien muss hier dessen besonderes Wirkungsumfeld berücksichtigt werden, wobei der Präfix ‚Cyber' im Allgemeinen

---

[13] Zum objektiven Element stellvertretend Walter (Fn. 11), der es unter rechtsvergleichenden Aspekten untersucht.
[14] Dazu statt vieler Friedländer (Fn. 11), 846.
[15] Vgl. „Defense Threat Reduction Agency" (U.S.-Department of Defense) (Hrsg.), *Terrorism: Concept, Causes, and Conflict Resolution*, 2003, 9.
[16] Siehe dazu Press Release SG/A/857 vom 4. November 2003, abrufbar unter: http://www.un.org/News/Press/docs/2003/sga857.doc.htm (Zugriff am 03. 01. 2005).
[17] So die vom *United Nations High-Level Panel* gemachten Ausführungen zur Definition des Terrorismus in seinem Bericht zum Umgang der Vereinten Nationen mit den neuen Herausforderungen. Der Bericht ist bisher noch nicht online verfügbar. Vgl. daher stellvertretend die Rezeption in den Medien: z. B. Süddeutsche Zeitung vom 1. Dezember 2004, 1.

die von Computern erzeugte Scheinwelt[18] beschreibt und eine virtuelle Aktivität andeutet, die in unmittelbarem Zusammenhang mit dem Informationszeitalter steht. Für den zusammengesetzten Begriff des Cyberterrorismus lässt sich daraus folgendes Begriffsverständnis ableiten:

> „Cyberterrorism is the politically motivated attack against information, computer systems, computer programs, and data which results in violence against noncombatant targets."[19]

Der computerbezogene Terrorismus zeichnet sich objektiv durch die Störung von Datensystemen und Computerabläufen aus, die mit der Absicht verfolgt wird, die privaten oder staatlichen Nutzer der Computersysteme einzuschüchtern und sie dadurch zu einem bestimmten Verhalten zu veranlassen. Eine trennscharfe Abgrenzung des Cyberterrorismus von anderen Formen der computerbezogenen Kriminalität ist demgegenüber nicht möglich. Cyberterrorismus muss vielmehr als eine besonders schwere Form der Cyberkriminalität verstanden werden, die sich durch seine subjektive Qualifikation – d. h. die terroristische Zielsetzung des Verhaltens – auszeichnet[20]. Für computerbezogene Angriffe von Terroristen ist charakteristisch, dass sie über die unmittelbaren Schäden hinaus mittelbar die privaten und staatlichen Informations- und Datensysteme insgesamt verletzen wollen. Indem sie das hoch sensible Informationsnetz angreifen, können sie mittels einer Unterbrechung der Abläufe die industrialisierte Gesellschaft ganz erheblich treffen und dadurch Angst und Schrecken verbreiten. In diesem Zusammenhang wird zum Teil sogar von „Cyberattacks"[21] gesprochen, womit die

---

[18] *Duden des Fremdwörterbuchs*, 2001: Stichwort Cyber: Verkürzt aus den englischen „Cybernatics", d. h. die Wissenschaft von den Steuerungs- und Regelungsorganen. Wortbildungselement mit der Bedeutung „die von Computern erzeugte virtuelle Scheinwelt".

[19] Marc Goodman/Susan Brenner, „The Emerging Consensus on Criminal Conduct in Cyberspace", in: *Journal of Law and Technology* 10 (2002), 139-201, 150; Mark M. Pollitt, *Cyberterrorism – Fact or Fancy?*, abrufbar unter http://www.cs.georgetown.edu/~denning/infosec/pollitt.html (Zugriff am 04. 12. 2004); dem sich anschließend Mohammad Iqbal, *„Defining Cyberterrorism", in:* Journal of Computer and Information Law *22 (2004), 397-408, 402 f.*

[20] Trachtman (Fn. 10), 4; ablehnend Iqbal (Fn. 20), 400, der für eine Unterscheidung zur Cyberkriminalität eintritt.

[21] Dorothy E. Denning, „Cyberterrorism – Testimony before the Special Oversight Panel on Terrorism", Committee on Armed Services, U.S. House of Representatives, vom 23. Mai 2000, abrufbar unter: http://www.cs.georgetown.edu/~denning/infosec/cyberterror.html (Zugriff am 14. 12. 2004); zur rechtlichen Bewertung Schmitt (Fn. 7), 178.

bewusste Störung der Computerabläufe mit dem Ziel, den Informationsfluss zu unterbrechen, zu verfälschen oder gar ganz auszusetzen umschrieben wird.

3 Funktion des internationalen Rechts für die Bekämpfung des Terrorismus

Eine effektive Bekämpfung des grenzüberschreitenden Terrorismus setzt die Zusammenarbeit der Staaten auf internationaler Ebene voraus. Vor allem internationale Konventionen stellen ein wichtiges völkerrechtliches Instrumentarium dar, um gegen die verschiedenen Formen terroristischer Gewalt wirksam vorgehen zu können[22]. Der Beitrag multilateraler Abkommen kann allerdings von Beginn an nur ein begrenzter sein. Terroristische Täter bewegen sich trotz ihrer globalen Organisation und der Nutzung zwischenstaatlicher Verflechtungen auch immer innerhalb einer bestimmten nationalen Rechtsordnung; sie müssen daher zunächst mit Mitteln des innerstaatlichen Rechts bekämpft werden[23]. Aufgrund der transnationalen Struktur terroristischer Organisationen und der damit einhergehenden Ablösung ihres Tätigkeits- und Wirkungsbereiches von nationalstaatlichen Beschränkungen stoßen rein innerstaatliche Regelungen allerdings rasch an ihre Grenzen[24]. An dieser Stelle gewinnen multilaterale Konventionen entscheidende Bedeutung, da sie auf internationaler Ebene einheitliche Regelungen zum Umgang mit den grenzüberschreitend agierenden Akteuren bereit stellen. Allerdings besteht bislang kein allgemeines internationales Abkommen zur Bekämpfung des grenzüberschreitenden Terrorismus. Obwohl es bereits frühzeitig Versuche gegeben hat, die Bekämpfung des Terrorismus auf der Basis internationaler Konventionen durchzuführen, blieben diese Ansätze bislang weitestgehend

---

[22] Thomas Oppermann, „Der Beitrag des Internationalen Rechts zur Bekämpfung des internationalen Terrorismus", in: *Festschrift für Hans-Jürgen Schlochauer*, 1981, 495-514; Boutros Boutros-Ghali, „The United Nations and Comprehensive Legal Measures for Combating International Terrorism", in: Karel Wellens (Hrsg.), *International Law: Theory and Practice*, 1998, 274-308, 287; Murphy (Fn. 5), 85; Erich Kussbach, „Die internationale Bekämpfung des Terrorismus mit Mitteln des Rechts", in: *European Integration Studies* 1 (2002), 47-63, 50.

[23] Zur Rechtslage in Deutschland etwa Martin Nolte, „Die Anti-Terror-Pakete im Lichte des Verfassungsrechts", in: *Deutsches Verwaltungsblatt* 2002, 573-578; zur Rechtslage in den Vereinigten Staaten näher Nathan C. Henderson, „The Patriot Act's Impact on the Government's Ability to Conduct Electronic Surveillance of ongoing Domestic Communications", in: *Duke Law Journal* 52 (2002), 179-209; Sean D. Murphy, „International Law, the United States, and the non-military ‚War' against Terrorism", in: *European Journal of Int'l Law* 14 (2003), 347-364.

[24] Boutros-Ghali (Fn. 23), 287.

erfolglos. Zu nennen ist hier vor allem die *Convention for the Prevention and Punishment of Terrorism* des Völkerbundes von 1937, die allerdings in Ermangelung einer ausreichenden Zahl von Ratifikationen niemals in Kraft trat[25]. Bedingt durch die unterschiedliche politische Bewertung der nach dem Zweiten Weltkrieg einsetzenden Entkolonialisierungsbemühungen und der damit verbundenen Gewalt wurde die Entwicklung eines umfassenden Übereinkommens gegen den internationalen Terrorismus unmöglich. Die internationale Staatengemeinschaft wählte statt dessen einen punktuellen Ansatz, nach dem als besonders verwerflich und gefährlich eingeordnete Begehungsformen der terroristischen Gewalt völkerrechtlich geächtet wurden. Denn über die Pönalisierung bestimmter terroristischer Handlungsformen konnten sich die Staatenvertreter leichter einigen als über die Bewertung terroristischer Gewalt im Allgemeinen[26]. Mit dem weitgehenden Abschluss der von Befreiungsbewegungen geführten Unabhängigkeitskriege (abgesehen von dem israelisch-palästinensischen Konflikt) und der Zunahme von transnationalen Terrornetzwerken, die von regionalen Zielen unabhängig agieren, ist die Entwicklung einer umfassenden Anti-Terrorismus-Konvention jedoch wieder in den Bereich des Vorstellbaren gerückt. Wie noch im Einzelnen nachzuweisen sein wird, lassen sich sogar schon erste Anzeichen für eine solche Entwicklung feststellen.

3.1 Überblick über bestehende Konventionen gegen den internationalen Terrorismus

In den vergangenen Jahren sind unter der Schirmherrschaft der Vereinten Nationen zwölf internationale Konventionen entstanden und durch regionale Übereinkommen ergänzt worden. Gemeinsam bilden sie ein sachbezogenes Netz gegen besonders häufig anzutreffende terroristische Aktivitäten[27]:

- Convention on Offences and Certain Other Acts Committed on Board Aircraft (Tokio) vom 14. September 1963;

---

[25] Die Konvention wurde überhaupt nur von Indien ratifiziert und erledigte sich dann mit dem Beginn des 2. Weltkrieges. Siehe dazu Doris König, „Terrorism", in: Rüdiger Wolfrum (Hrsg.), *United Nations: Law, Policies and Practice*, Vol. 1, 1995, 1220-1228, 1220.

[26] Rüdiger Wolfrum, „Die inhaltliche Ordnung der internationalen Gemeinschaft", in: Georg Dahm/Jost Delbrück/ders., *Völkerrecht*, Bd. I/3, 2002, 1110.

[27] Siehe dazu Jasper Finke/Christiane Wandscher, „Terrorismusbekämpfung jenseits militärischer Gewalt", in: *Vereinte Nationen* 49 (2001), 168-173, 169 f.; zum Regelungsgehalt der einzelnen Konventionen auch Kussbach (Fn. 23), 50 ff.; Wolfrum (Fn. 27), 1115.

- Convention for the Suppression of Unlawful Seizure of Aircraft (Den Haag) vom 16. Dezember 1970;
- Convention for the Suppression of Unlawful Acts against the Safety of Civil Aviation (Montreal) vom 23. September 1971;
- Convention on the Prevention and Punishment of Crimes against Internationally Protected Persons, including Diplomatic Agents (verabschiedet von der Generalversammlung der Vereinten Nationen) vom 14. Dezember 1973;
- International Convention against the Taking of Hostages (verabschiedet von der Generalversammlung der Vereinten Nationen) vom 17. Dezember 1979;
- Protocol on the Suppression of Unlawful Acts of Violence at Airports Serving International Civil Aviation (Montreal II) vom 24. Februar 1988;
- Convention on the Physical Protection of Nuclear Material (Wien) vom 3. März 1980;
- Convention for the Suppression of Unlawful Acts against the Safety of Maritime Navigation (Rom) vom 10. März 1988;
- Protocol for the Suppression of Unlawful Acts against the Safety of Fixed Platforms Located on the Continental Shelf (Rom) vom 10. März 1988;
- Convention on the Marking of Plastic Explosives for the Purpose of Detection (Montreal) vom 1. März 1991;
- International Convention for the Suppression of Terrorist Bombings (verabschiedet von der Generalversammlung der Vereinten Nationen) vom 15. Dezember 1997;
- International Convention for the Suppression of the Financing of Terrorism (verabschiedet von der Generalversammlung der Vereinten Nationen) vom 9. Dezember 1999 (die insoweit eine Sonderstellung einnimmt).

Allen diesen Konventionen ist gemeinsam, dass sie Straftatbestände für ein typischerweise terroristisches Verhalten formulieren. Die Vertragsstaaten verpflichten sich, diese Delikte unter Strafe zu stellen, und tragen somit zu einer Harmonisierung der unterschiedlichen nationalen Rechtsordnungen bei. In der Regel lassen die Konventionen den Staaten einen weiten Ermessensspielraum bei der Umsetzung der Vorgaben. Sie können ihren Verpflichtungen durch den Erlass bestimmter legislativer Maßnahmen oder die Angleichung bestehender Normen nachkommen. Die Konventionen verfolgen allesamt das Ziel, durch eine Angleichung sowohl der Tatbestände als auch der Strafrahmen hinsichtlich bestimmter terroristischer Verhaltensweisen Strafbarkeitslücken zu vermeiden. Durch einheitliche Regelungen soll weltweit die gleichförmige Strafverfolgung der terroristischen Täter gewährleistet werden. Auf diesem Weg soll außerdem die Entstehung von sog. „Safe Havens", d. h. von Staaten, die aufgrund fehlender oder weniger strenger nationaler Regelungen als Zufluchtsorte für in anderen Ländern verfolgte Terroristen dienen, vermieden werden.

Die verschiedenen Konventionen enthalten aber nicht nur Vorgaben hinsichtlich der Schaffung einheitlicher Straftatbestände und Strafrahmen, sondern verpflichten die Vertragsstaaten auch zu einer umfassenden Kooperation bei der Strafverfolgung und Rechtsdurchsetzung. Aus den Abkommen ergeben sich konkrete Verpflichtungen in Bezug auf Maßnahmen der Strafverfolgung gegen bestimmte terroristische Straftäter[28]. Durch entsprechende Regelungen wird das völkerrechtliche Prinzip des *aut dedere aut judicare* in den meisten der Abkommen rechtlich verankert. Demnach ist ein Staat verpflichtet, entweder selbst die Strafverfolgung durchzuführen oder aber die Tatverdächtigen an einen verfolgungswilligen Staat auszuliefern. Bedingt durch den oftmals politisch motivierten Charakter der terroristischen Taten enthalten die Abkommen ferner Vorschriften, nach denen die Vertragsstaaten ein Auslieferungsgesuch nicht mit der Begründung ablehnen können, es handele sich um eine politisch motivierte Straftat. Nur so kann sichergestellt werden, dass die Effektivität der Übereinkommen nicht beeinträchtigt wird. Den verschiedenen Anti-Terror-Konventionen ist zudem gemeinsam, dass sie die Staaten zur Zusammenarbeit und Gewährung von Rechtshilfe verpflichten[29].

Eine wesentliche Schwäche der Übereinkommen liegt in ihrem teilweise geringen Ratifikationsstand[30]. Selbst wenn es den Staaten gelingt, sich auf einen Vertrag zu einigen, kann sein Inkrafttreten noch lange auf sich warten lassen. Erst wenn eine bestimmte Mindestzahl von Staaten den Vertrag völkerrechtlich ratifiziert hat, tritt seine völkerrechtliche Bindungswirkung ein. Dazu kommt, dass völkerrechtliche Verträge *per definitionem* immer nur die Staaten binden können, die ihnen auch beigetreten sind[31]. Selbst wenn daher eine große Zahl von

---

[28] Finke/Wandscher (Fn. 28), 170; Wolfrum (Fn. 27), 1113.
[29] Dazu stellvertretend Volker Röben, „The Role of International Conventions and the General International Law in the Fight against International Terrorism", in: ders./Silja Vöneky/Volker Röben/Frank Schorkopf (Hrsg.), *Terrorism as a Challenge for National and International Law: Security versus Liberty?*, 2003, 12; abrufbar unter: http://edoc.mpil.de/conference-on-terrorism/index.cfm (Zugriff am 14. 01. 2005).
[30] Dazu Finke/Wandscher (Fn. 28), 170.
[31] Art. 34 Wiener Übereinkommen über das Recht der Verträge vom 23. Mai 1969 (BGBl. 1985 II S. 926) kodifiziert die Maxime *pacta tertiis nec nocent nec prosunt*. Weiterführend Wolfgang Graf Vitzthum, „Begriff, Geschichte und Quellen des Völkerrechts", in: ders. (Hrsg.), *Völkerrecht*, 2004, 58 Rn. 120.

Staaten die entsprechenden Konventionen ratifiziert hat, bleiben die übrigen – und es gibt keinen völkerrechtlichen Vertrag, der wirklich von allen Staaten dieser Welt vollständig ratifiziert worden wäre[32] – zumindest partiell als Zufluchtstätten für international agierende Terroristen erhalten[33]. Nach den Ereignissen des 11. September 2001 lässt sich freilich eine zunehmende Bereitschaft der Staaten konstatieren, den internationalen Übereinkommen zur Bekämpfung des Terrorismus beizutreten und deren völkerrechtliche Verbindlichkeit zu akzeptieren. Hier sei beispielhaft auf das Anti-Finanzierungs-Übereinkommen von 1999 verwiesen, das im September 2001 mangels ausreichender Ratifikationen noch nicht in Kraft getreten war. Nach den Anschlägen wurde das Übereinkommen jedoch schnell von der Mehrzahl der Staaten unterzeichnet und ratifiziert[34], sodass es am 10. April 2002 in Kraft treten konnte.

3.2 Unterscheidung der Konventionen nach ihrem Regelungsinhalt

Die bestehenden Abkommen lassen sich in drei verschiedene Gruppen unterteilen. Die erste Gruppe umfasst alle diejenigen internationalen Übereinkommen, die ein spezifisches terroristisches Verhalten unter Strafe stellen. Zu nennen sind hier beispielsweise die *Convention for the Suppression of Terrorist Bombings*(1997) und aufgrund einer ähnlichen Struktur auch die *Convention against the Taking of Hostages* (1979). Diese Konventionen zeichnen sich dadurch aus, dass sie als Anknüpfungspunkt für eine strafrechtliche Verfolgung neben dem besonderen Unwertgehalt der Tat auch die subjektive Gesinnung der Täter einzubeziehen. Die Absicht, staatliche Entscheidungsträger durch Einschüchterung der Zivilbevölkerung in ihrem Handeln zu beeinflussen, wird als ein die Strafbarkeit begründendes Tatbestandsmerkmal besonders herausgestellt. Die *Convention for the Suppression of Terrorist Bombings*sieht zudem ausdrücklich vor, dass eine Rechtfertigung aufgrund politischer, religiöser oder ethischer Gründe

---

[32] Selbst die UN-Charter ist bis heute nicht von allen Staaten unterzeichnet worden. Nachdem die Schweiz und Ost-Timor im Jahr 2002 den Vereinten Nationen beitraten, sind gegenwärtig der Staat der Vatikanstadt (und Taiwan) nicht Mitglieder der Vereinten Nationen.

[33] Hier ist die Einschränkung vorzunehmen, dass einzelne Teile dieser Konventionen möglicherweise inzwischen als (zwingendes) Völkergewohnheitsrecht anzusehen sind oder in Zukunft als solches anzusehen sein könnten. Als Völkergewohnheitsrecht würden sie dann auch die Nichtvertragsstaaten binden. Vgl. Vitzthum (Fn. 32), 58 Rn. 120.; allgemein zum Völkergewohnheitsrecht Antonio Cassese, *International Law*, 2005, 156-166.

[34] So unterzeichneten 82 der 132 Vertragsstaaten das Abkommen erst nach dem 11. September 2001; 113 von 117 Ratifikationen erfolgten danach.

ausgeschlossen ist, und kann damit als ein weiteres Indiz für das sich allmählich durchsetzende Verständnis herangezogen werden, nach dem terroristische Gewalt unter keinen Umständen zu rechtfertigen ist.

Dem steht die zweite und weitaus umfangreichere Gruppe von Abkommen gegenüber, die nicht in dem hier vertretenen Sinn als spezifisch antiterroristisches Recht qualifiziert werden kann. Statt dessen richten sie sich gegen eine als besonders gefährlich eingestufte kriminelle Handlungsform. Die Abkommen pönalisieren Taten, die sowohl von „regulären" Kriminellen als auch von Tätern mit einem terroristischen Hintergrund begangen werden können[35]. Zu dieser Gruppe von Konventionen gehören beispielsweise die Übereinkommen, die Handlungen gegen die Sicherheit der Zivilluftfahrt[36] oder Seeschifffahrt[37] betreffen. Auch das Übereinkommen zum Schutz von Diplomaten kann in diese Gruppe eingeordnet werden. Die besondere subjektive Gesinnung der Täter wird nicht zu einer Strafbarkeitsvoraussetzung erklärt. Statt dessen dienen sie dem Schutz eines von der Staatengemeinschaft als besonders schützenswert anerkannten Gemeinschaftsinteresses, das typischerweise durch terroristische Täter gefährdet wird. Es ist nicht ausgeschlossen, dass eine terroristische Gewalttat den Tatbestand mehrerer völkerrechtlicher Konventionen erfüllt. So kann etwa ein Anschlag gegen ein Zivilflugzeug mit terroristischem Hintergrund die Konventionen von Tokio (1963) und Montreal (1971) verletzen sowie die Voraussetzungen der *Convention for the Suppression of Terrorist Bombings* erfüllen. Die Konventionen sowohl der ersten als auch der zweiten Gruppe zeichnen sich dadurch aus, dass sie repressiv gegen ein als besonders gefährlich und verwerflich angesehenes Verhalten vorgehen. Damit stehen sie in einem engen Zusammenhang mit dem internationalen materiellen Strafrecht[38].

---

[35] Oppermann (Fn. 23), 507.

[36] Geschützt durch die Convention on Offences and Certain Other Acts Committed on Board Aircraft (Tokio) vom 14. September 1963; Convention for the Suppression of Unlawful Seizure of Aircraft (Den Haag) vom 16. Dezember 1970; Convention for the Suppression of Unlawful Acts against Safety of Civil Aviation (Montreal) vom 23. September 1971.

[37] Geschützt durch die Convention for the Suppression of Unlawful Acts against the Safety of Maritime Navigation (Rom) vom 10. März 1988. Der Bezug zu terroristischen Gewaltakten ergibt sich lediglich aus der Präambel: „*Deeply concerned* about the worldwide escalation of acts of terrorism in all its forms, which endanger or take innocent human lives, jeopardize fundamental freedoms and seriously impair the dignity of human beings [...]."

[38] Wolfrum (Fn. 27), 1114.

Schließlich gibt es eine weitere Gruppe multilateraler Konventionen, die sich von den Vorgenannten vor allem durch ihren präventiven Charakter unterscheidet. Dazu zählt insbesondere die *Convention for the Suppression of the Financing of Terrorism* vom 9. Dezember 1999, die einen Paradigmenwechsel hinsichtlich der Funktion von internationalen Übereinkommen bei der Bekämpfung des internationalen Terrorismus darstellt[39]. Die Konvention setzt den Schwerpunkt nicht mehr allein auf die repressive Verfolgung terroristischer Täter, sondern versucht, bereits präventiv die Entstehung und Ausbreitung terroristischer Organisationen zu verhindern. Dazu verbietet das Abkommen alle Tätigkeiten staatlicher, aber auch privater Organisationen, die direkt oder indirekt terroristische Anschläge unterstützen[40]. Das Neuartige dieser Konvention liegt darin, dass sie nicht nur die unmittelbaren terroristischen Aktivitäten, sondern auch die Tätigkeiten der hinter ihnen stehenden Netzwerke und Organisationen zum Gegenstand hat, die erfolgreichen Terrorismus erst ermöglichen. Durch die Strafbarkeit derartiger materieller Unterstützungshandlungen sollen dem internationalen Terrorismus die finanziellen Mittel entzogen werden, die dieser für die langfristige Erhaltung seiner globalen Netzwerke benötigt. Damit wendet sich zum ersten Mal ein Übereinkommen nicht mehr nur typischen Begehungsformen des Terrorismus zu, sondern richtet sich präventiv gegen seine eigentlichen Wurzeln – die finanziellen Quellen. Die Konvention ist im hier behandelten Kontext aus einem weiteren Grund von besonderem Interesse: Mit ihr wird erstmals auf internationaler Ebene eine rechtsverbindliche allgemeine Umschreibung des Begriffs Terrorismus vorgenommen. Diese war notwendig geworden, um bestimmte Formen der finanziellen Unterstützung terroristischer Aktivitäten zu einem strafbaren Delikt zu erklären. Terrorismus wird in der Konvention definiert als:

> „Any other act intended to cause death or serious bodily injury to a civilian, or to any other person not taking active part in the hostilities in a situation of armed conflict, when the purpose of such act, by its nature

---

[39] Dazu umfassend Sven Peterke, „Die Bekämpfung der Terrorismusfinanzierung unter Kapitel VII der UN-Charta", in: *Humanitäres Völkerrecht* 2001, 217-221; Anthony Aust, „Counter-Terrorism – a New Approach: The International Convention for the Suppression of the Financing of Terrorism", in: *Max Planck Yearbook of United Nations Law* 5 (2001), 285-306; Jonathan Charney, „The International Law of Terrorist Financing", in: *American Journal of Int'l Laws* 97 (2003), 315-333; Jean-Marc Sorel, „Some Questions about the Definition of Terrorism and the Fight against its Financing", in: *European Journal of Int'l Law* 14 (2003), 365-378; Ayers (Fn. 2), 449-459.

[40] Vgl. Art. 2 Abs. 1: „Any person commits an offence within the meaning of this Convention if that person by any means, directly or indirectly, unlawfully and willfully, provides or collects funds with the intention that they should be used [...] to carry out [...] any act intended to cause death or serious bodily injury to a civilian [...]."

or context, is to intimidate a population, or to compel a government or an international organization to do or to abstain from doing any act."[41]

Diese Begriffsbestimmung kann als ein erster Schritt zu einer allgemeinen Definition des Begriffs des Terrorismus verstanden werden, womit auch die Schaffung eines allgemeinen Abkommens zur Bekämpfung des internationalen Terrorismus nicht mehr völlig unrealistisch erscheint. Der Vollständigkeit halber sei hier noch die *Convention on the Physical Protection of Nuclear Material* vom 3. März 1980 genannt, die ebenfalls präventiven Charakter hat[42]. Mit ihr werden die Aneignung und der Erwerb nuklearen Materials verboten und somit die Strafbarkeit der terroristischen Handlungen auf Vorbereitungsakte ausgedehnt.

3.3 Eine internationale Konvention gegen den computerbezogenen Terrorismus?

Bislang existiert allerdings kein multilaterales Abkommen, das sich mit der spezifischen Begehungsform des Cyberterrorismus auseinander setzt. Die bestehenden Übereinkommen zur Terrorismusbekämpfung können nur begrenzt gegen den Cyberterrorismus angewandt werden. Ausgangspunkt des internationalen Vorgehens müssen vielmehr solche Abkommen bilden, die sich allgemein gegen die computerbezogene Kriminalität richten. In diesem Kontext ist vor allem auf die *Council of Europe Convention on Cybercrime* [43] vom November 2001 hinzuweisen, die sowohl von Mitgliedstaaten des Europarates als auch von weiteren Staaten, die nicht Mitglieder des Europarates[44] sind, unterzeichnet worden ist[45]. Obwohl diese Konvention keinen eigenen Tatbestand des Cyberterrorismus beinhaltet, kann computerbezogenes terroristisches Verhalten unter gewissen Umständen unter die bestehenden Tatbestände subsumiert werden. Das ist immer dann möglich, wenn die terroristischen Täter einen der dort aufgeführten computerspezifischen Tatbestände verwirklichen und ihr Handeln somit anderen Formen computerbezogener Kriminalität entspricht. Dieser Ansatz hat jedoch die Schwäche, dass er dem besonderen Charakter des computerbezogenen Terrorismus als politisch-ideologisch motivierter Straftat nur bedingt gerecht wird und

---

[41] Art. 2 Abs. 1 der Konvention.
[42] Siehe dazu auch Wolfrum (Fn. 27), 1122.
[43] Text der Konvention abrufbar unter: http://conventions.coe.int/Treaty/en/Treaties/Html/185.htm.
[44] Das sind die Vereinigten Staaten, Kanada, Japan und Südafrika.
[45] Umfassend dazu Mike Keyser, „The Council of Europe Convention on Cybercrime", in: *Journal of Transnational Law and Policy* 12 (2003), 287-326; Hopkins (Fn. 10), 101 ff.; Ryan M.F. Baron, „Critique of the International Cybercrime Treaty", in: *CommLaw Conceptus* 10 (2002), 263-278.

vor allem seinen besonderen Unwertgehalt sowie die verwerfliche Motivation der Täter nur unzureichend erfasst[46]. Cyberterroristen wollen mittels der Nutzung von Computersystemen einen „politischen Angriff" durchführen, indem sie die betroffenen Nutzer durch Einflussnahme auf Datenverarbeitungsprozesse einschüchtern und dadurch mittelbar zu einem bestimmten Handeln zwingen. Die unterschiedliche Motivation der Täter erfordert auch eine unterschiedliche rechtliche Reaktion, sodass die Konventionen gegen die Computerkriminalität nur als Grundlage für weitere spezielle völkerrechtliche Übereinkommen dienen können. In diese Richtung geht beispielsweise der Entwurf einer *Convention on Cyber Crime and Terrorism*[47] des Hoover Instituts der Universität Stanford aus dem Jahr 1999. Dieser trägt der Tatsache Rechnung, dass der Cyberterrorismus eine außerordentlich schwere und durch eine besonders verwerfliche subjektive Zielsetzung qualifizierte Form der Computerkriminalität darstellt. Der Konventionsentwurf enthält Vorgaben zur Schaffung von nationalen Straftatbeständen, die sich sowohl gegen computerbezogene Kriminalität als auch terroristische Aktivitäten richten.

4 Schlussbemerkungen

Das Vorgehen der Staatengemeinschaft gegen den internationalen Terrorismus wird nur dann erfolgreich sein, wenn es auf der Grundlage des internationalen Rechts erfolgt. Vor allem multilaterale Abkommen schaffen in diesem Bereich die Grundlage dafür, den vom grenzüberschreitenden Terrorismus ausgehenden Gefahren wirksam zu begegnen. Zusammenfassend sollen vor allem drei Aspekte herausgestellt werden, aufgrund derer internationale Konventionen einen wesentlichen Beitrag zur Bekämpfung des grenzüberschreitenden Terrorismus erbringen:

1. Indem sie die Vertragsstaaten zur Umsetzung bestimmter legislativer Maßnahmen verpflichten, tragen sie zu einer Harmonisierung der nationalen Rechtsordnungen hinsichtlich der Strafbarkeit bestimmter terroristischer Verhaltensweisen bei.

---

[46] Trachtman (Fn. 10), 4.
[47] Der Text des Entwurfs (August 2004) ist abgedruckt unter: http://www.iwar.org.uk/ law/resources/cybercrime/stanford/cisac-draft.htm. (Zugriff 10. 01. 2005). Zu einer rechtlichen Bewertung näher *Stein Schjolberg*, The Legal Framework – Unauthorized Access to Computer Systems, vom 7. April 2003, abrufbar unter: http://www. mosstingrett.no/info/legal.html (Zugriff am 14. 01. 2005), 3; Goodman/Brenner (Fn. 20), 191.

2. Internationale Übereinkommen erlegen den Staaten Kooperationspflichten bei der Strafverfolgung und dem Informationsaustausch auf und verhindern somit im Idealfall die Entstehung von Strafbarkeitslücken und „Safe Havens".
3. Schließlich begründen die völkerrechtlichen Übereinkommen für die Vertragsstaaten die Pflicht, entsprechend dem Grundsatz *aut dedere aut judicare* die Terrorismusverdächtigen entweder selbst strafrechtlich zu verfolgen oder aber an ein verfolgungswilliges Land auszuliefern.

Freilich nähern sich alle diese Maßnahmen dem Phänomen des internationalen Terrorismus jedoch vor allem aus repressiver Perspektive. Eine effektive Bekämpfung des internationalen Terrorimus setzt aber eine intensive Zusammenarbeit nicht nur auf dem Gebiet der Strafverfolgung, sondern auch im Bereich der präventiven Bekämpfung terroristischer Vorhaben voraus. Damit die Völkerrechtsordnung zu einem umfassend wirksamen Instrument im Vorgehen gegen den Terrorismus wird, ist eine Verstärkung der präventiven Maßnahmen erforderlich. Die *Convention for the Suppression of the Financing of Terrorism* stellt diesbezüglich ein richtigen Ansatzpunkt dar, da sie auch gegen die Ursachen und des internationalen Terrorismus vorgeht.

Hinsichtlich des hier nur exemplarisch untersuchten Aspekts des Cyberterrorismus ergibt sich kein anderes Resultat: Um wirksam gegen diese mit den Mitteln des nationalen Rechts nur schwer fassbare Form des Terrorismus vorgehen zu können, muss auf multilaterale Verträge zurückgegriffen werden. Im Gegensatz zum Umgang mit sonstigen terroristischen Handlungsformen bedarf es im Vorgehen gegen den Cyberterrorismus allerdings eines zweifachen Ansatzes. Da er eine besonders schwere Form der computerbezogenen Kriminalität darstellt, müssen die internationalen Konventionen gegen die computerbezogene Kriminalität als Ausgangspunkt zu Grunde gelegt werden. Auf ihrer Basis gilt es nunmehr, weitere spezialgesetzliche Übereinkommen zu erarbeiten, welche zusätzlich die besonderen Elemente jener Abkommen berücksichtigen, die man als spezifisches Anti-Terror-Recht bezeichnen kann.

Maßnahmen der Sicherheitsdienste

Measures of the Intelligence Agencies

Cooperation between National and International Security Services in Countering Global Terrorism

Ernst Uhrlau

Coordinator of the Intelligence Services
Federal Chancellery of the Federal Republic of Germany, Berlin

More than three years after 11 September 2001, the alarming threat posed by global terrorism still persists. All experts agree that the most serious threat emanates from al-Qaida's Islamist terrorism and related Islamist structures.

In the aftermath of the most devastating terrorist attack of modern times, there have been many acts of terrorism claiming hundreds of lives. Most recently, the events in Madrid in March 2004 made the public more aware of the threat posed by terrorism, also in Europe. It became clear that Europe is not just a possible, but an actual target.

Recent reports that Abu Musab al-Zarqawi has announced mega terrorist attacks in the near future add to the disquiet, even if the authenticity and seriousness of these announcements currently seem far from certain.

Security policy makers and Europe's security service operators were certainly aware of the threat even before 11 September 2001. Yet all were surprised by the scale of the attacks. Following Osama bin Laden's declaration of war on the "crusaders" in 1998, the attacks on the embassies in Nairobi and Dar es Salaam in 1998 and the one on the USS Cole in 2000 seemed like the writing on the wall.

Events in Germany around Christmas 2000 are to be seen in a similar light. German security services uncovered plans for attacks on the Strasbourg Christmas market and managed to prevent them. The perpetrators from Islamist circles have now been sentenced and are serving their time in German prisons. A key to this success was the intensive cooperation between intelligence services and the police, also across national borders.

Key features of Islamist terrorism are the international posture of its players, the transnational nature of the threat and the transnational preparation of attacks. Beyond the inner circle of its leadership, the mainstay of al-Qaida and the Islamist groups linked to it are a large number of so-called Afghanistan veterans. During the Taliban regime, these people, originating predominantly from Arab countries, were given military and terrorist training in al-Qaida camps. On returning to their countries of origin, these Afghanistan veterans now form part of a global, close-knit network.

Shared experiences and convictions nurture the emergence of a type of conspiratorial community that is prepared to use violence to press home the Islamist goals proclaimed by their leaders. It is not just the so-called West that they perceive as the enemy, first and foremost the US, Israel and Britain, and also Germany, but rather many of the regimes in Arab countries that the Islamists term "un-Islamic", for example Saudi Arabia, Jordan and Egypt.

The resulting threat is a global one. To successfully combat this terrorism and curb the subsequent danger, we need a complex set of measures integrating various spheres: intelligence services, police and judiciary, but also diplomatic, economic and development-policy measures, including, in exceptional cases, military action. Given the global transnational threat, the international cooperation of security services is an essential component of this set of measures.

For the required international cooperation to be effective, each state has to do its homework in the fight against terrorism. Germany has been very thorough here, even before 11 September 2001. Perhaps this is partly because we had gathered painful experience with terrorist groups in Germany and Europe in the 1970s and right up to the early 1990s. Besides the legal and material basis established at the time for the work of the security and law enforcement authorities, intensive cooperation between these bodies played a central role.

There was general consensus at the time amongst German authorities dealing with terrorism that cooperation was the only way to defeat it. Thus the intelligence services and law enforcement authorities contributed the advantages of their individual approaches and methods for the common cause. It was the state based on the rule of law and its representatives that had been challenged. And the security services of the Federation and the Länder (federal states) presented a united front in rising to that challenge.

Some of the cooperation and experience may have been lost once German terrorism had been defeated. But having recognized the increasing threat posed by Islamist terrorism prior to 11 September 2001, the security services of the Federation saw the need to resort to previous forms of cooperation and to intensively exchange information on terrorist issues.

With the "Information Board," a platform was created which gave all the authorities involved – Federal Intelligence Service (BND), Federal Office for the Protection of the Constitution (BfV) and Federal Criminal Police Office (BKA) – the opportunity to exchange findings within the bounds of the law and to agree on appropriate measures. After 11 September 2001, this cooperation was clearly stepped up once more, meetings became more frequent and technical links between the various authorities were improved to guarantee broader and quicker communication between the different stakeholders.

Including the heads of the Federal Criminal Police Office and the Federal Public Prosecution Office in the regular meetings at the Federal Chancellery on the intelligence situation was another important step taken to promote cooperation between the security services. Traditionally, this meeting has been used to coordinate the intelligence services of the Federation (that is the Federal Intelligence Service, the Federal Office for the Protection of the Constitution and the Military Counter-Intelligence Service). At this weekly meeting chaired by State Secretary Steinmeier, Head of the Federal Chancellery, the heads of the intelligence services, the state secretaries from the Federal Foreign Office, the Federal Ministry of the Interior, the Federal Ministry of Justice and the Federal Ministry of Defence come together to discuss aspects of national and international security and to exchange relevant information.

Even before 11 September 2001, the head of the Federal Criminal Police Office attended this meeting regularly, largely due to experience had with the Meliani group in Frankfurt/Main. This meant police findings and considerations could be fed into and reflected in the discussions. Since September 2001, the Federal Public Prosecutor General has been reporting once a month in person on the progress made in ongoing investigations concerning terrorism.

The federal system in Germany also requires the security services of the Länder to be duly coordinated both with each other and with the authorities at federal level. Particularly in recent weeks, there has been much talk of the 38 security services in Germany which, if you believe the critics, are all doing pretty much the same work. I feel that this criticism is very much exaggerated. Of course there have been occasions where criticism was justified – in both directions. I am not trying to gloss over the facts, but generalizations are rarely productive.

The Federal Criminal Police Office and the Federal Office for the Protection of the Constitution play a central role when it comes to coordinating with the police or the constitution-protection authorities of the Länder. The Federal Criminal Police Office as a clearing house helps the Länder police forces to prevent and prosecute offences involving two or more Länder or in cases of international or otherwise considerable importance, including of course international terrorism. Its function is to collate and evaluate all the necessary information to perform this task.

The Federal Office for the Protection of the Constitution has a similar coordinating function for the relevant offices at Land level. The scale and type of information-sharing practised by the constitution-protection authorities are governed by the Federal Act on the Protection of the Constitution. With this year's new regulation, the two-way obligation to pass on information on terrorism has been expanded. This means that the exchange of information between the constitution-protection authorities of the Federation and the Länder will improve further.

All in all, the national cooperation of our security services is working well. According to the security services themselves, they managed to prevent five attacks between late 2000 and late 2004, including most recently the planned attack on the Iraqi Prime Minister Allawi.

This is an impressive record. But of course we must not rest on our laurels. We have to continue to be vigilant and step up our efforts wherever possible. After all, the security services must continue to be successful in fighting terrorism, because one single success on the part of the terrorists is enough to make them come closer to their political and propagandist goals.

Therefore the Federal Government has in recent months launched a project to further improve and increase the efficiency of cooperation between the security services. In early December, a Joint Counter-Terrorism Centre was set up in Berlin-Treptow, which Interior Minister Otto Schily presented to the public in mid December 2004. In the Joint Centre, the specialist and analyst units of the Federal Criminal Police Office and the Federal Office for the Protection of the Constitution have been co-located.

The Federal Intelligence Service, the Federal Border Police, the Central Office of the German Customs Investigation Service and the Military Counter-Intelligence Office are thus involved in current work, just like the criminal police offices and constitution-protection offices of the Länder, which have been invited – and have mostly agreed – to cooperate. Furthermore, the Federal Public Prosecution Office as the authority responsible for prosecuting terrorist offences is also represented in this Joint Counter-Terrorism Centre.

Besides daily briefings on the current situation, the tasks performed there include:

- drawing up general threat assessments,
- exchanging information on operational matters,
- assessing concrete cases as well as structural analyses,
- gathering intelligence on potential Islamist terrorists and
- pooling available resources, for example technology and language capacities, thus making more effective use of them.

No new authority has been created with this Joint Centre. Rather, it is a further development of the cooperation previously practised as part of the "Information Boards." Full account has been taken of the – due to the peculiar German historical experience – indispensable need to separate police and intelligence services. But by increasing the physical proximity, the Federal Government hopes to promote more intensive, comprehensive and rapid exchange of information between the authorities dealing with the fight against terrorism.

Cooperation at national level will be further increased by means of a joint index database as well as temporary project files, to which the staff in the Joint Counter-Terrorism Centre will have access. And not just there. Legal amendments are required for this move, and the relevant bills are currently being agreed between the various authorities. With these shared files, data exchange will be even more targeted and effective.

International cooperation is absolutely indispensable to supplement this national cooperation between security services. While cooperation between security services on combating terrorism did exist prior to 11 September 2001, it was usually restricted to individual cases. In such operative cooperation, too, experience and trust built up through the transnational fight against German, European and Middle East terrorism played a major role.

11 September 2001 did however work as a catalyst in this field. It made abundantly clear to all that international terrorism poses a threat to the entire civilized world which must be resolutely countered. Since then, international cooperation of the security services has become much wider and deeper and reached an unprecedented scale. This is true of intelligence services as well as the police and judicial authorities. Nevertheless, international cooperation is very different in the various spheres. There are tangible reasons for this:

- Above all for the intelligence services, bilateral – in exceptional cases trilateral – cooperation remains by far the most effective form of cooperation, given the often sensitive nature of information sources. In comparison, multilateral approaches often only scratch the surface. Yet some forms of multilateral cooperation in the intelligence community have now developed which have been achieving good results with three, four or even five participating states.

- There is a similar attitude to multilateral cooperation in the policing sphere, albeit in a less pronounced form. Yet multilateral approaches have long been proving their worth with Interpol and Europol. For Germany, strengthening Europol in its tasks and capabilities is a particular priority.

- Turning to judicial cooperation, some procedures still seem somewhat cumbersome. Even within the European Union, national considerations occasionally seem to stand in the way of more rapid and improved information exchange between the judicial authorities. However, 11 September 2001 heralded positive developments here as well. It seems justified to hope for further improvements in the near future. The European arrest warrant enabling a state's own citizens to be extradited to other European states if certain conditions are fulfilled points in the right direction.

Persistent efforts to further improve this platform of cooperation are crucial. It cannot be that Europe is largely free of borders for terrorist groups, but that police and judicial authorities continue to encounter national frontiers. Therefore it is right and proper that the fight against terrorism remains a priority issue for the European Union.

This has been the case for the past few years. Both the European Security Strategy and the European Council Declaration of 25 March 2004 highlight the central importance of combating terrorism. Similarly, in the European Council Declaration of 17 December 2004 great store is set by the fight against international terrorism.

The priority attached to fighting terrorism in political circles has led to tangible improvements in the cooperation between security services. Within Europol, the Counter-Terrorist Task Force has been reactivated, while the role of Europol itself has been continually strengthened. Nevertheless, Germany hopes for further-reaching improvements.

Europe's domestic intelligence services are now cooperating closely in the Counter-Terrorism Group (CTG). The European Council approved an action plan clearly stating who has to do what and when. To help with the implementation and monitoring of this action plan, Javier Solana, High Representative for the Common Foreign and Security Policy, appointed Gijs de Vries as Counter-Terrorism Coordinator, who is in constant contact with the member states.

The EU views international cooperation as fundamental when it comes to combating terrorism. Therefore this cooperation is placed high on the EU's international agenda. The EU is for example ready to use its economic clout to push through anti-terrorism provisions in EU bilateral treaties with third countries.

The cooperation of the security services – whether national or international – is crucial to success in the fight against terrorism. But it is not enough on its own. As I mentioned earlier, we need a complex set of measures from a range of spheres. Security services are not isolated units in a society. They depend on people's trust and readiness to cooperate. Business is one of the crucial fields. Economic institutions are also always a potential target for terrorists. Cooperation between the security services and the economy is thus essential.

Shortly after 11 September, the Federal Government launched talks with the business and administration communities to make them more aware of the need for improved risk prevention, given the new threat situation. These talks and contacts are being continued to tackle the major, and in part new, challenges together. The Working Group for Security in the Economy, which has the aim of promoting information exchange between the economy and the security services, has made a major contribution.

In the long term, curbing the dangers of international terrorism has to start with the root causes. There is a whole set of motives for Islamist terrorism, including the Middle East conflict, the "ideological" rejection of the Westernisation of Islamic societies and not least the region's economic problems.

Furthermore, Islamist terrorists hold the USA (or the West) responsible for supporting the governments of their home countries and thus also for the suppression of the Islamist opposition. Therefore they target the USA – but always with the goal of toppling their home governments. With the Iraq war, the subsequent occupation and not least the images of Abu Ghraib, these motives – and the readiness to support them – have rather been strengthened.

According to most experts, the terrorist threat will be one of the major challenges of the coming years or even decades. Thus political solutions are needed above and beyond the work of the security services. As well as improving living standards and solving regional conflicts, we have to work in Islamic states towards a liberalization and democratization of Islamic societies to prevent the Islamist Opposition turning to terrorism.

Here we have to win over the many al-Qaida sympathizers. As we will always have a primary interest in the stability of the states in the region, this will be a major challenge as well as a tightrope act. Such a policy is, however, essential for a long-term stabilization of the region.

How this threat will develop is something not entirely in our control. But we must take it seriously. Yet we should not succumb to panic, either. Through broad international cooperation, our security services will do all in their power to prevent further attacks. However, no-one can guarantee that this will work every time.

The successes achieved by the security services around the world since 11 September 2001 could be a source of confidence, yet they are in stark contrast to the many other terrible attacks seen all over the world, even very recently. Against this backdrop, vigilance and cooperation remain the order of the day.

Die Rolle des Bundesnachrichtendienstes bei der Aufklärung des Internationalen Terrorismus

Dr. August Hanning

Präsident des Bundesnachrichtendienstes

Immer häufiger sehen wir uns mit einem Phänomen konfrontiert, das mittlerweile als islamistischer Terrorismus bezeichnet wird und welches, auch wenn Anschläge in Deutschland bislang verhindert werden konnten, bereits sichtbare Auswirkungen auch auf unser Handeln hat. In zweifacher Hinsicht spüren wir die Folgen. Anschläge, wie jene in Madrid, und Enthauptungen, wie sie im Irak an der Tagesordnung sind, beeinflussen zunehmend auch politische Entscheidungen europäischer Regierungen. Dabei sind es nicht nur konkrete Ereignisse, sondern bereits antizipierte Gefahren, die Reaktionen hervorrufen. Zudem sind in manchen Ländern, in denen terroristische Gruppen bewusst Ausländer mit Gewalt vertreiben wollen, natürlich auch deutsche Staatsbürger und Wirtschaftsunternehmen betroffen. Wir sind also zu einer intensiven Auseinandersetzung mit dem ‚Islamistischen Terrorismus' gezwungen.

Bevor ich zu der Frage komme, welchen Beitrag der Bundesnachrichtendienst bei dieser Auseinandersetzung leisten kann, möchte ich in aller Kürze den Versuch unternehmen, die Entstehung, die heutige Ausformung und die zu erwartende künftige Entwicklung des Problems zu analysieren. Die Möglichkeiten des BND seinen Teil zur Aufklärung und damit zur Bekämpfung dieser Form des Terrorismus zu leisten, hängen naturgemäß vom Charakter der Bedrohung ab.

Deutlich als Triebfeder des Handelns heutiger islamistisch orientierter Terroristen und Extremisten erkennbar sind tiefsitzende Minderwertigkeitsgefühle, die aus einer weit verbreiteten und über Jahrhunderte gewachsenen Empfindung westlicher Dominanz über die islamische Welt rühren. Diese Strömung löste schon vor Jahrzehnten grundsätzliche Überlegungen zu islamischem Staatswesen und Gesellschaftsformen aus, gleichsam als Antithese auf eine im Zuge der gesellschaftlichen Aufklärung in Europa geprägten Staatsauffassung. Das Missfallen mit der sowohl ausländischen Staaten als auch den eigenen Regimen angelasteten Situation ließ Personen wie die Ägypter Hassan Al Banna und Sayyid Qutb, um nur zwei Namen zu nennen, über alternative Konzepte nachdenken. Im Ergebnis gründete der erste 1928 die Muslimbrüder und rief der zweite in den 50er und 60er Jahren zum Sturz von Regierungen in der westlichen und islamischen Welt auf. Der Einfluss Qutbs auf islamistische Extremisten bis hin zu Al-Qa'ida-Größen hält unvermindert an. Das Streben dieser und anderer Ideologen galt und gilt ganz allgemein der Errichtung einer aus Koran und Sunna ableitbaren göttlichen Ordnung, die, folgt man der Logik ihrer Protagonisten, jeder von Menschen ausgedachten und entworfenen Staatsform überlegen sei.

Politische Vorgänge von teilweise epochaler Bedeutung, wie der Zerfall des osmanischen Reiches, die Gründung Israels und der Palästinenserkonflikt, die Revolution im Iran und die Golfkriege, die zu einer Stationierung amerikanischer Truppen in Saudi Arabien führten – Vorgänge also, die sozusagen die Schwäche der islamischen Welt auch politisch dokumentieren – beeinflussten die weitere Entwicklung.

Basierend auf diesen geistigen Ursachen formierte sich der internationale Terrorismus heutiger Prägung. Keimzelle war hierbei der Kampf von Teilen der afghanischen Bevölkerung gegen die sowjetische Besatzung ihres Landes. In diesem vom Westen anerkannten Befreiungskampf erfuhr auch die Gruppe um Bin Laden politische und materielle Unterstützung durch den Westen. Nach der erfolgreichen Vertreibung der sowjetischen Besatzer zog sich Bin Laden in der Folge in den Sudan zurück, wo er sich aufhielt, bis er auf Druck der USA zum Verlassen des Landes aufgefordert wurde.

Damals entstand in Pakistan die Bewegung der religiös fundamentalen Taliban. Ihre Anhänger entstammten Madrassen, die mit saudiarabischem Geld finanziert wurden. Mit dem Ziel in Afghanistan einen Gottesstaat zu errichten, eroberten sie weite Teile des Landes. Der Bundesnachrichtendienst beobachtete diese Entwicklungen seit Entstehung des Konfliktes sehr intensiv. Ein besonderes Augenmerk lag dabei auf den Ausbildungslagern, in denen radikales Gedankengut und Handwerkszeug vermittelt wurde, was bei Anschlägen außerhalb Afghanistans zum Einsatz kam. Parallel ging eine ‚Internationalisierung' der al-Qa'ida-Agenda einher, die zunehmend Ziele außerhalb Afghanistans anvisierte, wie es bei den Anschlägen von Dar Es Salaam und Nairobi der Fall war. Mit diesem Vorlauf kamen die Anschläge vom 11. September 2001 für den Bundesnachrichtendienst nicht ganz unerwartet. Überraschend war vielmehr die konkrete Zielauswahl, die Dimension des Angriffs und die zu Grunde liegende strategische Planung. Ein besonderes Merkmal bildete die langfristige und konspirative Vorbereitung.

Konflikte und Krisen wie in Bosnien, Tschetschenien, Algerien, Kashmir und Mindanao boten diesen Strukturen die Gelegenheit, ihre Netzwerke auszubauen. Dabei waren internationale Kämpfer, wie in Afghanistan, nie Hauptträger des Widerstandes. Ihr Prestige vor Ort gestaltete sich unterschiedlich; ihr Ansehen in der internationalen Sympathisantenszene dagegen stieg.

Mit den Entwicklungen im Irak scheint ein weiterer „Sozialisationsschritt" mit deutlichen Bezügen zu westlichen Staaten einherzugehen. Die Lage im Irak bietet mit der ausländischen Besetzung kernislamischen Territoriums genau jene Elemente, die der Agenda der Extremisten entsprechen.

Welche Bedrohung ergibt sich aus diesen Entwicklungen für Europa, und wie können wir diesen begegnen? Zunächst einmal möchte ich auf eine scheinbar paradoxe Situation hinweisen: trotz einer gestiegenen Anzahl von Antiterroroperationen und Festnahmen nahm die Zahl der Anschläge zu. Gründe hierfür sind strukturelle Veränderungen innerhalb der Terrorszene und die anhaltende Ausstrahlungskraft der Terrroragenda auf Sympathisanten.

Al Qa'ida wurde zwar strukturell und operativ geschwächt, bleibt aber handlungsfähig. Sie ist heute, nach verschiedenen Evolutionsschritten, als eine Art terroristisches Kernnetzwerk zu verstehen, mit Verbindungen zu vielen lokalen und regionalen Gruppierungen, Kleingruppen, Zellen, Einzelpersonen, aber auch Parteien und NGOs. Manchmal ist das einzig verbindende Element das gemeinsame Gedankengut. In der Regel bilden direkte und indirekte personelle Kennverhältnisse das Rückrat dieser Verbindungen, die ein grenzüberschreitendes Agieren erlauben.

Terroristische Ambitionen, möglichst spektakuläre und symbolträchtige Anschläge zu verüben, bestehen fort. Eine Möglichkeit zu einem spektakulären Anschlag besteht in der Verwendung von Massenvernichtungswaffen. Noch, zum Glück, waren wir nicht Zeugen eines Anschlages islamistischer Gruppierungen mit Waffen aus dem ABC-Arsenal. Die Möglichkeit eines solchen Vorgehens hat uns jedoch die japanische AUM-Sekte vorexerziert. Die Aufklärung derartiger Entwicklungen, die Verbindungen zum Waffenhandel, die Kenntnis, ob Massenvernichtungswaffen oder Vorprodukte auf illegalen Waffenmärkten verfügbar und durch Terroristen einsetzbar sind, sind ebenfalls Fragen, die bei der realistischen Einschätzung der Bedrohung eine Bedeutung haben.

Welche Rolle hat der Bundesnachrichtendienst nun bei der Aufklärung des internationalen Terrorismus?

Bereits seit Anfang der 90er Jahre beobachtet der Bundesnachrichtendienst Entwicklungen auf den Gebieten, die mit der Entstehung und Ausbreitung von Terrorismus in Verbindung stehen. Dabei stand im Vordergrund, die Ursachen des Phänomens zu analysieren und seine Ausprägungen zu untersuchen. Neben den ideologischen Grundlagen spielen natürlich regionale und ethnische Sachverhalte eine besondere Rolle. Darüber hinaus lassen sich terroristische Strukturen nur dann sinnvoll aufklären, wenn auch logistische Strukturen ihre Finanzierung ebenfalls beobachtet werden. Für den Bundesnachrichtendienst wirkt sich hier positiv aus, dass er auch bei der Aufklärung der Bereiche Waffenhandel, Drogenhandel und Geldwäsche seit über einem Jahrzehnt aktiv ist. Eine nicht zu vernachlässigende Rolle spielt auch die Beobachtung der illegalen Migration, da deren Strukturen zur Schleusung von Personen auch von terroristischen Netzwerken genutzt werden. Den Bundesnachrichtendienst kennzeichnet sein ganzheitlicher und interdisziplinärer Aufklärungsansatz. Alle diese Bereiche werden beobachtet, die Informationen themenübergreifend bewertet und zu Lagebildern verdichtet.

Zur Informationsgewinnung nutzen wir alle uns zur Verfügung stehenden Mittel. Wir werten in großem Umfang offenes Material aus, wir ergänzen dies durch die Beschaffung von Informationen mit menschlichen Quellen, unter Nutzung von Technik und unter Verwendung von Satellitenbildern. Doch die Beschaffung bildet nur den ersten Schritt. Eine besondere Bedeutung kommt der Analyse zu. Für uns ist diese besonders wichtig, um relevante Informationen als solche zu erkennen, sie richtig zu bewerten und somit Gefahren angemessen einzuschätzen. In all diesen Schritten arbeiten wir mit anderen Organisationen und Behörden im In- und Ausland zusammen. Zudem pflegen wir eine intensive Kooperation mit den anderen deutschen Sicherheitsbehörden. Bereits seit dem Jahr 2000 tauschen wir im Rahmen des Information Board regelmäßig Erkenntnisse mit den anderen deutschen Sicherheitsbehörden aus. Dieser Austausch wird durch die Einrichtung des Gemeinsamen Terrorismusabwehrzentrums im Berliner Stadtteil Treptow, das der Bundesminister des Innern Anfang der Woche eingeweiht hat, weiter verbessert werden. Wichtig ist in diesem Zusammenhang, dass hier keine neue Behörde eingerichtet wurde, sondern dass die Erkenntnisse der deutschen Sicherheitsorgane auf dem Gebiet des islamistischen Terrorismus unter Beibehaltung der jeweiligen Zuständigkeiten zusammengeführt werden. Auch aus meiner Sicht ist es zwingend erforderlich, nicht zuletzt wegen des im Grundgesetz verankerten Trennungsgebots, polizeiliche und nachrichtendienstliche Aufgaben strikt voneinander zu trennen. Ein Nachrichtendienst, wie der Bundesnachrichtendienst, übernimmt für seine Quellen oder Informanten eine besondere Verantwortung. Diese liegt darin begründet, dass die Quellen im besonderen Maße darauf vertrauen müssen, dass der Bundesnachrichtendienst sie schützen kann. Ein Nachrichtendienst muss daher selbst abwägen können, ob die von ihm beschafften Informationen geeignet sind, um sie in Verfahren von Strafverfolgungsbehörden einzuführen und sie damit der Öffentlichkeit zugänglich zu machen. Das in Treptow umgesetzte Modell berücksichtigt diesen Aspekt ausreichend.

Mit Treptow, wo auch die Länderbehörden eingebunden werden, sind wir bei der praktischen Gefahrenabwehr einen weiteren Schritt gegangen. Dies ist jedoch nur eine Seite der Medaille. Die andere hingegen fordert von uns, die Köpfe und Herzen der Menschen zu gewinnen, eine Gegenstrategie zur geistlichen Grundlage des Terrorismus zu entwickeln und einer von Globalisierung verunsicherten Jugend Perspektiven zu geben. Letztlich geht es darum, zu verhindern, dass eine Situation entsteht, in der vermeintliche Globalisierungsverlierer anfällig bleiben für eine intolerante, extremistische und Hass säende Weltsicht.

Information Sharing in Support of Strategic Intelligence

Peter J. Sharfman, PhD

The MITRE Corporation
McLean, Virginia, USA

As we plan and work to improve the quality and the quantity of intelligence to support actions to counter terrorism, we must distinguish between tactical intelligence and strategic intelligence. Tactical intelligence is sufficiently specific, sufficiently detailed, and sufficiently reliable to form the basis for immediate action; in fact, it is sometimes referred to as "actionable intelligence." Strategic intelligence, in contrast, lacks the specificity necessary to direct operations, but because its content is believed to be valid for a period of years, it can be used to support the allocation of resources – including decisions to invest in order to create future capabilities – or political measures which by their nature could be effective only over a period of time.

Some examples of tactical intelligence are: (1) information that a known terrorist intends to take a particular flight, so that he can be arrested; (2) information that a terrorist organization is storing weapons in a particular location, so that a police raid upon this location can be authorized and carried out; (3) information that terrorists are planning to attack a particular building on a particular day, so that vehicles and people approaching this building can be searched for weapons or explosives; (4) identification of an individual as the link among various cells of a terrorist organization, so that surveillance of this individual and identification of his contacts will lead to a short list of people to investigate; (5) identification of a particular bank account as a vehicle for terrorist financing, which could support a variety of useful counterterrorist actions. Some characteristics of tactical intelligence are: (a) it must be used quickly, or it loses its value; (b) its sources are fragile, meaning that if the terrorists learn enough about a tactical intelligence source they can eliminate it; (c) it becomes valueless if the terrorists learn that we know it before we use it; (d) in many cases, there can be serious disagreements about how best to use the intelligence, or even whether preservation of a critical source dictates that a particular item of tactical intelligence should not be used at all. Because of these characteristics, tactical intelligence is generally shared only when sharing is absolutely essential for effective action.

Some examples of strategic intelligence are: (1) information about the internal effectiveness (e.g. leadership cohesion, recruiting success, financial resources) of various terrorist groups, so that estimates can be made about which terrorist organizations or networks pose the greatest future threat and should therefore be priority counterterrorism targets; (2) information about collaborative arrangements among specific terrorist groups, so that tactical intelligence about one of them can be leveraged to obtain tactical intelligence about others; (3) information about state sponsorship of terrorism, so that pressure can be brought to bear against the offending state; (4) information about how the leadership of a particular terrorist organization defines its goals and thinks about the connections between terrorist acts and these goals, so that inferences can be drawn about the targets and techniques that this leadership would find most attractive; (5) information about the incentives a terrorist organization uses to obtain resources (recruits, money, and logistic support), so that its access to these resources can be disrupted or attenuated. Some characteristics of strategic intelligence are: (a) in many cases, accurate strategic intelligence remains useful for months or even years; (b) if the content of strategic intelligence is revealed to its terrorist subjects, they cannot easily act either to invalidate the intelligence or to shut off the sources and methods through which it was obtained; (c) it is obtained by the analysis of many pieces of fragmentary data, rather than from a single excellent source; (d) even when strategic intelligence analysis makes use of secret data about terrorists, it is valuable to consider it in the light of publicly available information and academic analysis.

It should be evident that to counter terrorism over a period of years, we require strategic as well as tactical intelligence. This fairly obvious point needs to be emphasized because the understandable public demand that terrorists be arrested and that terrorist operations be prevented has made it more difficult to see the value of building strategic intelligence by methods that would be quite unlikely to generate tactical "actionable" intelligence.

How, then, can better strategic intelligence be generated?

We should begin by acknowledging that terrorists do not generally think the way most intelligence analysts think. It is not just that terrorists have different objectives and different concepts of how human society ought to function; they also seem to have a different view of the relationships between ends and means, or the relationships between causes and effects. Furthermore, terrorists mobilize support from a population of sympathizers (that is, individuals who would not themselves commit a terrorist act but are willing to facilitate or tolerate terrorist acts by others) by means that are different from the ways in which democratic political organizations (or, for that matter, autocratic states) mobilize support.

Consequently, some of the standard approaches to strategic intelligence analysis, which work reasonably well when the subject of the analysis is a state, do not work well when the subject is terrorism. Analysts cannot reason from the objectives of the terrorist organization and the objective situation that faces the organization to a manageable list of options for action. Partly this is because the terrorists' appreciation of the objective situation they face may be quite different from that analyst's view. But even more, it is because the terrorists' concept of what actions will advance their objectives may be one that the analyst does not share and does not understand. To some extent this difference may arise because the terrorist has an idiosyncratic view of the vulnerabilities of the power structure he wishes to attack. To some extent it may arise because the analyst does not understand as well as the terrorists do what behavior by the terrorists will strengthen their support from sympathizers and add to their resources. But also, it seems that some terrorists have a concept of the nature of human society and human motivation quite different from what one would learn in a Western (or, for that matter, Japanese or Chinese) educational system.

Analysts must be very cautious about building a template of a hypothetical terrorist action and then looking for data that would fit into this template. This analytical method – which can be used very effectively to sort through large quantities of data in working many kinds of intelligence problem – fails when the analyst does not understand the adversary well enough to judge which possible strategies he would consider effective and appropriate. Similarly, the technique of seizing upon some data and inferring what additional data to look for – the technique of inferring that anybody who purchases an automobile must sooner or later purchase either gasoline or diesel fuel – fails to yield clues or warnings regarding a terrorist threat that we do not expect. Instead, strategic analysis must be based upon consideration of a very wide range of information, including information from a very wide range of sources. The metaphor of "connecting the dots" must be modified to recognize that strategic intelligence means reviewing several thousand dots in order to connect a few hundred of them.

In the light of these difficulties, there is a strong case to be made for departing from the traditional approaches to strategic intelligence. Ways must be found to consider simultaneously the information derived from secret sources and the information derived from open sources. Ways must be found to bring to bear simultaneously expertise regarding terrorists and terrorism and expertise regarding the societies and cultures from which terrorists and sympathizers are recruited. Ways must be found to expose tentative ideas or hypotheses to those with different backgrounds, skill sets, or pre-occupations in order to elicit the creative impulse to see the same facts from a different perspective. And, given the great difficulty we have in comprehending how terrorists view the world, analysis should involve collaboration of people from different cultures and educational systems who can effectively probe each other's assumptions and mental habits.

This would be a very substantial departure from the normal practices of generating intelligence. We would, to be sure, retain the existing staffs of intelligence analysts with security clearances, operating in a closed and secure environment and working to make sense of secret information gathered through a variety of sources and methods. (It is possible, however, that assigning a substantial number of them to work on strategic analysis, with no pressure whatever to produce tactical intelligence, would be a departure from existing practice.) But instead of having this tightly closed group produce its reports in secret and disseminate them directly to Government officials with security clearances and a need-to-know, we would ask this group of traditional intelligence analysts to work collaboratively with analysts drawing upon very different information sources and using very different analytical methods. Specifically, we would ask them to collaborate with academic experts – treating the academics not as "sources" to be queried and cited but as colleagues with whom to engage in a two-way give-and-take of ideas, perceptions, and interpretations. In addition, we would seek out experts in drawing information from the Internet and from the mass media. We would ask them to try to understand how the world appears to the sympathizers of the terrorists and to the communities from which these sympathizers are drawn – in the hope that this would offer insights and clues to how the terrorists themselves understand the world. Here, too, we would ask the traditional intelligence analysts to treat these experts not as sources but as collaborators.

Finally, in order to obtain the creativity that arises from the interaction of people with similar factual expertise and similar skills but with different educational backgrounds and different assumptions, we would try to make this collaborative effort to produce strategic intelligence a multi-national one.

This program would probably not look very attractive to an intelligence agency focused on generating actionable – hence tactical – intelligence. To attempt to review very large amounts of diverse data would lengthen the intelligence cycle. To work collaboratively with experts outside the tight community of secret intelligence would jeopardize security. Security – or at least the traditional approaches to security – would also be jeopardized by multinational collaboration. But perhaps the strongest challenge to normal intelligence methods would be the abandonment of the principle of need-to-know, based on the idea that so long as we don't really understand how our adversaries think, we cannot say who has a need to know any given fragment of intelligence.

Accordingly, the Governments of countries concerned with terrorism should give consideration to organizing strategic intelligence analysis separately from the processes that aim to produce actionable intelligence. Both the strategic and the tactical would pursue the same aims of counterterrorism, and both would draw upon the same streams of raw data, but they would function very differently. If both produce useful results, we should expect these results to complement each other and enhance each other's usefulness.

There are a number of Governments that might benefit from setting up separate strategic counterterrorism intelligence processes, and the most appropriate form of organization would no doubt vary from country to country. I would argue, however, that three characteristics are essential:

1. The strategic counterterrorism intelligence effort should have a certain degree of autonomy, so that the people leading the effort on a day-to-day basis would understand that their mission is strategic intelligence and not tactical, "actionable" intelligence. Otherwise the continuity of effort that is necessary for high-quality strategic intelligence would be jeopardized by the temptation to seek immediately useful results.

2. To make this autonomy secure, the strategic intelligence effort should have an identifiable stream of resources (people and money) that is separate from the resources devoted to tactical intelligence. Moreover, such a separate resource stream would allow the Government to consciously balance the strategic and the tactical. Readers of an early draft of this paper noted an implication that strategic intelligence deserves more resources than it is currently receiving. I must disclaim any such proposition – because I have no idea what resources are devoted to strategic intelligence.

3. The strategic intelligence effort needs a set of security rules that are more flexible than those appropriate for tactical intelligence. If strategic intelligence is to have any chance of "getting inside the heads" of the terrorist leadership or of understanding the world views of the communities from which the terrorists recruit, its practitioners must work collaboratively with their counterparts in many other countries. They must also be able to experiment with collaborative efforts with private citizens who share their ab-

horrence of terrorism, but whose backgrounds and motivations would disqualify them from receiving – or wanting – security clearances.

Following these suggestions would certainly not be free of cost, disruption, and even risk. I cannot demonstrate conclusively that the results would justify the effort. Nevertheless, given the importance and difficulty of the problem and the disappointing quality to date of strategic counterterrorism intelligence, there is a strong case that efforts along these lines would at the least be a worthwhile experiment.

Risiko-, Krisen- und Katastrophenmanagement

Risk, Crisis, and Catastrophe Management

Non-Conventional Terrorism: Challenge & Response

Yael Shahar

International Policy Institute for Counter-Terrorism
Herzliya, Israel

1 The Challenge

Non-conventional terrorism has become the bug-bear of modern society. The possibility that a group like al-Qaida – which is known to have no qualms about causing thousands of deaths – might acquire non-conventional weapons is the stuff of nightmares. Governments the world over have invested vast resources in preparing for "worst-case" scenarios. Municipal police, emergency services, and hospitals have participated in non-conventional scenario exercises, many of which have highlighted the woeful state of preparedness of many urban centers in the face of what is seen as an imminent threat. But how imminent is it?

Is non-conventional terrorism – in the form of mass poisoning of urban facilities or the spread of deadly contagion – the form that the next major terrorist outrage will take? This paper examines the threat of non-conventional terrorism as just one of a host of different methods that terrorists might employ to further their aims. Our ultimate goal is to come up with a predictive method that can help us decide which terrorist groups are most likely to employ non-conventional agents and what methods they are most likely to use – a task that requires us to "get into the mindset" of the terrorist organizations.

But to begin with, let us lay some groundwork. What exactly is non-conventional terrorism? Most security professionals would define non-conventional terrorism as any use by terrorist elements of Weapons of Mass Destruction (WMD's). Weapons of Mass Destruction include chemical agents that can cause death or injury upon being inhaled, absorbed or swallowed; biological agents that can cause illness and/or death; radiological agents that can contaminate a large area; and of course nuclear weapons. To these we could also add "weapons of mass disruption" – electronic weapons that can disrupt or destroy electronic equipment

However, as we shall see, there are a number of potentially deadly agents extant and readily available to terrorists which are not formally classified as WMD's. Materials such as pesticides and common industrial chemicals could potentially wreak as much havoc on an unprepared populace as could weapons-grade chemical substances. What is more, such common materials are potentially much easier for terrorists to get hold of and deploy.

Note that there is one characteristic that all the non-conventional agents have in common, and which separates them from traditional, or conventional, weaponry. Their common denominator is this: all the non-conventional methods cause damage indirectly; they all work by influencing our immediate environment. Thus, there may be a significant time lag between the deployment of a non-conventional agent and the time when its effects become obvious. While some agents may have an almost immediate effect, others may take days, or even weeks, to manifest their presence. Naturally, this time factor could play into the hands of the terrorists, by making it much more difficult for first responders to comprehend the nature of the attack, while giving the perpetrators time to escape.

1.1 Chemical Weapons

Chemical weapons are usually classified as vesicants, blood agents, nerve agents, and choking agents. A fifth category – toxins – could be classified either as chemical or biological agents.

Vesicants, also referred to as "blister agents" are highly reactive chemicals that combine with proteins, DNA, and other cellular components to cause cellular changes immediately after exposure. Examples include:

- HD –Sulfur Mustard (Yperite)
- HN – Nitrogen Mustard
- L – Lewisite
- CX – Phosgene Oximine

The most likely routes of exposure are inhalation, dermal contact, and ocular contact. Depending on the vesicant, clinical effects may occur immediately (as with phosgene oxime or lewisite) or may be delayed for two to 24 hours (as with mustards).

Blister agents have a relatively low lethality, but inflict painful burns and blisters requiring medical attention, even at low doses. The classic example is mustard gas, which is relatively easy to make, cost-effective, and persistent – meaning that it remains effective in the target area over time. Mustard gas on the skin causes no immediate sensation and symptoms normally do not appear until several hours after exposure. At incapacitating levels this may be as long as 12 hours. Mustard gas was used by Iraq in the Iran-Iraq War, where it caused horrible fatalities because Iranian soldiers, feeling no effects, continued to wear mustard-gas-soaked clothing and inhale its fumes.[1]

1.1.1 Blood Agents

Blood agents are typically cyanide-based or arsenic-based compounds that prevent the transfer of oxygen to bodily tissues. The most likely means of exposure is ingestion or inhalation of gas.

Many chemicals in this class are common by-products of standard manufacturing processes, and may be readily available to hostile elements. For example, hydrogen cyanide is currently manufactured worldwide as an intermediate in the manufacture of acrylic polymers, and could be diverted for other uses or separately manufactured with about the same investment.[2]

1.1.2 Choking/Lung/Pulmonary Agents

Choking agents are also known as lung agents or pulmonary agents. These are substances that damage the respiratory tract, causing extensive fluid build-up in the lungs (pulmonary oedema).

The most likely routes of exposure are inhalation, dermal contact, and ocular contact. Symptoms may not be noticed until several hours following exposure, which may be an attractive feature for terrorists.

Examples include:

- CF – Phosgene
- DP – Diphosgene
- CL – Chlorine
- PS – Chloropicrin
- CA – Bromine

---

[1] Federation of Atomic Scientists. "Chemical Weapons History & Characteristics." http://www.fas.org/nuke/intro/cw/intro.htm.

[2] Federation of Atomic Scientists. "Chemical Weapons History & Characteristics." http://www.fas.org/nuke/intro/cw/intro.htm.

- Osmium tetroxide

One such agent, phosgene, was used for the first time in 1915, and accounted for 80% of all chemical fatalities during World War I. Many choking agents are commonly available byproducts of manufacturing process. For example, phosgene is important in industry as a chlorinating material.

1.1.3 Nerve Agents or anticholinesterase agents

Nerve agents are organo-phosphorus compounds which block an enzyme (acetylcholinesterase) necessary for functions of the central nervous system. They are liquids at room temperature.

Nerve agents are divided into G- and V-agents. The "G" agents tend to be non-persistent, whereas the "V" agents are persistent. Nerve agents can be inhaled or absorbed by the skin. Similar in action to many pesticides, they are lethal in very low quantities. In general, the lower the material's volatility (and hence its inhalation threat) the greater is its percutaneous toxicity.

Examples of nerve agents include:

- GA (Tabun)
- GB (Sarin)
- GD (Soman)
- GF
- VX (methylphosponothioic acid)

1.1.4 Toxins

Toxins are yet another type of non-conventional material, sometimes classed as midway between biological and chemical agents. Although not living organisms themselves, these materials are usually products of living organisms, with complex molecular structures.

A wide variety of toxins exist, with an equally broad spectrum of chemical, physical, and physiological properties. The classic example is ricin, a potent toxin made from castor beans.

1.2 Biological Agents

Biological agents can be classified into contagious and non-contagious substances. The vast majority of the diseases that have been weaponized for use in war are non-contagious, although worst-case scenarios center around those that would continue to spread by contagion after their initial deployment.

Anthrax is perhaps the best-known biological agent. It affects the respiratory system and is 80% fatal if not treated. What makes anthrax particularly problematic is that its spores can survive for decades.

Other common biological agents include botulism (a classic form of "food poisoning"), which can cause paralysis & death but is treatable if caught early. Botulinum toxin can also be inhaled.

Of the variety of biological weapons that might be used for terrorism, anthrax and smallpox are the two with the greatest potential for mass casualties and civil disruption. Both are highly lethal, and both are stable for transmission in aerosol and relatively easy to manufacture in large quantities.[3] Smallpox, in particular, could cause a public health catastrophe because of its communicability. Even a single case could lead to 10 to 20 others. It is estimated that no more than 20% of the population has any immunity from prior vaccination.[4] There is no acceptable treatment. Furthermore, due to the disease's communicability by aerosol, smallpox patients would need to be kept in negative-pressure isolation facilities in order to avoid contagion. Limited isolation resources in medical facilities would be easily overwhelmed by any major outbreak.

Other infectious agents capable of causing major devastation and disruption include plague and tularemia. Plague, like smallpox and anthrax, can decimate a population, as occurred in Europe during the Middle Ages. Both plague and tularemia are potentially lethal without proper treatment, and both are infectious at low doses.[5]

1.3 Radiological Weapons

The threat of radiological terrorism usually takes the form of a Radioactive Dispersal Device (RDD), also known as a "dirty bomb." This type of apparatus is designed to contaminate a large area with radioactive material in order to cause maximum havoc and disruption. Radioactive material might be dispersed over

---

[3] Mark G. Kortepeter and Gerald W. Parker. "Potential Biological Weapons Threats," U.S. Army Medical Research Institute of Infectious Diseases, Fort Detrick, Maryland, USA.

[4] Henderson DA. "The looming threat of bioterrorism," *Science* 1999; 283:1279-82.

[5] Mark G. Kortepeter and Gerald W. Parker. "Potential Biological Weapons Threats," U.S. Army Medical Research Institute of Infectious Diseases, Fort Detrick, Maryland, USA.

a wide area using conventional explosives, though other means, such as aerial dissemination, could also be used.[6]

The amount of explosive needed for effective dispersion is low – only 2.5-5 kg is needed if the radioactive material is highly dispersible. However, the effectiveness of the dispersion is dependent on many other factors, including the quantity of the explosive charge, the physical state of the radioactive material, the amount of radioactive material, weather conditions, and the type of landscape.

In order to be effective as a radiological weapon the radioactive material used must have a reasonably long half-life, on the order of a year or more. The most obvious candidates are the beta-gamma (β,γ)-emitters cobalt-60 and caesium-137, and to a lesser extent the beta (β)-emitter strontium-90 and the beta-gamma emitter iridium-192. Some of the more "exotic"' radionuclides or mixtures cannot be excluded completely.[7]

Isotope	Half-life	Radiation
Manganese-54 (^{54}Mn)	312.1 days	γ
Cobalt-60 (^{60}Co)	5.3 years	β,γ
Strontium-90 (^{90}Sr)	28.78 years	β
Silver-110 (^{110}Ag)	249.8 days	β,γ
Cadmium-109 (^{109}Cd)	462.6 days	γ
Barium-133 (^{133}Ba)	10.53 years	γ
Caesium-137 (^{137}Cs)	30.07 years	β,γ
Europium-152 (^{152}Eu)	13.54 years	β,γ
Iridium-192 (^{192}Ir)	73.8 days	β,γ
Plutonium-238 (^{238}Pu)	87.7 years	α
Americium-241 (^{241}Am)	432.7 years	α
Californium-252 (^{252}Cf)	2.65 years	α

Source: Josef R. Parrington et al., Nuclides and Isotopes, 15th revised edn, Knolls Atomic Power Laboratory, San Jose, CA, 1996. Cited in Klaas van der Meer. "The radiological threat: verification at the source." Verification Yearbook 2003.

---

[6] Klaas van der Meer. "The radiological threat: verification at the source." Verification Yearbook 2003.

[7] Klaas van der Meer. "The radiological threat: verification at the source." Verification Yearbook 2003.

All of the isotopes listed above are frequently used in medical and industrial equipment. Cobalt-60 and caesium-137 are the most commonly-available isotopes. Strontium-90, iridium-192 and the alpha (α)-emitters plutonium-238, americium-241 and californium-252 are also available in large quantities. Some of the other isotopes listed are less likely to be used since they are not produced on an industrial scale.

The amount of radioactive material needed to contaminate a large area is estimated to be about 1,000 Curies (Ci). This would generally amount to several grams, depending on the isotope used.[8]

The physical state of material dispersed is one of the most important factors in gauging its effectiveness. Cobalt-60 is normally produced in metallic pellets. During an explosion it would be dispersed in small metallic fragments. Caesium-137 takes the form of a powdery salt and is thus highly dispersible. Strontium-90 also occurs in the form of a salt and is extremely dispersible. Iridium-192 is produced in the form of metallic pellets and has the same qualities as cobalt-60. Plutonium-238, americium-241 and californium-252 are produced in the form of oxide particles with a small diameter (10-50 μm), which makes them highly dispersible.

One of the impediments to the deployment of radioactive contaminants is the difficulty in transporting the material. For example the safe transport of a strong radioactive β, γ source requires some sort of shielding container. This would normally be made of lead, and might weigh as much as 1,000 kg. Such a container also has a considerable volume (20-80 liters), and would thus be difficult to conceal. Even suicidal terrorists would not be able to handle an unshielded radioactive source with a strength of 1,000 Ci for longer than one hour within a range of 1 meter from the source. Although a radiation requires hardly any shielding, most a-emitters also emit β, γ radiation and therefore would also require shielding.

1.3.1 Consequences of Use

The immediate consequences of use of an RDD would be loss of life through direct impact of the explosion and contamination. However, direct casualties due to the impact of the explosion are likely to be limited, and there would probably be no immediate casualties from radioactive contamination. In the long run, contamination might cause casualties through the "statistical" effects,

---
[8] Klaas van der Meer. "The radiological threat: verification at the source." Verification Yearbook 2003.

such as radiation-induced cancers and genetic defects in future generations. At the same time casualties would probably be fewer than commonly claimed in the media.

When inhaled or ingested, radioactive dust emits heavy particles that can cause great damage to the human body. β, γ radiation involves light particles (β) or electromagnetic radiation (similar to light, ultra-violet (UV) light or X-rays). These are more penetrating and therefore harmful for human health. β, γ radiation have a longer range, and the damage they inflict on the human body is spread over a larger area than is the case for a radiation.

Calculations have shown that a large area (0.28 square kilometer) can be contaminated by dispersing a radioactive substance with a strength on the order of only 1,000 Ci. This would likely cause widespread public panic, fear and uncertainty. Depending on the physical state of the radioactive material, the decontamination costs might be very high. Decontamination would be time-consuming and would need to take place immediately after the contamination occurred.

1.4 Non-Conventional terrorism – the historical record

Although non-conventional terrorism is high on just about every government's list of potential threats, very little is known about the actual threat. So far, the ratio of "hype" to reality with regard to the WMD terrorist threat is heavily weighted towards popular hysteria. Generally speaking, the threat of terrorists' using non-conventional substances to carry out an attack is much lower than the threat of the same group's using conventional explosives or other fairly low-tech means.[9] At the same time, the consequences of non-conventional terrorism are thought to be too great to relegate it to a lower place on the totem pole of potential threats; non-conventional terrorism is thus classed as a low-risk/high-consequence threat. Is there any basis for this classification?

Based on a database of non-conventional incidents maintained by the Center for Nonproliferation Studies at the Monterey Institute of International Studies in Monterey, California, researchers Jonathan B. Tucker and Amy Sands carried out a survey of historical incidents in which non-conventional agents were used

---

[9] Dr. Boaz Ganor, of the International Policy Institute for Counter-Terrorism in Herzliya, classifies non-conventional terror attacks into "limited" and "unlimited" attacks. Unlimited attacks would be those intended to wipe out whole populations. Such attacks are beyond the abilities of all but a few terrorist cells – or even nations – and are not discussed in this paper.

by terrorists.[10] They compiled a database of 520 global CBW incidents that occurred between 1900 and May 1999. These incidents included hoaxes, plots, efforts to acquire toxic materials, proven possession of materials, and actual attacks.

There were 282 terrorist cases (54 percent of the total) and 238 criminal cases (46 percent). Of the 282 terrorist incidents recorded, 263 were selected for analysis on the basis of their individual characteristics.

This analysis found that, "Contrary to the conventional wisdom about the catastrophic nature of chemical and biological terrorism, actual attacks were few in number, small in scale, and generally produced fewer casualties than conventional bombs."

A breakdown of the 263 cases revealed that:

- 26 percent were hoaxes or pranks.
- Eight percent involved an apparent conspiracy that did not proceed far.
- Four percent involved the attempted acquisition of dangerous materials.
- 10 percent involved the actual possession of dangerous materials.
- 21 percent concerned a threatened attack that did not materialize.
- Only 27 percent (71 incidents) included the actual use of a chemical or biological agent.

Chemical agents employed included cyanide (by far the most popular), rat poison, VX nerve agent, sarin nerve agent, butyric acid, mercury, and insecticide. Biological agents included anthrax, botulinum toxin, salmonella bacteria, and the HIV virus.

The 71 actual attacks between 1900 and May 1999 resulted in 123 fatalities and 3,774 injuries. The incidents that inflicted the largest numbers of fatalities were:

- Contamination of drinking water with pesticide in the Philippines in 1987, causing 19 deaths among new recruits to the Philippine Constabulary on the island of Mindanao.
- Use of an unknown poison gas against a Turkish village in 1994, possibly by the Kurdish Workers Party (PKK), causing 21 deaths.

Of the nonfatal casualties, 1,038 were associated with Aum Shinrikyo's release of sarin on the Tokyo subway in 1995.

---

[10] Jonathan B. Tucker and Amy Sands. "An Unlikely Threat." July/August 1999 pp. 46-52 (vol. 55, no. 04) 1999 *Bulletin of the Atomic Scientists.*

Another very significant factor was the identity of the perpetrators. For the most part, the terrorists implicated in the 71 actual attacks were not traditional terrorist organizations. A breakdown of the incidents showed the following:

- 24 attacks were perpetrated by religiously motivated groups.
- 15 were perpetrated by nationalist-separatist groups.
- 12 were perpetrated by single-issue groups such as anti-abortion or animal-rights advocates.
- The rest were committed by lone terrorists, right-wing or left-wing groups, and unknown actors.

2 Meeting the Challenge – Forecasting

What can we learn from this historical analysis? To begin with, this analysis shows that if historical precedent is any indication of future threat, there is a very real gap between reality and "hype" with regard to the consequences of non-conventional terrorism. Virtually every past incident of non-conventional terrorism involved fewer casualties than the same organization could have achieved using conventional explosives. This was not only due to the nature of the materials used, but was also a reflection of the difficulties in effectively deploying these materials.

Moreover, the majority of cases – including some of the more effective attacks – involved common poisons and pesticides rather than weapons-grade materials. This trend is often overlooked when preparing for "worst case" scenarios; the non-conventional attack of the near future is just as likely to involve the creative use of a commonly available "dual use" chemical rather than the type military-grade biological or chemical weapon for which most first-responders generally prepare.

In the absence of empirical data on threats, most planners and pundits fall back on "worst case" scenarios. However, this has often meant the over-allocation of resources to some of the least likely scenarios. Preparing for the "low risk / high consequence" attack is not the only (or even the best) response.

Scarce resources can be better exploited if a way is found to classify threats according to likelihood, and not just according to the severity of consequences.

Naturally, our assessment of which scenarios are most likely must be made from the point of view of the terrorist. We need to be on the same wavelength as our enemies; we need to know our enemies from the inside out, and this requires that any preparedness program be built on sound intelligence. The stages in preparing an operational counterterrorism plan vis-à-vis non-conventional terrorism would be, first, to identify those groups or individuals who are both motivated *and* capable of employing chemical or biological agents against civilians; secondly, to concentrate intelligence gathering resources on these groups in order discern possible methods and targets; and thirdly, to conduct tactical operations against these groups. At the same time, our understanding of who the enemy is and what he is likely to do should inform our defensive preparedness as well, allowing us to increase security around likely targets.

2.1 Towards a target-specific method of threat assessment

The probability of a terror attack on a particular target is dependant not only on the characteristics of the target – its symbolic or strategic value and its vulnerabilities – but also on the ambition, capabilities, and sensitivities of the relevant terrorist organizations.

I would like to present an overview of a statistical method for evaluating the threat presented by different types of terrorist groups to particular venues. The method builds on input regarding the known characteristics of the terrorist groups active in the region in question, combined with the characteristics of each potential *modus operandi*. The goal is not so much to give a precise prediction of who, how, and where; but rather to provide a better basis for deciding how best to allocate finite counterterrorism resources.

The stages used in the proposed model are:

1. *Organization-specific factors* – Develop a means of determining which organizations present the greatest threat.

2. *Venue-specific factors* – Categorize scenarios according to the target selection strategies of these particular organizations.

3. *Numerical synthesis* – Combine these two stages into a numerical analysis of what type of attack would appeal to which organization.

To evaluate the likelihood that any particular type of attack will be carried out by a particular terrorist organization, we identify factors relating to the difficulty of carrying out an attack, along with the desirability of the outcome of the attack from the point of view of the terrorist organization. For each terrorist organization type, we include factors to weigh the terrorists' sensitivity to these attack-specific factors. The result is a score that indicates the net "attractiveness" of a particular type of attack to a particular type of organization. For example, some organizations may be more deterred by physical difficulty or by attacks requiring years of planning, while others would be less so. Some may see achieving maximum casualties as part of their goals, while others may be unwilling to risk causing high casualties.

This method is useful for getting an idea of the types of attacks that each organization might be inclined to carry out on the selected venue, based on our understanding of the organization's target-selection methods. Thus, the method builds on considerable research into the characteristics of each organization.

The same care must be taken to examine the vulnerabilities of the venue in question, from the point of view of the potential terrorist – seeking weaknesses that might be exploited in the various scenarios under consideration.

Naturally, the resulting numbers are only as good as the information that goes into the model. In effect, the model should be viewed as merely a template for better organizing our knowledge; without that knowledge, the template is empty of all content. However, when based on reliable information, the model is a very useful tool for data visualization and risk assessment.

2.1.1 Organization-specific factors

The conclusions drawn by the authors of the Monterey study cited above was that non-conventional means were most likely to be used by groups motivated by religious fanaticism, supremacist or anti-government ideology, or millenarian prophecy. These groups were those that were cut off from any mainstream constituency, and often had a paranoid, conspiratorial worldview.

Such individuals and groups may view chemical or biological terrorism as a means to destroy a corrupt social structure, to fulfill an apocalyptic prophecy, to exact revenge against evil-doers or oppressors, or as a form of "defensive aggression" against outsiders seen as threats to the group's survival. [11]

These characteristics are, by and large, alien to the traditional "political" terrorist organizations, which were far more likely to be influenced by moral constraints. Such organizations were also more likely to be deterred by the possibility that indiscriminate casualties could alienate current or future supporters, and the concern that a non-conventional attack could bring the full repressive power of the affected government into play against them.

---

[11] Jonathan B. Tucker and Amy Sands. "An Unlikely Threat." July/August 1999 pp. 46-52 (vol. 55, no. 04) 1999 *Bulletin of the Atomic Scientists*.

These conclusions have been echoed by several other prominent studies on the threat of non-conventional terrorism, including one carried out by the International Policy Institute for Counter-Terrorism (ICT) between May 1998 and May 1999 in collaboration with the French institute CREST, and Interdisciplinary Center for Technological Analysis and Forecasting (ICTAF) at Tel-Aviv University. That research too found that there were very definite threat indicators that could be used to assess the likelihood that a terrorist organization would be attracted to non-conventional materials.

Based on these and other similar studies, we can compile a list of the main indicators that would point toward an organization's possible use of non-conventional materials. This list is summarized in Table 1.

Table 1: *Indications pointing toward possible use of non-conventional means*

Indicator	Relative Weight
Structure and reach	
Supported by a state or sub-state entity.	S_1
Part of international network of groups or cells.	S_2
Ability to blend in with local groups in the target country.	S_3
	Max: X
Attack History	
Past history of attacks outside its own sphere of influence.	H_1
Past attempts to acquire non-conventional substances	H_2
Past history of "non-standard attacks"	H_3
	Max: Y
Motivation	
Motivated by religion or quasi-religious ideology.	M_1
Has threatened to use non-conventional substances.	M_2
Has been, or expects to be, targeted by counter-terror campaign.	M_3
	Max: Z
Total (X + Y + Z)	**100**

The exact values of the above variables would be determined by the researchers, according to the nature of the venue under consideration. The total of all the variables should equal to 100.

2.1.2 Venue-specific factors affecting target selection

In order to evaluate the net "attractiveness" of a particular type of attack to a particular type of organization, each type of attack receives a combined Difficulty score, as well as three separate Impact scores, as shown below in Table 2:

Table 2: Attack-Type Parameters

Parameters	Relative Weight
Difficulty, based on:	
• Planning time required,	33
• Resources required,	33
• Physical difficulty	33
Impact, based on:	
• Physical/economic damage,	33
• Casualties,	33
• Symbolic value (includes psychological impact)	33

Example scenarios

The following scenarios illustrate how these factors are applied to particular scenarios. Since we are not dealing with a particular venue in these examples, these samples are very general in nature. An actual threat assessment would require that the specific vulnerabilities of the venue be factored into the scenario rating.

Poisoning – Restaurant, bar

Insert poison in food served at the restaurants dinning areas.	The agent is inserted into the served food. This can be done at the location where the food is prepared or in a buffet were the food is displayed. Since this would require access to restricted zones, inside help or false ID would probably be required.	Planning time: 5 Resources: 5 Difficulty: 5
	Result: • Undetermined number of casualties (larger if poison works slowly) • Complete closure of the hotel until source is found and area is isolated. • Damage to facility's reputation.	Physical/Economic Damage: 18 Casualties: 5 Symbolic: 5

Ingested Biological Agent or Toxin - Restaurant

Place toxin or biological agent in food or on utensils	A "sleeper" working in food service inserts the agents into the food or spreads them on utensils. The agent should be slow enough so that no symptoms are noticed immediately.	Planning time: 20 Resources: 30 Difficulty: 15

	Result: • Potential large number of casualties • Complete closure of facility for decontaminated (can take weeks) • Damage to facility's reputation	Physical/Economic Damage: 20 Casualties: 10 Symbolic: 10

Aerosol Suicide Attack – Public Spaces, Shopping Mall

Spray aerosol manually – suicide attack	The attacker uses an aerosol or pressurized canister to disperse a chemical agent in an enclosed space. This type of attack is one the simplest to carry out, but has several disadvantages: First, the attacker will suffer a terrible death Second, the attack is discovered as soon as it happens, reducing the effect of "secret" contamination.	Planning time: 30 Resources: 30 Difficulty: 20

	Result: • Potentially large number of casualties • Panic • Complete closure of facility until decontaminated (can take weeks)	Physical/Economic Damage: 26 Casualties: 28 Symbolic: 25

Evaluation of organizational sensitivities

Each category of terrorist organization receives four "sensitivity" scores, as shown in Table 3. These scores will be combined with each attack-type's Difficulty and Impact factors to determine the importance of these factors to the organization type. When the resulting "Weighted Difficulty" is subtracted from the resulting "Weighted Impact," the result is the "Attractiveness" of that attack to that organization type.

Table 3: *Sensitivity Parameters*
  (Negative interest indicates aversion to causing this type of damage.)

Parameters	Range
Sensitivity to Difficulty	0 – 100%
Interest in causing physical/economic damage	-100% – 100%
Interest in causing casualties	-100% – 100%
Interest in symbolic value of targets	-100% – 100%

Based on our familiarity with the various types of terror organization mentioned above, we can estimate their sensitivities. Table 3 below shows a sample of such a categorization, using three groups known to operate in major European cities. Note that this table is based only on a generic analysis; in order to be truly effective, it would require far more parameters than those shown – an analysis that is beyond the scope of this paper.

Table 4: *Organization-type Sensitivities*

	Al-Qaida "Central"	Local Islamists	Ad hoc Groups
Sensitivity to Difficulty	25%	60%	90%
Interest in Physical / Economic Damage	100%	60%	95%
Interest in Casualties	100%	80%	-70%
Interest in Symbolic Value of Targets	100%	100%	90%

2.1.3 Synthesis

Putting all these factors together, we can derive the following numerical breakdown, indicating the attractiveness of specific types of attack to the groups discussed above.

Attack Type	Al-Qaida	Local Islamist Groups	Ad Hoc Groups
Food Poisoning	24	11	5
Toxin in Food	26	-3	-29
Explosive Chemical Device	57	16	-40
Pressurized Chemical Device	55	13	-44
Bio-Agent in A/C	52	5	-56
Bio-Agent in Fire Sprinklers	52	4	-58
Suicide Chemical Aerosol	59	15	-44
Slow Radioactive Dispersal	25	-6	1
Radioactive in A/C	33	-11	-62

By graphing this information, we can get a more visually satisfying view of the data:

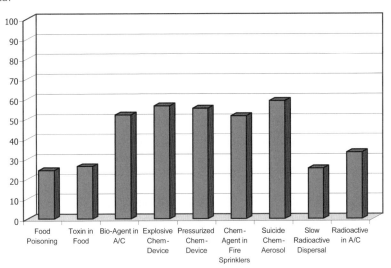

Figure 1: Attacks attractive to al-Qaida "Central"

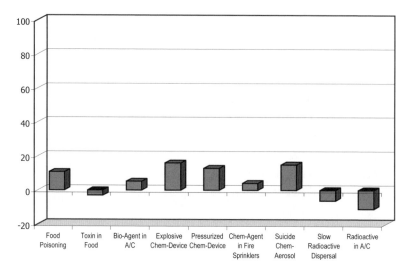

Figure 2: Attacks attractive to local Islamists

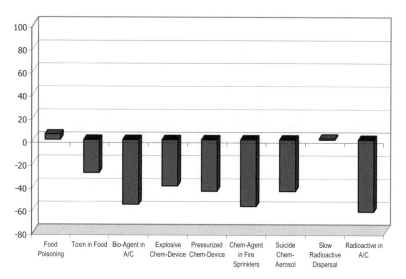

Figure 3: Attacks attractive to Ad hoc Groups

3 Conclusion

What can we learn from all this? Perhaps the most significant lesson is that – insofar as the premises on which our threat-assessment model is based are correct – non-conventional terrorism does not appeal to all terrorist groups, or even to some of those considered most dangerous in a particular area. For the most part, the terrorist groups discussed above, with the exception of al-Qaida's central command, would be more likely to rely on tried-and-true methods such as car-bombings than to attempt the more difficult and less certain methods of non-conventional attack.

Even where such groups are interested in non-conventional attacks, the emphasis would appear to be on low-tech methods, such as food poisoning or the use of conventional explosives to spread chemical agents; these modes of attack can deliver similar results without the uncertainties of more exotic methods.

Of the terrorist groups discussed here, only al-Qaida can be expected to show interest in the "weapons of mass destruction" aspect of non-conventional substances. Interestingly enough, the same characteristics that make al-Qaida a prime suspect for possible non-conventional weapons use can also be found in apocalyptic groups, such as the Japanese Aum Shinrikyo cult that carried out the 1995 Tokyo subway attack. The two groups have in common an extremist ideology that appeals to intelligent people of a certain mindset, together with a cult-like isolation and division of the world into "true believers" versus everyone else. This kind of paranoiac, messianic worldview makes every act an expression of divine command, and grants members the ability to view even the greatest atrocity as a necessary step toward the salvation of the individual and the group as a whole.

And yet, despite its many trained scientists, Aum Shinrikyo never made much headway in developing biological weapons. While Aum Shinrikyo's poison gas program fared better, it was rife with life-threatening production and dissemination accidents. After all of Aum Shinrikyo's extensive financial and intellectual investment, the Tokyo subway attack killed only a dozen people, seriously injured just over fifty more, and mildly injured just under 1,000.

The value of the model discussed here lies not in its ability to reveal new information, but rather in its usefulness as a planning and pedagogical aid: a means to visualize data so that trends may be readily apparent where they might otherwise have been lost in a sea of data. Such data-visualization tools are important in helping us better manage our resources.

However, such models, and the intelligence on which they are based, should be seen as only one component in the fight against terrorism – including non-conventional terrorism. We must never forget that terrorism is psychological warfare and its real targets are located not on the battlefield, but on the home front. Thus, a significant portion of our resources must go toward thwarting the effectiveness of terrorism here, at its true target. Terrorism works somewhat like a virus; by hijacking society's own means of communication – the news media – terrorism succeeds in disseminating its own messages. In a sense, the media plays a multi-level role in the chain of terrorism effectiveness – it carries scenes of death and destruction into the homes of every member of society, while at the same time carrying the fears and anxieties of society to the ears of the terrorists. By telling the terrorists what we are most afraid of, we play an active role in their selection of targets and modes of attack.

That terrorists use the media to further their own aims has become a cliché, and yet this knowledge is too often ignored in the heat of the moment. The reaction of the media toward the threat of non-conventional terrorism is a case in point. Education is the only way to break the chain of terrorism – by informing the public of the real extent of the threat. Here too, the media can play a role – this time a positive one. By helping citizens understand what terrorists can and cannot do, and what the individual can do to defend his or her society, we can decrease the effectiveness of terrorism as a means of policy-making. It is up to us, the counterterrorism professionals, to see that this information reaches both the media and the citizenry.

Bedrohungslage biologische Waffen – Identifizierung biologischer Kampfstoffe

Dr. Elisabeth Hauschild

Key Account Manager Homeland Security
Diehl BGT Defence GmbH & Co. KG

Bakterien, Viren oder Toxine als Waffen zu nutzen ist nicht neu. Bereits 1346 gab es die ersten Anschläge mit Pestbakterien in Kaffa, indem infizierte tote Körper über die Stadtmauer katapultiert wurden. Kürzlich hielten Milzbrandanschläge die USA in Atem und sorgten für Trittbrettfahrer in der westlichen Welt, Al Quaida hat mußmaßlich geplant, Toxine und Bakterien als Waffen einzusetzen, die RAF verfügte über Toxine, die Aum Shinrikyo Sekte führte diverse Versuche mit Anthrax- und Pestbakterien durch. Die Liste lässt sich beliebig verlängern. In den USA gibt es jedes Jahr mehrere Mordanschläge mit biologischen Agenzien, hinter denen in der Regel rechtsextreme Kreise stehen. Auf der anderen Seite stehen Staaten wie z. B. Russland, die in der Vergangenheit ein riesiges BW-Programm geführt haben, und Staaten, von denen man vermutet, dass sie an BW arbeiten, wie z. B. der Iran.

Die eigentliche Problematik sehe ich in möglichen Schläfern. Es ist bisher nicht möglich bzw. war es auch nicht Absicht, Doktoranden oder Technische Angestellte der Labore an Universitäten und zivilen Einrichtungen, in denen über bzw. mit Krankheitserregern geforscht wird, zu überprüfen. Hier schlummert unter Umständen der BW-Terrorist von morgen, ebenso wie Herr Atta unbehelligt in Hamburg studieren konnte. Viele Institute in den USA werden immer wieder angemahnt, Grundstandards der Biosafety-Regeln einzuhalten. Es ist nicht klar, wie viel Material aus diesen Labors tatsächlich verschwindet. Im Osten hingegen sind viele der ehemaligen B-Waffenschmieden in den zivilen Bereich überführt und offiziell geöffnet worden – unklar bleibt, wie es um die sichere Lagerung der hochpathogenen Substanzen bestellt ist. Zudem kann der Handel und Export von B-Substanzen und Zubehör nicht oder nur bedingt kontrolliert werden.

Biologische Substanzen als Waffen einzusetzen gewinnt an Attraktivität, da bedingt durch Fortschritte auf den Feldern Molekularbiologie und Biotechnologie sowie der Verfahrenstechnologie im Hinblick auf verbesserte Ausbringung die

Organismen und die Einsatzszenarien besser kontrolliert werden können. Einige Organismen sind per se sehr attraktiv als Waffensystem, wie der immer wieder genannte Anthraxerreger: Er ist im Überdauerungsstadium außerordentlich stabil, über Jahrzehnte lagerfähig und zudem bei entsprechender Inhalation zu einem hohen Prozentsatz tödlich. Andere Organismen wie die Pocken sind zwar ebenfalls sehr aggressiv, jedoch sehr empfindlich Umweltbedingungen gegenüber.

Hier ist schon zu erkennen, dass jeder Organismus eigene Parameter besitzt und damit auch ein jeweils anderes Waffensystem per se darstellt. Dies erschwert den Schutz und die Abwehr. Vor allem ist der Eintritt des Organismus in unseren Körper in der Regel nicht wahrnehmbar. Diese Aspekte machen BW zu einer psychologischen Waffe. Und was wollen Terroristen in der Regel erreichen? Angst schüren und damit lähmen – der Einsatz von BW führt zu Panik und ist aus dieser Sicht eine ideale Waffe. „Glücklicherweise" erscheint es jedoch für viele Terroristen bisher noch sehr attraktiv, mit einer großen Explosion hohen Schaden und hohe Aufmerksamkeit zu erzielen. Allerdings weisen viele Erkenntnisse darauf hin, dass der Sprung zum B-Waffeneinsatz unter Umständen nicht weit ist.

Da es nur wenig überzeugende Möglichkeiten hinsichtlich eines Schutzes mit Impfungen gibt, bemüht man sich seit Jahren, schnelle und spezifische Identifizierungsmethoden zu entwickeln, um dann auf die einmal erkannte Gefahr schnell mit medizinischer Versorgung antworten zu können. Dies gekoppelt mit einer guten Intelligence ist vermutlich die beste Antwort auf die reale und manchmal doch nur latent wahrnehmbare Gefahr („Die Kunst des Teufels ist, dass man ihn nicht sieht.").

Mittlerweile gibt es eine Reihe von Möglichkeiten zur Detektion biologischer Gefahrstoffe (genetische, immunologische, chromatographische etc.), jedoch sind viele dieser Methoden immer noch relativ langsam; wünschenswert ist eine Detektionszeit von unter einer Stunde – gekoppelt mit einer hohen Spezifität.

Zusätzlich sollten Messgeräte ein geringes Gewicht haben und unkompliziert zu bedienen sein, so dass jeder Soldat oder Feuerwehrmann das Gerät schnell an einen Ort bringen und dort sofort Messungen durchführen kann (oder via Roboter). Gefordert sind mithin Vor-Ort-Geräte zur schnellen und zuverlässigen Identifizierung biologischer Kampfstoffe, um wirkungsvolle Gegenmaßnahmen schnell einzuleiten.

Großveranstaltungen bieten eine besonders ideale Arena für potenzielle terroristische Angriffe oder Angriffe durch Extremisten, da sie mit großen Menschenmengen und somit großer Aufmerksamkeit – insbesondere bei Anwesenheit von prominenten Personen – verbunden sind. In Bezug auf Angriffe mit biologischen Waffen erzeugt die hohe Mobilität bei diesen Veranstaltungen letztlich für einen hohen Wirkungsradius, potenziert im Falle ansteckender Krankheiten. VIP- oder andere geschlossene Räume, die mit Klimaanlagen ausgestattet sind, eignen sich ebenfalls ideal für die wirksame Ausbreitung.

Nicht nur bei Großveranstaltungen, sondern generell im Falle eines Angriffs mit B-Waffen sind die Kräfte für Bevölkerungsschutz und Katastrophenhilfe sowie die Streitkräfte in einem besonders hohen Maß gefordert, miteinander ihre Aktionen und Gegenmaßnahmen aufeinander abzustimmen – zu kommunizieren, auf allen Ebenen. Insbesondere ist eine schnelle, flächendeckende Identifikation mit mobilen Geräten und eine schnelle, lückenlose und übergreifende Informationsverteilung prioritär.

Das Fraunhofer-Institut für Siliziumtechnologie (ISIT) hat sich dieser Herausforderung schon vor Jahren gestellt und auf der Basis der Siliziumtechnologie und der „klassischen" ELISA-Methode ein eBioChip-System entwickelt, das die oben genannten Anforderungen erfüllt. Zusammen mit Diehl BGT Defence wird das System derzeit weiter verbessert. Dieses Konsortium DBD-ISIT-eBioChip hat nun in einem ersten Schritt einen Labordemonstrator zur Detektion von B-Kampfstoffen, zunächst für Toxine, entwickelt, der nur zwei Kilogramm wiegt und sehr einfach zu bedienen ist.

Nach der Probenentnahme (die in Zukunft automatisch abläuft) findet die vollautomatische Messung statt. Parallel können derzeit 16 verschiedene Substanzen detektiert werden, in Zukunft 32. Gemessen wird nach folgendem Prinzip: Auf der Siliziumoberfläche sind in definierten und vorher festgelegten Spots die für einen Erreger oder ein Toxin spezifischen Antikörper angedockt. Wird die Oberfläche mit der Probenlösung überspült, heften sich die Toxine oder Erreger an die für sie spezifischen Antikörper an, in einer Folgelösung heften sich wiederum spezifische Antikörper an die Toxine, die jedoch im Unterschied zu den auf der Siliziumoberfläche sitzenden ein Enzym tragen. Dieses Enzym verändert eine im folgenden Schritt zugeführte Substanz, die durch die Veränderung einen Stromfluß initiert. Dieser Stromfluß wird gemessen. Aufgrund der Zuordnung der Antikörper zu den Strom leitenden Siliziumspots kann der gemessene Erreger/das Toxin exakt identifiziert und auch quantifiziert werden. Analog verläuft das Verfahren mit dem genetischen Material eines Erregers (Bindung einsträngiger DNA, Bildung von doppelsträngiger DNA) anstelle von Antikörpern.

Diese Methode erlaubt bei Toxinen eine Messempfindlichkeit im einstelligen Nanogramm-Bereich, also einen Faktor 10 unter der geforderten Empfindlichkeit. Das Verfahren dauert weniger als 30 Minuten. Das Gerät selbst ist Erschütterungen gegenüber robust und soll weiter miniaturisiert wie auch gegenüber Bakterien noch empfindlicher gestaltet werden.

Ich habe persönlich aufgrund meiner Tätigkeiten die technische Entwicklung der Detektionsverfahren im B-Bereich sehr eng verfolgt – und es ist außerordentlich, was die Forschung in den letzten Jahren hier geleistet hat. Noch vor kurzem gingen viele davon aus, einem B-Waffenangriff hilflos gegenüberzustehen. Schnelle und spezifische Methoden wie das eben skizzierte eBioChip-Verfahren und auch das Engagement auf Seiten der zivilen Behörden und militärischen Dienststellen in Bezug auf verbesserte Zusammenarbeit erlauben und ermöglichen, mit der potenziellen Gefahr und einem tatsächlichen Anschlag – ob bei Großveranstaltungen oder im Einsatzland – kompetent umgehen zu können.

Tools for Countering Future Terrorism

Eric Herren

International Policy Institute for Counter-Terrorism, Switzerland

What shape do we expect future terrorist activities to take? Most probably it will be a mixture of what we already see around us, enriched with some surprises we are afraid to think about.

This might include assassinations and direct action against governments, together with the more usual pressure on public opinion and psychological warfare. We may see suicide attacks combined with weapons of mass destruction, multiple attacks, and cyber terrorism. Terrorist actors may include known and ad hoc terrorist organizations that have yet to be formed. All of this and many possibilities that we have not yet thought of may be part of future terrorism. Are we ready to confront this threat?

I would like to focus on existing tools in counterterrorism, and some dilemmas and difficulties in countering terrorism. I would like to provoke some thinking in the direction of additional tools necessary in the fight against terrorism.

It all comes down to the question of the chicken and the egg: what do we do first, kill the crocodiles or drain the swamp?

1 The Structure of Terrorism

Let us take a closer look at the ingredients of a terrorist attack. I will concentrate on only few important aspects, taking a "top-down" approach, from the general to the specific. This list can be thought of as a kind of "infrastructure" for a terrorist attack.

Ideological/religious/political movement – Here we find the hotbeds of future terrorist organizations.

Terrorist organization – Included in the terrorist organization are radical supporters, the leadership, the masterminds, economic support activities – both legal and illegal –, and all logistic cover operations and institutions. More and more we see organizations networking with other terrorist organizations espousing the same cause.

Strategic planning – Terrorist organizations invest significant efforts in "meta activities," such as public relations, and often use sophisticated tools to steer internal public opinion. Extensive efforts are also directed toward influencing the world audience through psychological warfare. Strategic planning also includes logistics and basic training. Terrorist organizations need to maintain and continually upgrade their arsenals and fill the ranks of fighters. Fundraising is another characteristic operation on this level.

Operational activities – In order to be effective, terrorist organizatons need to have an intelligence-gathering capability. The use of open sources like the Internet aide in target selection. Terrorists also seek to get information by simply monitoring the grey area around private security organizations. The increasing tendency to outsource police and law enforcement tasks to the private sector may also allow terrorists to access information on vulnerabilities.

Tactical preparation – This includes recruiting operatives and planning terrorist attacks. A terror attack is a complex operation. The "shahid," or suicide attacker, is surrounded by several circles of activists who select and arm the human bomb, and send him on his mission. A successful attack is based on intelligence and the processing of real time information, knowledge management, and a certain degree of "dumb luck."

Attack – From the standpoint of the terrorist organizations, an attack is successful if it produces a high body count and maximum destruction, followed by extensive media coverage.

2   The Structure of Counterterrorism

Here, too, I will touch on only a few of the relevent factors in the counterterrorism "infrastructure," again going from the general to the specific. Keep in mind that this list is far from complete.

Public opinion – Terrorism is a kind of psychological warfare; its aim is to undermine the morale of the targeted nation as well as to influence international public opinion. Thus, counterterrorism must start at the true frontline – the level of the general public.

The media – The media is of crucial importance for both terrorist and counterterrorist strategies.

Political leadership – The leadership of the nation forms the policies and guidelines for counterterrorist organization and operations.

Think-tanks – Interdisciplinary think-factories can play a role in advising decision-makers and enhancing counterterrorist strategies.

Intelligence – Intelligence is of central importance in the war against terrorism.

Special operations – Special operations are the spearhead of counter terrorist efforts. They include rescue operations as well as law enforcement, security, and military operations.

3 Counterterrorism Tools

I would like to point out that counterterrorism begins with a strong and determined counterterrorism community. In order to effectively fight terrorism, it is necessary to build a community of interest that is single-minded and solution-oriented. This organization needs an efficient internal communication system; it needs a common language and a sense of trust and responsibility among members of the community.

Effective counterterrorism requires the establishment of operational platforms to exchange views, create training scenarios, and set up red-teams. All of the foregoing applies equally to the national and the international levels.

It is also necessary to invest extensive efforts in ensuring that new terrorist organizations do not sprout as quickly as we uproot the ones we now face. In other words, it is not enough to fight the alligators; we must drain the swamp.

We will now examine the dilemmas and difficulties of each aspect of counterterrorism in relation to the terrorist infrastructure. I will tackle this from the bottom up, beginning with the more specific and working up to the most general ingredients of counterterrorism.

4 Special Operations

Special operations are the fundamental activities of counterterrorism. As an example of the various factors involved, let us take the type of operations that may come into play in the case of a suicide terror attack.

Rescue operations – Once the human bomb is within his or her chosen target area, special operations will be limited to reducing the impact of the attack. Professional rescue operations will need to take into account that the attack may be a compound one, with secondary attacks planned to target rescue forces. Medical personnel are an integral part of the security plan and play the greatest role in mitigating the effects of the attack.

Security measures – Increased security measures can lead to the discovery of the attacker before he or she can reach the target zone, thus reducing the damage or preventing the attack altogether. Successful security measures include the designation of different security zones ranging from non-target to pre-target and target zones. Each zone is characterized by different security activities, ranging from electronic surveillance to physical barriers.

Defensive activities – This includes special operations against planning and recruiting efforts by specialised cells within the terrorist organizations. Defensive measures must be continually upgraded by constantly re-examining and testing security arrangements. Nothing is more dangerous in security operations than the establishing of routine procedures which lose their sensitivity.

Offensive strikes – Offensive counterterror operations are special operations directed against the close circle surrounding the suicide bomber – those who recruit the human bombs, equip them with the deadly explosives, instruct them about favourable targets, harbour them before sending them into action, and try to cover their footprints. Many nations that strike back at terrorists base such operations on the right to self-defense. The rationale is that the person who "arms and aims" the human bomb is no less culpable than the bomber, and must be held responsible.

Surgical operations – This aspect of counterterrorism includes counterintelligence activities as well as special operations against logistics and training infrastructure. Terrorist often hide their activities within legal business or social – even medical – or international organizations. Bomb factories have been found in the same building as nursery schools and hospitals. By the same token, procurement of weapons may take place under the legal auspices of a third state, and support and fundraising for terrorist organizations may be covered by legal business activities. This type of interaction between terrorist infrastructure and civilian institutions makes special operations against such activities extremely difficult and risky.

Coordinated strategies – Among the most important special operations are those that seek to stem the flow of sympathy and support to terrorist organizations. These operations attempt to knock the wind out of public outrage and hate, the glorification of suicide bombers, and the misleading of young men and women by religious indoctrination. Counterterrorism at the highest levels must counter disinformation and psychological warfare. Long-term counterterrorist strategies must include the winning of hearts and minds to successfully win the war against terrorism.

Preventive actions in the virtual world – Lastly, we come to preventive counterterrorist "street work," carried out by units specifically trained to deal with the "virtual infrastructure" of terrorism. Here intelligence is derived from the continual monitoring of internet forums, website, and other forms of digital communications. The goal is to enter the virtual battlefield to pick out potential future terrorists and attempt to open a window for them to integrate back into our society.

4.1 Conclusion for Future Terrorism

To deal with the threat of future terrorism, we will need to create multinational special operation teams. These teams will include regional intervention units who will be first on the scene to stabilize the situation and prepare the field for take-over units.

It would be useful to establish an international counterterrorist unit which would bring together the best counterterror solutions from around the world. At the same time, we must establish international and transnational centers of excellence, and create think-factories and knowledge-management organizations.

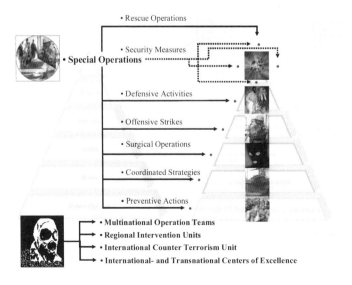

5 Intelligence

Intelligence is the sense-organ of the counterterrorist organism – the faculty that takes in and processes incoming information. As we did above, we will analyze the components of intelligence using the example of the threat of suicide attacks.

Identification of the threat – Intelligence is the key factor in preventing the attack. Once the potential suicide bomber is identified, security measures can be directed in a purposeful direction. The time factor here is critical; information processing procedures must work quickly and forward their analysis to the end users at special operations level.

Counterintelligence – Intelligence communities must upgrade their counterintelligence capabilities. Data security is vital to prevent terrorists from gaining access to information that could help in target selection. Intelligence agencies should be able to provide specific recommendations and advice to private institutions seen as being at risk of information theft, in order to prevent sensitive information from falling into the hands of terrorists.

Humint/Sigint/Elint – Intelligence gathered from the inner circle of the activists surrounding the "shahid" is based mainly on human sources. The running of such cells is a sensitive and risky business.

In many countries, human intelligence is very much a neglected artform. Too many efforts have been, and are being, invested to other means of intelligence gathering. We must come back to the human sources within our own organizations, including police and customs officers and other government employees. The police officer on his own beat must be successfully integrated into the information-gathering process; he has intimate knowledge of his own area and will be the first to know of any unusual activity.

Unfortunately the flow of information is often blocked by obstacles within the system. At the same time that we are collecting the best resources from our peripheries and bringing them together in federal institutions, we may be missing some of the best resources that are already available in our midst.

Psy Ops – Psychological operations involving the intelligence community should be directed not only against public relation efforts of the terrorist organization, but should also aim to disrupt the flow of communications within the levels of the terrorist organizations. This kind of activity can help to keep the terrorist organization busy preserving their own structures, and the risk of making mistakes will increase.

Multinational intelligence community – Intelligence aimed at terrorist organizations and their strategic efforts includes humint, sigint, and elint. The most important factor in this kind of activity is international cooperation. Often this part of the game is played on the international stage far from the "hot spots" and well protected from unwanted attention. Examples are operations to prevent terrorist fundraising and weapons procurement.

Thermostat – Intelligence agencies need to establish sensors within ideological, religious, and political movements that can sense the "temperature" of the more radical elements and put into play preventive activities. Dilemmas in the struggle against terrorist organizations often include the lack of cooperation between all the agencies involved. While healthy competition is part of the game on the national as well as the international level, it is clear that success in the war against terrorism is only reached through partnership and trust. Intelligence agencies are notorious for spreading their efforts far and wide. In order to avoid this, the intelligence community should be gathered under a common umbrella, coordinated and guided by political decisions.

Needless to say, intelligence is crucial to the success of special operations of all kinds. But more than this, it is the job of intelligence to create a round-table for the exchange of views and strive as far as possible to achieve an interdisciplinary approach.

I would like to highlight an issue often seen within intelligence communities: who is the end-user for all these sensitive products? Too often intelligence has been, and is, created merely to support old institutions and infrastructure within the intelligence agency.

Intelligence must be used by political decision-makers as part of their consultancy tools.

In many countries, the relation between intelligence and media is like cat-and-mouse, with the "right to know" and censorship producing a lot of frictions. Public opinion and intelligence are sometimes strange bedfellows; in times of threat, the public calls for visible results from the agencies. Here the dilemma is to explain what is being done without jeopardizing the success of intelligence operations.

5.1 Conclusion for Future Terrorism

The threat of future terrorism will force the intelligence community to establish multinational intelligence databases, with reasonable access for partner states. This will naturally lead to the dilemma of protecting the sources of the intelligence and establishing who gets access, and how much access. One simple rule could be: the more a state gives, the greater its access.

It will also be necessary to upgrade our ability to successfully process information under time pressure. It makes no sense to become a vacuum cleaner, sucking in all kinds of information, if the means of analyzing and interpreting this information lack. Analyzed information must be able to flow back to the end-users and other sensors of the counterterrorist community.

Here we will need to learn about and integrate better knowledge management processes. Do we fully recognize the power of open sources? We will need to have specialists analyzing open sources in all languages and in every open forum.

Human intelligence will be the main resource for effective intelligence gathering. The human factor must become our main concern. Intelligence officers will need to be offered purposeful career planning and feedback for successful activities. To be proud of his or her job is one of the main sources of motivation in a career that has little open reward or glory.

6 Think-Tanks

One of the most neglected of counterterrorist tools is the think-tank. Academic "think-factories" are helpful in providing a broader view of the phenomena of terrorism. They are removed from the actual stage of combat and are able to focus on the problem from all possible views and positions.

Think-tanks should concentrate on the actual threats, as well as learning from the overall history of terrorism. Their task should include attempting to foresee the future and "think the unthinkable."

Members of think-tanks should include former and present members of the counterterrorism community as well as anyone who can contribute to the vision. Think-tanks should become consultants and critical observers supplying feedback to the counterterrorism community, and providing forecasts and partnership in solution-oriented task forces. We will also have to learn to accept them as teachers and instructors.

6.1 Conclusion for Future Terrorism

What is needed is a successful network of think-tanks. These organizations are probably the only ones that can keep up with the pace of terrorist networking. Official governmental operations and coordinated strategies are often held back by office procedures, unnecessary bureaucracy, and political interests.

Think-tanks create the possibility of online brainstorming forums, bringing together huge resources of intellectual potential – a kind of creative solution-seeking that can be extremely helpful.

We will need interdisciplinary institutions whose activities are devoted to finding global strategies and who are willing to be part of a whole. We will need international centers of competence which will concentrate on specialized tasks as an interdisciplinary contribution to the fight against terror. An example is the recently established Center for the Study of Militant Islam.

Regarding future terrorist threats, it is likely enough that science fiction will become a relevant part of mental preparedness for future terrorism.

7 Politics

Politics and counterterrorism are at the head of virtually every national agenda today. Let me just point out several key issues with regard to successful measures against terrorism.

Political will – Political commitment to combat terrorism is the fundamental motor behind all counterterrorist activities. The will to fight terrorism – and especially to confront the gray areas where terrorism and organized crime meet – are crucial tasks for political decision-makers. But let us not be dreamers; today in many countries the gray areas are an integral part of the economic infrastructure of the nation. It will be hard to get countries to cut off funding to terrorists when this funding is seen as a legitimate part of the national economy.

Leadership – National and international leadership in the war against terrorism is necessary to concentrate the efforts of all relevant sources.

Definitions – An international definition of terrorism is crucial and fundamental. Such a definition will serve as a basis for counterterrorist activities and as an operational tool to expand our ability to combat terrorism on the international level. Too many groups that employ terrorism are still hiding behind expressions like "freedom fighters" and "insurgents."

Laws – Based on the political will of the leaders and supported by international definitions, nations must create and change their laws to be better prepared to meet the emerging threat of terrorism and organized crime.

Clear political decisions – We must demand that political leaders to make difficult decisions; in the absence of political guidance, counterterrorism organizations all too often become notorious institutions for managing problems rather than solving them. Politics is an important partner in counterterrorism, and is responsible for controlling and supporting counterterrorism tools.

Politicians must not only impress public opinion by their determination to fight terrorism, but they must also send clear signals to extremist groups. We further expect from politics a professional handling of the media.

7.1 Conclusion for Future Terrorism

The fight against future terrorism will demand political courage as well as perseverance to overcome the impact of future attacks. Future terrorism will also entail great political flexibility and the need to adapt. We will need political vision, and most of all our leaders will need the ability to learn and integrate reality into their decision-making processes.

8 Media

Most of the public knowledge about terrorism is transmitted through the media. Many international media outlets concentrate only on the most obvious stage of terrorist activities – the attack itself. In fact, it is often the media that is the first responder to a terrorist attack.

Using the example of a suicide attack, the media will home in on the scene of the attack, broadcasting images of death and destruction. These pictures are the strongest weapon in the hands of terrorist organizations. They show results on the targeted population and play to an international audience. These images prove the success of the operation to the terrorist organization while at the same time satisfying their sick motivation to kill innocents.

But where is the media's interest in backstage terrorist activities? Such activity is the real "bread and butter" of terrorism and deserves at least as much coverage as do terror attacks. However, this kind of coverage requires intensive investment, professionalism, and journalistic expertise, and the success of such TV documentaries is not guaranteed.

Many media agencies nowadays are using the term "infotainment." The average audience wants to know who is the bad guy and who is the good guy without investing too much thought. Information must be cut into small, tasty pieces which can be swallowed easily and cause no stomach-ache.

Modern terrorists try to influence decision-makers through public opinion. This kind of psychological warfare is often supported by the media by the lack of professionalism of on-scene journalists. They themselves become part of the action and lose their sense of objectivity. The terrorists' message is transmitted through the good offices of the international media. The effects of this reportage could be mitigated by paying the same attention to backstage terrorist activities.

8.1 Conclusion for Future Terrorism

It is in our interests to educate the media to their responsibilities as a first responder to terrorist attacks. The media can be used and/or misused as part of psychological operations. It can become a partner in counterterrorism if we learn how to cooperate and if we strictly draw the borders between responsible journalism and playing into the hands of terrorists.

Future terrorism may well include "media terrorism" – information channels could be hijacked and panic spread by pre-prepared pictures and scenes as well as fake political statements. This, too, is something for which we need to be prepared.

9 Public Opinion

Today's terrorist attacks target public opinion in several ways. First, a successful suicide attack aims to lower the morale and weaken the resistance of the targeted population. The terrorists' goal is to create a feeling of general vulnerability among the citizens. This psychological warfare results in enormous pressure on the government to take action (or over-reaction) and thus forces international condemnation of the targeted nation.

Secondly, the attack is also used by terrorist organizations to spread their message to the whole world. Unlike the old forms of terrorism, which sometimes had very clear political messages, today's terrorist strategy is twofold: it sends shockwaves through the civilized world; and it uses its "successes" to call for sympathizers to join the jihad. Each successful attack is another page written in the terrorist handbook used to teach a coming generation of extremists.

A successful counterterrorist strategy must include a powerful effort to educate and teach citizens about the dangers of terrorist manipulation and the impact of psychological warfare.

Security measures – Increased security measures can only be implemented if public opinion supports these actions. It is the general population that suffers from security checks and the loss of privacy. Therefore much more attention should be directed to this most vital part of counterterrorist strategy – with an emphasis on education. Terrorism is an attack on the public morale and the emotional balance of each individual. We must do all we can to strengthen this most important partner in counterterrorism.

9.1 Conclusion for Future Terrorism

Public support is critical for any long-term counterterrorist strategy. As Boaz Ganor has said, "Counter terrorist forces can win the battle but lose the war the moment that citizens are afraid to use public transportation or to go to public places."

Forecasting Terrorists' Warfare: 'Conventional' to CBRN

Dr. Joshua Sinai

Senior Terrorism Analyst, ANSER, Shirlington, Virginia, USA
Joshua.sinai@verizon.net

To assess the type or spectrum of warfare that a terrorist group is likely to conduct in its operations, this paper proposes an indications and warning (I&W) methodology to comprehensively and systematically map all the significant indicators (as well as sub-indicators and observables) that need to be examined.

A key proposition is that most of the current threat assessments fail to adequately assess the likelihood and magnitude of the types of threats posed by contemporary terrorism because of three fundamental problems in their approaches. First, many threat assessments focus exclusively on two types of warfare, "conventional" or CBRN, but not on three types of warfare that are more prevalent in terms of their actual or potential impact: conventional low-impact (CLI), conventional high-impact (CHI), and CBRN.[1]

Second, most of the current approaches do not adequately differentiate between the characteristics that define the types of warfare that terrorist groups are likely to resort to in order to achieve their objectives, particularly in terms of the leadership, motivation, strategy, and other factors as well as accelerators, triggers, and the numerous constraints involved in the transition by terrorist groups from CLI to CHI and to CBRN warfare.

Third, most of the current approaches fail to address the crucial factor of the spectrum of disincentives and constraints that are likely to deter most terrorist groups away from CBRN warfare, particularly when they can resort to conventional explosives which have become more lethal and "catastrophic" in their

---

[1] In this approach, CLI refers to 'low-impact' attacks involving relatively 'few' casualties or physical damage, such as detonating explosives or shootings; CHI refers to the use of conventional means to inflict massive casualties, such as 9/11-type attacks; while CBRN refers to the use of chemical, biological, radiological, and nuclear weapons and devices.

impact. As a result, most of the current approaches tend to lump all terrorist groups currently operating on the international scene as potential CBRN actors, without an adequate understanding of which terrorist groups are likely or unlikely to transition not only from CLI to CHI, but from CHI to CBRN warfare.

To forecast the type of warfare that a group is likely to choose, we must first gain an understanding of terrorism. Terrorism is a form of physical and psychological warfare by non-state actors against their more powerful state adversaries. In the terrorists' decision-making calculus, a localized incident is intended not only to cause casualties and physical damage, but to spread fear and anxiety throughout the larger society. Terrorists generally calibrate their warfare to maximize these objectives.

The simultaneous suicide attacks by al Qaida on 9/11 and the follow-on poisonous anthrax letter campaign by a still undetermined perpetrator ushered in the new era of catastrophic terrorist warfare. Since then, reports in the media about training by al Qaida operatives in chemical and biological warfare, and their interest in acquiring radiological and nuclear weapons, are strong indicators that the group possesses the intention and potential capability to carry out catastrophic warfare involving chemical, biological, radiological, and nuclear (CBRN) weapons and devices against their adversaries. Moreover, media reports about black market transactions by Russian and other organized criminal groups in trafficking various CBRN components are additional indicators that CBRN represents the next phase in catastrophic terrorist warfare. With the growing availability of CBRN weapons and devices, the final indicator to drive such catastrophic warfare is motivation. Leaders such as Usama bin Laden and his coterie of top advisers are considered most likely to engage in such warfare because of their ambition to propel their group and its affiliates on the international arena as a first order of magnitude technological destroyer and menace.

Thus, the threat of terrorist CBRN catastrophic warfare is real and imminent. It is also based on several historical cases where at least some of the indicators necessary to conduct such warfare have coalesced:

- the 1984 Rajneeshee salmonella poisonings of the salad bars of several restaurants in Oregon,

- the 1990 Tamil Tigers chlorine gas attack on the Sri Lankan military,

- the 1995 Aum Shinrikyo sarin gas attack against the Tokyo subway system,

- the post-9/11 poisonous anthrax letter campaign,

- the May 2002 arrest at Chicago O'Hare International Airport of Jose Padilla, an al Qaida operative charged with plotting to detonate a radiological "dirty" bomb in the U.S.,
- the January 2003 plot by an al Qaida cell to employ ricin to lace the food supply at a British military base, and
- captured al Qaida documents and training films that demonstrated the magnitude of its interest and training in employing chemical weapons.

Whether actually executed, thwarted, or nascent plots, these efforts by terrorist groups have cumulatively crossed the threshold from "conventional" to CBRN terrorism, about which terrorism experts have been warning with increasing frequency since the mid-1990s. As a result, governments around the world have been expending billions of dollars annually in homeland security-related protective training, technologies, new organizational structures, and pre-emptive response strategies.

In this approach, a trichotomous outcome (CLI, CHI, or CBRN warfare) is hypothesized to predict the types of warfare most likely to be engaged in by terrorist groups. The pre-incident activities by terrorist groups are the *independent variables* (X), while the trichotomous outcome is the *dependent variable* (Y). As discussed later on, the independent variables are related to each other, so they need to be correlated in combination. The premise is that if one can collect this type of intelligence information about terrorist groups, it will be possible to attain a sufficient predictive accuracy, while recognizing that there will always remain a certain percent of "real-world" uncertainty built into any I&W forecasting system.

This analysis is based on 31 I&W indicator categories generally considered to influence and shape a terrorist group's warfare proclivity.

The Pre-Incident Four Phases of Terrorism's 31 I&W Indicator Categories

Group Formation ⊃	Plan ⊃	Develop ⊃	Execute
Societal Conditions	Decisive Meeting	Acquisition	Tactics
Radical Subcultures	Recruitment	Development/ Production	Security
Types of Groups	Training	Testing	Communication
Leadership		Weaponization	Logistics
Motivation		Storage Facilities	Surveillance

Strategy			Targeting
Agenda			Accelerators
Front Organizations (political, economic, religious/charity)			Triggers
Organization			Internal Hurdles
Funding			External Hurdles
Constituency			
Foreign Group Linkages			
State Sponsor			

The following diagram displays the ordered grouping of the I&W indicators by phases along the lethality and propensity axes (the phased ordering of the indicators is for analytic purposes only):

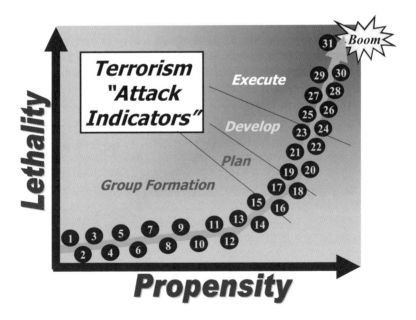

Developing an accurate, timely, and actionable I&W indicators system to forecast a terrorist group's warfare proclivity involves the following steps:

First, a threat assessment needs to be formulated that will generate warning "flags" that indicate a terrorist group's "attack potential." Several formulas can be used to derive a group's "attack potential."

- Intention + Capability = Threat
- Threat + Indicators (activities/observables) = Warning
- Warning + Adversary Vulnerability = Risk Assessment
- Intention + Capability + Accelerators/Triggers + Overcoming Hurdles + Adversary Vulnerability = Attack Indicators/Attack Potential

Second, a terrorist group's attack potential is derived from formulating hypotheses, which are broad explanatory statements that generate factors, which are more specific indicators suggesting a type of terrorist warfare proclivity. Indicators need to be considered in combination, because no single factor is likely to indicate a particular warfare proclivity. Indicators can be combined to generate a group's warfare proclivity by performing four tasks:

- *Task 1*: identifying the key observable CLI/CHI/CBRN characteristics concerning the 31 I&W indicator categories (i.e. information available to analysts from various sources) regarding terrorist group motivations, capabilities, and access to weapons, devices, and delivery systems as well as accelerators, triggers, and internal and external hurdles that would indicate a proclivity or disinclination to engage in "catastrophic" warfare.

- *Task 2*: determining how to properly weigh those indicators/observables in order to assign higher weights to those characteristics in order to assign lower or higher weights to potential CLI/CHI/CBRN proclivities that indicate a group is likely to embark on a particular type of warfare. For example, the indicators might be weighed by a rating system on a scale of 1 to 10, with 1 being the lowest and 10 being the highest threat potential, indicating the presence of the necessary motivation and operational capability by a terrorist group to carry out a particular type of attack.

- *Task 3*: providing a quantifiable system for aggregating the weights assigned to the observable characteristics in order to arrive at an overall CLI/CHI/CBRN threat rating, which accurately indicates the likelihood that a group is planning an attack exhibiting the characteristics of a particular type of warfare.

- *Task 4*: setting an appropriate numerical threshold for those aggregated weights to indicate a probability that a group will resort to CLI, CHI, or CBRN warfare, thus reaching a point to issue an appropriate warning concerning that group. The warning may take the form of distinct colors to indicate the spectrum of warfare, such as green, yellow, or red warnings.

However, unlike an I&W system for "conventional" terrorism that must effectively warn about a "conventional" type attack (for which there would also be a much higher probability), a CLI/CHI/CBRN-oriented I&W system must be customized to focus on the likelihood that a particular terrorist group has attained either of the three types of warfare operational capability and that it intends to carry out a CLI/CHI/or CBRN-type attack for which there is a spectrum of probabilities ranging from low to high, including lower to higher consequences in terms of casualties and panic throughout society caused by one of the three types of attack.

Moreover, there are significant differences between "conventional" and CBRN warfare in terms of their types of weapons, devices, and delivery systems that will affect the way an I&W system will be designed. For example, the lead-time needed by a terrorist group to develop the capability to launch a nuclear attack is much greater than the time needed to prepare for a biological, chemical, radiological, or conventional attack. Therefore, the I&W indicators for the former will probably be based on a much more comprehensive list of factors, developed over a longer period of time, than for the latter weapons, devices, and delivery systems. Similarly, the threshold for warning about a possible terrorist nuclear attack is probably lower than that for a biological, chemical, or radiological (BCR) and "conventional" attack, because the consequences of the former (and, therefore, the probable reactions of law enforcement agencies and military forces) are likely to be much more severe than for most terrorist attacks.

Thus, the I&W system for CLI/CHI/or CBRN warfare should be based on a series of databases and attributes for each of the CLI/CHI/or CBRN weapons and devices that the terrorist group under examination may be considering. As a result, one database of I&W attributes could examine the characteristics regarding motivations and operational capabilities by the terrorist group to determine which kinds of CLI/CHI/or CBRN weapons, devices, and delivery systems they are most likely to employ. The second database of I&W attributes would identify the key characteristics that an analyst should look for in determining whether a group is becoming more or less likely to actually launch an attack for which they have the theoretical capability.

The objective of developing such an I&W methodology is to provide the analytical community with a tool kit to chart as many significant indicators (including sub-indicators and observables) as possible against which to collect information and data that, once correlated, would provide the necessary aggregation to issue warnings, at the earliest possible timeframe, that a group is likely to embark on a "worrisome" type of warfare. Such an objective, however, is inherently limited in several respects. First, without penetrating a group with one's own operatives or debriefing defectors, it is difficult to obtain tactical intelligence about a terrorist group's intentions, capabilities, and targeting. Thus, without such optimal counterintelligence conditions, any predictive analytic tool can only raise a warning flag based on secondary, not "primary," indicators about a certain terrorist group to generate a spectrum of potential "worrisome" scenarios, as opposed to pinpointing the timeframe for an actual attack.

Second, some of the new terrorist groups are loosely affiliated, ad hoc groupings that coalesce for a single operation, leaving few 'footprints' or 'signatures' of their activity, thus making it difficult for an analyst to monitor their activities and intentions.[2]

Third, additional limitations include (1) the difficulty of monitoring CLI/CHI/or CBRN-associated activities by groups that engage in clandestine activities; (2) the need for significant lead time in tracking high technology-based terrorist attacks; and (3), even once information is gathered about a group's activities, the problem of aggregating all the indicators, because the likelihood of a group turning to CLI/CHI/or CBRN terrorism will probably be more a function of the interaction of several indicators than the force of any single indicator alone.

Nevertheless, despite these inherent shortcomings, an effective I&W methodology can provide analysts and counterterrorism planners with a conceptual approach "to collate diverse sources of information and to understand complex relationships and data."[3]

To display the pre-incident's processes, paths, and links involved in the likelihood that a terrorist group will resort to CLI/CHI/or CBRN warfare, this analysis groups the I&W indicators into four phases. These four phases are distinguished for analytical purposes and, in reality, some of the indicators or phases could be carried out contemporaneously or bypassed altogether. Moreover, within these four phases, the I&W indicators should be considered in combination, because no single factor has sufficient independent explanatory value.

---

[2] Stephen R. Bowers and Kimberly R. Keys, "Technology and Terrorism: The New Threat for the Millenium," *Conflict Studies*, No. 309, May 1998, p. 18.
[3] Ibid., p. 19.

Phase I – the Group Formation Phase
Phase II – the Planning Phase
Phase III – the Developmental Phase
Phase IV – the Execution Phase

These four phases of the pre-incident process can be further broken down into ten levels of analysis:

- First, which *geographic areas/states* require monitoring for precipitating *societal conditions* (#1) and the *proliferation of radical subcultures* (#2), from which terrorist groups emerge?
- Second, which *particular terrorist groups* (#3) are inclined, in terms of their *leadership* (#4), *motivation* (#5), *strategy* (#6), and *agenda* (#7), to transition from conventional to CBRN warfare, and why would they choose CBRN "catastrophic" warfare when "conventional" warfare might be sufficiently lethal?
- Third, what is the nature of the terrorist group's core *constituency* (#11) and how would it react to mass casualty/CBRN-type attacks as opposed to "low-casualty" attacks with conventional weapons (although certain CBRN weapons might result in few casualties but mass panic throughout society)?
- Fourth, what kinds of *accelerators* (#14) and *triggers* (#15) are likely to drive terrorist leaders to plan a "high casualty"- as opposed to a "low casualty"-type attack?
- Fifth, what kinds of *organizational* (#8), *funding* (#10), *recruitment* (#17), *acquisition* (#19), *development* (#20), and *logistical* (#27) capabilities will a terrorist group need to attain the operational capability to execute either a "conventional" or CBRN attack?
- Sixth, in terms of the terrorist group's targeting options, what *vulnerable 'key targeting* (#29) *points'* are they most interested in attacking and are there certain key anniversaries around which they are likely to attack?
- Seventh, how does a terrorist group's decision to attack a particular target affect their *choice of CBRN weapons, devices, and delivery systems*?
- Eighth, can the terrorist group embark on terrorist warfare *on its own* or with the *support of a state sponsor* (#13)?
- Ninth, what *internal* (#30) and *external* (#31) *hurdles* must terrorist groups overcome in order to execute a CBRN attack?
- Finally, what can the targeted adversary do during the pre-incident process to *harden its defenses* against the spectrum of terrorist attacks?

Applying these 31 indicator categories to currently operating or emerging terrorist groups will reveal whether a group is planning an attack, its motivation and strategy, the type (or types) of weapons it plans to use (particularly "conventional" or CBRN), and its likely targeting. In such a way, this methodology enables the analyst to correlate along the pre-incident's four phases a terrorist group's *internal factors* (such as the nature of its leadership, motivation and strategy, organization, funding, recruitment, training, front organizations, constituency, logistical network, and surveillance of potential targets) with *external factors* (such as linkages with foreign groups, state sponsors, and foreign suppliers), as well as potential *accelerators and triggers* (such as access on the grey or black markets to needed components or devices, or a dramatic event that would precipitate a group to take drastic action) and a group's capability to overcome various *internal and external hurdles* (such as defections, breakdowns in security, testing failures or accidents with devices, or monitoring or penetration of a group by external intelligence or counterterrorism organizations) in order to ascertain its *"attack potential."* Thus, if these indicator categories and their sub-indicators and observables could be *correlated* – recognizing that some indicators are more significant and have higher quantifiable weighting properties than others –, such analysis might indicate increasing threat possibilities, including the possible resort to conventional or single or multiple CBRN weapons and devices, and their likely targeting.

Once the methodology yields the appropriate I&W information concerning terrorist groups warfare proclivity, then the analyst can utilize a tiered approach to develop a spectrum of warnings. Filter sets can be used to focus attention on current or emerging terrorist groups most likely to embark on CLI/CHI/or CBRN-type warfare. A tiered approach can be used to identify groups likely to embark on CLI/CHI/or CBRN warfare, with increasingly "tight" filters for moving a group from CLI to CHI and the higher tier CBRN warfare.

Tier 1 (CBRN/CHI)	– Alert	1-3?
Tier 2 (CHI)	– Suspect	4-7?
Tier 3	– Possible	8-10?
Tier 4	– Potential	11-15?

Once sufficient "attack indicator" information and data coalesce to issue warnings about a group's imminent warfare proclivity, then other agencies or personnel would be tasked to operationally pre-empt or prevent a terrorist group from carrying out an attack, if such a governmental pre-emptive capability existed.

In such a way, a robust I&W methodology can be made sufficiently comprehensive and systematic to exhaust all possible relevant indicators involved in the pre-incident process, and yet not be too general or abstract to be of practical use.

CBRN terrorist warfare is likely to pose a significant threat in the 21st century as a result of the confluence of motivation, particularly in terms of less constraints, technical capabilities (especially in assembling crude devices), wider availability of CBRN materiel (from the republics of the former Soviet Union), and involvement by state sponsors (such as Iran or North Korea). This analysis is intended to highlight some of the internal and external factors, requirements, and hurdles that need to be considered in assessing a terrorist group's current and future development status and operational capability to conduct CBRN warfare. Correlating these internal and external factors and hurdles would make it possible to assess which terrorist groups and state sponsors are likely to embark on CBRN warfare, the types of adaptations and changes they would require to transition to such warfare, the types of weapons and targeting they are likely to pursue (including the possible resort to single or multiple CBRN weapons and devices), the timelines for such attacks, and vulnerabilities that could be exploited by foreign intelligence and counterterrorism agencies to constrain terrorist groups – and, when applicable, state sponsors – from embarking on such warfare.

Hopefully, such a conceptual approach will make it possible for the counterterrorism community, whether policy makers, warfighters, or analysts, to efficiently calibrate their resources to intervene at the earliest possible phases to influence, pre-empt, deter, prevent, and defeat terrorist actions, whether CLI, CHI, or CBRN.

Technologies against Terrorism

Burkhard Theile

Rheinmetall DeTec AG Düsseldorf

1 Introduction

Terrorism is a complex phenomenon. It can be caused by various motivations like reach for power, ideology, organized crime, hopelessness or hatred. Terrorism operates secretly, applies unexpected means and uses media coverage as a multiplying agent. The targets of terrorism are civil citizens and institutions as well as military facilities. Polls in Germany have shown that 57% of German citizens perceive terrorism as a threat.

Innovative solutions are needed to cope successfully with the terrorist threat. Terrorist attacks may be either single isolated or repetitive actions. The war like methods of terrorism is employed without declaring war and without regard of international or martial law. Suicide bombers and arms carrying children are almost impossible to deal with for western nations. Terrorists do not have well defined goals and there is no obvious end of a terrorist action plan. Terrorists do not commit much money. Counterterrorism is much more expensive than an act of terror.

Classical military means do not suffice to subdue terrorists. Counterterrorism has many aspects like institutional co-operation, training and exercises, equipment and prevention.

This paper will primarily address technologies and equipment. The scenario is depicted in Fig. 1.

Prevention and reaction are the two key capabilities against terrorism. Prevention has a political and an operational dimension. We will deal here only with the operational aspects and the related technologies. Prevention can be done at two different stages: The first stage is to make the perpetrators believe that their attack has no chance to succeed and the second stage is to physically thwart the terrorist's action. Reaction includes all measures to minimise the effects of a terrorist act and immediate countermeasures against the terrorists. A third aspect of reaction is "lessons learned" for future prevention.

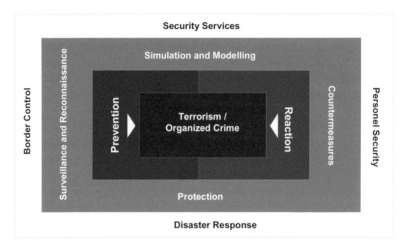

Figure 1: Scenario for counterterrorism

Prevention and reaction employ technologies for:

- Surveillance and intelligence
- Simulation and modelling
- Protection
- Countermeasures

These technical capabilities are complemented by organisational operational and personal measures to meet the objectives for site protection, personal safety and security, boarder control, and last but not least catastrophic relief. It is irrelevant for the relief actions weather a catastrophe was caused by humans or by nature.

2 Capabilities and Technologies

The four counterterrorist objectives are supported by various technologies. The DeTec capabilities matrix in Fig. 2 shows the relationship between capabilities and technologies. These technologies were developed for civil and military customers.

Civil *command and control* systems are derivatives of military systems. Command and control is essential in all four categories. *Surveillance and intelligence* are prerequisites for prevention and reaction. Surveillance and intelligence data must be available for command and control without time delay. Command and

	Border Control (Land and Coastal)	Personel Security (Individuals, Groups, and Events)	Security Services (Plants, Airports, and critical infrastructures)	Disaster Response
Command and Control	●	●	●	●
Surveillance and Reconnaissance	●	●	●	●
Special Vehicles	●	●	●	●
Effector Systems	●	●	●	
Passive Protection Systems	●	●	●	
Mobile Robotics	●	●	●	●
Modelling, Simulation and Training	●	●	●	●

Figure 2: DeTec Capability Matrix

control require flawless information. A key enabling technology, though not shown in the matrix, is networking. The networking of sensors and command and control provides the capability to immediately react to a terrorist attack.

Special vehicles are modified commercial vehicles for ABC reconnaissance, surveillance and intelligence missions and ambulance. The primary purpose of *effectors* or effector systems is the protection of military facilities against terror attacks. *Passive protection* systems are decoys means to impair sensor operation.

Simulation and modelling allows the set up of mock up scenarios to enable training and evaluation of operations a synthetic environment.

Technological standards in these different applications will be shown by the following examples. More information and imagery can be obtained through a visit of Rheinmetall DeTec's website http://www.rheinmetall-detec.com/.

2.1 Command and Controlsystems

Three different realisations of command and control systems are shown in Fig. 3. Command and control provides the situational awareness and the means to control and co-ordinate police forces fire brigades and engineers. The situational awareness is dependent on the number, quality and sensitivity of available sensors. Command and control systems display a mix of background data, like geographical information or maps, manpower information, and real time data of the scenario under observation. Sensor data include electro optical and infrared cameras, observations by humans, motion sensors and radars. All relief forces can be co-ordinated by the command and control system with the capability of an immediate response to a changing situation.

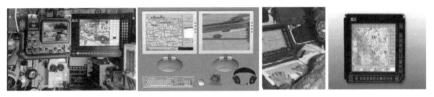

Figure 3: Command and control systems in different layouts

2.2 Surveillance and reconnaissance

Surveillance and reconnaissance is provided by a multitude of sensors. Fig. 4 shows a set of three different sensors: Electro optical, ground-based sensor, and radar. Optical sensors can detect objects of interest out of a distance of 15 kilometres and identify them at a distance of two thousand meters. These sensors can be operated in stationary or mobile modes. The co-ordinates of the object under observation are calculated automatically and delivered to the command and control system together with the imaging information. Ground bases sensors can measure acoustic signals local seismic signatures and magnetic field changes. These signatures single or correlated can deliver information to determine vehicles and small groups of people. Radars are well known sensors particularly for aerial surveillance. These sensors are mainly for prevention purposes in a way that a threat can be detected timely enough to launch countermeasures before the damage is done.

Figure 4: Electro optical Sensor, Ground based Sensor and Radar

NBC reconnaissance is a typical example for reaction. Fig. 5 shows two different vehicles, the Fox and the NBC explorer together with a field laboratory and an NBC situation map. The field laboratory determines the concentration of dangerous agents. The spreading and concentrations of hazardous materials in the air are determined by incorporation of meteorological data in a spread prediction model. This system allows timely warning for endangered areas.

Figure 5: Fox, NBC Explorer, Field Laboratory, NBC Situation Map

Unmanned aerial vehicles (UAV) or drones provide aerial reconnaissance and surveillance. They are particularly suited for missions with a highly repetitive flight path like border patrol and for missions which would unnecessary endanger a pilot's life. The UAV van be controlled by the command and control centre and the reconnaissance data can be made available to many users in real time. Fig. 6 shows unmanned air vehicles representing two different categories. KZO was developed for military reconnaissance, surveillance and target acquisition. However, it can be easily tailored down for border patrol and area surveillance. The mini drone Carolo can be man carried and is a close range surveillance tool.

Figure 6: KZO reconnaissance UAV for medium range, Carolo Mini UAV

2.3 Special Vehicles

Special vehicle are needed for ground-based mobile reconnaissance, ambulance, transport of relief teams and all other transportation needs. The design of these vehicles combine commercial and defence technologies. They provide protection against the kind of weapons most likely used by terrorists and against mine blasts.

2.4 Effector Systems

Effector Systems are primarily used to protect military facilities in foreign countries against terrorist attacks. The experience has shown a serious threat by attacks with small missiles, aerial vehicles or grenades. Rheinmetall DeTec's close range anti aircraft systems Skyshield, Asrad and MLG have proven to successfully counter such threats.

2.5 Passive Protection Systems (Fig. 7)

Passive protection methods use physical effects to impair the functioning of sensors and electronic systems. These effects are generated by pyrotechnics and electromagnetic energy. Pyrotechnically produced fog shows particular physical properties which disable optical and infrared sensors to see the desired target. These electro optical fogs can protect vehicles, facilities strike forces. Pyrotechnic devices are also available as decoys. The decoy is activated when a sensor guided weapon attacks by displaying the signature of the real target which results in sidetracking the missile.

Figure 7: Passive Protection. Microwaves to interfere with electronic equipment, Fog to blind electro optical sensors and decoys to produce a temporary mock target.

High Power Microwaves (HPM) can temporarily or permanently disrupt the operation of electronic devices. The example in Fig. 7 shows how a car can be stopped by electromagnetic interference through high power microwaves which disrupt the proper operation of the car's processors. HPM expertise is equally important to develop protection against microwave systems potentially used by terrorists.

2.6 Mobile Robotics

Fig. 8 shows a small robotic ground vehicle which has been in use for many years. It is remotely controlled and can handle challenging manipulations. It can be used to secure critical infrastructures, for monitoring of crowds and to handle dangerous tasks like discharging explosives.

Figure 8: *Small Robotic Ground Vehicle tEODor*

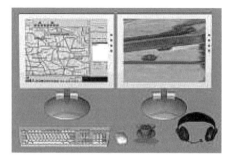

Figure 9: *TACSI Display (Telerob Explosive Ordnance Disposal and Observation*

2.7 Modelling, Simulation and Training

Simulation has gained a very high fidelity for pilot and driver training. Drivers for police, ambulances and fire brigades can develop high driving skills and equally learn their personal limits. They can handle the vehicles in demanding terrain and thus can handle their vehicle, even if roads are destroyed. Rheinmetall DeTec offers different driving trainers for various vehicle models.

Simulation and modelling enables the creation of virtual scenarios in which different institutions can act together to cope with a specific situation. This kind of simulation is provided by networking command and control, vehicles, administrative executive offices, the model of a catastrophic event, and operational forces. The system of Rheinmetall DeTec is a modular set up, which was developed for military tactical operations under the name TACSI. Fig. 9 shows an example of a TACSI display.

3 Actual Scenarios

DeTec technologies for counter terror have already been deployed and will be employed for various scenarios. A well known forum with high level attendance from around the world was protected, among other measures, by full radar coverage of the airspace to prevent potential attacks from the air.

German nuclear power plants will be protected by obscuring them by artificial fog, which drastically reduces the probability for a hit from the air. A framework agreement with the plant operators was signed in 2004. Fig. 10 shows the Effect of obscuration.

The tEODor robot (Fig. 8) was used in June 2003 to remove an IED (improvised explosive device) from Dresden's main station. The explosive filled suitcase was removed and disarmed by the robot with people at a safe distance.

Events which attract many people, like the soccer world championships in 2006, are potential targets for terrorists. Operational procedures, communications between the various persons in charge, surveillance and information management can be simulated well ahead of the event. The networking the nodes of such an event uses the same technologies as the simulation.

Figure 10: Plant obscuration

Non lethal weapons are well suited for the liberation of hostages. Microwave and electroshock devices can disable the perpetrator(s) without endangering the hostages.

The transportation of hazardous materials can be accompanied by aerial vehicles. The Carolo UAV can be hand launched to provide data ahead of the progress of the transport. Potential blockades or other problems can be handled in a timely manner.

4 Summary

Terrorism requires new means and measures to ensure safety and security of the population, secure critical infrastructures and protect military facilities home and abroad. Counter terror technologies are derivatives of civil and military technologies. Many problems can be successfully addressed today. The threats will increase requiring a continuous development of technologies.

Anforderungen an Informationen zum Schutz von kritischen Infrastrukturen

Matthias Holenstein und Daniel Bircher

Ernst Basler + Partner AG
Zollikerstrasse 65, 8702 Zollikon, Schweiz
matthias.holenstein@ebp.ch
daniel.bircher@ebp.ch

1 Einleitung

Eine zentrale Forderung zum Schutz der Kritischen Infrastrukturen (KRITIS)[1] ist der Informationsaustausch zwischen allen Beteiligten (privatwirtschaftliche Betreiber von Infrastrukturen, Behörden, internationale Stellen). Schon seit längerer Zeit existieren CERTs und CSIRTs, die sich schwergewichtig für Schwachstellen und Verletzlichkeiten von Soft- und Hardware interessieren, während sich Cyber-Crime-Units vor allem auch mit strafbaren Handlungen und Inhalten in elektronischen Medien beschäftigen. Spezifische Informationsdrehscheiben für den Schutz von Kritischen Infrastrukturen (KRITIS-Stellen) sind erst im Aufbau[2], wobei Fragen zur Architektur (Public Private Partnerships), dem Businessmodell und den gesetzlichen Rahmenbedingungen im Raum stehen.

Der vorliegende Artikel beleuchtet den Informationsbedarf zum Schutz von Kritischen Infrastrukturen und entwickelt Gedankenmodelle zu nutzbringenden Inhalten und Strukturierung der Informationen. Auf Rahmenbedingungen wie Vertraulichkeit und rechtliche Aspekte wird nur am Rande eingegangen.

---

[1] „Kritische Infrastrukturen sind Organisationen und Einrichtungen mit wichtiger Bedeutung für das staatliche Gemeinwesen, bei deren Ausfall oder Beeinträchtigung nachhaltig wirkende Versorgungsengpässe, erhebliche Störungen der öffentlichen Sicherheit oder andere dramatische Folgen eintreten würden." (http://www.bsi.de/fachthem/kritis/index.htm, letzter Besuch 8. Oktober 2004)

[2] Andere vergleichbare Stellen sind beispielsweise ISIDRAS (Australien), CIRCA (Österreich), CICS (Kanada), SITIC (Schweden), NatioNISCC (Grossbritannien) oder MELANI (Schweiz).

2 Risikomanagement für kritische Infrastrukturen

Verschiedene KRITIS-Stellen sind für das Funktionieren der jeweiligen Infrastrukturen verantwortlich (beispielsweise eines Telekommunikationsnetzwerkes). Diese Stellen betreiben ein explizites oder implizites Risikomanagement, um Risiken zu identifizieren, den Schutzbedarf zu ermitteln, Maßnahmen zu treffen und die Systeme fortlaufend zu überwachen. Dieses Risikomanagement lässt sich als Kreislauf darstellen von der Prävention und Vorsorge über den Einsatz und die Instandstellung bis zum Wiederaufbau. In den einzelnen Phasen müssen verschiedene Aufgaben durch unterschiedliche Akteure wahrgenommen werden. Für den hier diskutierten Schutz von kritischen Infrastrukturen sind primär die zwei Phasen „Prävention und Vorsorge" sowie der „Einsatz und die Instandstellung" von Bedeutung. Einen summarischen Überblick der dabei notwendigen Arbeiten und Akteure zeigt die Tabelle 1.

	Prävention und Vorsorge	Einsatz und Instandstellung
Aufgaben	• Gefährdungs- und Risikoanalysen in den einzelnen Sektoren • Erarbeiten von Policies/Massnahmenplänen • Aufbau von Netzwerken und Sicherheitskooperationen (PPP) • Aufbau von Informationsplattformen • Notfallplanung inkl. Kommunikation	• Analyse des Ereignisses • Koordination/Treffen von Massnahmen • Informationsfluss zwischen den Akteuren • Instandstellung organisieren • Strafverfolgung etablieren • Klären von juristischen/finanziellen Fragen
Akteure	• Betreiber von Kritischen Infrastrukturen • Verbände, Fachkreise, Arbeitsgruppen • Einsatzkräfte wie Polizei, FW, THW etc. • Nationale Behörden (BSI, BBK, BKA, ...) • Sicherheitsverantwortliche • Forschungsstellen	• Betreiber von Kritischen Infrastrukturen • Ereignisdienste wie Polizei, THW etc. • Strafverfolgungsbehörden • CERTs • Systemadministratoren • Versicherungen

Tabelle 1: *Aufgaben und Akteure in den einzelnen Phasen des Risikomanagements*

3 Informationen als zentrales Element des Risikomanagements

Um die einzelnen Elemente dieses Risikomanagements erfolgreich zu betreiben, benötigen die Verantwortlichen unterschiedliche Informationen auf sehr verschiedenen Ebenen: Strategische Informationen dienen der langfristigen Planung und ziehen auch übergeordnete sicherheitspolitische Aspekte mit ein. Sie sind vor allem in der Prävention wichtig. Elemente der Sicherheitsplanung untersuchen konkrete Fragestellungen zur Ausgestaltung von Systemen, z. B. das gesamte System des Finanzsektors. Schließlich müssen auf der operativen Ebene

Informationen vorhanden sein, um die einzelnen Systeme zu betreiben. Dies ist auch in der Ereigisbewältigung von größter Bedeutung. Von einer operativen zu einer strategischen Ebene wird zunehmend Information aggregiert und zu Übersichten zusammengezogen. Deshalb verringert sich dort die Informationsmenge, wie in Abbildung 1 dargestellt ist.

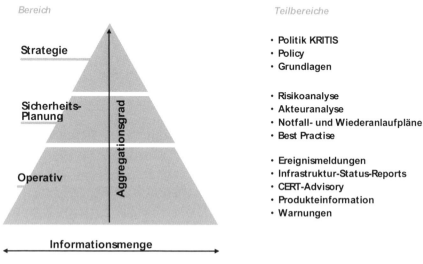

Abbildung 1: Ebenen und Menge der Information

Am Beispiel des Sektors „Wasserversorgung" lassen sich exemplarisch typische Fragestellungen und somit Hinweise auf den entstehenden Informationsbedarf für die drei Ebenen aufzeigen:

a) Strategie
  – Wie ist die Wasserversorgung in Deutschland organisiert?
  – Welches Versorgungs- und Sicherheitsniveau soll angestrebt werden?

b) Sicherheitsplanung
  – Wie sind die Netzstrukturen aufgebaut? Wo bestehen spezielle Gefährdungen etc.?
  – Welches sind die 20 wichtigsten Akteure (Betreiber, Personen)?
  – Wie stark ist die IT-Abhängigkeit des Sektors zu beurteilen?
  – Wie stark ist die Abhängigkeit von der Energie- und Telekommunikationsversorgung?

c) Operative Ebene

- Welche Sicherheitslöcher sind in den SCADA-Systemen bekannt?
- Welche Ereignisse sind bekannt (technische Defekte, Sabotage, ...)?
- Welche Notfallplanungen bestehen?

4 Informationsbedürfnisse von KRITIS-Stellen

KRITIS-Stellen haben zwei grundsätzliche Funktionen: Informationen innerhalb des KRITIS-Netzwerkes auszutauschen (im Sinne einer Clearingstelle) sowie die Informationen zu aggregieren und auszuwerten. Aus den bisherigen Überlegungen ergibt sich somit das zusammenfassende Gedankenmodell in Abbildung 2. Sowohl aus der Art der vorhandenen Informationen und Daten (linke Box) als auch den Informationsbedürfnissen (rechte Box) ergeben sich Anforderungen an den Informationsaustausch im KRITIS-Netzwerk. Im Gegensatz zur heutigen Vielfalt von Einzelmeldungen in sehr unterschiedlicher Art (angedeutet durch gepunktete Linien) kann durch eine Vereinheitlichung (dicke Pfeile) ein Mehrwert erzielt werden.

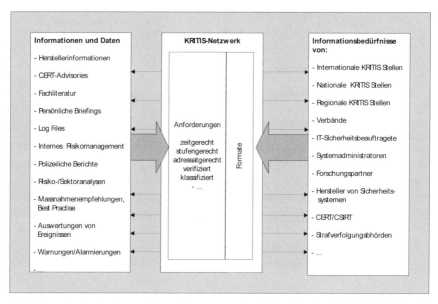

Abbildung 2: *Gedankenmodell zu Informationsbedarf und Informationsfluss im KRITIS-Netzwerk*

KRITIS-Stellen innerhalb des KRITIS-Netzwerkes werden unter anderem folgende Ansprüche an Informationen haben:

- zeitgerecht verfügbar (Zeitaspekt),
- stufengerecht aufbereitet (richtige Aggregationsstufe),
- adressatengerecht (die richtigen Informationen an den richtigen Empfänger),
- verifiziert (Korrektheit der Information) und
- klassifiziert (Vetraulichkeit und Verlässlichkeit sicherstellen).

Sie werden zudem die Aufgabe haben, Zusammenhänge zwischen Informationen zu analysieren und Konsequenzen zu formulieren.

Bezüglich Austauschformaten wurden in der letzten Zeit verschiedene Bemühungen zur Standardisierung von eingehenden oder ausgetauschten Informationen unternommen. Sie sollen zur Erleichterung der Aufgaben beitragen. So existieren heute für die Tätigkeit von CERTs Standards bezüglich Dienstleistungen und Datenaustauschformaten (z. B. RFC 3067: Incident Object Description and Exchange Format oder ISO/IEC JTC 1/SC 27 WD 18044: Security Incident Management)[3] Normen und Vorgaben. Für den Bereich der Cyberkriminalität sind in der Cyber-Crime-Convention gewisse Normierungen von Handlungen und Aktivitäten definiert.[4] Als weiteres Beispiel ist das Deutsche Advisory-Format (DAF) zu erwähnen. Analoge Standardisierungsansätze sind auch für den Informationsfluss von KRITIS-Stellen zu prüfen.

5 Fazit

Eine zentrale Voraussetzung, damit die Inhalte und Struktur der KRITIS-Meldungen überhaupt zum Tragen kommen, ist die Bereitschaft, solche Meldungen auszutauschen. Gerade für konkurrierende privatwirtschaftliche Betreiber von Kritischen Infrastrukturen kann dies ein Problem darstellen. Dem kann durch den sorgfältigen Aufbau eines Vertrauensnetzwerkes begegnet werden, wobei die nötige Vertraulichkeit garantiert werden kann. Eine zentrale Frage dabei ist, wie der Informationsaustausch erfolgen soll (via zentrale Clearingstelle, direkt zwischen den Unternehmen etc.).

Die Bemühungen und die gemachten Erfahrungen mit Meldungen und Informationsaustausch können aus einer technikfokussierten Sicht der IT-Sicherheit auf den umfassenden Schutz der Kritischen Infrastrukturen übertragen werden. Der Nutzen einer stärker formalisierten Struktur ist dabei:

---

[3] Vgl. die Incident Object Description and Exchange Format Working Group unter: http.terena.nl

[4] Vgl. dazu http://conventions.coe.int/Treaty/en/Reports/Html/185.htm

- eine einfachere und einheitliche Bearbeitung und Verarbeitung von Daten,
- eine klarere Darstellung der Bedürfnisse,
- transparentere statistische Auswertungen,
- möglicherweise eine erhöhte Qualität der Informationen,
- einfachere Spezifikation und Integration in bestehende IKT-Systeme und
- eine einfachere Zuordnung, welche Informationen auf einer Management- resp. auf der Technikerstufe benötigt werden.

Insgesamt lässt sich durch eine verstärkte inhaltliche und strukturelle Vereinheitlichung von Informationen in KRITIS-Netzwerken ein einfacherer Informationsaustausch und damit auch eine professionellere Nutzung der Informationen sicherstellen. Zudem kann der Informationsbedarf zwischen den Partnern klarer abgestimmt werden, was wiederum die Bereitschaft zur Meldung von Vorfällen bei den Betreiben von Kritischen Infrastrukturen erleichtern kann. Denn ohne die Bereitschaft zum Informationsaustausch kann der Schutz der Kritischen Infrastrukturen nur schwerlich gewährleistet werden.

I³BAT and Nomad Eyes™ – Modeling the "Design of Death" and Incorporating Terrorist Thinking into Countermethods of Sensing and Preventive Response

Martin Dudziak, PhD

Chief Scientist
TETRAD I3 Inc., Pompano Beach, Florida, USA

Abstract: Localizing, tracking and subverting terrorist plans in advance of their execution can benefit from techniques drawn from disciplines seemingly far removed from security and counterterrorism. Among the tools available to countermeasure designers are modeling methods that may be regarded as unconventional, non-traditional and "asymmetric." The I³BAT system is designed to complement existing preventive strategies by using patterns of behavior and concealment that match terrorist tactics and group dynamics, incorporating these patterns into active data collection networks. The data acquisition is based upon the use of distributed, mobile, wireless sensing (Nomad Eyes™) that incorporates public and private cellular communication devices. Back-end analysis and forecasting is based upon both Bayesian and non-linear statistical methods. I³BAT foundations include findings derived from field studies in terrorist-supportive cognitive, planning and decision-making models. Patterns of terrorist cadre formation and psychological training have been studied in depth through cultural assimilation and familiarization methods in order to develop an improved understanding and "expert skill set" with regard to conducting terrorist operations in large population centers such as cities and metropolitan transport networks.

The analytics include diffusion-attractor and inverse scattering surface imaging models drawn from medical imaging and surface/subsurface sensing. These are coupled with pseudo-random data collection and associative abductive techniques. The expected outcome is a faster production and validation of patterns linking persons, objects, transactions and targets. The mathematical basis derives from an integration of simulated annealing as employed in pattern recognition, Ramsey-theoretic sorting and matching of graphs representing events, players and relationships, and probabilistic surface fitting.

The theoretic development of I³BAT (Integrative Inverse Intelligence Behavior Analysis and Tracking) has proceeded in tandem with the design of an informatics architecture for real-time and near-real-time applications to counterterrorism. This architecture, Nomad Eyes™, is currently in the implementation, simulation and preliminary field testing stages, targeting high-volume metropolitan transportation networks and hubs such as metro and train stations for deployment of field tests in 2005. Key to the future deployment of a system such as Nomad Eyes™ is the ability to gain support for both passive and active data collection by large numbers of the general population and simultaneously the miniaturization of chemical and radiation sensors into industry standard low-power components that can be widely used by both formal agencies and members of the general population. The project has recently engendered the interest and support of a consortium of public sector and private corporate partners, including the Commonwealth of Virginia, Office of Emergency Preparedness.[1]

1 Introduction

Consider the following series of events: a shipment of ^{60}Co was enroute from Paris to Caracas. Intercepted in the Caracas airport after passing through customs, the shipment's absence is yet another event in the IAEA NEWS database and has generated alerts among a variety of security and investigation authorities. The shipment subsequently passed through Columbia, Panama, Costa Rica and upwards on the Pan-American Highway into Mexico and thence into the USA, crossing a series of borders without any radiological sensor checkpoints for private vehicles. A shielded container within the back seat of the vehicle provided ample protection for the vehicle occupants as well as deterrence from detection by passive gamma/neutron sensors.

Once in the USA, this shipment was transferred to a second private automobile and carried to a private home in the vicinity of Arlington, Virginia, outside Washington, DC. Within a week the containers were transferred to a rented commercial office site equipped with a primitive but sufficient workspace for handling hazardous materials and the contents were distributed into eight thin-walled steel cylinders, into which bar magnets had been affixed.

Four days later, a team of eight individuals carried the cylinders, one each, in their rucksacks to six different Washington metro stations and two major shopping malls. The cylinders were placed inside large metal waste disposal bins adjoining escalators that sustain high volumes of traffic, upwards of several thousand persons per day. The magnets on the cylinders provided a strong bond to the interior walls of the waste-bins and, thus placed, the cylinders were hidden from normal view including at the times when the plastic waste-bins would be replaced by maintenance workers.

---

[1] Contact information: martin@forteplan.com.

Three months later, a member of the Union Station cleaning crew, in the process of cleaning up a liquid waste spillage inside one of the waste-bins, noticed the odd cylinder and pulling it free also noticed that it was warm to the touch.

Some hours later, the implications of the event were beginning to reach the press and the public.

1.1 Reality 101

This series of events has not yet (hopefully) occurred in real life. It is a hypothetical act of radiation terrorism, a scenario presented for illustration. Nonetheless, it could be an act in progress, occurring at the very present time. This is a very easy way to conduct a very attractive form of radiation terrorism against a civilian population. It has the benefit, moreover (from the terrorist perspective), of being effective against large numbers of people and also producing a potentially large and long-lasting aftershock in public panic and general social-economic-political disruption.

Radiation terrorism is a potent terrorist weapon even without any "bang." Fission bombs and dirty bombs are not required to do any effective job at delivering disruption and fear along with some accessory effects of actual collateral damage to individuals. From the terrorist perspective it is one of the best tools in the workshop – make an impact upon very large numbers of people with uncertain fear and doubt. Who will not wonder about their possible exposure and the level of exposure? Who will not see and feel, in a visceral manner, some form of individual and collective vulnerability?

This form of radiation terrorism may be termed a Passive Radiation Exposure Device or PRED, as opposed to the classic "dirty bomb" or Radiation Dispersion Device (RDD) [1, 2] that would typically employ a conventional explosion as the medium for distributing a cloud of radioactive material in a populated area. Building an effective PRED does not have many requirements and need not involve even the scale of operative techniques suggested in the hypothetical example given here. Cadre members willing to sacrifice their lives or health for the Cause can reduce the need for complex protective precautions which could raise attention and notice among outsiders and draw perchance an investigation by civilian or government security forces.

The execution of a PRED would have a major impact on any major civilian population, regardless of the actual health implications for any individuals, short-term or long-term. It is possible that no one would die or even suffer major long-term adverse medical effects. It is possible that some individuals could have significant harm from sustained or repeated exposure to the PRED. Therein lies the power of the PRED within the terrorist value system; no one among the victim population would know for certain about their individual exposure or consequences, and all would know that if it happened in one instance, at one place, it could happen again, and again, and again...

A terrorist action such as a PRED could also be done with non-radiological means and different effects. The example drawn from the world of radiation terrorism is only one possible scenario for a general class of actions that can be among the most effective from the standpoint of generating social, economic and political disruption within the target society. Clearly there are chemical and biological agents that could be used in similar fashion. However, radioactive substances offer several advantages to the terrorist [3, 4].

First, they may be easier to conceal, given the present limitations of detectability within the general civilian sector. Second, they may be easier to handle, without specialized technology, especially if the perpetrators are willing to risk long-term and uncertain health effects to their own persons. Third and perhaps most significantly, radiation devices of the PRED variety can have the greatest impact in generating open-ended and irresolvable uncertainty and fear within the civilian population because of the impossibility of measuring individual exposure after the fact. There is no definitive test of any sort – no blood test, no antibody reaction, no biometric. There is no prophylactic, no vaccine, no palliative measures that can be dispensed. Only uncertainty and angst of a sort that is particular, in a psychological way, for nuclear radiation.

1.2 Applying Terrakt-Think as a Countermeasure

The reality of the PRED is presently undefined. It is certainly something that has been identified as being within the learning-space and plans of groups such as Al Qaeda and specifically has been among attempted actions by Chechen terrorist groups active inside the Russian Federation. However, a PRED or similar "secret action" attack is also something that can be countered, in not only its execution but planning stages, by use of technology and operative techniques that draw upon the same principles of stealth and pseudo-randomness. If the terrorists are operating outside the bounds of the "box" of customary transport, fabrication, delivery and attack with respect to different devices and weapons, so can similar asymmetric "outside-the-box" techniques be deployed as countermeasures.

This is what Nomad Eyes^{TM} is all about, as a methodology, architecture, and system. Sensors and data collectors that are in the least likely, unexpected, unpredictable places and times will be (collectively) a more powerful shield against attacks (and their planning operations) that are not in the usual places, not through the usual gateways and paths of transport and shipment, not in the usual and customary style.

A simple analogy may be helpful. A twenty-dollar bill is convenient, whereas a collection of pennies, nickels and dimes adding up to $20 is quite the opposite. However, $20 is $20 and pays for the same amount of goods as legal tender. A collection of radioisotopes acquired from a variety of sources, a mix-and-match assortment of industrial, medical and academic materials lost here, stolen there, disappearing into the "black hole" of being items on an Interpol registry but low in apparent significance, at least in comparison to military-grade ^{235}U or ^{239}Pu, is like that collection of pennies and nickels. It may be an inconvenient and slow process to build up a stockpile, and that stockpile may never be practical for an RDD, much less anything more dramatic for instantaneous destructive power. However, it may be the easiest, simplest, cheapest and most surreptitious way to build up a stockpile of PREDs that can be distributed throughout mass transit systems and in other public places.

Nomad Eyes™ is an architecture for collecting information that will signal alerts about the movement of terrorist-style weapons and their components, prior to and during assembly and preparation of the devices, and also during or after their deployment. With respect to PRED attacks in particular, Nomad Eyes™ offers the strongest deterrent to such a terrorist attack since it offers the highest level of probability for detection of the PRED components in the places and times when the terrorists themselves least expect or can least defend themselves against countermeasures – in transit, in the home or shop used as the workplace, and in the process of actual deployment. Nomad Eyes™ also offers the most probable detection of a PRED after it has been deployed, all because the sensing and detecting is not something that is limited to the airport or the shipping terminal, nor is it a system that is only in the hands of law enforcement and security forces.

Nomad Eyes™ indeed takes as a literal truth the words attributed to Osama bin Laden during a recent October 2004 videotape circulated as a warning message and overture to the American public in particular: "Your security is in your own hands." While the author and speaker of that message obviously had other intents in mind, the fact is that security against PRED and other forms of "quiet" terrorism using radiation, biological or chemical ingredients is most effective if the detection and response mechanism is in the hands of the general public as much as possible, literally and figuratively.

2 Operating Principles

Nomad Eyes™ is based upon the open-ended distribution and movement of many mobile wireless sensors and data collectors that feed asynchronously, based upon an improvisation of a classical MIMD parallel processing paradigm, into a server cluster. The latter in turn provides data management, itself a variant of industry-standard ETL[2] processing used in commercial database and data warehouse management. The analytics and forecasting applications are based upon inverse problem methods originally developed for surface and sub-surface (including ground-penetrating) sensing. Figure 1 on page 433 provides an overview of the architecture in the abstract.

Data is collected using sensors of different types (visual, audio, radiation, chemical), which communicate digital output to mobile, wireless communication devices including personal mobile phones. These transmit the data as conventional digital packets through both dedicated and public-access networks to servers which conduct the analytical processing and distribution of information. No special protocols are used, but only the standards employed for mobile internet and SMS.

Sensor types:
Sensors are of two types, "plug-in" and "built-in," with respect to the communication devices that will receive digital data from the sensor apparatus and transmit it to ultimately a server running analysis applications and database management.

The following are the sensor types planned for the full Nomad Eyes™ deployment. Generally biological, chemical and radiation sensors will be "plug-in" units whereas the others will be "built-in" devices. This is due to the nature or the technologies required for the different sensor types and also due to the development and dispersion of visual, audio and text consumer-class mobile wireless devices in the global marketplace.

Biological – registering the presence, through biochemical or in-vitro interactions in the sensor, of particular substances that indicate the presence in the ambient airborne environment of one or more types of harmful organisms. Output is a digital packet, each containing a small set of parameters indicating the results

---
[2] Extract-Transfer-Load, a mechanism for populating data warehouses real-time from transaction-intensive databases where down-time of the latter must be minimized in order to obviate disruption of the business processes of the organization. The ETL application within Nomad Eyes™ enables the use of agents or triggers for activating other responses, including those in security and first-responder teams.

of the sensing operation performed onboard the device. This is received by the mobile, wireless communication unit to which the sensor is electronically coupled.

Chemical – registering the presence of substances that indicate the presence in the ambient airborne environment of one or more types of chemical weapon or conventional explosive or the substantive components thereof. Note that chemical sensing is not limited to specific, recognized "chemical weapons" (e.g. organo-phosphates indicative of a sarin-type compound) but also to chemicals that may indicate the presence of a body-worn or hand-carried conventional explosive device. Output is as described above.

Radioactive – gamma and neutron sensors registering the presence of radioactive nuclear materials with a focus on simple detection, not dosimetry. Note that the object of the radiation sensing is to aid in the collection of data that may indicate any aspect of the construction, handling or transport of radioactive substances. Output is as described above.

Visual – images and video clips. The technology is mature, but there are additional developments in flat-surface (e.g. thin polymer-embedded lens) and extreme-low-power image capture that can enhance Nomad Eyes™. The current technology is well-deployed already within consumer-class devices (mobile phones) and other specialized units. Output is an image or series of images.

Audio – sound clips. The technology is mature and ubiquitous in consumer-class and specialized units. Output is in both analog and (increasingly, primarily) digital data.

Text – SMS text clips and e-mail. The technology is mature and well-established.

General characteristics of "plug-in" sensor units (mainly chem-bio-rad sensing):

- *Compact size and light-weight* – no larger or heavier than a contemporary mobile cell phone and optimally a device that can be literally plugged in to a mobile phone without adding significantly to the "human factors" of handling, carrying and general operation.
- *Low-power and long-life* – adaptable to the power supply of a standard mobile phone and not significantly degrading the performance life of the phone before recharging is necessary.
- *Low-cost* – the individual unit-cost of a sensor device must fit the constraints of the intended market, whether that cost is absorbed by an individual consumer (this is the less likely route of network dissemination and use) or a local, regional or national agency.

- *Low accuracy* – this is a surprising characteristic, but it is believed to be necessary in order to meet the many other extraordinary technical requirements. However, Nomad Eyes™ by first principles is designed to make use of large amounts of spatially and temporally distributed noisy, low-sensitivity and non-linear data, where some of the data is simply incomplete and inaccurate. The performance of the analysis is based upon statistical processing, and the inverse non-linear methods employed will be responsible for turning low-accuracy into high-probability results.

Note that specialized sensor units designed for interfacing with devices other than consumer-class mobile phones can have a much greater latitude and range in terms of size, weight, power consumption, rechargeability, etc. But the emphasis within Nomad Eyes™ is still and always upon sensing units being small, portable, low-cost, and allowing for some sacrifice in accuracy.

Data Collection Types:

Data is collected from the above types of sensors using mobile, wireless devices. These are of two types: "specialized" units and consumer units.

Consumer: a "standard" mobile phone. The "standard" for Nomad Eyes™ purposes is a camera-equipped device, of which there are many variants from virtually all phone manufacturers. Consumer-class units will typically be a mobile phone plus the sensor plug-in (for chem-bio-rad) or simply the mobile phone itself, enabled with additional on-phone software for the human as well as the autonomous interface. This device will be handled and operated by the human user (e.g. owner) of the phone. Through public education, advertising and general media public relations volunteers participate in the deployment and operation of Nomad Eyes™ in his or her community. Educational games and entertainment as well as commercial offerings are being designed as part of the consumer attraction model in order to gain volunteer subscriber-participants. In the case of chem-bio-rad sensing, the sensors will be "background-operating" devices not generally requiring any human interaction or response. In the case of video, audio and text data collection, this will require the conscious activity of the human user.

Specialized: units that are functionally equivalent to a standard mobile phone, capable of direct electronic interface with the chem-bio-rad or audio-video sensor, and coupled through either a cellular or wi-fi network. The interface and power requirements for such specialized units are more flexible than those of the consumer-class phones, but will be driven and impacted by some of the same basic constraints. These are also described further below.

These specialized units will typically be deployed in ad hoc configurations throughout a geographic region (e.g. building, complex, neighborhood, shipping port, industrial area) for a limited period of time by different security and maintenance staff. Devices will be either permanently powered (direct power, solar, or remote-rechargeable batteries) or will require battery replacement by maintenance staff.

Server-Side Information Processing and Analysis:
All data from the Nomad Eyes^{TM} sensors is ultimately received in digital message packets through the internet by servers. The data is moved in real time to a large database (data warehouse) and processed by several applications. One of these is known as I^{3}BAT. Using a combination of statistical, neural, inverse, abductive and Bayesian algorithms, I^{3}BAT makes probabilistic determinations, on the basis of very large datasets collected over space and time, of the likelihood that terrorist-like actions are indicated and meriting further attention by law enforcement and other security forces. Results from I^{3}BAT processing will be directly transmitted (and its databases made accessible in the fullest regard) to the "homeland security" information processing systems and personnel, who are charged with the further analysis and tactical response to potential terrorist activities.

Feedback to the Sensors and Collectors:
Nomad Eyes^{TM} has the capability built into its underlying architecture for feedback from the server-side analytical processing to the sensors in the field. This means that sensors, particularly those of the chem-bio-rad variety, could be designed to operate within servo-controlled devices for repositioning (3-axis rotation, mobile robots or airborne RPVs). Furthermore, consumer-class devices (sensors built into or plugged into mobile phones) can participate in the feedback network by means of simple audio and text alerts, commands and requests made to the human users, e.g. for collecting additional data, particularly images – as an example, a plug-in chem sensor reading received by the server may indicate a positive "hit" on a nitrite or organo-phosphate compound. The user may be alerted and requested (through his or her normal phone interface): to press a button for activating higher data collection rates or sensitivity (perhaps a higher power consumption process), to move the phone (and sensor) around an area more widely, to take random or directed-region snapshots, or simply to notify the nearest police or militia authorities.

3 Asymmetry and Asynchronicity

Nuclear and other materials for a dirty bomb may originate from and be trafficked through unpredictable paths. Tracking countermeasures based upon detection of trace radiation alone, even were it possible to measure every shipping container coming into a port or airport, are insufficient because of the precautions and intelligence that must be attributed as being within the power of the terrorist team to implement. However, the pseudo-random dispersal of mini- and micro-scale radiation sensors coupled with the integration of such information in a real-time knowledge discovery and inference environment that includes other classes of data (e.g. known or predicted purchases of materials by potential suspects, presence or absence of increased data traffic within suspect groups and centers, recorded orders and requests for building permits, licenses, or construction data that could be used in the planning of the terrakt campaign) – all of this will amplify the knowledge-value of what may otherwise seem to be insignificant variances and circumstantial evidence.

An illustration of the value of apparent outlier or irrelevant data and the value of the ADaM (Active Data Mover) ETL and the Nomad Eyes™ internal graph-theoretic pattern association model (I^3BAT) can be found in the case history of the World Trade Center attacks of September 2001. If the graph construct within I^3BAT (a data structure used to build and test similarities and differences among thousands of potential graphs linking known or suspect data such as reported locations of terrorist suspects, purchases or movements of terrakt device ingredients and some of the types of data referenced earlier) contains sufficient temporal and geographic logical arcs connecting nodes that may include:

> (potential-sec-terror-risk (person))
> (anomaly (financial transaction))
> (anomaly (public data))
> (potential-sec-terror-risk (target))
> (anomaly (information req))
> (potential-bomb-component (purchase))
> etc.,

there can be agent-driven triggers that simultaneously accomplish two things:

(a) data is brought to the attention of authorities responsible for next actions;
(b) automatic modifications are made to those mobile wireless data collection elements that are available and relevant for use in the monitoring and defense against terrorist actions including pre-terrakt planning. This, moreover, consists of two types of modification:

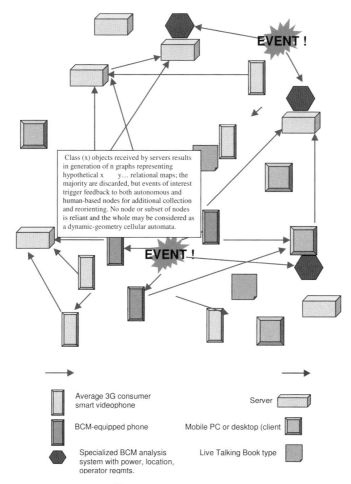

Figure 1: Nomad Eyes™ asymmetric threat event data flow (first stage).

- autonomous modulation of "robot" sensors – devices that are collecting images, audio, chemical or radiological sense-data and transmitting into the Nomad Eyes™ network, and which may be moveable, rotatable or otherwise tunable under remote control;

- messages to active and accessible participants in the broad general-public community of Nomad Eyes™ users.

Going back to September 2001, a linkage of data concerning the presence of known foreigners with immigration and documentation problems in the USA outside of their known areas of local residence, plus temporally contiguous requests by the same or probable-same persons for purchase of cell phones, plus data linking the social circle of the same with training at a flight school, plus travel of a number of individuals within the same general category could have raised a number of alerts and triggers resulting in a different morning of September 11, 2001.

4 The Role of the Public in Nomad Eyes™ as a Preventive Force

The Nomad Eyes™ model has been compared to the function of the compound eye in an insect visual system. Each data collector is very low-quality in performance compared to the mammalian or avian eye. However, taken together, the resulting array of sensors yields a spatially and temporally associable set of data points that actually is not available in the more sophisticated visual systems because of the number of orientations possible. This gives certain advantages to the insect eye, notably evident in the avoidance of obstacles by some insects while flying at high speed. Nomad Eyes™ aims to have as many collectors distributed throughout a community as possible, and to do so with a minimum of cost or maintenance. By doing so, the compound-eye effect can be achieved through I^3BAT. Furthermore, as a force of deterrence, when the terrorist forces do not know where there may be data collectors and observations, because it is no longer a matter of discrete and predictable sensors at airports, gates, or in the hands of uniformed police and security guards, but potentially a sensor-equipped mobile phone in the hands of the person next in line or across the hall or bar, then not only is the potential for early detection and disruption increased, but also the entire planning system and clandestine operational scheme of the terrorists is disrupted. Their work becomes more difficult, and that is part of the strategy for weakening their enterprise.

How can this be achieved in a practical sense? By employing large numbers of ordinary public users, focusing upon the incorporation of mobile phones that are already in use, connected and maintained.

In order to gather the active participation of thousands and even tens of thousands of people, there is a different psychology that must be employed, and for this reason Nomad Eyes™ is engaged in developing a method to make participation interesting through games, advertising, and in general entertainment.

Work by Klopfer, Jenkins and others at MIT has already demonstrated the feasibility of using cell phones in a variety of educational and socially-meaningful games [5, 6]. Nomad Eyes™ for the public sector is based upon the premise that increasing numbers of consumers are purchasing and using high-end mobile devices for entertainment, gaming, internet access and non-traditional phone communications, primarily visual in nature. Games such as those being developed in academia and industry plus commercial advertising can be used to engage a sufficient number of the public to participate productively in Nomad Eyes™ without the large number of such participants feeling like it is a dull or boring task, and with the use of plug-in sensors such as radiation monitors that can be "piggybacked" onto the mobile phone, the active engagement of the human user is minimized.

5 Nomad Eyes™ for First Responders and the Public in Post-Terrakt Recovery

Nomad Eyes™ is designed to assist also in having an improved response system for dealing with a PRED or other form of terrakt. Given a network that extends into the general public for data collection in the broad community, coupled with GPS locator functions enabled in many cellular networks (even without such the availability of clear and legible maps through current mobile phone high-res graphics), large numbers of people can be more easily notified and routed to safety. Going back to Figure 1 on page 433, the basic capability is illustrated. Sensors and data collectors including radiation monitors are assumed to be dispersed pseudo-randomly throughout a location of a terrakt incidence, and with additional resources available from the actual first-responder teams.

This data, routed into the Nomad Eyes™ servers, is then processed to generate broadcasts to the users of mobile phones in the public (commercial) networks and to the mobile autonomous devices that are deployed in the area of concern. The simple fact is that more people can be notified faster and with more intelligent and timely information than by any other means. Those without mobile devices will gather information from those around them who are thus equipped. The end result is more people moving in better directions and means away from the area of radiation (or other substance) hazard and a continuous stream of additional monitoring and sensing data coming from those people as they move and egress from the danger zones.

There are obvious dependencies for the success of the public elements of Nomad Eyes™. The objective is to minimize requirements upon the general user to do any action other than to carry their mobile wireless device; the goal is to make operations as seamless, hassle-free, and ubiquitous as possible. Critical, emergency events are high-stress and not the time for complex interactions.

6 Current Status

Currently the Nomad Eyes™ project has progressed to the stage of detailed design and prototyping, using a methodology of rapid application prototype derived from XP[3] and OOD[4] practices in the semiconductor and software industries. There are four stages to the work at present:

Sensor Configurations
Refinement of MIPI-compliant low-power compact-size plug-ins adaptable to a wide class of consumer mobile phones and also for specialized non-consumer devices.

Consumer Human Factors and Engagement
Design of educational and entertaining games for use on mobile and internet-accessible PDAs that cultivate the awareness, observation, and communication of counterterrorist-useful information through SMS, image, and voice to the Nomad Eyes™ acquisition servers.

I^{3}BAT
Modeling of terrorist planning and behavior for the construction of dynamic computing models that can be used alongside other models for identifying potential terrakt campaigns and neutralizing the threats.

Nomad Eyes™ Network and Database
Software development for the ADaM (Active Data Mover) ETL processing and the bi-directional communications with large arrays of mobile units, including the broadcast of appropriate evacuation map and route information to mobile phone users directly in the Nomad Eyes™ network and also those in the general commercial networks as well through their providers.

References

[1] Zimmerman, Peter and Loeb, Cheryl, "Dirty Bombs: The Threat Revisited," National Defense University, Defense, vol. 38, Jan. 2004, available online at http://www.ndu.

---

[3] Extreme Programming, a system for flexible, adaptive small-team design of intensive time-constrained tasks.
[4] Object Oriented Design (more widely known as OOP – Object Oriented Programing).

edu/ctnsp/DH38.pdf.
[2] Singer, Fred (Emeritus Professor, University of Virginia and Visiting Fellow, Hoover Institute (Stanford University)), available online at http://www.againstbombing.com/singer.htm.
[3] Cf proceedings and reports from the conference *Dirty Bombs II: Current Concepts in Radiation terror Preparedness and Response*, Johns Hopkins School of Public Health, Baltimore, MD, April 2004.
[4] Department of Homeland Security Working Group on Radiological Dispersal Device (RDD) Preparedness, Medical Preparedness and Response Sub-Group, http://www.productstewardship.us/supportingdocs/RadMat_BkgrdRpt.doc.
[5] MIT Comparative Media Studies Program (Henry Jenkins III, http://web.mit.edu/cms) and MIT Teacher Education Program (Eric Klopfer, http://education.mit.edu/).
[6] O'Driscoll, Alice, Tan, Philip, Targum, Elliot, Squire, Kurt and Miller, Heather, "On the Border of Life," MIT Comparative Media Studies Dept, 11/02.

Maßnahmen der Wirtschaft

Economic Measures

Internationaler Terrorismus als Herausforderung für die moderne Unternehmenssicherheit

Dr. Christoph Rojahn

Prevent AG, Hamburg

1 Einleitung

Dass die Anschläge des 11. September 2001 die Welt verändert haben, wird selbst von den größten Kritikern der westlichen Außen- und Sicherheitspolitik nicht ernsthaft in Frage gestellt. Die daraufhin eingeleitete Reaktion nationaler Stellen auf die Bedrohung durch Gruppen des internationalen Terrorismus deckt inzwischen ein Spektrum an Maßnahmen ab, das vom Einsatz militärischer Mittel gegen das Taliban-Regime in Afghanistan über die Stärkung der Nachrichtendienste bis zum Erlass eigener Gesetze reicht. Gemeinsames Ziel dieser Maßnahmen ist eine Verbesserung der Sicherheitslage und eine verstärkte Bekämpfung terroristischer Gruppen.

Eine demgegenüber weitaus weniger diskutierte Frage ist, wie sich die Privatwirtschaft mit der seit 2001 veränderten Bedrohungslage auseinandersetzen kann und muss. Traditionell wird die äußere Sicherheit nahezu ausschließlich durch staatliche Institutionen gewährleistet. Unternehmen beschränken sich demgegenüber auf den Schutz ihrer Interessen vor kriminell motivierten Tätern. Diese Einstellung spiegelt die Überzeugung wieder, dass die größte Gefahr für Unternehmen von Tätern ausgeht, die es auf die Ressourcen der Zielunternehmen abgesehen haben, während Terroristen ihre Aktivitäten auf politische Ziele konzentrieren würden.

Diese Sicht der Dinge muss nach heutigem Kenntnisstand als überholt betrachtet werden: Die Anschläge des 11. September galten nationalen Symbolen der Vereinigten Staaten von Amerika, sie verursachten aber zugleich erhebliche wirtschaftliche Schäden – die Wirtschaftsberatung Deloitte quantifizierte 2004 die direkten und indirekten Schäden der Anschläge auf 83 Mrd. US$.[1] Betreiber wie Nutzer des World Trade Center waren in der Mehrheit privatwirtschaftliche Un-

---

[1] Deloitte, *Erfolg in der Secure Economy* (deutsche Kurzfassung der Studie „Prospect in the Secure Economy"), ohne Ortsangabe 2004.

ternehmen, die nicht aufgrund ihrer jeweiligen Tätigkeit, sondern einzig und allein aufgrund ihres Geschäftssitzes zum Ziel wurden.

Grundsätzlich ist davon auszugehen, dass Unternehmen und ihre Interessen in weiter steigendem Maß von terroristischen Aktivitäten betroffen sein werden:

- Sie betreiben den größten Teil der gesamtgesellschaftlich genutzten Infrastrukturen, deren Störung sowohl Ziel als auch Begleiterscheinung von Anschlägen ist.
- Der globale Wiedererkennungswert von Großkonzernen und ihrer Marken macht Anschläge gegen sie zu medienwirksamen Ereignissen.
- Großkonzerne werden international als Vertreter der jeweiligen Heimatländer und ihrer Politik wahrgenommen.

Gerade angesichts der Tatsache, dass die Sicherheit von militärischen und politischen Anschlagszielen vor dem Hintergrund der militärischen Auseinandersetzungen in Afghanistan und im Irak weltweit gestärkt wurde, steht zu befürchten, dass terroristische Täter in zivilen Objekten mit entsprechendem Wiedererkennungswert eine attraktive Alternative sehen.

Gleichzeitig führt eine Kombination von zwei unterschiedlichen – wenn auch miteinander verbundenen – Faktoren dazu, dass die traditionelle Rolle des Staates als Gewährleister der Sicherheit für moderne Unternehmen nur noch bedingt Bestand hat. Einerseits zieht sich der Nationalstaat traditioneller Prägung zunehmend auch im Sicherheitsbereich auf als essenziell wahrgenommene Kernkompetenzen zurück, eine Entwicklung, die sich nicht zuletzt in der in der jüngeren Vergangenheit kontrovers diskutierten Auftragsvergabe an Private Military Companies (PMCs) widerspiegelt. Andererseits führen wirtschaftliche Globalisierungsprozesse dazu, dass sich für Unternehmen kritische Ressourcen an Orten befinden, die nicht notwendigerweise im Fokus der nationalen Außen- und Sicherheitspolitik liegen.

Thema des vorliegenden Beitrags ist die Frage, wie Unternehmen die durch eine gesteigerte Bedrohung einerseits und eine Neuorientierung staatlicher Aktivitäten andererseits entstehende Lücke im Sicherheitsbereich schließen können, um ihre eigenen Interessen zu schützen. Dabei soll einerseits die traditionelle Rolle von Unternehmenssicherheit skizziert und andererseits die oben angesprochenen Globalisierungsprozesse beispielhaft dargestellt werden.

2 Unternehmenssicherheit als privatwirtschaftliche Aufgabe

Die beschriebene Veränderung der Risikolage hat in zahlreichen Ländern zu einer erheblichen und häufig mit verstärktem Ressourceneinsatz verbundenen Neuorientierung des staatlichen Sicherheitsapparates geführt. Neben Gesetzesänderungen und einer verstärkten Beobachtung islamistischer Gruppierungen wurden zusätzliche Mittel bewilligt und die für die Terrorismusbekämpfung zuständigen Abteilungen der Polizeibehörden und der Nachrichtendienste gestärkt, in einigen Fällen wurden unter dem Eindruck der terroristischen Bedrohung sogar vollkommen neue Sicherheitsstrukturen geschaffen.

Anhand dieser Beispiele ist bereits deutlich erkennbar, in welche Richtung die Reaktion staatlicher Stellen auf die veränderte Gefährdungslage geht. Sie besteht in erster Linie in einer quantitativen Verbesserung der Terrorismusbekämpfung, teilweise ergänzt durch modifizierte Rahmenbedingungen. Grundlegende strukturelle Veränderungen bei der Ausgestaltung staatlicher Sicherheit sind die Ausnahme geblieben – und dort, wo sie umgesetzt oder diskutiert worden sind, wurden häufig Themen aufgegriffen, die bereits vor dem 11. September als möglicherweise erforderliche Reformen diskutiert worden waren. Beispielhaft sei an dieser Stelle auf die Einrichtung des Department of Homeland Security in den USA verwiesen, das bereits geraume Zeit vor den Anschlägen angedacht worden war.[2] Auch die Einsetzung eines nationalen Leiters der US-amerikanischen Nachrichtendienste war in der Vergangenheit als mögliche Maßnahme zur Reform der amerikanischen *Intelligence Community* thematisiert worden.

Dieser überwiegend quantitative Ansatz in der Auseinandersetzung mit dem internationalen Terrorismus spiegelt die Überzeugung des öffentlichen Sektors wider, dass das für die Lösung des Problems erforderliche Instrumentarium grundsätzlich vorhanden ist und lediglich in seiner Anwendung gestärkt werden muss. Die Aufgabe der Terrorismusbekämpfung mit polizeilichen, nachrichtendienstlichen und militärischen Mitteln ist an sich nicht neu. Betrachtet man allerdings den privatwirtschaftlichen Bereich, wird schnell deutlich, dass etablierte Strukturen im Bereich der Unternehmenssicherheit nur bedingt zur Minimierung von Terrorismusrisiken geeignet sind.

Dass Unternehmen ihre eigenen Vorkehrungen zum Schutz ihrer Interessen treffen, ist vermutlich so alt wie der organisierte Handel selbst. Heute reicht das Maßnahmenspektrum der Unternehmenssicherheit vom Zaun um das Werksgelände über den Pfortendienst im Verwaltungsgebäude bis zum Einsatz schwer

---

[2] Vgl. Richard Clarke, *Against All Enemies*, London 2004, S. 248ff.

bewaffneter Personenschützer bei der Projektabwicklung in Krisenregionen. Unternehmen haben im Grundsatz längst akzeptiert, dass sie aktive Schritte unternehmen müssen, um ihre Geld- und Warenbestände, ihre Produktionseinrichtungen und im Extremfall das Leben ihrer Mitarbeiter zu schützen.

Eine genauere Betrachtung der durch die Unternehmenssicherheit wahrgenommenen Aufgaben verdeutlicht, dass diese überwiegend auf die Abwehr *krimineller* Angriffe gegen die Unternehmensinteressen gerichtet sind. Diese Fokussierung ist unabhängig von einer – insbesondere im US-amerikanischen Raum zu beobachtenden – gesteigerten Bereitschaft, Sicherheitsfragen auf der Ebene der Unternehmensleitung zu berücksichtigen. Charles A. Sennewald verweist in diesem Zusammenhang auf die gestiegene interne Bedeutung der Unternehmenssicherheit, die seiner Meinung nach auf ihren Beitrag zu den Zielen des Unternehmens, insbesondere der Profitmaximierung, zurückzuführen ist.[3] Wenn man sich dieser Position anschließt, bedeutet dies aber auch, dass allenfalls ein indirekter Zusammenhang zwischen der Komplexität der Bedrohung und der unternehmensinternen Gewichtung von Sicherheitsfragen besteht.

Die Arbeitsschwerpunkte der Unternehmenssicherheit lassen sich in drei wesentlichen Tätigkeitsfeldern zusammenfassen:

1. physischer Schutz,

2. Ermittlungsführung,

3. Krisenmanagement.

Diese Aufstellung ist keineswegs erschöpfend – abhängig von den Strukturen des Unternehmens sowie den zu schützenden geschäftlichen Aktivitäten können weitere Tätigkeitsfelder hinzukommen. Zudem ist anzumerken, dass die beschriebenen Aufgaben nicht notwendigerweise von Mitarbeitern des Unternehmens erfüllt werden, sondern häufig in Form von spezialisierten Beratungs- und anderen Dienstleistungen zugekauft werden.

Diese Differenzierung ist allerdings im Zusammenhang der aktuellen Überlegungen insofern zu vernachlässigen, als die Frage, inwieweit ein Unternehmen im Zusammenhang mit der Bedrohung durch den internationalen Terrorismus Handlungsbedarf sieht, zunächst unabhängig von der Frage ist, inwieweit ein entsprechender Bedarf durch interne oder durch externe Kapazitäten abzudecken ist. Sie wird erst in dem Augenblick wesentlich, in dem ein Unternehmen

---

[3] Charles A. Sennewald, *Effective Security Management*, 4. Aufl., Burlington, Massachussetts, 2003, S. 19.

entweder aus Kostengesichtspunkten oder aus grundsätzlichen Überlegungen heraus eine Präferenz für eine externe oder eine interne Lösung entwickelt.

Diese Aktivitäten stehen nach wie vor in erster Linie in einem nationalstaatlichen Kontext. Wirtschaft wie Politik teilen die Welt in sichere und weniger sichere Länder auf, und die Entscheidung, in der einen oder anderen Region tätig zu werden, wird zumindest am oberen Ende des Risikospektrums durchaus von der Frage beeinflusst, welchen Gefahren sich ein dort engagiertes Unternehmen ausgesetzt sieht.

Die Freiheit, sich aus betriebswirtschaftlichen Überlegungen heraus weltweit nach Standorten, Märkten und – sofern die gesetzlichen Rahmenbedingungen auch dies zulassen – Mitarbeitern umzusehen, gehört zu den definitorischen Aspekten der Globalisierung, eines Begriffs, der in der Sicherheitsdebatte inzwischen wohl untrennbar mit dem Phänomen global operierender Terrorgruppen verbunden ist. In einem Vortrag vor der Clausewitz-Gesellschaft sprach beispielsweise der Vizepräsident des Bundesnachrichtendienstes vor kurzem selbstverständlich von „internationalem Terrorismus als klassischer Globalisierungsform".[4]

Diese Einschätzung eines Praktikers deckt sich in beinahe untypischem Ausmaß mit der entsprechenden wissenschaftlichen Diskussion. Denn in einer ansonsten nicht unbedingt durch besondere Einheitlichkeit der Positionen gekennzeichneten Debatte gehört die These, dass der moderne Terrorismus in Zusammenhang mit Globalisierungsprozessen stehen müsse, zu den wenigen gemeinsamen Nennern, auf die sich die Mehrheit der Teilnehmer verständigen kann.

Die Existenz einer solchen Kausalverbindung erscheint in sich durchaus schlüssig. Es wäre aber mit Sicherheit zu einfach, die Wurzeln des modernen Terrorismus vorwiegend in der Tatsache zu suchen, dass der Kontrast zwischen Arm und Reich in einer global mobilen Welt nicht in erster Linie zwischen Bürgern derselben Nation sichtbar wird. Die sozialrevolutionäre These, dass Terrorismus die Waffe der Unterprivilegierten sei, hat sich bereits in den siebziger Jahren des letzten Jahrhunderts in Westeuropa als nur bedingt tragfähig erwiesen. Sie wird kaum überzeugender angesichts einer Organisation wie der Al Qaida, deren Finanzmittel es ihr beispielsweise 1998 gestatteten, durch Börsenspekulationen an

---

[4] „Terrorismus und Massenvernichtungswaffen", Vortrag vor der Clausewitz-Gesellschaft, Hamburg, 23.11.2004.

den französischen Aktienmärkten kurzfristige Gewinne in Höhe von 20 Mio. US$ zu erzielen.[5]

Und auch wenn die Al Qaida in diesem Punkt aufgrund ihrer in der Person Osama Bin Ladens begründeten Mittel ein besonders herausragendes Beispiel darstellt, steht sie doch keineswegs ganz allein. Loretta Napoleoni verweist in ihrem aktuellen Buch *Modern Jihad* darauf, dass die zum damaligen Zeitpunkt als terroristische Vereinigung eingestufte UCK 1999 in der Lage war, Gelder in einer Gesamthöhe von etwa 10 Mio. US$ in der albanischen Exil-*Community* in den USA zu sammeln.[6] Angesichts der offensichtlichen Tatsache, dass dieser Betrag 1999 im Kosovo oder selbst in Albanien mit dieser Leichtigkeit im Sympathisantenumfeld der Organisation kaum zu beschaffen gewesen wäre, bleibt nur die nüchterne Feststellung, dass die Täterseite sich längst die Realitäten der Globalisierung zunutze macht, unabhängig davon, ob man dort bestimmte Aspekte derselben Prozesse als Rechtfertigung für den bewaffneten Kampf heranzieht.

3 Globalisierung und veränderte Referenzsysteme

Die Welt, in der Unternehmen und die für ihre Sicherheit verantwortlichen Mitarbeiter ihren jeweiligen Aufgaben nachgehen, hat sich im Verlauf der zweiten Hälfte des 20. Jahrhunderts dramatisch verändert. Die Zahl der selbstständigen Nationalstaaten hat sich vervielfacht, eine Entwicklung, die vermutlich – angesichts der zahlreichen nach wie vor in verschiedenen Teilen der Welt aktiven Separatistengruppen – noch keineswegs abgeschlossen ist. Das Ende des Ost-West-Konflikts hat dazu geführt, dass ein die Außen- und Sicherheitspolitik sämtlicher Staaten beherrschender Faktor verschwunden ist. In der Folge dieser Entwicklung haben lokale und regionale Konflikte erheblich an Bedeutung gewonnen.

Parallel dazu haben wirtschaftliche Globalisierungsprozesse eine Neuorientierung international tätiger Unternehmen mit sich gebracht. Während in der Vergangenheit der Stammsitz einer Firma gleichzeitig ein Indikator für die Lokalisierung ihrer Produktionsstätten und ihrer Absatzmärkte darstellte, bedeutet die weitgehende Loslösung betrieblicher Strukturen von nationalen Grenzen, dass ein Unternehmen mit scheinbar ausgeprägter nationaler Markenidentität zwar in einem Land offiziell ansässig ist, die gesamte Produktion aber auf einem an-

---

[5] Loretta Napoleoni, *Modern Jihad – Tracing the Dollars Behind the Terrorist Networks*, London 2003, S. 163.
[6] Loretta Napoleoni, *Modern Jihad – Tracing the Dollars Behind the Terrorist Networks*, London 2003, S. 167.

deren Kontinent durchführen lässt, während Gesellschafter die jeweils vorteilhafteste Rechtsform in einer ausschließlich auf die Ansiedlung von internationalen Holdings spezialisierten Region gewählt haben. Führungspositionen werden in weiten Teilen der Wirtschaft durch qualifizierte Personen unabhängig von nationaler oder ethnischer Zugehörigkeit besetzt, und die von Samuel Huntington beschriebene „Davos-Kultur" einer global aktiven, gemeinsame Ausbildungswege und Grundwerte teilenden Gruppierung ist zumindest partiell Wirklichkeit geworden.[7]

Die Internationalisierung von Märkten, Produktionsprozessen und Unternehmensstrukturen bringt gleichzeitig in mehrfacher Hinsicht ein gesteigertes Risikopotenzial mit sich.

Sowohl die Internationalisierung der Absatzmärkte als auch die gestiegene Bedeutung von Niedriglohnländern führen dazu, dass mehr und mehr kritische Prozesse in Regionen mit reduzierter politischer Stabilität verlagert werden. Dieselben sozioökonomischen Gegebenheiten, die Unternehmen den Zugang zu ausreichend vielen extrem kostengünstigen Mitarbeitern ermöglichen, können im nationalen und regionalen Kontext zu Spannungen mit erheblichen Konsequenzen führen. Dabei besteht die Gefahr, dass gerade ausländische Unternehmer nicht als positiver volkswirtschaftlicher Faktor, sondern als Profiteure der Ungleichheit wahrgenommen werden. Dort, wo sich die entsprechenden Spannungen gewaltsam entladen, sind die Einrichtungen dieser Unternehmen in besonderem Maße gefährdet.

4 Rückzug des Nationalstaates

Globalisierung bedeutet gleichzeitig nicht zuletzt auch eine Neudefinition der Rolle des Nationalstaates und seiner Aufgaben. Wirtschaftliche Prozesse lösen sich von Ländergrenzen. Gerade für Deutschland als Exportnation spielen geographische Grenzen in wirtschaftlicher Hinsicht eine untergeordnete Rolle: Grob geschätzt zwei Drittel des Umsatzes der 30 deutschen DAX-Unternehmen werden außerhalb der deutschen Landesgrenzen erzielt. Gleichzeitig gehört geschätzt ein Drittel ihres Kapitals nichtdeutschen Eigentümern.

Unternehmen profitieren offensichtlich von einer Entwicklung, die Handelshindernisse reduziert – in organisatorischer, personeller und demzufolge auch in finanzieller Hinsicht. Dieses an sich positive Ergebnis ist allerdings keineswegs unumstritten. Während sich aufgrund der spezifischen Gegebenheiten der deut-

---

[7] Vgl. Samuel P. Huntington, *Kampf der Kulturen*, München/Wien 1996, S. 78.

schen politischen Landschaft die diesbezügliche Diskussion hierzulande überwiegend auf die Frage konzentriert, ob ein deutsches Unternehmen politisch dazu verpflichtet ist, Arbeitsplätze in Deutschland zu schaffen oder zu erhalten, konzentriert sich die globale Debatte überwiegend auf die moralische Legitimität unternehmerischer Entscheidungen, Prozesse dorthin zu verlagern, wo Kosten gering und Margen vorteilhaft sind. Naomi Klein hat in *No Logo* das Unbehagen einer Generation von Konsumenten wiedergegeben und fokussiert, der beim Anblick des Schildchens „Made in China" eben *nicht* zuallererst die organisatorische Brillianz eines weltumspannend tätigen Herstellers einfällt, sondern das Bild einer einsamen Gestalt vor dem Panzer auf dem Tiannamen-Platz.[8]

Gleichzeitig stellt der Rückzug des Nationalstaates in unterschiedlichen Bereichen ein zentrales Merkmal der modernen Gesellschaft dar. Funktionen, die im Europa des 19. Jahrhunderts vollkommen selbstverständlich als hoheitliche Aufgaben verstanden wurden, standen bereits hundert Jahre später in vielen Ländern bereits auf dem Prüfstand, und der dahinter stehende Prozess hält vielerorts mehr oder weniger unvermindert an.

Aber während die Bereitschaft, Aufgaben im Interesse der Effizienz, der Qualität und nicht zuletzt der durch Steuergelder zu finanzierenden Aufwendungen in private Hand zu übertragen, Unternehmen zahlreiche neue Möglichkeiten eröffnet, führt sie im selben Atemzug zu unerwünschten Begleiterscheinungen. So kann sich ein Unternehmen, das weltweit nach neuen Märkten sucht, heute nur bedingt darauf verlassen, dass die in Frage kommenden Länder hohe Priorität in der Außen- und Sicherheitspolitik genießen.

Zwischen der Freiheit bei der Suche nach neuen Tätigkeitsfeldern einerseits und einer (verkürzt gesagt) auf das Wesentliche reduzierten Außen- und Sicherheitspolitik andererseits sind Unternehmen praktisch gezwungen, ihre eigenen Vorkehrungen zu treffen. Kaum ein Großkonzern verlässt sich heute vollständig darauf, dass im Krisenfall die Evakuierung der Mitarbeiter und ihrer Familien durch die diplomatische Vertretung vor Ort organisiert werden wird. Wer im Sicherheitsbereich international aktiv ist, weiß um das Arbeitspensum der Verbindungsbeamten deutscher Sicherheitsbehörden, die häufig bei allem guten Willen nur bedingt die Möglichkeit haben, den spezifischen Bedürfnissen einzelner Unternehmen Rechnung zu tragen. Wenn in diesem Zusammenhang die Arbeitsgemeinschaft für Sicherheit in der Wirtschaft in ihren Anmerkungen zur Sicherheitslage den ausdrücklichen Wunsch äußert, die Bundesregierung möge Unternehmen durch die Übermittlung von Lage- und Gefährdungsinformationen

---

[8] Naomi Klein, *No Logo*, London 2000.

unterstützen und diese Unterstützung intensivieren, so ist dies zwar verständlich, scheint aber vor dem Hintergrund der dargestellten Entwicklungen eher optimistisch.[9]

Es ist vielmehr davon auszugehen, dass die Belieferung der als *Global Player* agierenden Unternehmen mit sicherheitsrelevanten Informationen in demselben Maße abnehmen wird, in dem sich diese durch den globalen Wettbewerb gezwungen sehen, ihre Prozesse permanent anzupassen. Allenfalls dort, wo die Konzentration des wirtschaftlichen Engagements durch verschiedene Unternehmen eine kritische Masse erreicht, ist mittelfristig auch mit einem entsprechenden Engagement der Politik zu rechnen.

5 Abschließende Überlegungen

Die beschriebenen wirtschaftlichen und politischen Prozesse sind eine Realität, mit der sich heute sämtliche Teilbereiche eines Unternehmens in der einen oder anderen Form auseinandersetzen müssen. Dabei wird es zunehmend die Aufgabe der Konzernsicherheit sein, die beschriebene Sicherheitslücke zu füllen, entweder durch eigene Aktivitäten, durch den Einkauf externer Leistungen oder durch eine enge Abstimmung mit staatlichen Stellen in den jeweiligen Tätigkeitsländern.

Dabei kommt mit Blick auf die Gefährdung von Unternehmenswerten durch Aktivitäten des internationalen Terrorismus der Vorfeldaufklärung besondere Bedeutung zu. Denn trotz des in den Proklamationen der Al Qaida erkennbaren globalen Anspruchs sind viele der Anschläge sowohl ideologisch als auch operativ in einem regionalen oder sogar nationalen Kontext zu sehen. Eine entsprechende Beobachtung des Umfelds, in dem ein Unternehmen tätig ist, kann entscheidende Hinweise auf eine mögliche Veränderung der Risikosituation liefern. Hierbei darauf zu setzen, dass staatliche Stellen in der Lage sind, die für das Unternehmen relevanten Informationen zu sammeln, auszuwerten und entsprechend zuzuliefern, heißt, die ökonomischen Realitäten des 21. Jahrhunderts zu verkennen.

Unternehmenssicherheit bekommt damit quasinachrichtendienstlichen Fokus. Vor diesem Hintergrund gewinnt die Notwendigkeit zu einer qualifizierten Beobachtung und Analyse möglicher Risikotendenzen in Schlüsselregionen erheblich an Bedeutung, wobei die Ergebnisse ihren Nutzen nicht nur im Bereich der

---

[9] Arbeitsgemeinschaft für Sicherheit in der Wirtschaft, *Anmerkungen zur Sicherheitslage der deutschen Wirtschaft 2003/2004*, Berlin 2004, S. 7.

Terrorismusabwehr, sondern auch in anderen Aspekten der operativen Tätigkeit haben können. Eine Konzernsicherheit, die in der Lage ist, unter Nutzung firmeneigener Strukturen ein differenziertes und über die unmittelbare Sicherheitsfragestellung hinaus nutzbares Lagebild zu entwerfen, kann nicht nur dazu beitragen, Risiken für das Unternehmen zu reduzieren, sondern der Unternehmensleitung zudem wesentliche zusätzliche Informationen in strategischen Fragestellungen liefern. Diese Möglichkeit rückt sie näher an die Kernaktivitäten des Unternehmens und reduziert die häufig von beiden Seiten kritisch vermerkte Distanz zwischen Betreibern des operativen Geschäfts und den für ihre Sicherheit verantwortlichen Stellen.

Die mittel- bis langfristige Beobachtung potenziell risikobehafteter Entwicklungen setzt die Bereitschaft und die Fähigkeit voraus, neben rein kriminalitätsbezogenen Tendenzen das weitere politische, wirtschaftliche und soziale Umfeld zu beobachten. Denn während Kriminalität gegen Unternehmen kaum je ideologische Aspekte jenseits der Profitmaximierung aufweist, stehen die Terroranschläge der letzten Jahre zu einem erheblichen Teil auch im Kontext lokaler und regionaler Konflikte. Die Fähigkeit zur Einschätzung, wann ein Unternehmen aufgrund welcher Entwicklungen durch wen gefährdet ist, bildet damit eine essenzielle Komponente der Eigensicherung. In einer komplexen Welt, in der nachrichtendienstliche wie außenpolitische Schwerpunktsetzungen mit der Entscheidungsgeschwindigkeit globaler Konzerne aus gutem Grund weder mithalten können noch wollen, sind Unternehmen gut beraten, diese Kapazitäten selbst zu entwickeln.

Der beschriebene Ansatz ist politisch nicht unproblematisch. Trotz aller Bereitschaft moderner Gesellschaften, sich zunehmend mit der Privatisierung ehemals originär staatlicher Bereiche zu beschäftigen, stößt gerade die Übernahme von sicherheitlichen Aufgaben durch private Anbieter fast überall auf erhebliche Skepsis. Die entsprechenden Überlegungen stehen heute im weiteren Kontext einer Diskussion, die vom Einsatz privater Sicherheitsdienstleister in höherwertigen Einkaufsgegenden bis zu der Auseinandersetzung um den Einsatz privater Verhörspezialisten der Firma CACI im Gefängnis von Abu Ghraib reicht. Wer in der heutigen Zeit nicht nur für mehr Eigenverantwortung, sondern auch für mehr eigene Aktivitäten der Wirtschaft im Sicherheitsbereich plädiert, setzt sich leicht dem Vorwurf aus, das staatliche Gewaltmonopol zugunsten rein ökonomischer Interessen untergraben zu wollen.

Dem ist entgegenzuhalten, dass die beschriebene Sicherheits- und Informationslücke keineswegs ursächlich auf ein Bemühen der Wirtschaft um mehr Verantwortung in diesem Bereich zurückzuführen ist. Unabhängig davon, ob man die rechtliche Ausgestaltung der einzelnen Einsätze und der dabei involvierten Anbieter für ausreichend hält, ist die Tendenz des Staates unverkennbar, sich neben vielen anderen Bereichen auch in Sicherheitsfragen mehr und mehr auf als essenziell wahrgenommene Kernkompetenzen zurückzuziehen. Man kann diese Tendenz aus unterschiedlichen Blickwinkeln unterschiedlich bewerten, aber sie ist eine Realität, mit der sich global tätige Unternehmen auseinandersetzen müssen.

Dabei ist die Frage, wie weit man auf diesem Weg gehen will, berechtigt und notwendig. Aber grundsätzlich gilt, dass Unternehmen, die aktiv Maßnahmen für die Sicherheit ihrer Mitarbeiter einleiten, ihrer Verantwortung gerecht werden. In einer komplexen Welt endet diese Verantwortung weder mit dem Ende der Personalliste noch mit der Grenze des Betriebsgeländes. Insofern stellt eine bedarfsangepasste und zur Früherkennung möglicher Gefährdungen geeignete Sicherheitsstruktur die logische Konsequenz einer Entwicklung dar, die dazu führt, dass die Interessen von Unternehmen mit außen- und sicherheitspolitischer Schwerpunktsetzung nur noch partiell deckungsgleich sind.

Risikomanagement und Sicherheitsstrategien in der Wirtschaft

Enterprise Risk Management als Führungsinstrument für Vorstand und Aufsichtsrat

Günter Lessing

Lessing IRM GmbH, Altenburgerstr. 24, 52538 Gangelt

1 Zentrale Gedanken für ein Enterprise Risk Management

Unternehmungen und Staaten befinden sich zunehmend in den Spannungsfeldern unterschiedlicher Interessengruppen (die bis zu terroristischen Mitteln greifen) die den Handlungsspielraum zwischen Chancen und Risiken in einem immer größeren Ausmaß bestimmen.

Für diese ergeben sich daraus verschiedene Konsequenzen. So nehmen die Bedeutung und die Auswirkungen von Risiken stetig zu, da Entwicklungen immer häufiger nur sehr schwer prognostiziert werden können. Planungen müssen daher immer flexibler werden, gleichzeitig aber höchsten wirtschaftlichen Ansprüchen wie Effektivität und Effizienz genügen.

Durch die gestiegenen Anforderungen wird das Risikomanagement sehr komplex, die entsprechenden methodischen Vorgaben und die organisatorische Umsetzung müssen erarbeitet und implementiert werden. Des Weiteren muss die notwendige IT-Unterstützung und -Integration erarbeitet und vollzogen werden.

Aufgrund der rechtlichen Relevanz (Haftung der Einzelpersonen) müssen alle Komponenten (Organisation und Infrastruktur) der Anforderung der Gerichtsfestigkeit genügen.

In der jüngeren Vergangenheit wird an Universitäten und bei Unternehmensberatungen an neuartigen, integralen Ansätzen des Risikomanagements gearbeitet, welche diesen gestiegenen Anforderungen gerecht werden.

Gegenstand der Forschung und Entwicklung sind dabei die Zusammenführung der operativen, funktionalen und verdeckten Risiken, die Erarbeitung von methodischen Vorgaben zur Durchführung des Risikomanagements, die Projektorganisation der Einführung und Operationalisierung des Riskomanagements sowie die Entwicklung von IT-Tools zur effizienten Stützung der Prozesse.

Die modernen Ansätze unterscheiden sich vom klassischen Risikomanagement in erster Linie dadurch, dass sie der Leitungsaebene ständig und direkt bei der Entscheidungsfindung unterstützen können. Explizit werden verschiedenste Arten von Risiken aus allen Fachbereichen des Unternehmens berücksichtigt, so beispielsweise Produktrisiken, Produktionsrisiken, Absatzrisiken, Finanzrisiken, IT-Risiken sowie politische und sicherheitsrelevante Risiken.

Die Herausforderungen und Problemfelder eines Integralen Risk Management liegen in:

- der fachbereichsübergreifenden Analyse der Kritikalität der Einzelrisiken.
- der Überwindung der verteilten Risk Management und Sicherheitsorganisation.
- der permanenten und direkten Aufbereitung der unternehmensweiten Risikosituation für die Unternehmensführung zur Unterstützung der Entscheidungsfindung.
- der Einbezug von qualitativen Kontrollkreisläufen für nicht nummerisch-messbare Risikoveränderungen.
- der Berücksichtigung von Risiken aus allen Fachbereichen des Unternehmens, so beispielsweise Produktrisiken, Produktionsrisiken, Absatzrisiken, Finanzrisiken, IT-Risiken sowie politische und sicherheitsrelevante Risiken.

2 Zusammenführung von Integraler Sicherheit und traditionellem Risk Management zu einem Integralen Risk Management

Die traditionellen Instrumente der Risikoerfassung und -bewältigung umfassen die Organisationseinheiten der Integralen Sicherheit und des klassischen Risk Managements und Risk Controllings. Teilweise sind dies eigenständige, ausschließlich für die Sicherheit vor Operativen, Funktionalen und Verdeckten Risiken verantwortliche Organe. Andererseits übernehmen auch die entsprechenden Fachbereiche einen Großteil dieser Sicherheitsaufgaben.

Das Integrale Risk Management (IRM) stellt den zentralen Baustein für die gesamtheitliche, unternehmensweite und zusammenhängende Beurteilung aller Risiken und Chancen eines Unternehmens dar und ist als Voraussetzung eines Lagezentrums und eines Frühwarnsystems zu betrachten.

Das Integrale Risk Management ist die Instanz eines Unternehmens, die unternehmensweit alle verfügbaren Risikoinformationen der drei Risikobereiche OR, FR und VR in eine einheitliche Darstellung der Gefährdungslage zusammenführt. Hierbei werden ebenso Abhängigkeiten der Risiken untereinander, als auch ihre logische Struktur analysiert und in Gesamtszenarien, unter der Berücksichtigung der Vorgaben der Unternehmensführung, aufbereitet und konsolidiert.

Dabei liegt ein besonderes Augenmerk in der Erfassung von gegenseitigen Abhängigkeiten, Kumulationspotentialen und der Ursachen und Wirkungszusammenhänge von Einzelrisiken im Unternehmen. Aus diesen Zusammenhängen werden für das Unternehmen existenzielle Ursachenfaktoren (Einflussfaktoren) ermittelt und dem Frühwarnsystem als Frühwarnindikatoren übermittelt.

Die strukturelle Gesamtdarstellung einer solchen Architektur, mit seinen operativen Einheiten und funktionalen Prozessen, umfasst folgende elementare Kennzeichnungen:

- Strategische Konzernebene

    Es sind einheitliche und aufeinander abgestimmte Vorgaben in den Bereichen der Organisation des Integralen Risk Management, der Technikunterstützung (gerade im Hinblick auf den Informationsaustausch zwischen zentralen und dezentralen Einheiten) und der rechtlichen Erfüllung von Auflagen und Verantwortungen in einer einheitlichen Architektur zu beschreiben, als allgemein verbindlich zu verabschieden und zu pflegen.

- Management-/Unternehmensebene

    Die integrierte Betrachtung und Bearbeitung der Risiken aller Risikobereiche mit ihren spezifischen Risikoverflechtungen bzw. -interdependenzen (Integrales Sicherheitsmanagement und sicherheitsbezogenes Risikomanagement) muss methodisch folgerichtig zu einer integrierten, d. h. Gesamtheitlichen und zentralen Betrachtung und Bearbeitung aller Unternehmensrisiken (Integrales Risk Management) führen. In welchen Stufen, Arbeitsschritten und Zeiten die integrierte Bearbeitung aller Risiken erfolgen kann und wird, ist strategisch und taktisch flexibel zu bestimmen.

    Das Integrale Risk Management wird so zentraler Bestandteil der Corporate Governance. Es muss sichergestellt werden, daß alle Unternehmensrisiken in ihrer Gesamtheit bei der Führung des Unternehmens berücksichtigt werden. Auf diese Weise werden auch die Voraussetzungen für eine effiziente interne und externe Revision geschaffen.

- Prozessebene

Wesentlich für die erfolgreiche und effiziente Arbeit eines Integralen Risk Management sind die Durchführung von Risiko-Analysen, dezidierte Kontrolle & Beobachtung der Prozesse, der Einbezug des Controlling, die Anbindung an Interne Kontrollsysteme (IKS) und die Einbettung eines Frühwarnsystems.

- Technischen Umsetzungsebene

Die manipulationssichere Unterstützung eines Integralen Risk Management und seiner Teilbereiche und angeschlossenen Einheiten müssen den Anforderungen der technischen Gerichtsfestigkeit genügen. Qualitative und quantitative Kontrollkreisläufe sind unerläßlich für die Überwachung der Gefährdungs- und Chancenlage eines Unternehmen und bedürfen einer sorgfältigen Implemtierung, Durchführung und Kontrolle.

- Steuerungs- und Kontrollebene

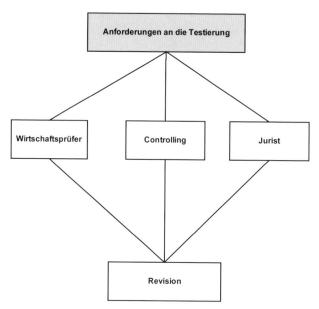

Integrales Risk Management und Risk Controlling müssen für alle unternehmensweiten und relevanten Geschäftsbereiche und Einheiten die Erfüllung der internen und externen Auflagen sicherstellen und den Anforderungen der

- Wirtschaftsprüfer (extern) – Wirtschaftlichkeit und Risikomanagement
- Controlling (intern) – Wirtschaftlichkeit und Effektivität

- Jurist (intern) – Gerichtsfestigkeit, Risikovorsorge, Einhaltung gesetzlicher Auflagen
- Revision – Kontrolle der Kosten und Rechnungsstellung

genügen.

3 Integrales Risk Management als Bestandteil eines Enterprise Risk Management

Ein Enterprise Risk Management Instrumentarium für die Führungsebene eines Unternehmens ist in Zukunft ein unerlässliches Werkzeug für die Entscheidungsfindung strategischer Vorgaben und deren Erfolg. Die zentrale Aufgabe eines „Enterprise Risk Management" besteht in der Sicherstellung einer tagesaktuellen Einschätzung der Risikosituation für ein Unternehmen. Die Erfüllung dieser Aufgabe stellt eine wesentliche Qualitätsanhebung von Risikoinformationen für die Führung eines Unternehmens dar.

Die Aufgabe eines Enterprise Risk Management besteht in der systematischen und konstruktiven Abwehr der Risiken eines Unternehmen als Ganzes, anstatt – wie bisher – den Umgang mit ihnen den einzelnen Unternehmensteilen allein zu überantworten.

Ein Enterprise Risk Mangement stellt ein Management System dar, welches eine allgemeine Dachorganisation für alle Risk Management Tätigkeiten in einem Unternehmen zur Verfügung stellt:

- geschäftsbereichübergreifend
  (von der Entwicklung bis zum Vertrieb und Service),
- hierarchieunabhängig
  (vom Verkäufer bis zum Geschäftsführer und Aufsichtsrat),
- standortübergreifend

und konzentriert sich hierbei auf den kontinuierlichen Betrieb eines hocheffizienten Prozesses vom Einzelrisiko bis zur Frühwarnung.

3.1 Aufbauorganisation mit einem Integralen Risk Management (Kernelemente)

Die Aufbauorganisation zur Sicherstellung dieses hocheffizienten Prozesses umfasst folgende wesentliche Kernelemente:

- Risk Management

Generische Risikoanalyse

- Informationsmanagementsystem (Knowledge Hub)

Der Knowledge Hub bildet die zentrale Beschaffungs-, Auswertungs-, Vervielfältigungs- und Verbreitungsinstanz der relevanten Nachrichten im Hinblick auf die zeitnahe Wahrung der Sicherheit von Kerngeschäftsprozessen und arbeitet eng mit dem Frühwarnsystem und dem Integralen Risk Management zusammen.

- Integrales Risk Management

Die zentralen Aufgaben eines Integralen Risk Managements bilden die Ermittlung und Feststellung von verdichteten Risikoszenarien (Gesamtszenarien) für OR/FR/VR, die angemessene Verfügbarkeit von Kompensationen und Maßnahmenkatalogen hinsichtlich der Sicherung eines störungsfreien Kerngeschäftsprozeßablaufs und dessen Funktionalität, die Steuerung und Kontrolle zeitnaher „Crisis Management"-Aufgaben sowie die organisatorische Zusammenführung der einzelnen Sicherheitsdienstleister eines Unternehmens (Informationsschutz, Objektschutz, Personenschutz, Finanzschutz, Qualitätsschutz, etc.).

- Frühwarnsystem

Die Ermittlung von Gesamtszenarien für OR/FR/VR ermöglicht es, hierauf aufbauend Beobachtungsbereiche und Frühindikatoren für Frühwarnindikatoren festzulegen, deren Erarbeitung, Überwachung und Kontrolle vom Frühwarnsystem sicherzustellen ist.

Es gilt die implizierte Annahme, daß im Normalfall Veränderungen nicht abrupt auftreten. Vielmehr sind Signale sichtbar, die herausstehende Änderungen signalisieren, sie also ankündigen.

- Der Lagebericht

Der Konzernlagebericht umfaßt eine konsolidierte Darstellung der aktuellen Risikoszenarien für ein Unternehmen mit entsprechenden Auswirkungen der Risikovarianten, Kompensationen und Maßnahmenvorschläge als Entscheidungsempfehlungen.

Risikomanagement und Sicherheitsstrategien in der Wirtschaft 459

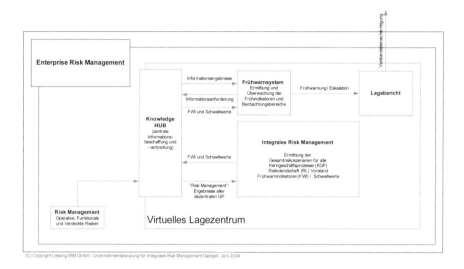

3.2 Ablauforganisation mit einem Integralen Risk Management (Kernelemente)

Die Ablauforganisation umfasst folgende wesentliche Kernelemente:

- Auf der lokalen Ebene:
  - Identifikation, Bewertung und Kontrolle der dezentralen Risiken
  - Beschreibung von Risikoszenarien
  - Dezentrale Planung von Crisis Management Maßnahmen
  - Regelmäßige Auditierung der Risk Management Ergebnisse
- Auf der zentralen Ebene:
  - Zentrale Zusammenführung der nicht tolerierbaren dezentralen Risiken
  - Überführung der zusammengeführten dezentralen Risiken zu zentralen Hauptrisikopotentialen und Beschreibung von zentralen Risikoszenarien
  - Zentrale Planung von Crisis Management Maßnahmen (zusätzlich zu den dezentralen)
  - Zentrale Beschaffung von zeitnahen Risikoinformationen und Überwachung der kritischsten Risiken aus der Perspektive des Gesamtunternehmens
  - Tägliche und zeitnahe Erstellung von Lageberichten für die betroffenen Entscheidungsträger

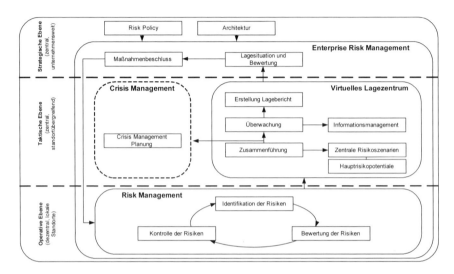

Die wesentlichen qualitativen Merkmale eines Enterprise Risk Management umfassen:

- Einzelrisiken und Gesamtrisikoszenarien

  Die gesamthafte Ermittlung der Gemeinsamkeiten der wichtigsten und kritischsten Risiken werden in einem oder mehreren Gesamtrisikoszenarien (GRS) unter Einbezug der Einfluß- und Wirkungsfaktoren abgebildet.

Risikomanagement und Sicherheitsstrategien in der Wirtschaft

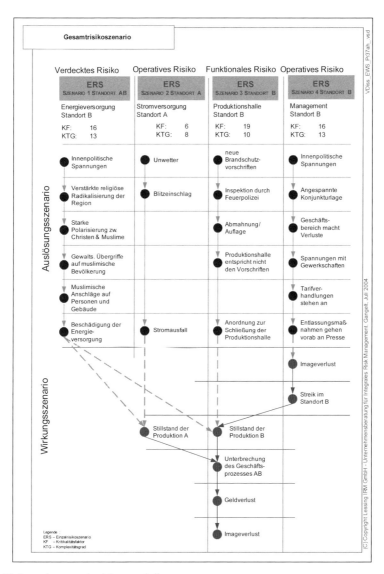

- Unternehmensstrukturmodelle

  Gesamtszenarien werden in einem Unternehmensstrukturmodell abgebildet. Dies ermöglicht, die Auslösungs- und Wirkungsfaktoren mit ihren Beobachtungsbereichen systematisch zu strukturieren.

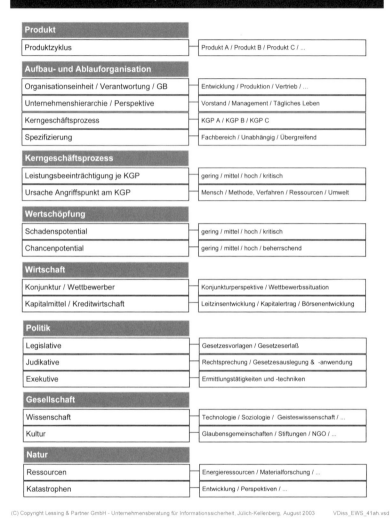

- Qualitative Kontrollkreisläufe

  Mithilfe der Gesamtrisikoszenarien und deren Verortung im Unternehmensstrukturmodell können integrale, berechenbare und steuerbare Erfassungen von qualitativen Zustandveränderungen kritischer Situationen innerhalb eines Frühwarnsystems ermittelt werden.

Risikomanagement und Sicherheitsstrategien in der Wirtschaft 463

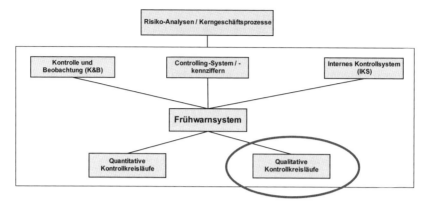

- Frühwarnsystem

    Das Ziel der Einrichtung eines Frühwarnsystems ist die gezielte Überwachung von Faktoren bzw. Ereignissen, welche zur Auslösung von unternehmenskritischen Risiken führen. Hierdurch wird das Unternehmen in die Lage versetzt, vor einem Schadenseintritt handeln zu können, d. h. Agieren zu können und nicht reagieren zu müssen.

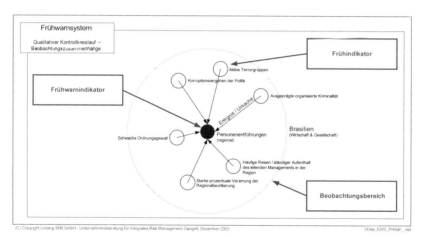

4 Zusammenfassung

Die Aufrechterhaltung der Äußeren Sicherheit (Internationale Organisationen, Internationale Beziehungen im Krisenmanagement), Inneren Sicherheit (Polizei, Nachrichtendienste, Infrastrukturen, Rechts- und Kriminalpolitik, Strafrecht) und der Gesellschaft (Wirtschaft, Ressourcen, Bürger, Medien, Freiheitsrechte) wird im zunehmenden Maße durch destabilisierende Gefährdungsentwicklungen (Naturkatastrophen, Terrorismus, Organisierte Kriminalität, präemptive Kriegsführung, Wertschöpfung um der Wertschöpfung Willen) herausgefordert.

Hierbei ist in der Regel ein verspätetes und unkoordiniertes Reagieren auf die Störfall- und Krisenereignisse hinsichtlich der Bewältigung zu beobachten. Dies betrifft nicht nur die Zusammenarbeit staatlicher und wirtschaftlicher Sicherheitsorgane, sondern gerade auch die Koordinierung der wirtschaftlichen Sicherheitsverantwortlichen untereinander (im Einzelunternehmen und in Zusammenarbeit mit anderen Unternehmen), als gleich in der staatlichen Sicherheitsorganisation (Krisenprävention der Länder, Städte und Gemeinden).

Eine effektive und ganzheitliche Risikovorsorge ist praktisch fast nicht gegeben. Die Krisenprävention verläuft sich in selektiven Einzelbetrachtungen, die zumeist ihre Eingebundenheit in den größeren Rahmen der Gesamtsicherheit (International, National, Regional) übersieht und zu einer Über- oder Unterschätzung der Gefahren führt und daher zu uneffektiv, redundant und kostenintensiv ist.

Insbesondere Kapitalgesellschaften sind durch Basel II und KonTraG (Gesetz zur Kontrolle und Transparenz im Unternehmensbereich) aufgefordert, sich intensiver denn je mit einem aktiven Risikomanagement zu beschäftigen. Dabei spielen die Themen Risikofrüherkennung und Risikoreduzierung eine wesentliche Rolle, während sich in der Vergangenheit viele Unternehmen nicht selten auf die reine Beobachtung von finanziellen Kennzahlen beschränkt haben.

Ein Integrales Risikomanagement (IRM) beschränkt sich dabei nicht etwa nur auf Basel II und KonTraG; vielmehr ist ein funktionierendes IRM Voraussetzung für den Erfolg und Wachstum sowohl von Unternehmen der Wirtschaft als auch von Einrichtungen der Öffentlichen Hand.

Ein Enterprise Risk Management soll der betreffenden Leitungsebene als Instrumentarium dienen, die Beherrschbarkeit seiner Risikolandschaft unter den Voraussetzungen der Rechtssicherheit, Praktikabilität, Effektivität und Effizienz zu ermöglichen. Es garantiert einen Zugewinn an sicherheitspolitischer Handlungshoheit in Gefährdungs- und Krisensituationen. Zentrale Fragen einer Unternehmung bzw. Öffentlichen Organs, dessen Teilaufgabe in der Sicherstellung seiner Funktionsfähigkeit liegt, d. h. Die Sicherstellung von Kernbereichen der Unternehmung und/oder öffentlichen Vorsorge und Verwaltung, werden mit Hilfe eines IRM, Lagezentrums und Frühwarnsystem zeitnah, kostenmindernd und effektiv beantwortet.

Wege zur Versicherung des Terrorrisikos

Dr. Bruno Gas

Vorstandsvorsitzender Extremus Versicherungs-AG

1 Terrorversicherung vor und nach dem 11. September

Vor dem 11. September 2001 galt das Terrorrisiko in den meisten Staaten, so auch in Deutschland, als ohne weiteres versicherbar. Mangels Ausschlussklauseln boten die Rückversicherer insoweit uneingeschränkten Versicherungsschutz, so dass Erstversicherer auch größte Risiken umfassend versichern konnten. Das Terrorrisiko fand keine Erwähnung in den Versicherungsbedingungen, auch wurden hierfür keine gesonderten Prämien in Rechnung gestellt.

Mit den Anschlägen vom 11. September, insbesondere auf das World Trade Center (WTC), änderte sich die Situation schlagartig. Die Rückversicherungsmärkte, die ca. 60% der Schadenleistungen zu erbringen hatten und zum Teil eine erhebliche Schwächung ihrer Solvenz hatten hinnehmen müssen, kündigten ihre Sachversicherungsverträge[1] zum Jahresschluss und boten Erneuerung bei Großrisiken nur noch mit Terrorausschluss an. Die Erstversicherer hatten dem zwangsläufig zu folgen, so dass in Staaten, in denen es nicht schon vorher Auffangregelungen gegeben hatte,[2] ein Versicherungsnotstand drohte.

2 Staat und Versicherungswirtschaft als Public Private Partnership

Während Frankreich bereits im Dezember 2001 eine Lösung fand, zogen sich nicht nur in den USA, sondern auch in Deutschland die Verhandlungen zwischen Vertretern der Regierung, der Industrie und der Versicherungswirtschaft über eine staatlich gestützte Versicherungslösung hin. Die Bundesregierung war zwar bereit, eine hinreichend große Haftung zur Verfügung zu stellen, doch erwartete sie von der Privatwirtschaft eine vorrangige Deckung in einer Höhe, wie sie

---

[1] Vom Ausschluss des Terrorrisikos wurden neben der Sachversicherung durchaus auch weitere Versicherungszweige erfasst. Die Auswirkungen des Terroranschlags auf andere Sparten wie z. B. die Haftpflicht- oder die Lebensversicherung würde jedoch den Rahmen dieser Untersuchung sprengen.

[2] So z. B. Großbritannien und Spanien.

die – geschwächten – internationalen Märkte nicht erbringen konnten. Schließlich einigte man sich nach siebenmonatigen Verhandlungen auf eine privatwirtschaftliche Deckung in Höhe von 3 Mrd. €, der der Staat mit einer nachrangigen Haftung von 10 Mrd. € zu folgen versprach. Die hiernach bereitgestellte Gesamthaftung von 13 Mrd. € hatte die gleichen Dimensionen wie der gesamte Sachschaden am WTC[3] und deckte damit einen Schadenaufwand, den man sich in Deutschland gegenwärtig nur nach einer Serie schwerster Schadenereignisse innerhalb eines Jahres vorstellen kann.

Deutschland verfügt mit dieser Zusammenarbeit von Staat und Versicherungswirtschaft wie inzwischen auch etliche andere Industriestaaten über eine stabile Terrordeckung, die auch eine hinreichende Standfestigkeit gegenüber Schwankungen der Terrorgefahr gewährleistet.

3 Zum Start von Extremus

Auf der Basis der Vereinbarung mit der Bundesregierung gründeten 16 in Deutschland besonders engagierte Erst- und Rückversicherungsgruppen die Extremus Versicherungs-Aktiengesellschaft, deren einziger Zweck der Abschluss von Terrorversicherungen für in Deutschland belegene Großrisiken[4] ist. Durch die gewährte Rückdeckung von 13 Mrd. € war man sicher, die erwartete Nachfrage trotz des geringen Startkapitals von Extremus (60 Mio. €) uneingeschränkt bedienen zu können.

Bedingt durch die langen Verhandlungen und den nur mit Mühe möglich gewesenen Erwerb der privatwirtschaftlichen Deckung von 3 Mrd. € kam es erst im November 2002 zur Aufnahme des Geschäftsbetriebes. Das Geschäftsmodell basierte auf Schätzungen, wonach ca. 60% der Großunternehmen[5], 40% der mittelgroßen Unternehmen und weniger als 20% der „kleineren"[6] Unternehmen Terrorversicherungsschutz nachsuchen würden. Von den 40.000 Feuerpolicen, bei denen inzwischen das Terrorrisiko ausgeschlossen worden war, sollten damit ca. 7.000 durch Wiedereinschluss bei Extremus auf den bisher gewohnten Deckungsstandard gebracht werden. Aufgrund der Prämienforderungen der

---

[3] Die im Allgemeinen genannte Zahl von ca. 40 Mrd. US$ enthält in großem Umfang auch Personenschäden sowie Schäden aus mittelbarer Betriebsunterbrechung, die in dem hier vorgenommenen Vergleich außer Acht bleiben.

[4] Extremus zeichnet nur Sachversicherungspolicen mit einer Versicherungssumme von über 25 Mio. €. Bei kleineren Risiken wird Terrorversicherungsschutz nach wie vor von der privaten Versicherungswirtschaft allein geboten.

[5] Unternehmen mit einer Versicherungssumme von über 5 Mrd. €.

[6] Unternehmen mit einer Versicherungssumme von bis zu 1 Mrd. €.

Rückversicherer und der vom Staat für die Haftung erwarteten Vergütung wurde ein Umsatz von über 500 Mio. € kalkuliert, was etwa einem Sechstel der gewerblichen Sachversicherungsprämien in Deutschland entsprach. Dies schien angesichts der nach dem WTC-Schaden empfundenen Bedrohung durchaus als angemessen. Gleichwohl wurde von diesen Zahlen noch ein Sicherheitsabschlag von 50% vorgenommen.

In den vom 11. September 2001 bis zur Aufnahme des Geschäftsbetriebes vergangenen 14 Monaten hatte sich allerdings das Gefühl der Bedrohung bei den Versicherungsnehmern erheblich zurückgebildet. In der Zeit von November 2002 bis zum Jahresschluss 2003 kam es lediglich zu etwas mehr als 1.000 Vertragsabschlüssen mit einem Prämienvolumen von 105 Mio. €. Es gelang indessen, die Rückversicherer davon zu überzeugen, dass die deutlich geringere Risikoexponierung auch geringere Beitragsabgaben zur Folge haben müsse. Hierdurch konnte die sich zunächst abzeichnende große Diskrepanz zwischen den Kosten des Rückversicherungsschutzes und den Beitragseinnahmen und damit ein gravierendes Existenzrisiko beseitigt werden, so dass lediglich ein kleiner Bilanzverlust nicht mehr zu verhindern war.[7]

4 Die weitere Entwicklung der Terrorversicherung in Deutschland

Internationale Maßnahmen zur Terrorabwehr sowie die Verlagerung des Schwerpunkts von Terrorakten in arabische Staaten sorgten in Europa für scheinbare Ruhe, und selbst die Attentate in Madrid vom 11. März 2004 führten nicht dazu, dass die Bedrohung in Deutschland wieder stärker empfunden wurde. Etliche Großkunden entschlossen sich sogar, auf eine Terrorversicherung gänzlich zu verzichten, wobei dies oft damit begründet wurde, dass Extremus nur im Inland Versicherungsschutz bieten könne, was allerdings bei allen staatlich gestützten Terrorversicherungslösungen in der Welt der Fall ist. Hinzu kam die wachsende Bereitschaft einiger Versicherer, in gewissem Umfang wieder Terrorversicherungen auf rein privatwirtschaftlicher Basis anzubieten, so dass das Angebot von Extremus im Jahre 2004 noch schwächer angenommen wurde als 2003. Zwar kam es zu etwa gleich vielen Vertragsabschlüssen, doch sank das Prämienvolumen durch den Fortfall wenn auch nur weniger Großkunden auf unter 80 Mio. € ab.

---

[7] Die Bilanzen 2002 und 2003 schlossen insgesamt mit einem Verlust von 2,5 Mio. € ab, der dem Organisationsfonds entnommen wurde.

Extremus reagierte auf diese Entwicklung, indem die Haftung von 13 Mrd. € auf 10 Mrd. € unterjährig gesenkt wurde.[8] Damit ging eine Reduzierung der Rückversicherungsprämien einher, eine erneute Existenzgefährdung konnte in 2004 deshalb verhindert werden.

Jüngste Konditionsverbesserungen seitens der Rückversicherer gewährleisten über das Jahr 2004 hinaus ein stabiles und zuverlässiges Terrorversicherungsangebot auch für Zeiten geringer Nachfrage. Um das Angebot an die sich wandelnde Nachfrage anzupassen, hat Extremus überdies die bislang starre Regelung der Selbstbehalte[9] gelockert. Unternehmen mit entsprechend hoher Finanzkraft können ab 2005 größere Teile des Terrorrisikos selbst tragen und hierfür Versicherungsprämie einsparen. Dieses Angebot stößt auf großes Interesse.

5 Zur Zukunft der Terrorversicherung

Angesichts der zunehmenden Spannungen in der Welt ist die Wahrscheinlichkeit nicht groß, dass die Terrorgefahr anhaltend abnimmt und die Versicherungswirtschaft sich auf Dauer wieder in die Lage versetzt sieht, das Terrorrisiko in voller Höhe allein und ohne staatliche Mitwirkung zu tragen. Die Terrorgefahr gehört zu den politischen Risiken, die allesamt grundsätzlich als nicht versicherbar gelten, und man muss sich eher die Frage stellen, wieso deren Sonderstellung bis zum Jahr 2001 möglich war.

Der vorstehenden Aussage steht nicht entgegen, dass es Perioden geben mag, in denen eine Rückkehr zu rein privatwirtschaftlichen Deckungen möglich erscheint. Diese Deckungen bleiben indessen volatil; sie werden bei erhöhtem Terrorrisiko so schnell vom Markt verschwinden, wie sie gekommen sind.

Einer Ausweitung privatwirtschaftlicher Terrordeckungen stehen auch die weltweit immer schärferen gesetzlichen Anforderungen an das Risikomanagement, an die Solvabilität von Versicherungsunternehmungen und an die Eigenkapitalunterlegung von risikoreicheren Geschäften entgegen. Hinzu kommen externe

---

[8] Ab 1. März 2004 beträgt die privatwirtschaftlich gewährte Rückdeckung 2 anstatt wie bisher 3 Mrd. €, der Staat haftet anschließend mit 8 Mrd. € (bisher 10 Mrd. €).

[9] Zurzeit beträgt der Selbstbehalt des Versicherungsnehmers 1% der so genannten Jahreshöchstentschädigung. Dieser Wert wird vom Versicherungsnehmer frei gewählt; er liegt oft unter der Versicherungssumme, insbesondere dann, wenn ein Versicherungsnehmer mehrere Risiken versichert, er aber nur mit einem Anschlag auf ein Risiko rechnet. Nach oben ist die Jahreshöchstentschädigung auf 1,5 Mrd. € je Versicherungsnehmer begrenzt, weshalb bislang keine Selbstbeteiligungen in größerer Höhe als 15 Mio. € wählbar waren.

Bewertungen von Versicherungsunternehmungen durch Ratingagenturen sowie durch die Kapitalmärkte, die dazu neigen, eine hohe Risikoexponierung bei der Terrorgefahr negativ zu bewerten.

Nach alledem wird eine Zusammenarbeit von Staat und Versicherungswirtschaft am Rande der Unversicherbarkeit von Risiken[10] weiterhin erforderlich sein. Zwar wird eine solche Zusammenarbeit von etlichen Nationalökonomen als Eingriff in einen Markt gesehen, der sich dadurch nicht richtig entwickeln kann, was zwangsläufig Fehlallokationen zur Folge hat. Ein auch nur temporärer Versicherungsnotstand kann hingegen noch größere Nachteile für die Volkswirtschaft eines Staates zur Folge haben, weshalb letztlich doch die Zusammenarbeit als kleineres Übel gesehen wird. Speziell in Bezug auf das Terrorrisiko ist deshalb zu beobachten, dass Regierungen in der Regel nur einer temporären Zusammenarbeit zugestimmt haben, diese aber im Regelfall langfristig anhält.[11]

6 Terrorbekämpfung durch Terrorversicherung?

In nahezu allen Versicherungszweigen beschränkt sich die Versicherungswirtschaft nicht auf die Gewährung von Versicherungsschutz. Vielmehr bringt sie ihre Erfahrungen aus Schadenfällen ein, um hieraus Maßnahmen zur Schadenverhütung abzuleiten. Als herausragende Ergebnisse auf diesem Gebiet sind die Erkenntnisse der Brandursachen- und der Unfallforschung zu nennen. Die heutigen Standards des Brandschutzes und der Verkehrssicherheit wären ohne die von der Versicherungswirtschaft initiierte Forschung nicht erreicht worden.

Im Bereich der Terrorschäden tut sich die Versicherungswirtschaft ungleich schwerer. Zunächst fehlt es an der wichtigsten Voraussetzung einer effizienten Schadenverhütungsarbeit: einer gewissen Menge und Streuung der Schadenereignisse. Nur hierdurch lassen sich Erkenntnisse von allgemeiner Aussagekraft für etwaige künftige Schadenfälle ableiten. Selbst wenn man dieses Problem negieren wollte, so verbleibt ein anderes. Während die Versicherungswirtschaft bei Schadenfällen im Allgemeinen alles über den Hergang erfährt, pflegen Staaten bei Terroranschlägen die Hintergründe aus ermittlungstechnischen Gründen geheim zu halten. Die Versicherer werden im Regelfall nicht in die Details der Anschläge einbezogen. Dies ist verständlich, es muss jedoch gesagt werden, dass damit den Versicherern auch hierdurch die Grundlage für eine vorbeugende Schadenverhütungsarbeit entzogen wird.

---
[10] Hierunter fällt durchaus nicht nur die Terrorversicherung. Auch bezüglich Naturkatastrophen gibt es in etlichen Staaten solche Kooperationen.
[11] Die spanische Lösung stammt aus dem Jahre 1941.

Mangels hinreichender Erkenntnisse über spezifische Terrorgefährdungen fehlt es der Terrorversicherung an einem wichtigen Regulativ, über den Einfluss auf das Schadengeschehen den Prämienbedarf zu differenzieren und dadurch Versicherungsnehmer durch Prämienanreize für Schaden verhütende Maßnahmen zu interessieren. Zwar werden – schon aus Gründen des Personenschutzes – erhebliche Mittel zum Zwecke des Objektschutzes aufgewandt, doch hat dies bei weitem nicht den unmittelbaren Zusammenhang zum realen Schadengeschehen und zur Prämienkalkulation wie z. B. bei Brandschutzmaßnahmen.

Der eingeschränkte Einblick der Versicherer in das Schadengeschehen unterstreicht, dass letztlich doch meist der Staat Adressat etwaiger Anschläge ist und nur selten ein betroffenes Unternehmen. Dies mag ein Hinweis dafür sein, dass die Mitwirkung des Staates bei der Bereitstellung von Versicherungsschutz nicht nur durch die Grenzen der Leistungsfähigkeit der privaten Versicherungswirtschaft begründet sein könnte, sondern auch dadurch geboten ist, dass hier der Staat das eigentliche Ziel ist und Unternehmen nur mehr oder weniger zufällig ins Visier geraten. Schließlich haben verschiedene Staaten – auch Deutschland – gerade in jüngster Zeit unter Beweis gestellt, dass sie aufgrund ihrer Möglichkeiten und Erfahrungen durchaus im Stande sind, Anschläge zu vereiteln.

Lösung städtischer Krisen

Solutions of Urban Crisis

Bekämpfung von großen Schadensereignissen durch kommunale Sicherheitsbehörden im Rahmen der föderalen Struktur Deutschlands

Gegenwärtige Situation und künftige Erfordernisse

Ursus Fuhrmann

Abteilungsleiter im Deutschen Städtetag Verfassung, Recht und Sicherheit

1 Gegenwärtige Situation

1.1 Verteilung der Kompetenzen für den Katastrophenschutz zwischen Bund und Ländern

Nach der Kompetenzordnung der Bundesrepublik Deutschland gliedert sich der Katastrophenschutz in zwei Teile. Der eine Teil befindet sich als Komponente des Zivilschutzes in der Zuständigkeit des Bundes, während der andere Teil zur originären Kompetenz der deutschen Länder gehört.

Der Katastrophenschutz im Zivilschutz erwächst grundsätzlich nur im Verteidigungsfall zur operativen Aufgabe. Der in der originären Kompetenz der Länder stehende Katastrophenschutz dient der Bekämpfung von Schadensereignissen im Frieden.

Im Hinblick auf die Bekämpfung von Gefahren in einem Verteidigungsfall ist die Struktur des Katastrophenschutzes des Bundes und der Länder dergestalt angelegt, dass der Bund die Einheiten und Einrichtungen des Katastrophenschutzes der Länder um zusätzliche Ressourcen der Gefahrenabwehr ergänzt.

Das bedeutet, dass in einem Verteidigungsfall sowohl die Ressourcen des Katastrophenschutzes des Bundes als auch der Länder zum Einsatz kämen. Andererseits hat es der Bund den Ländern gestattet, seine ergänzenden Ressourcen des Katastrophenschutzes auch zur Bekämpfung von Gefahren im Frieden zu nutzen.

Da der Bund mit Ausnahme des Technischen Hilfswerks über keine eigenen operativen Einheiten verfügt und die Länder selbst keine staatlichen Einheiten des Katastrophenschutzes vorhalten, ist die Hauptlast der operativen Katastrophenbekämpfung der kommunalen Ebene zugewiesen worden.

Auf die kommunale Ebene greift der Bund zu, indem er von seinem Recht Gebrauch macht, den Ländern, denen die kommunale Ebene zugeordnet ist, die Aufgabe des Katastrophenschutzes in einem Verteidigungsfall zur Ausführung zu übertragen; d. h., der Bund hat auf der Basis der Kompetenzordnung der Deutschen Verfassung die Länder beauftragt, die im Verteidigungsfall drohenden Gefahren abzuwehren.

In Deutschland nehmen 323 Kreise und 117 kreisfreie Städte den Katastrophenschutz im Verteidigungsfall wahr. Diesen 440 kommunalen Gebietskörperschaften obliegt zugleich auch die Aufgabe des Katastrophenschutzes im Frieden, denn die Länder haben jenen durch ihre Gesetzgebung diese Aufgabe zugewiesen. Die drei Stadtstaaten in Deutschland, Berlin, Bremen und Hamburg, nehmen den Katastrophenschutz als Komponente des Zivilschutzes des Bundes und den friedensmäßigen Katastrophenschutz als Einheit wahr. Eine Delegation dieser beiden Aufgaben kommt infolge der städtischen Struktur dieser Länder naturgemäß nicht in Betracht.

Dies zur Struktur der Verteilung der Kompetenzen zwischen Bund und Ländern auf dem Gebiet des Katastrophenschutzes.

1.2 Gravierende Mängel aufgrund der Zweigliedrigkeit des Katastrophenschutzes in Deutschland

Die dargestellte Zweigliedrigkeit des Katastrophenschutzes in Deutschland wies im Hinblick auf dessen erforderliche Schlagkraft in der Vergangenheit immer gravierende Mängel auf, die bis zur Gegenwart nicht behoben worden sind. Neue Bedrohungen, wie etwa durch Klimaänderungen bewirkte, Ländergrenzen überschreitende Hochwasser oder ein Land überfordernde Schadensereignisse, wie beispielsweise die Waldbrandkatastrophe auf dem Gebiet des Landes Niedersachsen im Jahre 1975, oder von Terroristen bewirkte Anschläge in den USA bzw. in Spanien, die gemessen an ihrer Dimension durchaus kriegerische Anzeichen zeigen, offenbaren die in Deutschland vorhandenen Mängel der Katastrophenabwehr überdeutlich.

Die wesentlichen, in der Vergangenheit festzustellenden und bis heute fortwirkenden Mängel sind folgende:

- Bund und Länder haben immer – gemessen an ihrem Aufgabenteil im Bereich des Katastrophenschutzes – mögliche Bedrohungen isoliert, d. h. im Wesentlichen unabgestimmt definiert und danach die Finanzierung der Ressourcen für ihren jeweiligen Katastrophenschutz ausgerichtet.

Je mehr sich das Ende des Kalten Krieges abzeichnete, umso mehr fuhr der Bund seine Ausgaben für den Zivilschutz zurück. Während im Jahre 1990 diese Ausgaben noch 940 Mio. DM oder ca. 470 Mio. € betrugen, wurden im Jahre 2001 nur noch 335 Mio. DM oder ca. 167,5 Mio. € aufgebracht. Dies ist eine Verringerung der Finanzierung um etwa 65 %. Im Zuge der Verringerung seiner Finanzierung löste der Bund die von ihm unterhaltenen Zentralwerkstätten zur Reparatur von Fahrzeugen und Gerät des ergänzenden Katastrophenschutzes auf, stellte die Finanzierung von Maßnahmen zur Unterrichtung der Bevölkerung im Selbstschutz ein, gab 160 Hilfskrankenhäuser mit ca. 80.000 Betten auf, beseitigte Lager für die Bevorratung von Sanitätsmitteln, stellte die Ausbildung der Bevölkerung in Erster Hilfe ein, schaltete das bundesweit bestehende Sirenennetz ab, reduzierte die Ausstattung des ergänzenden Katastrophenschutzes und die Zahl der ehrenamtlichen Kräfte in den Einheiten des Katastrophenschutzes, löste seine Schulen für die Ausbildung der ehrenamtlichen Kräfte in den Einheiten des Katastrophenschutzes auf Länderebene auf, verzichtete bei vorhandenem Wohlwollen der Länder auf einheitliche Dienstvorschriften der Führung des Katastrophenschutzes und schloss das von ihm unterhaltene Bundesamt für Zivilschutz.

Begründet wurden alle diese Maßnahmen, wie im begleitenden Text zur Novelle des Zivilschutzgesetzes im Jahre 1997 nachzulesen ist, mit folgendem Satz: „Der Zivilschutz muss nicht mehr in der Lage sein, praktisch aus dem Stand alle Kräfte des Staates zur Abwehr einer existenzbedrohenden Aggression zu mobilisieren". Daraus wurde mit Blick auf mögliche Bedrohungen Folgendes abgeleitet:

> Es muss nur noch von punktuellen Schadensereignissen ausgegangen werden; es ist insbesondere nicht mehr mit großflächigen Zerstörungen der Infrastruktur zu rechnen, die Kräfte zur Abwehr von Gefahren können sich darauf einstellen, dass sie nur noch mit ausreichendem zeitlichem Vorlauf ihre volle Leistungsfähigkeit erreichen müssen, so dass Planungen und die Bevorratung von Sonderressourcen eingestellt werden können.

- Die Länder haben in der Vergangenheit – und dies wirkt angesichts ihrer prekären Finanzlage weiterhin nach – die ihren friedensmäßigen Katastrophenschutz ergänzenden Ressourcen des Bundes immer gerne angenommen, um sie auch bei Schadensereignissen im Frieden einzusetzen. D. h., sie haben auf die Anschaffung eigener Ressourcen insoweit verzichtet und konnten somit eigenes Geld einsparen. So haben sie beispielsweise vom Bund zum Zwecke des Brandschutzes beschaffte Fahrzeuge den zu ihrem

Kompetenzbereich gehörenden Freiwilligen Feuerwehren überlassen. Weitere, vergleichbare Beispiele könnten angeführt werden. Die Beschaffungen von Fahrzeugen und Gerät sowie die Ausrichtung des Personalkörpers der Einheiten der Gefahrenabwehr der Länder orientierten und orientieren sich weitgehend immer noch an der Bewältigung von Großbränden und der Versorgung von 50 Verletzten. Das Szenario ist hier das Busunglück.

Wie bereits zuvor angedeutet, nahmen die Länder wohlwollend den Verzicht des Bundes auf eine einheitliche Dienstvorschrift für die Führung der Einheiten des Katastrophenschutzes auf – mit der Folge, dass die meisten Länder eigene Führungsvorschriften und -konzepte entwickelten und dabei auch unterschiedliche Begriffe verwendeten. Ein derartiger Separatismus oder – man kann auch sagen – Provinzialismus muss naturgemäß dazu führen, dass aus mehreren Teilen Deutschlands bei länderübergreifenden oder ein Land überfordernden Großschadenslagen eingesetzte Führungskräfte sich naturgemäß nur noch eingeschränkt verständigen können. Fehler in der Führung müssen zwangsläufig eintreten.

Die unterschiedlichen Führungsvorschriften und -konzepte der Länder verursachten zudem erhebliche Probleme für die vom Bund unterhaltene Bundesakademie für Notfallvorsorge und Zivilschutz, die die Aufgabe hatte und hat, Ausbildung der Führung des Katastrophenschutzes im Zivilschutz zu betreiben.

- Die von den meisten Ländern bewusst verfolgte Abtrennung des in ihrer Zuständigkeit stehenden Katastrophenschutzes hat darüber hinaus zu erheblichen Unterschieden in der Ausrüstung der Einheiten mit Fahrzeugen und Geräten geführt. Diese Unterschiede, die die Austauschbarkeit solcher Ressourcen behindern, reduzieren die Schlagkraft der Einheiten bei Großschadenslagen, die sich über die Grenzen der Länder hinweg ausbreiten.
- Eine der vollkommen ungelösten Kernfragen im Hinblick auf die Bekämpfung von außergewöhnlichen Schadenslagen ist, dass in Deutschland keine verlässlichen, funktionstüchtigen Strukturen vorhanden sind, die in der Lage wären, im Falle von die Grenzen der Länder überschreitenden oder ein Land überfordernden Schadensereignissen Einheiten des Katastrophenschutzes mit unterschiedlichen Aufgaben der Gefahrenabwehr aus mehreren Ländern gezielt und zeitnah zum Schadensereignis heranzuführen und stabsmäßig zu leiten. Mit anderen Worten: Es existiert in Deutschland kein Stab, der sehr schnell gebildet werden könnte, um den Herausforderungen der erwähnten großen Schadensereignisse begegnen zu können. Deshalb musste in der Vergangenheit, so bei der Waldbrandkatastrophe in Niedersachsen und zuletzt auch beim Hochwasser der Elbe, jeweils die Armee hin-

zugezogen werden, um mit ihren festgefügten Strukturen der Leitung zu helfen. Alleiniger Grund für diesen gravierenden Mangel ist die immer wieder geäußerte Furcht mancher großer Länder, im Besonderen eines süddeutschen Landes, der Bund werde den vorhandenen Mangel in der Stabsarbeit ausfüllen wollen, um seine auf den Verteidigungsfall begrenzte Zuständigkeit des Katastrophenschutzes auf Zuständigkeiten für die Bekämpfung bestimmter, im Frieden auftretender Schadensereignisse zu erweitern, die bislang ausschließlich den Ländern obliegen. Diese Haltung verkennt, dass die Mehrzahl der kleinen Länder in Deutschland für den Fall sie überfordernder großer Schadensereignisse das erforderliche gut ausgebildete Führungspersonal schon aus finanziellen Gründen nicht wird vorhalten können. Schlimmer ist aber noch, das diejenigen, die eine Erweiterung der Bundeskompetenz auf die Bekämpfung von bestimmten großen Schadensereignissen im Frieden befürchten, bisher überhaupt noch keine Alternative entwickelt haben, wie das bestehende Vakuum in der Leitung großer Verbände, die aus Einheiten des Katastrophenschutzes mehrer Länder bestehen, ausgefüllt werden könnte.

- Ein weiteres großes Defizit besteht darin, dass es für den Fall plötzlich im Gebiet einer Katastrophenschutzbehörde örtlich eintretender außergewöhnlicher Schadensereignisse keine fest geplanten und organisierten Strukturen der Zusammenarbeit zwischen örtlichen, d. h. kommunalen Katastrophenschutzbehörden und der staatlichen Polizei gibt. Die staatliche Polizei plant und organisiert die von ihr wahrzunehmenden präventiven und repressiven Maßnahmen des Schutzes vor Gefahren grundsätzlich isoliert von den Maßnahmen der Gefahrenabwehr des Katastrophenschutzes. Dies gilt sogar für mit großem zeitlichen Vorlauf planbare Maßnahmen, die Sicherheit bei großen Veranstaltungen – wie beispielsweise der Fußballweltmeisterschaft 2006 – gewährleisten sollen. Bis zum gegenwärtigen Zeitpunkt ist noch immer keine konkrete Zusammenarbeit zur Abstimmung der Konzepte der Gefahrenabwehr der staatlichen Polizei und der kommunalen Katastrophenschutzbehörden aufgenommen worden.

- Ein in großen Teilen ungelöstes Problem ist nach wie vor die Bewältigung eines Massenanfalls von Verletzten durch eine entsprechende Planung in den Krankhäusern. Vorab ist nochmals kurz zu erwähnen, dass die verschiedenen Gesundheitsreformen in Deutschland zu einem Abbau von ca. 30.000 Betten mit dem dazugehörenden Personal geführt haben. Die jüngste Gesundheitsreform wird nach allen Prognosen zu einer weiteren Schließung zahlreicher Krankenhäuser führen. Erwähnt werden soll auch noch einmal, dass im Rahmen der Reduzierung des Zivilschutzes des Bundes 160 Hilfskrankenhäuser mit ca. 80.000 Betten aufgegeben worden sind. In diesem Kontext ist zugleich zu beachten, dass die Krankenhausplanung der Länder Krankenhäuser unterschiedlicher Versorgungsstufen vorsieht. Zu aller Letzt ist auch noch darauf hinzuweisen, dass in Deutschland täglich nur zwischen 25 und 30 Betten für Brandschwerstverletzte organisierbar sind.

Die geschilderte Situation lässt sehr klar erkennen, dass angesichts bestehender Planungen für die Bewältigung eines Anfalls von 50 Verletzten – orientiert am Busunglück – die Versorgung von Verletzten bis zu einer Zahl von 500 oder gar 1.000 ein gewaltiges Problem sein wird. Eine dafür ausgelegte Alarm- bzw. Organisationsplanung existiert im Krankenhauswesen Deutschlands bislang nicht. Bei der Bewältigung eines Massenanfalls von Verletzten in dem hier in Frage stehenden Umfang, der vor allem von kleineren Ländern alleine nicht beherrschbar wäre, würden die Länder einander zwar helfen, jedoch wäre die Hilfe ungeplant und dementsprechend nicht hinreichend organisiert: Erhebliche zeitliche Verzögerungen in der Zuführung von Verletzten unter Berücksichtigung der Art von Verletzungen zu entsprechend leistungsfähigen Krankenhäusern wären die Folge.

- Im Bereich der Bekämpfung biologischer und chemischer Gefahren existieren Defizite in der Messbarkeit bzw. Aufspürbarkeit solcher Gefahren.

2 Künftige Erfordernisse

Der Deutsche Städtetag, der als größter kommunaler Verband in Deutschland alle Städte als Träger des Katastrophenschutzes unter seinem Dach vereinigt, hat die geschilderten, seit langem bestehenden Defizite immer wieder angemahnt. Die verheerenden Wirkungen der terroristischen Angriffe in New York und Washington vom 11. September 2001 waren für ihn Anlass, mit ausgewiesenen Fachleuten des kommunalen Bereichs ein Konzept zur „Reform des Zivil- und Katastrophenschutzes in der Bundesrepublik Deutschland" mit großem Nachdruck zu erarbeiten. Er legte dieses Konzept Bund und Ländern bereits am 31. März 2002, also exakt ein halbes Jahr nach der Katastrophe in den USA, vor. Er hoffte darauf, dass diese Katastrophe einen nachhaltigen Eindruck auf die führenden Politiker in Bund und Ländern hinterlassen und sie zu einer grundlegenderen Reform des Zivil- und Katastrophenschutzes in Deutschland bewegen würde. Die Reaktion der Politik verlief aber nach dem üblichen Muster, das bereits in der Folge der Waldbrandkatastrophe im Jahr 1975 im Land Niedersachsen und auch bei weiteren vergleichbar großen Schadensereignissen zu beobachten gewesen war. Die staatlichen Einrichtungen der Gefahrenabwehr wurden sehr schnell mittels organisatorischer und finanzieller Maßnahmen gestärkt, während die staatsferneren Einrichtungen der Gefahrenabwehr, d. h. Einrichtungen des kommunalgetragenen Katastrophenschutzes, keine wesentlichen Verbesserungen erfuhren. Anders ausgedrückt: Polizeien und Verfassungsschutz des Bundes und der Länder und insbesondere der im Katastrophenschutz operativ mitwirkende Dienst des Bundes, dieser ist das Technische Hilfswerk des Bundes, wurden personell und technisch enorm verstärkt. Der kommunale Katastrophenschutz erhielt zwar einige Fahrzeuge für die Bereiche der Erkundung atomarer, biologischer und chemischer Gefahren und des Krankentransports zusätzlich, die allein auch noch der Bund zur Verfügung stellte. Gemessen an der Verstärkung der staatlichen Einrichtungen waren dies aber eher unbedeutende Maßnahmen.

Im Ergebnis kann festgestellt werden, dass bis heute, d. h. mehr als drei Jahre nach den Terroranschlägen vom 11. September 2001 in den USA, nur eines der geschilderten Defizite des Katastrophenschutzes in Deutschland behoben worden ist: Bund und Länder haben sich auf die Einführung einheitlicher Dienstvorschriften der Führung des Katastrophenschutzes verständigt.

Diese Führungsvorschriften sind aber noch nicht in allen Ländern verbindlich eingeführt worden. Dort, wo sie eingeführt wurden, sind bereits wieder Abweichungen bei den verwendeten Begriffen feststellbar. Erkenntnisse eines Konfuzius zum Sprachgebrauch, der immerhin vor ca. 2.500 Jahren gelebt hat und dessen Lehren nach wie vor aktuell sind, finden infolge eines eigentümlichen Staatsverständnisses mancher Länder keine Berücksichtigung.

Konfuzius wurde von seinen Schülern einmal gefragt, was er für das Wichtigste in einem Staatswesen halte. Konfuzius antwortete schlicht:

> Das Wichtigste in einem Staatswesen ist es, den Sprachgebrauch zu verbessern. Denn wenn die Menschen die Begriffe, die sie verwenden, nicht verstehen, verstehen sie sich nicht. Wenn sie sich nicht verstehen, gedeihen die Werke nicht. Wenn die Werke nicht gedeihen, gedeihen Justiz und Moral nicht.

Also, so seine Schlussfolgerung: Das Wichtigste in einem Staatswesen sei es, den Sprachgebrauch zu verbessern.

Neben der nunmehr realisierten Forderung der deutschen Städte, einheitliche Dienstvorschriften für die Führung des Katastrophenschutzes zu erlassen, sind in dem Reformkonzept des Deutschen Städtetages noch folgende weitere, grundlegende Forderungen erhoben worden:

1. Die bisherige faktische Trennung zwischen dem Katastrophenschutz als Teil des Zivilschutzes des Bundes und dem Katastrophenschutz der Länder muss

überwunden werden. Die Aufgabe des Katastrophenschutzes ist zukünftig von allen in Frage kommenden Stellen ganzheitlich wahrzunehmen. Überörtliche, überregionale und bundesweite Hilfe ist in dem erforderlichen Umfang zu leisten.

2. Entsprechend der im Grundgesetz vorgesehenen Aufteilung der Kompetenzen und Aufgaben des Katastrophenschutzes sind Planung und Durchführung des Katastrophenschutzes grundsätzlich dreistufig aufzubauen und auch hinreichend sicher und kontinuierlich zu finanzieren, nämlich auf der kommunalen Ebene, der Ebene der Länder und der des Bundes. Der Aufbau des Katastrophenschutzes muss aber durch die drei Ebenen verzahnt erfolgen.

- Die kommunale Ebene hat die alltägliche lokale Gefahrenbekämpfung bis hin zur überörtlichen Unterstützung, d. h. zur Unterstützung benachbarter kommunaler Gebietskörperschaften, sicherzustellen. Hierfür sind insbesondere den örtlichen Gegebenheiten entsprechend leistungsfähige Feuerwehren und Rettungsdienste einzurichten und zu unterhalten.
- Den Ländern obliegt die Sicherstellung der Gefahrenbekämpfung für ihr Gebiet bis hin zur Hilfeleistung bei großen Schadenslagen, die sich über die Landesgrenzen hinweg auswirken. Hierfür haben die Länder den kommunalen Gebietskörperschaften ergänzende Komponenten des Katastrophenschutzes zur Verfügung zu stellen und gegebenenfalls auf Landesebene Spezialeinheiten zum überregionalen Einsatz einzurichten.
- Der Bund hat demgegenüber die Bekämpfung von solchen großen Schadenslagen sicherzustellen, mit denen ein Land überfordert ist oder von denen mehrere Länder betroffen sind, sofern die Ursachen der Gefahrenbekämpfung kriegerische Handlungen oder terroristische Anschläge sind. Hierfür hat der Bund den Ländern und den Gemeinden als Trägern des Katastrophenschutzes die erforderlichen Komponenten zur Verstärkung des Katastrophenschutzes zu leisten.

3. Die Organisation und Ausstattung des Katastrophenschutzes muss die vorhandenen, im Bundesgebiet unterschiedlich verteilten Gefahrenpotenziale berücksichtigen. Das Gebiet der Bundesrepublik Deutschland ist einer Gefährdungsanalyse oder -abschätzung zu unterziehen und sollte in drei Risikokategorien aufgeteilt werden. Dabei sollte der Grundsatz anerkannt werden, dass die größten Risiken dort bestehen, wo die meisten Menschen leben. Für die Gefahrenanalyse ist ein einheitliches Planungsinstrumentarium zu entwickeln und einzusetzen.

Die Risikokategorien sollten nach folgender Grundstruktur ausgerichtet werden:

- Die Risikokategorie I sollten Städte oder Ballungsräume mit mehr als 1 Mio. Personen bilden, zu denen Einwohner und auch Pendler zu rechnen sind, und die internationale Bedeutung als Handels-, Industrie- und Wirtschaftsstandort oder Verkehrsknotenpunkt haben.
- Als Risikokategorie II kämen Städte oder Ballungsräume mit 500.000 bis 1 Mio. Personen (Einwohner und Pendler) mit besonderen industriellen oder verkehrstechnischen Risiken in Betracht.
- Unter der Risikokategorie III wären Städte oder Ballungsräume von 100.000 bis 500.000 Personen (Einwohner und Pendler) mit geringen industriellen oder verkehrstechnischen Risiken und Landkreise auszuweisen.

Die Verteilung der Ressourcen des Zivil-/Katastrophenschutzes hat sich dann neben einer Ausstattung aller Risikokategorien mit Standardkomponenten eines Grundschutzes an den speziellen Bedarfen der jeweiligen Risikokategorie zu orientieren.

Die Strukturen müssen so gegliedert werden, dass spezielle Einheiten, d. h. Spezialeinsatzgruppen oder „Task Forces", nur in den Risikokategorien I oder II vorgehalten werden, jedoch in allen Bereichen der Gefahrenabwehr eingesetzt werden können.

Zivil- und Katastrophenschutz sind daher zukünftig aufeinander abgestimmt in der Art zu konzipieren, dass ein flächendeckender Grundschutz sichergestellt wird, der unter Berücksichtigung von Risikoschwerpunkten in den Ballungszentren und Großstädten durch einen bundesweit einsetzbaren Spezialschutz ergänzt wird.

Konkret bedeutet dies, dass der Bund den Ländern im Rahmen seiner Kompetenz einerseits zum Grundschutz erforderliche Standardkomponenten und andererseits zum besonderen Schutz erforderliche Spezialkomponenten zuweist. Mit der Weiterverteilung der Komponenten an die kommunalen Gebietskörperschaften entsprechend der sie betreffenden Risikokategorie sind diese zum bundesweit möglichen Einsatz verpflichtet.

4. Die Ausstattung des Katastrophenschutzes ist zu modernisieren und an den tatsächlichen Bedarf anzupassen. Dazu gehört insbesondere Folgendes:
   - Der Brandschutz ist mit neuen, bereits auf dem Markt vorhandenen Wasserfördersystemen, die gegenüber den herkömmlichen Systemen sehr viel größere Wassermengen fördern können, auszustatten.
   - Die Einheiten, die der Bekämpfung von atomaren, biologischen und chemischen Gefahren dienen, sind mit Messleitfahrzeugen und hochwertigen Mess- und Analysegeräten zu versorgen. Darüber hinaus müssen

sie auch mit den erforderlichen Komponenten der Dekontaminierung ausgestattet werden.

- Der Sanitätsdienst des Katastrophenschutzes muss enger mit dem Rettungsdienst, der der täglichen medizinischen Versorgung akut erkrankter oder verletzter Personen im Vorfeld der Krankenhäuser dient, verzahnt werden.

5. Zur Verbesserung der Führung des Katastrophenschutzes sind professionell besetzte, mobile Stäbe für besondere, große Schadenslagen aufzustellen, die auf Anforderung der örtlichen Leitung des Katastrophenschutzes zum Einsatz gelangen können. Angesichts der Mehrzahl kleiner Länder in Deutschland, die für den Fall besonders großer Schadenslagen infolge des Fehlens einer hinreichenden Zahl professionell ausgebildeter Führungskräfte nicht noch zusätzlich einen mobilen Stab aufstellen können, sollten sich mehrere Länder zur Einrichtung eines solches Stabes zusammenschließen.

6. Der in kommunaler Trägerschaft befindliche Katastrophenschutz muss an Erkenntnissen zur Sicherheitslage der für den präventiven Gefahrenschutz zuständigen staatlichen Behörden – dies sind Polizei und Verfassungsschutz – zeitnah teilhaben, damit er seine der Gefahrenabwehr dienende Aufbauorganisation rechtzeitig auf nahe liegende Schadensszenarien einrichten kann. Der kommunale Bereich muss immer wieder feststellen, dass sich die staatlichen Dienste lieber mit sich und ihrer Aufgabenstellung beschäftigen als eine kontinuierliche Zusammenarbeit mit den kommunalen Katastrophenschutzbehörden zu pflegen. Die gegenwärtig laufenden Maßnahmen zur Gewährleistung der erforderlichen Sicherheit im Rahmen der Fußballweltmeisterschaft 2006 bestätigen diesen Befund.

7. In Deutschland muss angesichts seiner föderalen Struktur zumindest für die Bewältigung großer Schadenslagen, die ein Land überfordern oder die sich auf mehrere Länder auswirken, eine Stelle verlässlich eingerichtet werden, die die Logistik und Leitung zur Bewältigung solcher Schadensereignisse verbindlich übernimmt. Ob diese Stelle mit Zustimmung der Länder beim Bund angesiedelt wird oder ob die Länder diese Stelle etwa durch Staatsvertrag selbst einrichten, ist eine nachrangige Frage. Wichtig ist nur, dass sie tatsächlich geschaffen wird. Allerdings lehrt die Erfahrung, dass die Länder weder politisch noch finanziell die Kraft aufbringen werden, eine solche Stelle gemeinsam kontinuierlich zu unterhalten und sie mit den notwendigen Rechten zur Bewältigung der in Frage stehenden großen Schadensereignisse auszustatten.

3 Schlussbemerkung

Die im Konzept zur Reform des Zivil- und Katastrophenschutzes in Deutschland von kommunaler Seite aufgestellten Forderungen sind von Bund und Ländern als richtig anerkannt worden. Dieser Prozess hat ca. zwei Jahre gedauert. Bis auf eine Forderung, nämlich die Einführung einheitlicher Dienstvorschriften für die Führung des Katastrophenschutzes, sind drei Jahre nach den Anschlägen in den USA keine weiteren Forderungen realisiert worden. Im Bereich der staatlichen Dienste erfolgten erhebliche Verstärkungen. Die staatsferneren kommunalen Einrichtungen des Katastrophenschutzes sind, gemessen an dem Potenzial, das den Staatsdiensten zur Verfügung gestellt wurde, bislang stiefmütterlich behandelt worden. Die Länder haben sich schwer damit getan, begreifen zu müssen, dass der Bund seine Unterstützung des Katastrophenschutzes der Länder, die zuvor alle 440 kommunalen Katastrophenschutzbehörden gleichermaßen bediente, in eine an Gefahrenschwerpunkten orientierte Unterstützung umstellen will. Dies bedeutet zugleich, dass die Länder zusätzliches Geld werden aufbringen müssen, um die erforderliche Sicherheit in Deutschland zu gewährleisten. Dies entspricht andererseits aber auch ihrer originären Kompetenz für den Katastrophenschutz bei Schadenslagen im Frieden. Die drei Jahre andauernde Verzögerung notwendiger Reformen des Katastrophenschutzes resultiert in erster Linie aus dem von den Ländern initiierten Streit darüber, wer was bezahlt.

Jedermann weiß, dass mehr Sicherheit nicht zum Nulltarif zu haben ist. Mehr Sicherheit kostet mehr Geld.

Einsatzkonzept ÜMANV – „MANV überörtlich"
Organisation rettungsdienstlicher Großschadenslagen in Nordrhein-Westfalen

Dr. Jörg Schmidt

Berufsfeuerwehr, Amt für Feuerschutz, Rettungsdienst und Bevölkerungsschutz
Scheibenstraße 13, 50737 Köln

Die neue Bedrohung durch terroristische Anschläge hat die Berufsfeuerwehr Köln veranlasst, zusammen mit mehreren rheinischen Städten und Kreisen ein Konzept zur gegenseitigen Unterstützung bei Schadensfällen von bis 1.000 Verletzten aufzustellen und umzusetzen.

Der Massenanfall von Verletzten (MANV) ist gekennzeichnet durch einen Ressourcenmangel über einen unklaren Zeitraum. In Nordrhein-Westfalen sind durch die Arbeitsgemeinschaft der Leiter der Berufsfeuerwehren (AGBF) und die Hilfsorganisationen in den vergangenen 15 Jahren Konzepte zur Versorgung von 50 Patienten entwickelt worden (MANV 50 = Reisebusunfall).

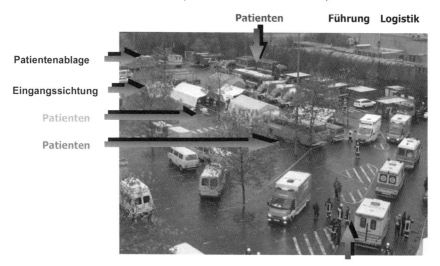

Abbildung 1: Behandlungsplatz in Nordrhein-Westfalen (Beispiel Köln)

Diese Konzepte fußen auf einer Bündelung der (Behandlungs-)Ressourcen, einer Aufgabenpriorisierung (d. h. Patientensichtung) und einer Pufferung des Patientenflusses. Im Ergebnis erhält man ein Dreistufenmodell aus Patientenablage, Behandlungsplatz und Patientenverteilung. Die Patientenablage ist Schnittstelle zur technischen Rettung aus dem Schadensort und erster Puffer durch lebensrettende Sofortmaßnahmen, der anschließende Behandlungsplatz die Bündelung der Behandlungsressourcen zur weiteren Pufferung. Sichtungen unterschiedlicher Qualität finden an den jeweiligen Ein- und Ausgängen statt. Dieses System für 50 Patienten ist in Nordrhein-Westfalen weit verbreitet und einsatzprobt.

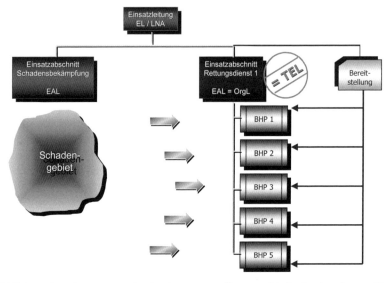

Abbildung 2: *Führungsorganisation im Konzept ÜMANV (bis fünf Behandlungsplätze)*

Im Konzept ÜMANV werden die Komponenten der beteiligten Kreise und Städte zusammengeführt. Dazu werden Leistungen standardisiert, die angefordert werden können (Erstversorgung, Behandlung, Transport) – die technische Ausgestaltung ist örtlich unterschiedlich und wird nicht angetastet. Die Leistung Erstversorgung umfasst drei Rettungsmittel und einen Notarzt, die Leistung Transport variiert, verfügt jedoch über ein genormtes Anforderungsverfahren. Behandlungsplätze sind die größte Leistung und werden als autarke unteilbare Einheit entsandt und zusammen mit vor Ort zugewiesenen Patientenablagen und Transportmitteln über den mitentsandten Verbandsführer geführt (= taktische Einheit Behandlungsplatz). Sie bekommen durch die örtliche Einsatzleitung einen festen Einsatzabschnitt zugewiesen und versorgen auf max. 2.000 m² mindestens 50 Patienten in 60 bis 90 Minuten. Nur die limitierten Klinikkapazitäten für akut Lebensbedrohte werden zentral durch die Einsatzleitung verteilt, alle anderen Patienten werden durch die Behandlungsplätze in die Umgebung, vorzugsweise das eigene Kreisgebiet, verteilt.

Das Konzept konnte in zwei Übungen mit 150 und 250 Patienten erfolgreich erprobt werden.

Optimierungsbedarf ergibt sich noch in der Verteilung der akut Lebensbedrohten sowie dem Führen und der notwendigen Logistik bei diesen Großeinsätzen: Heranführung von Marschverbänden und Rettungsmitteln über Sammelplätze und Bereitstellungsräume, Routenvergaben an Rettungstransporte sowie Zuteilung von Klinikressourcen und frühzeitigen Transportmitteln. Die Projektgruppe der rheinischen Städte und Kreise setzt ihre Arbeit zusammen mit der Akademie für Krisenmanagement, Notfallplanung und Zivilschutz (AKNZ) fort.

Sicherheitsmaßnahmen in unterirdischen Verkehrsanlagen

Peer Rechenbach

Am Beedenkamp 2, 22559 Hamburg
rechenbach@t-online.de

Der internationale Wandel der Gesellschaften hat in den vergangenen Jahrzehnten auch zu einer ständigen Zunahme von terroristischen Anschlägen geführt. Mit dem Auftreten der Selbstmordattentäter ist vor ca. 20 Jahren eine neue Dimension im Terrorismus entstanden. Täter und Tätergruppen, die aufgrund extremer fanatischer Anschauungen das Leben unbeteiligter Menschen als Ziel auswählen und dabei auch das eigene Leben bereitwillig opfern, sind besonders gefährlich und verursachen, wie wir an vielen Beispielen erfahren mussten, erhebliche Wirkungen.

Wesentliche Ziele der international agierenden Terroristen sind:

- Destabilisierung der Gesellschaft durch die Verbreitung von Angst und Schrecken,
- Erzeugung von fatalen Wirkungen mit möglichst hohen Opferzahlen,
- Nutzung international bedeutsamer Objekte oder Ereignisse.

Aus den Erfahrungen der vergangenen Jahre erkennen wir, dass auch unterirdische Verkehrsanlagen als Ziel von Terroristen, Kriminellen und Psychopathen ausgewählt wurden. Die folgende exemplarische Übersicht zeigt die fatalen Wirkungen:

- 8. Januar 1977, Moskau: Explosion mit sieben Toten;
- 19. März 1994, Baku: Explosion mit 13 Toten und über 50 verletzten Personen;
- 3. Mai 1994, Baku: Explosion und Brand mit sieben Toten und über zehn verletzten Personen;
- 20. März 1995, Tokio: Anschlag mit dem Nervengas Sarin durch die Aum-Sekte mit zwölf Toten und über 3.800 verletzten Personen;

- 25. Juli 1995, Paris: Explosion mit acht Toten und über 100 verletzten Personen.

Neben diesen Terroranschlägen wird beispielhaft auch auf Schadenereignisse infolge technischer Mängel (Brand in der U-Bahnstation King's Cross 1987 in London mit 31 Toten) oder der Brandstiftung eines Psychopathen (Brand zweier U-Bahnzüge in Südkorea mit 198 Toten) hingewiesen. Dabei wird deutlich, welche fatalen Wirkungen bei Schadenereignissen in unterirdischen Verkehrsanlagen eintreten können.

In nahezu allen Ballungsräumen und Großstädten sind unterirdische Verkehrsanlagen und umfangreiche unterirdische Ver- und Entsorgungseinrichtungen vorhanden. Folgende Differenzierungen zeigen die Nutzungsvarianten und die damit verbundene Infrastruktur auf:

- Straßentunnelanlagen im innerstädtischen Verkehr;
- Straßentunnelanlagen im Fernverkehr;
- Tunnelanlagen für den schienengebundenen öffentlichen Personennahverkehr;
- Fußgängertunnelanlagen;
- Verkaufsstellen in unterirdischen Verkehrstunnelanlagen.

Dabei sind auch unterschiedliche Kombinationen in mehreren miteinander verbundenen Ebenen realisiert worden.

Schadenereignisse, in denen gefährliche chemische Stoffe freigesetzt werden, oder solche infolge von Bränden und Explosionen haben eine hohe Dynamik. Den betroffenen noch handlungsfähigen Menschen bleibt in der Regel nur ein Zeitraum von wenigen Minuten zur Flucht. Andernfalls sind schwere irreversible Gesundheitsschäden oder der Tod zu befürchten. Der Erfolg der Rettungsaktion für die nicht mehr handlungsfähigen Menschen hängt wesentlich von der Leistungsfähigkeit der gefahrenbegrenzenden Anlagen und Einrichtungen ab. Anschläge, bei denen biologische oder radioaktive Kontaminationen ohne initiale Explosion ausgebracht werden, haben in der Regel eine niedrigere Dynamik, weil die gesundheitlichen Schäden erst zeitlich verzögert eintreten. Bei diesen Terroranschlägen steht für die Rettung und notfallmedizinische Versorgung mehr Zeit zur Verfügung.

Terroranschläge lösen grundsätzlich folgende Effekte – auch in Kombination – aus:

- Betriebsstörung,

- Brand,
- Rauchausbreitung,
- Wassereinbruch,
- Explosion,
- Freisetzung gefährlicher chemischer, biologischer oder radioaktiver Stoffe.

Diese Effekte verursachen insbesondere folgende Wirkungen:

- temporäre Schäden an Anlagen und Einrichtungen,
- irreversible Schäden an Anlagen und Einrichtungen,
- Unruhe bei den beteiligten/betroffenen Menschen,
- unkontrolliertes Handeln der betroffenen Menschen,
- Fluchtreaktionen,
- Panikreaktionen,
- Kontamination mit chemischen, biologischen oder radioaktiven gefährlichen Stoffen,
- akute Vergiftung durch Rachgase oder sonstige toxische chemische Stoffe,
- akute mechanische Verletzungen.

Unabhängig von den genannten Gefahren durch technische Störungen, kriminelle Handlungen oder Terroranschläge hat jeder Betreiber (öffentliche oder gewerbliche Einrichtungen) einer unterirdischen Verkehrsanlage insbesondere folgende Ziele oder Pflichten:

- Die verschiedenen Nutzergruppen (Kunden, Fahrgäste, Kraftfahrer und dergleichen) sollen sich in der unterirdische Verkehrsanlage sicher fühlen.
- Die Benutzergruppen sollen die Anlage weiterhin (intensiv) nutzen.
- Unvermeidbare Schadenereignisse dürfen keine nachhaltige Störung der Funktionsfähigkeit verursachen.

Um diese Ziele oder Pflichten zu gewährleisten, werden Gefahrenabwehrmaßnahmen zur Schadenvermeidung bzw. -begrenzung geplant und umgesetzt. Dazu gehören insbesondere folgende Elemente:

- effektives Sicherheitsmanagement,
- Risikoanalysen,
- Identifizierung der Verwundbarkeiten,

- bauliche Sicherheitseinrichtungen und -anlagen,
- betriebliche Sicherheitsmaßnahmen,
- Sicherstellung einer kontinuierlichen Abwehrbereitschaft,
- regelmäßige Sicherheitszirkel mit allen beteiligten Stellen (Anlagenbetreiber, Polizei, Rettungsdienst, Feuerwehr, Katastrophenschutz und dergleichen),
- effektives Krisenmanagement.

Die vorhandenen Sicherheitseinrichtungen dienen in der Regel folgenden Zielen:

- schnelle Identifizierung einer Störung,
- schnelle Information und Aktivierung der zur Rettung oder Störungsbeseitigung erforderlichen Ressourcen,
- Aktivierung automatischer Systeme zur Schadenbekämpfung (z. B. Löschanlagen),
- Aktivierung automatischer Systeme zur Schadensbegrenzung (z. B. Rauchabführung).

Diese beispielhaft genannten Sicherheitseinrichtungen sind grundsätzlich für die wahrscheinlichen Störfälle ausgelegt. Gezielte Anschläge oder Schadenereignisse, die die Sicherheitseinrichtungen nachhaltig beeinträchtigen (z. B. infolge einer Bombenexplosion), verursachen nicht kalkulierbare Wirkungen.

Auf der Basis einer Schutzzieldefinition müssen in einer Analyse insbesondere folgende Fragen untersucht werden:

- Wo besteht welche Ereigniswahrscheinlichkeit?
- Wo und warum sind räumliche, inhaltliche oder personelle Verwundbarkeiten gegeben?

Auf dieser Basis ist zu untersuchen, welche Maßnahmen ergriffen werden müssen, um das Schutzziel zu erreichen, und welche Personen, Personengruppen, Anlagen, Einrichtungen oder Prozesse vor Verlust, Ausfall oder Beschädigung nachhaltig geschützt werden, damit die jeweilige negative Wirkung minimiert wird.

Bei der Beurteilung der Eintrittswahrscheinlichkeit werden folgende Differenzierungen diskutiert:

- *sehr hoch*: Das Ereignis kann jederzeit eintreten und hat sich vielfach ereignet (z. B. Person verunglückt, Kraftfahrzeugunfall);

- *wahrscheinlich*: Der Eintritt ist zu erwarten und ist mehrfach aufgetreten (z. B. Brand);
- *gelegentlich*: Mit dem Eintreten ist zu rechnen (z. B. Ausfall der Energieversorgung);
- *denkbar*: Mit dem Eintreten des Ereignisses ist grundsätzlich nicht zu rechnen, es ist jedoch nicht auszuschließen (z. B. Wassereinbruch);
- *unvorstellbar*: Der Eintritt ist extrem unwahrscheinlich und noch nicht vorgekommen.

Dabei ist anzumerken, dass die Ereignisse am 11. September 2001 bis zu diesem Zeitpunkt als unvorstellbar eingestuft worden wären.

Bei der Umsetzung eines effektiven Sicherheitsmanagements sind insbesondere die verschiedenen Handlungsfelder, wie z. B.

- Betriebspersonal,
- Kooperationsnetzwerke,
- Benutzer/Gäste,
- Kommunikation,
- Sicherheitstechnik,
- passive Schutzmaßnahmen,
- technische Sicherheit,
- Training/Übung sowie
- organisatorische Maßnahmen,

dahingehend zu untersuchen, wo und wie die effektivste Steuerung erfolgen kann. Weiterhin ist regelmäßig im gesamten Kontext zu analysieren, ob die Funktionalität tatsächlich noch gegeben ist.

Mit der erfolgreichen Realisierung eines Sicherheitsmanagements sind die wesentlichen Bedingungen erfüllt, um Schadensfälle zu vermeiden bzw. die Wirkungen zu begrenzen. Für die Bewältigung eines tatsächlich eingetretenen Ereignisses muss jedoch zusätzlich ein effektives Krisenmanagement vorbereitet sein. Dabei müssen insbesondere vorbereitete trainierte Handlungsabläufe abrufbar sein. Diese Handlungsabläufe müssen sich weitgehend an den vorhandenen Standardprozessen orientieren, weil nur so gewährleistet wird, dass die Mitarbeiter auch in Krisen richtig handeln. Die Handlungsprozesse müssen redundant ausgelegt sein, weil im Falle des Ereignisses höchstwahrscheinlich einzelne Funktionselemente (z. B. Kommunikationswege) ausfallen werden.

Grundsätzlich ist im Krisenfall davon auszugehen, dass

- ein Informationsdefizit,
- ein Handlungsschock,
- ein Kontrollverlust sowie
- ein erheblicher Druck seitens der Medien und der Angehörigen der Opfer

gegeben sind. Die Erfahrung lehrt, dass individuell zu entwickelnde Reaktionsmechanismen eines trainierten Krisenmanagements frühestens nach ca. vier Stunden etabliert werden können. Das Krisenmanagement muss durch entsprechend etablierte Handlungsanweisungen sicherstellen, dass im Zeitraum, bis individuelle Anweisungen greifen können, eine sachgerechte Aufgabenwahrnehmung weitgehend gesichert ist. Dabei muss gewährleistet sein, dass alle Schnittstellen harmonisiert sind.

Das Krisenmanagement muss im Ereignisfall auf der Basis unzureichender Informationen, unter erheblichem Zeitdruck und angesichts fehlenden Ressourcen Entscheidungen treffen, die immer auch erhebliche Nachteile für bestimmte Bereiche verursachen.

Autorinnen und Autoren / Contributors

Dr. Rudolf Adam

Dr. Rudolf Adam ist seit April 2004 Präsident der Bundesakademie für Sicherheitspolitik in Berlin. Er war zuvor in verschiedenen Positionen für das Auswärtige Amt tätig und in den Jahren 2001 bis 2004 Vizepräsident des Bundesnachrichtendienstes.

Dr. Rudolf Adam has been president of the Bundesakademie für Sicherheitspolitik, Berlin. Before, he worked for the German State Department in different positions, and was vice-president of the Federal Intelligence Service between 2001 and 2004.

Col. Eithan Azani

Colonel Eithan Azani ist Mitarbeiter des International Policy Institute for Counter-Terrorism (ICT) am Interdisciplinary Center (IDC) in Herzliya, Israel.

Colonel Eithan Azani is a member of the International Policy Institute for Counter-Terrorism (ICT) at the Interdisciplinary Center (IDC) in Herzliya, Israel.

Daniel Bircher

Daniel Bircher arbeitet seit 1996 bei Ernst Basler + Partner AG als Leiter des Tätigkeitsfelds Risikomanagement und Informationssicherheit. Er ist Beirat der Stiftung InfoSurance und Mitglied des International Institute for Strategic Studies (IISS).

Daniel Bircher has been working for Ernst Basler + Partner AG as head of risk management and information security since 1996. He is an adviser to the InfoSurance foundation and member of the International Institute for Strategic Studies (IISS).

Michael E. G. Chandler

Michael E. G. Chandler ist Inhaber des Risks Management Solutions (RMS) Visiting Fellowship am Institute for Defence and Strategic Studies in Singapur. Er ist zudem Mitglied des International Advisory Council am International Policy Institute for Counter-Terrorism (ICT) in Herzliya, Israel.

Daniel Bircher has been working for Ernst Basler + Partner AG as head of risk management and information security since 1996. He is an adviser to the InfoSurance foundation and member of the International Institute for Strategic Studies (IISS).

Prof. Dr. Martin van Creveld

Prof. Dr. Martin van Creveld ist Professor für Geschichte an der Hebräischen Universität in Jerusalem. Darüber hinaus ist er als militärischer Berater und Referent tätig.

Prof. Dr. Martin van Creveld is Professor of History at Hebrew University, Jerusalem. In addition, he works as military adviser and lecturer.

Dr. Martin Dudziak

Dr. Martin Dudziak ist Gründer und Managing Director der TETRAD i3 Inc., Florida, USA.

Dr. Martin Dudziak ist founder und Managing Director of TETRAD i3 Inc., Florida, USA.

Ursus Fuhrmann

Ursus Fuhrmann ist Abteilungsleiter für Verfassung, Recht und Sicherheit beim Deutschen Städtetag in Köln.

Ursus Fuhrmann is head of the department of constitution, law and security at Deutscher Städtetag, Cologne.

Boaz Ganor, PhD

Dr. Boaz Ganor ist Direktor des International Policy Institute for Counter-Terrorism (ICT) am Interdisciplinary Center (IDC) in Herzliya, Israel.

Dr. Boaz Ganor is director of the International Policy Institute for Counter-Terrorism (ICT) at the Interdisciplinary Center (IDC) in Herzliya, Israel.

Dr. Bruno Gas

Dr. Bruno Gas ist seit 2002 Vorstandsvorsitzender der Extremus Versicherungs-AG.

Dr. Bruno Gas has been chairman of the board of directors of Extremus Versicherungs-AG since 2002.

Dr. August Hanning

Dr. August Hanning ist seit 1998 Präsident des Bundesnachrichtendienstes. Zuvor war er in verschiedenen Positionen für das Bundesinnenministerium und das Bundeskanzleramt tätig.

Dr. August Hanning has been president of the Federal Intelligence Service since 1998. Before, he worked for the Federal Ministry of the Interior and the Federal Chancellery in different positions.

Dr. Elisabeth Hauschild

Dr. Elisabeth Hauschild ist Key Account Manager Homeland Security bei der Diehl BGT Defence und hat zuvor die Abteilung Strategie bei der Rheinmetall Defence Electronics geleitet. Sie ist Mitinitiatorin von „Women In International Security Deutschland e.V.", dessen Vorstand sie bis 2004 als Schatzmeisterin angehörte.

Dr. Elisabeth Hauschild is Key Account Manager Homeland Security at Diehl BGT Defence. Before, she was head of the strategy department at Rheinmetall Defence Electronics. She is co-initiator of "Women In International Security Deutschland e.V." and was its treasurer until 2004.

Eric Herren

Eric Herren ist Mitarbeiter und Senior Research Fellow am International Policy Institute for Counter-Terrorism (ICT) in Israel. Er unterrichtet am Supreme Headquarter Allied Powers Europe (SHAPE), der NATO-Schule in Deutschland und am Royal United Services Institute for Defence Studies in England. Darüber hinaus ist er Mitarbeiter am International Institute for Strategic Studies (IISS).

Eric Herren is Senior Research Fellow at the International Policy Institute for Counter-Terrorism (ICT) in Israel. He teaches at the Supreme Headquarter Allied Powers Europe (SHAPE), the NATO-school in Germany and the Royal United Services Institute for Defence Studies in England. Moreover, he works at the International Institute for Strategic Studies (IISS).

Matthias Holenstein

Matthias Holenstein ist seit 1999 bei der Ernst Basler + Partner AG als Projektleiter im Geschäftsbereich Sicherheit tätig. Er ist Mitglied der Swiss Austrian German Simulation And Gaming Association (SAGSAGA), im Präsidium der ETH Alumni Umweltwissenschaften tätig sowie als Milizoffizier im Stab Bundesrat der Nationalen Alarmzentrale eingeteilt.

Matthias Holenstein has been project leader in security matters at Ernst Basler + Partner AG since 1999. Apart from being a member of the Swiss Austrian German Simulation And Gaming Association (SAGSAGA), he is part of the committee of the ETH Alumni Umweltwissenschaften and detailed for the staff Bundesrat der Nationalen Alarmzentrale as a militia officer.

Thomas H. Johnson

Thomas H. Johnson ist Senior Research Associate am Center for Contemporary Conflict und Associate Research Professor am Institut für National Security Affairs an der Naval Postgraduate School in Monterey, Kalifornien, USA. Er unterrichtet im Bereich Südostasien und betreibt Forschung im Auftrag zahlreicher Einrichtungen der US-Regierung.

Thomas H. Johnson is Senior Research Associate at the Center for Contemporary Conflict and Associate Research Professor at the Institute for National Security Affairs at the Naval Postgraduate School in Monterey, California, USA. He teaches about South-East Asia and does research on behalf of numerous institutions of the US government.

Katharina von Knop

Katharina von Knop promoviert zum Thema Counter- und Antiterrorismen am Institut für Politikwissenschaft der Leopold-Franzens-Universität Innsbruck, Österreich.

Katharina von Knop is currently working on a PhD (Counter- und Antiterrorismen) at the department of political science, Leopold-Franzens-Universität Innsbruck, Austria.

Prof. Dr. Jan von Knop

Prof. Dr. Jan von Knop ist Professor für Informatik und Direktor des Universitätsrechen- und Medienzentrums der Heinrich-Heine-Universität Düsseldorf. Zudem ist er Mitglied des Arbeitskreises Schutz von Infrastrukturen (AKSIS).

Prof. Dr. Jan von Knop ist Professor of Informatics und director of the computer center at Heinrich-Heine-Universität Düsseldorf. Moreover, he is a member of the study-group "Arbeitskreis Schutz von Infrastrukturen" (AKSIS).

Prof. Dr. Aleksandr A. Kovalev

Prof. Dr. Aleksandr A. Kovalev ist Lehrstuhlinhaber für Internationales Recht der Diplomatischen Akademie des Innenministeriums der Russischen Föderation.

Prof. Dr. Aleksandr A. Kovalev holds the chair of international law at the Diplomatic Academy of the Ministry of the Interior of the Russian Federation.

General Anatolji Kulikov

Anatolji Kulikov ist ehemaliger Innenminister Russlands und ehemaliger stellvertretender Regierungschef. Er ist zurzeit stellvertretender Vorsitzender des Sicherheitsausschusses der Staatsduma sowie Vorsitzender des Unterausschusses der Staatsduma für internationale Zusammenarbeit und Gesetzgebung im Bereich der Terrorismusbekämpfung und der Bekämpfung der grenzüberschreitenden Kriminalität. Zudem ist er Präsident des Internationalen Antiterroristischen Forums.

Anatolji Kulikov, former Minister of the Interior and former Deputy Head of the Russian governement, is deputy chairman of the security committee of the State Duma as well as chairman of the sub-committee of the State Duma for international cooperation and legislation with regard to the fight against terrorism and against cross-border crime. Moreover, he is the president of the International Forum against Terrorism.

Günter Lessing

Günter Lessing ist Geschäftsführender Gesellschafter der Lessing IRM GmbH – Unternehmensberatung für Integrales Risk-Management.

Günter Lessing is executive partner of Lessing IRM GmbH – management consulting for integral risk management.

Sabine Leutheusser-Schnarrenberger, MdB

Sabine Leutheusser-Schnarrenberger ist Mitglied des Präsidiums der FDP-Bundespartei, Landesvorsitzende der FDP in Bayern und europapolitische Sprecherin der FDP-Fraktion. Sie war von 1992 bis 1996 Bundesministerin der Justiz.

Sabine Leutheusser-Schnarrenberger is a member of the executive committee of the German Free Democratic Party (FDP), leader of the FDP in Bavaria and spokeswoman of the FDP faction in matters concerning European politics. She was Minister of Justice from 1992 to 1996.

Prof. Dr. Ralph Alexander Lorz, LL.M.

Prof. Dr. Ralph Alexander Lorz ist Lehrstuhlinhaber für deutsches und ausländisches öffentliches Recht, Völkerrecht und Europarecht an der Heinrich-Heine-Universität Düsseldorf sowie Vorstandsmitglied des Düsseldorfer Instituts für Außen- und Sicherheitspolitik.

Prof. Dr. Ralph Alexander Lorz holds the chair of German and foreign public law, international law and European law at Heinrich-Heine-Universität Düsseldorf. He is member of the board of the Düsseldorf Institute for Foreign and Security Politics.

Lars Mammen

Lars Mammen ist wissenschaftlicher Mitarbeiter am Lehrstuhl für deutsches und ausländisches öffentliches Recht, Völkerrecht und Europarecht an der Heinrich-Heine-Universität Düsseldorf.

Lars Mammen is Assistant Lecturer in the department of German and foreign public law, international law and European law at Heinrich-Heine-Universität Düsseldorf.

Dr. Stephan Maninger

Dr. Stephan Maninger ist Politikwissenschaftler und unter anderem Lehrbeauftragter an der Friedrich-Schiller-Universität Jena.

Dr. Stephan Maninger is political scientist and, inter alia, lecturer at Friedrich-Schiller-Universität Jena.

Prof. Dr. Heinrich Neisser

Prof. Dr. Heinrich Neisser hält die Jean-Monnet-Professur am Institut für Polititikwissenschaft an der Leopold-Franzens-Universität Innsbruck, Österreich.

Prof. Dr. Heinrich Neisser holds the Jean-Monnet-Chair at the department of political science, Leopold-Franzens-Universität Innsbruck, Austria.

Peter S. Probst

Peter S. Probst ist ehemaliger Mitarbeiter der CIA und im Büro des Verteidigungsministeriums tätig. Er ist Berater der US-Regierung und des Privatsektors in Fragen des Terrorismus.

Peter S. Probst, a former member of the CIA, works in the office of the United States Department of Defense. He is an adviser to the US government as well as the private sector on terrorism issues.

Peer Rechenbach

Peer Rechenbach ist Leitender Branddirektor der Feuerwehr Hamburg.

Peer Rechenbach is chief of the fire department Hamburg.

Dr. Christoph Rojahn

Dr. Christoph Rojahn, Politikwissenschaftler, ist Berater bei der Prevent AG in Hamburg mit den Tätigkeitsschwerpunkten Ermittlung und Risikomanagement.

Dr. Christoph Rojahn, political scientist, is adviser to Prevent AG, Hamburg, where he concentrates on investigation and risk management.

James A. Russell

James A. Russell ist Senior Lecturer am Department of National Security Affairs an der Naval Postgraduate School, Monterey, Kalifornien, USA. Er unterrichtet im Bereich Nahost-Sicherheitsstudien und betreibt Forschung im Auftrag zahlreicher Einrichtungen der US-Regierung.

James A. Russell is Senior Lecturer at the Department of National Security Affairs at Naval Postgraduate School, Monterey, California, USA. He teaches in the field of security studies from the Middle East and does research on behalf of numerous institutions of the US government.

Marc Sageman, MD, PhD

Dr. Marc Sageman ist klinischer Assistenzprofessor an der Universität von Pennsylvania. Er war jahrelang für die CIA tätig und ist Autor der wissenschaftlichen Studie „Understanding Terror Networks". Darüber hinaus berät er zahlreiche Regierungseinrichtungen der USA und anderer Staaten.

Dr. Marc Sageman is Clinical Assistant Professor at the University of Pennsylvania. He worked for the CIA for many years and is the author of the scientific study "Understanding Terror Networks." In addition, he is an adviser to numerous institutions of the US government and other states.

Dr. Jörg Schmidt

Dr. Jörg Schmidt ist Brandrat und arbeitet am Institut für Notfallmedizin der Berufsfeuerwehr der Stadt Köln.

Dr. Jörg Schmidt is fire inspector and works at the Institute for Emergency Medicine, fire department Cologne.

Yael Shahar

Yael Shahar ist Leiterin des Database and Internet Projects am International Policy Institute for Counter-Terrorism (ICT) in Herzliya in Israel.

Yael Shahar ist head of the Database and Internet Project at the International Policy Institute for Counter-Terrorism (ICT) in Herzliya, Israel.

Peter J. Sharfman, PhD

Dr. Peter J. Sharfman ist Director of Policy Analysis, The MITRE Corporation, und Adjunct Professor im Science, Technology, and International Affairs Program der Georgetown University, Washington, DC.

Dr. Peter J. Sharfman is Director of Policy Analysis, The MITRE Corporation, and Adjunct Professor in the Science, Technology, and International Affairs Program of Georgetown University, Washington, DC.

Autorinnen und Autoren / Contributors

Dr. Joshua Sinai

Dr. Joshua Sinai ist Senior Terrorism Analyst bei ANSER in Shirlington, Virginia, USA. Darüber hinaus ist er zurzeit für die Regierung der USA tätig.

Dr. Joshua Sinai is Senior Terrorism Analyst for ANSER in Shirlington, Virginia, USA. Moreover, he is currently working for the US government.

Dr. Burkhard Theile

Dr. Burkhard Theile ist Hauptabteilungsleiter für Strategische Unternehmensplanung und Technologie bei der Rheinmetall DeTec AG in Düsseldorf.

Dr. Burkhard Theile is chief head of department for strategic business planning and technology at Rheinmetall DeTec AG, Düsseldorf.

Prof. Dr. Bassam Tibi

Prof. Dr. Bassam Tibi ist Leiter der Abteilung für Internationale Beziehungen an der Universität Göttingen und seit 1988 Research Associate an der Harvard University, USA. Darüber hinaus ist er Visiting Professor für Islamologie an der Universität St. Gallen, Schweiz.

Prof. Dr. Bassam Tibi is head of the department of international relations at the university of Göttingen. He has been Research Associate at Harvard University since 1988 and is Visiting Professor of Islamic studies at the university of St. Gallen, Switzerland.

Ernst Uhrlau

Ernst Uhrlau ist Koordinator der Nachrichtendienste im Bundeskanzleramt der Bundesrepublik Deutschland. Zuvor war er unter anderem Vizechef des Hamburger Landesamtes für Verfassungsschutz sowie Polizeipräsident in Hamburg.

Ernst Uhrlau is coordinator of intelligence in the Chancellery of the Federal Republic of Germany. Before, he was vice-head of the Hamburg Landesamt für Verfassungsschutz (office responsible for defending the constitution) and chief of the Hamburg police.

Prof. Dr. Gabriel Weimann

Prof. Dr. Gabriel Weimann ist Professor für Kommunikationswissenschaft am Institut für Kommunikation an der Universität von Haifa in Israel.

Prof. Dr. Gabriel Weimann is Professor of communication studies at the Institute of Communication, University of Haifa, Israel.